THE MKTG SOLUTION

Every 4LTR Press solution includes:

Heading Numbers Connect Print & eBook

Visually Engaging Textbook

Online Study Tools

Tear-out Review Cards

Interactive eBook

STUDENT RESOURCES:

- Interactive eBook
- Auto-Graded Quizzes
- Flashcards
- Media Quizzing
- Games: Crossword Puzzles, Beat the Clock, & Who Wants to Be a Marketer?
- Audio and Visual Summary

- KnowNOW! Blog
- Career Transitions
- PowerPoint® Slides
- Videos
- Part and Chapter Cases
- Marketing Plan and Planning worksheets
- Review Cards

INSTRUCTOR RESOURCES:

- All Student Resources
- Engagement Tracker
- First Day of Class Instructions
- Instructor's Manual
- Test Bank
- PowerPoint® Slides
- Instructor Prep Cards

Students sign in at **www.cengagebrain.com**

Instructors sign in at **www.cengage.com/login**

> "I used all aspects of the 4LTR Press solutions. I found them very helpful study tools."
> – **Consuelo Seda**, Student, *Valencia Community College*

JULY 2010

Engagement Tracker launches, giving faculty a window into student usage of digital tools.

4LTR Press adds eBooks in response to a 10% uptick in digital learning preferences.

AUGUST 2010

1 out of every 3 (1,400) schools has adopted a 4LTR Press solution.

750,000 students are IN.

NOVEMBER 2010

Third party research confirms that 4LTR Press digital solutions improve retention and outcomes.

IN 2011

60 unique solutions across multiple course areas validates the 4LTR Press concept.

CourseMate

Students access the 4LTR Press website at 4x's the industry average.

APRIL 2011

1 out of every 2 (2,000) schools has a 4LTR Press adoption.

IN 2011

2,000

AUGUST 2011

Over 1 million students are IN.

We're always evolving. Join the 4LTR Press In-Crowd on Facebook at www.facebook.com/4ltrpress

2012 AND BEYOND

SOUTH-WESTERN
CENGAGE Learning™

MKTG7

Charles W. Lamb
Texas Christian University

Joseph F. Hair, Jr.
Kennesaw State University

Carl McDaniel
University of Texas–Arlington

SVP, Learning Acquisitions & Solutions
   Planning: Jack W. Calhoun

Editorial Director, Business and
   Economics: Erin Joyner

Publisher: Mike Schenk

Executive Editor: Michael Roche

Developmental Editor: Laura Rush,
   B-books, Ltd.

Editorial Assistant: Megan Fischer

VP 4LTR & Learning Solutions Strategy,
   Institutional: Neil Marquardt

Sr. Brand Manager: Robin LeFevre

Sr. Product Development Manager,
   4LTR Press: Steven E. Joos

Sr. Marketing Development Manager:
   Courtney Sheldon

Marketing Coordinator: Michael A. Saver

Production Director: Amy McGuire,
   B-books, Ltd.

Sr. Content Project Manager:
   Tamborah Moore

Media Editor: John Rich

Manufacturing Planner: Ron Montgomery

Production Service: B-books, Ltd.

Sr. Rights Acquisitions Specialist:
   Deanna Ettinger

Rights Acquisitions Specialist: Audrey
   Pettengill

Photo Researcher: Terri Miller/E-Visual
   Communications, Inc.

Text Permissions Researcher: Kalpana
   Nagaraju, PreMedia Global

Sr. Art Director: Stacy Jenkins Shirley

Internal Designer: KeDesign, Mason, OH

Cover Designer: KeDesign, Mason, OH

For product information and technology assistance, contact us at
Cengage Learning Customer & Sales Support, 1-800-354-9706.

For permission to use material from this text or product,
submit all requests online at **www.cengage.com/permissions**.
Further permissions questions can be emailed to
permissionrequest@cengage.com.

Library of Congress Control Number: 2012955793

Student Edition ISBN-13: 978-1-285-09186-0
Student Edition ISBN-10: 1-285-09186-0

South-Western
5191 Natorp Boulevard
Mason, OH 45040
USA

Cengage Learning products are represented in Canada by
Nelson Education, Ltd.

For your course and learning solutions, visit **www.cengage.com**.
Purchase any of our products at your local college store or at our
preferred online store **www.CengageBrain.com**.

Cover and Page i Photography Credits:
Cover Image: © iStockphoto.com/Robert Churchill
Inside Front Cover: © iStockphoto.com/sdominick;
© iStockphoto.com/alexsl; © iStockphoto.com/A-Digit
Page i: © iStockphoto.com/CostinT; © iStockphoto.com/photovideostock;
© iStockphoto.com/Leontura
Back Cover: © iStockphoto.com/René Mansi

Printed in the United States of America
1 2 3 4 5 6 7 17 16 15 14 13

MKTG7

Lamb | Hair | McDaniel

BRIEF CONTENTS

CONTENTS

Part 1
THE WORLD OF MARKETING

© iStockphoto.com/Roger Branch

© Thinkstock Images/Jupiterimages

© Dasha Rusanenko/Shutterstock.com

3 ETHICS AND SOCIAL RESPONSIBILITY 32

4 THE MARKETING ENVIRONMENT 42

Part 2
ANALYZING MARKETING OPPORTUNITIES

© Dasha Rusanenko/Shutterstock.com

© Katherine Welles/Shutterstock.com

© Wuttichok/Shutterstock.com

9 MARKETING RESEARCH 144

Part 3 PRODUCT DECISIONS

© bloomua/Shutterstock.com

10 PRODUCT CONCEPTS 164

© Oleksiy Mark/Shutterstock.com

11 DEVELOPING AND MANAGING PRODUCTS 178

12 SERVICES AND NONPROFIT ORGANIZATION MARKETING 194

© Blue Lemon Photo/Shutterstock.com

© James Steidl/Shutterstock.com

Part 4
DISTRIBUTION DECISIONS

Part 5
PROMOTION AND COMMUNICATION STRATEGIES

15 MARKETING COMMUNICATIONS 246

© Dragana Gerasimoski/Shutterstock.com

© iStockphoto.com/Neustockimages

© Eric Isselée/Shutterstock.com

Part 6 PRICING DECISIONS

19 PRICING CONCEPTS 324

18 SOCIAL MEDIA AND MARKETING 306

© iStockphoto.com/NoDerog

© iStockphoto.com/NoDerog

20 SETTING THE RIGHT PRICE 342

1-1 WHAT IS MARKETING?

What does the term *marketing* mean to you? Many people think it means personal selling. Others think marketing means advertising. Still others believe marketing has to do with making products available in stores, arranging displays, and maintaining inventories of products for future sales. Actually, marketing includes all of these activities and more.

"Marketing is too important to be left only to the marketing department." David Packard

marketing the activity, set of institutions, and processes for creating, communicating, delivering, and exchanging offerings that have value for customers, clients, partners, and society at large

Marketing has two facets. First, it is a philosophy, an attitude, a perspective, or a management orientation that stresses customer satisfaction. Second, marketing is an organization function and a set of processes used to implement this philosophy.

The American Marketing Association's definition of marketing focuses on the second facet. **Marketing** is the activity, set of institutions, and processes for creating, communicating, delivering, and exchanging offerings that have value for customers, clients, partners, and society at large.[1]

Marketing involves more than just activities performed by a group of people in a defined area or department. In the often-quoted words of David Packard, co-founder of Hewlett-Packard, "Marketing is too important to be left only to the marketing department." Marketing entails processes that focus on delivering value and benefits to customers, not just selling goods, services, and/or ideas. It uses communication, distribution, and pricing strategies to provide customers and other stakeholders with the goods, services, ideas, values, and benefits they desire when and where they want them. It involves building long-term, mutually rewarding relationships when these benefit all parties concerned. Marketing also entails an understanding that organizations have many connected stakeholder "partners," including employees, suppliers, stockholders, distributors, and others.

Research shows that companies that reward employees with incentives and recognition on a consistent basis are those that perform best.[2] Google captured the number one position in *Fortune*'s "100 Best Companies to Work For in 2011." The company pays 100 percent of health care premiums, offers paid sabbaticals, and provides boccie courts, a bowling alley, and twenty-five cafés, for free. Google has also never had a layoff. One so-called Googler reported that "employees are never more than 150 feet away from a well-stocked pantry."[3]

An Overview of Marketing

Learning Outcomes

After you finish this chapter go to
p13 *for* **STUDY TOOLS** ------->

exchange people giving up something in order to receive something they would rather have

production orientation a philosophy that focuses on the internal capabilities of the firm rather than on the desires and needs of the marketplace

Google offers many amenities to its employees, one reason *Fortune* ranked it as the best company to work for in 2011.

© ZUMA Wire Service/Alamy

One desired outcome of marketing is an **exchange**, people giving up something in order to receive something they would rather have. Normally, we think of money as the medium of exchange. We "give up" money to "get" the goods and services we want. Exchange does not require money, however. Two (or more) people may barter or trade such items as baseball cards or oil paintings. An exchange can take place only if the following five conditions exist:

1. **There must be at least two parties.**

2. **Each party has something that might be of value to the other party.**

3. **Each party is capable of communication and delivery.**

4. **Each party is free to accept or reject the exchange offer.**

5. **Each party believes it is appropriate or desirable to deal with the other party.**[4]

Exchange will not necessarily take place even if all these conditions exist. They are, however, necessary for exchange to be possible. For example, you may place an advertisement in your local newspaper stating that your used automobile is for sale at a certain price. Several people may call you to ask about the car, some may test-drive it, and one or more may even make you an offer. All five conditions are necessary for an exchange to exist. But unless you reach an agreement with a buyer and actually sell the car, an exchange will not take place. Notice that marketing can occur even if an exchange does not occur. In the example just discussed, you would have engaged in marketing by advertising in the local newspaper even if no one bought your used automobile.

Four competing philosophies strongly influence an organization's marketing processes. These philosophies are commonly referred to as production, sales, market, and societal marketing orientations.

1-2a Production Orientation

A **production orientation** is a philosophy that focuses on the internal capabilities of the firm rather than on the desires and needs of the marketplace. A production orientation means that management assesses its resources and asks these questions: "What can we do best?" "What can our engineers design?" "What is easy to produce, given our equipment?" In the case of a service organization, managers ask, "What services are most convenient for the firm to offer?" and "Where do our talents lie?" Some have referred to this orientation as a *Field of Dreams* orientation, from the well-known movie line, "If we build it, they will come." The furniture industry is infamous for its disregard of customers and for its slow cycle times. For example, most traditional furniture stores (think Ashley or Havertys) carry the same styles and varieties of furniture that they have carried for many years. They always produce and stock sofas, coffee tables, arm chairs, and end tables for the living room. Master bedroom suites always include at least a queen- or king-sized bed, two dressers, and two side tables. Regardless of what customers may actually be looking for, this is what they will find at these stores—and it works because what the stores produce has matched up with customer expectations. This has always been a production-oriented industry.

There is nothing wrong with assessing a firm's capabilities; in fact, such assessments are major considerations in strategic marketing planning (see Chapter 2). A production orientation falls short because it does not consider whether the goods and services that the firm produces most efficiently also meet the needs of the marketplace. Sometimes what a firm can best produce is exactly what the market wants. Apple has a history of production orientation, creating computers, operating systems, and other gadgetry because it can and hoping to sell the result. Some items have found a waiting market (early computers, iPod, iPhone). Other products, like the Newton, one of the first versions of a PDA, were simply flops. In other situations, as when competition is weak or demand exceeds supply, a production-oriented firm can survive and even prosper. More often, however, firms that succeed in competitive markets have a clear understanding that they must first determine what customers want and then produce it, rather than focus on what company management thinks should be produced and hope that product is something customers want.

1-2b Sales Orientation

A **sales orientation** is based on the ideas that people will buy more goods and services if aggressive sales techniques are used and that high sales result in high profits. Not only are sales to the final buyer emphasized, but intermediaries are also encouraged to push manufacturers' products more aggressively. To sales-oriented firms, marketing means selling things and collecting money.

The fundamental problem with a sales orientation, as with a production orientation, is a lack of understanding of the needs and wants of the marketplace. Sales-oriented companies often find that, despite the quality of their sales force, they cannot convince people to buy goods or services that are neither wanted nor needed.

One of the dangers of a sales orientation is failing to understand what is important to the firm's customers. When that occurs, sales-oriented firms sometimes use aggressive incentives to drive sales. For example, after Nintendo faced

a steep decline in Wii and 3DS sales, the company slashed the price on the portable, glasses-free 3DS from $250 to $170, hoping to spark sales of the game platform before releasing new games.[5]

1-2c Market Orientation

The **marketing concept** is a simple and intuitively appealing philosophy that articulates a market orientation. It states that the social and economic justification for an organization's existence is the satisfaction of customer wants and needs while meeting organizational objectives. What a business thinks it produces is not of primary importance to its success. Instead, what customers think they are buying—the perceived value—defines a business. The marketing concept includes the following:

» **Focusing on customer wants and needs so that the organization can distinguish its product(s) from competitors' offerings**

» **Integrating all the organization's activities, including production, to satisfy customer wants**

» **Achieving long-term goals for the organization by satisfying customer wants and needs legally and responsibly**

The recipe for success is to develop a thorough understanding of your customers and your competition, your distinctive capabilities that enable your company to execute plans on the basis of this customer understanding, and how to deliver the desired experience using and integrating all of the resources of the firm.[6]

Firms that adopt and implement the marketing concept are said to be **market oriented**, meaning they assume that a sale does not depend on an aggressive sales force but rather on a customer's decision to purchase a product. Achieving a market orientation involves obtaining information about customers, competitors, and markets; examining the information from a total business perspective; determining how to deliver superior customer

sales orientation the ideas that people will buy more goods and services if aggressive sales techniques are used and that high sales result in high profits

marketing concept the idea that the social and economic justification for an organization's existence is the satisfaction of customer wants and needs while meeting organizational objectives

market orientation a philosophy that assumes that a sale does not depend on an aggressive sales force but rather on a customer's decision to purchase a product; it is synonymous with the marketing concept value; and implementing actions to provide value to customers.

Some firms are known for delivering superior customer value and satisfaction. The 2011 National Retail Federation Foundation/American Express Customer Service Survey listed Zappos.com, Amazon.com, L.L.Bean, Overstock.com, and Lands' End as the top five U.S. retailers for customer service.[7]

Understanding your competitive arena and competitors' strengths and weaknesses is a critical component of a market orientation. This includes assessing what existing or potential competitors might be intending to do tomorrow and what they are doing today. Western Union failed to define its competitive arena as telecommunications, concentrating instead on telegraph services, and was eventually outflanked by fax technology. Had Western Union been a market-oriented company, its management might have better understood the changes taking place, seen the competitive threat, and developed strategies to counter the threat. In contrast, American Express's success has rested largely on the company's ability to focus on customers and adapt to their changing needs over the past 160 years.[8]

1-2d Societal Marketing Orientation

The **societal marketing orientation** extends the marketing concept by acknowledging that some products that customers want may not really be in their best interests or in the best interests of society as a whole. This philosophy states that an organization exists not only to satisfy customer wants and needs and to meet organizational objectives but also to preserve or enhance individuals' and society's long-term best interests. Marketing products and containers that are less toxic than normal, are more durable, contain reusable materials, or are made of recyclable materials is consistent with a societal marketing orientation. The American Marketing Association's definition of marketing recognizes the importance of a societal marketing orientation by including "society at large" as one of the constituencies for which marketing seeks to provide value.

Although the societal marketing concept has been discussed for more than thirty years, it did not receive widespread support until the early 2000s. Concerns such as climate change, the depleting of the ozone layer, fuel shortages, pollution, and health concerns have caused consumers and legislators to be more aware of the need for companies and consumers to adopt measures that conserve resources and that cause less damage to the environment.

Studies reporting consumers' attitudes toward, and intentions to buy, environmentally friendly products show widely varying results. A Nielsen study found that while 83 percent of consumers worldwide believe companies should have environmental programs, only 22 percent would pay more for an eco-friendly product. The key to consumer purchasing lies beyond labels proclaiming sustainability, natural ingredients, or "being green." Customers want sustainable products that perform better than their unsustainable counterparts.[9]

1-2e Who's in Charge?

The Internet and the widespread use of social media have accelerated the shift in power from manufacturers and retailers to consumers and business users. This shift began when customers started using books, electronics, and the Internet to access information, goods, and services. Customers use their widespread knowledge to shop smarter, leading executives such as former Procter & Gamble CEO A.G. Lafley to conclude that "the customer is boss."[10]

Sam Walton echoed this sentiment when he reportedly once said, "There is only one boss. The customer. And he can fire everybody in the company from the chairman on down, simply by spending his money somewhere else."[11] Walmart's chief

NOW THAT IS A GREAT DEAL!

marketing officer, Stephen Quinn, agrees. "It starts with the customer. You've got to be incredibly customer-focused nowadays because—it's been said many times—the customer is in control."[12] And as Internet use and mobile devices become increasingly pervasive, that control will continue to grow. This means that companies must create strategy from the outside in by offering distinct and compelling customer value.[13] This can only be accomplished by carefully studying customers and using deep market insights to inform and guide companies' outside-in view.[14] Jeff Bezos, founder and chairman of Amazon.com, calls this a "working backward" mentality.[15]

1-3 DIFFERENCES BETWEEN SALES AND MARKET ORIENTATIONS

The differences between sales and market orientations are substantial. The two orientations can be compared in terms of five characteristics: the organization's focus, the firm's business, those to whom the product is directed, the firm's primary goal, and the tools used to achieve the organization's goals.

1-3a The Organization's Focus

Personnel in sales-oriented firms tend to be inward looking, focusing on selling what the organization makes rather than making what the market wants. Many of the historic sources of competitive advantage—technology, innovation, economies of scale—allowed companies to focus their efforts internally and prosper. But that same inward focus characteristic of the sales orientation has also led to the demise of firms like 3D Realms, Steve and Barry's, and SeeqPod.

Today, many successful firms derive their competitive advantage from an external, market-oriented focus. A market orientation has helped companies such as Zappos.com and Bob's Red Mill Natural Foods outperform their competitors. These companies put customers at the center of their business in ways most companies do poorly or not at all.

CUSTOMER VALUE The relationship between benefits and the sacrifice necessary to obtain those benefits is known as **customer value**. Customer value is not simply a matter of high quality. A high-quality product that is available only at a high price will not be perceived as a good value, nor will bare-bones service or low-quality goods selling for a low price. Instead, customers value goods and services that are of the quality they expect and that are sold at prices they are willing to pay. Value can be used to sell a Mercedes-Benz as well as a Tyson frozen chicken dinner.

Lower-income consumers are price sensitive, but they will pay for products if they deliver a benefit that is worth the money.[16] While price conveys value (a $4,000 handbag is perceived as being more luxurious and of higher quality than one selling for $100), value is about more than just price. For example, the social shopping scene has been expanding for several years, but wealthy customers with money to spend are being courted by a new breed of social shopping site. The basic premise is that a well-known fashion name (be it a fashion editor, an elite socialite, or a celebrity) moderates sites by handpicking pieces from favorite retailers, such as Barneys New York or Saks Fifth Avenue. Shoppers then purchase the curated items, and the site receives a commission for each purchase. There are many of these sites: Moda Operandi has highlighted (and sold out of) woven skirts for $4,000 apiece, Motilo focuses on French fashion (including couture pieces), and *Fino File* is an online, shopable magazine, with pieces ranging from $80 tops to $1,000 boots. With reports of growing subscribers and sold-out merchandise, it is clear that these sites are attracting customers who value curated style.[17]

Marketers interested in customer value:

▸ **OFFER PRODUCTS THAT PERFORM: This is the bare minimum requirement. After grappling with the problems associated with its Vista operating system, Microsoft listened to its customers and made drastic changes for Windows 7, which received greatly improved reviews.**

▸ **EARN TRUST: A stable base of loyal customers can help a firm grow and prosper. Residents in Brooklyn are fiercely loyal to their neighborhood's businesses. So, as part of their product introductions, Sixpoint Craft Ales brewery and Crop to Cup coffee did extensive sidewalk brand introduction in Brooklyn, offering passersby samples and personally developing relationships with local retailers to get their products on shelves and in restaurants. Both have made a huge market impact in Brooklyn through their constant presence, and Crop to Cup has opened its first store.[18]**

▸ **AVOID UNREALISTIC PRICING: E-marketers are leveraging Internet technology to redefine how prices are set and negotiated. With lower costs,** e-marketers can often offer lower prices than their brick-and-mortar counterparts. The enormous popularity of auction sites such as eBay and the customer-bid model used by Priceline and uBid.com illustrates that online customers are interested in bargain prices. In fact, as Smartphone usage grows, brick-and-mortar stores are fighting customers who price compare using their Smartphones and purchase items for less online while standing in the store.

▸ **GIVE THE BUYER FACTS:** Today's sophisticated consumer wants informative advertising and knowledgeable salespeople. It is becoming very difficult for business marketers to differentiate themselves from competitors. Rather than trying to sell products, salespeople need to find out what the customer needs, which is usually a combination of products, services, and thought leadership.[19] In other words, salespeople need to start with the needs of the customer and work toward the solution.

▸ **OFFER ORGANIZATION-WIDE COMMITMENT IN SERVICE AND AFTER-SALES SUPPORT:** The Arizona Cardinals realized that their competitors were not only other NFL teams but also every organization that competes for the customers' entertainment dollars. The team hired Disney Institute, the professional development unit of The Walt Disney Company that helps other companies learn how to adopt Disney best practices and transform how they approach business. The Cardinals wanted Disney Institute to show them how to keep everyone in the organization focused on great customer service and help them draw in more customers.[20]

▸ **CO-CREATION:** Some companies and products allow customers to help create their own experience. For example, Case-Mate, a firm that makes formfitting cases for cell phones, laptops, and other personal devices, allows customers to design their own cases by uploading their own photos. Customers who don't have designs of their own can manipulate art from designers using the "design with" feature at case-mate.com. Either way, customers produce completely unique covers for their devices.

CUSTOMER SATISFACTION The customers' evaluation of a good or service in terms of whether that good or service has met their needs and expectations is called **customer satisfaction**. Failure to meet needs and expectations results in dissatisfaction with the good or service. Some companies, in their passion to drive down costs, have damaged their relationships with customers. Comcast, Bank of America, and Sprint Nextel are examples of companies where executives lost track of the delicate balance between efficiency and service.[21] Firms that have a reputation for delivering high levels of customer satisfaction do things differently from their competitors. Top management is obsessed with customer satisfaction, and employees throughout the organization understand the

AMAZON.COM'S PLOY AGAINST PHYSICAL RETAILERS

Amazon.com is a target for bargain-minded shoppers. The Internet retailer offers great prices and quick shipping from the comfort of home. But now, it wants customers to find the lowest prices on the go. Amazon's latest Smartphone app, Price Check, allows customers to scan a barcode and compare store prices to other locations and on Amazon.com. To encourage customers to use the app and to increase its pricing database, Amazon offered a promotion—scan a barcode at any store, buy the product from Amazon instead, and get 5 percent off that item. Brick-and-mortar stores cried foul, stating that Amazon is encouraging customers to use stores as show rooms, where customers try out products while comparison shopping on Smartphones. But with customers placing a premium on getting the best value and being able to access prices from mobile devices, Amazon may prove to be the first of many price-comparison apps.

Source: Janet Novack, "Amazon Price Check Flap Is No Strategic Blunder," *Forbes*, December 12, 2011, www.forbes.com/sites /janetnovack/2011/12/12/amazon-price-check-flap-is-no-strategic-blunder (Accessed March 27, 2012).

link between their job and satisfied customers. The culture of the organization is to focus on delighting customers rather than on selling products.

Coming back from customer dissatisfaction can be tough, but there are some key ways that companies begin to improve customer satisfaction. Forrester Research discovered that when companies experience gains in the firm's Customer Experience Index (CxPi), they have implemented one of two major changes. Aetna, a major health insurance provider, executed the first type of change—changing its decentralized part-time customer service group into a full-time, centralized customer service team. Aetna's CxPi score rose six points in one year. Office Depot executed the second type of change—addressing customer "pain points" and making sure that what customers need is always available to them. By streamlining its supply chain and adding more stylish office products, Office Depot satisfied business customers and female shoppers, increasing its CxPi by nine points.[22]

BUILDING RELATIONSHIPS Attracting new customers to a business is only the beginning. The best companies view new-customer attraction as the launching point for developing and enhancing a long-term relationship. Companies can expand market share in three ways: attracting new customers, increasing business with existing customers, and retaining current customers. Building relationships with existing customers directly addresses two of the three possibilities and indirectly addresses the other.

Relationship marketing is a strategy that focuses on keeping and improving relationships with current customers. It assumes that many consumers and business customers prefer to have an ongoing relationship with one organization rather than switch continually among providers in their search for value. USAA is a good example of a company focused on building long-term relationships with customers. In an annual Customer Service Champs survey conducted by *Bloomberg Businessweek* and J.D. Power and Associates, USAA has been the only company to be ranked in the top two for four years running. Not only does USAA have an incredible 97.8 percent client retention rate, but 87 percent of the respondents in the survey said they would purchase from USAA again. Clearly, USAA provides services to its customers that make their lives easier, and the customers respond very positively.[23]

Most successful relationship marketing strategies depend on customer-oriented personnel, effective training programs, employees with authority to make decisions and solve problems, and teamwork.

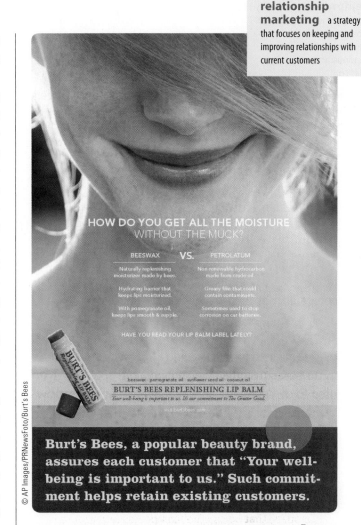

Burt's Bees, a popular beauty brand, assures each customer that "Your well-being is important to us." Such commitment helps retain existing customers.

CUSTOMER-ORIENTED PERSONNEL For an organization to be focused on building relationships with customers, employees' attitudes and actions must be customer oriented. An employee may be the only contact a particular customer has with the firm. In that customer's eyes, the employee is the firm. Any person, department, or division that is not customer oriented weakens the positive image of the entire organization. For example, a potential customer who is greeted discourteously may well assume that the employee's attitude represents the whole firm.

Customer-oriented personnel come from an organizational culture that supports its people. Southwest Airlines has been operating with high levels of customer satisfaction for forty years (forty years of love, as the airline quips). Not only does the airline have low fares, charge few fees (first two bags fly free!), and apologize via e-mail or phone for any delays or mishaps, it also receives tons of fan mail about its employees. The secret? Executives say they "hire nice people" and "empower employees to make decisions, and we support them."[24] Listed on several customer service "Best of" lists, Southwest's nice people are definitely popular with their customers.

Some companies, such as Coca-Cola, Delta Air Lines, Hershey, Kellogg, Nautilus, and Sears, have appointed chief customer officers (CCOs). These customer advocates provide an executive voice for customers and report directly to the CEO. Their responsibilities include ensuring that the company maintains a customer-centric culture and that all company employees remain focused on delivering customer value.

THE ROLE OF TRAINING Leading marketers recognize the role of employee training in customer service and relationship building. Sales staff at The Container Store receive over 240 hours of training and generous benefits compared to an industry average of 8 hours of training and modest benefits.

EMPOWERMENT In addition to training, many market-oriented firms are giving employees more authority to solve customer problems on the spot. The term used to describe this delegation of authority is **empowerment**. Employees develop ownership attitudes when they are treated like part-owners of the business and are expected to act the part. These employees manage themselves, are more likely to work hard, account for their own performance and that of the company, and take prudent risks to build a stronger business and sustain the company's success. In an attempt to change Cadillac's image, General Motors is looking to wow its customers with excellent, fast, and reliable service. Emulating Ritz-Carlton hotels, Cadillac service chiefs are given $300 to $500 to spend on individual customers. A chief can reduce rates, give free maintenance, or reduce service fees for unhappy customers—all at his or her discretion.[25]

Empowerment gives customers the feeling that their concerns are being addressed and gives employees the feeling that their expertise matters. The result is greater satisfaction for both customers and employees.

TEAMWORK Many organizations that are frequently noted for delivering superior customer value and providing high levels of customer satisfaction, such as Southwest Airlines and Walt Disney World, assign employees to teams and teach them team-building skills. **Teamwork** entails collaborative efforts of people to accomplish common objectives. Job performance, company performance, product value, and customer satisfaction all improve when people in the same department or work group begin supporting and assisting each other and emphasize cooperation instead of competition. Performance is also

An emphasis on cooperation over competition can help a company's performance improve. That's why many companies have moved to using teams to get jobs done.

enhanced when cross-functional teams align their jobs with customer needs. For example, if a team of telecommunications service representatives is working to improve interaction with customers, back-office people such as computer technicians or training personnel can become part of the team with the ultimate goal of delivering superior customer value and satisfaction.

1-3b The Firm's Business

A sales-oriented firm defines its business (or mission) in terms of goods and services. A market-oriented firm defines its business in terms of the benefits its customers seek. People who spend their money, time, and energy expect to receive benefits, not just goods and services. This distinction has enormous implications. As a senior executive noted, Coca-Cola is in the hydration business.[26]

Because of the limited way it defines its business, a sales-oriented firm often misses opportunities to serve customers whose wants can be met through a wide range of product offerings instead of through specific products. For example, in 1989, 220-year-old Britannica had estimated revenues of $650 million and a worldwide sales force of 7,500. Just five years later, after three consecutive years of losses, the sales force had collapsed to as few as 280 representatives. How did this respected company sink so low? Britannica managers saw that competitors were beginning to use CD-ROMs to store huge masses of information but chose to ignore the new computer technology as well as an offer to team up with Microsoft. In 2012, the company announced that it would stop printing its namesake books and instead focus on selling its reference works to subscribers through its Web site and apps for tablets and Smartphones.[27]

Having a market orientation and a focus on customer wants does not mean offering customers everything they want. It is not possible, for example, to profitably manufacture and market automobile tires that will last for 100,000 miles for twenty-five dollars. Furthermore, customers' preferences must be mediated by sound professional judgment as to how to deliver the benefits they seek. As Henry Ford once said, "If I had listened to the marketplace, I would have built a faster, cheaper horse."[28] Consumers have a limited set of experiences. They are unlikely to request anything beyond those experiences because they are not aware of benefits they may gain from other potential offerings. For example, before the Internet, many people thought that shopping for some products was boring and time-consuming but could not express their need for electronic shopping.

WHAT IS THIS FIRM'S BUSINESS?

Answering the question "What is this firm's business?" in terms of the benefits customers seek, instead of goods and services, offers at least three important advantages:

▸▸ It ensures that the firm keeps focusing on customers and avoids becoming preoccupied with goods, services, or the organization's internal needs.

▸▸ It encourages innovation and creativity by reminding people that there are many ways to satisfy customer wants.

▸▸ It stimulates an awareness of changes in customer desires and preferences so that product offerings are more likely to remain relevant.

1-3c Those to Whom the Product Is Directed

A sales-oriented organization targets its products at "everybody" or "the average customer." A market-oriented organization aims at specific groups of people. The fallacy of developing products directed at the average user is that relatively few average users actually exist. Typically, populations are characterized by diversity. An average is simply a midpoint in some set of characteristics. Because most potential customers are not "average," they are not likely to be attracted to an average product marketed to the average customer. Consider the market for shampoo as one simple example. There are shampoos for oily hair, dry hair, and dandruff. Some shampoos remove the gray or color hair. Special shampoos are marketed for infants and elderly people. There are even shampoos for people with average or normal hair (whatever that is), but this is a fairly small portion of the total market for shampoo.

A market-oriented organization recognizes that different customer groups want different features or benefits. It may therefore need to develop different goods, services, and promotional appeals. A market-oriented organization carefully analyzes the market and divides it into groups of people who are fairly similar in terms of selected characteristics. Then the organization develops marketing programs that will bring about mutually satisfying exchanges with one or more of those groups. For example, during the recession, Target modified the pieces offered by its Merona brand to focus on basic wardrobe staples. Target knew Merona shoppers were moms who wanted to look nice without trying too hard and were also pulling back on fashion spending. By offering nice, basic pieces, Merona remained a strong seller throughout the recession.[29]

CUSTOMER RELATIONSHIP MANAGEMENT Beyond knowing to whom it is directing its products or services, today, a company must develop a deeper understanding of its customers. One way of doing this is through *customer relationship management*. **Customer relationship management (CRM)** is a company-wide business strategy designed to optimize profitability, revenue, and customer satisfaction by focusing on highly defined and precise customer groups. This is accomplished by organizing the company around customer segments, establishing and tracking customer interactions with the company, fostering customer-satisfying behaviors, and linking all processes of the company from its customers through its suppliers. The difference between CRM and traditional mass marketing can be compared to shooting a rifle versus a shotgun. Instead of scattering messages far and wide across the spectrum of mass media (the shotgun approach), CRM marketers now are homing in

customer relationship management (CRM) a company-wide business strategy designed to optimize profitability, revenue, and customer satisfaction by focusing on highly defined and precise customer groups on ways to effectively communicate with each customer (the rifle approach).

Companies that adopt CRM systems are almost always market oriented, customizing product and service offerings based on data generated through interactions between the customer and the company. This strategy transcends all functional areas of the business, producing an internal system where all of the company's decisions and actions are a direct result of customer information. We will examine specific applications of CRM in several chapters throughout this book.

1-3d The Firm's Primary Goal

A sales-oriented organization seeks to achieve profitability through sales volume and tries to convince potential customers to buy, even if the seller knows that the customer and product are mismatched. Sales-oriented organizations place a higher premium on making a sale than on developing a long-term relationship with a customer. In contrast, the ultimate goal of most market-oriented organizations is to make a profit by creating customer value, providing customer satisfaction, and building long-term relationships with customers. The exception is so-called nonprofit organizations that exist to achieve goals other than profits. Nonprofit organizations can and should adopt a market orientation. Nonprofit organization marketing is explored further in Chapter 12.

1-3e Tools the Organization Uses to Achieve Its Goals

Sales-oriented organizations seek to generate sales volume through intensive promotional activities, mainly personal selling and advertising. In contrast, market-oriented organizations recognize that promotion decisions are only one of four basic marketing mix decisions that have to be made: product decisions, place (or distribution) decisions, promotion decisions, and pricing decisions. A market-oriented organization recognizes that each of these four components is important. Furthermore, market-oriented

Using the correct tool for the job will help an organization ACHIEVE ITS GOALS. Marketing tools are covered throughout this book!

organizations recognize that marketing is not just a responsibility of the marketing department. Interfunctional coordination means that skills and resources throughout the organization are needed to create, communicate, and deliver superior customer service and value.

1-3f Word of Caution

This comparison of sales and market orientations is not meant to belittle the role of promotion, especially personal selling, in the marketing mix. Promotion is the means by which organizations communicate with present and prospective customers about the merits and characteristics of their organization and products. Effective promotion is an essential part of effective marketing. Salespeople who work for market-oriented organizations are generally perceived by their customers to be problem solvers and important links to supply sources and new products. Chapter 17 examines the nature of personal selling in more detail.

1-4 WHY STUDY MARKETING?

Now that you understand the meaning of the term *marketing*, why it is important to adopt a marketing orientation, and how organizations implement this philosophy, you may be asking, "What's in it for me?" or "Why should I study marketing?" These are important questions whether you are majoring in a business field other than marketing (such as accounting, finance, or management information systems) or a nonbusiness field (such as journalism, education, or agriculture). There are several important reasons to study marketing: Marketing plays an important role in society, marketing is important to businesses, marketing offers outstanding career opportunities, and marketing affects your life every day.

1-4a Marketing Plays an Important Role in Society

The total population of the United States exceeds 310 million people.[30] Think about how many transactions are needed each day to feed, clothe, and shelter a population of this size. The number is huge. And yet it all works quite well, partly because the well-developed

U.S. economic system efficiently distributes the output of farms and factories. A typical U.S. family, for example, consumes 2.5 tons of food a year.[31] Marketing makes food available when we want it, in desired quantities, at accessible locations, and in sanitary and convenient packages and forms (such as instant and frozen foods).

1-4b Marketing Is Important to Businesses

The fundamental objectives of most businesses are survival, profits, and growth. Marketing contributes directly to achieving these objectives. Marketing includes the following activities, which are vital to business organizations: assessing the wants and satisfactions of present and potential customers, designing and managing product offerings, determining prices and pricing policies, developing distribution strategies, and communicating with present and potential customers.

All businesspeople, regardless of specialization or area of responsibility, need to be familiar with the terminology and fundamentals of accounting, finance, management, and marketing. People in all business areas need to be able to communicate with specialists in other areas. Furthermore, marketing is not just a job done by people in a marketing department. Marketing is a part of the job of everyone in the organization. Therefore, a basic understanding of marketing is important to all businesspeople.

© Richard Levine/Alamy

Marketing surrounds you in many ways— even beyond billboards and television ads!

1-4c Marketing Offers Outstanding Career Opportunities

Between one-fourth and one-third of the entire civilian workforce in the United States performs marketing activities. Marketing offers great career opportunities in such areas as professional selling, marketing research, advertising, retail buying, distribution management, product management, product development, and wholesaling. Marketing career opportunities also exist in a variety of nonbusiness organizations, including hospitals, museums, universities, the armed forces, and various government and social service agencies.

1-4d Marketing in Everyday Life

Marketing plays a major role in your everyday life. You participate in the marketing process as a consumer of goods and services. About half of every dollar you spend pays for marketing costs, such as marketing research, product development, packaging, transportation, storage, advertising, and sales expenses. By developing a better understanding of marketing, you will become a better-informed consumer. You will better understand the buying process and be able to negotiate more effectively with sellers. Moreover, you will be better prepared to demand satisfaction when the goods and services you buy do not meet the standards promised by the manufacturer or the marketer.

STUDY TOOLS 1

LOCATED AT BACK OF THE TEXTBOOK
☐ *Rip out Chapter Review Card*

LOCATED AT WWW.CENGAGE.COM/LOGIN
☐ *Review Key Terms Flashcards (print or online)*
☐ *Download audio and visual summaries to review on the go*
☐ *Complete both Practice Quizzes to prepare for tests*
☐ *Play "Beat the Clock" and "Quizbowl" to master concepts*
☐ *Complete "Crossword Puzzle" to review key terms*
☐ *Watch Video on "Geoffrey B. Small" for a real company example*

Strategic planning is the managerial process of creating and maintaining a fit between the organization's objectives and resources and the evolving market opportunities. The goal of strategic planning is long-run profitability and growth. Thus, strategic decisions require long-term commitments of resources.

"There are a lot of great ideas that have come and gone in [the digital advertising] industry. Implementation many times is more important than the actual idea." *David Moore*

strategic planning
the managerial process of creating and maintaining a fit between the organization's objectives and resources and the evolving market opportunities

A strategic error can threaten a firm's survival. On the other hand, a good strategic plan can help protect and grow the firm's resources. For instance, if the March of Dimes had decided to focus only on fighting polio, the organization would no longer exist, because polio is widely viewed as a conquered disease. The March of Dimes survived by making the strategic decision to switch to fighting birth defects.

Strategic marketing management addresses two questions: What is the organization's main activity at a particular time? How will it reach its goals? Here are some examples of strategic decisions.

▶▶ **Target, which has always had a strong apparel history, is moving away from its popular designer partnerships or expanding them into non-apparel parts of the store (such as home goods). The company is now focusing on developing its owned and exclusive brands, such as Merona, to make sure that those brands fit what customers are looking for.**[1]

▶▶ **Disney is trying to capture the two- to seven-year-old demographic, hoping to steal viewership from Viacom, which owns powerhouse shows *Dora the Explorer* and *SpongeBob SquarePants*. To do so, Disney is shuttering its twelve-year-old SOAPnet channel, which was devoted to soap operas, to create the new Disney Junior channel. The channel will feature shows such as *Doc McStuffins*, an animated show about a young girl who fixes up ailing stuffed animals.**[2]

▶▶ **To attract positive attention to its restaurants, Darden Restaurants Inc. is pledging to offer healthier fare in accordance with First Lady Michelle Obama's initiative to fight childhood obesity. Olive Garden, one of Darden's chains, will make fruit or vegetables the default side dish for kids' meals and is promising to reduce calories and sodium by 20 percent over ten years.**[3]

All these decisions have affected or will affect each organization's long-run course, its allocation of resources, and ultimately its financial success. In contrast, an operating decision, such as changing the package design for Post Toasties or altering the

Chapter 2

Strategic Planning for Competitive Advantage

Learning Outcomes

After you finish this chapter go to
p30 for **STUDY TOOLS**

sweetness of a Kraft salad dressing, probably won't have a big impact on the long-run profitability of the company.

2-2 STRATEGIC BUSINESS UNITS

Large companies may manage a number of very different businesses, called strategic business units (SBUs). Each SBU has its own rate of return on investment, growth potential, and associated risks, and requires its own strategies and funding. When properly created, an SBU has the following characteristics:

» **A distinct mission and a specific target market**

» **Control over its resources**

» **Its own competitors**

» **A single business or a collection of related businesses**

» **Plans independent of the other SBUs in the total organization.**

In theory, an SBU should have its own resources for handling basic business functions: accounting, engineering, manufacturing, and marketing. In practice, however, because of company tradition, management philosophy, and production and distribution economies, SBUs sometimes share manufacturing facilities, distribution channels, and even top managers.

2-3 STRATEGIC ALTERNATIVES

There are several tools available that a company, or SBU, can use to manage the strategic direction of its portfolio of businesses. Three of the most commonly used tools are Ansoff's strategic opportunity matrix, the Boston Consulting Group model, and the General Electric model. Selecting which strategic alternative to pursue depends on which of two philosophies a company maintains about when to expect

profits—right away or after increasing market share. In the long run, market share and profitability are compatible goals. For example, Michelin, the tire producer, consistently sacrifices short-term profits to achieve market share. On the other hand, IBM stresses profitability and stock valuation over market share, quality, and customer service. As you can see, different firms may view the same strategic alternative entirely differently.

2-3a Ansoff's Opportunity Matrix

One method for developing alternatives is Ansoff's strategic opportunity matrix (see Exhibit 2.1), which matches products with markets. Firms can explore these four options:

» **MARKET PENETRATION: A firm using the market penetration alternative would try to increase market share among existing customers. Amazon.com introduced a streaming movie and television service for its Amazon Prime customers, hoping to increase streaming media market share by encouraging current Prime subscribers to use the new service instead of Netflix.[4] Customer databases, discussed in Chapter 9, would help managers implement this strategy.**

» **MARKET DEVELOPMENT: Market development means attracting new customers to existing products. Ideally, new uses for old products stimulate additional sales among existing customers while also bringing in new buyers. McDonald's, for example, has opened restaurants in Russia, China, and Italy and is eagerly expanding into Eastern European countries. In the nonprofit arena, the growing emphasis on continuing education and executive development by colleges and universities is a market development strategy.**

» **PRODUCT DEVELOPMENT: A product development strategy entails the creation of new products**

Exhibit 2.1
ANSOFF'S STRATEGIC OPPORTUNITY MATRIX

	Present Product	New Product
Present Market	*Market Penetration* Starbucks sells more coffee to customers who register their reloadable Starbucks cards.	*Product Development* Starbucks develops powdered instant coffee called Via.
New Market	*Market Development* Starbucks opens stores in Brazil and Chile.	*Diversification* Starbucks launches Hear Music and buys Ethos Water.

© Cengage Learning

This ad for Daisy Brand cottage cheese shows five different ways to use the product. Daisy is hoping to increase market share among existing customers by encouraging its use as an ingredient in various meals.

A diversification strategy can be risky when a firm is entering unfamiliar markets. However, it can be very profitable when a firm is entering markets with little or no competition.

Critics of Ansoff's matrix mention that the matrix doesn't reflect the reality of how businesses grow—that modern businesses plan growth in a more fluid manner based on current capabilities rather than the clear-cut sectors outlined by the opportunity matrix. To reflect this, Bansi Nagji and Geoff Tuff, global innovation managers at Monitor Group, have recently developed a system that enables a company to see exactly what types of assets need to be developed and what types of markets are possible to grow into (or create) based on the company's core capabilities, as shown in Exhibit 2.2.

The layout of the innovation matrix demonstrates that as a company moves away from its core capabilities (the lower left) it traverses a range of change and innovation rather than choosing one of the four sectors in Ansoff's matrix. These ranges are broken down into three levels:

1. **CORE INNOVATION:** Represented by the yellow circle in Exhibit 2.2, these decisions implement changes that

for present markets. Reckitt Benckiser Group, which gets the bulk of its revenue from home and personal care products, also produces Suboxone, a drug that helps heroin addicts manage their habit. The company recently lost its patent protection and is now releasing Suboxone as a thin film that dissolves on the tongue (like Listerine PocketPaks). Reckitt Benckiser hopes to convert current Suboxone tablet users to the film before the generic tablets are released.[5]

▸ **DIVERSIFICATION:** Diversification is a strategy of increasing sales by introducing new products into new markets. For example, UGG, the popular footwear brand known for its casual boots, has introduced an upscale men's footwear collection. The shoes are inspired by rock'n'roll legends such as Jimi Hendrix and Jim Morrison, and meant to appeal to a new customer. "There are some UGG customers that will be interested in the Collection product, but it will also bring in new customers for us," says UGG's vice president.[6]

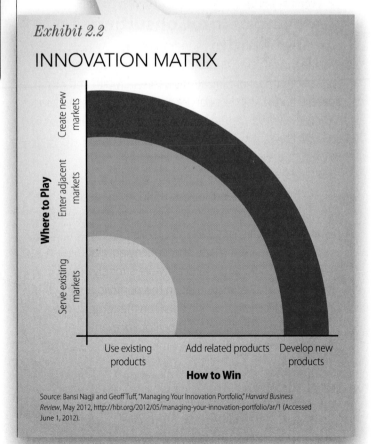

Exhibit 2.2

INNOVATION MATRIX

Source: Bansi Nagji and Geoff Tuff, "Managing Your Innovation Portfolio," *Harvard Business Review*, May 2012, http://hbr.org/2012/05/managing-your-innovation-portfolio/ar/1 (Accessed June 1, 2012).

use existing assets to provide added convenience to existing customers and potentially entice customers from other brands. Packaging changes, such as Tide's laundry detergent Pods, fall into this category.

2. **ADJACENT INNOVATION:** Represented by the orange arc in Exhibit 2.2, these decisions are designed to take company strengths into new markets. This space uses existing abilities in new ways. For example, Botox, the popular cosmetic surgery, was originally developed to treat intestinal problems and to treat crossed eyes. Leveraging the drug into cosmetic surgery has dramatically increased the market for Botox.

3. **TRANSFORMATIONAL INNOVATION:** Represented by the red arc in Exhibit 2.2, these decisions result in brand-new markets, products, and often new businesses. The company must rely on new, unfamiliar assets to develop the type of breakthrough decisions that fall in this category. Apple's iTunes is a prime example of developing an immature market with a brand-new experience.[7]

2-3b The Boston Consulting Group Model

Management must find a balance among the SBUs that yields the overall organization's desired growth and profits with an acceptable level of risk. Some SBUs generate large amounts of cash, and others need cash to foster growth. The challenge is to balance the organization's portfolio of SBUs for the best long-term performance.

To determine the future cash contributions and cash requirements expected for each SBU, managers can use the Boston Consulting Group's portfolio matrix. The **portfolio matrix** classifies each SBU by its present or forecast growth and market share. The underlying assumption is that market share and profitability are strongly linked. The measure of market share used in the portfolio approach is *relative market share*, the ratio between the company's share and the share of the largest competitor. For example, if a firm has a 50 percent share and the competitor has 5 percent, the ratio is 10 to 1. If a firm has a 10 percent market share and the largest competitor has 20 percent, the ratio is 0.5 to 1.

Exhibit 2.3 is a hypothetical portfolio matrix for a computer manufacturer. The size of the circle in each cell of the

Exhibit 2.3

PORTFOLIO MATRIX FOR A LARGE COMPUTER MANUFACTURER

Market growth rate (in constant dollars)

High — Netbooks, handheld computers, and tablet PCs (stars)

Integrated phone/palm device (problem child or question mark)

10

Low — Laptop and personal computers (cash cows)

Mainframe computer (dog)

Market share dominance (share relative to largest competitor): 10x High — 1x Low 0.1x

© Cengage Learning

matrix represents dollar sales of the SBU relative to dollar sales of the company's other SBUs. The portfolio matrix breaks SBUs into four categories:

▸ **STARS:** A **star** is a fast-growing market leader. For example, the iPad is Apple's current star. Star SBUs usually have large profits but need lots of cash to finance rapid growth. The best marketing tactic is to protect existing market share by reinvesting earnings in product improvement, better distribution, more promotion, and production efficiency. Management must capture new users as they enter the market.

▸ **CASH COWS:** A **cash cow** is an SBU that generates more cash than it needs to maintain its market share. It is in a low-growth market, but the product has a dominant market share. Personal computers and laptops are categorized as cash cows in Exhibit 2.3. The basic strategy for a cash cow is to maintain market dominance by being the

© Thinkstock Images/Jupiterimages

price leader and making technological improvements in the product. Managers should resist pressure to extend the basic line unless they can dramatically increase demand. Instead, they should allocate excess cash to the product categories where growth prospects are the greatest. For example, Heinz has two cash cows: ketchup and Weight Watchers frozen dinners.

▸ **PROBLEM CHILDREN:** A problem child, also called a question mark, shows rapid growth but poor profit margins. It has a low market share in a high-growth industry. Problem children need a great deal of cash. Without cash support, they eventually become dogs. The strategy options are to invest heavily to gain better market share, acquire competitors to get the necessary market share, or drop the SBU. Sometimes a firm can reposition the products of the SBU to move them into the star category. Elixir guitar strings, made by W.L. Gore & Associates, maker of Gore-Tex and Glide floss, were originally tested and marketed to Walt Disney theme parks to control puppets. After trial and failure, Gore repositioned and marketed heavily to musicians, who have loved the strings ever since.

▸ **DOGS:** A dog has low growth potential and a small market share. Most dogs eventually leave the marketplace. In the computer manufacturer example, the mainframe computer has become a dog. Other examples include Warner-Lambert's Reef mouthwash and Campbell's Red Kettle soups. The strategy options for dogs are to harvest or divest.

After classifying the company's SBUs in the matrix, the next step is to allocate future resources for each. The four basic strategies are to:

▸ **BUILD:** If an organization has an SBU that it believes has the potential to be a star (probably a problem child at present), building would be an appropriate goal. The organization may decide to give up short-term profits and use its financial resources to achieve this goal. Apple postponed further work on the iPad to pursue the iPhone. The wait paid off when Apple was able to repurpose much of the iOS software and the iPhone's App Store for the iPad, making development less expensive and getting the product into the marketplace more quickly.[8]

▸ **HOLD:** If an SBU is a very successful cash cow, a key goal would surely be to hold or preserve market share so that the organization can take advantage of the very

positive cash flow. Apple plans to add new features, such as built-in projectors, to its Macintosh line to keep its market share growing.[9]

▸ **HARVEST:** This strategy is appropriate for all SBUs except those classified as stars. The basic goal is to increase the short-term cash return without too much concern for the long-run impact. It is especially worthwhile when more cash is needed from a cash cow with long-run prospects that are unfavorable because of a low market growth rate. For instance, Lever Brothers has been harvesting Lifebuoy soap for a number of years with little promotional backing.

▸ **DIVEST:** Getting rid of SBUs with low shares of low-growth markets is often appropriate. Problem children and dogs are most suitable for this strategy. Procter & Gamble dropped Cincaprin, a coated aspirin, because of its low growth potential.

2-3c The General Electric Model

The third model for selecting strategic alternatives was originally developed by General Electric. The dimensions used in this model—market attractiveness and company strength—are richer and more complex than those used in the Boston Consulting Group model but are harder to quantify.

Exhibit 2.4 presents the GE model. The horizontal axis, Business Position, refers to how well positioned the organization is to take

Exhibit 2.4

GENERAL ELECTRIC MODEL

Market Attractiveness	Low Business Position	Med Business Position	High Business Position
High	CAUTIOUSLY INVEST	INVEST/GROW	INVEST/GROW
Med	HARVEST/DIVEST	CAUTIOUSLY INVEST	INVEST/GROW
Low	HARVEST/DIVEST	HARVEST/DIVEST	CAUTIOUSLY INVEST

planning the process of anticipating future events and determining strategies to achieve organizational objectives in the future

marketing planning designing activities relating to marketing objectives and the changing marketing environment

marketing plan a written document that acts as a guidebook of marketing activities for the marketing manager

advantage of market opportunities. Business position answers questions such as: Does the firm have the technology it needs to effectively penetrate the market? Are its financial resources adequate? Can manufacturing costs be held down below those of the competition? Can the firm cope with change? The vertical axis measures the attractiveness of a market, which is expressed both quantitatively and qualitatively. Some attributes of an attractive market are high profitability, rapid growth, a lack of government regulation, consumer insensitivity to a price increase, a lack of competition, and availability of technology. The grid is divided into three overall attractiveness zones for each dimension: high, medium, and low.

Those SBUs (or markets) that have low overall attractiveness (indicated by the red cells in Exhibit 2.4) should be avoided if the organization is not already serving them. If the firm is in these markets, it should either harvest or divest those SBUs. The organization should selectively maintain markets with medium attractiveness (indicated by the yellow cells in Exhibit 2.4). If attractiveness begins to slip, then the organization should withdraw from the market.

Conditions that are highly attractive—an attractive market plus a strong business position (the green cells in Exhibit 2.4)—are the best candidates for investment. For

example, the DVD kiosk company Redbox more than doubled the number of kiosks it operates since 2008 to capitalize on convenient placement of new rentals available to customers. However, to continue its growth, Redbox has invested in digital technology that is further spurring its growth with Smartphones. Currently, the Redbox app allows users to find kiosks nearby and reserve movies, but reports suggest that Redbox is looking to team up with Blockbuster to release a streaming service through the popular app.[10]

2-4 THE MARKETING PLANNING PROCESS

Based on the company's or SBU's overall strategy, marketing managers can create a marketing plan for individual products, brands, lines, or customer groups. Planning is the process of anticipating future events and determining strategies to achieve organizational objectives in the future. **Marketing planning** involves designing activities relating to marketing objectives and the changing marketing environment. Marketing planning is the basis for all marketing strategies and decisions. Issues such as product lines, distribution channels, marketing communications, and pricing are all delineated in the **marketing plan**. The marketing plan is a written document that acts as a guidebook of marketing activities for the marketing manager. In this chapter, you will learn the importance of writing a marketing plan and the types of information contained in a marketing plan.

2-4a Why Write a Marketing Plan?

By specifying objectives and defining the actions required to attain them, you can provide in a marketing plan the basis by which actual and expected performance can be compared. Marketing can be one of the most expensive and complicated business activities, but it is also one of the most important. The written marketing plan provides clearly stated activities that help employees and managers understand and work toward common goals.

Writing a marketing plan allows you to examine the marketing environment in conjunction with the inner workings of the business. Once the marketing plan is written, it serves as a reference point for the success of future activities. Finally, the marketing plan allows the marketing manager to enter the marketplace with an awareness of possibilities and problems.

2-4b Marketing Plan Elements

Marketing plans can be presented in many different ways. Most businesses need a written marketing plan because a marketing plan is large and can be complex. Details about tasks and activity assignments may be lost if communicated orally. Regardless of the way a marketing plan is presented, some elements are common to all marketing plans. Exhibit 2.5 shows these elements, which include defining the business mission, performing a situation analysis, defining objectives, delineating a target market, and establishing components of the marketing mix. Other elements that may be included in a plan are budgets, implementation timetables, required marketing research efforts, or elements of advanced strategic

Exhibit 2.5
ELEMENTS OF A MARKETING PLAN

- Business Mission Statement
- Situation or SWOT Analysis
- Objectives
- Marketing Strategy
  - Target Market Strategy
  - Marketing Mix
    - Product
    - Distribution
    - Promotion
    - Price
- Implementation Evaluation Control

© Cengage Learning

planning. Log in to the CourseMate for MKTG at cengagebrain.com for a marketing planning outline and an example of a marketing plan.

2-4c Writing the Marketing Plan

The creation and implementation of a complete marketing plan will allow the organization to achieve marketing objectives and succeed. However, the marketing plan is only as good as the information it contains and the effort, creativity, and thought that went into its creation. Having a good marketing information system and a wealth of competitive intelligence (covered in Chapter 9) is critical to a thorough and accurate situation analysis. The role of managerial intuition is also important in the creation and selection of marketing strategies. Managers must weigh any information against its accuracy and their own judgment when making a marketing decision.

Note that the overall structure of the marketing plan (Exhibit 2.5) should not be viewed as a series of sequential planning steps. Many of the marketing plan elements are decided on simultaneously and in conjunction with one another. Further, every marketing plan has different content, depending on the organization, its mission, objectives, targets, and marketing mix components. There is not one single correct format for a marketing plan. Many organizations have their own distinctive format or terminology for creating a marketing plan. Every marketing plan should be unique to the firm for which it was created. Remember, however, that although the format and order of presentation should be flexible, the same types of questions and topic areas should be covered in any marketing plan.

2-5 DEFINING THE BUSINESS MISSION

The foundation of any marketing plan is the firm's mission statement, which answers the question "What business are we in?" The way a firm defines its business mission profoundly affects the firm's long-run resource allocation, profitability, and survival. The mission statement is based on a careful analysis of benefits sought by present and potential customers and an analysis of existing and anticipated environmental conditions. The firm's

mission statement
a statement of the firm's business based on a careful analysis of benefits sought by present and potential customers and an analysis of existing and anticipated environmental conditions

mission statement establishes boundaries for all subsequent decisions, objectives, and strategies.

A mission statement should focus on the market or markets the organization is attempting to serve rather than on the good or service offered. Otherwise, a new technology may quickly make the good or service obsolete and the mission statement irrelevant to company functions. Business mission statements that are stated too narrowly suffer from **marketing myopia**—defining a business in terms of goods and services rather than in terms of the benefits customers seek. In this context, *myopia* means narrow, short-term thinking. For example, Frito-Lay defines its mission as being in the snack-food business rather than in the corn chip business. The mission of sports teams is not just to play games but also to serve the interests of the fans.

Alternatively, business missions may be stated too broadly. "To provide products of superior quality and value that improve the lives of the world's consumers" is probably too broad a mission statement for any firm except Procter & Gamble. Care must be taken when stating what business a firm is in. For example, the mission of Ben & Jerry's centers on three important aspects of its ice cream business: (1) Product: "To make, distribute and sell the finest quality all natural ice cream and euphoric concoctions with a continued commitment to incorporating wholesome, natural ingredients and promoting business practices that respect the Earth and the Environment"; (2) Economic: "To operate the Company on a sustainable financial basis of

JUST AS MYOPIA NEGATIVELY AFFECTS HOW PEOPLE SEE, MARKETING MYOPIA NEGATIVELY AFFECTS HOW BUSINESSES SEE THEMSELVES AND THEIR ENVIRONMENT.

profitable growth, increasing value for our stakeholders and expanding opportunities for development and career growth for our employees"; and (3) Social: "To operate the Company in a way that actively recognizes the central role that business plays in society by initiating innovative ways to improve the quality of life locally, nationally, and internationally."[11] By correctly stating the business mission in terms of the benefits that customers seek, the foundation for the marketing plan is set. Many companies are focusing on designing more appropriate mission statements because these statements are frequently displayed on the companies' Web sites.

2-6 CONDUCTING A SITUATION ANALYSIS

Marketers must understand the current and potential environment in which the product or service will be marketed. A situation analysis is sometimes referred to as a **SWOT analysis**—that is, the firm should identify its internal strengths (**S**) and weaknesses (**W**) and also examine external opportunities (**O**) and threats (**T**).

When examining internal strengths and weaknesses, the marketing manager should focus on organizational resources such as production costs, marketing skills, financial resources, company or brand image, employee capabilities, and available technology. For example, Dell's stock has fallen 42 percent since January 2007, so management needs to examine strengths and weaknesses in the company and its competition. Dell has a $6 billion server business (strength), but the shrinking PC market accounts for a significant 24 percent of sales (weakness). Competitors like IBM and Hewlett-Packard (HP) are moving heavily into software and consulting, so to avoid them, Dell might instead consider the $7.1 billion networking equipment market.[12] Another issue to consider in this section of the marketing plan is the historical background of the firm—its sales and profit history.

When examining external opportunities and threats, marketing managers must analyze aspects of the marketing environment. This process is called **environmental scanning**—the collection and interpretation of information about

SALTWATER PEARL: $$$$$

CHINESE FRESHWATER PEARL: $$

forces, events, and relationships in the external environment that may affect the future of the organization or the implementation of the marketing plan. Environmental scanning helps identify market opportunities and threats and provides guidelines for the design of marketing strategy. The six most often studied macroenvironmental forces are social, demographic, economic, technological, political and legal, and competitive. These forces are examined in detail in Chapter 4. PepsiCo has been trying to increase SoBe Lifewater's market share since 2001, but when Coca-Cola purchased **vitamin**water in 2007, urgency skyrocketed. With the help of Tom Silk, a Web-savvy marketer who oversaw the marketing for the *Call of Duty* and *Guitar Hero* video game series, Lifewater has refocused on the market that made SoBe popular: millennials. Understanding youth's love of viral marketing, SoBe tests television ads on YouTube before airing them. To drive sales, SoBe dropped the price per bottle by four cents as competitor **vitamin**water raised prices by four cents. The changes are working. Understanding who buys Lifewater and making marketing changes to address the environment doubled the market share of Lifewater.[13]

2-7 COMPETITIVE ADVANTAGE

Performing a SWOT analysis allows firms to identify their competitive advantage. A competitive advantage is a set of unique features of a company and its products that are perceived by the target market as significant and superior to those of the competition. It is the factor or factors that cause customers to patronize a firm and not the competition. There are three types of competitive advantage: cost, product/service differentiation, and niche.

2-7a Cost Competitive Advantage

Cost leadership can result from obtaining inexpensive raw materials, creating an efficient scale of plant operations, designing products for ease of manufacture, controlling overhead costs, and avoiding marginal customers. For example, saltwater pearls have always sold at a premium price, particularly those classed as "gem" quality. However, a Chinese man has recently flooded the pearl market with freshwater pearls that are gem quality, causing the price of pearls to fall 30 percent. In addition to these high-quality pearls, the company also produces lower-quality, inexpensive pearls for costume jewelry. The traditional Tahitian saltwater pearl producers are losing revenue because of the inexpensive pearls, but they have no choice but to compete in price with the Chinese pearls.[14] Having a **cost competitive advantage** means being the low-cost competitor in an industry while maintaining satisfactory profit margins. Costs can be reduced in a variety of ways:

▸ **EXPERIENCE CURVES:** Experience curves tell us that costs decline at a predictable rate as experience with a product increases. The experience curve effect encompasses a broad range of manufacturing, marketing, and administrative costs. Experience curves reflect learning by doing, technological advances, and economies of scale. Firms like Boeing use historical experience curves as a basis for predicting and setting prices. Experience curves allow management to forecast costs and set prices based on anticipated costs as opposed to current costs.

▸ **EFFICIENT LABOR:** Labor costs can be an important component of total costs in low-skill, labor-intensive industries such as product assembly and apparel manufacturing. Many U.S. publishers and software developers send data entry, design, and formatting tasks to India, where skilled engineers are available at lower overall cost.

▸ **NO-FRILLS GOODS AND SERVICES:** Marketers can lower costs by removing frills and options from a product or service. Southwest Airlines, for example, offers low fares but no seat assignments or meals. Low costs give Southwest a higher load factor and greater economies of scale, which, in turn, mean lower prices.

▸ **GOVERNMENT SUBSIDIES:** Governments can provide grants and interest-free loans to target industries. Such government assistance enabled Japanese semiconductor manufacturers to become global leaders.

▸ **PRODUCT DESIGN:** Cutting-edge design technology can help offset high labor costs. BMW is a world leader in designing cars for ease of manufacture and assembly. Reverse engineering—the process of disassembling a product piece by piece to learn its components and obtain clues as to the manufacturing process—can also mean savings. Reverse engineering a low-cost competitor's product can save research and design costs. Japanese engineers have reversed many products, such as computer chips from Silicon Valley.

▸ **REENGINEERING:** Reengineering entails fundamental rethinking and redesign of business processes to achieve dramatic improvements in critical measures of performance. It often involves reorganizing functional departments, such as sales, engineering, and production, into cross-disciplinary teams.

▸ **PRODUCTION INNOVATIONS:** Production innovations such as new technology and simplified production techniques help lower the average cost of production. Technologies such as computer-aided design (CAD) and computer-aided manufacturing (CAM) and increasingly sophisticated robots help companies such as Boeing, Ford, and General Electric reduce their manufacturing costs.

▸ **NEW METHODS OF SERVICE DELIVERY:** Medical expenses have been substantially lowered by the use of outpatient surgery and walk-in clinics. Online-only magazines deliver great savings, and even some print magazines are exploring ways to go online to save material and shipping costs.

2-7b Product/Service Differentiation Competitive Advantage

Because cost competitive advantages are subject to continual erosion, product/service differentiation tends to provide a longer-lasting competitive advantage. The durability of this strategy tends to make it more attractive to many top managers. A **product/service differentiation competitive advantage** exists when a firm provides something that is unique and valuable to buyers beyond simply offering a lower price than that of the competition. Examples include brand names (Lexus), a strong dealer network (Caterpillar for construction work), product reliability (Maytag appliances), image (Neiman Marcus in retailing), or service (FedEx). Duane Reade recently opened a new luxury outlet on Wall Street, and the drugstore is working to appeal to the masses through excellent service in an upscale space. Not only does the drugstore have a juice bar and sushi, it offers an express salon that analyzes scalps, suggests shampoo, and offers treatments, as well as a full nail bar. Even if customers aren't looking for services, they will still be able to consult a beauty adviser (on hand twenty-four hours a day) and test out most products in the store before purchase. With this level of service, Duane Reade outdoes CVS and other drugstores in the area.[15]

2-7c Niche Competitive Advantage

A **niche competitive advantage** seeks to target and effectively serve a single segment of the market (see Chapter 8). For small companies with limited resources that potentially face giant competitors, niche targeting may be the only viable option. A market segment that has good growth potential but is not crucial to the success of major competitors is a good candidate for developing a niche strategy.

Many companies using a niche strategy serve only a limited geographic market. Buddy Freddys is a very successful restaurant, but it is found only in Plant City, Florida. Migros is the dominant grocery chain in Switzerland. It has no stores outside that small country.

The Chef's Garden, a 225-acre Ohio farm, specializes in growing and shipping rare artisan vegetables directly to its customers. Chefs from all over the world call to order or to request a unique item, which is grown and shipped by The Chef's Garden. The farm provides personal services and specialized premium vegetables that aren't available anywhere else and relies on its customers to supply it with ideas for what they would like to be able to offer in their restaurants. The excellent service and feeling of contribution keep chefs coming back.[16]

2-7d Building Sustainable Competitive Advantage

The key to having a competitive advantage is the ability to sustain that advantage. A **sustainable competitive advantage** is one that cannot be copied by the competition. For example, Netflix, the online movie subscription service, has a steady hold over the movie rental market. No company has come close to the incomparable depth of titles available to be sent directly to homes or streamed online. Blockbuster tried to set up a similar online subscription service tied to new releases, but so far it has not been able to compete with the convenience and selection offered by Netflix. Netflix's fourteen million subscribers have a twenty-eight-day delay on most of the latest movies, but Netflix says that only a couple hundred customers have complained about the delay. Up-and-comer Hulu just released a new subscription service, and Netflix is hoping to maintain its advantage with its iPhone app that lets you carry Netflix in your pocket.[17] In contrast, when Datril was introduced into the pain-reliever market, it was touted as being exactly like Tylenol, only cheaper. Tylenol responded by lowering its price, thus destroying Datril's competitive advantage and ability to remain on the market. In this case, low price was not a sustainable competitive advantage. Without a competitive advantage, target customers don't perceive any reason to patronize an organization instead of its competitors.

The notion of competitive advantage means that a successful firm will stake out a position unique in some manner from its rivals. Imitation by competitors indicates a lack of competitive advantage and almost ensures mediocre performance. Moreover, competitors rarely stand still, so it is not surprising that imitation causes managers to feel trapped in a seemingly endless game of catch-up. They are regularly surprised by the new accomplishments of their rivals.

Rather than copy competitors, companies need to build their own competitive advantages. The sources of tomorrow's competitive advantages are the skills and assets of the organization. Assets include patents, copyrights, locations, equipment, and technology that are superior to those of the competition. Skills are functions such as customer service and promotion that the firm performs better than its competitors. Marketing managers should continually focus the firm's skills and assets on sustaining and creating competitive advantages.

Remember, a sustainable competitive advantage is a function of the speed with which competitors can imitate a leading company's strategy and plans. Imitation requires a competitor to identify the leader's competitive advantage, determine how it is achieved, and then learn how to duplicate it.

2-8 SETTING MARKETING PLAN OBJECTIVES

Before the details of a marketing plan can be developed, objectives for the plan must be stated. Without objectives, there is no basis for measuring the success of marketing plan activities.

A **marketing objective** is a statement of what is to be accomplished through marketing activities. To be useful, stated objectives should be:

▸ **REALISTIC: Managers should develop objectives that have a chance of being met. For example, it may be unrealistic for start-up firms or new products to command dominant market share, given other competitors in the marketplace.**

▸ **MEASURABLE: Managers need to be able to quantitatively measure whether or not an objective has been met. For example, it would be difficult to determine success for an objective that states, "To increase sales of cat food." If the company sells 1 percent more cat food, does that mean the objective was met? Instead, a specific number should be stated, "To increase sales of Purina brand cat food from $300 million to $345 million."**

▸ **TIME SPECIFIC: By what time should the objective be met? "To increase sales of Purina brand cat food between January 1, 2013, and December 31, 2013."**

▸ **COMPARED TO A BENCHMARK: If the objective is to increase sales by 15 percent, it is important to know the baseline against which the objective will be measured. Will it be current sales? Last year's sales? For example, "To increase sales of Purina brand cat food by 15 percent over 2012 sales of $300 million."**

Therefore, a successful marketing objective would include all four elements. For example, a strong marketing objective for Purina might be: "To increase sales of Purina brand cat food by 15 percent, compared to 2012

sales of $300 million, between January 1, 2013, and December 31, 2013."

Objectives must also be consistent with and indicate the priorities of the organization. Specifically, objectives flow from the business mission statement to the rest of the marketing plan.

Carefully specified objectives serve several functions. First, they communicate marketing management philosophies and provide direction for lower-level marketing managers so that marketing efforts are integrated and pointed in a consistent direction. Objectives also serve as motivators by creating something for employees to strive for. When objectives are attainable and challenging, they motivate those charged with achieving the objectives. Additionally, the process of writing specific objectives forces executives to clarify their thinking. Finally, objectives form a basis for control; the effectiveness of a plan can be gauged in light of the stated objectives.

2-9 DESCRIBING THE TARGET MARKET

Marketing strategy involves the activities of selecting and describing one or more target markets and developing and maintaining a marketing mix that will produce mutually satisfying exchanges with target markets.

2-9a Target Market Strategy

A market segment is a group of individuals or organizations who share one or more characteristics. They therefore may have relatively similar product needs. For example, parents of newborn babies need formula, diapers, and special foods.

The target market strategy identifies the market segment or segments on which to focus. This process begins with a **market opportunity analysis (MOA)**—the description and estimation of the size and sales potential of market segments that are of interest to the firm and the assessment of key competitors in these market segments. After the firm describes the market segments, it may target one or more of them. There are three general strategies for selecting target markets.

Target market(s) can be selected by appealing to the entire market with one marketing mix, concentrating on

© aniad/Shutterstock.com

one segment, or appealing to multiple market segments using multiple marketing mixes. The characteristics, advantages, and disadvantages of each strategic option are examined in Chapter 8. Target markets could be eighteen- to twenty-five-year-old females who are interested in fashion (Nintendo DS and Wii game developers), people concerned about sugar and calories in their soft drinks (Diet Pepsi), or parents without the time to potty train their children (Booty Camp classes where kids are potty trained).

Any market segment that is targeted must be fully described. Demographics, psychographics, and buyer behavior should be assessed. Buyer behavior is covered in Chapters 6 and 7. If segments are differentiated by ethnicity, multicultural aspects of the marketing mix should be examined. If the target market is international, it is especially important to describe differences in culture, economic and technological development, and political structure that may affect the marketing plan. Global marketing is covered in more detail in Chapter 5.

2-10 THE MARKETING MIX

The term marketing mix refers to a unique blend of product, place (distribution), promotion, and pricing strategies (often referred to as the four Ps) designed to produce mutually satisfying exchanges with a target market. The marketing manager can control each component of the marketing mix, but the strategies for all four components must be blended to achieve optimal results. Any marketing mix is only as good as its weakest component. For example, the first pump toothpastes were distributed over cosmetics counters and failed. Not until pump toothpastes were distributed the same way as tube toothpastes did the products succeed. The best promotion and the lowest price cannot save a poor product. Similarly, excellent products with poor placing, pricing, or promotion will likely fail.

Successful marketing mixes have been carefully designed to satisfy target markets. At first glance, McDonald's and Wendy's may appear to have roughly identical marketing mixes because they are both in the fast-food hamburger business. However, McDonald's has been most successful at targeting parents with young children for lunchtime meals, whereas Wendy's targets the adult crowd for lunches and dinner. McDonald's has playgrounds, Ronald McDonald the clown, and children's Happy Meals. Wendy's has salad bars, carpeted restaurants, and no playgrounds.

Variations in marketing mixes do not occur by chance. Astute marketing managers devise marketing strategies to gain advantages over competitors and best serve the needs and wants of a particular target market segment. By manipulating elements of the marketing mix, marketing managers can fine-tune the customer offering and achieve competitive success.

2-10a Product Strategies

Of the four Ps, the marketing mix typically starts with the product. The heart of the marketing mix, the starting point, is the product offering and product strategy. It is hard to design a place strategy, decide on a promotion campaign, or set a price without knowing the product to be marketed.

The product includes not only the physical unit but also its package, warranty, after-sale service, brand name, company image, value, and many other factors. A Godiva chocolate has many product elements: the chocolate itself, a fancy gold wrapper, a customer satisfaction guarantee, and the prestige of the Godiva brand name. We buy things not only for what they do (benefits) but also for what they mean to us (status, quality, or reputation).

Products can be tangible goods such as computers, ideas like those offered by a consultant, or services such as medical care. Products should also offer customer value. Product decisions are covered in Chapters 10 and 11, and services marketing is detailed in Chapter 12.

2-10b Place (Distribution) Strategies

Place, or distribution, strategies are concerned with making products available when and where customers want them. Would you rather buy a kiwi fruit at the 24-hour grocery store within walking distance or fly to Australia to pick your own? A part of this P—place—is physical distribution, which involves all the business activities concerned with storing and transporting raw materials or finished products. The goal is to make sure products arrive in usable condition at designated places when needed. Place strategies are covered in Chapters 13 and 14.

2-10c Promotion Strategies

Promotion includes advertising, public relations, sales promotion, and personal selling. Promotion's role in the marketing mix is to bring about mutually satisfying exchanges with target markets by informing, educating, persuading, and reminding them of the benefits of an organization or a product. A good promotion strategy, like using a beloved cartoon character such as SpongeBob SquarePants to sell gummy snacks, can dramatically increase sales. Each element of this P—promotion—is coordinated and managed with the others to create a promotional blend or mix. These integrated marketing communications activities are described in Chapters 15, 16, and 17. Technology-driven and social media aspects of promotional marketing are covered in Chapter 18.

2-10d Pricing Strategies

Price is what a buyer must give up in order to obtain a product. It is often the most flexible of the four Ps—the quickest element to change. Marketers can raise or lower prices more frequently and easily than they can change other marketing mix variables. Price is an important competitive weapon and is very important to the organization because price multiplied by the number of units sold equals total revenue for the firm. Pricing decisions are covered in Chapters 19 and 20.

2-11 FOLLOWING UP ON THE MARKETING PLAN

One of the keys to success overlooked by many businesses is to actively follow up on the marketing plan. The time spent researching, developing, and writing a useful and accurate marketing plan goes to waste if the plan is not used by the organization. One of the best ways to get the most out of a marketing plan is to correctly implement it. Once the first steps to implementation are taken, evaluation and control will help guide the organization to success as laid out by the marketing plan.

2-11a Implementation

Implementation is the process that turns a marketing plan into action assignments and ensures that these assignments are executed in a way that accomplishes the plan's objectives. Implementation activities may involve detailed job assignments, activity descriptions, time lines, budgets, and lots of communication. Implementation requires delegating authority and responsibility, determining a time frame for completing tasks, and allocating resources. Sometimes a strategic plan also requires task force management. A *task force* is a tightly organized unit under the direction of a manager who, usually, has broad authority. A task force is established to accomplish a single goal or mission

THE GAME OF ORGANIZING E-MAIL

E-mail has become a necessity for students and business professionals, as well as an integral part of many personal lives. With so much riding on e-mail, inboxes can overflow, and important e-mails can fall by the wayside. One company is out to change that. Baydin is a software developer that sells Boomerang, a product that allows users to "snooze" e-mails. The user sets the time for the e-mail to reappear in the inbox, and Boomerang moves it into a folder out of the inbox until the specified time. To promote their e-mail management products for Outlook, Baydin also developed *The Email Game*. The game sets a timer for each message and accrues points for decisions made in a timely manner. Baydin guarantees the game will get you through your e-mail 40 percent faster or your money back.

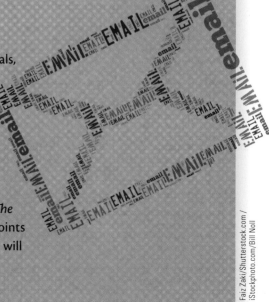

Source: "How to Play the Email Game," *The Email Game*, http://emailgame.baydin.com/index.html (Accessed March 28, 2012).

and thus works against a deadline. AT&T assigned a task force to develop marketing plans that would protect its long-distance market from MCI and Sprint.

Implementing a plan has another dimension: gaining acceptance. New plans mean change, and change creates resistance. One reason people resist change is that they fear they will lose something. For example, when new-product research is taken away from marketing research and given to a new-product department, the director of marketing research will naturally resist this loss of part of his or her domain. Misunderstanding and lack of trust also create opposition to change, but effective communication through open discussion and teamwork can be one way of overcoming resistance to change.

Although implementation is essentially "doing what you said you were going to do," many organizations repeatedly experience failures in strategy implementation. Brilliant marketing plans are doomed to fail if they are not properly implemented. These detailed communications may or may not be part of the written marketing plan. If they are not part of the plan, they should be specified elsewhere as soon as the plan has been communicated. Strong, forward-thinking leadership can overcome resistance to change, even in large, highly integrated companies where change seems very unlikely.

2-11b Evaluation and Control

After a marketing plan is implemented, it should be evaluated. **Evaluation** entails gauging the extent to which marketing objectives have been achieved during the specified time period. Four common reasons for failing to achieve a marketing objective are unrealistic marketing objectives, inappropriate marketing strategies in the plan, poor implementation, and changes in the environment after the objective was specified and the strategy was implemented.

Once a plan is chosen and implemented, its effectiveness must be monitored. **Control** provides the mechanisms for evaluating marketing results in light of the plan's objectives and for correcting actions that do not help the organization reach those objectives within budget guidelines. Firms need to establish formal and informal control programs to make the entire operation more efficient.

Perhaps the broadest control device available to marketing managers is the **marketing audit**—a thorough, systematic, periodic evaluation of the objectives, strategies, structure, and performance of the marketing

organization. A marketing audit helps management allocate marketing resources efficiently.

Although the main purpose of the marketing audit is to develop a full profile of the organization's marketing effort and to provide a basis for developing and revising the marketing plan, it is also an excellent way to improve communication and raise the level of marketing consciousness within the organization. It is a useful vehicle for selling the philosophy and techniques of strategic marketing to other members of the organization.

2-11c Postaudit Tasks

After the audit has been completed, three tasks remain. First, the audit should profile existing weaknesses and inhibiting factors, as well as the firm's strengths and the new opportunities available to it. Recommendations have to be

evaluation gauging the extent to which the marketing objectives have been achieved during the specified time period

control provides the mechanisms for evaluating marketing results in light of the plan's objectives and for correcting actions that do not help the organization reach those objectives within budget guidelines

marketing audit a thorough, systematic, periodic evaluation of the objectives, strategies, structure, and performance of the marketing organization

FOUR CHARACTERISTICS OF A MARKETING AUDIT:

▸ **COMPREHENSIVE:** The marketing audit covers all the major marketing issues facing an organization—not just trouble spots.

▸ **SYSTEMATIC:** The marketing audit takes place in an orderly sequence and covers the organization's marketing environment, internal marketing system, and specific marketing activities. The diagnosis is followed by an action plan with both short-run and long-run proposals for improving overall marketing effectiveness.

▸ **INDEPENDENT:** The marketing audit is normally conducted by an inside or outside party that is independent enough to have top management's confidence and has the ability to be objective.

▸ **PERIODIC:** The marketing audit should be carried out on a regular schedule instead of only in a crisis. Whether it seems successful or is in deep trouble, any organization can benefit greatly from such an audit.

judged and prioritized so that those with the potential to contribute most to improved marketing performance can be implemented first. The usefulness of the data also depends on the auditor's skill in interpreting and presenting the data so decision makers can quickly grasp the major points.

The second task is to ensure that the role of the audit has been clearly communicated. It is unlikely that the suggestions will require radical change in the way the firm operates. The audit's main role is to address the question "Where are we now?" and to suggest ways to improve what the firm already does.

The final postaudit task is to make someone accountable for implementing recommendations. All too often, reports are presented, applauded, and filed away to gather dust. The person made accountable should be someone who is committed to the project and who has the managerial power to make things happen.

2-12 EFFECTIVE STRATEGIC PLANNING

Effective strategic planning requires continual attention, creativity, and management commitment. Strategic planning should not be an annual exercise in which managers go through the motions and forget about strategic planning until the next year. It should be an ongoing process because the environment is continually changing and the firm's resources and capabilities are continually evolving.

Sound strategic planning is based on creativity. Managers should challenge assumptions about the firm and the environment and establish new strategies. For example, major oil companies developed the concept of the gasoline service station in an age when cars needed frequent and rather elaborate servicing. These major companies held on to the full-service approach, but independents were quick to respond to new realities and moved to lower-cost self-service and convenience store operations. Major companies took several decades to catch up.

Perhaps the most critical element in successful strategic planning is top management's support and participation. For example, when Michael Anthony was CEO of Brookstone Inc. he and the Brookstone buying team earned hundreds of thousands of frequent-flyer miles searching the world for manufacturers and inventors of unique products that could be carried in Brookstone's retail stores and catalogs and on its Web site. Anthony co-developed some of these products and also was active in remodeling efforts for Brookstone's 250 permanent and seasonal stores.

© iStockphoto.com/Niko Guido

STUDY TOOLS 2

LOCATED AT BACK OF THE TEXTBOOK

☐ *Rip out Chapter Review Card*

LOCATED AT WWW.CENGAGE.COM/LOGIN

☐ *Review Key Terms Flashcards (print or online)*

☐ *Download audio and visual summaries to review on the go*

☐ *Complete both Practice Quizzes to prepare for tests*

☐ *Play "Beat the Clock" and "Quizbowl" to master concepts*

☐ *Complete "Crossword Puzzle" to review key terms*

☐ *Watch Video on "The Nederlander Organization" for a real company example*

3-1 THE CONCEPT OF ETHICAL BEHAVIOR

It has been said that ethics is something everyone likes to talk about but nobody can define. Others have suggested that defining ethics is like trying to nail Jello to the wall. You begin to think that you understand it, but that's when it starts squirting out between your fingers.

> If you have ever resented a line-cutter, then you understand ethics and have applied ethical standards in life.

ethics the moral principles or values that generally govern the conduct of an individual or a group

Ethics refers to the moral principles or values that generally govern the conduct of an individual or a group. Ethics also can be viewed as the standard of behavior by which conduct is judged. Standards that are legal may not always be ethical, and vice versa. Laws are the values and standards enforceable by the courts. Ethics, then, consists of personal moral principles. For example, there is no legal statute that makes it a crime for someone to "cut in line." Yet, if someone doesn't want to wait in line and cuts to the front, it often makes others very angry.

If you have ever resented a line-cutter, then you understand ethics and have applied ethical standards in life. Waiting your turn in line is a social expectation that exists because lines ensure order and allocate the space and time needed to complete transactions. Waiting your turn is an expected but unwritten behavior that plays a critical role in an orderly society.[1]

So it is with ethics. Ethics consists of those unwritten rules we have developed for our interactions with one another. These unwritten rules govern us when we are sharing resources or honoring contracts. "Waiting your turn" is a higher standard than the laws that are passed to maintain order. Those laws apply when physical force or threats are used to push to the front of the line. Assault, battery, and threats are forms of criminal conduct for which the offender can be prosecuted. But the law does not apply to the stealthy line-cutter who simply sneaks to the front, perhaps using a friend and a conversation as a decoy. No laws are broken, but the notions of fairness and justice are offended by one individual putting himself or herself above others and taking advantage of others' time and position.

Ethical questions range from practical, narrowly defined issues, such as a businessperson's obligation to be honest with customers, to broader social and philosophical questions, such as whether a company is responsible for preserving the environment and protecting employee rights. Many ethical conflicts develop from conflicts between the differing interests of company owners and their workers, customers, and surrounding community. Managers must balance the ideal against the practical—that

Chapter 3

Ethics and Social Responsibility

Learning Outcomes

3-1 *Explain the concept of ethical behavior* 32–34

3-2 *Describe ethical behavior in business* 34–37

3-3 *Discuss corporate social responsibility* 37–41

3-4 *Explain cause-related marketing* 41

After you finish this chapter go to
p41 *for* **STUDY TOOLS** - - - - - ->

© iStockphoto.com / Kenneth C. Zirkel

is, the need to produce a reasonable profit for the company's shareholders against honesty in business practices and concern for environmental and social issues.

3-2 ETHICAL BEHAVIOR IN BUSINESS

Morals are the rules people develop as a result of cultural values and norms. Culture is a socializing force that dictates what is right and wrong. Moral standards may also reflect the laws and regulations that affect social and economic behavior. Thus, morals can be considered a foundation of ethical behavior.

Morals are usually characterized as good or bad. "Good" and "bad" have many different connotations. One such connotation is "effective" and "ineffective." A good salesperson makes or exceeds the assigned quota. If the salesperson sells a new stereo or television set to a disadvantaged consumer—knowing full well that the person can't keep up the monthly payments—is that still a good salesperson? What if the sale enables the salesperson to exceed his or her quota?

"Good" and "bad" can also refer to "conforming" and "deviant" behaviors. A doctor who runs large ads offering discounts on open-heart surgery would be considered bad, or unprofessional, because he or she is not conforming to the norms of the medical profession. "Bad" and "good" also express the distinction between criminal and law-abiding behavior. And finally, different religions

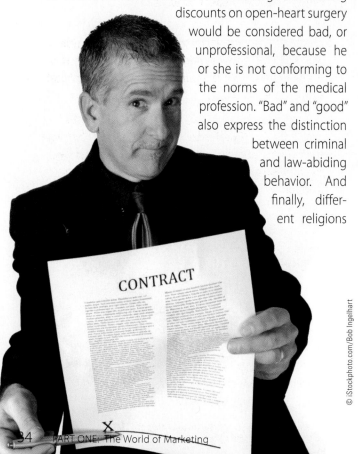

© iStockphoto.com/Bob Ingelhart

define "good" and "bad" in markedly different ways. A Muslim who eats pork would be considered bad, as would a fundamentalist Christian who drinks whiskey. Religion is just one of the many factors that affect a businessperson's ethics.

3-2a Morality and Business Ethics

Today's business ethics actually consist of a subset of major life values learned since birth. The values businesspeople use to make decisions have been acquired through family, educational, and religious institutions.

Ethical values are situation specific and time oriented. Everyone must have an ethical base that applies to conduct in the business world and in personal life. One approach to developing a personal set of ethics is to examine the consequences of a particular act. Who is helped or hurt? How long do the consequences last? What actions produce the greatest good for the greatest number of people? A second approach stresses the importance of rules. Rules come in the form of customs, laws, professional standards, and common sense. "Always treat others as you would like to be treated" is an example of a rule.

Another approach emphasizes the development of moral character within individuals. Ethical development can be thought of as having three levels:[2]

▸ **Preconventional morality, the most basic level, is childlike. It is calculating, self-centered, and even selfish, based on what will be immediately punished or rewarded. Fortunately, most businesspeople have progressed beyond the self-centered and manipulative actions of preconventional morality.**

▸ **Conventional morality moves from an egocentric viewpoint toward the expectations of society. Loyalty and obedience to the organization (or society) become paramount. A marketing decision maker would be concerned only with whether the proposed action is legal and how it will be viewed by others.**

▸ **Postconventional morality represents the morality of the mature adult. At this level, people are less concerned about how others might see them and more concerned about how they see and judge themselves over the long run. A marketing decision maker who has attained a postconventional level of morality might ask, "Even though it is legal and will increase company profits, is it right in the long run? Might it do more harm than good in the end?"**

recover or reactivate.

reactivate with twice the power. regenerist

OLAY

Olay Regenerist transforms tired skin into skin that looks beautifully regenerated. What better way to reactivate your skin. And your life. Without the drastic measures.

OLAY
love the skin you're in™

Some beauty companies sell products using exaggerated language, claiming their creams or powders hide lack of sleep or erase age lines.

Image courtesy of The Advertising Archives

© iStockphoto.com/Bill Noll

3-2b Ethical Decision Making

There is rarely a cut-and-dried answer to ethical questions. Studies show that the following factors tend to influence ethical decision making and judgments:[3]

▸▸ **EXTENT OF ETHICAL PROBLEMS WITHIN THE ORGANIZATION:** Marketing professionals who perceive fewer ethical problems in their organizations tend to disapprove more strongly of "unethical" or questionable practices than those who perceive more ethical problems. Apparently, the healthier the ethical environment, the more likely it is that marketers will take a strong stand against questionable practices.

▸▸ **TOP MANAGEMENT'S ACTIONS ON ETHICS:** Top managers can influence the behavior of marketing professionals by encouraging ethical behavior and discouraging unethical behavior. Researchers found that when top managers develop a strong ethical culture, there is reduced pressure to perform unethical acts, fewer unethical acts are performed, and unethical behavior is reported more frequently.[4]

▸▸ **POTENTIAL MAGNITUDE OF THE CONSEQUENCES:** The greater the harm done to victims, the more likely it is that marketing professionals will recognize a problem as unethical.

▸▸ **SOCIAL CONSENSUS:** The greater the degree of agreement among managerial peers that an action is harmful, the more likely it is that marketers will recognize a problem as unethical. Research found that a strong ethical culture among coworkers decreases observations of ethical misconduct. In companies with strong ethical cultures, 8 percent of employees observed misconduct, compared with 31 percent in companies with weaker cultures.[5]

▸▸ **PROBABILITY OF A HARMFUL OUTCOME:** The greater the likelihood that an action will result in a harmful outcome, the more likely it is that marketers will recognize a problem as unethical.

▸▸ **LENGTH OF TIME BETWEEN THE DECISION AND THE ONSET OF CONSEQUENCES:** The shorter the length of time between the action and the onset of negative consequences, the more likely it is that marketers will perceive a problem as unethical.

FTC: ETHICAL MARKETING POLICE

The Federal Trade Commission (FTC) monitors unsubstantiated marketing claims by companies that may be misleading and **ethically questionable**. For example, product labels are not allowed to make medical or health claims if they are not backed by specific types of studies. Nivea's Silhouette skin cream claimed to reduce customer body size with regular use, and the company paid for ads to appear at the top of Google searches for "stomach fat" and "thin waist." The Federal Trade Commission fined Nivea $900,000 for making the weight-loss claims and has prohibited the company from making further claims on other products.

Source: Kristi Ellis, "FTC Prohibits Nivea's Claims," *Women's Wear Daily*, June 30, 2011.

FOLLOWING A SET OF ETHICAL GUIDELINES...WILL IMPROVE THE CHANCES THAT A DECISION WILL BE ETHICAL.

» **NUMBER OF PEOPLE TO BE AFFECTED:** The greater the number of persons affected by a negative outcome, the more likely it is that marketers will recognize a problem as unethical.

As you can see, many factors determine the nature of an ethical decision.

3-2c Ethical Guidelines

Many organizations have become more interested in ethical issues. One sign of this interest is the increase in the number of large companies that appoint ethics officers—from virtually none several years ago to almost 33 percent of large corporations today. In addition, many companies of various sizes have developed a **code of ethics** as a guideline to help marketing managers and other employees make better decisions. Creating ethics guidelines has several advantages:

» **The guidelines help employees identify what their firm recognizes as acceptable business practices.**

» **A code of ethics can be an effective internal control on behavior, which is more desirable than external controls such as government regulation.**

» **A written code helps employees avoid confusion when determining whether their decisions are ethical.**

» **The process of formulating the code of ethics facilitates discussion among employees about what is right and wrong and ultimately leads to better decisions.**

PepsiCo, like virtually all major corporations, has a code of ethics, sometimes referred to as a "code of conduct." PepsiCo has a single code of conduct for Pepsi and all of its subsidiaries around the world. Major topics include respect for employees, global relations, health and safety, the environment, and a number of other factors.

Businesses, however, must be careful not to make their code of ethics too vague or too detailed. Codes that are too vague give little or no guidance to employees in their day-to-day activities. Codes that are too detailed encourage employees to substitute rules for judgment. For instance, if

employees are involved in questionable behavior, they may use the absence of a written rule as a reason to continue behaving that way, even though their conscience may be telling them to stop. Following a set of ethical guidelines will not guarantee the "rightness" of a decision, but it will improve the chances that the decision will be ethical.

Although many companies have issued policies on ethical behavior, marketing managers must still put the policies into effect. They must address the classic "matter of degree" issue. For example, marketing researchers often resort to deception to obtain unbiased answers to their research questions. Asking for a few minutes of a respondent's time is dishonest if the researcher knows the interview will last forty-five minutes. Unless there are examples of ethical and unethical behavior relating to each item in the code, an employee may not apply a certain item to the appropriate situation. Moreover, top management must stress to all employees the importance of adhering to the company's code of ethics. Without an appropriately detailed code of ethics and top management's support, creating ethical guidelines becomes an empty exercise.

Ethics training is an effective way to help employees put good ethics into practice. Because of various scandals, such as Bernard Madoff's financial trickery that cost investors billions, more and more companies are offering ethics training to their employees. Today, about 70 percent of all large employers (over 500 employees) provide ethics training.[6] Simply giving employees a long list of "dos and don'ts" is a start, but it doesn't really help employees navigate the gray areas or adapt to a changing world market. Walmart has switched from simply listing "dos and don'ts" for its employees to a value-based culture. This involves educating employees in all the cultural values that Walmart stands for and trusting them to do the right thing based on that knowledge.[7]

Do ethics training programs work? The National Business Ethics survey (NBES) found that in 2011, misconduct witnessed by U.S. workers was the lowest it has ever been and that reporting of violations was at an all-time high. However, the number of employees who said they had felt pressure to commit an ethics violation—to cut corners or worse—rose from 8 to 13 percent in 2011.[8] The NBES suggests that working with employees who avidly use social networks may be the next big step in ethics training. The survey found that despite a tendency to be tolerant of questionable activities, most social network users are more likely to report violations than non-social media users. Social network users are also more likely to post positive statements about coworkers and employers.[9]

3-2d Ethics in Other Countries

Studies suggest that ethical beliefs vary little from culture to culture. Certain practices, however, such as the use of illegal payments and bribes, are far more acceptable in some places than in others, though increasingly enforced laws are making the practice less accepted. One such law, the **Foreign Corrupt Practices Act (FCPA)**, was enacted because Congress was concerned about U.S. corporations' use of illegal payments and bribes in international business dealings. This act prohibits U.S. corporations from making illegal payments to public officials of foreign governments to obtain business rights or to enhance their business dealings in those countries. The act has been criticized for putting U.S. businesses at a competitive disadvantage. Many contend that bribery is an unpleasant but necessary part of international business, especially in countries such as China, where business gift giving is widely accepted and expected. But, as prosecutions under the FCPA have increased worldwide, some countries are implementing their own anti-bribery laws. For example, even though China is among the three countries with the most international corruption cases prosecuted under

© bloomua/Shutterstock.com

My job is awesome! 👍

the FCPA, the country is working to develop its own anti-bribery laws. In 2010, Chinese courts sentenced four employees of Rio Tinto, a mining company with headquarters in London, to prison for taking bribes.[10]

3-3 CORPORATE SOCIAL RESPONSIBILITY

Corporate social responsibility (CSR) is a business's concern for society's welfare. This concern is demonstrated by managers who consider both the long-range best interests of the company and the company's relationship to the society within which it operates.

CSR can be a divisive issue. Some analysts believe that a business should focus on making a profit and leave social and environmental problems to nonprofit organizations and government. Economist Milton Friedman believed that the free market, and not companies, should decide what is best for the world.[11] Friedman argued that when business executives spend more money than necessary—to purchase delivery vehicles with hybrid engines, pay higher wages in developing countries, or even donate company funds to charity—they are spending shareholders' money to further their own agendas. It would be better to pay dividends and let the shareholders give the money away if they choose.

On the other hand, CSR has an increasing number of supporters based on several compelling factors. One is that it is simply the right thing to do. Some societal problems, such as pollution and poverty-level wages have been brought about by corporations' actions; it is the responsibility of business to right these wrongs. Businesses also have the resources, so businesses should be given the chance to solve social problems. For example, businesses can provide a fair work environment, safe products, and informative advertising.

Another, more pragmatic, reason for being socially responsible is that if businesses don't act responsibly, then government will create new regulations and perhaps levy fines against corporations.

Finally, social responsibility can be a profitable undertaking. Smart companies can prosper and build value by tackling global problems. Reebok is developing an ultra-inexpensive sneaker to sell in India as a way to help the incredibly poor move from bare feet or flip-flops to sneakers. While the company may not turn much profit on the actual sales of the sneakers, it is hoping to increase brand awareness and goodwill for the company.[12]

Total CSR has four components: economic, legal, ethical, and philanthropic.[13] The **pyramid of corporate social responsibility**, as shown in Exhibit 3.1, portrays economic performance as the foundation for the other three responsibilities. At the same time that it pursues profits (economic responsibility), however, a business is expected to obey the law (legal responsibility); to do what is right, just, and fair (ethical responsibility); and to be a good corporate citizen (philanthropic responsibility). These four components are distinct but together constitute the whole. Still, if the company doesn't make a profit, then the other three responsibilities are moot.

3-3a Sustainability

The newest theory in social responsibility is called **sustainability**. This refers to the idea that socially responsible companies will outperform their peers by focusing

Exhibit 3.1

PYRAMID OF CORPORATE SOCIAL RESPONSIBILITY

Philanthropic responsibilities
Be a good corporate citizen.
Contribute resources to the community; improve the quality of life.

Ethical responsibilities
Be ethical.
Do what is right, just, and fair. Avoid harm.

Legal responsibilities
Obey the law.
Law is society's codification of right and wrong. Play by the rules of the game.

Economic responsibilities
Be profitable.
Profit is the foundation on which all other responsibilities rest.

© Cengage Learning

PATAGONIA PUSHING AWAY SALES?

In the face of Black Friday ads with door-buster events and low, low prices, Patagonia's common-sense full-page ad that ran in the *New York Times* raised a few eyebrows. The ad pictured a Patagonia R2 jacket and said in large capital letters, **"Don't Buy This Jacket."** Despite appearances, the company was not trying to drive away sales. Rather, it was encouraging customers to think carefully about purchases. The full copy of the ad revealed how much of an environmental footprint that R2 jacket left (135 liters of water and 20 pounds of CO_2) and asked customers to be aware of the environmental price of each purchase they make. Patagonia wants to create highly useful, functional, long-lasting items and to encourage consumers to purchase with the same high standards.

Source: Marc Gunther, "Patagonia's Conscientious Response to Black Friday Consumer Madness," *GreenBiz.com*, November 28, 2011, www.greenbiz.com/blog/2011/11/28/patagonias-conscientious-response-black-friday-consumer-madness (Accessed February 29, 2012).

© Olga Danylenko/Shutterstock.com

on the world's social problems and viewing them as opportunities to build profits and help the world at the same time. The movement has enough momentum that many companies are hiring chief sustainability officers (CSOs) to ensure that the company saves energy, meets standards, and qualifies for federal stimulus money.[14]

When an organization focuses on sustainability, it is acting with long-term consequences in mind and managing its business in such a way that its processes or overall state can be maintained indefinitely. A company that believes in sustainability will integrate long-term economic, environmental, and social factors into its business strategies while maintaining its competitiveness and brand reputation. To do so, a company must have effective planning for long-run economic growth. This requires focusing on product and service innovation and building customer loyalty. It also means having the highest ethical standards and a meaningful code of conduct. Sustainability also demands that human resources be managed in a way that maintains workforce capabilities and employee satisfaction. Some companies that excel in their sustainability philosophies are Adidas, BMW, Kingfisher, Nokia, and Unilever.[15]

Sustainability is not simply "green marketing," though environmental sustainability is an important component of the sustainability philosophy. An environmentally sustainable process contributes to keeping the environment healthy by using renewable resources and by avoiding actions that depreciate the environment.

3-3b Growth of Social Responsibility

Social responsibility of businesses is growing around the world. A recent study of social responsibility in selected countries asked the following: "Does your company consider social responsibility factors when making business decisions?" The percentage of firms that said yes in each country was as follows: Brazil, 62 percent; Canada, 54 percent; Australia, 52 percent; the United States, 47 percent; India, 38 percent; China, 35 percent; and Mexico, 26 percent.[16] Another survey found that companies around the globe are coming

under increasing pressure from governments, advocacy groups, investors, prospective employees, employees, and consumers to make their organizations more socially responsible. In turn, firms are seeing social responsibility as an opportunity. Eighty-seven percent of the respondents believed that social responsibility can aid in improving operational efficiency, and 69 percent felt that it will lead to new revenue opportunities.[17]

UNITED NATIONS GLOBAL COMPACT One way that U.S. firms can do more is by joining the United Nations Global Compact (UNGC). The UNGC, the world's largest global corporate citizenship initiative, has seen its ranks swell over the past few years. In 2001—the first full year after its launch—just sixty-seven companies joined, agreeing to abide by ten principles covering, among other

Ben & Jerry's fun flavors are paired with a commitment to social responsibility that gives the company a highly unique selling point.

things, human rights, labor practices, and the environment. In its tenth-anniversary Annual Review, the UNGC boasts more than 8,000 participants in 135 countries.[18]

Firms realize that CSR isn't easy or quick. It doesn't work without a long-term strategy, effort, and coordination throughout the enterprise. It doesn't always come cheap, either. And the payoff, both to society and to the business itself, isn't always immediate. Businesses say they want to be responsible citizens, but that's often not their only reason for taking action. In a recent survey, the UNGC asked members why they had joined. "Networking opportunities" was the second most popular reason; "addressing humanitarian concerns" was third. The first was to "increase trust in the company."[19]

3-3c Green Marketing

An outgrowth of the social responsibility movement is green marketing. **Green marketing** is the development and marketing of products designed to minimize negative effects on the physical environment or to improve the environment.[20] A study by PricewaterhouseCoopers states that in twenty-five years the earth will run out of raw materials, assuming the top 500 global companies grow at 4 to 5 percent annually.[21]

Not only can a company aid the environment through green marketing, but it can often help its bottom line as well. Environmentally aware consumers tend to earn more and are willing to pay more for green products. However, only a very small percentage of customers make their buying decisions based primarily on the environmentally friendly qualities of a product.[22] Also, marketers may have to educate the consumer about the green product if its environmental benefit is not readily apparent. To make the sale, the green marketer may even use a traditional, nongreen benefit. For example, General Electric's energy-efficient CFL floodlights are better for the environment than incandescent lightbulbs. However, the promotion theme is "Long life for hard to reach places." GE is selling convenience because the floodlight doesn't need to be replaced as often.[23]

Some green products have practical consumer benefits that are readily apparent to consumers. A few examples are energy-efficient appliances (cut electric bills), heat-reflective windows (cut air-conditioning costs), and organic foods (no pesticides poisoning the food or planet). Preserve toothbrushes have handles made from recycled yogurt cups and come in mail-back packs. Once the used toothbrushes are returned to the company, Preserve makes them into picnic tables![24]

BOURJOIS
PARIS
www.bourjois.co.uk

FORMULA
98.8%
OF NATURAL ORIGIN

ECO CERT
ORGANIC COSMETIC

CHLOROPHYLL FROM PLANTS
BRINGS OXYGEN & FILTERS POLLUTION

Foundation Bio DETOX ORGANIC
Pure, fresh and even complexion
DETOXIFY YOUR SKIN!

Model is wearing Foundation Bio Detox Organic #51 and concealer Bio Detox Organic #02

Bourjois advertises a natural makeup that filters pollution to detoxify skin.

Image courtesy of The Advertising Archives

cause-related marketing the cooperative marketing efforts between a for-profit firm and a nonprofit organization

Recent surveys have found that consumers and many firms are still not motivated by the green movement. One survey of 1,500 consumers found that while 75 percent said that buying energy-efficient products is important to them, less than half have bought a green electronic product. Thirty-five percent said they are unwilling to pay any premium for green products.[25] On the business side, a separate survey of 270 corporate communications professionals found that 43 percent expect to increase their marketing of their sustainability programs. However, only 36 percent said that their businesses embraced recycling, and only 20 percent were actively pursuing more efficient electric energy usage.[26]

3-4 CAUSE-RELATED MARKETING

A sometimes controversial subset of social responsibility is cause-related marketing. Sometimes referred to as simply "cause marketing," it is the cooperative efforts of a for-profit firm and a nonprofit organization for mutual benefit. Any marketing effort for social or other charitable causes can be referred to as cause-related marketing.

Cause marketing differs from corporate giving (philanthropy), as the latter generally involves a specific donation that is tax deductible, whereas cause marketing is a marketing relationship not based on a straight donation.

Cause-related marketing is very popular and is estimated to generate about $7 billion a year in revenue. It creates good public relations for the firm and will often stimulate sales of the brand. Nevertheless, the huge growth of cause-related marketing can lead to a case of consumer cause fatigue. Researchers have found that businesses need to guard against being perceived as cause exploitative, or using a cause simply to sell more of a product.[27]

Examples of cause-related marketing used by large companies are abundant. Arby's asked customers for a $1 donation to help Big Brothers Big Sisters. In turn, the customer received a coupon valued at a dollar. Whirlpool donated a range and refrigerator to every home built by Habitat for Humanity for a year. However, companies also participate on a smaller, more local scale. For example, Nantucket Bookworks, an independent bookstore in Nantucket, Massachusetts, ran "Love Month" in February 2012. Throughout the month, the bookstore donated 10 percent of its sales to a nonprofit pulled from a hat each day. The twenty-nine participating nonprofits promoted the event through their mailing lists. The extra word of mouth and advertising benefited the store by increasing sales during a traditionally slow month and showing the store's dedication to community.[28]

STUDY TOOLS 3

LOCATED AT BACK OF THE TEXTBOOK
- ☐ *Rip out Chapter Review Card*

LOCATED AT WWW.CENGAGE.COM/LOGIN
- ☐ *Review Key Terms Flashcards (print or online)*
- ☐ *Download audio and visual summaries to review on the go*
- ☐ *Complete both Practice Quizzes to prepare for tests*
- ☐ *Play "Beat the Clock" and "Quizbowl" to master concepts*
- ☐ *Complete "Crossword Puzzle" to review key terms*
- ☐ *Watch Video on "Zappos" for a real company example*

4-1 THE EXTERNAL MARKETING ENVIRONMENT

Perhaps the most important decisions a marketing manager must make relate to the creation of the marketing mix. Recall from Chapters 1 and 2 that a marketing mix is the unique combination of product, place (distribution), promotion, and price strategies. The marketing mix is, of course, under the firm's control and is designed to appeal to a specific group of potential buyers, or target market. A **target market** is a group of people or organizations for which an organization designs, implements, and maintains a marketing mix intended to meet the need of that group, resulting in mutually satisfying exchanges.

⌐Although managers can control the marketing mix, they cannot control elements in the external environment.⌐

target market a group of people or organizations for which an organization designs, implements, and maintains a marketing mix intended to meet the need of that group, resulting in mutually satisfying exchanges

Managers must alter the marketing mix because of changes in the environment in which consumers live, work, and make purchasing decisions. Also, as markets mature, some new consumers become part of the target market; others drop out. Those who remain may have different tastes, needs, incomes, lifestyles, and buying habits than the original target consumers. Technology, and the resulting change in buying habits, meant that consumers no longer have those "Kodak Moments" when taking pictures of a birthday party or an exceptional sunset. Digital photography has sent thirty-five-millimeter film the way of the horse and buggy. Unfortunately, shifting technology ultimately led to the bankruptcy of Eastman Kodak.

Although managers can control the marketing mix, they cannot control elements in the external environment that continually mold and reshape the target market. Controllable and uncontrollable variables affect the target market, whether it consists of consumers or business purchasers. The uncontrollable elements in the center of the environment continually evolve and create changes in the target market. In contrast, managers can shape and reshape the marketing mix to influence the target market. That is, managers react to changes in the external environment and attempt to create a more effective marketing mix.

Chapter **4**

The Marketing Environment

© iStockphoto.com/ Ugurhan Betin

Learning Outcomes

After you finish this chapter go to
p57 *for* **STUDY TOOLS** - - - - - - - >

This ad targets upwardly mobile customers by suggesting that owning the Baby Phat product offers upward mobility and a reward for hard work.

Image courtesy of The Advertising Archives

4-1a **Understanding the External Environment**

Unless marketing managers understand the external environment, the firm cannot intelligently plan for the future. Thus, many organizations assemble a team of specialists to continually collect and evaluate environmental information, a process called environmental scanning. The goal in gathering the environmental data is to identify future market opportunities and threats.

4-1b **Environmental Management**

No single business is large or powerful enough to create major change in the external environment. Thus, marketing managers are basically adapters rather than agents of change. For example, despite the huge size of firms like General Electric, Walmart, Apple, and Caterpillar, they don't control social change, demographics, or other factors in the external environment.

Just because a firm cannot fully control the external environment, however, doesn't mean that it is helpless. Sometimes a firm can influence external events. For example, extensive lobbying by FedEx has enabled it to acquire virtually all the Japanese routes it has sought. When a company implements strategies that attempt to shape the external environment within which it operates, it is engaging in **environmental management**.

The factors within the external environment that are important to marketing managers can be classified as social, demographic, economic, technological, political and legal, and competitive.

4-2 SOCIAL FACTORS

Social change is perhaps the most difficult external variable for marketing managers to forecast, influence, or integrate into marketing plans. Social factors include our attitudes, values, and lifestyles. Social factors influence the products people buy; the prices paid for products; the effectiveness of specific promotions; and how, where, and when people expect to purchase products.

4-2a **American Values**

A *value* is a strongly held and enduring belief. During the United States' first 200 years, four basic values strongly influenced attitudes and lifestyles:

- **SELF-SUFFICIENCY:** Every person should stand on his or her own two feet.

- **UPWARD MOBILITY:** Success would come to anyone who got an education, worked hard, and played by the rules.

- **WORK ETHIC:** Hard work, dedication to family, and frugality were moral and right.

- **CONFORMITY:** No one should expect to be treated differently from everybody else.

These core values still hold for a majority of Americans today. A person's values are key determinants of what is important and not important, what actions to take or not to take, and how one behaves in social situations.

People typically form values through interaction with family, friends, and other influencers such as teachers, religious leaders, and politicians. The changing environment can also play a key role in shaping one's values.

Values influence our buying habits. Today's consumers are demanding, inquisitive, and discriminating. No longer willing to tolerate products that break down, they are insisting on high-quality goods that save time, energy, and often calories. U.S. consumers rank the characteristics of product quality as (1) reliability, (2) durability, (3) easy maintenance, (4) ease of use, (5) a trusted brand name, and (6) a low price. Shoppers are also concerned about nutrition and want to know what's in their food, and many have environmental concerns.

The Natural Marketing Institute has marked some burgeoning **trends** that are apparently becoming American **values.** Some of them are:

▶▶ **Getting off the grid: Consumers are pursuing ways to become more self-sufficient, including household-generated energy, water conservation and purification, and private gardens.**

▶▶ **Meaningful green: Green initiatives must be distinctive, memorable, and measurable to have an impact on environmental, social, and economic dimensions.**

▶▶ **EcoTechMed: New economic realities are motivating many to take greater steps toward proactive health care rather than sick care and to take greater responsibility for their own health and wellness.**

Source: Partial list of trends projected by the Natural Marketing Institute, "Healthy, Green, Simple—Trends to Watch in the Next Ten Years," *Quirk's Marketing Research Review*, May 2010, 6.

4-2b The Growth of Component Lifestyles

People in the United States today are piecing together **component lifestyles**. A lifestyle is a mode of living; it is the way people decide to live their lives. With component lifestyles, people are choosing products and services that meet diverse needs and interests rather than conforming to traditional stereotypes.

In the past, a person's profession—for instance, banker—defined his or her lifestyle. Today, a person can be a banker and also a gourmet, fitness enthusiast, dedicated single parent, and Internet guru. Each of these lifestyles is associated with different goods and services and represents a target audience. Component lifestyles increase the complexity of consumers' buying habits. Each consumer's unique lifestyle can require a different marketing mix.

component lifestyles the practice of choosing goods and services that meet one's diverse needs and interests rather than conforming to a single, traditional lifestyle

4-2c How Social Media Have Changed the Way People and Businesses Communicate

Social media are Web-based and mobile technologies that allow the creation and exchange of user-generated content. Social media encompass a wide variety of content formats including text, video, photos, audio, PDF files, and PowerPoint. These media allow for one-to-one, one-to-many, and many-to-many (going viral) communications. Social media participants can create content, comment on content, or simply observe.

By the beginning of 2012, one minute out of every five spent on the Internet worldwide was dedicated to social networking. This statistic is based upon data from 1.2 billion people around the globe, or 82 percent of the world's Internet population.[1] Facebook, YouTube, and Twitter are the most-used social networking sites worldwide, and Facebook, by far, is the world's most popular with 92 percent of all social networking site users signing in. Fifteen percent of Facebook users update their own status, 22 percent comment on another's post or status, 20 percent comment on another user's photos, 26 percent "like" another user's content, and 10 percent send another user a private message.[2]

Are social networking site users more socially connected? Looking at how much total support, emotional support, companionship, and instrumental aid adults receive, the average American scores 75 out of 100 on a scale of total support, 75 out of 100 on emotional support (such as receiving advice), 76 out of 100 in companionship (such as having people to spend time with), and 75 out of 100 in instrumental aid (such as having someone to help if they are sick in bed).[3]

Internet users in general score three points higher in companionship and four points higher in instrumental support. A Facebook user who uses the site multiple

© Roz Woodward/PhotoDisc/Jupiterimages

times per day tends to score an additional five points higher in total support, emotional support, and companionship than Internet users of similar demographic characteristics.[4]

At one time, Myspace had far more customers than Facebook. What enabled Facebook to grow so rapidly? The company has a different design philosophy than the rest of Silicon Valley. Instead of obsessing about making tasks like posting a photo easier or making the interface more beautiful, Facebook is getting its product out of the way. Most designers in the computer industry have focused on helping humans interact with machines. But Facebook is about human-to-human interaction. "We don't want people to remember their interactions with Facebook," says director of design Kate Aronowitz. "We want them to remember their interactions with their friends and family." Chris Cox, director of product, calls this "social design." "It's more like designing a plaza or a restaurant," he explains. "The best building is one where the people inside get it and work together and are connected. That connectivity is created by how everything is arranged."[5]

HOW FIRMS USE SOCIAL MEDIA There are many categories and types of social media that will be discussed in Chapter 16. You will learn how businesses are using these tools to engage and retain customers, acquire new customers, and understand the marketplace. There are several examples of how Facebook has been used successfully by businesses:

▸▸ **Target ran a Valentine's Day promotion called "Super Love Sender" that allowed people to send personalized valentines and to vote on (and track) the charity to which Target would donate $1 million.**

▸▸ **Corona put the faces of its Facebook fans onto a Times Square billboard, generating 1.5 million impressions**

per day and feeding into 200,000 more "likes" for the brand.

▸▸ **L'Oréal's Salon Facebook Program provided a kit to local salons that the salons then used on their own Facebook pages. More than 6,000 salons now improve their own Facebook pages with L'Oréal-supplied elements such as how-to videos, an appointment booking engine, information on products, and a Facebook advertising credit. Was L'Oréal's Facebook program "worth it"? Since it has reached 1.7 million clients, it appears that it was.**

▸▸ **Bacardi created a promotion on Facebook called "Like It Live, Like It Together." In a six-week period, Bacardi fans "liked" randomly featured items on the brand's Facebook page (for example, one promotion asked people to "like" a pizza truck or a taco truck). The promotion gained Bacardi more than 145,000 fans in the United States and boosted its YouTube channel views by 67 percent.[6]**

None of these companies settled for simple "likes" for the company or brand. Instead, each found a creative way to engage customers and potential customers.

4-3 DEMOGRAPHIC FACTORS

Another uncontrollable variable in the external environment—also extremely important to marketing managers—is demography, the study of people's vital statistics, such as age, race and ethnicity, and location. Demographics are significant because the basis for any market is people. Demographic characteristics are strongly related to consumer buyer behavior in the marketplace.

4-3a Population

People are directly or indirectly the basis of all markets, making population the most basic statistic in marketing. The world's population hit 7 billion in 2012. China has the largest population with 1.3 billion persons; India is second with 1.2 billion.[7] The latest Census (2010) puts the U.S. population at 308 million. The country grew

© diego Cervo/Shutterstock.com

by 27 million from 2000 to 2010. But growth was un-evenly distributed. Metropolitan areas, defined as the collection of small cities and suburbs that surround an urban core with at least 50,000 people, accounted for most of the gain, growing 10.8 percent over the decade to 257.7 million people.[8]

Rural areas, meanwhile, grew just 4.5 percent to 51 million. Many regions—from the Great Plains to the Mississippi delta to rural New England—saw population declines. About 46 percent of rural counties lost population in the decade, including almost 60 percent of rural counties that aren't adjacent to a metro area.[9]

Population is a broad statistic that is particularly useful when broken into smaller increments. Age groups present opportunities to focus on a section of the population and offer opportunities for marketers. These groups are called tweens, teens, Generation Y, Generation X, and baby boomers. You will find that each cohort group has its own needs, values, and consumption patterns.

4-3b Tweens

America's tweens (ages eight to twelve) are a pop-ulation of more than 20 million. With attitudes, ac-cess to information, sophistication well beyond their years, and purchasing power to match, these young consumers spend over $200 billion annually. Tweens directly spend about $50 billion per year, and the remainder is spent by parents and family members for them.[10] For example, the average family budget for back-to-school clothes is $225.[11]

With such spending power, many markets are striv-ing to attract this age group. One of the fastest-growing tween markets is home décor. Both boys and girls want their rooms to be more than just rooms, and retailers such as Pottery Barn, Pier 1 Imports, and other home goods re-tailers sell bedding, furniture, and wall art designed spe-cifically for tweens. By introducing tweens to home fur-nishings at a younger age, these firms hope to keep their business as they change their fashion sense and need to furnish dorms or apartments for college.[12]

4-3c Teens

There are approximately 25 million teens in the United States. They spend approximately seventy-two hours

WHAT'S YOUR ADVANTAGE?

90% less sugar and 70% more protein and fiber than PowerBar.*

PROTEIN:17g   FIBER:6g   SUGARS:1g
SEE THE NEW LOOK OF NUTRITION AT ATKINS.COM

GIVE YOURSELF AN **A**

Atkins is targeting Gen Y's active lifestyles and adventurous spirit with ads like this one.

per week tuned in electronically. This includes television, Internet, music, video games, and cell phones. About 93 percent of U.S. teens are on the Internet, 75 percent own a cell phone, and 66 percent say they text. Seventy-three percent of teens in the United States are into social networking, and 50 million teens worldwide post their profiles on Facebook. Only 14 percent of American teens blog, but about half post comments on blogs. Only 8 per-cent of teens use Twitter.[13]

For teens, shopping has become a social sport whether online or at the mall, though most teens prefer to shop in stores instead of online.[14] The average teen spends about forty-five dollars per week (25 percent report work-ing part time, and 70 percent work odd jobs).[15] Thirty-one percent of teen spending goes toward clothing, shoes, and accessories, and the biggest purchase influence comes from friends.[16]

4-3d Generation Y

Generation Y, also called the millennial generation, is made up of people born between 1979 and 1994. Initially, Generation Y was a smaller cohort than baby boomers (discussed below). However, due to immigration and the aging of the boomer generation, Gen Y passed the boomers in total population in 2010. Millennials are currently in two different stages of the life cycle. The youngest members of Gen Y, born in 1994, are in their late teens and fit the cohort group above. In contrast, the oldest Gen Yers, born in 1979, were thirty-four years old in 2013. They have started their careers, and many have become parents for the first time, leading to dramatic lifestyle changes. They care for their babies rather than go out, and they spend money on baby products. Gen Yers already spend more than $200 billion annually and over their lifetimes will likely spend about $10 trillion. No group was hit harder by the recent Great Recession than the Millennials. Many found their newly launched careers stalled or their jobs eliminated. An estimated 24 percent had to move home with their parents at least once.[17] The lucky ones have been able to keep their jobs during the difficult economic times and are making major purchasing decisions such as cars and homes; at the very least, they are buying computers, MP3 players, Smartphones, tablet computers, and sneakers.

Millennials may be the tech-savviest generation yet, spending more time surfing the Web and on social media than they do watching television, listening to radio, or reading newspapers, but they still use and value traditional media. Gen Yers expect brands to be on social media. Two-thirds say a brand being on social media shows it cares about their generation, and 56 percent think social media are a great way to find out what's new with brands they like. That may be why 64 percent have "liked" a brand on Facebook and follow an average of ten brands or companies.[18]

4-3e Generation X

Generation X—people born between 1965 and 1978—consists of 40 million consumers. It was the first generation of latchkey children—products of dual-career households or, in roughly half of the cases, of divorced or separated parents. Gen Xers often spent more time without adult support and guidance than any other age cohort. This experience made them independent, resilient, adaptable, cautious, and skeptical.[19]

Marketing to Gen Xers has often been described as difficult. Yet understanding their needs, wants, and attitudes can make the task much easier. Gen Xers, now in their thirties and forties, are reaching the age when they are planning to send their kids off to college. Seventy-one percent of Gen Xers still have children under the age of eighteen.[20] Gen Xers, like the Millennials, have also been hit hard by the Great Recession. As one Gen Xer noted, "I don't know anyone in my age group who's 'quote' where they want to be 'unquote' from a financial perspective." Around 18 percent of Gen Xers carry credit card debt exceeding 20 percent of their annual salary.[21] Difficult financial times have made Gen Xers big spenders at discounters such as Walmart.

© incamerastock/Alamy

4-3f Baby Boomers

In 2012, there were approximately 75 million **baby boomers** (persons born between 1946 and 1964). Today, their ages range from the late-forties to the mid-sixties. With average life expectancy at an all-time high of 77.4 years, more and more Americans over fifty consider middle age a new start on life. Boomers purchase iPads, redecorate, go on vacation, and postpone retirement.[22] They control about 80 percent of personal wealth in the United States and spend about $50 billion on their grandchildren alone.[23] Boomers spend $1.8 trillion annually on food, cars, personal care, and other personal products. In addition, they are willing to change brands and try new things, making them an ideal group—affluent, experienced, and flexible.[24] Clearly, boomers and seniors are still a huge market with significant needs. In fact, many advertisers are homing in on the boomer market. For example, Procter & Gamble teamed up with NBCUniversal to launch a group of Web sites targeted at boomers using the phrase "life goes strong." The sites cover topics such as technology and health, and hope to catch boomers' fancy as well as some of their $1 trillion in spending power.[25]

4-4 GROWING ETHNIC MARKETS

In 2015, it is estimated that Hispanics will wield $1.5 trillion in purchasing power. In the same year, African Americans will have $1.2 trillion, followed by Asian Americans at $775 billion. Native American spending is expected to increase more than 30 percent to $90.4 billion.[26]

The minority population of the United States reached 110 million in 2011. About one in three U.S. residents is a member of a minority group. By 2050, about one in three U.S. residents will be Hispanic. Currently, nonwhite minorities account for 49 percent of the children born in the United States.[27] Hawaii (75 percent), the District of Columbia (68 percent), New Mexico (58 percent), California (58 percent), and Texas (53 percent) are all majority-minority areas in the United States.[28] The United States will flip to "majority minority" in 2041, meaning whites of European ancestry will make up less than 50 percent of the population. Ten states are already there; in six of them—Arizona, Florida, Georgia, Maryland, Mississippi and Nevada—whites became a minority in the last decade.[29] Today there are more Hispanics living in the United States than there are Canadians in Canada. Hispanics accounted for most of the population growth in the 2010 census. Without Hispanics, America's under-eighteen population would have actually declined.[30]

As you'll see in the following sections, minority populations embrace other cultures while continuing to patronize companies that understand their native cultural preferences.[31] Smart marketers are reaching out and tapping these dynamic, growing markets with a wide range of products and targeted advertising. For example, JCPenney spent 16.4 percent of its media advertising budget on the Hispanic market.[32]

4-4a Marketing to Hispanic Americans

The term *Hispanic* encompasses people of many different backgrounds. Nearly 60 percent of Hispanic Americans are of Mexican descent. Puerto Ricans, the next largest group, make up just under 10 percent of Hispanics. Other groups, including Central Americans, Dominicans, South Americans, and Cubans, each account for less than 5 percent of all Hispanics.

The diversity of the Hispanic population and the language differences create many challenges for those trying to target this market. Hispanics, especially recent immigrants, often prefer products from their native country. Therefore, many retailers along the southern U.S. border

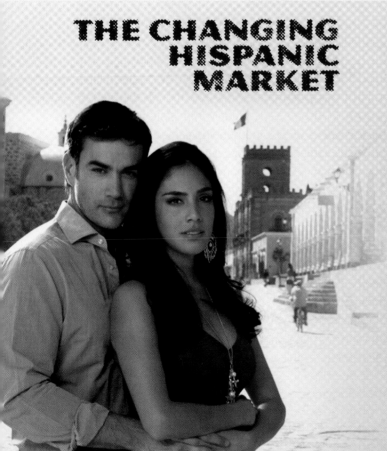

THE CHANGING HISPANIC MARKET

For many years, broadcast media have assumed that immigrants, as they settled into the United States, would move away from Hispanic channels to mainstream media. However, there are key changes in the Hispanic market that are challenging that assumption. Over the last decade, the largest growth in the Hispanic population has come from births, not immigration. With such a large number of children being raised inside the United States, it should come as little surprise to researchers that 80 percent of the Latino population prefers English or bilingual programming. Univision and Telemundo, the largest Hispanic broadcast television networks, both have English subtitles on their prime-time telenovelas, and Univision broke with its all-Spanish programming by interviewing Republican presidential hopefuls in English with a Spanish translation. The new assumption seems to be that Hispanics have acculturated and are maintaining the best parts of their cultures while adapting some aspects of American culture.

Source: Greg Allen, "Media Outlets Adapt to Growing Hispanic Audience," NPR, April 3, 2012, www.npr.org /2012/04/03/149845056/media-outlets-adapt-to-growing-hispanic-audience (Accessed April 10, 2012).

import goods from Mexico. If the brands found in their homeland are not available, Hispanics will choose brands that reflect their native values and culture.

Procter & Gamble has increasingly targeted Hispanic Americans, and as the Hispanic population continues to gain market share, additional companies are hoping to grab these consumers.

4-4b Marketing to African Americans

African Americans are nearly six years younger on average than all consumers; 47 percent are between eighteen and forty-nine years old, which is considered the top-spending age demographic by marketers. Although their population is smaller, there are more African American households in the United States than Hispanic households because the latter tend to have larger families.[33] Nearly 30 percent of African American households are headed by single women.[34]

Several companies owned by African Americans—such as SoftSheen-Carson and Pro-Line—target the African American market for health and beauty aids. Huge corporations like Revlon, Gillette, and Alberto Culver have either divisions or major product lines for this market as well. The promotional dollars spent on African Americans continue to rise, as does the number of black media choices. BET, the Black Entertainment Television network, has over 80 million viewers. The forty-five-year-old *Essence* magazine reaches one-third of all black females aged eighteen to forty-nine. African Americans spend considerable time with radio (an astounding 4 hours a day versus 2.8 hours for other groups), and urban audiences have an intensely personal relationship with the medium. ABC Radio Networks' Tom Joyner reaches an audience of more than 8 million in 115 markets, and Doug Banks is heard by 1.5 million listeners in 36 markets. Recent research shows that more African Americans than ever before are achieving the American dream. In 2012, there were 2.8 million African Americans earning more than $75,000 annually.[35]

4-4c Marketing to Asian Americans

Asian Americans, who represent only 5 percent of the U.S. population, have the highest average family income of all groups. At $68,780, it exceeds the average U.S. household income by roughly $15,000. Fifty percent of all Asian Americans have at least a bachelor's degree.[36] Because Asian Americans are younger (the average age is 34), better educated, and have higher incomes than average, they are sometimes called a "marketer's dream." Asian Americans are heavy users of technology. Moreover, they are early adopters of the latest digital gadgets. A staggering 95 percent of Asian Americans own PCs.[37]

A number of products have been developed specifically for the Asian American market. For example, the Kayla Beverly Hills salon draws Asian American consumers because the firm offers cosmetics formulated for them. Cultural diversity within the Asian American market complicates promotional efforts, however, and marketers must understand the differences among the Chinese, Filipino, Japanese, Vietnamese, Korean, Indian, and Pakistani markets.

4-5 ECONOMIC FACTORS

In addition to social and demographic factors, marketing managers must understand and react to the economic environment. The three economic areas of greatest concern to most marketers are consumers' incomes, inflation, and recession.

4-5a Consumers' Incomes

As disposable (or after-tax) incomes rise, more families and individuals can afford the "good life." In recent years, however, U.S. incomes have risen at a rather slow pace. The annual median household income in the United States in 2012 was approximately $50,000, though the median household income varies widely from state to state. This means half of all U.S. households earned less, and the other half earned more.[38] Two percent of the U.S. population earns $250,000 a year or more.[39]

Education is the primary determinant of a person's earning potential. For example, only 1 percent of those with only a high school education earn over $100,000 annually. By comparison, 13 percent of college-educated workers earn six figures or more. People with a bachelor's degree take home an average of 38 percent more than those with just a high school diploma. Over a lifetime, an individual with a bachelor's degree will earn twice as much total income as a nondegree holder.[40] Along with "willingness to buy," or "ability to buy," income is a key determinant of target markets. A marketer who knows where the money is knows where the markets are. If you are seeking a new store location for Dollar General, a retail chain that caters to lower-income consumers, you would probably concentrate on the South and Midwest, because most households with annual incomes of less than $45,000 are concentrated in these areas.

4-5b Purchasing Power

Rising incomes don't necessarily mean a higher standard of living. Increased standards of living are a function of purchasing power. **Purchasing power** is measured by comparing income to the relative cost of a standard set of goods and services in different geographic areas, usually referred to as the cost of living. Another way to think of purchasing power is income minus the cost of living (i.e., expenses). In general, a cost of living index takes into account housing, food and groceries, transportation, utilities, health care, and miscellaneous expenses such as clothing, services, and entertainment. HomeFair.com's salary calculator uses these metrics when it figures that the cost of living in New York City is almost three times the cost of living in Youngstown, Ohio. This means that a worker living in New York City must earn nearly $279,500 to have the same standard of living as someone making $100,000 in Youngstown.

When income is high relative to the cost of living, people have more discretionary income. That means they have more money to spend on nonessential items (in other words, on wants rather than needs). This information is important to marketers for obvious reasons. Consumers with high purchasing power can afford to spend more money without jeopardizing their budget for necessities like food, housing, and utilities. They also have the ability to purchase higher-priced necessities—for example, a more expensive car, a home in a more expensive neighborhood, or a designer handbag versus a purse from a discount store.

4-5c Inflation

Inflation is a measure of the decrease in the value of money, generally expressed as the percentage reduction in value since the previous year, which is the rate of inflation. Thus, in simple terms, an inflation rate of 5 percent means you will need 5 percent more units of money than you would have needed last year to buy the same basket of products. If inflation is 5 percent, you can expect that, on average, prices have risen by about 5 percent since the previous year. Of course, if pay raises are matching the rate of inflation, then employees will be no worse off in terms of the immediate purchasing power of their salaries.

Walmart is known as a low-price retailer, but brands such as OP are often found in Walmart stores serving higher-income markets.

purchasing power a comparison of income versus the relative cost of a standard set of goods and services in different geographic areas

inflation a measure of the decrease in the value of money, expressed as the percentage reduction in value since the previous year

In times of low inflation, businesses seeking to increase their profit margins can do so only by increasing their efficiency. If they significantly increase prices, no one will purchase their goods or services. The recent recession brought inflation rates to almost zero.

In creating marketing strategies to cope with inflation, managers must realize that, regardless of what happens to the seller's cost, the buyer is not going to pay more for a product than the subjective value he or she places on it. No matter how compelling the justification might be for a 10 percent price increase, marketers must always examine its impact on demand. Many marketers try to hold prices level for as long as is practical.

© iStockphoto.com/james steidl

4-5d Recession

A **recession** is a period of economic activity characterized by negative growth. More precisely, a recession is defined as occurring when the gross domestic product falls for two consecutive quarters. Gross domestic product is the total market value of all final goods and services produced during a period of time. The official beginning of the 2007–2009 recession was December 2007. While the causes of the recession are very complex, this one began with the collapse of inflated housing prices. Those high prices led people to take out mortgages they couldn't afford from banks that should have known the money would not be repaid. By 2008, the recession had spread around the globe. A very slow economic recovery began in July 2009.

The 2007–2009 recession, called "the Great Recession" by some, was the largest economic downturn since the Great Depression of 1929 to 1939. Unemployment rose from slightly over 4 percent to over 10 percent.[41] The unemployment rate has been slowly falling since mid-2010 due to job creation and people leaving the workforce entirely.

Uncertain economic times have caused many consumers to shift to store brands—60 percent of shoppers buy only private label bread or baked goods![42] More consumers than ever before are using coupons. Researchers found that during the recession, consumers were sticking very close to shopping lists and doing their best to completely empty their pantries before restocking. Also, consumers were going to fewer stores but selecting stores where they could get the widest array of products at the best value. Many people, for the first time, prepared their lunches to take to work.[43]

4-6 TECHNOLOGICAL FACTORS

The recent economic downturn and slow recovery have had an impact on research and development (R&D) spending. In order to cut costs and boost short-term profits, many companies, particularly in the auto and drug industries, slashed R&D, product design, and laboratory spending. Other firms have taken a different tack and either increased or held R&D spending steady, hoping that they will be able to compete more effectively when the economy improves. Companies such as 3M, Microsoft, Google, Intel, and Cisco Systems have followed this strategy. Without investment in R&D, the United States cannot compete in a knowledge-based global economy.

4-6a Research

The United States, historically, has excelled at both basic and applied research. **Basic research** (or *pure research*) attempts to expand the frontiers of knowledge but is not aimed at a specific, pragmatic problem. Basic research aims to confirm an existing theory or to learn more about a concept or phenomenon. For example, basic research might focus on high-energy physics. **Applied research**, in contrast, attempts to develop new or improved products. The United States has dramatically improved its track record in applied research. For example, the United States leads the world in applying basic research to aircraft design and propulsion systems.

4-6b Stimulating Innovation

Companies attempting to innovate often limit their searches to areas they are already familiar with. This can help lead to incremental progress but rarely leads to a dramatic breakthrough. Companies are now using several approaches to keeping innovation strong. These include:

- **BUILD SCENARIOS:** Some firms use teams of writers to imagine detailed opportunities and threats for their companies, partners, and collaborators in future markets.

- **ENLIST THE WEB:** A few companies have created Web sites that act as literal marketplaces of ideas where they can go to look for help with scientific and business challenges.

- **TALK TO EARLY ADOPTERS:** Early adopters tend to be innovators themselves. They are risk takers and look for new things or wish for something better to help in daily tasks at home and work.

- **USE MARKETING RESEARCH:** Firms find out what customers like and dislike about their products and competitors' products.

- **CREATE AN INNOVATIVE ENVIRONMENT:** Companies let employees know that they have the "freedom to fail." They create intranets to encourage sharing ideas. Most importantly, top management must lead by example to create an atmosphere where innovation is encouraged and rewarded.

- **CATER TO ENTREPRENEURS:** Policies that reserve blocks of time for scientists or engineers to explore their own ideas have worked well at some companies. At 3M, scientists can spend 15 percent of their time on projects they dream up themselves, and the company has set procedures for taking bright ideas forward, including grants and venture funding.[44]

Although developing new technology internally is a key to creating and maintaining a long-term competitive advantage, external technology is also important to managers for two reasons. First, by acquiring the technology, the firm may be able to operate more efficiently or create a better product. Second, a new technology may render existing products obsolete.

Recently, China has been rolling out an array of interlocking regulations and state spending aimed at making the country a global technology powerhouse by 2020.

The new initiatives—shaped by rising nationalism and a belief that foreign companies unfairly dominate key technologies—range from big investments in national industries to patent laws that favor Chinese companies and mandates that essentially require foreign companies to transfer technology to China if they hope to sell in that

© leedsn/Shutterstock.com

market. The U.S. Chamber of Commerce, a business trade group, calls China's actions "an intricate web of new rules considered by many international technology companies to be a blueprint for technology theft on a scale the world has never seen before."[45] This issue promises to dominate relations between the two countries for years to come.

4-7 POLITICAL AND LEGAL FACTORS

Business needs government regulation to protect innovators of new technology, the interests of society in general, one business from another, and consumers. In turn, government needs business because the marketplace generates taxes that support public efforts to educate our youth, pave our roads, protect our shores, and the like.

Every aspect of the marketing mix is subject to laws and restrictions. It is the duty of marketing managers or their legal assistants to understand these laws and conform to them, because failure to comply with regulations can have major consequences for a firm. Sometimes just sensing trends and taking corrective action before a government agency acts can help avoid regulation.

4-7a Federal Legislation

Federal laws that affect marketing fall into several categories of regulatory activity: competitive environment, pricing, advertising and promotion, and consumer privacy. The key pieces of legislation in these areas are summarized in Exhibit 4.1. The primary federal laws that protect consumers are shown in Exhibit 4.2.

In 2010, Congress passed the Restoring American Financial Stability Act that brought sweeping changes to bank and financial market regulations. The legislation created the Consumer Financial Protection Bureau to oversee checking accounts, private student loans, mortgages, and other financial products. The agency deals with unfair, abusive, and deceptive practices.

4-7b State Laws

Legislation that affects marketing varies state by state. Oregon, for example, limits utility advertising to 0.5 percent of the company's net income. California has forced industry to improve consumer products and has enacted legislation to lower the energy consumption of refrigerators, freezers, and air conditioners. Several states, including California and North Carolina, are considering levying a tax on all in-state commercial advertising.

Many states and cities are attempting to fight obesity by regulating fast-food chains and other restaurants. For example, California has passed a law banning trans fats in restaurants and bakeries, New York City chain restaurants must now display calorie counts on menus, and Boston has banned trans fats in restaurants.

4-7c Regulatory Agencies

Although some state regulatory bodies actively pursue violators of their marketing statutes, federal regulators generally have the greatest clout. The Consumer Product Safety Commission, the Federal Trade Commission, and the Food and Drug Administration are the three federal agencies most directly and actively involved in marketing affairs. These agencies, plus others, are discussed throughout the book, but a brief introduction is in order at this point.

The sole purpose of the **Consumer Product Safety Commission (CPSC)** is to protect the health and safety of consumers in and around their homes. The CPSC has the power to set mandatory safety standards for almost all products consumers use (about 15,000 items) and can

Exhibit 4.1

PRIMARY U.S. LAWS THAT AFFECT MARKETING

Legislation	Impact on Marketing
Sherman Act of 1890	Makes trusts and conspiracies in restraint of trade illegal; makes monopolies and attempts to monopolize misdemeanors.
Clayton Act of 1914	Outlaws discrimination in prices to different buyers; prohibits tying contracts (which require the buyer of one product to also buy another item in the line); makes illegal the combining of two or more competing corporations by pooling ownership of stock.
Federal Trade Commission Act of 1914	Created the Federal Trade Commission to deal with antitrust matters; outlaws unfair methods of competition.
Robinson-Patman Act of 1936	Prohibits charging different prices to different buyers of merchandise of like grade and quantity; requires sellers to make any supplementary services or allowances available to all purchasers on a proportionately equal basis.
Wheeler-Lea Amendments to FTC Act of 1938	Broadens the Federal Trade Commission's power to prohibit practices that might injure the public without affecting competition; outlaws false and deceptive advertising.
Lanham Act of 1946	Establishes protection for trademarks.
Celler-Kefauver Antimerger Act of 1950	Strengthens the Clayton Act to prevent corporate acquisitions that reduce competition.
Hart-Scott-Rodino Act of 1976	Requires large companies to notify the government of their intent to merge.
Foreign Corrupt Practices Act of 1977	Prohibits bribery of foreign officials to obtain business.

© Cengage Learning

fine offending firms up to $500,000 and sentence their officers to up to a year in prison. It can also ban dangerous products from the marketplace. The CPSC oversees about 400 recalls per year. In 2008, Congress passed the Consumer Product Safety Improvement Act. The law is aimed primarily at children's products, which are defined as those used by individuals twelve years old or younger. The law addresses items such as cribs, electronics and video games, school supplies, science kits, toys, and pacifiers. The law requires mandatory testing and labeling and increases fines and prison time for violators.

The **Food and Drug Administration (FDA)**, another powerful agency, is charged with enforcing regulations against selling and distributing adulterated, misbranded, or hazardous food and drug products. In 2009, the Tobacco Control Act was passed. This act gave the FDA authority to regulate tobacco products, with a special emphasis on preventing their use by children and young people and reducing the impact of tobacco on public health. Another recent FDA action is the "Bad Ad" program. It is geared toward health care providers to help them recognize misleading prescription drug promotions and gives them an easy way to report the activity to the FDA.

The **Federal Trade Commission (FTC)** consists of five members, each holding office for seven years. Over

Food and Drug Administration (FDA) a federal agency charged with enforcing regulations against selling and distributing adulterated, misbranded, or hazardous food and drug products

Federal Trade Commission (FTC) a federal agency empowered to prevent persons or corporations from using unfair methods of competition in commerce

Exhibit 4.2

PRIMARY U.S. LAWS PROTECTING CONSUMERS

Legislation	Impact on Marketing
Federal Food and Drug Act of 1906	Prohibits adulteration and misbranding of foods and drugs involved in interstate commerce; strengthened by the Food, Drug, and Cosmetic Act (1938) and the Kefauver-Harris Drug Amendment (1962).
Federal Hazardous Substances Act of 1960	Requires warning labels on hazardous household chemicals.
Kefauver-Harris Drug Amendment of 1962	Requires that manufacturers conduct tests to prove drug effectiveness and safety.
Consumer Credit Protection Act of 1968	Requires that lenders fully disclose true interest rates and all other charges to credit customers for loans and installment purchases.
Child Protection and Toy Safety Act of 1969	Prevents marketing of products so dangerous that adequate safety warnings cannot be given.
Public Health Smoking Act of 1970	Prohibits cigarette advertising on television and radio and revises the health hazard warning on cigarette packages.
Poison Prevention Labeling Act of 1970	Requires safety packaging for products that may be harmful to children.
National Environmental Policy Act of 1970	Established the Environmental Protection Agency to deal with various types of pollution and organizations that create pollution.
Public Health Cigarette Smoking Act of 1971	Prohibits tobacco advertising on radio and television.
Consumer Product Safety Act of 1972	Created the Consumer Product Safety Commission, which has authority to specify safety standards for most products.
Child Protection Act of 1990	Regulates the number of minutes of advertising on children's television.
Children's Online Privacy Protection Act of 1998	Empowers the FTC to set rules regarding how and when marketers must obtain parental permission before asking children marketing research questions.
Aviation Security Act of 2001	Requires airlines to take extra security measures to protect passengers, including the installation of stronger cockpit doors, improved baggage screening, and increased security training for airport personnel.
Homeland Security Act of 2002	Protects consumers against terrorist acts; created the Department of Homeland Security.
Do Not Call Law of 2003	Protects consumers against unwanted telemarketing calls.
CAN-SPAM Act of 2003	Protects consumers against unwanted e-mail, or spam.
Credit Card Act of 2009	Provides many credit card protections.
Restoring American Financial Stability Act of 2010	Created the Consumer Financial Protection Bureau to protect consumers against unfair, abusive, and deceptive financial practices.

© Cengage Learning

the years, Congress has greatly expanded the powers of the FTC. Its responsibilities have grown so large that the FTC has created several bureaus to better organize its operations. One of the most important is the Bureau of Competition, which promotes and protects competition. The Bureau:

» reviews mergers and acquisitions, and challenges those that would likely lead to higher prices, fewer choices, or less innovation;

» seeks out and challenges anti-competitive conduct in the marketplace, including monopolization and agreements between competitors;

» promotes competition in industries where consumer impact is high, such as health care, real estate, oil and gas, technology, and consumer goods; and

© Vjom/Shutterstock.com

» provides information and holds conferences and workshops for consumers, businesses, and policy makers on competition issues for market analysis.[46]

The FTC's Bureau of Consumer Protection works for the consumer to prevent fraud, deception, and unfair business practices in the marketplace. The Bureau claims that it:

» enhances consumer confidence by enforcing federal laws that protect consumers,

» empowers consumers with free information to help them exercise their rights and to spot and avoid fraud and deception, and

» wants to hear from consumers who want to get information or file a complaint about fraud or identity theft.[47]

Another important FTC Bureau is the Bureau of Economics. It provides economic analysis and support to antitrust and consumer protection investigations. Many consumer protection issues today involve the Internet.

CONSUMER PRIVACY The popularity of the Internet for direct marketing, for collecting consumer data, and as a repository for sensitive consumer data has alarmed privacy-minded consumers. The U.S. Congress passed the CAN-SPAM Act in an attempt to regulate unsolicited e-mail advertising. The act prohibits commercial e-mailers from using false addresses and presenting false or misleading information, among other restrictions.

Internet users who once felt fairly anonymous when using the Web are now disturbed by the amount of information marketers collect about them and their children as they visit various sites in cyberspace. The FTC, with jurisdiction under the Children's Online Privacy Protection Act, requires Web site operators to post a privacy policy on the home page and a link to the policy on every page where personal information is collected. An area of growing concern to privacy advocates is called behavioral targeting, which is discussed in more detail in Chapter 9. Behavioral targeting is used by researchers to better target advertising to Web surfers and users of search engines and social media.

In 2012, the FTC called for online data collectors to adopt better privacy policies and asked Congress to pass comprehensive privacy legislation. The FTC wants data collectors to implement a "Do Not Track" button in Web browsers. "No one has the right to put anything on [your

THE EYES OF THE E-BOOK

Online privacy is a fairly common discussion today, particularly in U.S. legislation. But few people mention e-reader privacy, despite the ever increasing numbers of e-books sold each year. However, the companies that sell e-books are able to track how people read, what they read, the amount of time spent in each book, and even what passages they underline and bookmark. While Amazon touts this feature as a "collective intelligence," the Electronic Frontier Foundation (EFF) is concerned that this data could be used against individuals. In California, the EFF has worked to implement legislation requiring a warrant before personal e-reader data is released for investigation. The EFF hopes to encourage other states to enact the same legislation in order to safeguard consumer privacy.

Source: Alexandra Alter, "Your E-Book is Reading You," *Wall Street Journal*, July 19, 2012 (Accessed September 3, 2012) http://online.wsj.com/article/SB10001424052702304870304577490950051438304.html

© iStockphoto.com/Bill Noll

computer] that you don't want," said Jon Leibowitz, chairman of the FTC.[48]

The agency also turned its attention to off-line data brokers—which buy and sell names, addresses, and other personal information—calling on them to create a centralized Web site providing consumers with better access to their data. The agency also wants legislation requiring data brokers to give consumers the right to see and make corrections to their information.[49]

4-8 COMPETITIVE FACTORS

The competitive environment encompasses the number of competitors a firm must face, the relative size of the competitors, and the degree of interdependence within the industry. Management has little control over the competitive environment confronting a firm.

4-8a Competition for Market Share and Profits

As U.S. population growth slows, global competition increases, costs rise, and available resources tighten, firms find that they must work harder to maintain their profits and market share regardless of the form of the competitive market. Sometimes technology advances can usher in a whole new set of competitors that can change a firm's business model. In the single-serve coffee brewing market, Keurig and Green Mountain have the lion's share of the market, but Starbucks is hoping to cash in on some of that market share by working with Green Mountain to package its super-premium coffee into the single-serve pods used in the Keurig machines. Dunkin' Donuts coffee is also offered by Green Mountain, but Starbucks would represent the only super-premium coffee offered by the company. This is one of several moves Starbucks is making to add profit growth by selling in consumer goods markets beyond its retail coffee shops.[50]

4-8b Global Competition

Boeing is a very savvy international business competitor. Many foreign competitors also consider the United States to be a ripe target market. Thus, a U.S. marketing manager can no longer focus only on domestic competitors. In automobiles, textiles, watches, televisions, steel, and many other areas, foreign competition has been strong. In the past, foreign firms penetrated U.S. markets by concentrating on price, but today the emphasis has switched to product quality. Nestlé, Sony, and Rolls-Royce are noted for quality, not cheap prices. Global competition is discussed in much more detail in Chapter 5.

STUDY TOOLS 4

↑ LOCATED AT BACK OF THE TEXTBOOK
☐ *Rip out Chapter Review Card*

LOCATED AT WWW.CENGAGE.COM/LOGIN
☐ *Review Key Terms Flashcards (print or online)*
☐ *Download audio and visual summaries to review on the go*
☐ *Complete both Practice Quizzes to prepare for tests*
☐ *Play "Beat the Clock" and "Quizbowl" to master concepts*
☐ *Complete "Crossword Puzzle" to review key terms*
☐ *Watch Video on "GaGa's Inc." for a real company example*

5-1 REWARDS OF GLOBAL MARKETING

Today, global revolutions are under way in many areas of our lives: management, politics, communications, and technology. The word *global* has assumed a new meaning, referring to a boundless mobility and competition in social, business, and intellectual arenas. **Global marketing**—marketing that targets markets throughout the world—has become an imperative for business.

> Over the past two decades, world trade has climbed from $200 billion a year to over $12.5 trillion.

global marketing
marketing that targets markets throughout the world

global vision recognizing and reacting to international marketing opportunities, using effective global marketing strategies, and being aware of threats from foreign competitors in all markets

U.S. managers must develop a global vision not only to recognize and react to international marketing opportunities but also to remain competitive at home. Often a U.S. firm's toughest domestic competition comes from foreign companies. Moreover, a global vision enables a manager to understand that customer and distribution networks operate worldwide, blurring geographic and political barriers and making them increasingly irrelevant to business decisions. In summary, having a **global vision** means recognizing and reacting to international marketing opportunities, using effective global marketing strategies, and being aware of threats from foreign competitors in all markets.

Over the past two decades, world trade climbed from $200 billion a year to over $12.5 trillion in 2009. This was a 12 percent contraction from 2008 sparked by the global economic crisis. As the world slowly began to emerge from the Great Recession, world trade grew by 14 percent in 2010.[1]

Today's marketers face many challenges to their customary practices. Product development costs are rising, the life of products is getting shorter, and new technology is spreading around the world faster than ever. But marketing winners relish the pace of change instead of fear it.

Adopting a global vision can be very lucrative for a company. Caterpillar, one of the world's largest manufacturers of construction and mining equipment, diesel and natural gas engines, and industrial turbines, has sales of over $33 billion annually. Almost $21 billion comes from sales outside the United States.[2]

Despite the increasing availability of foreign customers, small businesses still account for only approximately 30 percent of U.S. exporting volume. Whether global business is daunting because of the various trade laws or tariffs, or because the markets are unfamiliar, small businesses are taking only slow, hesitant steps into the global market.[3]

Global marketing is not a one-way street whereby only U.S. companies sell their wares and services throughout the world. Foreign competition in the domestic market was once relatively rare but now is found in almost every industry. In fact, in many industries, U.S.

Developing a Global Vision

Learning Outcomes

After you finish this chapter go to
p78 *for* STUDY TOOLS ----→

businesses have lost significant market share to imported products. In electronics, cameras, automobiles, fine china, tractors, leather goods, and a host of other consumer and industrial products, U.S. companies have struggled at home to maintain their market shares against foreign competitors.

5-1a Importance of Global Marketing to the United States

Many countries depend more on international commerce than the United States does. For example, France, Britain, and Germany all derive more than 19 percent of their gross domestic product from world trade, which is considerably more than the United States does. **Gross domestic product (GDP)** is the total market value of all final goods and services produced in a country for a given time period (usually a year or a quarter of a year). *Final* in the definition refers to final products that are sold, not to intermediate products used in the assembly of a final product. For example, if the value of a brake (an intermediate product) and that of a car (the final product) were both counted, the brake would be counted twice. Therefore, GDP counts only the final goods and services to get the true value of a country's production.

Nevertheless, the impact of international business on the U.S. economy is still impressive:

▸▸ **The United States exports about a fifth of its industrial production.**

▸▸ **More than 10 million Americans hold jobs that are supported by exports, accounting for 7 percent of employment.**

▸▸ **Exports represent approximately 13 percent of our GDP.[4]**

▸▸ **Every U.S. state has realized net employment gains directly attributed to foreign trade.**

▸▸ **The United States exports over $1.7 trillion in goods and services each year.[5]**

About 85 percent of all U.S. exports of manufactured goods are shipped by 250 companies, and less than 10 percent of all manufacturing businesses, or around 25,000 companies, export their goods on a regular basis. Most small- and medium-sized firms are essentially nonparticipants in global trade and marketing. Only the very large multinational companies have seriously attempted to compete worldwide. Fortunately, more small companies are now aggressively pursuing international markets. To increase U.S. exports, in March 2010 President Barack Obama created the National Export Initiative (NEI). The NEI's goal is to double U.S. exports over the next five years and support 2 million U.S. jobs.

5-1b The Impact of Trade and Globalization

The protests during meetings of the World Trade Organization, the World Bank, and the International Monetary Fund (the three organizations are discussed later in the chapter) show that many people fear world trade and globalization. What do they fear? The negatives of global trade are as follows:

▸▸ **Millions of Americans have lost jobs due to imports, production shifts abroad, or outsourcing of tech jobs. Some find new jobs, but they often pay less.**

▸▸ **Millions of others fear losing their jobs, especially at those companies operating under competitive pressure.**

▸▸ **Employers often threaten to outsource jobs if workers do not accept pay cuts.**

▸▸ **Service and white-collar jobs are increasingly vulnerable to operations moving offshore.**

JOB OUTSOURCING The notion of **job outsourcing** (sending U.S. jobs abroad) has been highly controversial for the past several years. Many executives say that it leads to corporate growth, efficiency, productivity, and revenue growth. Most companies see cost savings as a key driver in outsourcing. Detroit has suffered as many factories in the auto industry have been shut down and

© Max Earey/Shutterstock.com

FORD'S FIESTA IS ONE EXAMPLE OF AN OUTSOURCED JOB.

relocated around the world. For example, Ford's newly reintroduced line of compact sedans and hatchbacks, called the Fiesta, is being built in several countries, including Mexico.

BENEFITS OF GLOBALIZATION Traditional economic theory says that globalization relies on competition to drive down prices and increase product and service quality. Business goes to the countries that operate most efficiently and/or have the technology to produce what is needed. In summary, globalization expands economic freedom, spurs competition, and raises the productivity and living standards of people in countries that open themselves to the global marketplace. For less developed countries, globalization also offers access to foreign capital, global export markets, and advanced technology while breaking the monopoly of inefficient and protected domestic producers. Faster growth, in turn, reduces poverty, encourages democratization, and promotes higher labor and environmental standards. Though government officials may face more difficult choices as a result of globalization, their citizens enjoy greater individual freedom. In this sense, globalization acts as a check on governmental power by making it more difficult for governments to abuse the freedom and property of their citizens.

Globalization deserves credit for helping lift many millions out of poverty and for improving standards of living of low-wage families. In developing countries around the world, globalization has created a vibrant middle class that has elevated the standard of living for hundreds of millions of people.

5-2 MULTINATIONAL FIRMS

The United States has a number of large companies that are global marketers. Many of them have been very successful. A company that is heavily engaged in international trade, beyond exporting and importing, is called a **multinational corporation**. A multinational corporation moves resources, goods, services, and skills across national boundaries without regard to the country in which its headquarters is located.

Multinationals often develop their global business in stages. In the first stage, companies operate in one country and sell in others. Second-stage multinationals set up foreign subsidiaries to handle sales in one country. In the third stage, multinationals operate an entire line of business in another country. The fourth stage has evolved primarily due to the Internet and involves mostly high-tech companies. For these firms, the executive suite is virtual. Their top executives and core corporate functions are in different countries, wherever the firms can gain a competitive edge through the availability of talent or capital, low costs, or proximity to their most important customers.

A multinational company may have several worldwide headquarters, depending on where certain markets or technologies are. Britain's APV, a maker of food-processing equipment, has a different headquarters for each of its worldwide businesses.

Many U.S.-based multinationals earn a large percentage of their total revenue abroad. Exhibit 5.1 shows revenue abroad for some industrial companies. Caterpillar, the construction-equipment company, receives 67 percent of its revenue from overseas, and General Electric earns 54 percent of its revenue abroad.

5-2a Are Multinationals Beneficial?

Although multinationals comprise far less than 1 percent of U.S. companies, they account for about 19 percent of all private jobs, 25 percent of all private wages, 48 percent of total exports of goods, and a remarkable 74 percent of nonpublic R&D spending. For decades, U.S. multinationals have driven an outsized share of U.S. productivity growth, the foundation of rising standards of living for everyone. They are responsible for 41 percent of the increase in

multinational corporation a company that is heavily engaged in international trade, beyond exporting and importing

Exhibit 5.1

INDUSTRIAL COMPANIES WITH THE LARGEST OVERSEAS REVENUE

Company	Percent Foreign Revenue	Percent Growth of International Exposure (April 2008–April 2009)
Caterpillar	67	120
General Electric	54	64
United Technologies	46	59
Deere	35	57
Honeywell	39	58

Source: David MacDougall, "Caterpillar Makes the Case for Going Abroad," *TheStreet*, April 27, 2010.

capital intensive
using more capital than labor in the production process

global marketing standardization
production of uniform products that can be sold the same way all over the world

private labor productivity since 1990. More investment and employment abroad have tended to create more American investment and jobs as well. From 1988 to 2007, employment in foreign affiliates rose to 10 million from 4.8 million. During that same period, employment in U.S. parent companies rose to 22 million from 17.7 million.[6] Some multinationals have shifted income to low-tax countries, which has reduced corporate income tax payments in America. The multinationals claim that this was necessary because the United States has a very complicated tax structure with one of the highest corporate income tax rates among industrialized nations.

The role of multinational corporations in developing nations is a subject of controversy. The ability of multinationals to tap financial, physical, and human resources from all over the world and combine them economically and profitably can be of benefit to any country. They also often possess and can transfer the most up-to-date technology. Critics, however, claim that often the wrong kind of technology is transferred to developing nations. Usually, it is **capital intensive** (requiring a greater expenditure for equipment than for labor) and thus does not substantially increase employment. A "modern sector" then emerges in the nation, employing a small proportion of the labor force with relatively high productivity and income levels and with increasingly capital-intensive technologies. In addition, multinationals sometimes support reactionary and oppressive regimes if it is in their best interests to do so. Other critics say that the firms take more wealth out of developing nations than they bring in, thus widening the gap between rich and poor nations. The petroleum industry in particular has been heavily criticized in the past for its actions in some developing countries.

To counter such criticism, more and more multinationals are taking a proactive role in being good global citizens. Sometimes companies are spurred to action by government regulation, and in other cases multinationals are attempting to protect their good brand names.

5-2b Global Marketing Standardization

Traditionally, marketing-oriented multinational corporations have operated somewhat differently in each country. They use a strategy of providing different product features, packaging, advertising, and so on. However, Ted Levitt, a former Harvard professor, described a trend toward what he referred to as "global marketing," with a slightly different meaning.[7] He contended that communication and technology have made the world smaller so that almost all consumers everywhere want all the things they have heard about, seen, or experienced. Thus, he saw the emergence of global markets for standardized consumer products on a huge scale, as opposed to segmented foreign markets with different products. In this book, global marketing is defined as individuals and organizations using a global vision to effectively market goods and services across national boundaries. To make the distinction, we can refer to Levitt's notion as **global marketing standardization**.

Global marketing standardization presumes that the markets throughout the world are becoming more alike. Firms practicing global marketing standardization

McDonald's has been cited as an example of global marketing standardization, but menus like this one indicate that McDonald's also relies on variation.

© China Economy/Alamy

produce "globally standardized products" to be sold the same way all over the world. Uniform production should enable companies to lower production and marketing costs and increase profits. Levitt cited Coca-Cola, Colgate-Palmolive, and McDonald's as successful global marketers. His critics point out, however, that the success of these three companies is really based on variation, not on offering the same product everywhere. McDonald's, for example, changes its salad dressings and provides self-serve espresso for French tastes. It sells bulgogi burgers in South Korea and falafel burgers in Egypt. Further, the fact that Coca-Cola and Colgate-Palmolive sell some of their products in more than 160 countries does not signify that they have adopted a high degree of standardization for all their products globally. Only three Coca-Cola brands are standardized, and one of them, Sprite, has a different formulation in Japan.

Companies with separate subsidiaries in other countries can be said to operate using a multidomestic strategy. A **multidomestic strategy** occurs when multinational firms enable individual subsidiaries to compete independently in domestic markets. Simply put, multidomestic strategy is how multinational firms use strategic business units (see Chapter 2). Colgate-Palmolive uses both strategies: Axion paste dishwashing detergent, for example, was formulated for developing countries, and La Croix Plus detergent was custom made for the French market—examples of multidomestic strategies. Colgate toothpaste is marketed the same way globally, using global marketing standardization.

Nevertheless, some multinational corporations are moving toward a degree of global marketing standardization. Kraft's popular Tang drink, which has dropped off most Americans' radars, is incredibly popular around the world. Kraft markets the beverage in the same way everywhere, and orange is still the most popular flavor.[8]

© HANDOUT/KRT/Newscom

5-3 EXTERNAL ENVIRONMENT FACED BY GLOBAL MARKETERS

A global marketer or a firm considering global marketing must consider the external environment. Many of the same environmental factors that operate in the domestic market also exist internationally. These factors include culture, economic and technological development, political structure and actions, demographic makeup, and natural resources.

5-3a Culture

Central to any society is the common set of values shared by its citizens that determines what is socially acceptable. Culture underlies the family, the educational system, religion, and the social class system. The network of social organizations generates overlapping roles and status positions. These values and roles have a tremendous effect on people's preferences and thus on marketers' options. A company that does not understand a country's culture is doomed to failure in that country. Cultural blunders lead to misunderstandings and often perceptions of rudeness or even incompetence. For example, when people in India shake hands, they sometimes do so rather limply. This isn't a sign of weakness or disinterest; instead, a soft handshake conveys respect. Avoiding eye contact is also a sign of deference in India.

American culture often fascinates other countries, making reality and news programs as broadcast in the United States popular. Several companies such as News Corporation (which operates Fox News) have begun exporting their channels to English-speaking countries such as Britain. Most recently, PBS has been exported to Britain as an alternative to other American programming there. David Lyons, who spearheaded the arrangement, hopes that PBS will help show a different, more historical side of American culture. American audiences can receive a similar cultural exchange through Britain's BBC programming.[9]

Language is another important aspect of culture that can create problems for marketers. Marketers must take care in translating product names, slogans, instructions, and promotional messages so as not to convey the wrong meaning. Free translation software, such as babelfish.com or Google Translate, allows users to input text in one language and output in another language. But marketers must take care using the software, as it can have unintended results—the best being unintelligible, the worst being insulting.

Each country has its own customs and traditions that determine business practices and influence negotiations with foreign customers. In many countries, personal relationships are more important than financial considerations. For instance, skipping social engagements in Mexico may lead to lost sales. Negotiations in Japan often include long evenings of dining, drinking, and entertaining, and only after a close personal relationship has been formed do business negotiations begin.

Making successful sales presentations abroad requires a thorough understanding of the country's culture. Germans, for example, don't like risk and need strong reassurance. A successful presentation to a German client will emphasize three points: the bottom-line benefits of the product or service, that there will be strong service support, and that the product is guaranteed. In southern Europe, it is an insult to show a price list. Without negotiating, you will not close the sale. The English want plenty of documentation for product claims and are less likely to simply accept the word of the sales representative. Scandinavian and Dutch companies are more likely to approach business transactions as Americans do than are companies in any other country.

5-3b Economic Factors

A second major factor in the external environment facing the global marketer is the level of economic development in the countries where it operates. In general, complex and sophisticated industries are found in developed countries, and more basic industries are found in less developed nations. Average family incomes are higher in the more developed countries compared to the less developed countries. Larger incomes mean greater purchasing power and demand not only for consumer goods and services but also for the machinery and workers required to produce consumer goods.

According to the World Bank, the average *gross national income (GNI)* per capita for the world is $10,341.[10] GNI is a country's GDP (defined earlier) together with its income received from other countries (mainly interest and dividends) less similar payments made to other countries. The United States' GNI per capita is $46,790, but it is not the world's highest. That honor goes to Luxembourg at $52,770. Of course, there are many very poor countries: Guinea, $970; Malawi, $810; Mozambique, $771; Sierra Leone, $770; Niger, $680; and Eritrea, $640.[11] GNI per capita is one measure of the ability of a country's citizens to buy various goods and services. A marketer with a global vision can use these data to aid in measuring market potential in countries around the globe.

Not only is per capita income a consideration when going abroad, but so is the cost of doing business in a country. Although it is not the same as the cost of doing business, we can gain insights into expenses by examining the cost of living in various cities. The most expensive cities in the world are Luanda, Angola; Tokyo, Japan; and N'Djamena, Chad. N'Djamena is mired in unrest and violence, and appropriately secure accommodations for both employees and businesses are very hard to come by. Such instability makes N'Djamena a place where it is very expensive to do business. Conditions are similar in Luanda, where a two-bedroom apartment rents for $7,000 a month.[12]

5-3c The Global Economy

A global marketer today must be fully aware of the intertwined nature of the global economy. In the past, the size of the U.S. economy was so large that global markets tended to move up or down depending on its health. It was said, "If America sneezes, then the rest of the world catches a cold." This is still true today. The U.S. housing market collapse and speculative financing led to a major global recession in 2008. It was, in fact, America's deepest decline in economic activity since the Great Depression. As the world slowly pulled itself out of the recession, the possibility of Greece defaulting on its national debt nearly stifled global economic recovery. The Greek crisis was followed by concern about other debt crises in Spain and Portugal. Moreover, the world now looks to other economies such as China, India, and Brazil to help jump-start economic growth. The lesson for the global marketer is clear: forecasting global demand and economic growth requires an understanding of what is happening economically in countries around the globe.

DOING BUSINESS IN CHINA AND INDIA The two countries of growing interest to many multinationals are India and China because of their huge economic potential. They have some of the highest growth rates in the world and are emerging as megamarkets. China and India also have the world's two largest populations, two of the world's largest geographic areas, greater linguistic and sociocultural diversity than any other country, and among the highest levels of income disparity in the world—some people are extremely poor whereas others are very rich. Given this scale and variety, there is no "average Chinese customer" or "average Indian customer."

Both India and China have exploded in spending power, particularly in the upper classes. By 2020, China will likely be the largest luxury market in the world, with sales exceeding $100 billion.[13] Driving this growth are Chinese below the age of forty-five, a demographic that constitutes 73 percent of China's luxury buyers. One market research firm reported a staggering 95 percent increase in online sales in China during 2010, marking another avenue for companies to reach shoppers.[14] Starbucks is hoping to mimic its success in China (where it plans to triple its stores) in India. Affluent Indians often have experienced Starbucks outside of India and would welcome the coffee giant. It is a burgeoning market: coffee consumption increased roughly 90 percent from 1998 to 2008 because the Indian consumer enjoys the casual café atmosphere. Starbucks hopes to increase the distribution of its Indian coffee beans and to open premium locations in Tata's super-luxurious Taj hotels.[15]

Relations between the United States and China have not always been smooth, however. China is committed to protecting its businesses and asserting new global strength, which has resulted in several legislative stalemates with the United States. China has the power and draw of a country with steadily increasing consumption and high growth potential, making it particularly attractive to U.S. firms. China is the fastest-growing importer of U.S. goods—up 330 percent since 2000. The rest of the world increased imports from the United States by only 29 percent. If trade fails, China loses significant U.S. imports, and the United States loses a rapid-growth market.[16]

5-3d Political Structure and Actions

Political structure is a third important variable facing global marketers. Government policies run the gamut from no private ownership and minimal individual freedom to little central government and maximum personal freedom. As rights of private property increase, government-owned industries and centralized planning tend to decrease. But a political environment is rarely at one extreme or the other. India, for instance, is a republic with elements of socialism, monopoly capitalism, and competitive capitalism in its political ideology.

A recent World Bank study found that the least amount of business regulation fosters the strongest economies.[17] The least regulated and most efficient economies are concentrated among countries with well-established common-law traditions, including Australia, Canada, New Zealand, the United Kingdom, and the United States. On a par with the best performers are Singapore and Hong Kong. Not far behind are Denmark, Norway, and Sweden, social democracies that recently streamlined their business

FOOD FIGHTS IN CHINA

In recent years, China has faced a number of **deadly food scares**. One incident killed 6 infants and sickened 300,000 when they drank formula that contained melamine, a material used to make plastics and adhesives. Other incidents involve companies such as Walmart and Carrefour **mislabeling** regular products as organic or natural. Now, offenders will be banned from investing in or operating any food-related businesses for up to five years. The ways an operation can violate a food-safety law are increasing as well, making it harder for companies to operate in China. However, the country is focused on trying to protect its consumers from mislabeled products and food sold past its "best-by" dates. The first year of the new regulations, China will crack down heavily on non-food additives, such as melamine. Each change is a new piece of information to add to the Chinese external environment that global marketers must face.

Source: Yidi Zhao, "Beijing Tightens Food Safety Control with Life Ban in New Rules," *Bloomberg Businessweek*, April 9, 2012, www.businessweek.com/news/2012-04-09/beijing-tightens-food-safety-control-with-life-ban-in-new-rules (Accessed April 11, 2012).

regulation. India, infamous for infrastructure troubles and avoiding international investment, recently made some regulation changes that should help global companies enter the huge Indian market. The major change offers companies such as Walmart more options for establishing business. Before, the company could only wholesale joint ventures. Now, it can own up to 51 percent of joint ventures in India.[18]

LEGAL CONSIDERATIONS Closely related to and often intertwined with the political environment are legal considerations. In France, nationalistic sentiments led to a law that requires pop music stations to play at least 40 percent of their songs in French (even though French teenagers love American and English rock and roll).

Many legal structures are designed to either limit or encourage trade:

▸ **TARIFF:** a tax levied on the goods entering a country. Because a tariff is a tax, it will either reduce the profits of the firms paying the tariff or raise prices to buyers, or both. Normally, a tariff raises prices of the imported goods and makes it easier for domestic firms to compete. The United States maintains tariffs as high as 27 percent on Canadian softwood lumber because the Canadian government allegedly subsidizes the industry.

▸ **QUOTA:** a limit on the amount of a specific product that can enter a country. Several U.S. companies have sought quotas as a means of protection from foreign competition.

▸ **BOYCOTT:** the exclusion of all products from certain countries or companies. Governments use boycotts to exclude companies from countries with which they have a political dispute. Several Arab nations boycotted Coca-Cola because it maintained distributors in Israel.

▸ **EXCHANGE CONTROL:** a law compelling a company earning foreign exchange from its exports to sell it to a control agency, usually a central bank. A company wishing to buy goods abroad must first obtain a foreign currency exchange from the control agency. For instance, Avon Products drastically cut back new production lines and products in the Philippines because exchange controls prevented the company from converting pesos to dollars to ship back to the home office. The pesos had to be used in the Philippines.

▸ **MARKET GROUPING** (also known as a common trade alliance): occurs when several countries agree to work together to form a common trade area that enhances trade opportunities. The best-known market grouping is the European Union (EU).

▸ **TRADE AGREEMENT:** an agreement to stimulate international trade. Not all government efforts are meant to stifle imports or investment by foreign corporations. The largest Latin American trade agreement is **Mercosur**, which includes Argentina, Bolivia, Brazil, Chile, Colombia, Ecuador, Paraguay, Peru, Uruguay, and Venezuela. The elimination of most tariffs among the trading partners has resulted in trade revenues of more than $16 billion annually. The economic boom created by Mercosur will undoubtedly cause other nations to seek trade agreements on their own or to enter Mercosur.

THE URUGUAY ROUND, THE FAILED DOHA ROUND, AND BILATERAL AGREEMENTS The **Uruguay Round** is an agreement that has dramatically lowered trade barriers worldwide. Adopted in 1994, the agreement has been signed by 151 nations. It is the most ambitious global trade agreement ever negotiated. The agreement has reduced tariffs by one-third worldwide—a move that has raised global income by $235 billion annually. Perhaps most notable is the recognition of new global realities. For the first time, an agreement covers services, intellectual property rights, and trade-related investment measures such as exchange controls.

The Uruguay Round made several major changes in world trading practices.

▸ **ENTERTAINMENT, PHARMACEUTICALS, INTEGRATED CIRCUITS, AND SOFTWARE:** The rules protect patents, copyrights, and trademarks for twenty years. Computer programs receive fifty years of protection, and semiconductor chips receive ten years of protection. But many developing nations were given a decade to phase in patent protection for drugs. France, which limits the number of U.S. movies and television shows that can be shown, refused to liberalize market access for the U.S. entertainment industry.

▸ **FINANCIAL, LEGAL, AND ACCOUNTING SERVICES:** Services came under international trading rules for the first time, creating a vast opportunity for these competitive U.S. industries. Now it is easier for managers and key personnel to be admitted to a country. Licensing standards for professionals, such as doctors, cannot discriminate against foreign applicants. That is, foreign applicants cannot be held to higher standards than domestic practitioners.

▸ **AGRICULTURE:** Europe is gradually reducing farm subsidies, opening new opportunities for such U.S. farm exports as wheat and corn. Japan and Korea are beginning to import rice. But U.S. growers of sugar and citrus fruit have had their subsidies trimmed.

▸ **TEXTILES AND APPAREL:** Strict quotas limiting imports from developing countries are being phased out, causing further job losses in the U.S. clothing trade. But retailers and consumers are the big winners, because past quotas have added $15 billion a year to clothing prices.

▸ **A NEW TRADE ORGANIZATION:** The **World Trade Organization (WTO)** replaced the old **General Agreement on Tariffs and Trade (GATT)**, which was created in 1948. The WTO eliminated the extensive loopholes of which GATT members took advantage. Today, all WTO members must fully comply with all agreements under the Uruguay Round. The WTO also has an effective dispute settlement procedure with strict time limits to resolve disputes.

The latest round of WTO trade talks began in Doha, Qatar, in 2001. For the most part, the periodic meetings of WTO members under the Doha Round have been very contentious. One of the most contentious goals of the round was for the major developing countries, known collectively as BRIC (Brazil, Russia, India, and China), to lower tariffs on industrial goods in exchange for European and American tariff and subsidy cuts on farm products. Concerned that lowering tariffs would result in an economically damaging influx of foreign cotton, sugar, and rice, China and India demanded a safeguard clause that would allow them to raise tariffs on those crops if imports surged. Unable to agree on what percentage increase constituted a surge in imports, the countries remain at an impasse.[19]

In addition to the slow progress of the Doha Round, many countries have moved toward protectionism after the global recession of 2008–2009. This movement discourages new trade agreements, which are designed to encourage international trade. Ecuador, for instance, has hiked tariffs on more than 600 categories of imports. Chinese companies have made several allegations that the United States is engaging in protectionism and blocking companies from participating in bids for work or companies for sale.[20]

However, the move toward protectionism has not reversed the agreements and organizations that arose from the period of increased globalization before the economic crisis in 2008: the North American Free Trade Agreement, the Central America Free Trade Agreement, the European Union, the World Bank, and the International Monetary Fund.

NORTH AMERICAN FREE TRADE AGREEMENT At the time it was instituted, the **North American Free Trade Agreement (NAFTA)** created the world's largest free trade zone. Ratified by the U.S. Congress in 1993, the agreement includes Canada, the United States, and Mexico, with a combined population of 441 million and an economy of $17 trillion.

The main impact of NAFTA was to open the Mexican market to U.S. companies. When the treaty went into effect,

World Trade Organization (WTO) a trade organization that replaced the old General Agreement on Tariffs and Trade (GATT)

General Agreement on Tariffs and Trade (GATT) a trade agreement that contained loopholes enabling countries to avoid trade-barrier reduction agreements

North American Free Trade Agreement (NAFTA) an agreement between Canada, the United States, and Mexico that created the world's then-largest free trade zone

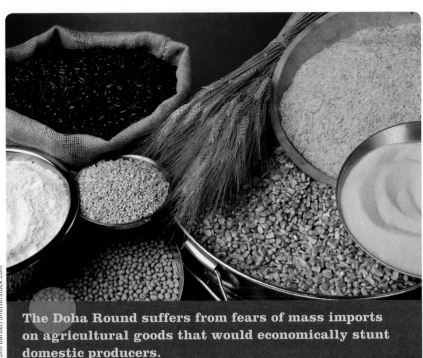

The Doha Round suffers from fears of mass imports on agricultural goods that would economically stunt domestic producers.

© Jim Barber/Shutterstock.com

tariffs on about half the items traded across the Rio Grande disappeared. The pact removed a web of Mexican licensing requirements, quotas, and tariffs that limited transactions in U.S. goods and services. For instance, the pact allowed U.S. and Canadian financial-services companies to own subsidiaries in Mexico.

In August 2007, the three member countries met in Canada to tweak NAFTA but not make substantial changes. For example, the members agreed to further remove trade barriers on hogs, steel, consumer electronics, and chemicals. They also directed the North American Steel Trade Committee, which represents the three governments, to focus on subsidized steel from China.

The real question is whether NAFTA can continue to deliver rising prosperity in all three countries. America has certainly benefited from cheaper imports and more investment opportunities abroad. According to the World Trade Organization, trade between the three countries comprised 51 percent of total trade, whereas 49 percent of exports went to other countries.[21]

NAFTA has also created millions of jobs for all three nations. It is estimated that Canada has gained almost 5 million jobs, the United States has picked up 25 million jobs, and Mexico has created nearly 10 million jobs.[22]

CENTRAL AMERICA FREE TRADE AGREEMENT The **Central America Free Trade Agreement (CAFTA)** was instituted in 2005. Besides the United States, the agreement includes Costa Rica, the Dominican Republic, El Salvador, Guatemala, Honduras, and Nicaragua.

Between 2005 and 2007, trade between the United States and CAFTA countries grew 18 percent. The United States exported $23 billion of goods and services to CAFTA nations in 2007, up 33 percent since 2005. The United States imported $19 billion of goods and services from CAFTA nations, up 4 percent since 2005.[23] CAFTA has been an unqualified success. It has created new commercial opportunities for its members, has promoted regional stability, and is an impetus for economic development for an important group of U.S. neighbors.

EUROPEAN UNION The **European Union (EU)** is one of the world's most important free trade zones and now encompasses most of Europe. More than a free trade

zone, it is also a political and economic community. As a free trade zone, it guarantees the freedom of movement of people, goods, services, and capital between member states. It also maintains a common trade policy with outside nations and a regional development policy. The EU represents member nations in the WTO. Recently, the EU also began venturing into foreign policy as well, getting involved in issues such as Iran's refining of uranium.

The European Union currently has twenty-seven member states: Austria, Belgium, Bulgaria, Cyprus, the Czech Republic, Denmark, Estonia, Finland, France, Germany, Greece, Hungary, Ireland, Italy, Latvia, Lithuania, Luxembourg, Malta, the Netherlands, Poland, Portugal, Romania, Slovakia, Slovenia, Spain, Sweden, and the United Kingdom. There are currently six official candidate countries: Croatia, Iceland, the Republic of Macedonia, Montenegro, Serbia, and Turkey. In addition, the western Balkan countries of Albania and Bosnia-Herzegovina are officially recognized as potential candidates.[24]

In early 2010, Greece entered a financial crisis that highlighted the challenges of a large currency union where member nations maintain responsibility for their own fiscal policies. Unable to devalue its currency to boost sales of products without injuring other member nations, Greece turned to member states for a bailout. The crisis has highlighted debt problems in other EU nations such as Spain and Ireland. Ireland, after a burst property bubble, may also need a bailout, while Greece faces protests as it imposes austerity measures in order to receive continued bailout money.[25]

The European Union Commission and the courts have not always been kind to multinationals. For example, the EU fined Procter & Gamble, Unilever, and Henkel for running a cartel that fixed laundry detergent prices. The EU investigated the three companies and found that they formed the cartel after joining in efforts to reduce packaging materials for Ariel and Tide (P&G), OMO and Radiant (Unilever), and Persil (Henkel). In that meeting, the three companies agreed on pricing and respective market share, which the EU determined unfairly limited competition and forced consumers to pay higher prices. All three companies agreed to cooperate with the investigation and are paying the fine.[26]

The EU is the largest economy in the world. The EU is also a huge market, with a population of nearly 500 million and a GDP of $18 trillion. The United States and the EU have the largest bilateral trade and investment relationship

World Bank an international bank that offers low-interest loans, advice, and information to developing nations

International Monetary Fund (IMF) an international organization that acts as a lender of last resort, providing loans to troubled nations, and also works to promote trade through financial cooperation

Despite the country's dire financial situation, Greeks are protesting the austerity measures imposed by the government. Many of the measures directly impact huge portions of the population.

in world history. Together, they account for more than half of the global economy, while bilateral trade accounts for 7 percent of the world total. U.S. and EU companies have invested an estimated $2 trillion in each other's economies, employing directly and indirectly as many as 14 million workers. Nearly every U.S. state is involved with exporting to, importing from, or working for European firms.[27]

The EU is an attractive market, with purchasing power almost equal to that of the United States. But the EU presents marketing challenges because, even with standardized regulations, marketers will not be able to produce a single European product for a generic European consumer. With more than fourteen different languages and individual national customs, Europe will always be far more diverse than the United States. Thus, product differences will continue to be necessary.

An entirely different type of problem facing global marketers is the possibility of a protectionist movement by the EU against outsiders. For example, European automakers have proposed holding Japanese imports at roughly their current 10 percent market share. The Irish, Danes, and Dutch don't make cars and have unrestricted home markets; they would be unhappy about limited imports of Toyotas and Nissans. But France has a strict quota on Japanese cars to protect Renault and Peugeot. These local carmakers could be hurt if the quota is raised at all.

THE WORLD BANK, THE INTERNATIONAL MONETARY FUND, AND THE G-20 Two international financial organizations are instrumental in fostering global trade. The **World Bank** offers low-interest loans to developing nations. Originally, the purpose of the loans was to help these nations build infrastructure such as roads, power plants, schools, drainage projects, and hospitals. Now the World Bank offers loans to help developing nations relieve their debt burdens. To receive the loans, countries must pledge to lower trade barriers and aid private enterprise. In addition to making loans, the World Bank is a major source of advice and information for developing nations. The **International Monetary Fund (IMF)** was founded in 1945, one year after the creation of the World Bank, to promote trade through financial cooperation and eliminate trade barriers in the process. The IMF makes short-term loans to member nations that are unable to meet their budgetary expenses. It operates as a lender of last resort for troubled nations, such as Greece. In exchange for these emergency loans, IMF lenders frequently extract significant commitments from the borrowing nations to address the problems that led to the crises. These steps may include curtailing imports or even devaluing the currency. Greece, working with both the IMF and the EU, has raised taxes to unprecedented levels, cut government spending (including pensions), and implemented labor reforms such as reducing the minimum wage, as part of its austerity measures to receive loans from the IMF and the EU.[28]

The **Group of Twenty (G-20)** finance ministers and central bank governors was established in 1999 to bring together industrialized and developing economies to discuss key issues in the global economy. The G-20 is a forum for international economic development that promotes discussion between industrial and emerging-market countries on key issues related to global economic stability. By contributing to the strengthening of the international financial system and providing opportunities for discussion on national policies, international cooperation, and international financial institutions, the G-20 helps to support growth and development across the globe. The members of the G-20 are shown in Exhibit 5.2.

In 2009, the G-20 met in Pittsburgh, Pennsylvania, where it adopted President Obama's proposed *Framework for Strong, Sustainable, and Balanced Growth*. The document outlined a process to help avoid other financial crises such as the one that started in the financial markets in the United States in 2007. It also provided recommendations for long-term global growth.

5-3e Demographic Makeup

The three most densely populated nations in the world are China, India, and Indonesia. But that fact alone is not particularly useful to marketers. They also need to know whether the population is mostly urban or rural, because marketers may not have easy access to rural consumers. Belgium, with about 90 percent of the population living in urban settings, is an attractive market.

Exhibit 5.2

MEMBERS OF THE G-20

Argentina	European Union	Italy	Saudi Arabia
Australia	France	Japan	South Africa
Brazil	Germany	Mexico	Turkey
Canada	India	Republic of Korea	United Kingdom
China	Indonesia	Russia	United States

Another key demographic consideration is age. There is a wide gap between the older populations of the industrialized countries and the vast working-age populations of developing countries. This gap has enormous implications for economies, businesses, and the competitiveness of individual countries. It means that while Europe and Japan struggle with pension schemes and the rising cost of health care, countries like Brazil, China, and Mexico can reap the fruits of a demographic dividend: falling labor costs, a healthier and more educated population, and the entry of millions of women into the workforce. The demographic dividend is a gift of falling birthrates, and it causes a temporary bulge in the number of working-age people. Population experts have estimated that one-third of East Asia's economic miracle can be attributed to a beneficial age structure. But the miracle occurred only because the governments had policies in place to educate their people, create jobs, and improve health.

5-3f Natural Resources

A final factor in the external environment that has become more evident in the past decade is the shortage of natural resources. For example, petroleum shortages have created huge amounts of wealth for oil-producing countries such as Norway, Saudi Arabia, and the United Arab Emirates. Both consumer and industrial markets have blossomed in these countries. Other countries—such as Indonesia, Mexico, and Venezuela—were able to borrow heavily against oil reserves in order to develop more rapidly. On the other hand, industrial countries such as Japan, the United States, and much of Western Europe experienced an enormous transfer of wealth to the petroleum-rich nations. The high price of oil has created inflationary pressures in petroleum-importing nations. It also created major problems for airlines and other petroleum-dependent industries. Petroleum is not the only natural resource that affects international marketing. Warm climate and lack of water mean that many of Africa's countries will remain importers of foodstuffs. The United States, on the other hand, must rely on Africa for many precious metals. Vast differences in natural resources create international dependencies, huge shifts of wealth, inflation and recession, export opportunities for countries with abundant resources, and even a stimulus for military intervention.

© Cengage Learning

5-4 GLOBAL MARKETING BY THE INDIVIDUAL FIRM

A company should consider entering the global marketplace only after its management has a solid grasp of the global environment.

Companies decide to "go global" for a number of reasons. Perhaps the most important is to earn additional profits. Managers may feel that international sales will result in higher profit margins or more added-on profits. A second stimulus is that a firm may have a unique product or technological advantage not available to other international competitors. Such advantages should result in major business successes abroad. In other situations, management may have exclusive market information about foreign customers, marketplaces, or market situations not known to others. While exclusivity can provide an initial motivation for international marketing, managers must realize that competitors can be expected to catch up with the firm's information advantage. Finally, saturated domestic markets, excess capacity, and potential for economies of scale can also be motivators to "go global." Economies of scale mean that average per-unit production costs fall as output is increased.

Many firms form multinational partnerships—called strategic alliances—to assist them in penetrating global markets; strategic alliances are examined in Chapter 7. Five other methods of entering the global marketplace are, in order of risk, exporting, licensing and franchising, contract manufacturing, joint venture, and direct investment (see Exhibit 5.3).

5-4a Exporting

When a company decides to enter the global market, exporting is usually the least complicated and least risky alternative. **Exporting** is selling domestically produced products to buyers in other countries. A company can sell directly to foreign importers or buyers. The United States is the world's largest exporter.

Instead of selling directly to foreign buyers, a company may decide to sell to intermediaries located in its domestic market. The most common intermediary is the export merchant, also known as a **buyer for export**, which is usually treated like a domestic customer by the domestic manufacturer. The buyer for export assumes all risks and sells internationally for its own account. The domestic firm is involved only to the extent that its products are bought in foreign markets.

A second type of intermediary is the **export broker**, who plays the traditional broker's role by bringing buyer and seller together. The manufacturer still retains title and assumes all the risks. Export brokers operate primarily in agricultural products and raw materials.

Export agents, a third type of intermediary, are foreign sales agents/distributors who live in the foreign country and perform the same functions as domestic manufacturers' agents, helping with international financing, shipping, and so on. The U.S. Department of Commerce has an agent/distributor service that helps

exporting selling domestically produced products to buyers in other countries

buyer for export an intermediary in the global market who assumes all ownership risks and sells globally for its own account

export broker an intermediary who plays the traditional broker's role by bringing buyer and seller together

export agent an intermediary who acts like a manufacturer's agent for the exporter; the export agent lives in the foreign market

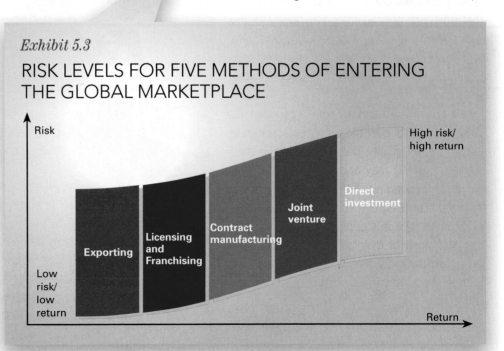

Exhibit 5.3

RISK LEVELS FOR FIVE METHODS OF ENTERING THE GLOBAL MARKETPLACE

© Cengage Learning

about 5,000 U.S. companies each year find an agent or distributor in virtually any country of the world. A second category of agents resides in the manufacturer's country but represents foreign buyers. This type of agent acts as a hired purchasing agent for foreign customers operating in the exporter's home market.

5-4b Licensing and Franchising

Another effective way for a firm to move into the global arena with relatively little risk is to sell a license to manufacture its product to someone in a foreign country. **Licensing** is the legal process whereby a licensor allows another firm to use its manufacturing process, trademarks, patents, trade secrets, or other proprietary knowledge. The licensee, in turn, pays the licensor a royalty or fee agreed on by both parties.

For example, the owners of the rights to Broadway plays, such as Disney's *The Lion King*, have seen increasing revenue from foreign markets through licensing. The rights to produce the plays internationally have different price points, but foreign presenters begin by paying $200,000 in advance to stage a U.S. production. Replica shows, using licensed sets and costumes, cost the most; nonreplica shows, which pay for the rights to the play but not sets or costuming, cost less. Foreign revenue for licensing nonreplica shows grew more than 10 percent between 2008 and 2010.[29]

A licensor must make sure it can exercise sufficient control over the licensee's activities to ensure proper quality, pricing, distribution, and so on. Licensing may also create a new competitor in the long run, if the licensee decides to void the license agreement. International law is often ineffective in stopping such actions. Two common ways of maintaining effective control over licensees are shipping one or more critical components from the United States or locally registering patents and trademarks to the U.S. firm, not to the licensee. Garment companies maintain control by delivering only so many

labels per day; they also supply their own fabric, collect the scraps, and do accurate unit counts.

Franchising is a form of licensing that has grown rapidly in recent years. More than 400 U.S. franchisors operate more than 40,000 outlets in foreign countries, bringing in sales of over $9 billion.[30] Over half of the international franchises are for fast-food restaurants and business services.

CONTRACT MANUFACTURING Firms that do not want to become involved in licensing or to become heavily involved in global marketing may engage in **contract manufacturing**, which is private label manufacturing by

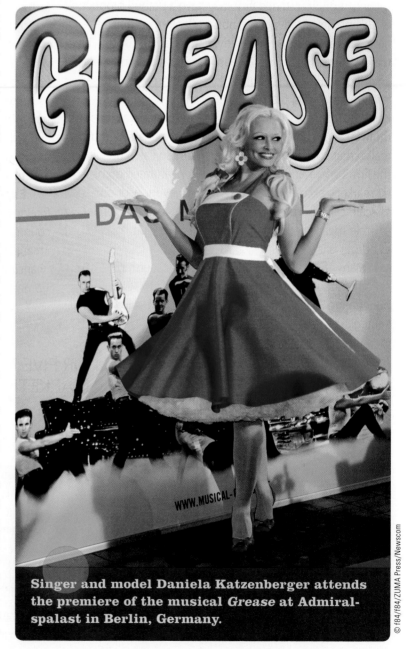

Singer and model Daniela Katzenberger attends the premiere of the musical *Grease* at Admiralspalast in Berlin, Germany.

a foreign company. The foreign company produces a certain volume of products to specification, with the domestic firm's brand name on the goods. The domestic company usually handles the marketing. Thus, the domestic firm can broaden its global marketing base without investing in overseas plants and equipment. After establishing a solid base, the domestic firm may switch to a joint venture or direct investment.

5-4c Joint Venture

Joint ventures are somewhat similar to licensing agreements. In an international **joint venture**, the domestic firm buys part of a foreign company or joins with a foreign company to create a new entity. A joint venture is a quick and relatively inexpensive way to go global and to gain needed expertise. Chronicle Books joined the existing Abrams marketing and sales team in the United Kingdom in a joint venture called Abrams & Chronicle Books to expand its presence in the UK market.[31]

Joint ventures can be very risky, however. Many fail; others fall victim to a takeover in which one partner buys out the other. Sometimes joint venture partners simply can't agree on management strategies and policies.

5-4d Direct Investment

Active ownership of a foreign company or of overseas manufacturing or marketing facilities is called **direct foreign investment**. Direct foreign investment by U.S. firms is currently about $2.1 trillion. Direct investors have either a controlling interest or a large minority interest in the firm. Thus, they have the greatest potential reward and the greatest potential risk. Because of problems with contract manufacturing and joint ventures in China, multinationals are going it alone. Today, nearly five times as much foreign direct investment comes into China in the form of stand-alone efforts as comes in for joint ventures.

A firm may make a direct foreign investment by acquiring an interest in an existing company or by building new facilities. It might do so because it has trouble transferring some resource to a foreign operation or getting that resource locally. One important resource is personnel, especially managers. If the local labor market is tight, the firm may buy an entire foreign firm and retain all its employees instead of paying higher salaries than competitors.

The United States is a popular place for direct investment by foreign companies. In 2008, the value of foreign-owned businesses in the United States was more than $650 billion. For example, in 2007, Taiwan-based Acer bought U.S. computer maker Gateway.

joint venture when a domestic firm buys part of a foreign company or joins with a foreign company to create a new entity

direct foreign investment active ownership of a foreign company or of overseas manufacturing or marketing facilities

5-5 THE GLOBAL MARKETING MIX

To succeed, firms seeking to enter into foreign trade must still adhere to the principles of the marketing mix. Information gathered on foreign markets through research is the basis for the four Ps of global marketing strategy: product, place (distribution), promotion, and price. Marketing managers who understand the advantages and disadvantages of different ways of entering the global market and the effect of the external environment on the firm's marketing mix have a better chance of reaching their goals.

The first step in creating a marketing mix is developing a thorough understanding of the global target market. Often this knowledge can be obtained through the same types of marketing research used in the domestic market (see Chapter 9). However, global marketing research is conducted in vastly different environments. Conducting a survey can be difficult in developing countries, where telephone ownership is growing but is not always common and mail delivery is slow or sporadic. Drawing samples based on known population parameters is often difficult because of the lack of data. In some cities in Africa, Asia, Mexico, and South America, street maps are unavailable, streets are unidentified, and houses are unnumbered. Moreover, the questions a marketer can ask may differ in other cultures. In some cultures, people tend to be more private than in the United States and will not respond to personal questions on surveys. For instance, in France, questions about one's age and income are considered especially rude.

5-5a Product Decisions

With the proper information, a good marketing mix can be developed. One important decision is whether to alter

Offering a free sample of a product with another purchase, can be useful all over the world, such as Tide's promotions in China.

the product or the promotion for the global marketplace. Other options are to radically change the product or to adjust either the promotional message or the product to suit local conditions.

ONE PRODUCT, ONE MESSAGE The strategy of global marketing standardization, which was discussed earlier, means developing a single product for all markets and promoting it the same way all over the world. For instance, Procter & Gamble uses the same product and promotional themes for Head & Shoulders in China as it does in the United States. The advertising draws attention to a person's dandruff problem, which stands out in a nation of black-haired people. Head & Shoulders is now the best-selling shampoo in China despite costing over 300 percent more than local brands. Buoyed by its success with Head & Shoulders, P&G is using the same product and same promotion strategy with Tide detergent in China. It also used another common promotion tactic that has been successful in the United States. The company spent half a million dollars to reach agreements with local washing machine manufacturers, which now include a free box of Tide with every new washer.

Global media—especially satellite and cable television networks such as CNN International, MTV Networks, and British Sky Broadcasting—make it possible to beam advertising to audiences unreachable a few years ago. Eighteen-year-olds in Paris often have more in common with eighteen-year-olds in New York than with their own parents. Almost all of MTV's advertisers run unified,

English-language campaigns in the twenty-eight nations the firm reaches. The audiences buy the same products, go to the same movies, listen to the same music, and sip the same colas. Global advertising merely works on that premise. Although teens throughout the world prefer movies above all other forms of television programming, they are closely followed by music videos, stand-up comedy, and then sports.

Global marketing standardization can sometimes backfire. Unchanged products may fail simply because of cultural factors. Any type of war game tends to do very poorly in Germany, even though Germany is by far the world's biggest game-playing nation. A successful game in Germany is highly detailed and has a thick rulebook.

Sometimes the desire for absolute standardization must give way to practical considerations and local market dynamics. For example, because of the feminine connotations of the word *diet*, the European version of Diet Coke is Coca-Cola Light. Even if the brand name differs by market—as with Lay's potato chips, which are called Sabritas in Mexico—a strong visual relationship may be created by uniform application of the brandmark and graphic elements on packaging.

PRODUCT INVENTION In the context of global marketing, product invention can be taken to mean either creating a new product for a market or drastically changing an existing product. For example, Dunkin' Donuts offers American-style donuts in Korea, but the firm created a number of new items for Korean tastes. The company offers sweet potato donuts, glutinous rice donuts, and several varieties of tofu donuts.[32]

McDonald's was once vilified for pushing its American-created fast food on the world. Now it is taking a different approach and selling more than ever in the global marketplace.

GLOBAL MEDIA MAKE IT POSSIBLE TO BEAM ADVERTISING TO AUDIENCES UNREACHABLE A FEW YEARS AGO.

PRODUCT ADAPTATION Another alternative for global marketers is to slightly alter a basic product to meet local conditions. Unilever's Rexona brand deodorant sticks sell for sixteen cents and up. They are big hits in Bolivia, India, Peru, and the Philippines—where Unilever has grabbed 60 percent of the deodorant market. In many cases, the company makes smaller packages, often single-use packages, to accommodate lower-income areas.

Fast-food restaurants often adapt products to fit the needs of their foreign customers. In India, Domino's sells a pizza called the Peppy Paneer, which features the popular Indian cheese paneer and spicy red peppers. McDonald's, known for its foreign adaptations, sells Chicken Maharaja Macs instead of Big Macs, out of respect for the cow's sacred status for Hindus.[33]

5-5b Promotion Adaptation

Another global marketing strategy is to maintain the same basic product but alter the promotional strategy. Bicycles are mainly pleasure vehicles in the United States. In many parts of the world, however, they are a family's main mode of transportation. Thus, promotion in these countries should stress durability and efficiency. In contrast, U.S. advertising may emphasize escaping and having fun.

Language barriers, translation problems, and cultural differences have generated numerous headaches for international marketing managers. For example, a toothpaste claiming to give users white teeth was especially inappropriate in many areas of Southeast Asia, where the well-to-do chew betel nuts and black teeth are a sign of higher social status.

5-5c Place (Distribution)

Solving promotional and product problems does not guarantee global marketing success. The product still has to get adequate distribution. For example, Europeans don't play sports as much as Americans do, so they don't visit sporting-goods stores as often. Realizing this, Reebok started selling its shoes in about 800 traditional shoe stores in France. In one year, the company doubled its French sales.

To combat distribution problems, companies are using creative strategies. A small company in India is setting up a unique distribution system that will allow large and small companies to distribute their goods to very small retailers in villages of 5,000 people or less. The company, Universal Village, uses a large sales staff, often from the villages they work with, to take orders from the small retailers. The staff then send the orders through a mobile application to a warehouse. The warehouse packs the order into small boxes, and those boxes are delivered to each retailer. Not only does the system help distribute a wider range of products, but it also allows these small retailers to operate more efficiently because they don't have to leave their shops to travel large distances to restock their stores.[34]

In many developing nations, channels of distribution and the physical infrastructure are inadequate. In Africa, the continent's GDP is growing rapidly, and African businesses want to expand. Unfortunately, they face high tariffs, weak infrastructure, and severely impoverished populations. To expand into neighboring countries, Notore Chemical Industries Ltd., a Nigerian fertilizer company, appealed directly to the governments to develop a distribution chain across twenty African nations. Some East African countries are even developing a regional trade zone to encourage growth.[35]

American companies importing goods from overseas facilities to the United States are facing other problems. Logistics has been a growing challenge for U.S. companies seeking to cut costs by shifting more production to countries where manufacturing is cheaper. Now, however, the rising costs for shipping goods are adding to their profit pressures. The surge in global trade in recent years has added to strains and charges for all forms of transport. As a result, some manufacturers are developing costly buffer stocks—which can mean setting up days' or weeks' worth of extra components—to avoid shutting down production lines and failing to make timely deliveries. Others are shifting to more expensive but more reliable modes of transport, such as airfreight, which is faster and less prone to delays than ocean shipping.

5-5d Pricing

Once marketing managers have determined a global product and promotion strategy, they can select the remainder of the marketing mix. Pricing presents some unique problems in the global sphere. Exporters must not only cover their production costs but also consider transportation costs, insurance, taxes, and tariffs. When deciding on a final price, marketers must also determine how much customers are willing to spend on a particular product. Marketers also need to ensure that their foreign buyers will pay the price. Because developing nations lack mass purchasing power, selling to them often poses special pricing problems. Sometimes a product can be simplified in order to lower the price. The firm must not assume low-income countries are willing to accept lower quality, however. L'Oréal was unsuccessful selling cheap shampoo in India, so the company targets the rising class. It now sells a $17 Paris face powder and a $25 Vichy sunscreen. Both products are very popular.

EXCHANGE RATES The exchange rate is the price of one country's currency in terms of another country's currency. If a country's currency *appreciates*, less of that country's currency is needed to buy another country's currency. If a country's currency *depreciates*, more of that currency will be needed to buy another country's currency.

How do appreciation and depreciation affect the prices of a country's goods? If, say, the U.S. dollar depreciates relative to the Japanese yen, U.S. residents will have to pay more dollars to buy Japanese goods. To illustrate, suppose the dollar price of a yen is $0.012 and that a Toyota is priced at 2 million yen. At this exchange rate, a U.S. resident pays $24,000 for a Toyota ($0.012 x 2 million yen = $24,000). If the dollar depreciates to $0.018 to 1 yen, then the U.S. resident will have to pay $36,000 for the same Toyota.

As the dollar depreciates, the prices of Japanese goods rise for U.S. residents, so they buy

fewer Japanese goods—thus, U.S. imports may decline. At the same time, as the dollar depreciates relative to the yen, the yen appreciates relative to the dollar. This means prices of U.S. goods fall for the Japanese, so they buy more U.S. goods—and U.S. exports rise.

Currency markets operate under a system of **floating exchange rates**. Prices of different currencies "float" up and down based on the demand for and the supply of each currency. Global currency traders create the supply of and demand for a particular country's currency based on that country's investment, trade potential, and economic strength.

DUMPING **Dumping** is the sale of an exported product at a price lower than that charged for the same or a like product in the "home" market of the exporter. This practice is regarded as a form of price discrimination that can potentially harm the importing nation's competing industries. Dumping may occur as a result of exporter business strategies that include (1) trying to increase an overseas market share, (2) temporarily distributing products in overseas markets to offset slack demand in the home market, (3) lowering unit costs by exploiting large-scale production, and (4) attempting to maintain stable prices during periods of exchange rate fluctuations.

Historically, the dumping of goods has presented serious problems in international trade. As a result, dumping has led to significant disagreements among countries and diverse views about its harmfulness. Some trade economists view dumping as harmful only when it involves the use of "predatory" practices that intentionally try to eliminate competition and gain monopoly

IF A COUNTRY'S CURRENCY DEPRECIATES, MORE OF THAT CURRENCY WILL BE NEEDED TO BUY ANOTHER COUNTRY'S CURRENCY.

© Otna Ydur/Shutterstock.com

power in a market. They believe that predatory dumping rarely occurs and that antidumping rules are a protectionist tool whose cost to consumers and import-using industries exceeds the benefits to the industries receiving protection.

COUNTERTRADE Global trade does not always involve cash. Countertrade is a fast-growing way to conduct global business. In **countertrade**, all or part of the payment for goods or services is in the form of other goods or services. Countertrade is thus a form of barter (swapping goods for goods), an age-old practice whose origins have been traced back to cave dwellers. The U.S. Department of Commerce says that roughly 30 percent of all global trade is countertrade. In fact, both India and China have made billion-dollar government purchasing lists, with most of the goods to be paid for by countertrade.

One common type of countertrade is straight barter. For example, PepsiCo sends Pepsi syrup to Russian bottling plants and in payment gets Stolichnaya vodka, which is then marketed in the West. Another form of countertrade is the compensation agreement. Typically, a company provides technology and equipment for a plant in a developing nation and agrees to take full or partial payment in goods produced by that plant. For example, General Tire Company supplied equipment and know-how for a Romanian truck tire plant. In turn, General Tire sold the tires it received from the plant in the United States under the Victoria brand name. Both sides benefit even though they don't use cash.

5-6 THE IMPACT OF THE INTERNET

In many respects, "going global" is easier than it has ever been before. Opening an e-commerce site on the Internet immediately puts a company in the international marketplace. Sophisticated language translation software can make any site accessible to people around the world. Global shippers such as UPS, FedEx, and DHL help solve international e-commerce distribution complexities. E4X Inc. offers software to ease currency conversions by allowing customers to pay in the currency of their choice. E4X collects the payment from the customer and then pays the site in U.S. dollars. Nevertheless, the promise of "borderless commerce" and the global "Internet economy" are still being restrained by the old brick-and-mortar rules, regulations, and habits. For example, Lands' End is not allowed to mention its unconditional refund policy on its e-commerce site in Germany because German retailers, which normally do not allow returns after fourteen days, sued and won a court ruling blocking mention of it.

5-6a Social Media in Global Marketing

Because Facebook, YouTube, and other social media are popular around the world, firms both large and small have embraced social media marketing. Tim Hortons, a Canadian fast-casual restaurant chain known for its coffee

countertrade a form of trade in which all or part of the payment for goods or services is in the form of other goods or services

blog a publicly accessible Web page that functions as an interactive journal, where readers can post comments on the author's entries

and donuts, has over 3,000 stores. To engage its Facebook fans, the company will occasionally post a picture of one of its restaurants on Facebook, and its 1.4 million fans guess the location. Every time a fan makes a guess, Facebook posts a Tim Hortons branded message to that fan's and his friends' news feeds. The Sacred Ride is a bicycle shop in the small town of Nelson, British Columbia. The firm created a Facebook page, purchased Facebook ads, and targeted the ads to mountain bike enthusiasts. Within a short time, The Sacred Ride had over $40,000 in incremental sales from outside its regular market.

Accor, a French company operating over 4,400 hotels worldwide, uses a company called TrustYou to monitor online reviews, tweets (comments posted on Twitter), and blog posts. A **blog** is a publicly accessible Web page that functions as an interactive journal, where readers can post comments on the author's entries. TrustYou continuously gathers information in fifteen different languages from travel review and social media sites, including Facebook,

Foursquare, Google Places, TripAdvisor, HolidayCheck, Twitter, Qype, Yelp, and blogs, for user-generated content pertaining to a particular hotel or restaurant. TrustYou takes opinions from all online reviews, tweets, and posts and creates a comprehensive Trust Score that reflects the global sentiment for a specific hotel or restaurant. By monitoring social media via TrustYou, Accor hotels can see where they stand against competitors and identify strength and weaknesses.[36]

Global marketers use social media not only for understanding consumers but also to build their brands as they expand internationally. Uniqlo is a Japanese retailer of low-cost, quality casual wear targeted to young adults that competes directly with Zara and H&M. In 2006, the company began to shift its promotional focus to the Internet and away from traditional media such as newspapers and television. The creative campaigns emphasize dance, music, and color rather than the spoken word. This enables Uniqlo to overcome language barriers as it expands globally.

One of the company's first online campaigns was called "Uniqlock," which was designed to build brand awareness internationally. It featured a clock with spliced clips of well-choreographed dancing and catchy lounge music. It ran all year round, 24/7. In summer the girls dancing wore polo shirts; in winter, cashmere; and at midnight they slept.

The Uniqlock contained a blog widget so the clock could be embedded into blog sites. After a year, over 27,000 bloggers from seventy-six countries had picked up the Uniqlock. Between the blogs and the Web site that accompanied the campaign, the Uniqlock had been viewed 68 million times in 209 countries.[37] Sales increased worldwide by 49 percent. By 2020, the firm hopes to have 4,000 stores worldwide and be the world's leading clothing retailer.[38]

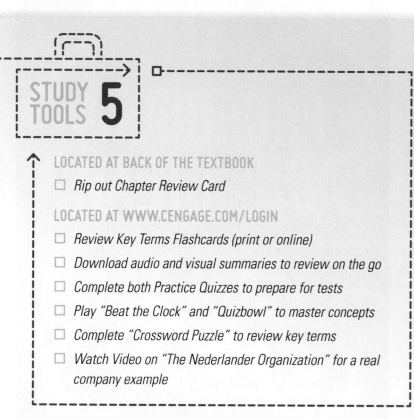

STUDY TOOLS 5

↑ LOCATED AT BACK OF THE TEXTBOOK

☐ *Rip out Chapter Review Card*

LOCATED AT WWW.CENGAGE.COM/LOGIN

☐ *Review Key Terms Flashcards (print or online)*

☐ *Download audio and visual summaries to review on the go*

☐ *Complete both Practice Quizzes to prepare for tests*

☐ *Play "Beat the Clock" and "Quizbowl" to master concepts*

☐ *Complete "Crossword Puzzle" to review key terms*

☐ *Watch Video on "The Nederlander Organization" for a real company example*

ANATOMY OF A MULTINATIONAL COMPANY: STARBUCKS

CANADA

USA

MEXICO

PERU

BRAZIL

CHILE

UNITED KINGDOM
IRELAND
NETHERLANDS
DENMARK
GERMANY
POLAND
CZECH REPUBLIC
AUSTRIA
SWITZERLAND
ROMANIA
FRANCE
SPAIN
GREECE
TURKEY
LEBANON
EGYPT
SAUDI ARABIA
KUWAIT
UNITED ARAB EMIRATES
RUSSIA
CHINA
THAILAND
SHANGHAI
BEIJING
HONG KONG
MALAYSIA
TAIWAN
SINGAPORE
PHILIPPINES
SOUTH KOREA
JAPAN
AUSTRALIA
NEW ZEALAND

> **STARBUCKS**
Starbucks has coffee shops in 44 different countries.

Local Culture
Adapting to local culture helps maintain global business.

Strategic Fit
Starbucks chooses locations with shared values and strategic fit.

Familiar logo
A familiar logo ensures global marketing standardization.

$9.4 billion annual revenue
15,000+ stores
170,000 partners (employees)

Customer Experience
Starbucks maintains control of its customer experience through joint ventures and company-owned operations.

79

6-1 THE IMPORTANCE OF UNDERSTANDING CONSUMER BEHAVIOR

Consumers' product and service preferences are constantly changing. Marketing managers must understand these desires in order to create a proper marketing mix for a well-defined market. So it is critical that marketing managers have a thorough knowledge of consumer behavior. **Consumer behavior** describes how consumers make purchase decisions and how they use and dispose of the purchased goods or services. The study of consumer behavior also includes factors that influence purchase decisions and product use.

"You've got to be incredibly customer focused because the customer is in control." Steve Quinn, CEO, Walmart

consumer behavior
processes a consumer uses to make purchase decisions, as well as to use and dispose of purchased goods or services; also includes factors that influence purchase decisions and product use

consumer decision-making process a five-step process used by consumers when buying goods or services

Understanding how consumers make purchase decisions can help marketing managers in several ways. For example, if a manager knows through research that gas mileage is the most important attribute for a certain target market, the manufacturer can redesign a car to meet that criterion. If the firm cannot change the design in the short run, it can use promotion in an effort to change consumers' decision-making criteria, for example, by promoting style, durability, and cargo capacity.

6-2 THE CONSUMER DECISION-MAKING PROCESS

When buying products, particularly new or expensive items, consumers generally follow the consumer decision-making process shown in Exhibit 6.1: (1) need recognition, (2) information search, (3) evaluation of alternatives, (4) purchase, and (5) postpurchase behavior. These five steps represent a general process that can be used as a guide for studying how consumers make decisions. It is important to note, though, that consumers' decisions do not always proceed in order through all of these steps. In fact, the consumer may end the process at any time or may not even make a purchase. The section on the types of consumer buying decisions later in the chapter discusses why a consumer's progression through these steps may vary. We begin, however, by examining the basic purchase process in greater detail.

Chapter 6

Consumer Decision Making

Learning Outcomes

After you finish this chapter go to
p106 *for* **STUDY TOOLS** �- - - - - - →

need recognition
result of an imbalance between actual and desired states

want recognition of an unfulfilled need and a product that will satisfy it

stimulus any unit of input affecting one or more of the five senses: sight, smell, taste, touch, hearing

> Most college students feel the need to decorate according to personal style.

6-2a Need Recognition

The first stage in the consumer decision-making process is need recognition. **Need recognition** is the result of an imbalance between actual and desired states. The imbalance arouses and activates the consumer decision-making process. A **want** is the recognition of an unfulfilled need and a product that will satisfy it. For example, have you ever gotten blisters from an old running shoe? Or maybe you have seen a television commercial for a new sports car and wanted to buy it. Need recognition is triggered when a consumer is exposed to either an internal or an external **stimulus**, which is any unit of input affecting one or more of the five senses: sight, smell, taste, touch, and hearing. *Internal stimuli* are occurrences you experience, such as hunger or thirst. For example, you may hear your stomach growl and then realize you are hungry. *External stimuli* are influences from an outside source such as someone's recommendation of a new restaurant, the color of an automobile, the design of a package, a brand name mentioned by a friend, or an advertisement on television or radio.

The imbalance between actual and desired states is sometimes referred to as the "want-got gap." That is, there is a difference between what a customer has and what he or she would like to have. This gap doesn't always trigger consumer action. The gap must be large enough to drive the consumer to do something. Just because your stomach growls once doesn't mean that you necessarily will stop what you are doing and go eat.

A marketing manager's objective is to get consumers to recognize this want-got gap. Advertising and sales promotion often provide this stimulus. Surveying buyer preferences provides marketers with information about consumer needs and wants that can be used to tailor products and services. Marketing managers can create wants on the part of the consumer. For example, when college students move into their own apartment or dorm room, they often need to furnish them and want new furniture rather than hand-me-downs from their parents. A want can be for a specific product, or it can be for a certain attribute or feature of a product. In this example, the college students not only need home furnishings but also want items that reflect their personal sense of style. Similarly, consumers may want ready-to-eat meals, drive-through dry-cleaning service, and Internet shopping to fill their need for convenience.

UNDERSTANDING NEEDS AND WANTS If marketers don't properly understand the target market's needs, the chances are good that the right good or service may not be produced. An excellent way to understand needs is to view them as job statements or outcome statements.[1] A job is a fundamental

Exhibit 6.1
CONSUMER DECISION-MAKING PROCESS

Cultural, social, individual, and psychological factors affect all steps

1. Need recognition
2. Information search
3. Evaluation of alternatives
4. Purchase
5. Postpurchase behavior

goal that consumers are trying to accomplish or a problem they are trying to resolve. Examples include: prevent mildew in a shower, hang a picture, or prepare income taxes. Desired outcome statements help marketers understand what consumers are seeking from a job. A desired outcome might be to minimize the time it takes to file an accurate income tax form that finds all possible legitimate deductions. People then can solve this problem several different ways: do the work themselves using government-provided information, do it themselves using software such as TurboTax, or hire a CPA to do it.

Marketers selling their products in global markets must carefully observe the needs and wants of consumers in various regions. RIM, maker of once ubiquitous BlackBerry Smartphones, observed that middle-class consumers in Indonesia were a huge potential category for its BlackBerry handsets. Research indicated that offering fixed pre-pay rates was very desirable for this market, so RIM decreased the price of its handsets to $200 (other Smartphones go for an average of $500) and offered pre-pay rates on a monthly, weekly, and daily basis. Customers have since flocked to RIM's handsets. In 2009 RIM had only 9 percent of the Indonesian Smartphone market. Today, it has 47 percent market share.[2]

6-2b Information Search

After recognizing a need or want, consumers search for information about the various alternatives available to satisfy it. For example, you know you are interested in seeing a movie, but you aren't sure what to see. So you visit Rotten Tomatoes to see what is getting great reviews by both critics and your peers on Facebook. This is a type of information search, which can occur internally, externally, or both. In an **internal information search**, the person recalls information stored in the memory. This stored information stems largely from previous experience with a product. For example, while traveling with your family, you may choose to stay at a hotel you have stayed in before because you remember that the hotel had clean rooms and friendly service.

In contrast, an **external information search** seeks information in the outside environment. There are two basic types of external information sources: nonmarketing-controlled and marketing-controlled. A **nonmarketing-controlled information source** is a product information source that is not associated with marketers promoting a product. These information sources include personal experiences (trying or observing a new

product), personal sources (family, friends, acquaintances, and coworkers who may recommend a product or service), and public sources (such as Rotten Tomatoes, *Consumer Reports*, and other rating organizations that comment on products and services). Once you have read reviews on Rotten Tomatoes to decide which movie to see (public source), you may search your memory for positive theater experiences to determine where you'll go (personal experience). Or, you might rely on a friend's recommendation to try out a new theater (personal source). Marketers gather information on how these information sources work and use it to attract customers. For example, car manufacturers know that younger customers are likely to get information from

internal information search the process of recalling past information stored in the memory

external information search the process of seeking information in the outside environment

nonmarketing-controlled information source a product information source that is not associated with advertising or promotion

Consumer Reports is a nonmarketing-controlled information source where consumers can find objective reviews of products. *Consumer Reports* magazines are available with a specific focus, in this case, car reviews.

© iStockphoto.com/Stephen Strathdee / © tavi/Shutterstock.com

marketing-controlled information source
a product information source that originates with marketers promoting the product

friends and family, so they try to develop enthusiasm for their products via word of mouth.

Living in the digital age has changed the way consumers get nonmarketing-controlled information. It can be from blogs, bulletin boards, activists, Web sites, Web forums, or consumer opinion sites such as www.consumerreview.com, www.tripadvisor.com, or www.epinions.com. Nearly 97 percent of U.S. consumers regularly or occasionally research products online before making a purchase, and on average, customers are looking at eight sources for product information.[3] To give you an idea of the number of searches this implies, in the United States alone there were 23.7 billion searches in April 2010.[4]

The latest research has examined how consumers use information picked up on the Internet. For example, in Web forums, the information seeker has normally never met the information provider or ever interacted with the person before. Hui Chen found that online reviewers presenting full accounts of their entire online shopping experience influenced other shoppers to promote the company through word of mouth the most. Reviews about pricing and quality of product influenced other shoppers the second most, and reviews discussing customer service by the company affected new consumers the least. Essentially, if other information seekers had found the provider trustworthy and kind, then the current seeker tended to believe the information, make a purchase, and then promote the company through other reviews.[5]

A **marketing-controlled information source** is biased toward a specific product because it originates with marketers promoting that product. Marketing-controlled information sources include mass media advertising (radio, newspaper, television, and magazine advertising), sales promotion (contests, displays, premiums, and so forth), salespeople, product labels and packaging, and the Internet. Many consumers, however, are wary of the information they receive from marketing-controlled sources, believing that most marketing campaigns stress the product's positive attributes and ignore its faults. These sentiments tend to be stronger among better-educated and higher-income consumers. Some marketing-controlled information sources can shift out of marketers' control, however, when there is bad news to report. For example, in 2011, *Consumer Reports* dropped the 2012 Honda Civic off its "recommended" list, the first time in recent memory. The news spread like wildfire, and Honda's only response was that the new Civic was entirely a step forward.[6]

LOST LUGGAGE WILL LIKELY CAUSE CUSTOMERS NOT TO CHOOSE THAT AIRLINE AGAIN.

The extent to which an individual conducts an external search depends on his or her perceived risk, knowledge, prior experience, and level of interest in the good or service. Generally, as the perceived risk of the purchase increases, the consumer enlarges the search and considers more alternative brands. For example, suppose that you want to purchase a surround sound system for your home stereo. The decision is relatively risky because of the expense and technical nature of the stereo system, so you are motivated to search for information about models, prices, options, compatibility with existing entertainment products, and capabilities. You may decide to compare attributes of many speaker systems because the value of the time expended finding the "right" stereo will be less than the cost of buying the wrong system.

A consumer's knowledge about the product or service will also affect the extent of an external information search. A consumer who is knowledgeable and well informed about a potential purchase is less likely to search for additional information. In addition, the more knowledgeable consumers are, the more efficiently they will conduct the search process, thereby requiring less time to search. For example, many consumers know that AirTran and other discount airlines have much lower fares, so they generally use the discounters and do not even check fares at other airlines.

The extent of a consumer's external search is also affected by confidence in one's decision-making ability. A confident consumer not only has sufficient stored information about the product but also feels self-assured about making the right decision. People lacking this confidence will continue an information search even when they know a great deal about the product. Consumers with prior experience in buying a certain product will have less perceived risk than inexperienced consumers. Therefore, they will spend less time searching and limit the number of products they consider.

A third factor influencing the external information search is product experience. Consumers who have had a positive prior experience with a product are more likely to limit their search to items related to the positive experience. For example, when flying, consumers are likely to choose airlines with which they have had positive experiences, such as consistent on-time arrivals, and avoid airlines with which they have had a negative experience, such as lost luggage.

Finally, the extent of the search is positively related to the amount of interest a consumer has in a product. A consumer who is more interested in a product will spend more time searching for information and alternatives. For example, suppose you are a dedicated runner who reads jogging and fitness magazines and catalogs. In searching for a new pair of running shoes, you may enjoy reading about the new brands available and spend more time and effort than other buyers in deciding on the right shoe.

The consumer's information search should yield a group of brands, sometimes called the buyer's **evoked set** (or **consideration set**), which are the consumer's most preferred alternatives. From this set, the buyer will further evaluate the alternatives and make a choice. Consumers do not consider all brands available in a product category, but they do seriously consider a much smaller set. For example, from the many brands of pizza available, consumers are likely to consider only the alternatives that fit their price range, location, take-out/delivery needs, and taste preferences. Having too many choices can, in fact, confuse consumers and cause them to delay the decision to buy, or, in some instances, cause them not to buy at all.

6-2c Evaluation of Alternatives and Purchase

After getting information and constructing an evoked set of alternative products, the consumer is ready to make a decision. A consumer will use the information stored in memory and obtained from outside sources to develop a set of criteria. Recent research has shown that exposure to certain cues in your everyday environment can affect decision criteria and purchase. For example, when NASA landed the *Pathfinder* spacecraft on Mars, it captured media attention worldwide. The candy maker Mars also noted a rather unusual increase in sales. Although the Mars bar takes its name from the company's founder and not the planet, consumers apparently responded to news about the planet Mars by purchasing more Mars bars. Further research also suggests that consumer reviews are influenced by existing reviews—if there

are existing one-star ratings, even positive consumer reviews will have fewer stars. Additionally, if consumers see large variations in consumer reviews, they are more likely to purchase the item and make a post-purchase evaluation on that site.[7]

The environment, internal information, and external information help consumers evaluate and compare alternatives. One way to begin narrowing the number of choices in the evoked set is to pick a product attribute and then exclude all products in the set that don't have that attribute. For example, assume Jane and Jill, both college sophomores, are looking for their first apartment. They need a two-bedroom apartment, reasonably priced and located near campus. They want the apartment to have a swimming pool, washer and dryer, and covered parking. Jane and Jill begin their search with all fifty apartments in the area and systematically eliminate complexes that lack the features they need. Hence, they may reduce their list to ten apartments that possess all of the desired attributes. Now they can use cutoffs to further narrow their choices. Cutoffs are either minimum or maximum levels of an attribute that an alternative must pass to be considered. Suppose Jane and Jill set a maximum of $1,000 per month for rent. Then all apartments with rent higher than $1,000 will be eliminated, further reducing the list of apartments from ten to eight. A final way to narrow the choices is to rank the attributes under consideration in order of importance and evaluate the products based on how well each performs on the most important attributes. To reach a final decision on one of the remaining eight apartments, Jane and Jill may decide proximity to campus is the most important attribute. As a result, they will choose to rent the apartment closest to campus.

If new brands are added to an evoked set, the consumer's evaluation of the existing brands in that set changes. As a result, certain brands in the original set may become more desirable. Suppose Jane and Jill find two apartments located equal distance from campus, one priced at $800 and the other at $750. Faced with this choice, they may decide that the $800 apartment is too expensive given that a comparable apartment is cheaper. If they add a $900 apartment to the list, however, then they may perceive the $800 apartment as more reasonable and decide to rent it.

The purchase decision process described above is a piecemeal process. That is, the evaluation is made by examining alternative advantages and disadvantages along important product attributes. A different way consumers can evaluate a product is according to a categorization process. The evaluation of an alternative depends upon the particular category to which it is assigned. Categories can be very general (motorized forms of transportation), or they can be very specific (Harley-Davidson motorcycles). Typically, these categories are associated with some degree of liking or disliking. To the extent that the product can be assigned membership in a particular category, it will receive an evaluation similar to that attached to the category. If you go to the grocery store and see a new organic food on the shelf, you may evaluate it on your liking and opinions of organic food.

So, when consumers rely on a categorization process, a product's evaluation depends on the particular category to which it is perceived as belonging. Given this, companies need to understand whether consumers are using categories that evoke the desired evaluations. Indeed, how a product is categorized can strongly influence consumer demand. For example, what products come to mind when you think about the "morning beverages" category? To the soft drink industry's dismay, far too few consumers include sodas in this category. Several attempts have been made at getting soft drinks on the breakfast table but with little success.

Brand extensions, in which a well-known and respected brand name from one product category is extended into other product categories, is one way companies employ categorization to their advantage. Brand extensions are a common business practice. For example, Qualcomm, maker of radio chips for many Smartphones, is trying to build demand for its radio chips outside the mobile phone market. How? By developing a line of tracking devices for pet collars. Tagg monitors pets and sends text messages to owners if the pet leaves a designated area.[8]

TO BUY OR NOT TO BUY Ultimately, the consumer has to decide whether to buy or not buy. Specifically, consumers must decide:

1. **Whether to buy**
2. **When to buy**
3. **What to buy (product type and brand)**
4. **Where to buy (type of retailer, specific retailer, online or in store)**
5. **How to pay**

When a person is buying an expensive or complex item, it is often a *fully planned purchase* based upon a lot of information. People rarely buy a new home simply on impulse. Often consumers will make a *partially planned purchase*, when they know the product category they want to buy (shirts, pants, reading lamp, car floor mats) but wait until they get to the store to choose a specific style or brand. Finally, there is the *unplanned purchase*, which people buy on impulse. Research has found that up to 68 percent of the items bought during major shopping trips and 54 percent on smaller shopping trips are unplanned.[9]

6-3 POSTPURCHASE BEHAVIOR

When buying products, consumers expect certain outcomes from the purchase. How well these expectations are met determines whether the consumer is satisfied or dissatisfied with the purchase. For example, if a person bids on a used car stereo from eBay and wins, he may have fairly low expectations regarding performance. If the stereo's performance turns out to be of superior quality, then the person's satisfaction will be high because his expectations were exceeded. Conversely, if the person bid on a new car stereo expecting superior quality and performance, but the stereo broke within one month, he would be very dissatisfied because his expectations were not met. Price often influences the level of expectations for a product or service.

For the marketer, an important element of any postpurchase evaluation is reducing any lingering doubts that the decision was sound. When people recognize inconsistency between their values or opinions and their behavior, they tend to feel an inner tension called **cognitive dissonance**. For example, say someone is looking to purchase an e-reader. After evaluating her options, she has decided to purchase an iPad, even though it is much more expensive than other dedicated e-readers. Prior to choosing the iPad, the shopper may experience inner tension or anxiety because she is worried that the current top-of-the-line technology, which costs much more than the middle-of-the-line technology, will be obsolete in a couple of months. That feeling of dissonance arises as her worries over obsolescence battle her practical nature, which is focused on the lower cost of a NOOK Color and its adequate—but less fancy—technology.

Consumers try to reduce dissonance by justifying their decision. They may seek new information that reinforces positive ideas about the purchase, avoid information that contradicts their decision, or revoke the original decision by returning the product. In some instances, people deliberately seek contrary information in order to refute it and reduce dissonance. Dissatisfied customers sometimes rely on word of mouth to reduce cognitive dissonance by letting friends and family know they are displeased.

Marketing managers can help reduce dissonance through effective communication with purchasers. For example, a customer service manager may slip a note inside the package congratulating the buyer on making a wise decision. Postpurchase letters sent by manufacturers and dissonance-reducing statements in instruction booklets may help customers feel at ease with their purchase. Advertising that displays the product's superiority over competing brands or guarantees can also help relieve the possible dissonance of someone who has already bought the product. Apple's Genius Bar and customer service will ease cognitive dissonance for purchasers of an iPad because they know that the company is there to support them.

6-4 TYPES OF CONSUMER BUYING DECISIONS AND CONSUMER INVOLVEMENT

All consumer buying decisions generally fall along a continuum of three broad categories: routine response behavior, limited decision making, and extensive decision making (see Exhibit 6.2). Goods and services in these three categories can best be described in terms of five factors: level of consumer involvement, length of time to make a decision, cost of the good or service, degree of information search, and the number of alternatives considered. The level of consumer involvement is perhaps the most significant determinant in classifying buying decisions. **Involvement** is the amount of time and effort a buyer invests in the search, evaluation, and decision processes of consumer behavior.

Frequently purchased, low-cost goods and services are generally associated with **routine response behavior**. These goods and services can also be called low-involvement products because consumers spend little time on search and decision before making the purchase. Usually, buyers are familiar with several different brands in the product category but stick with one brand. For example, a person may routinely buy Tropicana orange juice. Consumers engaged in routine response behavior normally don't

Exhibit 6.2

CONTINUUM OF CONSUMER BUYING DECISIONS

	Routine	Limited	Extensive
Involvement	Low	Low to moderate	High
Time	Short	Short to moderate	Long
Cost	Low	Low to moderate	High
Information Search	Internal only	Mostly internal	Internal and external
Number of Alternatives	One	Few	Many

© Cengage Learning

limited decision making the type of decision making that requires a moderate amount of time for gathering information and deliberating about an unfamiliar brand in a familiar product category

extensive decision making the most complex type of consumer decision making, used when buying an unfamiliar, expensive product or an infrequently bought item; requires use of several criteria for evaluating options and much time for seeking information

experience need recognition until they are exposed to advertising or see the product displayed on a store shelf. Consumers buy first and evaluate later, whereas the reverse is true for extensive decision making. A consumer who has previously purchased whitening toothpaste and was satisfied with it will probably walk to the toothpaste aisle and select that same brand without spending twenty minutes examining all other alternatives.

Limited decision making typically occurs when a consumer has previous product experience but is unfamiliar with the current brands available. Limited decision making is also associated with lower levels of involvement (although higher than routine decisions) because consumers expend only moderate effort in searching for information or in considering various alternatives. But what happens if the consumer's usual brand of whitening toothpaste is sold out? Assuming that toothpaste is needed, the consumer will be forced to choose another brand. Before making a final decision, the consumer will likely evaluate several other brands based on their active ingredients, their promotional claims, and the consumer's prior experiences.

Consumers practice **extensive decision making** when buying an unfamiliar, expensive product or an infrequently bought item. This process is the most complex type of consumer buying decision and is associated with high involvement on the part of the consumer. This process resembles the model outlined in Exhibit 6.1. These consumers want to make the right decision, so they want to know as much as they can about the product category and available brands. People usually experience the most cognitive dissonance when buying high-involvement products. Buyers use several criteria for evaluating their options and spend much time seeking information. Buying a home or a car, for example, requires extensive decision making.

The type of decision making that consumers use to purchase a product does not necessarily remain constant. For instance, if a routinely purchased product no longer satisfies, consumers may practice limited or extensive decision making to switch to another brand. And people who first use extensive decision making may then use limited or routine decision making for future purchases. For example, when a family gets a new puppy, they will spend a lot of time and energy trying out different toys to determine which one the dog prefers. Once the new owners learn that the dog prefers a bone to a ball, however, the purchase no longer requires extensive evaluation and will become routine.

6-4a Factors Determining the Level of Consumer Involvement

The level of involvement in the purchase depends on the following factors:

▸▸ **PREVIOUS EXPERIENCE:** When consumers have had previous experience with a good or service, the level of involvement typically decreases. After repeated product trials, consumers learn to make quick choices. Because consumers are familiar with the product and know whether it will satisfy their needs, they become less involved in the purchase. For example, a consumer purchasing cereal has many brands

Purchase involvement depends on level of interest. If this shopper is looking to use a bike as her main mode of transportation, then she is highly involved in this purchase decision.

© Cultura RM/Alamy

to choose from—just think of any grocery store cereal aisle. If the consumer always buys the same brand because it satisfies his hunger, then he has a low level of involvement. When a consumer purchases cereal for the first time, however, it likely will be a much more involved purchase.

▸ **INTEREST:** Involvement is directly related to consumer interests, as in cars, music, movies, bicycling, or electronics. Naturally, these areas of interest vary from one individual to another. A person highly involved in bike racing will be more interested in the type of bike she owns and will spend quite a bit of time evaluating different bikes. If a person wants a bike only for recreation, however, he may be fairly uninvolved in the purchase and just look for a bike from the most convenient location.

▸ **PERCEIVED RISK OF NEGATIVE CONSEQUENCES:** As the perceived risk in purchasing a product increases, so does a consumer's level of involvement. The types of risks that concern consumers include financial risk, social risk, and psychological risk.

  ▸ Financial risk is exposure to loss of wealth or purchasing power. Because high risk is associated with high-priced purchases, consumers tend to become extremely involved. Therefore, price and involvement are usually directly related: As price increases, so does the level of involvement. For example, someone who is purchasing a new car for the first time (higher perceived risk) will spend a lot of time and effort making this purchase. Financial risk may carry greater weight today because of the Great Recession of 2008–2009. The loss of jobs and potential loss of jobs meant that prices did not necessarily have to be high to have high involvement. A study by the SunAmerica Financial Group found that eight out of ten people say they exercise more caution with their finances, particularly investing and saving.[10]

  ▸ Social risks occur when consumers buy products that can affect people's social opinions of them (for example, driving an old, beat-up car or wearing unstylish clothes).

  ▸ Psychological risks occur if consumers feel that making the wrong decision might cause some concern or anxiety. For example, some consumers feel guilty about eating foods that are not healthy, such as regular ice cream rather than fat-free frozen yogurt.

▸ **SOCIAL VISIBILITY:** Involvement also increases as the social visibility of a product increases. Products often on social display include clothing (especially designer labels), jewelry, cars, and furniture. All these items make a statement about the purchaser and, therefore, carry a social risk.

NOT ALL INVOLVEMENT IS THE SAME High involvement means that the consumer cares about a product category or a specific good or service. The product or service is relevant and important, and means something to the buyer. High involvement can take a number of different forms. The most important types are discussed below:

▸ **PRODUCT INVOLVEMENT** means that a product category has high personal relevance. Product enthusiasts are consumers with high involvement in a product category. The fashion industry has a large segment of product enthusiasts. These people are seeking the latest fashion trends and want to wear the latest clothes.

▸ **SITUATIONAL INVOLVEMENT** means that the circumstances of a purchase may temporarily transform a low-involvement decision into a high-involvement one. High involvement comes into play when the consumer perceives risk in a specific situation. For example, an individual might routinely buy low-priced brands of liquor and wine. When the boss visits, however, the consumer might make a high-involvement decision and buy more prestigious brands.

▸ **SHOPPING INVOLVEMENT** represents the personal relevance of the process of shopping. There is a group of modern shoppers that tend to browse less and make fewer impulse buys because they shop on a mission. With armloads of research from the Internet, shoppers go into the store, buy what they came for, and get out. To these shoppers, the physical shopping is not as important as doing the research at home. Retailers must do their best to engage these mission shoppers in order to get them involved in the store and the shopping experience.[11]

▸ **ENDURING INVOLVEMENT** represents an ongoing interest in some product or activity. The consumer is always searching for opportunities to consume the product or participate in the activity. Enduring involvement typically gives personal gratification to consumers as they continue to learn about, shop for, and consume these goods and services. Therefore, there is often linkage between enduring involvement and shopping and product involvement.

▸ **EMOTIONAL INVOLVEMENT** represents how emotional a consumer gets during some specific consumption activity. Emotional involvement is closely related to enduring involvement because the things that consumers care most about will eventually create high emotional involvement. Sports fans typify consumers with high emotional involvement. The Olympics are one example of high emotional involvement in sporting outcomes.[12]

6-4b Marketing Implications of Involvement

Marketing strategy varies according to the level of involvement associated with the product. For high-involvement product purchases, marketing managers have several responsibilities. First, promotion to the target market should be extensive and informative. A good ad gives consumers the information they need for making the purchase decision and specifies the benefits and unique advantages of owning the product. For example, Ford has a vehicle with many custom options that is marketed to small business owners. One example of a recent print ad appears on this page, showing how one entrepreneur customized his Ford

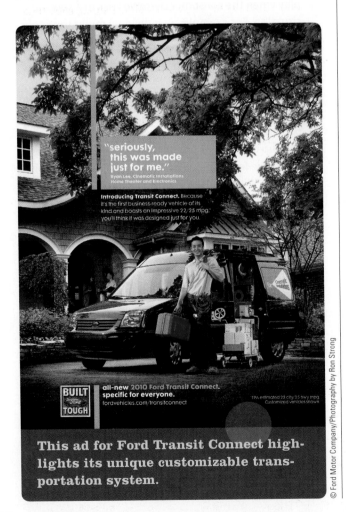

"seriously, this was made just for me."
Ryan Lee, Cinematic Installations Home Theater and Electronics

Introducing Transit Connect. Because it's the first business-ready vehicle of its kind and boasts an impressive 22/25 mpg.* you'll think it was designed just for you.

BUILT Ford TOUGH

all-new 2010 Ford Transit Connect. specific for everyone.
fordvehicles.com/transitconnect

*EPA-estimated 22 city/25 hwy mpg. Customized vehicles shown

This ad for Ford Transit Connect highlights its unique customizable transportation system.

© Ford Motor Company/Photography by Ron Strong

Transit Connect to help him have better efficiency for his home theater and electronics installation business. Ford highlights the fact that unique businesses need unique and customizable transportation. This ad not only demonstrates the customer's satisfaction but also shows the hauling capacity of the vehicle.

For low-involvement product purchases, consumers may not recognize their wants until they are in the store. Therefore, in-store promotion is an important tool when promoting low-involvement products. Marketing managers focus on package design so the product will be eye-catching and easily recognized on the shelf. Examples of products that take this approach are Campbell's soups, Tide detergent, Velveeta cheese, and Heinz ketchup. In-store displays also stimulate sales of low-involvement products. A good display can explain the product's purpose and prompt recognition of a want. Displays of health and beauty aid items in supermarkets have been known to increase sales many times above normal. Coupons, cents-off deals, and two-for-one offers also effectively promote low-involvement items.

Linking a product to a higher-involvement issue is another tactic that marketing managers can use to increase the sales or positive publicity of a low-involvement product. For example, Hyatt advertises that its hotels and resorts offer healthier kids' meals with fruit, vegetables, and milk as the default sides and drink. The company made the change in direct response to First Lady Michelle Obama's coalition to fight childhood obesity.[13]

*****

It is important to understand that the consumer decision-making process does not occur in a vacuum. On the contrary, underlying cultural, social, individual, and psychological factors strongly influence the decision process. These factors have an effect from the time a consumer perceives a stimulus through postpurchase behavior. Cultural factors, which include culture and values, subculture, and social class, exert a broad influence over consumer decision making. Social factors sum up the social interactions between a consumer and influential groups of people, such as reference groups, opinion leaders, and family members. Individual factors, which include gender, age, family life cycle stage, personality, self-concept, and lifestyle, are unique to each individual and play a major role in the type of products and services consumers want. Psychological factors determine how consumers perceive and interact with their environments and influence the ultimate decisions consumers make.

They include perception, motivation, learning, beliefs, and attitudes. Exhibit 6.3 summarizes these influences, and the following sections cover each in more detail.

6-5 CULTURAL INFLUENCES ON CONSUMER BUYING DECISIONS

Of all the factors that affect consumer decision making, cultural factors exert the broadest and deepest influence. Marketers must understand the way people's culture and its accompanying values, as well as their subculture and social class, influence their buying behavior.

6-5a Culture and Values

Culture is the set of values, norms, attitudes, and other meaningful symbols that shape human behavior and the artifacts, or products, of that behavior as they are transmitted from one generation to the next. It is the essential character of a society that distinguishes it from other cultural groups. The underlying elements of every culture are the values, language, myths, customs, rituals, and laws that shape the behavior of the people, as well as the material artifacts, or products, of that behavior as they are transmitted from one generation to the next.

Culture is pervasive. Cultural values and influences are the ocean in which individuals swim, and yet most are completely unaware that it is there. What people eat, how they dress, what they think and feel, and what language they speak are all dimensions of culture. It encompasses all the things consumers do without conscious choice because their culture's values, customs, and rituals are ingrained in their daily habits.

Culture is functional. Human interaction creates values and prescribes acceptable behavior for each culture. By establishing common expectations, culture gives order to society. Sometimes these expectations are enacted into laws. For example, drivers in our culture must stop at a red light. Other times these expectations are taken for granted: Grocery stores and hospitals are open twenty-four hours, whereas banks are open only during bankers' hours.

Culture is learned. Consumers are not born knowing the values and norms of their society. Instead, they must learn what is acceptable from family and friends. Children learn the values that will govern their behavior from parents, teachers, and peers. As members of our society, they learn to shake hands when they greet someone,

culture the set of values, norms, attitudes, and other meaningful symbols that shape human behavior and the artifacts, or products, of that behavior as they are transmitted from one generation to the next

Exhibit 6.3

FACTORS THAT AFFECT THE CONSUMER DECISION-MAKING PROCESS

Social Factors
Reference groups
Opinion leaders
Family

Cultural Factors
Culture and values
Subculture
Social class

Buy? Don't Buy?

Consumer Decision-Making Process

Individual Factors
Gender
Age and family life cycle stage
Personality, self-concept, and lifestyle

Psychological Factors
Perception
Motivation
Learning
Beliefs and attitudes

© Photodisc/Getty Images

to drive on the right-hand side of the road, and to eat pizza and drink Coca-Cola.

Culture is dynamic. It adapts to changing needs and an evolving environment. The rapid growth of technology in today's world has accelerated the rate of cultural change. Television has changed entertainment patterns and family communication and has heightened public awareness of political and other news events. Automation has increased the amount of leisure time we have and, in some ways, has changed the traditional work ethic. Cultural norms will continue to evolve because of our need for social patterns that solve problems.

The most defining element of a culture is its values. A **value** is an enduring belief shared by a society that a specific mode of conduct is personally or socially preferable to another mode of conduct. People's value systems have a great effect on their consumer behavior. Consumers with similar value systems tend to react alike to prices and other marketing-related inducements. Values also correspond to consumption patterns. For example, Americans place a high value on convenience. This value has created lucrative markets for products such as breakfast bars, energy bars, and nutrition bars that allow consumers to eat on the go. Values can also influence consumers' television viewing habits or the magazines they read. For instance, people who strongly object to violence avoid crime shows, and those who oppose pornography do not buy *Hustler*.

6-5b Understanding Cultural Differences

As more companies expand their operations globally, the need to understand the cultures of foreign countries becomes more important. A firm has little chance of selling products in a culture that it does not understand. Like people, products have cultural values and rules that influence their perception and use. Culture, therefore, must be understood before the behavior of individuals within the cultural context can be understood. Colors, for example, may have different meanings in global markets than they do at home. In China, white is the color of mourning and

brides wear red. In the United States, black is for mourning and brides wear white.

Language is another important aspect of culture that global marketers must consider. When translating product names, slogans, and promotional messages into foreign languages, they must be careful not to convey the wrong message. General Motors discovered too late that Nova (the name of an economical car) literally means "doesn't go" in Spanish; Coors encouraged its English-speaking customers to "Turn it loose," but the phrase in Spanish means "Suffer from diarrhea."

Although marketers expanding into global markets generally adapt their products and business formats to the local culture, some fear that increasing globalization, as well as the proliferation of the Internet, will result in a homogeneous world culture of the future. U.S. companies in particular, they fear, are Americanizing the world by exporting bastions of American culture, such as McDonald's fast-food restaurants, Starbucks coffeehouses, Microsoft software, and American movies and entertainment.

6-5c Subculture

A culture can be divided into subcultures on the basis of demographic characteristics, geographic regions, national and ethnic background, political beliefs, and religious beliefs. A **subculture** is a homogeneous group of people who share elements of the overall culture as well as cultural elements unique to their own group. Within subcultures, people's attitudes, values, and purchase decisions are even more similar than they are within the broader culture. Subcultural differences may result in considerable variation within a culture in what, how, when, and where people buy goods and services.

In the United States alone, countless subcultures can be identified. Many are concentrated geographically. People who belong to the Church of Jesus Christ of Latter-Day Saints, for example, are clustered mainly in Utah; Cajuns are located in the bayou regions of southern Louisiana. Many Hispanics live in states bordering Mexico, whereas the majority of Chinese, Japanese, and Korean Americans are found on the West Coast. Other subcultures are geographically dispersed. Computer hackers, people

© bloody/Shutterstock.com

SCENTS *such as Lavender and Thai Orchid tested well with Hispanics, which helped P&G boost sales.*

who are hearing or visually impaired, Harley-Davidson bikers, military families, and university professors may be found throughout the country. Yet they have identifiable attitudes, values, and needs that distinguish them from the larger culture.

Once marketers identify subcultures, they can design special marketing to serve their needs. Some companies launch simultaneous campaigns to reach different subcultures. P&G is targeting the Hispanic population due to the tendency of the group to have younger and larger families, a boon for the company looking to boost sales of Pampers diapers and Tide detergent. Additionally beneficial to P&G are several of the characteristics of the group. Hispanics are willing to spend more for premium products because they believe they work better. So P&G is adding Spanish to most packaging and is also creating some additional fragrances for Febreze products that research shows Hispanic consumers prefer.[14]

6-5d Social Class

The United States, like other societies, has a social class system. A **social class** is a group of people who are considered nearly equal in status or community esteem, who regularly socialize among themselves both formally and informally, and who share behavioral norms.

A number of techniques have been used to measure social class, and a number of criteria have been used to define it. One view of contemporary U.S. status structure is shown in Exhibit 6.4.

As you can see from Exhibit 6.4, the upper and upper middle classes comprise the small segment of affluent and wealthy Americans. In terms of consumer buying patterns, the affluent are more likely to own their own home and purchase new cars and trucks and are less likely to smoke. The very rich flex their financial muscles by spending more on vacation homes, vacations and cruises, and housekeeping and gardening services. The most affluent consumers are more likely to attend art auctions and galleries, dance performances, operas, the theater, museums, concerts, and sporting events. Marketers often pay attention to the superwealthy. The luxury book market is targeting superwealthy collectors with books sporting price tags that rival original artwork.

> **social class** a group of people in a society who are considered nearly equal in status or community esteem, who regularly socialize among themselves both formally and informally, and who share behavioral norms

Exhibit 6.4

U.S. SOCIAL CLASSES

Upper Classes		
Capitalist class	1%	People whose investment decisions shape the national economy; income mostly from assets, earned or inherited; university connections
Upper middle class	14%	Upper-level managers, professionals, owners of medium-sized businesses; well-to-do, stay-at-home homemakers who decline occupational work by choice; college educated; family income well above national average
Middle Classes		
Middle class	33%	Middle-level white-collar, top-level blue-collar; education past high school typical; income somewhat above national average; loss of manufacturing jobs has reduced the population of this class
Working class	32%	Middle-level blue-collar, lower-level white-collar; income below national average; largely working in skilled or semi-skilled service jobs
Lower Classes		
Working poor	11–12%	Low-paid service workers and operatives; some high school education; below mainstream in living standard; crime and hunger are daily threats
Underclass	8–9%	People who are not regularly employed and who depend primarily on the welfare system for sustenance; little schooling; living standard below poverty line

Sources: Adapted from Richard P. Coleman, "The Continuing Significance of Social Class to Marketing," *Journal of Consumer Research*, December 1983, 267; Dennis Gilbert and Joseph A. Kahl, *The American Class Structure: A Synthesis* (Homewood, IL: Dorsey Press, 1982), ch. 11.

For example, ten limited edition copies of an autobiography by Indian cricket star Sachin Tendulkar feature a page with his blood mixed into the paper pulp. Even though a copy of the book cost $75,000, all ten sold! Taschen, another novelty publisher, sold pieces of the moon with twelve copies of its photography book of the lunar landing. One sold for $112,500.[15]

The majority of Americans today define themselves as middle class, regardless of their actual income or educational attainment. This phenomenon most likely occurs because working-class Americans tend to aspire to the middle-class lifestyle, while some of those who do achieve affluence may downwardly aspire to respectable middle-class status as a matter of principle.

The working class is a distinct subset of the middle class. Interest in organized labor is one of the most common attributes among the working class. This group often rates job security as the most important reason for taking a job. The working-class person depends heavily on relatives and the community for economic and emotional support.

Lifestyle distinctions between the social classes are greater than the distinctions within a given class. The most significant difference between the classes occurs between the middle and lower classes, where there is a major shift in lifestyles. Members of the lower class have incomes at or below the poverty level.

Social class is typically measured as a combination of occupation, income, education, wealth, and other variables. For instance, affluent upper-class consumers are more likely to be salaried executives or self-employed professionals with at least an undergraduate degree. Working-class or middle-class consumers are more likely to be hourly service workers or blue-collar employees with only a high school education. Educational attainment, however, seems to be the most reliable indicator of a person's social and economic status. Those with college degrees or graduate degrees are more likely to fall into the upper classes, while those people with some college experience fall closest to traditional concepts of the middle class.

Marketers are interested in social class for two main reasons. First, social class often indicates which medium to use for advertising. Suppose an insurance company seeks to sell its policies to middle-class families. It might advertise during the local evening news because middle-class families tend to watch more television than other classes do. If the company wanted to sell more policies to upscale individuals, it might place an ad in a business publication like the *Wall Street Journal*. The Internet, long the domain of more educated and affluent families, is becoming an increasingly important advertising outlet for advertisers hoping to reach blue-collar workers and homemakers. As the middle class rapidly adopts the medium, marketers have to do more research to find out which Web sites will reach their audience.

Second, knowing what products appeal to which social classes can help marketers determine where to best distribute their products. Affluent Americans, a fifth of the U.S. population, have changed their buying habits since the recession. They now are willing to spend more of their discretionary income for unique one-of-a-kind items. They are also spending more per item than in previous years. Saks Fifth Avenue's most expensive item in 2008 was a pair of suede boots that sold for $1,575 a pair. In 2011, the most expensive item was also a pair of suede boots, but those retailed for $2,495 a pair.[16]

This shift has caused many full-priced and upscale retailers to demonstrate larger gains in revenue than discount chains. Because many lower-income consumers are still struggling to recover from job loss, retailers such as Walmart are selling smaller packages of items because customers do not have enough cash to buy more standard-size products. Apparel stores that target the middle class are raising prices by only pennies for fear of driving away customers.[17]

6-6 SOCIAL INFLUENCES ON CONSUMER BUYING DECISIONS

Many consumers seek out the opinions of others to reduce their search and evaluation effort or uncertainty, especially as the perceived risk of the decision increases. Consumers may also seek out others' opinions for guidance on new products or services, products with image-related attributes, or products for which attribute information is lacking or uninformative. Specifically, consumers interact socially with reference groups, opinion leaders, and family members to obtain product information and decision approval.

6-6a Reference Groups

People interact with many reference groups. A **reference group** consists of all the formal and informal groups that influence the buying behavior of an individual. Consumers may use products or brands to identify with or become a member of a group. They learn from observing how members of their reference groups consume, and they use the same criteria to make their own consumer decisions.

Reference groups can be categorized very broadly as either direct or indirect (see Exhibit 6.5). Direct reference groups are face-to-face membership groups that touch people's lives directly. They can be either primary or secondary. A **primary membership group** includes all groups with which people interact regularly in an informal, face-to-face manner, such as family, friends, and coworkers. Today, they may also communicate by e-mail, text messages, Facebook, Skype, or other electronic means. In contrast, people associate with a **secondary membership group** less consistently and more formally. These groups might include clubs, professional groups, and religious groups.

Consumers also are influenced by many indirect, nonmembership reference groups to which they do not belong. An **aspirational reference group** is a group a person would like to join. To join an aspirational group, a person must at least conform to the norms of that group. (A **norm** consists of the values and attitudes deemed acceptable by the group.) Thus, a

person who wants to be elected to public office may begin to dress more conservatively, as other politicians do. He or she may go to many of the restaurants and social engagements that city and business leaders attend and try to play a role that is acceptable to voters and other influential people. Similarly, teenagers today may dye their hair and experiment with body piercing and tattoos. Athletes are an aspirational group for several market segments. To appeal to the younger market, Coca-Cola signed basketball star LeBron James to be the spokesperson for its Sprite and PowerAde brands, and Nike signed a sneaker deal with him reportedly worth $90 million. Coca-Cola and Nike assumed James would encourage consumers to drink Coke brands and buy Nike shoes because they would like to identify with him.

Nonaspirational reference groups, or dissociative groups, influence our behavior when we try to maintain distance from them. A consumer may avoid buying some types of clothing or cars, going to certain restaurants or stores, or even buying a home in a certain neighborhood in order to avoid being associated with a particular group.

The activities, values, and goals of reference groups directly influence consumer behavior. For marketers, reference groups have three important implications: (1) They serve as information sources and influence perceptions; (2) they affect an individual's aspiration levels; and (3) their norms either constrain or stimulate consumer behavior. For example, research firms devoted to uncovering what's cool in the teen market have identified a couple of influential groups among today's teens based on their interests in clothes, music, and activities. Tracking these groups reveals

Exhibit 6.5

TYPES OF REFERENCE GROUPS

Reference groups

Direct Face-to-face membership
- **Primary** Small, informal group
- **Secondary** Large, formal group

Indirect Nonmembership
- **Aspirational** Group that someone would like to join
- **Nonaspirational** Group with which someone wants to avoid being identified

© Cengage Learning

how products become cool and how groups influence the adoption of cool products by other groups. A trend or fad often starts with teens who have the most innovative tastes. These teens are on the cutting edge of fashion and music, and they wear their attitude all over their bodies in the form of tattoos, body piercings, studded jewelry, or colored tresses. Certain fads embraced by these "edgers" will spark an interest in the small group of teens researchers call "influencers," who project the look other teens covet. Influencers also create their own trends in music and clothing choices. Once a fad is embraced and adopted by influencers, the look becomes cool and desirable. The remaining groups that comprise the majority of the teen population will not embrace a fad until it gets its seal of approval from the influencers.

Research has shown that reference groups are particularly powerful in influencing purchases of fragrances, wine, snack food, candy, clothing, and sodas.[18] LG Electronics and General Electric are using the sustainable green-living movement as a reference group to encourage green homeowners to functionally and stylistically "keep up with the Joneses." Once hidden away, boilers and water heaters are now designed to be aesthetically pleasing as well as energy efficient. After purchasing an expensive solar-powered water heater, homeowners want to show it off, so it must be stylish. In-room air conditioners look like sculptures, and the Everun water heater has a shelf that hides wires and holds decorative objects. Some consumers even consider the mechanical room to be like a wine cellar or library—a place to demonstrate how you fit in with your peers and the eco-friendly movement.[19] People with well-formed networks of somewhat overlapping reference groups and those with strong personal values are less susceptible to reference group influences.[20]

6-6b Opinion Leaders

Reference groups frequently include an individual known as a group leader, or **opinion leader**—a person who influences others. Obviously, it is important for marketing managers to persuade such people to purchase their goods or services. Many products and services that are integral parts of Americans' lives today got their initial boost from opinion leaders. For example, Kindles and iPads were purchased by opinion leaders well ahead of the general public.

Opinion leaders are often the first to try new products and services out of pure curiosity. They tend to possess more accurate knowledge and to be more innovative.[21] Technology companies have found that teenagers, because of their willingness to experiment, are key opinion leaders for the success of new technologies.

BEGINNING BRANDED TELEVISION

Ford has opened a new reality television door—branded television shows. The car company's show *Escape Routes* airs on NBC and features a slew of Internet celebrities such as iJustine competing in small challenges. The show is also interactive, allowing the celebrities to enlist their armies of fans to help them complete challenges such as finding a location without using the Ford Escape's GPS. The fans are given limited information as the show is filmed, and they watch how their participation affects the contestants when the show airs. This unique blending of social media and television fulfills the fans' desire to interact with a celebrity as well as interact and affect a show that others will watch. Essentially, *Escape Routes* reaches a new market for its 2013 Escape and adds that vehicle to their aspirational reference group of YouTube and Internet celebrities.

Source: Ari Karpel, "The Brand Content Breakdown: Behind Ford 'Escape Routes,'" *Fast Company*, April 24, 2012, www.fastcocreate.com/1680555/the-brand-content-breakdown-behind-ford-escape-routes (Accessed April 24, 2012).

© Ritu Manoj Jethani/Shutterstock.com / © iStockphoto.com/Bill Noll

socialization process how cultural values and norms are passed down to children

Opinion leadership is a casual phenomenon and is usually inconspicuous, so locating opinion leaders can be a challenge. Thus, marketers often try to create opinion leaders. They may use high school cheerleaders to model new fall fashions or civic leaders to promote insurance, new cars, and other merchandise. On a national level, companies sometimes use movie stars, sports figures, and other celebrities to promote products, hoping they are appropriate opinion leaders. The effectiveness of celebrity endorsements varies, though, depending largely on how credible and attractive the spokesperson is and how familiar people are with him or her. Endorsements are most likely to succeed if a reasonable association between the spokesperson and the product can be established.

Respected organizations such as the American Heart Association and the American Cancer Society may also serve as opinion leaders. Marketers may seek endorsements from them as well as from schools, churches, cities, the military, and fraternal organizations as a form of group opinion leadership. Salespeople often ask to use opinion leaders' names as a means of achieving greater personal influence in a sales presentation.

Increasingly, marketers are looking to social media to find opinion leaders, but the sheer volume of posts and platforms makes determining true opinion leaders challenging. So, marketers are focusing their attention on platforms frequented by teens (such as Facebook, Pinterest, and Tumblr) because those sites better identify the social trends that are shaping consumer behavior. With their unprecedented ability to network and communicate with each other, young people rely on each other's opinions more than marketing messages when making purchase decisions. And social media are becoming a key way that teens communicate their opinions. Consequently, today's marketers are reading teen posts, developing products that meet the very specific needs that teens express there, and learning unique and creative ways to put key influencers in charge of marketing their brands for them.[22] Marketers are also using other social networking and online media to determine and attract opinion leaders, which will be discussed in Chapter 18.

6-6c Family

The family is the most important social institution for many consumers, strongly influencing values, attitudes, self-concept, and buying behavior. For example, a family that strongly values good health will have a grocery list distinctly different from that of a family that views every dinner as a gourmet event. Moreover, the family is responsible for the **socialization process**, the passing down of cultural values and norms to children. Children learn by observing their parents' consumption patterns, so they tend to shop in similar patterns.

Decision-making roles among family members tend to vary significantly, depending on the type of item purchased. Family members assume a variety of roles in the purchase process. *Initiators* suggest, initiate, or plant the seed for the purchase process. The initiator can be any member of the family. For example, Sister might initiate the product search by asking for a new bicycle as a birthday present. *Influencers* are

Yes. She checks herself out in the mirror.

1 in 5 Americans will develop skin cancer in their lifetime. That's why Jennifer Garner made a promise to herself to examine her skin every month and see her dermatologist for a screening every year.

The Neutrogena Partnership for Skin Health, working with the American Academy of Dermatology (AAD), invites you to join them in their mission to stop skin cancer before it strikes. Empower their cause by wearing broad-spectrum sun protection, covering up and seeking shade between 10:00 am and 4:00 pm. Perform self-examinations regularly and report any changes in existing moles or birthmarks to your doctor. Because with early detection, skin cancer is 99% curable. And that's a statistic we love to share.

Protect yourself starting today.
The AAD and the Neutrogena Partnership for Skin Health encourage you to **get a free skin cancer screening** in May, June or July. Find one in your area by visiting aad.org or neutrogenaskinhealth.com. Mark the date of your screening on this slip as a healthy reminder.

Neutrogena PARTNERSHIP FOR SKIN HEALTH

Celebrity Jennifer Garner functions as an opinion leader for Neutrogena.

those members of the family whose opinions are valued. In our example, Mom might function as a price-range watchdog, an influencer whose main role is to veto or approve price ranges. Brother may give his opinion on certain makes of bicycles. The *decision maker* is the family member who actually makes the decision to buy or not to buy. For example, Dad or Mom is likely to choose the final brand and model of bicycle to buy after seeking further information from Sister about cosmetic features such as color and then imposing additional criteria of his or her own, such as durability and safety. The *purchaser* (probably Dad or Mom) is the one who actually exchanges money for the product. Finally, the *consumer* is the actual user—Sister, in the case of the bicycle.

Marketers should consider family purchase situations along with the distribution of consumer and decision-maker roles among family members. Ordinary marketing views the individual as both decision maker and consumer. Family marketing adds several other possibilities: Sometimes more than one family member or all family members are involved in the decision, sometimes only children are involved in the decision, sometimes more than one consumer is involved, and sometimes the decision maker and the consumer are different people. In most households, when parental joint decisions are being made, spouses consider their partner's needs and perceptions to maintain decision fairness and harmony. This tends to minimize family conflict. Research also shows that in harmonious households, the spouse who has "won" a previous decision is less likely to use strong influence in a subsequent decision.[23] This balancing factor is key in maintaining long-term family harmony.

Children can have great influence over the purchase decisions of their parents. In many families, with both parents working and short on time, children are encouraged to participate. In addition, children in single-parent households become more involved in family decisions at an earlier age. Children influence purchase decisions for many products and services. They are most influential in purchase decisions for products with which they will be directly involved or will be the primary user. Among the products about which children exhibit greatest influence are breakfast cereal, juice, mobile phones, and soft drinks.[24] Children also often participate in decisions about many other products, including toys, clothes, vacations, recreation, and automobiles, even though they usually are not the actual purchasers of such items. What if those children happen to be teenagers? In 2011, a poll of more than 1,000

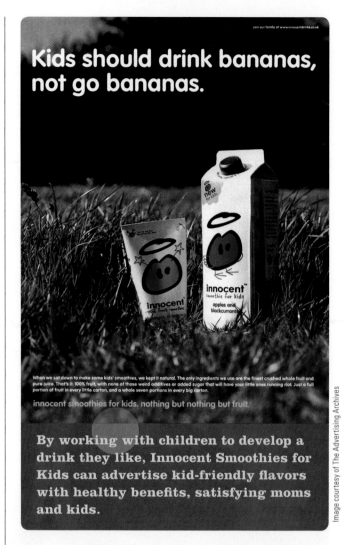

Image courtesy of The Advertising Archives

By working with children to develop a drink they like, Innocent Smoothies for Kids can advertise kid-friendly flavors with healthy benefits, satisfying moms and kids.

sixteen- to eighteen-year-olds found that, on average, these teens spend more than $18 a week.[25]

Traditionally, children learned about consumption from their parents. In today's technologically overloaded world, that trend is reversing for some topics. Teenagers and adult children often contribute information and influence the purchase of parents' technology products.[26] Often they even help with installation and show the parents how to use the product!

6-7 INDIVIDUAL INFLUENCES ON CONSUMER BUYING DECISIONS

A person's buying decisions are also influenced by personal characteristics that are unique to each individual, such as gender; age and life cycle stage;

and personality, self-concept, and lifestyle. Individual characteristics are generally stable over the course of one's life. For instance, most people do not change their gender, and the act of changing personality or lifestyle requires a complete reorientation of one's life. In the case of age and life cycle stage, these changes occur gradually over time.

6-7a Gender

Physiological differences between men and women result in different needs, such as health and beauty products. Just as important are the distinct cultural, social, and economic roles played by men and women and the effects that these have on their decision-making processes. For example, the wedding industry is overwhelmingly focused on brides and what they want. But Chris Easter and Bob Horner thought that the groom should be able to register for gifts he would like as well. So they began The Man Registry (www.themanregistry.com), a Web site with thousands of guy-friendly gifts for which grooms can register. The Man Registry also offers advice to grooms about groomsmen gifts and local vendors.[27]

Trends in gender marketing are influenced by the changing roles of men and women in society. For example, men used to rely on the women in their lives to shop for them. Today, however, more men are shopping for themselves. Fifty-seven percent of men shopped online in 2007, up from 38 percent in 2006. In 2009, 7.4 percent of fathers with children younger than eighteen years stayed at home while their wives worked. That is the highest recorded percentage, up 2 percentage points from 2008.[28] Whether because of the advent of online shopping or retailers becoming aware of the way men like to shop, today more men are comfortable shopping for themselves. A study commissioned by *GQ* found that 84 percent of men said they purchased their own clothes, up from 65 percent four years earlier.[29]

Technology companies are working to develop new high-tech products that resonate with women. For example, Barnes & Noble markets everything about its e-reader, NOOK, to the ideal customer, whom they call "Julie." She is between twenty-five and forty-five years old, lives within fifteen minutes of a Barnes & Noble, enjoys family-friendly stores because she has a family, uses NOOK's apps because she doesn't have to worry about data consumption, and loves that NOOK has apps for her kids too. Based on this information, Barnes & Noble stores have short tables for kids to play with sample NOOKs, and the app store caters to topics that interest women, such as puzzles, fashion, health, fitness, and travel. The strategy is successful in that 70 percent of NOOK purchasers are women.[30]

6-7b Age and Family Life Cycle Stage

The age and family life cycle stage of a consumer can have a significant impact on consumer behavior. How old a consumer is generally indicates what products he or she may be interested in purchasing. Consumer tastes in food, clothing, cars, furniture, and recreation are often age related.

Related to a person's age is his or her place in the family life cycle. As Chapter 8 explains in more detail, the *family life cycle* is an orderly series of stages through which consumers' attitudes and behavioral tendencies evolve through maturity, experience, and changing income and status. Marketers often define their target markets in terms of family life cycle, such as "young singles," "young married couples with children," and "middle-aged married couples without children." For instance, young singles spend more than average on alcoholic beverages, education, and entertainment. New parents typically increase their spending on health care, clothing, housing, and food and decrease their spending on alcohol, education, and transportation. Households with older children spend more on food, entertainment, personal care products, and education, as well as cars and gasoline. After their children leave home, spending by older couples on vehicles, women's clothing, health care, and long-distance calls typically increases. For instance, the presence of children in the home is the most significant determinant of the type of vehicle that's driven off the new car lot. Parents are the ultimate need-driven car consumers, requiring larger cars and trucks to haul their children and all their belongings. It comes as no surprise then that for all households with children, SUVs rank either first or second among new-vehicle purchases, followed by minivans.

Marketers should also be aware of the many nontraditional life cycle paths that are common today and provide insights into the needs and wants of such consumers as divorced parents, lifelong singles, and childless couples. Three decades ago, married couples with children under the age of eighteen accounted for about half of U.S. households. Today, such families make up only 23 percent of all households, while people living alone or with nonfamily members represent more than 30 percent. Furthermore, according to the U.S. Census Bureau, the

personality a way of organizing and grouping the consistencies of an individual's reactions to situations

self-concept how consumers perceive themselves in terms of attitudes, perceptions, beliefs, and self-evaluations

ideal self-image the way an individual would like to be perceived

real self-image the way an individual actually perceives himself or herself

number of single-mother households grew by 25 percent over the last decade. The shift toward more single-parent households is part of a broader societal change that has put more women on the career track. Although many marketers continue to be wary of targeting nontraditional families, Charles Schwab targeted single mothers in an advertising campaign featuring Sarah Ferguson, the Duchess of York and a divorced mom. The idea was to appeal to single mothers' heightened awareness of the need for financial self-sufficiency.

LIFE EVENTS Another way to look at the life cycle is to look at major events in one's life over time. Life-changing events can occur at any time. A few examples are death of a spouse, moving, birth or adoption of a child, retirement, job loss, divorce, and marriage. Typically, such events are quite stressful, and consumers will often take steps to minimize that stress. Many times, life-changing events will mean new consumption patterns. For example, a recently divorced person may try to improve his or her appearance by joining a health club and dieting. Someone moving to a different city will need a new dentist, grocery store, auto service center, and doctor, among other things. Marketers realize that life events often mean a chance to gain a new customer. The Welcome Wagon offers free gifts and services for area newcomers. Lowe's sends out a discount coupon to those moving to a new community. And when you put your home on the market, very quickly you start getting flyers from moving companies promising a great price on moving your household goods.

6-7c Personality, Self-Concept, and Lifestyle

Each consumer has a unique personality. **Personality** is a broad concept that can be thought of as a way of organizing and grouping how an individual typically reacts to situations. Thus, personality combines psychological makeup and environmental forces. It includes people's underlying dispositions, especially their most dominant characteristics. Although personality is one of the least useful concepts in the study of consumer behavior, some marketers believe personality influences the types and brands of products purchased. For instance, the type of car, clothes,

or jewelry a consumer buys may reflect one or more personality traits.

Self-concept, or self-perception, is how consumers perceive themselves. Self-concept includes attitudes, perceptions, beliefs, and self-evaluations. Although self-concept may change, the change is often gradual. Through self-concept, people define their identity, which in turn provides for consistent and coherent behavior.

Self-concept combines the **ideal self-image** (the way an individual would like to be perceived) and the **real self-image** (how an individual actually perceives himself or herself). Generally, we try to raise our real self-image toward our ideal (or at least narrow the gap). Consumers seldom buy products that jeopardize their self-image. For example, someone who sees herself as a trendsetter wouldn't buy clothing that doesn't project a contemporary image.

Human behavior depends largely on self-concept. Because consumers want to protect their identity as individuals, the products they buy, the stores they patronize, and the credit cards they carry support their self-image. No other product quite reflects a person's self-image as much as the car he or she drives. For example, many young consumers do not like family sedans like the Honda Accord or Toyota Camry and say they would buy one for their mom but not for themselves. Likewise, younger parents may avoid purchasing minivans because they do not want to sacrifice the youthful image they have of themselves just because they have new responsibilities. To combat decreasing sales, marketers of the Nissan Quest minivan decided to reposition it as something other than a "mom mobile" or "soccer mom car." They chose the ad copy "Passion built it. Passion will fill it up," followed by "What if we made a minivan that changed the way people think of minivans?"

© Dasha Rusanenko/Shutterstock.com

By influencing the degree to which consumers perceive a good or service to be self-relevant, marketers can affect consumers' motivation to learn about, shop for, and buy a certain brand. Marketers also consider self-concept important because it helps explain the relationship between individuals' perceptions of themselves and their consumer behavior.

Many companies now use psychographics to better understand their market segments. For many years, marketers selling products to mothers conveniently assumed that all moms were fairly homogeneous and concerned about the same things—the health and well-being of their children—and that they could all be reached with a similar message. But recent lifestyle research has shown that there are traditional, blended, and nontraditional moms, and companies like Procter & Gamble and General Mills are using strategies to reach these different types of mothers. Psychographics is also effective with other market segments. Psychographics and lifestyle segmentation are discussed in more detail in Chapter 8.

6-8 PSYCHOLOGICAL INFLUENCES ON CONSUMER BUYING DECISIONS

An individual's buying decisions are further influenced by psychological factors: perception, motivation, learning, and beliefs and attitudes. These factors are what consumers use to interact with their world. They are the tools consumers use to recognize their feelings, gather and analyze information, formulate thoughts and opinions, and take action. Unlike the other three influences on consumer behavior, psychological influences can be affected by a person's environment because they are applied on specific occasions. For example, you will perceive different stimuli and process these stimuli in different ways depending on whether you are sitting in class concentrating on the instructor, sitting outside of class talking to friends, or sitting in your dorm room watching television.

6-8a Perception

The world is full of stimuli. A stimulus is any unit of input affecting one or more of the five senses: sight, smell, taste, touch, and hearing. The process by which we select, organize, and interpret these stimuli into a meaningful and coherent picture is called **perception**. In essence, perception is how we see the world around us and how we recognize that we need some help in making a purchasing decision.

People cannot perceive every stimulus in their environment. Therefore, they use **selective exposure** to decide which stimuli to notice and which to ignore. A typical consumer is exposed to more than 2,500 advertising messages a day but notices only between 11 and 20.

The familiarity of an object, contrast, movement, intensity (such as increased volume), and smell are cues that influence perception. Consumers use these cues to identify and define products and brands. The shape of a product's packaging, such as Coca-Cola's signature contour bottle, can influence perception. Color is another cue, and it plays a key role in consumers' perceptions. Packaged foods manufacturers use color to trigger unconscious associations for grocery shoppers who typically make their shopping decisions in the blink of an eye. Ampacet, a world leader in color additives for plastics, reported in 2007 that nature-inspired colors and organic values were becoming more popular as the economy and global focus shifted from the tech boom to the bio or eco boom. Ecological consequences and concerns have resulted in marketing initiatives such as "going green." Colors like natural greens, earthy browns, and strong yellows, as well as metallics such as steely silver, carbon black, gold, and copper, are popular for packaging. Color researchers speculate that technological overload has led to a resurgence in the appreciation of simple luxury. Color names for fabrics and makeup reflect that trend with names such as Grounded, Champagne Chic, and Serene Blue.[31]

What is perceived by consumers may also depend on the stimuli's vividness or shock value. Graphic warnings of the hazards associated with a product's use are perceived more readily and remembered more accurately than less vivid warnings or warnings that are written in text. "Sexier" ads excel at attracting the attention of younger consumers. Companies like American Apparel and Abercrombie & Fitch appeal to the eight-to-eighteen age group with ads that push the envelope by setting models in provocative poses and highlighting their intimates collections with push-up bras and panties saying "Eye Candy."[32]

perception the process by which people select, organize, and interpret stimuli into a meaningful and coherent picture

selective exposure the process whereby a consumer notices certain stimuli and ignores others

selective distortion
a process whereby a consumer changes or distorts information that conflicts with his or her feelings or beliefs

selective retention
a process whereby a consumer remembers only that information that supports his or her personal beliefs

Two other concepts closely related to selective exposure are selective distortion and selective retention. **Selective distortion** occurs when consumers change or distort information that conflicts with their feelings or beliefs. For example, suppose a college student buys a Microsoft Zune MP3 player. After the purchase, if the student gets new information about an alternative brand, such as an Apple iPod, he or she may distort the information to make it more consistent with the prior view that the Microsoft Zune is just as good as the iPod, if not better. Business travelers who fly often may distort or discount information about plane crashes because they must use air travel constantly in their jobs.

Selective retention is remembering only information that supports personal feelings or beliefs. The consumer forgets all information that may be inconsistent. After reading a pamphlet that contradicts one's political beliefs, for instance, a person may forget many of the points outlined in it. Similarly, consumers may see a news report on suspected illegal practices by their favorite retail store but soon forget the reason the store was featured on the news.

Which stimuli will be perceived often depends on the individual. People can be exposed to the same stimuli under identical conditions but perceive them very differently. For example, two people viewing a television commercial may have different interpretations of the advertising message. One person may be thoroughly engrossed by the message and become highly motivated to buy the product. Thirty seconds after the ad ends, the second person may not be able to recall the content of the message or even the product advertised.

MARKETING IMPLICATIONS OF PERCEPTION
Marketers must recognize the importance of cues, or signals, in consumers' perception of products. Marketing managers first identify the important attributes, such as price or quality, that the targeted consumers want in a product and then design signals to communicate these attributes. For example, consumers will pay more for candy in expensive-looking foil packages. But shiny labels on wine bottles signify less expensive wines; dull labels indicate more expensive wines. Marketers also often use price as a signal to consumers that the product

is of higher quality than competing products. Of course, brand names send signals to consumers. The brand names of Close-Up toothpaste, DieHard batteries, and Caress moisturizing soap, for example, identify important product qualities. Names chosen for search engines and sites on the Internet, such as Yahoo!, Amazon.com, and Excite, are intended to convey excitement, intensity, and vastness.

Consumers also associate quality and reliability with certain brand names. Companies watch their brand identity closely, in large part because a strong link has been established between perceived brand value and customer loyalty. Brand names that consistently enjoy high perceived value from consumers include Disney, National Geographic, Mercedes-Benz, and Fisher-Price. Naming a product after a place can also add perceived value by association. Brand names using the words Santa Fe, Dakota, or Texas convey a sense of openness, freedom, and youth, but products named after other locations might conjure up images of pollution and crime. Marketing managers are also interested in the *threshold level of perception*, the minimum difference in a stimulus that the consumer will notice. This concept is sometimes referred to as the "just-noticeable difference." For example, how much would Apple have to drop the price of its iPod Shuffle before consumers recognize it as a bargain—$25? $50? or more? One study found that the just-noticeable difference in a stimulus is about a 20 percent change. For example, consumers will likely notice a 20 percent price decrease more quickly than one of only 15 percent. This marketing principle can be applied to other marketing variables as well, such as package size or loudness of a broadcast advertisement.[33]

Besides changing such stimuli as price, package size, and volume, marketers can change the product or attempt to reposition its image. But marketers must be careful when adding features. How many new services

© Matthew Cole/Shutterstock.com

Consumers are willing to **PAY MORE** *for candy in expensive-looking foil packages.*

will discounter Target need to add before consumers perceive it as a full-service department store? How many sporty features will General Motors have to add to a basic two-door sedan before consumers start perceiving it as a sports car?

Marketing managers who intend to do business in global markets should be aware of how foreign consumers perceive their products. For instance, in Japan, product labels are often written in English or French, even though they may not translate into anything meaningful. Many Japanese associate foreign words on product labels with the exotic, the expensive, and high quality.

Marketers have often been suspected of sending advertising messages subconsciously to consumers in what is known as *subliminal perception*. The controversy began when a researcher claimed to have increased popcorn and Coca-Cola sales at a movie theater after flashing "Eat popcorn" and "Drink Coca-Cola" on the screen every five seconds for 1/300th of a second, although the audience did not consciously recognize the messages. Almost immediately, consumer protection groups became concerned that advertisers were brainwashing consumers, and this practice was pronounced illegal in California and Canada. Although the researcher later admitted to making up the data and scientists have been unable to replicate the study since, consumers are still wary of hidden messages that advertisers may be sending.

6-8b Motivation

By studying motivation, marketers can analyze the major forces influencing consumers to buy or not buy products. When you buy a product, you usually do so to fulfill some kind of need. These needs become motives when aroused sufficiently. For instance, suppose this morning you were so hungry before class that you needed to eat something. In response to that need, you stopped at Subway for a breakfast sandwich. In other words, you were motivated by hunger to stop at Subway. A **motive** is the driving force that causes a person to take action to satisfy specific needs.

Why are people driven by particular needs at particular times? One popular theory is **Maslow's hierarchy of needs**, shown in Exhibit 6.6, which arranges needs in ascending order of importance: physiological, safety, social, esteem, and self-actualization.

© Cengage Learning

As a person fulfills one need, a higher-level need becomes more important.

The most basic human needs—that is, the needs for food, water, and shelter—are *physiological*. Because they are essential to survival, these needs must be satisfied first. Ads showing a juicy hamburger or a runner gulping down Gatorade after a marathon are examples of appeals to satisfy the physiological needs of hunger and thirst.

Safety needs include security and freedom from pain and discomfort. Marketers sometimes appeal to consumers' fears and anxieties about safety to sell their products. For example, aware of the aging population's health fears, the retail medical imaging centers Heart Check America and HealthScreen America advertise that they offer consumers a full body scan for early detection of health problems such as coronary disease and cancer. Some companies or industries advertise to allay consumer fears. For example, in the wake of the September 11 terrorist attacks, the airline industry found itself having to conduct an image campaign to reassure consumers about the safety of air travel.

After physiological and safety needs have been fulfilled, *social needs*—especially love and a sense of belonging—become the focus. Love includes acceptance by one's peers, as well as sex

motive a driving force that causes a person to take action to satisfy specific needs

Maslow's hierarchy of needs a method of classifying human needs and motivations into five categories in ascending order of importance: physiological, safety, social, esteem, and self-actualization

Exhibit 6.6

MASLOW'S HIERARCHY OF NEEDS

Self-actualization needs
Self-development, self-realization

Esteem needs
Self-esteem, recognition, status

Social needs
Sense of belonging, love

Safety needs
Security, protection

Physiological needs
Hunger, thirst

and romantic love. Marketing managers probably appeal more to this need than to any other. Ads for clothes, cosmetics, and vacation packages suggest that buying the product can bring love. The need to belong is also a favorite of marketers, especially those marketing products to teens. Teens consider Apple's iPod to be not only their favorite branded product but also something that defines their generation. Given the group's need for customization within a controlled environment, this love for Apple makes sense. Millennials' relationship with their parents is completely different from that of previous generations, and staying connected with family and friends is a priority. For marketers, this means understanding how to maximize crowdsourcing and peer-to-peer networks. For example, RelayRides offers the first peer-to-peer car-sharing where a person can borrow a neighbor's car for a quick trip to the store, and lenders can make up to $250 a month loaning out their cars.[34]

Love is acceptance without regard to one's contribution. Esteem is acceptance based on one's contribution to the group. *Self-esteem needs* include self-respect and a sense of accomplishment. Esteem needs also include prestige, fame, and recognition of one's accomplishments. Montblanc pens, Mercedes-Benz automobiles, and Neiman Marcus stores all appeal to esteem needs.

The highest human need is *self-actualization*. It refers to finding self-fulfillment and self-expression, reaching the point in life at which "people are what they feel they should be." Maslow felt that very few people ever attain this level. Even so, advertisements may focus on this type of need. For example, American Express ads convey the message that acquiring its card is one of the highest attainments in life. Microsoft appealed to consumers' needs for self-actualization when it chose "I'm a PC and Windows 7 was my idea" as the slogan for Windows 7; similarly, the U.S. Army changed its slogan from "Be all that you can be" to "Army of One."

CUSTOMERS WHO INSIST THEY TASTE A DIFFERENCE BETWEEN COKE AND PEPSI EXPERIENCE STIMULUS DISCRIMINATION.

6-8c Learning

Almost all consumer behavior results from **learning**, which is the process that creates changes in behavior through experience and practice. It is not possible to observe learning directly, but we can infer when it has occurred by a person's actions. For example, suppose you see an advertisement for a new and improved cold medicine. If you go to the store that day and buy that remedy, we infer that you have learned something about the cold medicine.

There are two types of learning: experiential and conceptual. *Experiential learning* occurs when an experience changes your behavior. For example, if the new cold medicine does not relieve your symptoms, you may not buy that brand again. *Conceptual learning*, which is not acquired through direct experience, is the second type of learning. Assume, for example, that you are standing at a soft drink machine and notice a new diet flavor with an artificial sweetener. Because someone has told you that diet beverages leave an aftertaste, you choose a different drink. You have learned that you would not like this new diet drink without ever trying it.

Reinforcement and repetition boost learning. Reinforcement can be positive or negative. If you see a vendor selling frozen yogurt (stimulus), buy it (response), and find the yogurt to be quite refreshing (reward), your behavior has been positively reinforced. On the other hand, if you buy a new flavor of yogurt and it does not taste good (negative reinforcement), you will not buy that flavor of yogurt again (response). Without positive or negative reinforcement, a person will not be motivated to repeat the behavior pattern or to avoid it. Thus, if a new brand evokes neutral feelings, some marketing activity, such as a price change or an increase in promotion, may be required to induce further consumption. Learning theory is helpful in reminding marketers that concrete and timely actions are what reinforce desired consumer behavior.

Repetition is a key strategy in promotional campaigns because it can lead

© iStockphoto.com/Donald Erickson

to increased learning. Most marketers use repetitious advertising so that consumers will learn what their unique advantage is over the competition. Generally, to heighten learning, advertising messages should be spread out over time rather than clustered together.

A related learning concept useful to marketing managers is **stimulus generalization**. In theory, stimulus generalization occurs when one response is extended to a second stimulus similar to the first. Marketers often use a successful, well-known brand name for a family of products because it gives consumers familiarity with and knowledge about each product in the family. Such brand name families spur the introduction of new products and facilitate the sale of existing items. OXO relies on consumers' familiarity with its popular kitchen and household products to sell office and medical supplies; Sony's film division relies on name recognition from its home technology, such as the PlayStation. Clorox bathroom cleaner relies on familiarity with Clorox bleach, and Dove shampoo relies on familiarity with Dove soap. Branding is examined in more detail in Chapter 10.

Another form of stimulus generalization occurs when retailers or wholesalers design their packages to resemble well-known manufacturers' brands. Such imitation often confuses consumers, who buy the imitation thinking it's the original.

The opposite of stimulus generalization is **stimulus discrimination**, which means learning to differentiate among similar products. Consumers may perceive one product as more rewarding or stimulating. For example, some consumers prefer Coca-Cola and others prefer Pepsi. Many insist they can taste a difference between the two brands.

With some types of products—such as aspirin, gasoline, bleach, and paper towels—marketers rely on promotion to point out brand differences that consumers would otherwise not recognize. This process, called *product differentiation*, is discussed in more detail in Chapter 8. Usually, product differentiation is based on superficial differences. For example, Bayer tells consumers that it's the aspirin "doctors recommend most."

6-8d Beliefs and Attitudes

Beliefs and attitudes are closely linked to values. A **belief** is an organized pattern of knowledge that an individual holds as true about his or her world. A consumer may believe that Sony's Cyber-shot camera takes the best HD

video, is easiest to use, and is the most reasonably priced. These beliefs may be based on knowledge, faith, or hearsay. Consumers tend to develop a set of beliefs about a product's attributes and then, through these beliefs, form a *brand image*—a set of beliefs about a particular brand. In turn, the brand image shapes consumers' attitudes toward the product.

An **attitude** is a learned tendency to respond consistently toward a given object, such as a brand. Attitudes rest on an individual's value system, which represents personal standards of good and bad, right and wrong, and so forth; therefore, attitudes tend to be more enduring and complex than beliefs.

For an example of the nature of attitudes, consider the differing attitudes of consumers around the world toward the practice of purchasing on credit. Americans have long been enthusiastic about charging goods and services and are willing to pay high interest rates for the privilege of postponing payment. To many European consumers, doing what amounts to taking out a loan—even a small one—to pay for anything seems absurd. Germans especially are reluctant to buy on credit. Italy has a sophisticated credit and banking system well suited to handling credit cards, but Italians prefer to carry cash, often huge wads of it. Although most Japanese consumers have credit cards, card purchases amount to less than 1 percent of all consumer transactions. The Japanese have long looked down on credit purchases but acquire cards to use while traveling abroad.

If a good or service is meeting its profit goals, positive attitudes toward the product merely need to be reinforced. If the brand is not succeeding, however, the marketing manager must strive to change target consumers' attitudes toward it. Changes in attitude tend to grow out of an individual's attempt to reconcile long-held values with a constant stream of new information. This change can be accomplished in three ways: changing beliefs about the brand's attributes, changing the relative importance of these beliefs, and adding new beliefs.

CHANGING BELIEFS ABOUT ATTRIBUTES The first approach is to turn neutral, negative, or incorrect beliefs about product attributes into positive ones. Hotmail, which debuted in 1996 and quickly garnered wide usage,

stimulus generalization a form of learning that occurs when one response is extended to a second stimulus similar to the first

stimulus discrimination a learned ability to differentiate among similar products

belief an organized pattern of knowledge that an individual holds as true about his or her world

attitude a learned tendency to respond consistently toward a given object is now perceived as less modern than other e-mail services, such as Gmail. To combat growing negative perceptions, Microsoft revamped the Hotmail site to make it more modern and to integrate it as part of its Windows Live program. The Windows Live program offers free, modern programs that allow users to manage multimedia, chatting, blogs, and e-mail. The new Windows Live Hotmail features include the ability to watch videos from YouTube and Hulu from within your e-mail, and even automatically track U.S. Postal Service packages when an e-mail contains a tracking number. These features make Hotmail an updated, modern choice for personal e-mail. To change people's lingering beliefs about Hotmail, Microsoft launched a massive marketing campaign to demonstrate Hotmail's updated, modern features.[35]

Changing beliefs about a service can be more difficult because service attributes are intangible. Convincing consumers to switch hairstylists or lawyers or to go to a mall dental clinic can be much more difficult than getting them to change brands of razor blades. Image, which is also largely intangible, significantly determines service patronage. Service marketing is explored in detail in Chapter 12.

CHANGING THE IMPORTANCE OF BELIEFS The second approach to modifying attitudes is to change the relative importance of beliefs about an attribute. J.Crew was suffering from plummeting sales in 2003, due in part to a frumpy, preppy persona but has risen to new profits by offering luxurious basics, such as tailored basic dresses and cashmere sweaters. An endorsement from Michelle Obama further elevated the brand.[36] Marketers can also emphasize the importance of some beliefs over others. For example, McDonald's has been fingered as the culprit for Americans' obesity. But the chain now offers a large line of salads and healthy meals and side options, hoping to demonstrate its ability to serve healthier options to customers who want them.[37]

ADDING NEW BELIEFS The third approach to transforming attitudes is to add new beliefs. Although changes in consumption patterns often come slowly, cereal marketers are betting that consumers will eventually warm up to the idea of cereal as a snack. A print ad for General Mills' Cookie Crisp cereal features a boy popping the sugary nuggets into his mouth while he does his homework. Koch Industries, the manufacturer of Dixie paper products, is also attempting to add new beliefs about the uses of its paper plates and cups with an advertising campaign aimed at positioning its product as a "home cleanup replacement." Commercials pitch Dixie paper plates as an alternative to washing dishes after everyday meals and not just for picnics.

U.S. companies attempting to market their goods overseas may need to help consumers add new beliefs about a product in general. Coca-Cola and PepsiCo have both found it challenging to sell their diet cola brands to consumers in India partly because diet foods of any kind are a new concept in that country where malnutrition was widespread until recently. Indians also have deep-rooted attitudes that anything labeled "diet" is meant for a sick person, such as a diabetic. As a general rule, most Indians are not diet conscious, preferring food prepared in the traditional manner that tastes good. Indians are also suspicious of the artificial sweeteners used in diet colas. India's Health Ministry has required warning labels on cans and bottles of Diet Coke and Diet Pepsi saying "Not Recommended for Children."[38]

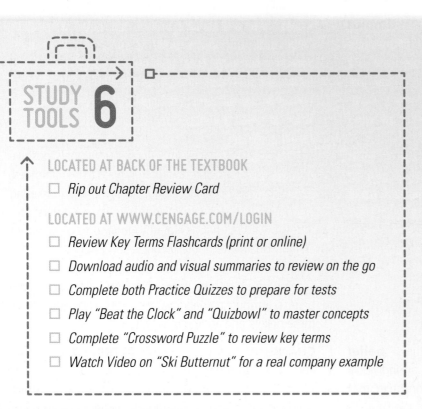

STUDY TOOLS 6

LOCATED AT BACK OF THE TEXTBOOK
☐ *Rip out Chapter Review Card*

LOCATED AT WWW.CENGAGE.COM/LOGIN
☐ *Review Key Terms Flashcards (print or online)*
☐ *Download audio and visual summaries to review on the go*
☐ *Complete both Practice Quizzes to prepare for tests*
☐ *Play "Beat the Clock" and "Quizbowl" to master concepts*
☐ *Complete "Crossword Puzzle" to review key terms*
☐ *Watch Video on "Ski Butternut" for a real company example*

ANATOMY OF A BUYING DECISION: CAR

SOCIAL FACTORS

Before deciding to buy a car, this woman may seek out others' opinions or observe what others purchase.

ADVICE FROM HER REFERENCE GROUP

EXAMPLE OF OPINION LEADER

INDIVIDUAL FACTORS:

LIFESTYLE

SELF-CONCEPT

Her buying decision will be influenced by her personality, self-concept, and lifestyle.

PSYCHOLOGICAL FACTORS:

The consumer's perception, motivation, learning, values, beliefs, and attitudes will influence her decision on which car to buy, too.

ATTITUDE

"Should I try a new brand, or stick with the familiar one?"

7-1 WHAT IS BUSINESS MARKETING?

Business marketing (also called industrial marketing) is the marketing of goods and services to individuals and organizations for purposes other than personal consumption. The sale of a PC to your college or university is an example of business marketing. Business products include those that are used to manufacture other products, become part of another product, or aid the normal operations of an organization. The key characteristic distinguishing business products from consumer products is intended use, not physical characteristics.

> The key characteristic distinguishing business products from consumer products is intended use, not physical form.

business marketing (industrial marketing) the marketing of goods and services to individuals and organizations for purposes other than personal consumption

How do you distinguish between a consumer product and a business product? A product that is purchased for personal or family consumption or as a gift is a consumer good. If that same product, such as a PC or a cell phone, is bought for use in a business, it is a business product. Some common items that are sold as both consumer goods and business products are office supplies (e.g., pens, paper, staple removers). Some items, such as forklifts, are more commonly sold as business products than as consumer goods. A survey by HubSpot revealed that the two primary marketing goals of U.S. business marketers' Web sites are making sales and attracting customers, clients, and other new business.[1]

The size of the business market in the United States and most other countries substantially exceeds that of the consumer market. In the business market, a single customer can account for a huge volume of purchases. For example, IBM's purchasing department spends more than $40 billion annually on business products. Procter & Gamble, Apple, Merck, Dell, and Kimberly-Clark each spend more than half of their annual revenue on business products.[2]

Some large firms that produce goods such as steel, computer memory chips, or production equipment market exclusively to business customers. Other firms market to both businesses and to consumers. Hewlett-Packard marketed exclusively to business customers in the past but now markets laser printers and personal computers to consumers. Sony, traditionally a consumer marketer, now sells office automation products to businesses. Both companies have had to make organizational and marketing changes to expand into the new market categories.

Chapter **7**

Business Marketing

Learning Outcomes

After you finish this chapter go to
p125 *for* **STUDY TOOLS** 📁 ------→

business-to-business electronic commerce (B-to-B or B2B e-commerce) the use of the Internet to facilitate the exchange of goods, services, and information between organizations

7-2 BUSINESS MARKETING ON THE INTERNET

The use of the Internet to facilitate activities between organizations is called business-to-business electronic commerce (B-to-B or B2B e-commerce). This method of conducting business has evolved and grown rapidly throughout its short history. In 1995, the commercial Web sites that did exist were static. Only a few had data-retrieval capabilities. Frames, tables, and styles were not available. Security of any sort was rare, and streaming video did not exist. Today, B-to-B sites look more like consumer sites with social media, valuable content, and community building applications. Before the Internet, customers had to call Dow Chemical and request a specification sheet for the products they were considering. The information would arrive a few days later by mail. After choosing a product, the customer could then place an order by calling Dow (during business hours, of course). Now, such information is available through MyAccount@Dow, which provides information tailored to the customer's requirements, such as secure internal monitoring of a customer's chemical tank levels. When tanks reach a predetermined level, reordering can be automatically triggered.[3]

Companies selling to business buyers face the same challenges as all marketers, including determining who, exactly, the market is and how best to reach it. This is particularly difficult in business marketing because

> "If we send a white paper with information about our industry, we might get more Web traffic."

business has rapidly moved online. A recent report from Forrester Research, "B2B US Interactive Marketing Forecast 2009–2014," predicted that interactive spending by B-to-B marketers will reach $4.8 billion by 2014. Some of the expected increase can be attributed to companies looking to bypass more expensive offline tactics and use more measurable online tactics.[4] Content marketing is becoming more and more important to B-to-B marketing. Content marketing is based on the idea of developing valuable content for interested audience members—namely through videos, white papers, e-mail newsletters, webinars, and blog posts—and subsequently using e-mail marketing, search engine optimization, paid search, and display advertising to "pull" customers to the site. For example, Kelly Outsourcing & Consulting Group spends about 60 percent of its B-to-B marketing budget on the creation and dissemination of content designed to provide useful information to executives about staffing and outsourcing. Indeed, one recent study found that 82 percent of B-to-B marketers used content marketing—the key is making it valuable to users.[5]

The reviews on social media are mixed. Some B-to-B marketers feel that social media are not as useful to them as to business-to-consumer (B-to-C) marketers.[6] But other experts see growth in social media use as B-to-B marketers use opportunities to generate quality leads. Overall, one study shows that 93 percent of B-to-B marketers use social media, primarily LinkedIn. Most of the spending is allocated to create and manage online customer communities (32 percent), podcasts (20 percent) and blogs (18 percent) to convey thought leadership, Facebook (71 percent), and Twitter (67 percent).[7] It is clear from some companies' Web sites that they are embracing new tools and applications. The primary tools used by B-to-B marketers are blogs, social networking sites, Twitter, video streaming sites, and mobile marketing. B-to-B marketers are experimenting with how to successfully use these media to build relationships with business customers. For example, YouTube offers a guide for B-to-B marketers to effectively use online videos to promote their brands. LinkedIn, a social networking site for professionals, is seen as a repository for finding new talent for companies.[8] Other companies are using social media listening tools to determine strategic topics to include in newsletters and videos. The key to making social media use effective is to combine it with other digital assets such as e-mail marketing and content marketing. For example, a marketer can drive e-mail subscriptions through Facebook or use Twitter to promote an upcoming e-mail newsletter that features an interview with an industry expert.

likely to purchase again in the near future than are customers who haven't purchased for a while. *Frequency* data help marketers identify frequent purchasers who are most likely to repeat their purchasing behavior in the future. The monetary value of sales is important because big spenders can be the most profitable customers for a business. As such, there are literally thousands of metrics that can then be utilized depending on the conversion task. The *conversion task* is the behavior that the marketer wants the visitor to

STICKINESS = FREQUENCY x DURATION x SITE REACH

Each year, BtoBonline.com identifies ten business marketing Web sites that are particularly good examples of how companies can use the Web to communicate with customers. Exhibit 7.1 identifies the ten great Web sites for 2011. The key is to design Web sites with the end user in mind. Many sites are designed with logic behind them, but people don't necessarily search in a logical manner. Personalization is an important element in the winning sites. Marketers are also focusing on zero-click Web sites, sites that bring visitors right to where they want and need to be (e.g., optimized landing pages). Many of these companies have also been recognized in past years for effectively communicating with their target markets.[9]

7-2a Measuring Online Success

Most marketers use some sort of Web analytics (such as Google Analytics or an enterprise system like Omniture) to determine which activities generate leads and then use that information to make their Web sites more effective. Metrics include external search traffic, internal search engine analytics, and key word search results. Three of the most important measurements of online success are recency, frequency, and monetary value. *Recency* relates to the fact that customers who have made a purchase recently are more

take—such as signing up for e-mails, watching a video, calling for more information, signing up for a webinar, and a host of others. This sets up the conversion rate, which is another important metric for digital marketing. The *conversion rate* is defined as a ratio of the number of people who visited the site to the number of people who went on to complete the desired action.

One common way of evaluating a Web application, Web site, or other piece of interactive technology is to evaluate its **stickiness** factor by combining frequency data with the length of time a visitor spent on the Web site (duration) and the number of site pages viewed during each visit (total site reach). For example, Apple's iCloud, which allows users to remotely store all content in the cloud and access it from any Apple device, increases user stickiness in the Apple software systems, meaning users will use all Apple software for longer periods of time.[10]

By measuring the stickiness factor of a Web site before and after a design or function change, the marketer can quickly determine whether visitors embrace the change. By adding purchase information to determine the level of stickiness needed to provide a desired purchase volume, the marketer gains an even more precise understanding of how a site change affects business. An almost endless number of factor combinations can be created to provide a

Exhibit 7.1

TEN COMPANIES WITH GREAT B-TO-B WEB SITES

1.	American Express OPEN Forum
2.	Approva Corp.
3.	Carnival Cruise Line's GoCCL.com
4.	Citrix Online's GoToWebinar
5.	Grainger Inc
6.	Groupon Inc.'s GrouponWorks for Businesses
7.	Heroku
8.	Shopify
9.	Siemens Corp
10.	U.S.Xpress

Source: Karen Bannan, "10 Great BtoB Sites," *BtoB Magazine*, September 19, 2011, 8.

disintermedi-ation the elimination of intermediaries such as wholesalers or distributers from a marketing channel

quantitative method for determining buyer behavior online. First, though, the marketer must determine what measures are required and which factors can be combined to arrive at those measurements.[11]

7-2b Trends in B-to-B Internet Marketing

Social media usage in B-to-B marketing and B-to-C marketing has been the largest marketing trend in the past five years. It requires vigilant adjustment to keep track of new applications and platforms, as well as constant evaluation to determine whether these new avenues are beneficial to (or used by) customers.

Many marketers use social media to create awareness and build relationships and community rather than to generate leads. As various platforms such as mobile and video grow, marketers must develop new ways to measure campaign effectiveness across those platforms. According to a survey by *BtoB* and the Web

13% OF B2B MKTRS <3 TWITTER!

Analytics Association, social media measurement was low for mobile (17 percent) and video (14 percent) and high for Web site traffic (88 percent) and e-mail campaigns (76 percent).[12] Because e-mail and Web sites have been in use by marketers longer, analytics to measure various metrics are more developed for those platforms. Some metrics that are particularly useful for social media are awareness, engagement, and conversion. Awareness is the attention that social media attracts, such as the number of followers or fans. Engagement refers to the interactions between the brand and the audience such as comments, retweets, and searches. Conversions occur when action is taken.[13] Each of these metrics affects the return on investment.

As the increasing use of social media indicates, over the past decade marketers have become more and more sophisticated in the use of the Internet. Exhibit 7.2 compares three prominent Internet business marketing strategy initiatives from the late 1990s to five that are currently being pursued. Companies have had to transition from "We have a Web site because our customer does" to having a site that attracts, interests, satisfies, informs, and retains customers. New applications that provide additional information about present and potential customers; increase efficiency; lower costs; increase supply chain efficiency; or enhance customer retention, loyalty, and trust are being developed each year. Increasingly, business customers expect suppliers to know them personally, keep tabs on people's movement within their company, and offer personal interaction through social media, e-mail, and personal mailers.[14]

One term in Exhibit 7.2 that may be unfamiliar is **disintermediation**, which means eliminating intermediaries such as wholesalers or distributors from a marketing channel.[15] A prime example of disintermediation is Dell, which sells directly to business buyers and consumers. Dell is now using Twitter to sell its overstock inventory. Large retailers such as Walmart use a disintermediation strategy to help reduce costs and prices.

A few years ago, many people thought the Internet would eliminate the need for distributors. Why would customers pay a distributor's markup when they could buy directly from the manufacturer with a few mouse clicks? Yet Internet disintermediation has occurred less frequently than many expected. The reason is that distributors often perform important functions such as providing credit,

TOP SOCIAL MEDIA PLATFORMS FOR B-TO-B MARKETERS

BtoB Magazine surveyed 577 B-to-B marketers on their favorite social media platforms at work, and while LinkedIn, Facebook, and Twitter were used by nearly all of the marketers, **LinkedIn** was their favorite social media tool (chosen by 26 percent of respondents). Runners up were **Facebook** (20 percent), blogs (19 percent), customer communities (14 percent), Twitter, (13 percent), and YouTube (7 percent).

Those who didn't use social media marketing cited difficulty in convincing top management of its usefulness. This could be due in part to lack of measurable success metrics or simply poor understanding of the media.

Source: "Emerging Trends in B-to-B Social Media Marketing: Insights from the Field," *BtoB Magazine*, April 2011, 6–9.

aggregation of supplies from multiple sources, delivery, and processing returns.

Many business customers, especially small firms, depend on knowledgeable distributors for information and advice that is not available to them online. You will notice in Exhibit 7.2 that building channel partnerships and trust has replaced aggressive disintermediation initiatives as a priority for most firms. Some firms have followed disintermediation with **reintermediation**, the reintroduction of an intermediary between producers and users. They realized that providing only direct online purchasing was similar to having only one store in a city selling a popular brand. For example, Cisco is dropping its direct-to-consumer line of products and services to focus entirely on helping corporate customers expand consumer offerings, including offering networking products and solutions.[16]

reintermediation
the reintroduction of an intermediary between producers and users

strategic alliance (strategic partnership)
a cooperative agreement between business firms

Exhibit 7.2

EVOLUTION OF E-BUSINESS INITIATIVES

- Revenue generation
- Aggressive disintermediation initiatives
- Basic marketing communication strategies

- Reduce costs
- Build channel partnerships and trust
- Customer-focused technology and systems
- Brand building and development
- Integrate online and traditional media

Time

Past initiatives   Present initiatives

Source: Andrew J. Rohm and Fareena Sultan, "The Evolution of E-Business," *Marketing Management*, January/February 2004, 35. Used by permission.

7-3 RELATIONSHIP MARKETING AND STRATEGIC ALLIANCES

As explained in Chapter 1, relationship marketing is a strategy that entails seeking and establishing ongoing partnerships with customers. Relationship marketing has become an important business marketing strategy as customers have become more demanding and competition has become more intense. Loyal customers are also more profitable than those who are price sensitive and perceive little or no difference among brands or suppliers.

Relationship marketing is increasingly important as business suppliers use platforms like Facebook, Twitter, and other social networking sites to advertise themselves to businesses. Social networking sites encourage businesses to shop around and research options for all their needs. This means that for many suppliers, retaining their current customers has become a primary focus, whereas acquiring new customers was the focus in the past. Maintaining a steady dialogue between the supplier and the customer is a proven way to gain repeat business.[17]

Building long-term relationships with customers offers companies a way to build competitive advantage that is hard for competitors to copy. For example, the FedEx PowerShip program includes a series of automated shipping, tracking, and invoicing systems that save customers time and money while solidifying their loyalty to FedEx. This produces a win-win situation.

7-3a Strategic Alliances

A **strategic alliance**, sometimes called a **strategic partnership**, is a cooperative agreement between business firms. Strategic alliances can take the form of licensing or distribution agreements, joint ventures, research and development consortia, and partnerships. They may be between manufacturers, manufacturers and customers, manufacturers and suppliers, and manufacturers and channel intermediaries.

Business marketers form strategic alliances to strengthen operations and better compete. eBay's popular online payment system, PayPal, has grown rapidly worldwide. However, adoption has been slow in Japan where there are other more popular forms of electronic payment. However, eBay is partnering with Softbank to bring PayPal to Japan. The two companies are hoping to capitalize on the burgeoning mobile shopping movement and to increase credit card usage in Japan.[18]

Sometimes alliance partners are fierce competitors. For instance, in the face of rising fuel prices and increasing business competition from Delta Air Lines, Singapore Airlines and Virgin Australia have teamed up to offer greater range for both airlines. Virgin's expansive Australian and Pacific routes will give Singapore Airlines access to the lucrative Australia–United States route, and Virgin will have access to seventy new routes. The companies will also collaborate on pricing and a frequent-flyer program, hoping to increase their share in the business traveler market.[19]

Other alliances are formed between companies that operate in completely different industries. For example, MasterCard and Avis Budget Group formed an alliance to provide MasterCard users discounts on services provided by Budget and Avis car rental services. MasterCard users prefer discounts in the travel sector, and the alliance gives Budget and Avis an opportunity to increase market share in the $4 billion-a-year U.S. car rental market.[20] Exhibit 7.3 demonstrates the benefits Starbucks and Green Mountain Coffee receive from each other through their strategic alliance.

For an alliance to succeed in the long term, it must be built on commitment and trust. **Relationship commitment** means that a firm believes an ongoing relationship with some other firm is so important that it warrants maximum efforts at maintaining it indefinitely.[21] A perceived breakdown in commitment by one of the parties often leads to a breakdown in the relationship.

Trust exists when one party has confidence in an exchange partner's reliability and integrity.[22] Some alliances fail when participants lack trust in their trading partners. For instance, General Motors, Ford, DaimlerChrysler, Nissan Motor Company, and Renault SA created an Internet automobile parts exchange, called Covisint, that they hoped would make $300 billion in sales per year. But the auto industry is characterized by mistrust between buyers and sellers, and the alliance never got a strong foothold. After three years and hundreds of millions of dollars invested, the exchange was floundering. The investment money was nearly gone, and the workforce had been reduced by 35 percent. Automobile industry suppliers did not trust Covisint, resulting in its failure.

7-3b Relationships in Other Cultures

Although the terms *relationship marketing* and *strategic alliances* are fairly new and popularized mostly by American business executives and educators, the concepts have long been familiar in other cultures. Businesses in China, Japan, Korea, Mexico, and much of Europe rely heavily on personal relationships. Customer relationship management is covered throughout the text.

In Japan, for example, exchange between firms is based on personal relationships that are developed through what is called *amae*, or indulgent dependency. *Amae* is the feeling of nurturing concern for, and dependence upon, another. Reciprocity and personal relationships contribute to *amae*. Relationships between companies can develop into a **keiretsu**—a network of interlocking corporate affiliates. Within a *keiretsu*, executives may sit on the boards of their customers or their suppliers. Members

IF YOU ORDER IT, WE WILL COME.

FOOD AND DRINKS ON DEMAND. THIS IS HOW TO FLY.

↳ GRAB A SEAT AT VIRGINAMERICA.COM
SAN FRANCISCO · LAS VEGAS · LOS ANGELES · NEW YORK · SAN DIEGO · SEATTLE · WASHINGTON, D.C.

Virgin america

Virgin Airlines is known as a luxurious business airline and has added more routes thanks to an alliance with Singapore Airlines.

of a *keiretsu* trade with each other whenever possible and often engage in joint product development, finance, and marketing activity. For example, the Toyota Group *keiretsu* includes 14 core companies and another 170 that receive preferential treatment. Toyota holds an equity position in many of these 170 member firms and is represented on many of their boards of directors.

Many firms have found that the best way to compete in Asian countries is to form relationships with Asian firms. For example, German automaker Volkswagen has an alliance with Suzuki Motor Corporation to work on developing new hybrid and electric vehicles under both brands.[23]

7-4 MAJOR CATEGORIES OF BUSINESS CUSTOMERS

The business market consists of four major categories of customers: producers, resellers, governments, and institutions.

7-4a Producers

The producer segment of the business market includes profit-oriented individuals and organizations that use purchased goods and services to produce other products, to incorporate into other products, or to facilitate the daily operations of the organization. Examples of producers include construction, manufacturing, transportation, finance, real estate, and food service firms. In the United States, there are more than 13 million firms in the producer segment of the business market. Some of these firms are small, and others are among the world's largest businesses.

Producers are often called **original equipment manufacturers** or **OEMs**. This term includes all individuals and organizations that buy business goods and incorporate them into the products they produce for eventual sale to other producers or to consumers. Companies such as General Motors that buy steel, paint, tires, and batteries are said to be OEMs.

original equipment manufacturers (OEMs) individuals and organizations that buy business goods and incorporate them into the products they produce for eventual sale to other producers or to consumers

Exhibit 7.3

STRATEGIC ALLIANCE: STARBUCKS AND GREEN MOUNTAIN

Gives		Gets	
Starbucks Branded Coffee Starbucks ground coffee has worldwide recognition and a strong market share.		*Market Share* Starbucks's worldwide recognition allows Green Mountain to steal market share from other single-pod brands that don't carry Starbucks brand coffee.	
Starbucks Customers Starbucks customers are willing to brew at home and tend to be affluent.		*Stronger Brand Recognition* By offering the high-value Keurig brewing machine at Starbucks stores, Green Mountain is able to give its Keurig line stronger branding.	
Existing Green Mountain Customers Current Green Mountain customers own Keurig machines and brew single-pod coffee.		*Market Share* Focused access to Keurig machine users in homes and businesses increases Starbucks's presence in those markets.	
Technology Keurig machines and single-pod brewing technology		*Expanded Product Offering* By selling Keurig machines and coffee pods in retail stores, Starbucks can offer more products and more ways to drink Starbucks coffee.	

7-4b Resellers

The reseller market includes retail and wholesale businesses that buy finished goods and resell them for a profit. A retailer sells mainly to final consumers; wholesalers sell mostly to retailers and other organizational customers. There are approximately 1.5 million retailers and 500,000 wholesalers operating in the United States. Consumer product firms like Procter & Gamble, Kraft Foods, and Coca-Cola sell directly to large retailers and retail chains and through wholesalers to smaller retail units. Retailing is explored in detail in Chapter 14.

Business product distributors are wholesalers that buy business products and resell them to business customers. They often carry thousands of items in stock and employ sales forces to call on business customers. Businesses that wish to buy a gross of pencils or a hundred pounds of fertilizer typically purchase these items from local distributors rather than directly from manufacturers such as Empire Pencil or Dow Chemical.

7-4c Governments

A third major segment of the business market is government. Government organizations include thousands of federal, state, and local buying units. They make up what may be the largest single market for goods and services in the world, estimated at $5.5 trillion in 2010.[24]

Marketing to government agencies can be an overwhelming undertaking, but companies that learn how the system works can position themselves to win lucrative contracts and build lasting, rewarding relationships.[25] Contracts for government purchases are often put out for bid. Interested vendors submit bids (usually sealed) to provide specified products during a particular time. Sometimes the lowest bidder is awarded the contract. When the lowest bidder is not awarded the contract, strong evidence must be presented to justify the decision. Grounds for rejecting the lowest bid include lack of experience, inadequate financing, or poor past performance.

Bidding allows all potential suppliers a fair chance at winning government contracts and helps ensure that public funds are spent wisely.

FEDERAL GOVERNMENT Name just about any good or service and chances are that someone in the federal government uses it. The U.S. federal government buys goods and services valued at more than $600 billion per year, making it the world's largest customer.

Although much of the federal government's buying is centralized, no single federal agency contracts for all the government's requirements, and no single buyer in any agency purchases all that the agency needs. We can view the federal government as a combination of several large companies with overlapping responsibilities and thousands of small independent units. One popular source of information about government procurement is *FedBizOpps*. Until recently, businesses hoping to sell to the federal government found the document (until recently called *Commerce Business Daily*) unorganized, and it often arrived too late to be useful. The online version (www.cbd-net.com) is timelier and lets contractors find leads using key word searches. Other examples of publications designed to explain how to do business with the federal government include *Doing Business with the General Services Administration*, *Selling to the Military*, and *Selling to the U.S. Air Force*.

STATE, COUNTY, AND CITY GOVERNMENT Selling to states, counties, and cities can be less frustrating for both small and large vendors than selling to the federal government. Paperwork is typically simpler and more manageable than it is at the federal level. But vendors must decide which of the more than 82,000 government units are likely to buy their wares. State and local buying agencies include school districts, highway departments, government-operated hospitals, and housing agencies.

7-4d Institutions

The fourth major segment of the business market consists of institutions that seek to achieve goals other than the standard business goals of profit, market share, and return on investment. This segment includes schools, hospitals, colleges and universities, churches, labor unions, fraternal organizations, civic clubs, foundations, and other so-called nonbusiness organizations. Xerox offers educational and medical institutions the same prices as government agencies (the lowest that Xerox offers) and has a separate sales force that calls on these customers.

7-5 THE NORTH AMERICAN INDUSTRY CLASSIFICATION SYSTEM

The North American Industry Classification System (NAICS) is an industry classification system introduced in 1997 to replace the standard industrial classification system (SIC). NAICS (pronounced *nakes*) is a system for classifying North American business establishments. The system, developed jointly by the United States, Canada, and Mexico, provides a common industry classification system for the North American Free Trade Agreement (NAFTA) partners. Goods- or service-producing firms that use identical or similar production processes are grouped together.

NAICS is an extremely valuable tool for business marketers engaged in analyzing, segmenting, and targeting markets. Each classification group is relatively homogeneous in terms of raw materials required, components used, manufacturing processes employed, and problems faced. The more digits in a code, the more homogeneous the group. Therefore, if a supplier understands the needs and requirements of a few firms within a classification, requirements can be projected for all firms in that category. The number, size, and geographic dispersion of firms can also be identified. This information can be converted to market potential estimates, market share estimates, and sales forecasts. It can also be used for identifying potential new customers. NAICS codes can help identify firms that may be prospective users of a supplier's goods and services. A sample of how NAICS codes function is listed in Exhibit 7.4. For a complete listing of all NAICS codes, see www.naics.com/search.htm.

© Cengage Learning

7-6 BUSINESS VERSUS CONSUMER MARKETS

The basic philosophy and practice of marketing are the same whether the customer is a business organization

or a consumer. Business markets do, however, have characteristics different from consumer markets.

7-6a Demand

Consumer demand for products is quite different from demand in the business market. Unlike consumer demand, business demand is derived, inelastic, joint, and fluctuating.

DERIVED DEMAND The demand for business products is called **derived demand** because organizations buy products to be used in producing their customers' products. For instance, the number of drills or lathes that a manufacturing firm needs is derived from, or based upon the demand for, products that are produced using these machines. Because demand is derived, business marketers must carefully monitor demand patterns and changing preferences in final consumer markets, even though their customers are not in those markets. Moreover, business marketers must carefully monitor their customers' forecasts, because derived demand is based on expectations of future demand for those customers' products.

Some business marketers not only monitor final consumer demand and customer forecasts but also try to influence final consumer demand. Aluminum producers use television and magazine advertisements to point out the convenience and recycling opportunities that aluminum offers to consumers who can choose to purchase soft drinks in either aluminum or plastic containers.

> **North American Industry Classification System (NAICS)**
> a detailed numbering system developed by the United States, Canada, and Mexico to classify North American business establishments by their main production processes
>
> **derived demand**
> the demand for business products

Exhibit 7.4

HOW NAICS WORKS

The more digits in the NAICS code, the more homogeneous the groups at that level.

NAICS Level	NAICS Code	Description
Sector	51	Information
Subsector	513	Broadcasting and telecommunications
Industry group	5133	Telecommunications
Industry	51332	Wireless telecommunications carriers, except satellite
Industry subdivision	513321	Paging

joint demand the demand for two or more items used together in a final product

multiplier effect (accelerator principle) phenomenon in which a small increase or decrease in consumer demand can produce a much larger change in demand for the facilities and equipment needed to make the consumer product

INELASTIC DEMAND The demand for many business products is inelastic with regard to price. *Inelastic demand* means that an increase or decrease in the price of the product will not significantly affect demand for the product. This will be discussed further in Chapter 19.

The price of a product used in the production of, or as part of, a final product is often a minor portion of the final product's total price. Therefore, demand for the final consumer product is not affected. If the price of automobile paint or spark plugs rises significantly, say, 200 percent in one year, do you think the number of new automobiles sold that year will be affected? Probably not.

JOINT DEMAND **Joint demand** occurs when two or more items are used together in a final product. For example, a decline in the availability of memory chips will slow production of microcomputers, which will in turn reduce the demand for disk drives. Likewise, the demand for Apple operating systems exists as long as there is demand for Apple computers. Sales of the two products are directly linked.

FLUCTUATING DEMAND The demand for business products—particularly new plants and equipment—tends to be less stable than the demand for consumer products. A small increase or decrease in consumer demand can produce a much larger change in demand for the facilities and equipment needed to make the consumer product. Economists refer to this phenomenon as the **multiplier effect** (or **accelerator principle**).

Cummins Inc., a producer of heavy-duty diesel engines, uses sophisticated surface grinders to make parts. Suppose Cummins is using twenty surface grinders. Each machine lasts about ten years. Purchases have been timed so two machines will wear out and be replaced annually. If the demand for engine parts does not change, two grinders will be bought this year. If the demand for parts declines slightly, only eighteen grinders may be needed, and Cummins won't replace the worn ones. However, suppose that next year demand returns to previous levels plus a little more. To meet the new level of demand, Cummins will need to replace the two machines that wore out in the previous year, the two that wore out in the current year, plus one or more additional

machines. The multiplier effect works this way in many industries, producing highly fluctuating demand for business products.

7-6b Purchase Volume

Business customers buy in much larger quantities than consumers. Just think how large an order Kellogg's typically places for the wheat bran and raisins used to manufacture Raisin Bran. Or, consider that Enterprise Rent-A-Car purchases 500 electric cars from Nissan at one time.[26]

7-6c Number of Customers

Business marketers usually have far fewer customers than consumer marketers. The advantage is that it is a lot easier to identify prospective buyers, monitor current customers' needs and levels of satisfaction, and personally attend to existing customers. The main disadvantage is that each customer becomes crucial—especially for those manufacturers that have only one customer. In many cases, this customer is the U.S. government. The success or failure of one bid can make the difference between prosperity and bankruptcy. Boeing, trying to regain its position as the dominant tanker plane developer, vied for more than three years to win the U.S. Air Force's $35 billion bid to supply refueling planes. Its main competition was European Aeronautic Defence and Space Company, the world's other leading supplier of tanker planes.[27]

7-6d Location of Buyers

Business customers tend to be much more geographically concentrated than consumers. For instance, more than half the nation's business buyers are located in California, Illinois, Michigan, New Jersey, New York, Ohio, and Pennsylvania. The aircraft and microelectronics industries are concentrated on the West Coast, and many of the firms that supply the automobile manufacturing industry are located in and around Detroit.

7-6e Distribution Structure

Many consumer products pass through a distribution system that includes the producer, one or more wholesalers, and a retailer. In business marketing, however, because of many of the characteristics already mentioned, channels of distribution for business marketing are typically shorter. Direct channels, where manufacturers market directly to

business-to-business online exchange an electronic trading floor that provides companies with integrated links to their customers and suppliers

users, are much more common. The use of direct channels has increased dramatically in the past decade with the introduction of various Internet buying and selling schemes. One such technique is called a **business-to-business online exchange**, which is an electronic trading floor that provides companies with integrated links to their customers and suppliers. The goal of B-to-B exchanges is to simplify business purchasing and to make it more efficient. For example, Exostar claims more than half of the aerospace industry's firms as its customers and has more than 70,000 registered companies to support those customers.[28] Exchanges such as Exostar facilitate direct channel relationships between producers and their customers.

7-6f Nature of Buying

Unlike consumers, business buyers usually approach purchasing rather formally. Businesses use professionally trained purchasing agents or buyers who spend their entire career purchasing a limited number of items. They get to know the items and the sellers well. Some professional purchasers earn the designation of Certified Purchasing Manager (CPM) after participating in a rigorous certification program.

7-6g Nature of Buying Influence

Typically, more people are involved in a single business purchase decision than in a consumer purchase. Experts from fields as varied as quality control, marketing, and finance, as well as professional buyers and users, may be grouped in a buying center (discussed later in this chapter).

7-6h Type of Negotiations

Consumers are used to negotiating price on automobiles and real estate. In most cases, however, American consumers expect sellers to set the price and other conditions of sale, such as time of delivery and credit terms. In contrast, negotiating is common in business marketing. Buyers and sellers negotiate product

MODIFYING CORPORATE MOOD TOWARD APPLE RETAILERS

When he was at Apple, Steve Jobs was notorious for not catering to large companies that wanted him to modify his designs to accommodate business needs. When Apple was asked to add some features to the iPhone to make it work better in a corporate environment, Jobs expressed how small the business market was in comparison to the overall cell phone market. Today, however, the new CEO of Apple, Tim Cook, sees the business market as a growth opportunity for the company. Now offering apps and software capabilities that make the iPhone and iPad more compatible with common business software such as Microsoft Exchange (used for e-mail), the popular consumer products are being evaluated for use by more than 90 percent of Fortune 500 companies. Already airlines, technology firms, and engineers have adopted the technology because it is easy to call up references and checklists for jobs. Overall, Apple is working to meet the needs of both the consumer and business markets with the same products.

Source: Nick Wingfield, "A Corporate Yen for iTools," *New York Times*, November 16, 2011, B1, B4.

© Katherine Welles/Shutterstock.com / © iStockphoto.com/Bill Noll specifications, delivery dates, payment terms, and other pricing matters. Sometimes these negotiations occur during many meetings over several months. Final contracts are often very long and detailed.

7-6i Use of Reciprocity

Business purchasers often choose to buy from their own customers, a practice known as **reciprocity**. For example, General Motors buys engines for use in its automobiles and trucks from BorgWarner, which in turn buys many of the automobiles and trucks it needs from General Motors. This practice is neither unethical nor illegal unless one party coerces the other and the result is unfair competition. Reciprocity is generally considered a reasonable business practice. If all possible suppliers sell a similar product for about the same price, doesn't it make sense to buy from those firms that buy from you?

7-6j Use of Leasing

Consumers normally buy products rather than lease them. But businesses commonly lease expensive equipment such as computers, construction equipment and vehicles, and automobiles. Leasing allows firms to reduce capital outflow, acquire a seller's latest products, receive better services, and gain tax advantages.

The lessor, the firm providing the product, may be either the manufacturer or an independent firm. The benefits to the lessor include greater total revenue from leasing compared to selling and an opportunity to do business with customers who cannot afford to buy.

7-6k Primary Promotional Method

Business marketers tend to emphasize personal selling in their promotion efforts, especially for expensive items, custom-designed products, large-volume purchases, and situations requiring negotiations. The sale of many business products requires a great deal of personal contact. Personal selling is discussed in more detail in Chapter 17.

7-7 TYPES OF BUSINESS PRODUCTS

Business products generally fall into one of the following seven categories, depending on their use: major equipment, accessory equipment, raw materials, component parts, processed materials, supplies, and business services.

7-7a Major Equipment

Major equipment includes capital goods such as large or expensive machines, mainframe computers, blast furnaces, generators, airplanes, and buildings. (These items are also commonly called **installations**.) Major equipment is depreciated over time rather than charged as an expense in the year it is purchased. In addition, major equipment is often custom designed for each customer.

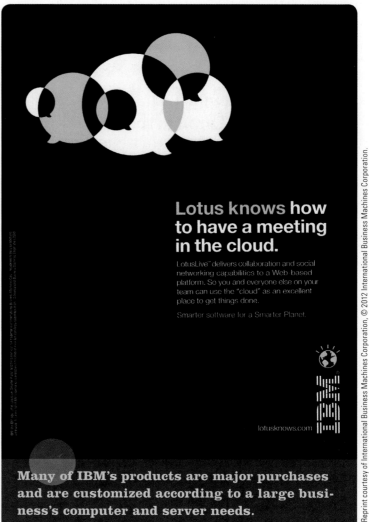

Lotus knows how to have a meeting in the cloud.

LotusLive™ delivers collaboration and social networking capabilities to a Web-based platform. So you and everyone else on your team can use the "cloud" as an excellent place to get things done.

Smarter software for a Smarter Planet.

lotusknows.com

Many of IBM's products are major purchases and are customized according to a large business's computer and server needs.

Personal selling is an important part of the marketing strategy for major equipment because distribution channels are almost always direct from the producer to the business user.

7-7b Accessory Equipment

Accessory equipment is generally less expensive and shorter-lived than major equipment. Examples include portable drills, power tools, microcomputers, and fax machines. Accessory equipment is often charged as an expense in the year it is bought rather than depreciated over its useful life. In contrast to major equipment, accessories are more often standardized and are usually bought by more customers. These customers tend to be widely dispersed. For example, all types of businesses buy microcomputers.

Local industrial distributors (wholesalers) play an important role in the marketing of accessory equipment because business buyers often purchase accessories from them. Regardless of where accessories are bought, advertising is a more vital promotional tool for accessory equipment than for major equipment.

7-7c Raw Materials

Raw materials are unprocessed extractive or agricultural products—for example, mineral ore, lumber, wheat, corn, fruits, vegetables, and fish. Raw materials become part of finished products. Extensive users, such as steel or lumber mills and food canners, generally buy huge quantities of raw materials. Because there is often a large number of relatively small sellers of raw materials, none can greatly influence price or supply. Thus, the market tends to set the price of raw materials, and individual producers have little pricing flexibility. Promotion is almost always via personal selling, and distribution channels are usually direct from producer to business user.

7-7d Component Parts

Component parts are either finished items ready for assembly or products that need very little processing before becoming part of some other product. Caterpillar diesel engines are component parts used in heavy-duty trucks. Other examples include spark plugs, tires, and electric motors for automobiles. A special feature of component parts is that they can retain their identity after becoming part of the final product. For example, automobile tires are clearly recognizable as part of a car. Moreover, because component parts often wear out, they may need to be replaced several times during the life of the final product. Thus, there are two important markets for many component parts: the original equipment manufacturer (OEM) market and the replacement market.

The availability of component parts is often a key factor in OEMs meeting their production deadlines. For example, Boeing had to delay final assembly of Boeing 787 Dreamliners by more than three years because of slower than expected completion of components prior to their arrival at the final assembly line. In addition to delayed sales and customer disappointment and dissatisfaction, Boeing paid billions in penalties and damaged its credibility with customers. Despite the setbacks and the fact that there were only six Dreamliners flying in 2010, Boeing had 866 of the planes on back-order at that time.[29]

The difference between unit costs and selling prices in the OEM market is often small, but profits can be substantial because of volume buying.

The replacement market is composed of organizations and individuals buying component parts to replace worn-out parts. Because components often retain their identity in final products, users may choose to replace a component part with the same brand used by the manufacturer—for example, the same brand of automobile tires or battery. The replacement market operates differently from the OEM market, however. Whether replacement buyers are organizations or individuals, they tend to demonstrate the characteristics of consumer markets that were shown in Learning Outcome 6. Consider, for example, an automobile replacement part. Purchase volume is usually small, and there are many customers, geographically dispersed, who typically buy from car dealers or parts stores. Negotiations do not occur, and neither reciprocity nor leasing is usually an issue.

Manufacturers of component parts often direct their advertising toward replacement buyers. Cooper Tire & Rubber, for example, makes and markets component parts—automobile and truck tires—for the replacement market only. General Motors and other carmakers compete with independent firms in the market for replacement automobile parts.

accessory equipment goods, such as portable tools and office equipment, that are less expensive and shorter-lived than major equipment

raw materials unprocessed extractive or agricultural products, such as mineral ore, lumber, wheat, corn, fruits, vegetables, and fish

component parts either finished items ready for assembly or products that need very little processing before becoming part of some other product

7-7e Processed Materials

Processed materials are products used directly in manufacturing other products. Unlike raw materials, they have had some processing. Examples include sheet metal, chemicals, specialty steel, treated lumber, corn syrup, and plastics. Unlike component parts, processed materials do not retain their identity in final products.

Most processed materials are marketed to OEMs or to distributors servicing the OEM market. Processed materials are generally bought according to customer specifications or to some industry standard, as is the case with steel and plywood. Price and service are important factors in choosing a vendor.

7-7f Supplies

Supplies are consumable items that do not become part of the final product—for example, lubricants, detergents, paper towels, pencils, and paper. Supplies are normally standardized items that purchasing agents routinely buy. Supplies typically have relatively short lives and are inexpensive compared to other business goods. Because supplies generally fall into one of three categories—maintenance, repair, or operating supplies—this category is often referred to as MRO items. Competition in the MRO market is intense. Bic and Paper Mate, for example, battle for business purchases of inexpensive ball-point pens.

7-7g Business Services

Business services are expense items that do not become part of a final product. Businesses often retain outside providers to perform janitorial, advertising, legal, management consulting, marketing research, maintenance, and other services. Contracting an outside provider makes sense when it costs less than hiring or assigning an employee to perform the task and when an outside provider is needed for particular expertise.

7-8 BUSINESS BUYING BEHAVIOR

As you probably have already concluded, business buyers behave differently from consumers. Understanding how purchase decisions are made in organizations is a first step in developing a business selling strategy. Business buying behavior has five important

Aluminum ore is a raw material.

An extruding machine is major equipment.

A tool cart is accessory equipment.

Extruded metal is a processed material.

A propeller blade is a component part.

Paper is a supply.

Uniforms are often a contracted service.

Photos courtesy chapel house photography

aspects: buying centers, evaluative criteria, buying situations, business ethics, and customer service.

7-8a Buying Centers

In many cases, more than one person is involved in a purchase decision. Identifying who these people are and the roles they play greatly enhances the salesperson's chances for success.[30]

A **buying center** includes all those people in an organization who become involved in the purchase decision. Membership and influence vary from company to company. For instance, in engineering-dominated firms like Bell Helicopter, the buying center may consist almost entirely of engineers. In marketing-oriented firms like Toyota and IBM, marketing and engineering have almost equal authority. In consumer goods firms like Procter & Gamble, product managers and other marketing decision makers

may dominate the buying center. In a small manufacturing company, almost everyone may be a member.

The number of people involved in a buying center varies with the complexity and importance of a purchase decision. The composition of the buying group will usually change from one purchase to another and sometimes even during various stages of the buying process. To make matters more complicated, buying centers do not appear on formal organization charts.

For example, even though a formal committee may have been set up to choose a new plant site, it is only part of the buying center. Other people, like the company president, often play informal yet powerful roles. In a lengthy decision-making process, such as finding a new plant location, some members may drop out of the buying center when they can no longer play a useful role. Others whose talents are needed then become part of the center. No formal announcement of "who is in" and "who is out" is ever made.

IMPLICATIONS OF BUYING CENTERS FOR THE MARKETING MANAGER Successful vendors realize the importance of identifying who is in the decision-making unit, each member's relative influence in the buying decision, and each member's evaluative criteria. Successful selling strategies often focus on determining the most important buying influences and tailoring sales presentations to the evaluative criteria most important to these buying center members. For example, Henkel, the manufacturer of Super Glue and industrial adhesives and sealants, found that engineers were the most important influencers and deciders in adhesive and sealant purchase decisions. As a result, Henkel focused its marketing efforts on production and maintenance engineers.

ROLES IN THE BUYING CENTER

As in family purchasing decisions, several people may each play a role in the business purchase process.

» **INITIATOR:** the person who first suggests making a purchase.

» **INFLUENCERS/EVALUATORS:** people who influence the buying decision. They often help define specifications and provide information for evaluating options. Technical personnel are especially important as influencers.

» **GATEKEEPERS:** group members who regulate the flow of information. Frequently, the purchasing agent views the gatekeeping role as a source of his or her power. A secretary may also act as a gatekeeper by determining which vendors get an appointment with a buyer.

» **DECIDER:** the person who has the formal or informal power to choose or approve the selection of the supplier or brand. In complex situations, it is often difficult to determine who makes the final decision.

» **PURCHASER:** the person who actually negotiates the purchase. It could be anyone from the president of the company to the purchasing agent, depending on the importance of the decision.

» **USERS:** members of the organization who will actually use the product. Users often initiate the buying process and help define product specifications.

7-8b Evaluative Criteria

Business buyers evaluate products and suppliers against three important criteria: quality, service, and price—in that order.

QUALITY In this case, quality refers to technical suitability. A superior tool can do a better job in the production process, and superior packaging can increase dealer and consumer acceptance of a brand. Evaluation of quality also applies to the salesperson and the salesperson's firm. Business buyers want to deal with reputable salespeople and companies that are financially responsible. Quality improvement should be part of every organization's marketing strategy.

SERVICE Almost as much as they want satisfactory products, business buyers want satisfactory service. A purchase offers several opportunities for service. Suppose a vendor is selling heavy equipment. Prepurchase service could include a survey of the buyer's needs. After thorough analysis of the survey findings, the vendor could prepare a report and recommendations in the form of a purchasing proposal. If a purchase results, postpurchase service might consist of installing the equipment and training those who will be using it. Postsale services may also include maintenance and repairs. Another service that business buyers seek is dependability of supply. They must be able to count on delivery of what was ordered when it is scheduled to be delivered. Buyers also welcome services that help them sell their finished products. Services of this sort are especially appropriate when the seller's product is an identifiable part of the buyer's end product.

PRICE Business buyers want to buy at low prices—at the lowest prices, under most circumstances. However, a buyer who pressures a supplier to cut prices to a point at which the supplier loses money on the sale almost forces shortcuts on quality. The buyer also may, in effect, force the supplier to quit selling to him or her. Then a new source of supply will have to be found.

7-8c Buying Situations

Often, business firms, especially manufacturers, must decide whether to make something or buy it from an outside supplier. The decision is essentially one of economics. Can an item of similar quality be bought at a lower price elsewhere? If not, is manufacturing it in-house the best use of limited company resources? For example, Briggs & Stratton Corporation, a major manufacturer of four-cycle engines, might be able to save $150,000 annually on outside purchases by spending $500,000 on the equipment needed to produce gas throttles internally. Yet Briggs & Stratton could also use that $500,000 to upgrade its carburetor assembly line, which would save $225,000 annually. If a firm does decide to buy a product instead of making it, the purchase will be a new buy, a modified rebuy, or a straight rebuy.

NEW BUY A **new buy** is a situation requiring the purchase of a product for the first time. For example, suppose a manufacturing company needs a better way to page its managers while they are working on the shop floor. Currently, each of the several managers has a distinct ring—for example, two short and one long—that sounds over the plant intercom whenever he or she is being paged by anyone in the factory. The company decides to replace its buzzer system of paging with handheld wireless radio technology that will allow managers to communicate immediately with the department initiating the page. This situation represents the greatest opportunity for new vendors. No long-term relationship has been established for this product, specifications may be somewhat fluid, and buyers are generally more open to new vendors.

If the new item is a raw material or a critical component part, the buyer cannot afford to run out of supply. The seller must be able to convince the buyer that the seller's firm can consistently deliver a high-quality product on time.

MODIFIED REBUY A **modified rebuy** is normally less critical and less time-consuming than a new buy. In a modified rebuy situation, the purchaser wants some change in the original good or service. It may be a new color, greater tensile strength in a component part, more respondents in a marketing research study, or additional services in a janitorial contract.

Because the two parties are familiar with each other and credibility has been established, the buyer and seller can concentrate on the specifics of the modification. But in some cases, modified rebuys are open to outside bidders. The purchaser uses this strategy to ensure that the new terms are competitive. An example would be the manufacturing company buying radios with a vibrating feature for managers who have trouble hearing the ring over the factory noise. The firm may open the bidding to examine the price and quality offerings of several suppliers.

STRAIGHT REBUY A **straight rebuy** is a situation vendors prefer. The purchaser is not looking for new information or other suppliers. An order is placed and the product is provided as in previous orders. Usually, a straight rebuy is routine because the terms of the purchase have been agreed to in earlier negotiations. An example would be the previously cited manufacturing company purchasing additional radios for new managers from the same supplier on a regular basis.

One common instrument used in straight rebuy situations is the purchasing contract. Purchasing contracts are used with products that are bought often and in high volume. In essence, the purchasing contract makes the buyer's decision making routine and promises the salesperson a sure sale. The advantage to the buyer is a quick, confident decision and, to the salesperson, reduced or eliminated competition. Suppliers must remember not to take straight rebuy relationships for granted. Retaining existing customers is much easier than attracting new ones.

7-8d Business Ethics

As we noted in Chapter 3, ethics refers to the moral principles or values that generally govern the conduct of an individual or a group. Ethics can also be viewed as the standard of behavior by which conduct is judged.

Although we have heard a lot about corporate misbehavior in recent years, most people, and most companies, follow ethical practices. To help achieve this, over half of all major corporations offer ethics training to employees. Many companies also have codes of ethics that help guide buyers and sellers. For example, Home Depot has a clearly written code of ethics available on its corporate Web site that acts as an ethical guide for all its employees.

7-8e Customer Service

Business marketers are increasingly recognizing the benefits of developing a formal system to monitor customer opinions and perceptions of the quality of customer service. Companies such as McDonald's, L.L.Bean, and Lexus build their strategies not only around products but also around a few highly developed service skills. These companies understand that keeping current customers satisfied is just as important as attracting new ones, if not more so. Leading-edge firms are obsessed not only with delivering high-quality customer service but also with measuring satisfaction, loyalty, relationship quality, and other indicators of nonfinancial performance.

Most firms find it necessary to develop measures unique to their own strategies, value propositions, and target markets. For example, Andersen Corporation assesses the loyalty of its trade customers by their willingness to continue carrying its windows and doors, recommend its products to colleagues and customers, increase their volume with the company, and put its products in their own homes. Basically, each firm's measures should not only ask "What are your expectations?" and "How are we doing?" but should also reflect what the firm wants its customers to do.

Some customers are more valuable than others. They may have greater value because they spend more, buy higher-margin products, have a well-known name, or have the potential of becoming a bigger customer in the future. Some companies selectively provide different levels of service to customers based on their value to the business.

By giving the most valuable customers superior service, a firm is more likely to keep them happy, hopefully increasing retention of these high-value customers and maximizing the total business value they generate over time.

To achieve this goal, the firm must be able to divide customers into two or more groups based on their value. It must also create and apply policies that govern how service will be allocated among groups. Policies might establish which customers' phone calls get "fast tracked" and which customers are directed to use the Web and/or voice self-service, how specific e-mail questions are routed, and who is given access to online chat and who isn't.[31]

Providing different customers with different levels of service is a very sensitive matter. It must be handled very carefully and very discreetly to avoid offending lesser-value, but still important, customers.

STUDY TOOLS 7

LOCATED AT BACK OF THE TEXTBOOK
- ☐ *Rip out Chapter Review Card*

LOCATED AT WWW.CENGAGE.COM/LOGIN
- ☐ *Review Key Terms Flashcards (print or online)*
- ☐ *Download audio and visual summaries to review on the go*
- ☐ *Complete both Practice Quizzes to prepare for tests*
- ☐ *Play "Beat the Clock" and "Quizbowl" to master concepts*
- ☐ *Complete "Crossword Puzzle" to review key terms*
- ☐ *Watch Video on "Zappos" for a real company example*

8-1 MARKET SEGMENTATION

The term *market* means different things to different people.
We are all familiar with the supermarket, stock market, labor market, fish market, and flea market. All these types of markets share several characteristics. First, they are composed of people (consumer markets) or organizations (business markets). Second, these people or organizations have wants and needs that can be satisfied by particular product categories. Third, they have the ability to buy the products they seek. Fourth, they are willing to exchange their resources, usually money or credit, for desired products. In sum, a **market** is (1) people or organizations with (2) needs or wants and with (3) the ability and (4) the willingness to buy. A group of people or an organization that lacks any one of these characteristics is not a market.

Market segmentation plays a key role in the marketing strategy of almost all successful organizations.

market people or organizations with needs or wants and the ability and willingness to buy

market segment a subgroup of people or organizations sharing one or more characteristics that cause them to have similar product needs

market segmentation the process of dividing a market into meaningful, relatively similar, and identifiable segments or groups

Within a market, a **market segment** is a subgroup of people or organizations sharing one or more characteristics that cause them to have similar product needs. At one extreme, we can define every person and every organization in the world as a market segment because each is unique. At the other extreme, we can define the entire consumer market as one large market segment and the business market as another large segment. All people have some similar characteristics and needs, as do all organizations.

From a marketing perspective, market segments can be described as somewhere between the two extremes. The process of dividing a market into meaningful, relatively similar, and identifiable segments or groups is called **market segmentation**. The purpose of market segmentation is to enable the marketer to tailor marketing mixes to meet the needs of one or more specific segments.

Segmenting and Targeting Markets

After you finish this chapter go to
p142 *for* **STUDY TOOLS**

© iStockphoto.com/OSTILL

8-2 THE IMPORTANCE OF MARKET SEGMENTATION

Until the 1960s, few firms practiced market segmentation. When they did, it was more likely a haphazard effort than a formal marketing strategy. Before 1960, for example, the Coca-Cola Company produced only one beverage and aimed it at the entire soft drink market. Today, Coca-Cola offers more than a dozen different products to market segments based on diverse consumer preferences for flavors and calorie and caffeine content. Coca-Cola offers traditional soft drinks, energy drinks (including POWERade), flavored teas, fruit drinks (Fruitopia), and water (Dasani).

Market segmentation plays a key role in the marketing strategy of almost all successful organizations and is a powerful marketing tool for several reasons. Most important, nearly all markets include groups of people or organizations with different product needs and preferences. Market segmentation helps marketers define customer needs and wants more precisely. Because market segments differ in size and potential, segmentation helps decision makers to more accurately define marketing objectives and better allocate resources. In turn, performance can be better evaluated when objectives are more precise.

To try and woo the up-and-coming technology-savvy younger generation of drivers, German luxury car manufacturers are adding a green side to their portfolios. BMW's i3 and i8 cars are electric hybrids built on aluminum chassis that have a top speed of 93 MPH. The cars are designed to appeal to a younger customer living in a congested city. Audi also has a line of cars designed for "mobility," emphasizing information sharing that notes efficient routes in congested cities, finds parking spaces, and uses Smartphone apps to arrange car-sharing.[1]

8-3 CRITERIA FOR SUCCESSFUL SEGMENTATION

Marketers segment markets for three important reasons. First, segmentation enables marketers to identify groups of customers with similar needs and to analyze the characteristics and buying behavior of these groups. Second, segmentation provides marketers with information to help them design marketing mixes specifically matched with the characteristics and desires of one or more segments. Third, segmentation is consistent with the marketing concept of satisfying customer wants and needs while meeting the organization's objectives.

To be useful, a segmentation scheme must produce segments that meet four basic criteria:

1. **SUBSTANTIALITY: A segment must be large enough to warrant developing and maintaining a special marketing mix. This criterion does not necessarily mean that a segment must have many potential customers. Marketers of custom-designed homes and business buildings, commercial airplanes, and large computer systems typically develop marketing programs tailored to each potential customer's needs. In most cases, however, a market segment needs many potential customers to make commercial sense. In the 1980s, home banking failed because not enough people owned personal computers. Today, a larger number of people own computers, and home banking is a thriving industry.**

2. **IDENTIFIABILITY AND MEASURABILITY: Segments must be identifiable and their size measurable. Data about the population within geographic boundaries, the number of people in various age categories, and other social and demographic characteristics are often easy to get, and they provide fairly concrete measures of segment size. Suppose that a social service agency wants to identify segments by their readiness to participate in a drug and alcohol program or in prenatal care. Unless the agency can measure how many people are willing, indifferent, or unwilling to participate, it will have trouble gauging whether there are enough people to justify setting up the service.**

3. **ACCESSIBILITY: The firm must be able to reach members of targeted segments with customized marketing mixes. Some market segments are hard to**

© Patrick Poendl/Shutterstock.com

BMW i8 Concept

reach—for example, senior citizens (especially those with reading or hearing disabilities), individuals who don't speak English, and the illiterate.

4. **RESPONSIVENESS:** Markets can be segmented using any criteria that seem logical. Unless one market segment responds to a marketing mix differently than other segments, however, that segment need not be treated separately. For instance, if all customers are equally price conscious about a product, there is no need to offer high-, medium-, and low-priced versions to different segments.

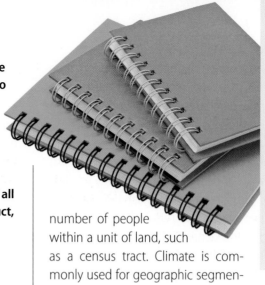

8-4 BASES FOR SEGMENTING CONSUMER MARKETS

Marketers use segmentation bases, or variables, which are characteristics of individuals, groups, or organizations, to divide a total market into segments. The choice of segmentation bases is crucial because an inappropriate segmentation strategy may lead to lost sales and missed profit opportunities. The key is to identify bases that will produce substantial, measurable, and accessible segments that exhibit different response patterns to marketing mixes.

Markets can be segmented using a single variable, such as age group, or several variables, such as age group, gender, and education. Although it is less precise, single-variable segmentation has the advantage of being simpler and easier to use than multiple-variable segmentation. The disadvantages of multiple-variable segmentation are that it is often harder to use than single-variable segmentation; usable secondary data are less likely to be available; and as the number of segmentation bases increases, the size of individual segments decreases. Nevertheless, the current trend is toward using more rather than fewer variables to segment most markets. Multiple-variable segmentation is clearly more precise than single-variable segmentation.

Consumer goods marketers commonly use one or more of the following characteristics to segment markets: geography, demographics, psychographics, benefits sought, and usage rate.

8-4a **Geographic Segmentation**

Geographic segmentation refers to segmenting markets by region of a country or the world, market size, market density, or climate. Market density means the number of people within a unit of land, such as a census tract. Climate is commonly used for geographic segmentation because of its dramatic impact on residents' needs and purchasing behavior. Snowblowers, water and snow skis, clothing, and air-conditioning and heating systems are products with varying appeal, depending on climate.

Consumer goods companies take a regional approach to marketing for four reasons. First, many firms need to find new ways to generate sales because of sluggish and intensely competitive markets. Second, computerized checkout stations with scanners give retailers an accurate assessment of which brands sell best in their region. Third, many packaged-goods manufacturers are introducing new regional brands intended to appeal to local preferences. Fourth, a more regional approach allows consumer goods companies to react more quickly to competition. At Target, local store managers pull school supply lists from all the nearby schools and stock extra of the items on those lists. If ten out of fifteen schools require composition notebooks instead of spiral notebooks, that Target will stock more composition notebooks in greater variety.[2]

8-4b **Demographic Segmentation**

Marketers often segment markets on the basis of demographic information because it is widely available and often related to consumers' buying and consuming behavior. Some common bases of **demographic segmentation** are age, gender, income, ethnic background, and family life cycle.

AGE SEGMENTATION Marketers use a variety of terms to refer to different age groups. Examples include newborns, infants, young children, tweens, Generation Y (teens, young adults), Generation X, baby boomers, and seniors. Age segmentation can be an important tool, as a brief exploration of the market potential of several age segments illustrates.

Through allowances, earnings, and gifts, children account for and influence a great deal of consumption. For

segmentation bases (variables) characteristics of individuals, groups, or organizations

geographic segmentation segmenting markets by region of a country or the world, market size, market density, or climate

demographic segmentation segmenting markets by age, gender, income, ethnic background, and family life cycle example, young shoppers in the United States spend more than $200 billion of their own money and their parents' money each year on purchases for themselves and also have considerable influence over major family purchase decisions.[3] Teens in particular are technology savvy and very social consumers. Tweens desire to be kids but also want some of the fun of being a teenager. Many retailers serve this market with clothing that is similar in style to that worn by teenagers and young adults.

The members of the Generation Y market, or the millennial generation, were born between 1979 and 2003 and make up almost one-third of the U.S. population. This group not only has formidable purchasing power but is also more civic-minded than the baby boom generation. Seventy-four percent of Millennials say they are more likely to pay attention to a company's overall message if the company has a deep commitment to a cause. The vast majority of this cohort was hit hard by the recession. Many, having just started in career path jobs, have found their opportunities stalled, if they didn't lose their jobs. Companies who were relying on Gen Yers to make up for decreasing boomer interest, such as Disney and Sony Pictures, or Gap and Abercrombie & Fitch, have found themselves without a market as Gen Yers shut their wallets. Even typical life events, such as marriage and starting a family, have been postponed while the youngest generation struggles to find its footing on the treacherous economic ground. Only companies able to offer very steep discounts have found purchase with the thrifty group. MGM Resorts International recently began offering rooms at $29 a night with $25 buckets of beer and $1 Jell-O shots to lure spring breakers. With success from its lower priced properties, the company steeply discounted rooms at its upscale Mandalay Bay and MGM Grand to $65 a night.[4]

Generation X is the group that was born after the baby boomers. Members of Generation X tend to be disloyal to brands and skeptical of big business. Many of them are parents, and they make purchasing decisions with thought for and input from their families. Gen Xers desire an experience, not just a product. The desire to have an experience has led to an increase in multifunctional boutiques, particularly in Manhattan's Lower East Side, where the small shops vie for high-end shoppers. The Dressing Room, for example, is a bi-level store with a boutique upstairs, vintage clothing downstairs, and a full bar where customers can hang out.[5]

People born between 1946 and 1964 are often called baby boomers. Boomers spend $2.1 trillion a year and represent half of all spending in the United States. For the next eighteen years, one baby boomer will turn sixty every seven seconds. Boomers make up 49 percent of affluent households, and they want attention and service when they shop.[6] This group spends big money on goods and services such as travel, electronics, and automobiles. Baby boomers are not particularly brand loyal, and they are a very diverse group. Some are parents to infant children, and others are empty nesters.

Consumers born before 1946 represent people who are part of the war generation (ages sixty-one to sixty-six), the Great Depression generation (ages sixty-seven to seventy-six), and the G.I. generation (age seventy-seven and up). Many in this group view retirement not as a passive time, but as an active time they use to explore new knowledge, travel, volunteer, and spend time with family and friends. They are living longer and are healthier than older consumers twenty years ago. As consumers age, they do require some shopping modifications. Tesco, a British grocery store chain, is considering designing a store specifically to meet the needs of older shoppers. Music, nonslip floors, extra-wide aisles, brighter than usual lighting, and steps to assist older consumers in reaching high shelves are some of the features being examined for inclusion.

GENDER SEGMENTATION In the United States, women make 85 percent of purchases of consumer goods each year.[7] They are an experienced purchasing group with the responsibility of purchasing the majority of household items. They also are increasingly part of what were once considered all-male markets, such as the video game market. In 2010, 40 percent of women owned some type of video game console, though the Wii, with its fitness games, was the most used of the consoles.[8] The video game industry has been forced to respond by developing more games with female protagonists and changing its advertising strategy. Design, fashion, and weight-loss games such as *Style Savvy* or *The Biggest Loser* are increasingly popular

© ZUMA Wire Service/Alamy

among women.[9] Marketers of products such as clothing, cosmetics, personal-care items, magazines, jewelry, and gifts still commonly segment markets by gender, and many of these marketers are going after the less-traditional male market. For example, Russell Simmons is developing a yoga line for men called Tantris, which will include clothes, mats, and even candles.[10] Even weight-loss programs, which currently have 90 percent female consumption, are starting to target men. Weight Watchers is trying to increase the number of men using its program to lose weight by offering a men-only version of its Web site and mobile applications, which research shows men prefer over attending traditional Weight Watchers meetings. Men's programs have higher point totals (reflecting the male tendency to have leaner body mass) and more "cheat sheets" telling them how many points various foods cost.[11]

INCOME SEGMENTATION Income is a popular demographic variable for segmenting markets because income level influences consumers' wants and determines their buying power. Many markets are segmented by income, including the markets for housing, clothing, automobiles, and food. Wholesale clubs Costco and Sam's Club appeal to many income segments. Harrison Group researchers found that the favorite stores of affluent households (those earning more than $100,000 annually) are Costco and Target.[12] High-income customers looking for luxury want outstanding customer service. For example, fashion companies use computer technology to customize upscale products that are designed specifically for their wealthy customers' needs.[13]

ETHNIC SEGMENTATION In the past, ethnic groups in the United States were expected to conform to a

Colgate uses a Hispanic woman and Spanish to advertise specifically to Hispanic populations.

homogenized, Anglo-centric ideal. This was evident both in the marketing of mass-marketed products and in the selective way that films, television, advertisements, and popular music portrayed America's diverse population. Until the 1970s, ethnic foods were rarely sold except in specialty

MISSING THE MIDDLE CLASS

Starting in 2008, P&G saw losses, a rare occurrence for the home and health brand giant. The change, however, wasn't that customers stopped buying, but that they downgraded to the basic bargain brands offered by P&G. P&G then re-evaluated its portfolios and took another look at the market. P&G's global strategy involves classifying customers into income groups called ones, twos, and threes. Ones are traditionally P&G's American target market, consisting of consumers who are not price sensitive and are easily persuaded by claims of superior product performance. Twos are P&G's new American target market—lower-income consumers who don't want to pay for extra features. Threes are a very small part of the American market, consisting of the poverty-level consumer who is generally subsidized by the government. P&G's new products appeal to high-end customers with products like the Olay Pro-X skin care kit for $60 and Gillette Glide razors for $12, but also to the twos—with Charmin basic and a new Gain dish soap that is half as expensive per ounce as Dawn Renewal dish soap.

Source: Ellen Byron, "As Middle Class Shrinks, P&G Aims High and Low," *Wall Street Journal*, September 12, 2011, A1.

stores. The racial barrier in entertainment lasted nearly as long, except for supporting movie and television roles—often based on stereotypes dating back to the nineteenth century.[14] Increasing numbers of ethnic minorities and increased buying power have changed this. Hispanic Americans, African Americans, and Asian Americans are the three largest ethnic groups in the United States. In the American Southwest, Caucasian populations comprise less than half the population and have become the minority to other ethnic groups combined. To meet the needs and wants of expanding ethnic populations, some companies, such as McDonald's and Kmart, make products geared toward a specific group. Kmart has teamed up with Sofia Vergara, a popular Colombian actress, to develop a clothing line to appeal to Hispanics.[15]

FAMILY LIFE CYCLE SEGMENTATION The demographic factors of gender, age, and income often do not sufficiently explain why consumer buying behavior varies. Frequently, consumption patterns among people of the same age and gender differ because they are in different stages of the family life cycle. The **family life cycle (FLC)** is a series of stages determined by a combination of age, marital status, and the presence or absence of children.

The life cycle stage consisting of the married-couple household used to be considered the traditional family in the United States. Today, however, married couples make up less than half of households, down from nearly 80 percent in the 1950s. Single adults are increasingly in the majority. Already, unmarried Americans make up 42 percent of the workforce, 40 percent of home buyers, and one of the most potent consumer groups on record. Exhibit 8.1 on page 133 illustrates numerous FLC patterns and shows how families' needs, incomes, resources, and expenditures differ at each stage. The horizontal flow shows the traditional FLC. The lower part of the exhibit gives some of the characteristics and purchase patterns of families in each stage of the traditional life cycle. The exhibit also acknowledges that about half of all first marriages end in divorce. If young marrieds move into the young divorced stage, their consumption patterns often revert back to those of the young single stage of the cycle. About four out of five divorced persons remarry by middle age and reenter the traditional life cycle, as indicated by the "recycled flow" in

the exhibit. Research has found that the overriding factor in describing baby boomer subsegments is the presence of children in the house. A Nielsen study discovered eight specific segments: four segments with children younger than eighteen represented about 40 percent of the boomers, and four segments without children represented 60 percent.[16] Consumers are especially receptive to marketing efforts at certain points in the life cycle.

8-4c Psychographic Segmentation

Age, gender, income, ethnicity, FLC stage, and other demographic variables are usually helpful in developing segmentation strategies, but often they don't paint the entire picture. Demographics provide the skeleton, but psychographics add meat to the bones. **Psychographic segmentation** is market segmentation on the basis of the following psychographic segmentation variables:

» **PERSONALITY:** Personality reflects a person's traits, attitudes, and habits. Clothing is the ultimate personality descriptor. Fashionistas wear high-end, trendy clothes, and hipsters enjoy jeans and T-shirts with tennis shoes. People buy clothes that they feel represent their personalities and give others an idea of who they are.

» **MOTIVES:** Marketers of baby products and life insurance appeal to consumers' emotional motives—namely, to care for their loved ones. Using appeals to economy, reliability, and dependability, carmakers like Subaru and Suzuki target customers with rational motives. Carmakers like Mercedes-Benz, Jaguar, and Cadillac appeal to customers with status-related motives.

» **LIFESTYLES:** Lifestyle segmentation divides people into groups according to the way they spend their time, the importance of the things around them, their beliefs, and socioeconomic characteristics such as income and education. For example, record stores specializing in vinyl are targeting young people who are listening to independent labels and often pride themselves on being independent of big business. LEED-certified appliances appeal to environmentally conscious "green" consumers. PepsiCo is promoting its no-calorie, sugar-free flavored water, Aquafina Sparkling, to consumers who are health conscious.

» **GEODEMOGRAPHICS:** Geodemographic segmentation clusters potential customers into

Exhibit 8.1

FAMILY LIFE CYCLE

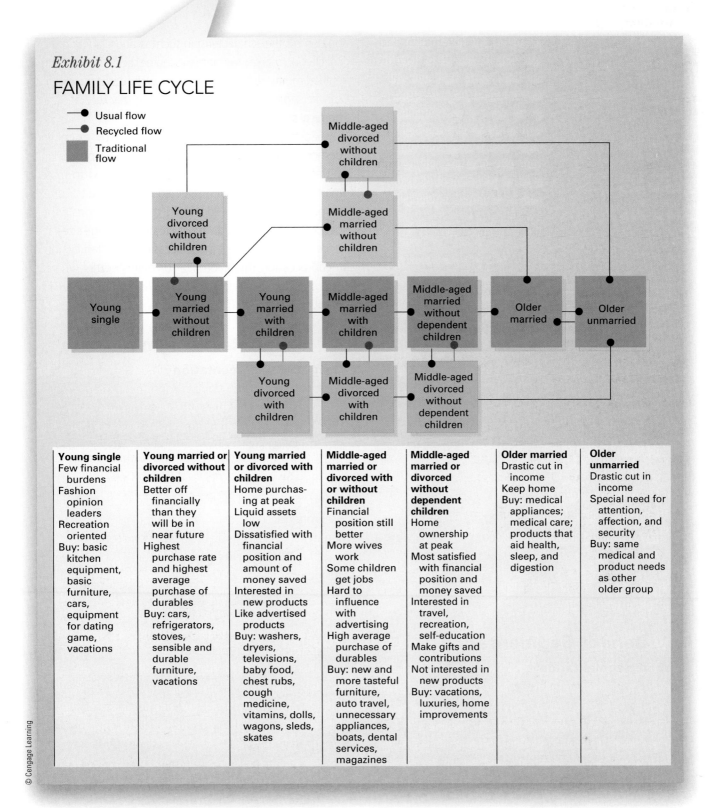

Young single
Few financial burdens
Fashion opinion leaders
Recreation oriented
Buy: basic kitchen equipment, basic furniture, cars, equipment for dating game, vacations

Young married or divorced without children
Better off financially than they will be in near future
Highest purchase rate and highest average purchase of durables
Buy: cars, refrigerators, stoves, sensible and durable furniture, vacations

Young married or divorced with children
Home purchasing at peak
Liquid assets low
Dissatisfied with financial position and amount of money saved
Interested in new products
Like advertised products
Buy: washers, dryers, televisions, baby food, chest rubs, cough medicine, vitamins, dolls, wagons, sleds, skates

Middle-aged married or divorced with or without children
Financial position still better
More wives work
Some children get jobs
Hard to influence with advertising
High average purchase of durables
Buy: new and more tasteful furniture, auto travel, unnecessary appliances, boats, dental services, magazines

Middle-aged married or divorced without dependent children
Home ownership at peak
Most satisfied with financial position and money saved
Interested in travel, recreation, self-education
Make gifts and contributions
Not interested in new products
Buy: vacations, luxuries, home improvements

Older married
Drastic cut in income
Keep home
Buy: medical appliances; medical care; products that aid health, sleep, and digestion

Older unmarried
Drastic cut in income
Special need for attention, affection, and security
Buy: same medical and product needs as other older group

© Cengage Learning

neighborhood lifestyle categories. It combines geographic, demographic, and lifestyle segmentations. Geodemographic segmentation helps marketers develop marketing programs tailored to prospective buyers who live in small geographic regions, such as neighborhoods, or who have very specific lifestyle and

demographic characteristics. For example, companies looking to win government manufacturing or technology contracts post cryptic billboards and posters on Washington, D.C. buses and Metro trains, as well as advertising their capabilities on local radio stations. The average commuter doesn't understand the cryptic

benefit segmentation
the process of grouping customers into market segments according to the benefits they seek from the product

usage-rate segmentation
dividing a market by the amount of product bought or consumed

80/20 principle
a principle holding that 20 percent of all customers generate 80 percent of the demand

acronyms, but government decision makers who see or hear the ads understand them and will award federal projects based on the ads—or so companies such as Northrop Grumman hope. Such a campaign could work only in an area where high levels of government decision makers commute regularly.[17]

Psychographic variables can be used individually to segment markets or be combined with other variables to provide more detailed descriptions of market segments. One approach is for marketers and advertisers to purchase information from a collector, such as eXelate Media, in order to reach the audience they want. eXelate, part of consumer research firm Nielsen, gathers information about Web-browsing habits through cookies placed on Web sites. Nielsen, using eXelate, organizes groups according to this information. One group, the "young digerati," includes twenty-four- to forty-four-year-olds who

- are tech savvy,
- are affluent,
- live in trendy condos,
- read the *Economist*, and
- have an annual income of $88,000.

An automaker can purchase that list and the list of people who visit car blogs and then target ads to the young digerati interested in cars.[18]

8-4d Benefit Segmentation

Benefit segmentation is the process of grouping customers into market segments according to the benefits they seek from the product. Most types of market segmentation are based on the assumption that this variable and customers' needs are related. Benefit segmentation is different because it groups potential customers on the basis of their needs or wants rather than

on some other characteristic, such as age or gender. The snack-food market, for example, can be divided into six benefit segments: nutritional snackers, weight watchers, guilty snackers, party snackers, indiscriminate snackers, and economical snackers.

Customer profiles can be developed by examining demographic information associated with people seeking certain benefits. This information can be used to match marketing strategies with selected target markets. For example, Coca-Cola has identified thirty "occasions" when people would drink soda and is creating package sizes and price points for each of those occasions. The "family home meal" occasion might be a 2- or 3-liter bottle, whereas a "gotta have it to go" occasion calls for either a 16- or 20-ounce bottle.[19]

8-4e Usage-Rate Segmentation

Usage-rate segmentation divides a market by the amount of product bought or consumed. Categories vary with the product, but they are likely to include some combination of the following: former users, potential users, first-time users, light or irregular users, medium users, and heavy users. Segmenting by usage rate enables marketers to focus their efforts on heavy users or to develop multiple marketing mixes aimed at different segments. Because heavy users often account for a sizable portion of all product sales, some marketers focus on the heavy-user segment.

The **80/20 principle** holds that 20 percent of all customers generate 80 percent of the demand. Although the percentages usually are not exact, the general idea often holds true. For example, in the fast-food industry, the heavy user accounts for only one of five fast-food patrons but makes about 60 percent of all visits to fast-food restaurants. The needs of heavy users differ from the needs of other usage-rate groups. They have intense needs for product and service selection and a variety of types of information, as well as an emotional attachment to the product category.[20]

Developing customers into heavy users is the goal behind many frequency/loyalty programs like the airlines' frequent-flyer programs. Many supermarkets and other retailers have also designed loyalty programs that reward the heavy-user segment with deals available only to them, such as in-store coupon dispensing systems, loyalty card programs, and special price deals on selected merchandise.

© Eric Carr/Alamy

8-5 BASES FOR SEGMENTING BUSINESS MARKETS

The business market consists of four broad segments: producers, resellers, government, and institutions. (For a detailed discussion of the characteristics of these segments, see Chapter 7.) Whether marketers focus on only one or on all four of these segments, they are likely to find diversity among potential customers. Thus, further market segmentation offers just as many benefits to business marketers as it does to consumer product marketers.

8-5a Company Characteristics

Company characteristics, such as geographic location, type of company, company size, and product use, can be important segmentation variables. Some markets tend to be regional because buyers prefer to purchase from local suppliers, and distant suppliers may have difficulty competing in terms of price and service. Therefore, firms that sell to geographically concentrated industries benefit by locating close to their markets.

Segmenting by customer type allows business marketers to tailor their marketing mixes to the unique needs of particular types of organizations or industries. For example, Round Table Companies teamed with SmarterComics to produce fifty-page illustrated versions of the most popular business books such as *The Long Tail* by Chris Anderson and *How to Master the Art of Selling* by Tom Hopkins. Corey Michael Blake, founder of Round Table, wanted to make the most-read business books available to time-pressed businesspeople. By condensing and illustrating popular business texts, Blake found a new market for comic books and extended the business book market.[21] Volume of purchase (heavy, moderate, light) is a commonly used basis for business segmentation. Another is the buying organization's size, which may affect its purchasing procedures, the types and quantities of products it needs, and its responses to different

marketing mixes. Banks frequently offer different services, lines of credit, and overall attention to commercial customers based on their size. Many products, especially raw materials like steel, wood, and petroleum, have diverse applications. How customers use a product may influence the amount they buy, their buying criteria, and their selection of vendors. For example, a producer of springs may have customers who use the product in applications as diverse as making machine tools, bicycles, surgical devices, office equipment, telephones, and missile systems.

8-5b Buying Processes

Many business marketers find it helpful to segment customers and prospective customers on the basis of how they buy. For example, companies can segment some business markets by ranking key purchasing criteria, such as price, quality, technical support, and service. Atlas Overhead Door has developed a commanding position in the industrial door market by providing customized products in just four weeks, which is much faster than the industry average of twelve to fifteen weeks. Atlas's primary market is companies with an immediate need for customized doors.

The purchasing strategies of buyers may provide useful segments. Two purchasing profiles that have been

L'Oréal is a well-known mass market makeup brand sold by most CVS and Walgreens stores. Smaller and more prestige makeup brands are not usually available outside of stores such as Sephora, Macy's, or other upscale retailers.

satisficers business customers who place an order with the first familiar supplier to satisfy product and delivery requirements

optimizers business customers who consider numerous suppliers (both familiar and unfamiliar), solicit bids, and study all proposals carefully before selecting one

identified are satisficers and optimizers. **Satisficers** contact familiar suppliers and place the order with the first one to satisfy product and delivery requirements. **Optimizers** consider numerous suppliers (both familiar and unfamiliar), solicit bids, and study all proposals carefully before selecting one.

The personal characteristics of the buyers themselves (their demographic characteristics, decision style, tolerance for risk, confidence level, job responsibilities, and so on) influence their buying behavior and thus offer a viable basis for segmenting some business markets. For example, because customers who shop prestige beauty stores want to know they are getting the best and most prestigious brands, companies with a long history in the industry bring in more brands and more customers. CVS found that out the hard way when trying to move from mass beauty in its drugstores into the prestige beauty market by opening a boutique-style concept store called Beauty 360. After opening only 25 of the proposed 500 stores and seeing sales drop, CVS shuttered the brand. However, Duane Reade (with its new upscale Look Boutique) and Macy's (with its new Impulse Beauty concept) continue to see increasing sales for their prestige beauty brands because the companies have been involved in the upscale beauty market for years.[22]

8-6 STEPS IN SEGMENTING A MARKET

The purpose of market segmentation, in both consumer and business markets, is to identify marketing opportunities.

1. **SELECT A MARKET OR PRODUCT CATEGORY FOR STUDY:** Define the overall market or product category to be studied. It may be a market in which the firm already competes, a new but related market or product category, or a totally new market.

2. **CHOOSE A BASIS OR BASES FOR SEGMENTING THE MARKET:** This step requires managerial insight, creativity, and market knowledge. There are no scientific procedures for selecting segmentation variables. However, a successful

segmentation scheme must produce segments that meet the four basic criteria discussed earlier in this chapter.

3. **SELECT SEGMENTATION DESCRIPTORS:** After choosing one or more bases, the marketer must select the segmentation descriptors. Descriptors identify the specific segmentation variables to use. For example, if a company selects demographics as a basis of segmentation, it may use age, occupation, and income as descriptors. A company that selects usage-rate segmentation needs to decide whether to go after heavy users, nonusers, or light users.

4. **PROFILE AND ANALYZE SEGMENTS:** The profile should include the segments' size, expected growth, purchase frequency, current brand usage, brand loyalty, and long-term sales and profit potential. This information can then be used to rank potential market segments by profit opportunity, risk, consistency with organizational mission and objectives, and other factors important to the firm.

5. **SELECT TARGET MARKETS:** Selecting target markets is not a part of the segmentation process but a natural outcome of that process. It is a major decision that influences and often directly determines the firm's marketing mix. This topic is examined in greater detail later in this chapter.

6. **DESIGN, IMPLEMENT, AND MAINTAIN APPROPRIATE MARKETING MIXES:** The marketing mix has been described as product, place (distribution), promotion, and pricing strategies intended to bring about mutually satisfying exchange relationships with target markets. These topics are explored in detail in Chapters 10 through 20.

Markets are dynamic, so it is important that companies proactively monitor their segmentation strategies over time. Often, once customers or prospects have been assigned to a segment, marketers think their task is done. Once customers are assigned to an age segment, for example, they stay there until they reach the next age bracket or category, which could be ten years in the future. Thus, the segmentation classifications are static, but the customers and prospects are changing. Dynamic segmentation approaches adjust to fit the changes that occur in customers' lives. For example, American Eagle mainly targets ten-year-old boys and girls with its 77 kids stores. However, some segments have too many players, and choosing to enter those kinds of segments can be particularly challenging. For example, with the popularity of Web sites that drive traffic using flash sales, which are sales occurring at a certain time that offer previously un-announced products at a heavy discount, there are so many to choose from that the *New York Times* put together a list of sites that it thinks are actually worth visiting.[23]

8-7 STRATEGIES FOR SELECTING TARGET MARKETS

So far, this chapter has focused on the market segmentation process, which is only the first step in deciding whom to approach about buying a product. The next task is to choose one or more target markets. A **target market** is a group of people or organizations for which an organization designs, implements, and maintains a marketing mix intended to meet the needs of that group, resulting in mutually satisfying exchanges. Because most markets will include customers with different characteristics, lifestyles, backgrounds, and income levels, it is unlikely that a single marketing mix will attract all segments of the market. Thus, if a marketer wishes to appeal to more than one segment of the market, it must develop different marketing mixes. For example, Subaru's customer base consists of eco-conscious individuals who value freedom and buy experiences, not things. To attract younger, sportier consumers with similar values, Subaru is developing a small car, as well as a hybrid.[24] The three

general strategies for selecting target markets—undifferentiated, concentrated, and multisegment targeting—are illustrated in Exhibit 8.2, which also illustrates the advantages and disadvantages of each targeting strategy.

8-7a Undifferentiated Targeting

A firm using an **undifferentiated targeting strategy** essentially adopts a mass-market philosophy, viewing the market as one big market with no individual segments. The firm uses one marketing mix for the entire market. A firm that adopts an undifferentiated targeting strategy assumes that individual customers have similar needs that can be met with a common marketing mix.

The first firm in an industry sometimes uses an undifferentiated targeting strategy. With no competition, the firm may not need to tailor marketing mixes to the preferences of market segments. Henry Ford's famous comment about the Model T is a classic example of an undifferentiated targeting strategy: "They can have their car in any color they want, as long as it's black." At one time, Coca-Cola used this strategy with a single product and a single size of its familiar green bottle. Marketers of commodity products, such as flour and sugar, are also likely to use an undifferentiated targeting strategy.

target market
a group of people or organizations for which an organization designs, implements, and maintains a marketing mix intended to meet the needs of that group, resulting in mutually satisfying exchanges

undifferentiated targeting strategy
a marketing approach that views the market as one big market with no individual segments and thus uses a single marketing mix

Exhibit 8.2

ADVANTAGES AND DISADVANTAGES OF TARGET MARKETING STRATEGIES

Targeting Strategy	Advantages	Disadvantages
Undifferentiated Targeting	• Potential savings on production/ marketing costs	• Unimaginative product offerings • Company more susceptible to competition
Concentrated Targeting	• Concentration of resources • Can better meet the needs of a narrowly defined segment • Allows some small firms to better compete with larger firms • Strong positioning	• Segments too small or changing • Large competitors may more effectively market to niche segment
Multisegment Targeting	• Greater financial success • Economies of scale in producing/ marketing	• High costs • Cannibalization

One advantage of undifferentiated marketing is the potential for saving on production and marketing. Because only one item is produced, the firm should be able to achieve economies of mass production. Also, marketing costs may be lower when there is only one product to promote and a single channel of distribution. Too often, however, an undifferentiated strategy emerges by default rather than by design, reflecting a failure to consider the advantages of a segmented approach. The result is often sterile, unimaginative product offerings that have little appeal to anyone.

Another problem associated with undifferentiated targeting is that it makes the company more susceptible to competitive inroads. Hershey lost a big share of the candy market to Mars and other candy companies before it changed to a multisegment targeting strategy. Coca-Cola forfeited its position as the leading seller of cola drinks in supermarkets to PepsiCo in the late 1950s, when Pepsi began offering several sizes of containers.

You might think a firm producing a standard product such as toilet tissue would adopt an undifferentiated strategy. However, this market has industrial segments and consumer segments. Industrial buyers want an economical, single-ply product sold in boxes of a hundred rolls. The consumer market demands a more versatile product in smaller quantities. Within the consumer market, the product is differentiated with designer print or no print, as cushioned or noncushioned, and as economy priced or luxury priced. Fort Howard Corporation, the market share leader in industrial toilet paper, does not even sell to the consumer market.

Undifferentiated marketing can succeed in certain situations, though. A small grocery store in a small, isolated town may define all of the people who live in the town as its target market. It may offer one marketing mix and generally satisfy everyone in town. This strategy is not likely to be as effective if there are three or four grocery stores in town.

8-7b Concentrated Targeting

With a **concentrated targeting strategy**, a firm selects a market **niche** (one segment of a market) for targeting its marketing efforts. Because the firm is appealing to a single segment, it can concentrate on understanding the needs, motives, and satisfactions of that segment's members and on developing and maintaining a highly specialized marketing mix. Some firms find that concentrating resources and meeting the needs of a narrowly defined market segment is more profitable than spreading resources over several different segments.

Intelligentsia Coffee & Tea, a Chicago-based coffee roaster/retailer, targets serious coffee drinkers with hand-roasted, ground, and poured super-gourmet coffee or tea served by seriously educated baristas. The company also offers training classes for the at-home or out-of-town coffee aficionado. Starting price—$200 per class. Additionally, America Online became one of the world's leading Internet providers by targeting Internet newcomers.

Small firms often adopt a concentrated targeting strategy to compete effectively with much larger firms. For example, Enterprise Rent-A-Car rose to number one in the car rental industry by catering to people with cars in the shop. It then expanded into the airport rental market. Some other firms use a concentrated strategy to establish a strong position in a desirable market segment. Porsche, for instance, targets an upscale automobile market through "class appeal, not mass appeal."

Concentrated targeting violates the old adage "Don't put all your eggs in one basket." If the chosen segment is too small or if it shrinks because of environmental changes, the firm may suffer negative consequences. For instance, OshKosh B'gosh was highly successful selling children's wear in the 1980s. It was so successful, however, that the children's line came to define OshKosh's image to the extent that the company could not sell clothes to anyone else. Attempts at marketing older children's clothing, women's casual clothes, and maternity wear were all abandoned. Recognizing it was in the children's wear business, the company expanded into products such as kids' shoes, children's eyewear, and plush toys.

A concentrated strategy can also be disastrous for a firm that is not successful in its narrowly defined target market. Before Procter & Gamble introduced Head & Shoulders shampoo, several small firms were already selling antidandruff shampoos. Head & Shoulders was introduced with a large promotional campaign, and the new brand captured over half the market immediately. Within a year, several of the firms that had been concentrating on this market segment went out of business.

8-7c Multisegment Targeting

A firm that chooses to serve two or more well-defined market segments and develops a distinct marketing mix for each has a **multisegment targeting strategy**. The P&G example discussed earlier in the chapter is one example of a multisegment strategy because the company targets both ones and twos. Harley-Davidson has recently switched to a multisegment strategy by targeting women and younger riders as its traditional "born-to-be-wild" market ages out of motorcycles. For women, Harley hosts "garage parties" and is developing a slightly smaller bike. For young adults, the company is toning down the chrome and offering a "dark custom" look.[25]

Multisegment targeting offers many potential benefits to firms, including greater sales volume, higher profits, larger market share, and economies of scale in manufacturing and marketing. Yet it may also involve greater product design, production, promotion, inventory, marketing research, and management costs. Before deciding to use this strategy, firms should compare the benefits and costs of multisegment targeting to those of undifferentiated and concentrated targeting.

Another potential cost of multisegment targeting is **cannibalization**, which occurs when sales of a new product cut into sales of a firm's existing products. For example, sales of peripherals for Apple's iPhone and iPad have eclipsed the total revenue from laptop and desktop Macs. In this case, however, the incredible increase in sales growth of both the iPhone and iPad reassure Apple that, while some people may choose to buy an iPad over a Mac, more people are choosing to buy an iPad over a PC.[26]

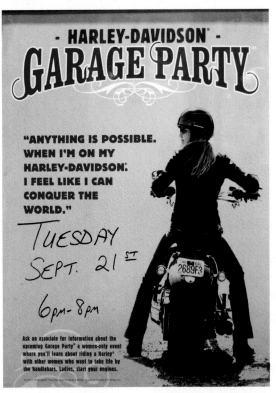

© Tim Boyle/Bloomberg via Getty Images

- HARLEY-DAVIDSON -
GARAGE PARTY

"ANYTHING IS POSSIBLE. WHEN I'M ON MY HARLEY-DAVIDSON. I FEEL LIKE I CAN CONQUER THE WORLD."

TUESDAY
SEPT. 21ST

6pm - 8pm

Ask an associate for information about the upcoming Garage Party™ a women-only event where you'll learn about riding a Harley® with other women who want to take life by the handlebars. Ladies, start your engines.

data generated through interactions between carefully defined groups of customers and the company.

For example, in Charlottesville, Virginia, Bill Crutchfield owns and operates a small electronics retailer called Crutchfield. In the age of Internet shopping and bargain hunting, Crutchfield has learned that people respond best to receiving product support from knowledgeable customer service representatives. When customers get home with a new electronics product and have no idea how to install it, they call the store in a panic. But all 500 employees can help a customer install or troubleshoot any of its products over the phone because Crutchfield engineers dissect each product and develop booklets with the product's specifications. Customer service representatives, salespeople, and tech support all receive the detailed information and use it to calm anxious customers or to direct new customers to the products that best fit their needs.[27] In the end, Crutchfield keeps its existing customers and generates new ones because it knows how to adapt its service to fit customer needs.

As many firms have discovered, a detailed and segmented understanding of customers can be advantageous. There are at least four trends that will lead to the continuing growth of CRM: personalization, time savings, loyalty, and technology.

8-8 CRM AS A TARGETING TOOL

Recall from Chapter 1 that CRM entails tracking interactions with customers to optimize customer satisfaction and long-term company profits. Companies that successfully implement CRM tend to customize the goods and services offered to their customers based on

▶ **PERSONALIZATION:** One-size-fits-all marketing is no longer relevant. Consumers want to be treated as the individuals they are, with their own unique sets of needs and wants. By its personalized nature, CRM can fulfill this desire.

▶ **TIME SAVINGS:** Direct and personal marketing efforts will continue to grow to meet the needs of consumers who no longer have the time to spend shopping and making purchase decisions. With the personal and targeted nature of CRM, consumers can

positioning
developing a specific marketing mix to influence potential customers' overall perception of a brand, product line, or organization in general

position the place a product, brand, or group of products occupies in consumers' minds relative to competing offerings

product differentiation
a positioning strategy that some firms use to distinguish their products from those of competitors

spend less time making purchase decisions and more time doing the things that are important to them.

‣ **LOYALTY:** Consumers will be loyal only to those companies and brands that have earned their loyalty and reinforced it at every purchase occasion. CRM techniques focus on finding a firm's best customers, rewarding them for their loyalty, and thanking them for their business.

‣ **TECHNOLOGY:** Mass-media approaches will decline in importance as advances in market research and database technology allow marketers to collect detailed information on their customers. New technology offers marketers a more cost-effective way to reach customers and enables businesses to personalize their messages. For example, My.Yahoo.com greets each user by name and offers information in which the user has expressed interest. Similarly, RedEnvelope .com helps customers keep track of special occasions and offers personalized gift recommendations. With the help of database technology, CRM can track a business's customers as individuals, even if they number in the millions.

CRM is a huge commitment and often requires a 180-degree turnaround for marketers who spent the last half of the twentieth century developing and implementing mass-marketing efforts. Although mass marketing will probably continue to be used, especially to create brand awareness or to remind consumers of a product, the advantages of CRM cannot be ignored.

8-9 POSITIONING

The development of any marketing mix depends on positioning, a process that influences potential customers' overall perception of a brand, product line, or organization in general. Position is the place a product, brand, or group of products occupies in consumers' minds relative to competing offerings. Consumer goods marketers are particularly concerned with positioning. Procter & Gamble, for example, markets eleven different laundry detergents, each with a unique position, such as allergen-free, softening, or ultra-concentrated.

Positioning assumes that consumers compare products on the basis of important features. Marketing efforts that emphasize irrelevant features are therefore likely to misfire. For example, Crystal Pepsi and a clear version of Coca-Cola's Tab failed because consumers perceived the "clear" positioning as more of a marketing gimmick than a benefit.

Effective positioning requires assessing the positions occupied by competing products, determining the important dimensions underlying these positions, and choosing a position in the market where the organization's marketing efforts will have the greatest impact. Jim Beam, a popular whiskey brand, is positioning its other beverages as part of "the girlfriend connection," the social setting in which women tend to share drinks and purchase mixers and spirits. The low-calorie Skinnygirl cocktails and Courvoisier cognac infused with red wine are just two examples of Jim Beam products positioned for women.[28] As the previous example illustrates, **product differentiation** is a positioning strategy that many firms use to distinguish their products from those of competitors. The distinctions can be either real or perceived. Tandem Computers designed machines with two central processing units and two memories for users who cannot afford for their computer systems to be down or databases to be lost (e.g., an airline reservation system). In this case, Tandem used product differentiation to create a product with very real advantages for the target market. However, many everyday products, such as bleaches, aspirin, unleaded regular gasoline, and some soaps, are differentiated by such trivial means as brand names, packaging, color, smell, or "secret" additives. The marketer attempts to convince consumers that a particular brand is distinctive and that they should demand it over competing brands.

Some firms, instead of using product differentiation, position their products as being similar to competing products or brands. Two examples of this positioning are artificial sweeteners advertised as tasting like sugar and margarine as tasting like butter.

8-9a Perceptual Mapping

Perceptual mapping is a means of displaying or graphing, in two or more dimensions, the location of products, brands, or groups of products in customers' minds. For example, Saks Incorporated, the department store chain, stumbled in sales when it tried to attract a younger core customer. To recover, Saks invested in research to determine its core customers in its fifty-four stores across the country. The perceptual map in Exhibit 8.3 below shows how Saks uses customer demographics, such as age, spending habits, and shopping patterns, to build a matrix that charts the best mix of clothes and accessories to stock in each store.

8-9b Positioning Bases

Firms use a variety of bases for positioning, including the following:

perceptual mapping a means of displaying or graphing, in two or more dimensions, the location of products, brands, or groups of products in customers' minds

▸ **ATTRIBUTE:** A product is associated with an attribute, product feature, or customer benefit. In engineering its products, Seventh Generation focuses on removing common toxins and chemicals from household products to make them safe for everyone in the household.

▸ **PRICE AND QUALITY:** This positioning base may stress high price as a signal of quality or emphasize low price as an indication of value. Neiman Marcus uses the high-price strategy; Walmart has successfully followed the low-price and value strategy. The mass merchandiser Target has developed an interesting position based on price and quality. It is an "upscale discounter," sticking to low prices but offering higher quality and design than most discount chains.

▸ **USE OR APPLICATION:** Stressing uses or applications can be an effective means of positioning a product with buyers. Danone introduced its Kahlúa liqueur using advertising to point out 228 ways to consume the product. Snapple introduced a new drink called "Snapple a Day" that is intended for use as a meal replacement.

▸ **PRODUCT USER:** This positioning base focuses on a personality or type of user. Gap Inc. has several different brands: Gap stores offer basic casual pieces, such as jeans and T-shirts to middle-of-the-road consumers at mid-level prices; Old Navy offers low-priced, trendy casual wear geared to youth and college-age groups; and Banana Republic is a luxury brand offering fashionable, luxurious business and casual wear to twenty-five- to thirty-five-year-olds.[29]

▸ **PRODUCT CLASS:** The objective here is to position the product as being associated with a particular category of products—for example, positioning a margarine brand with butter. Alternatively, products can be disassociated with a category.

Exhibit 8.3

PERCEPTUAL MAP AND POSITIONING STRATEGY FOR SAKS DEPARTMENT STORES

Source: Adapted from Vanessa O'Connell, "Park Avenue Classic or Soho Trendy?" *Wall Street Journal*, April 20, 2007, B1.

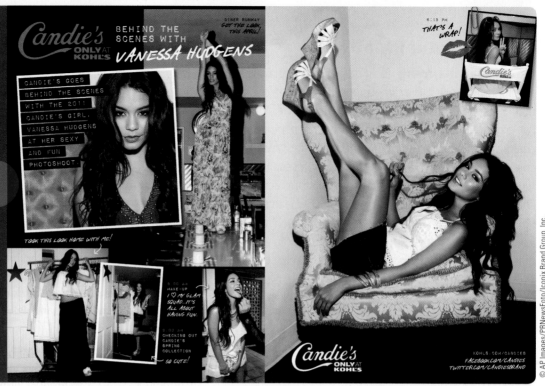

© AP Images/PRNewsFoto/Iconix Brand Group, Inc.

Kohl's positions its Candie's brand to trendy youth and college-aged consumers using recording artist Vanessa Hudgens.

▸▸ **COMPETITOR:** Positioning against competitors is part of any positioning strategy. Avis Car Rental's positioning as number two compared to Hertz exemplifies positioning against specific competitors.

▸▸ **EMOTION:** Positioning using emotion focuses on how the product makes customers feel. A number of companies use this approach. For example, Nike's "Just Do It" campaign didn't tell consumers what "it" is, but most got the emotional message of achievement and courage. The creators of iPhone game Bumpy Road not only created a new way to play a game (by manipulating the world around a car, rather than manipulating the car), they relied on a simple story about a precious little couple to differentiate Bumpy Road from other games.[30]

8-9c Repositioning

Sometimes products or companies are repositioned in order to sustain growth in slow markets or to correct positioning mistakes. **Repositioning** is changing consumers' perceptions of a brand in relation to competing brands. L'Oréal Paris has been a paragon of cosmetics since it began making hair dye in 1909. Hoping to encourage men to see the company as part of their grooming routine, L'Oréal launched a campaign called "Men Expert," which featured a manly expert (sometimes atop an armored elephant with volcanoes in the background) detailing how to tie a tie or how to pick a lock.[31]

STUDY TOOLS 8

↑ LOCATED AT BACK OF THE TEXTBOOK
- ☐ *Rip out Chapter Review Card*

LOCATED AT WWW.CENGAGE.COM/LOGIN
- ☐ *Review Key Terms Flashcards (print or online)*
- ☐ *Download audio and visual summaries to review on the go*
- ☐ *Complete both Practice Quizzes to prepare for tests*
- ☐ *Play "Beat the Clock" and "Quizbowl" to master concepts*
- ☐ *Complete "Crossword Puzzle" to review key terms*
- ☐ *Watch Video on "Numi Organic Tea" for a real company example*

WHY CHOOSE?

Every 4LTR Press solution comes complete with a visually engaging textbook in addition to an interactive eBook. Go to CourseMate for MKTG to begin using the eBook. Access at **www.cengagebrain.com**

Complete the Speak Up survey in CourseMate at **www.cengagebrain.com**

 Follow us at
www.facebook.com/4ltrpress

Accurate and timely information is the lifeblood of marketing decision making. Good information can help an organization maximize sales and efficiently use scarce company resources. To prepare and adjust marketing plans, managers need a system for gathering everyday information about developments in the marketing environment—that is, for gathering **marketing information**. The system most commonly used these days for gathering marketing information is called a *marketing decision support system*.

Whether a research project costs $200 or $2 million, the same general process should be followed.

marketing information everyday information about developments in the marketing environment that managers use to prepare and adjust marketing plans

decision support system (DSS) an interactive, flexible, computerized information system that enables managers to obtain and manipulate information as they are making decisions

database marketing the creation of a large computerized file of customers' and potential customers' profiles and purchase patterns

A marketing **decision support system (DSS)** is an interactive, flexible, computerized information system that enables managers to obtain and manipulate information as they are making decisions. A DSS bypasses the information-processing specialist and gives managers access to useful data from their own desks.

These are the characteristics of a true DSS:

▸▸ **INTERACTIVE:** Managers give simple instructions and see immediate results. The process is under their direct control. Managers don't have to wait for scheduled reports.

▸▸ **FLEXIBLE:** A DSS can sort, regroup, total, average, and manipulate the data in various ways. It will shift gears as the user changes topics, matching information to the problem at hand.

▸▸ **DISCOVERY ORIENTED:** Managers can probe for trends, isolate problems, and ask "what if" questions.

▸▸ **ACCESSIBLE:** Managers who aren't skilled with computers can easily learn how to use a DSS. Novice users should be able to choose a standard, or default, method of using the system. They can bypass optional features so they can work with the basic system right away while gradually learning to apply its advanced features.

Perhaps the fastest-growing use of a DSS is for **database marketing**, which is the creation of a large computerized file of customers' and potential customers' profiles and purchase patterns. It is usually the key tool for successful one-to-one marketing, which relies on very specific information about a market.

Chapter 9

Marketing Research

Learning Outcomes

9-1 *Explain the concept and purpose of a marketing decision support system* 144

9-2 *Define marketing research and explain its importance to marketing decision making* 146

9-3 *Describe the steps involved in conducting a marketing research project* 146–157

9-4 *Discuss the profound impact of the Internet on marketing research* 157–160

9-5 *Discuss the growing importance of scanner-based research* 160–161

9-6 *Explain when marketing research should be conducted* 161–163

9-7 *Explain the concept of competitive intelligence* 163

After you finish this chapter go to
p163 *for* **STUDY TOOLS**

marketing research the process of planning, collecting, and analyzing data relevant to a marketing decision

9-2 THE ROLE OF MARKETING RESEARCH

Marketing research is the process of planning, collecting, and analyzing data relevant to a marketing decision. The results of this analysis are then communicated to management. Thus, marketing research is the function that links the consumer, customer, and public to the marketer through information. Marketing research plays a key role in the marketing system. It provides decision makers with data on the effectiveness of the current marketing mix and insights for necessary changes. Furthermore, marketing research is a main data source for both management information systems and DSS. In other words, the findings of a marketing research project become data in a DSS.

Marketing research has three roles: descriptive, diagnostic, and predictive. Its *descriptive* role includes gathering and presenting factual statements. For example, what is the historic sales trend in the industry? What are consumers' attitudes toward a product and its advertising? Its *diagnostic* role includes explaining data, such as determining the impact on sales of a change in the design of the package. Its *predictive* function is to address "what if" questions. For example, how can the researcher use the descriptive and diagnostic research to predict the results of a planned marketing decision?

9-3 STEPS IN A MARKETING RESEARCH PROJECT

Virtually all firms that have adopted the marketing concept engage in some marketing research because it offers decision makers many benefits. Some companies spend millions on marketing research; others, particularly smaller firms, conduct informal, limited-scale research studies.

Whether a research project costs $200 or $2 million, the same general process should be followed. The marketing research process is a scientific approach to decision making that maximizes the chance of getting accurate and meaningful results. Exhibit 9.1 traces the seven steps in the research process, which begins with the recognition of a marketing problem or opportunity. As changes occur in the firm's external environment, marketing managers are faced with the questions, "Should we change the existing marketing mix?" and, if so, "How?" Marketing research may be used to evaluate product, promotion, distribution, or pricing alternatives.

Procter & Gamble has been struggling to keep its once megabrand Pantene in the black as many mass-market hair care brands struggle to stay on shelves in large retailers such as Walmart and Target. P&G has redone packaging and ad strategies for Pantene twice in the past five years. The first repackaging in 2007 did little to stop losses. In 2009, Pantene's U.S. sales dropped 9 percent, more than the 3 percent decline for the shampoo market as a whole. To try and reverse the downward trend, P&G executed another re-launch in 2010 that was designed to rethink the product from the ground up.

Pantene researchers delved into women's reactions to "bad hair days," a challenging, subjective area that is lightly touched on by only a few other hair care companies. But P&G faced the problem head on, surveying women about their feelings when using certain hair products. The ultimate goal for Pantene was to help women have "good hair days." After one week of using Pantene products, women using the new formula reported more joy than the control group. However, the new packaging strayed too far from what customers wanted: hair care packaging that focused on solutions (more volume, shinier hair, smoother hair). Instead, Pantene alienated customers with its focus on hair type and by discontinuing long-standing favorites, such as two-in-one shampoo and conditioner. In 2011, P&G brought back the two-in-one conditioner and changed packaging to be more readable

Exhibit 9.1

THE MARKETING RESEARCH PROCESS

1 Identify and formulate the problem/opportunity.

2 Plan the research design and gather secondary data.

3 Specify the sampling procedures.

4 Collect primary data.

5 Analyze the data.

6 Prepare and present the report.

7 Follow up.

© Cengage Learning

PANTENE'S MODIFIED PACKAGING BROUGHT BACK MORE FAMILIAR ELEMENTS, SUCH AS TELLING CUSTOMERS THAT A PARTICULAR SHAMPOO IS DESIGNED TO MOISTURIZE HAIR.

and more in line with consumer expectations. The corrections have reversed some losses thanks to Walmart's willingness to accept more products on shelves.[1]

The Pantene story illustrates an important point about problem/opportunity definition. The **marketing research problem** is information oriented. It involves determining what information is needed and how that information can be obtained efficiently and effectively. The **marketing research objective**, then, is to provide insightful decision-making information. This requires specific pieces of information needed to solve the marketing research problem. Managers must combine this information with their own experience and other information to make proper decisions. Initially, Procter & Gamble's marketing research problem was to gather specific information about how a woman's hair affects her feelings and mood. The marketing research objectives were to reformulate Pantene to affect women's hair more positively and to reposition the brand as an antidote to bad hair days. When sales continued slipping after the 2010 launch, the marketing research problem became gathering information about what shampoo customers were buying and how the changes to Pantene's products affected former customers. The marketing research objectives were to reposition the brand as a value brand against salon brands through modified packaging and to bring popular products out of retirement to regain lost sales.

In contrast, the **management decision problem** is action oriented. Management problems tend to be much broader in scope and far more general than marketing research problems, which must be narrowly defined

and specific if the research effort is to be successful. Sometimes several research studies must be conducted to solve a broad management problem. For Pantene, the management decision problem was deciding how to win sales back after the recession and several rebranding attempts.

9-3a Secondary Data

A valuable tool throughout the research process but particularly in the problem/opportunity identification stage is **secondary data**—data previously collected for any purpose other than the one at hand. Secondary information originating within the company includes documents such as annual reports, reports to stockholders, product testing results perhaps made available to the news media, and house periodicals composed by the company's personnel for communication to employees, customers, or others. Often this information is incorporated into a company's internal database.

Innumerable outside sources of secondary information also exist, principally in the forms of government departments and agencies (federal, state, and local) that compile and publish summaries of business data. Trade and industry associations also publish secondary data. Still more data are available in business periodicals and other news media that regularly publish studies and articles on the economy, specific industries, and even individual companies. The unpublished summarized secondary information from these sources corresponds to internal reports, memos, or special-purpose analyses with limited circulation. Economic considerations or priorities in the organization may preclude publication of these summaries. Most of the sources listed above can be found on the Internet.

Secondary data save time and money if they help solve the researcher's problem. Even if the problem is not solved, secondary data have other advantages. They can aid in formulating the problem statement and suggest research methods and other types of data needed for solving the problem. In addition, secondary data can pinpoint the kinds of people to approach and their locations and serve as a basis of comparison for other data. The disadvantages of secondary data stem mainly from a mismatch between

marketing research problem
determining what information is needed and how that information can be obtained efficiently and effectively

marketing research objective
the specific information needed to solve a marketing research problem; the objective should be to provide insightful decision-making information

management decision problem
a broad-based problem that uses marketing research in order for managers to take proper actions

secondary data
data previously collected for any purpose other than the one at hand

marketing research aggregator a company that acquires, catalogs, reformats, segments, and resells reports already published by marketing research firms

research design specifies which research questions must be answered, how and when the data will be gathered, and how the data will be analyzed

the researcher's unique problem and the purpose for which the secondary data were originally gathered, which are typically different. For example, a company wanted to determine the market potential for a fireplace log made of coal rather than compressed wood by-products. The researcher found plenty of secondary data about total wood consumed as fuel, quantities consumed in each state, and types of wood burned. Secondary data were also available about consumer attitudes and purchase patterns of wood by-product fireplace logs. The wealth of secondary data provided the researcher with many insights into the artificial log market. Yet nowhere was there any information that would tell the firm whether consumers would buy artificial logs made of coal.

The quality of secondary data may also pose a problem. Often secondary data sources do not give detailed information that would enable a researcher to assess their quality or relevance. Whenever possible, a researcher needs to address these important questions: Who gathered the data? Why were the data obtained? What methodology was used? How were classifications (such as heavy users versus light users) developed and defined? When was the information gathered?

THE NEW AGE OF SECONDARY INFORMATION: THE INTERNET Although necessary in almost any research project, gathering secondary data has traditionally been a tedious and boring job. The researcher often had to write to government agencies, trade associations, or other secondary data providers and then wait days or weeks for a reply that might never come. Often, one or more trips to the library were required, and the researcher might have found that needed reports were checked out or missing. Now, however, the rapid development of the Internet has eliminated much of the drudgery associated with the collection of secondary data.

9-3b Marketing Research Aggregators

The **marketing research aggregator** industry is a $120 million business that is growing about 6 percent a year. Companies in this field acquire, catalog, reformat, segment, and resell reports already published by large and small marketing research firms. Even Amazon.com has added a marketing research aggregation area to its high-profile e-commerce site.

The role of aggregator firms is growing because their databases of research reports are getting bigger and more comprehensive—and more useful—as marketing research firms get more comfortable using resellers as a sales channel. Meanwhile, advances in Web technology are making the databases easier to search and deliveries speedier. By slicing and repackaging research reports into narrower, more specialized sections for resale to small- and medium-sized clients who often cannot afford to commission their own studies or buy full reports, the aggregators are essentially nurturing a new target market for the information. Some major aggregators are marketresearch.com, aarkstore.com, and usadata.com.

9-3c Planning the Research Design and Gathering Primary Data

Good secondary data can help researchers conduct a thorough situation analysis. With that information, researchers can list their unanswered questions and rank them. Researchers must then decide the exact information required to answer the questions. The **research design** specifies which research questions must be answered, how and when the data will be gathered, and how the data will be analyzed. Typically, the project budget is finalized after the research design has been approved.

Sometimes research questions can be answered by gathering more secondary data; otherwise,

© Supri Suharjoto/Shutterstock.com

primary data may be needed. **Primary data**, or information collected for the first time, are used for solving the particular problem under investigation. The main advantage of primary data is that they will answer a specific research question that secondary data cannot answer. In 2009, when Procter & Gamble was doing intensive research for Pantene, managers used a psychological questionnaire to determine how hair products affected women's daily attitudes. For one week, one group of women used the old Pantene formula, and the other group used the new formula. These primary data revealed that women using the new Pantene felt more excited, proud, interested, and attentive than the other group—positive emotions that the Pantene research group could not have discovered through secondary research.[2] Moreover, primary data are current, and researchers know the source. Sometimes researchers gather the data themselves rather than assign projects to outside companies. Researchers also specify the methodology of the research. Secrecy can be maintained because the information is proprietary. In contrast, much secondary data is available to all interested parties for relatively small fees or free.

Gathering primary data is expensive; costs can range from a few thousand dollars for a limited survey to several million for a nationwide study. For instance, a nationwide, fifteen-minute telephone interview with 1,000 adult males can cost $50,000 for everything, including a data analysis and report. Because primary data gathering is so expensive, firms may cut back on the number of in-person interviews to save money and use an Internet study instead. Larger companies that conduct many research projects use another cost-saving technique. They *piggyback studies*, or gather data on two different projects using one questionnaire. Nevertheless, the disadvantages of primary data gathering are usually offset by the advantages. It is often the only way of solving a research problem. And with a variety of techniques available for research—including surveys, observations, and experiments—primary research can address almost any marketing question.

SURVEY RESEARCH The most popular technique for gathering primary data is **survey research**, in which a researcher interacts with people to obtain facts, opinions, and attitudes. Exhibit 9.2 summarizes the characteristics of traditional forms of survey research.

primary data
information that is collected for the first time; used for solving the particular problem under investigation

survey research
the most popular technique for gathering primary data, in which a researcher interacts with people to obtain facts, opinions, and attitudes

Exhibit 9.2

CHARACTERISTICS OF TRADITIONAL FORMS OF SURVEY RESEARCH

Characteristic	In-Home Personal Interviews	Mall Intercept Interviews	Central-Location Telephone Interviews	Self-Administered and One-Time Mail Surveys	Mail Panel Surveys	Executive Interviews	Focus Groups
Cost	High	Moderate	Moderate	Low	Moderate	High	Low
Time span	Moderate	Moderate	Fast	Slow	Relatively slow	Moderate	Fast
Use of interviewer probes	Yes	Yes	Yes	No	Yes	Yes	Yes
Ability to show concepts to respondent	Yes (also taste tests)	Yes (also taste tests)	No	Yes	Yes	Yes	Yes
Management control over interviewer	Low	Moderate	High	N/A	N/A	Moderate	High
General data quality	High	Moderate	High to moderate	Moderate to low	Moderate	High	Moderate
Ability to collect large amounts of data	High	Moderate	Moderate to low	Low to moderate	Moderate	Moderate	Moderate
Ability to handle complex questionnaires	High	Moderate	High, if computer aided	Low	Low	High	N/A

© Cengage Learning

mall intercept interview a survey research method that involves interviewing people in the common areas of shopping malls

computer-assisted personal interviewing an interviewing method in which the interviewer reads questions from a computer screen and enters the respondent's data directly into the computer

computer-assisted self-interviewing an interviewing method in which a mall interviewer intercepts and directs willing respondents to nearby computers where each respondent reads questions off a computer screen and directly keys his or her answers into a computer

central-location telephone (CLT) facility a specially designed phone room used to conduct telephone interviewing

executive interview a type of survey that involves interviewing businesspeople at their offices concerning industrial products or services

IN-HOME PERSONAL INTERVIEWS Although in-home personal interviews often provide high-quality information, they tend to be very expensive because of the interviewers' travel time and mileage costs. Therefore, they are rapidly disappearing from the American and European researchers' survey toolbox. They are, however, still popular in many countries around the globe.

MALL INTERCEPT INTERVIEWS The **mall intercept interview** is conducted in the common area of a shopping mall or in a market research office within the mall. To conduct this type of interview, the research firm rents office space in the mall or pays a significant daily fee. One drawback is that it is hard to get a representative sample of the population. One advantage is the ability of the interviewer to probe when necessary—a technique used to clarify a person's response and ask for more detailed information.

Mall intercept interviews must be brief. Only the shortest ones are conducted while respondents are standing. Usually, researchers invite respondents into the office for interviews, which are still generally less than fifteen minutes long. The overall quality of mall intercept interviews is about the same as telephone interviews.

Marketing researchers are applying computer technology in mall interviewing. The first technique is **computer-assisted personal interviewing**. The researcher conducts in-person interviews, reads questions to the respondent off a computer screen, and directly keys the respondent's answers into the computer. A second approach is **computer-assisted self-interviewing**. A mall interviewer intercepts and directs willing respondents to nearby computers. Each respondent reads questions off a computer screen and directly keys his or her answers into a computer. The third use of technology is fully automated self-interviewing. Respondents are guided by interviewers or independently approach a centrally located computer station or kiosk, read questions off a screen, and directly key their answers into the station's computer.

TELEPHONE INTERVIEWS Telephone interviews cost less than personal interviews, but cost is rapidly increasing due to respondent refusals to participate. Most telephone interviewing is conducted from a specially designed phone room called a **central-location telephone (CLT) facility**. A CLT facility has many phone lines, individual interviewing stations, headsets, and sometimes monitoring equipment. The research firm typically will interview people nationwide from a single location. The federal "Do Not Call" law does not apply to survey research.

Most CLT facilities offer computer-assisted interviewing. The interviewer reads the questions from a computer screen and enters the respondent's data directly into the computer, saving time. Hallmark Cards found that an interviewer administered a printed questionnaire for its Shoebox greeting cards in twenty-eight minutes. The same questionnaire administered with computer assistance took only eighteen minutes. The researcher can stop the survey at any point and immediately print out the survey results, allowing the research design to be refined as necessary.

MAIL SURVEYS Mail surveys have several benefits: relatively low cost, elimination of interviewers and field supervisors, centralized control, and actual or promised anonymity for respondents (which may draw more candid responses). A disadvantage is that mail questionnaires usually produce low response rates because certain elements of the population tend to respond more than others. The resulting sample may therefore not represent the surveyed population. Another serious problem with mail surveys is that no one probes respondents to clarify or elaborate on their answers.

Mail panels offer an alternative to the one-shot mail survey. A mail panel consists of a sample of households recruited to participate by mail for a given period. Panel members often receive gifts in return for their participation. Essentially, the panel is a sample used several times. In contrast to one-time mail surveys, the response rates from mail panels are high. Rates of 70 percent (of those who agree to participate) are not uncommon.

EXECUTIVE INTERVIEWS An **executive interview** involves interviewing businesspeople at their offices concerning industrial products or services, a process that is very expensive. First, individuals involved in the purchase decision for the product in question must be identified and located, which can itself be expensive and time-consuming. Once a qualified person is located, the next step is to get that person to agree to be interviewed and to set a time for the interview.

Finally, an interviewer must go to the particular place at the appointed time. Long waits are frequently encountered; cancellations are not uncommon. This type of survey requires the very best interviewers because they frequently are interviewing on topics that they know very little about.

FOCUS GROUPS A **focus group** is a type of personal interviewing. Often recruited by random telephone screening, seven to ten people with certain desired characteristics form a focus group. These qualified consumers are usually offered an incentive (typically $30 to $50) to participate in a group discussion. The meeting place (sometimes resembling a living room, sometimes featuring a conference table) has audiotaping and perhaps videotaping equipment. It also likely has a viewing room with a one-way mirror so that clients (manufacturers or retailers) can watch the session. During the session, a moderator, hired by the research company, leads the group discussion. Focus groups can be used to gauge consumer response to a product or promotion and are occasionally used to brainstorm new-product ideas or to screen concepts for new products. Focus groups also represent an efficient way of learning how products are actually used in the home. Panelists' descriptions of how they perform tasks highlight need gaps, which can improve an existing product or demonstrate how a new product might be received. In 2011, there were approximately 263,000 focus groups conducted in the United States. Focus groups are increasingly conducted through the Web using Web cameras, the use of which increased 133 percent from 2010 to 2011.[3]

QUESTIONNAIRE DESIGN All forms of survey research require a questionnaire. Questionnaires ensure that all respondents will be asked the same series of questions. Questionnaires include three basic types of questions: open-ended, closed-ended, and scaled-response. An **open-ended question** encourages an answer phrased in the respondent's own words. Researchers get a rich array of information based on the respondent's frame of reference (What do you think about the new flavor?). In contrast, a **closed-ended question** asks the respondent to make a selection from a limited list of responses. Closed-ended questions can either be what marketing researchers call *dichotomous* (Do you like the new flavor? Yes or No.) or *multiple choice*. A **scaled-response question** is a closed-ended question designed to measure the intensity of a respondent's answer.

focus group seven to ten people who participate in a group discussion led by a moderator

open-ended question an interview question that encourages an answer phrased in the respondent's own words

closed-ended question an interview question that asks the respondent to make a selection from a limited list of responses

scaled-response question a closed-ended question designed to measure the intensity of a respondent's answer

A DAY IN THE LIFE OF THE CUSTOMER

Martin Lindstrom, a business consultant, has **revitalized ailing brands** and taught CEOs how to tweak products or target them in just the right way to make sales soar. His secret is simple: live with your customers. When Lindstrom is hired by a company, he goes and lives with its target audience—eats, sleeps, and plays with them. As a result, he can tell companies that 37 percent of teenagers eat cereal on their first day of college in order to feel closer to home, and that 4 percent of people brush their teeth in the shower. Up close and personal market research gives marketers a true look into how their customers live and, properly applied, helps give them exactly what they need.

Source: Martin Lindstrom, "Want to Sell Product? Sleep with Your Customers," *Fast Company*, June 9, 2011, www.fastcompany.com/1758288/familiar-microscopic-consumer-insights-yet-to-be-discovered (Accessed May 23, 2012).

© Tyler Olson/Shutterstock.com / © iStockphoto.com/Bill Noll

observation research a research method that relies on four types of observation: people watching people, people watching an activity, machines watching people, and machines watching an activity

mystery shoppers researchers posing as customers who gather observational data about a store

behavioral targeting (BT) a form of observation marketing research that combines a consumer's online activity with psychographic and demographic profiles compiled in databases

Closed-ended and scaled-response questions are easier to tabulate than open-ended questions because response choices are fixed. On the other hand, unless the researcher designs the closed-ended question very carefully, an important choice may be omitted.

A good question must be clear and concise and avoid ambiguous language. The answer to the question "Do you live within ten minutes of here?" depends on the mode of transportation (maybe the person walks), speed, perceived time, and other factors. Language should also be clear. As such, jargon should be avoided, and wording should be geared to the target audience. A question such as "What is the level of efficacy of your preponderant dishwasher powder?" would probably be greeted by a lot of blank stares. It would be much simpler to say "Are you (1) very satisfied, (2) somewhat satisfied, or (3) not satisfied with your current brand of dishwasher powder?"

Stating the survey's purpose at the beginning of the interview may improve clarity, but it may also increase the chances of receiving biased responses. Many times, respondents will try to provide answers that they believe are "correct" or that the interviewer wants to hear. To avoid bias at the question level, researchers should avoid leading questions and adjectives that cause respondents to think of the topic in a certain way.

Finally, to ensure clarity, the interviewer should avoid asking two questions in one—for example, "How did you like the taste and texture of the Pepperidge Farm coffee cake?" This should be divided into two questions, one concerning taste and the other texture.

OBSERVATION RESEARCH In contrast to survey research, **observation research** depends on watching what people do. Specifically, it can be defined as the systematic process of recording the behavioral patterns of people, objects, and occurrences without questioning them. A market researcher using the observation technique witnesses and records information as events occur or compiles evidence from records of past events. Carried a step further, observation may involve watching people or phenomena and may be conducted by human observers or machines. Examples of these various observational situations are shown in Exhibit 9.3.

Exhibit 9.3
OBSERVATIONAL SITUATIONS

Situation	Example
People watching people	Observers stationed in supermarkets watch consumers select frozen Mexican dinners; the purpose is to see how much comparison shopping people do at the point of purchase.
People watching an activity	An observer stationed at an intersection counts traffic moving in various directions.
Machines watching people	Movie or videotape cameras record behavior as in the people-watching-people example above.
Machines watching an activity	Traffic-counting machines monitor traffic flow.

© Cengage Learning

Two common forms of people-watching-people research are one-way mirror observations and mystery shoppers. A one-way mirror allows the researchers to see the participants, but the participants cannot see the researchers.

MYSTERY SHOPPERS **Mystery shoppers** are researchers posing as customers who gather observational data about a store (e.g., are the shelves neatly stocked?) and collect data about customer/employee interactions. The interaction is not an interview, and communication occurs only so that the mystery shopper can observe the actions and comments of the employee. Mystery shopping is, therefore, classified as an observational marketing research method even though communication is often involved.

BEHAVIORAL TARGETING **Behavioral targeting (BT)** began as a simple process by placing cookies on users' browsers to track which Web sites they visited and ultimately match the users with ads they would most likely investigate. Today, BT combines a consumer's online activity with psychographic and demographic profiles compiled in databases (discussed in Chapters 4 and 8). Because of the potential effectiveness of BT advertising, its popularity is skyrocketing.

Social networking, which is discussed in depth in Chapter 18, is the fastest-growing area of BT. The information that a member of Google+ or Facebook shares, in combination with his or her demographic and psychographic

ethnographic
research the study of
human behavior in its natural
context; involves observation of
behavior and physical setting

information, becomes a very powerful tool for ad placement. Critics call this form of BT *conversational eavesdropping analysis,* but advocates call it *user-declared information targeting.*[4] It is an apt description because the information is posted by members in their profiles. Say Alex posts kayaking as an interest on his profile. Because he declared his interest, it is more concrete marketing knowledge. A note that someone from that computer's address visited a kayaking Web site is less concrete because anyone could have been using that computer. Both Facebook and MySpace allow marketers to target ads to members based upon profile information. Many large companies use BT. When PepsiCo wanted to promote Aquafina Alive on the Web, the company placed ads only on sites visited by people interested in healthy lifestyles.

ETHNOGRAPHIC RESEARCH Ethnographic research comes to marketing from the field of anthropology. The technique is becoming increasingly popular in commercial marketing research. **Ethnographic research,** or the study of human behavior in its natural context, involves observation of behavior and physical setting. Ethnographers directly observe the population they are studying. As "participant observers," ethnographers can use their intimacy with the people they are studying to gain richer, deeper insights into culture and behavior—in short, what makes people do what they do.

The at-home consumption market is one that eludes much research. Anthropologists and other observational researchers can't sit in people's homes and monitor which electronic devices they are using and how they use them. Questionnaires rely on one-time truthful responses and the respondent's memory. However, some of the nation's biggest media companies got a look into people's homes by using iPhones to monitor media consumption. The Coalition for Innovative Media Measurement (CIMM), a collaboration between media and ad industries to determine how consumers view media and which devices they use, sponsored the study. The company gave 1,000 participants iPhones with a special app that they would log into every thirty minutes and answer questions about their media activities. Respondents gave frequent updates on what and how they consumed music and television, whether through streaming or downloading, on computers or television, or from subscription services or free sources. The results offered myriad breakdowns of information, but one key segment is mothers. CIMM compared

USING FACEBOOK TO DRIVE ONLINE SALES AT WALMART

Walmart is working to become the **largest online retailer** (in spite of Amazon's current prowess). Hoping to encourage virtual shoppers to patronize Walmart.com, Walmart has developed a new Facebook app called Shopycat. Shopycat accesses information from your Facebook friends' pages and displays a list of items that would make great gifts for those people. For example, if your brother had the Green Bay Packers listed as his favorite sports team and also noted he loved breakfast, Shopycat would suggest a Green Bay Packers Toaster as a great gift for him. The program links to Walmart.com and lists the prices of all the suggested items. One bonus of the program is that it also links to unique items that are not sold by Walmart, which makes the gift list developed by Shopycat even more useful and benefits Walmart by building trust with its consumers.

Source: Chuck Salter, "How to Connect People and Products via Social Media," *Fast Company,* June 2012, 125.

© Yanik Chauvin/Shutterstock.com / © iStockphoto.com/Bill Noll three generations of mothers to determine when each group was most receptive to television, print, and digital advertising. This type of research may be the closest researchers have come to living with research participants and to understanding how Americans consume media. Knowing how and when Americans watch programs allows the media and ad industries to tailor delivery to the consumer and use the Internet to their advantage rather than be left behind with outdated business models.[5]

VIRTUAL SHOPPING Advances in computer technology have enabled researchers to simulate an actual retail store environment on a computer screen. Depending on the type of simulation, a shopper can "pick up" a package by touching its image on the monitor and rotate it to examine all sides. Like buying on most online retailers, the shopper touches the shopping cart to add an item to the basket. During the shopping process, the computer unobtrusively records the amount of time the consumer spends shopping in each product category, the time the consumer spends examining each side of a product, the quantity of the product the consumer purchases, and the order in which items are purchased.

Computer-simulated environments like this one offer a number of advantages over older research methods. First, the virtual store duplicates the distracting clutter of an actual market. Layouts can even be modified to reflect various types of retailers, such as drugstores or supermarkets, meaning that consumers can shop in an environment with a realistic level of complexity and variety. Second, researchers can set up and alter the tests very quickly. Data collection is also fast and error free because the information generated by the purchase is automatically tabulated and stored by the computer. Third, production costs are low because displays are created electronically. Once the hardware and

software are in place, the cost of a test is largely a function of the number of respondents, who generally are given a small incentive to participate. Fourth, the simulation has a high degree of flexibility. It can be used to test entirely new marketing concepts or to fine-tune existing programs.[6]

Virtual shopping research is growing rapidly as companies such as Cadbury, Nestlé, PepsiCo, and Clorox realize the benefits from this type of observation research.[7] About 150,000 new consumer packaged goods were introduced in the United States in 2010.[8] All are vying for very limited retail shelf space. Any process, such as virtual shopping, that can speed product development time and lower costs is always welcomed by manufacturers.

EXPERIMENTS An **experiment** is a method a researcher can use to gather primary data. The researcher alters one or more variables—price, package design, shelf space, advertising theme, advertising expenditures—while observing the effects of those alterations on another variable (usually sales). The best experiments are those in which all factors are held constant except the ones being manipulated. The researcher can then observe what changes in sales, for example, result from changes in the amount of money spent on advertising.

9-3d Specifying the Sampling Procedures

Once the researchers decide how they will collect primary data, their next step is to select the sampling procedures they will use. A firm can seldom take a census of all possible users of a new product, nor can they all be interviewed. Therefore, a firm must select a sample of the group to be interviewed. A **sample** is a subset from a larger population.

Several questions must be answered before a sampling plan is chosen. First, the population, or **universe**,

SAMPLE

UNIVERSE

of interest must be defined. This is the group from which the sample will be drawn. It should include all the people whose opinions, behavior, preferences, attitudes, and so on, are of interest to the marketer. For example, in a study whose purpose is to determine the market for a new canned dog food, the universe might be defined to include all current buyers of canned dog food.

After the universe has been defined, the next question is whether the sample must be representative of the population. If the answer is yes, a probability sample is needed. Otherwise, a nonprobability sample might be considered.

PROBABILITY SAMPLES A **probability sample** is a sample in which every element in the population has a known statistical likelihood of being selected. Its most desirable feature is that scientific rules can be used to ensure that the sample represents the population.

One type of probability sample is a **random sample**—a sample arranged in such a way that every element of the population has an equal chance of being selected as part of the sample. For example, suppose a university is interested in getting a cross section of student opinions on a proposed sports complex to be built using student activity fees. If the university can acquire an up-to-date list of all the enrolled students, it can draw a random sample by using random numbers from a table (found in most statistics books) to select students from the list. Common forms of probability and nonprobability samples are shown in Exhibit 9.4.

NONPROBABILITY SAMPLES Any sample in which little or no attempt is made to get a representative cross section of the population can be considered a **nonprobability sample**. Therefore the probability of selection of each sampling unit is not known. A common form of a nonprobability sample is the **convenience sample**, which uses respondents who are convenient or readily accessible to the researcher—for instance, employees, friends, or relatives.

Nonprobability samples are acceptable as long as the researcher

probability sample a sample in which every element in the population has a known statistical likelihood of being selected

random sample a sample arranged in such a way that every element of the population has an equal chance of being selected as part of the sample

nonprobability sample any sample in which little or no attempt is made to get a representative cross section of the population

convenience sample a form of nonprobability sample using respondents who are convenient or readily accessible to the researcher—for example, employees, friends, or relatives

Exhibit 9.4

TYPES OF SAMPLES

Probability Samples	
Simple Random Sample	Every member of the population has a known and equal chance of selection.
Stratified Sample	The population is divided into mutually exclusive groups (such as gender or age); then random samples are drawn from each group.
Cluster Sample	The population is divided into mutually exclusive groups (such as geographic areas); then a random sample of clusters is selected. The researcher then collects data from all the elements in the selected clusters or from a probability sample of elements within each selected cluster.
Systematic Sample	A list of the population is obtained—e.g., all persons with a checking account at XYZ Bank—and a skip interval is obtained by dividing the sample size by the population size. If the sample size is 100 and the bank has 1,000 customers, then the skip interval is 10. The beginning number is randomly chosen within the skip interval. If the beginning number is 8, then the skip pattern would be 8, 18, 28, ...
Nonprobability Samples	
Convenience Sample	The researcher selects the easiest population members from which to obtain information.
Judgment Sample	The researcher's selection criteria are based on personal judgment that the elements (persons) chosen will likely give accurate information.
Quota Sample	The researcher finds a prescribed number of people in several categories—e.g., owners of large dogs versus owners of small dogs. Respondents are not selected on probability sampling criteria.
Snowball Sample	Additional respondents are selected on the basis of referrals from the initial respondents. This method is used when a desired type of respondent is hard to find—e.g., persons who have taken round-the-world cruises in the last three years. This technique employs the old adage "Birds of a feather flock together."

© Cengage Learning

understands their nonrepresentative nature. Because of their lower cost, nonprobability samples are the basis of much marketing research.

TYPES OF ERRORS Whenever a sample is used in marketing research, two major types of errors may occur: measurement error and sampling error. **Measurement error** occurs when there is a difference between the information desired by the researcher and the information provided by the measurement process. For example, people may tell an interviewer that they purchase Crest toothpaste when they do not. Measurement error generally tends to be larger than sampling error.

Sampling error occurs when a sample somehow does not represent the target population. Sampling error can be one of several types. Nonresponse error occurs when the sample actually interviewed differs from the sample drawn. This error happens because the original people selected to be interviewed either refused to cooperate or were inaccessible.

Frame error, another type of sampling error, arises if the sample drawn from a population differs from the target population. For instance, suppose a telephone survey is conducted to find out Chicago beer drinkers' attitudes toward Coors. If a Chicago telephone directory is used as the *frame* (the device or list from which the respondents are selected), the survey will contain a frame error. Not all Chicago beer drinkers have phones, and many phone numbers are unlisted. An ideal sample (e.g., a sample with no frame error) matches all important characteristics of the target population to be surveyed. Could you find a perfect frame for Chicago beer drinkers?

Random error occurs when the selected sample is an imperfect representation of the overall population. Random error represents how accurately the chosen sample's true average (mean) value reflects the population's true average (mean) value. For example, we might take a random sample of beer drinkers in Chicago and find that 16 percent regularly drink Coors beer. The next day we might repeat the same sampling procedure and

discover that 14 percent regularly drink Coors beer. The difference is due to random error. Error is common to all surveys, yet it is often not reported or is underreported. Typically, the only error mentioned in a written report is sampling error.

9-3e Collecting the Data

Marketing research field service firms collect most primary data. A **field service firm** specializes in interviewing respondents on a subcontracted basis. Many have offices, often in malls, throughout the country. A typical marketing research study involves data collection in several cities, which requires the marketer to work with a comparable number of field service firms. Besides conducting interviews, field service firms provide focus group facilities, mall intercept locations, test product storage, and kitchen facilities to prepare test food products.

9-3f Analyzing the Data

After collecting the data, the marketing researcher proceeds to the next step in the research process: data analysis. The purpose of this analysis is to interpret and draw conclusions from the mass of collected data. The marketing researcher tries to organize and analyze those data by using one or more techniques common to marketing research: one-way frequency counts, cross-tabulations, and more sophisticated statistical analysis. Of these three techniques, one-way frequency counts are the simplest. One-way frequency tables simply record the responses to a question. For example, the answers to the question "What brand of microwave popcorn do you buy most often?" would provide a one-way frequency distribution. One-way frequency tables are always done in data analysis, at least as a first step, because they provide the researcher with a general picture of the study's results. A **cross-tabulation** lets the analyst look at the responses to one question in relation to the responses to one or more other questions. For example, in Exhibit 9.5, what is the association between gender and the brand of microwave popcorn bought most frequently?

Researchers can use many other more powerful and sophisticated statistical techniques, such as hypothesis testing, measures of association, and regression analysis. A description of these techniques goes beyond the scope of this book but can be found in any good marketing research textbook. The use of sophisticated statistical

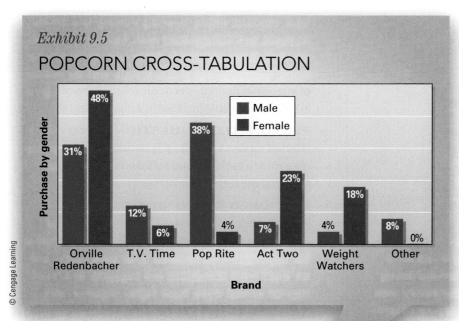

Exhibit 9.5

POPCORN CROSS-TABULATION

techniques depends on the researchers' objectives and the nature of the data gathered.

9-3g Preparing and Presenting the Report

After data analysis has been completed, the researcher must prepare the report and communicate the conclusions and recommendations to management. This is a key step in the process. If the marketing researcher wants managers to carry out the recommendations, he or she must convince them that the results are credible and justified by the data collected.

Researchers are usually required to present both written and oral reports on the project. Today, the written report is no more than a copy of the PowerPoint slides used in the oral presentation. Both reports should be tailored to the audience. They should begin with a clear, concise statement of the research objectives, followed by a complete but brief and simple explanation of the research design or methodology employed. A summary of major findings should come next. The conclusion of the report should also present recommendations to management.

Most people who enter marketing will become research users rather than research suppliers. Thus, they must know what to notice in a report. As with many other items we purchase, quality is not always readily apparent. Nor does a high price guarantee superior quality. The basis for measuring the quality of a marketing research report is the research proposal. Did the report meet the objectives established in the proposal? Was the methodology

outlined in the proposal followed? Are the conclusions based on logical deductions from the data analysis? Do the recommendations seem prudent, given the conclusions?

9-3h Following Up

The final step in the marketing research process is to follow up. The researcher should determine why management did or did not carry out the recommendations in the report. Was sufficient decision-making information included? What could have been done to make the report more useful to management? A good rapport between the product manager, or whoever authorized the project, and the market researcher is essential. Often they must work together on many studies throughout the year.

Typically, the research process flows rather smoothly from one step to the next in the United States. However, conducting research in international markets can create a whole host of problems and challenges.

9-4 THE PROFOUND IMPACT OF THE INTERNET ON MARKETING RESEARCH

Today, about one-fifth of the world's population is online. In the United States, 71 percent of the population is online, spanning every ethnic, socioeconomic, and educational divide.[9] Most managers accept that online research can, under appropriate conditions, accurately represent U.S. consumers as a whole. Non-adopters of the Internet tend to be older, low-income consumers (aged sixty-five and over with household income less than $30,000), who do not tend to be the target market for many goods and services.[10]

More than 90 percent of America's marketing research companies conduct some form of online research. Online survey research has replaced computer-assisted telephone interviewing (CATI) as the most popular mode of data collection, though there is no evidence of this or other traditional survey methods being completely replaced by online surveys.[11] Internet data collection is also rated as having the greatest potential for further growth.

9-4a Advantages of Internet Surveys

The huge growth in the popularity of Internet surveys is the result of the many advantages offered by the Internet. The specific advantages of Internet surveys are related to many factors:

‣ **RAPID DEVELOPMENT, REAL-TIME REPORTING:** Internet surveys can be broadcast to thousands of potential respondents simultaneously. Respondents complete surveys simultaneously; then results are tabulated and posted for corporate clients to view as the returns arrive. The result: survey results can be in a client's hands in significantly less time than would be required for traditional surveys.

‣ **DRAMATICALLY REDUCED COSTS:** The Internet can cut costs by 25 to 40 percent and provide results in half the time it takes to do traditional telephone surveys. Traditional survey methods are labor-intensive efforts incurring training, telecommunications, and management costs. Electronic methods eliminate these completely. While costs for traditional survey techniques rise proportionally with the number of interviews desired, electronic solicitations can grow in volume with little increase in project costs.

‣ **PERSONALIZED QUESTIONS AND DATA:** Internet surveys can be highly personalized for greater relevance to each respondent's own situation, thus speeding the response process.

‣ **IMPROVED RESPONDENT PARTICIPATION:** Internet surveys take half as much time to complete as phone interviews, can be accomplished at the respondent's convenience (after work hours), and are much more stimulating and engaging. As a result, Internet surveys enjoy much higher response rates.

‣ **CONTACT WITH THE HARD-TO-REACH:** Certain groups—doctors, high-income professionals, top management in Global 2000 firms—are among the most surveyed on the planet and the most difficult to reach. Many of these groups are well represented online. Internet surveys provide convenient anytime/anywhere access that makes it easy for busy professionals to participate.

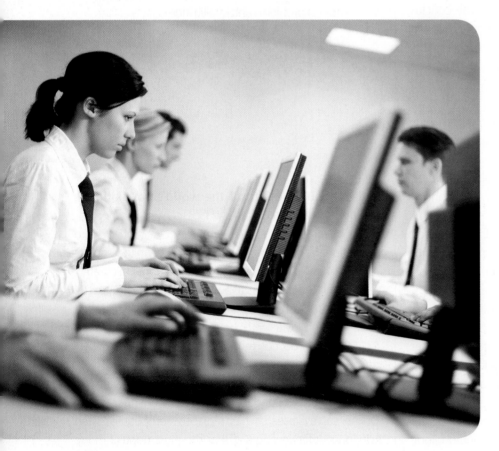

9-4b Uses of the Internet by Marketing Researchers

Marketing researchers are using the Internet to administer surveys, conduct focus groups, and perform a variety of other types of marketing research.

METHODS OF CONDUCTING ONLINE SURVEYS There are several basic methods for conducting online surveys: Web survey systems, survey design and Web hosting sites, and online panel providers.

WEB SURVEY SYSTEMS Web survey systems are software systems specifically designed for Web questionnaire construction and delivery. They consist of an integrated questionnaire designer, Web server, database, and data delivery program, designed for use by nonprogrammers. The Web server distributes the questionnaire and files responses in a database. The user can query the server at any time via the Web for completion statistics, descriptive statistics on responses, and graphical displays of data. Some popular online survey research software packages are Sawtooth CiW, Infopoll, SurveyMonkey, and SurveyPro.

SURVEY DESIGN AND WEB HOSTING SITES
Several Web sites allow the researcher to design a survey online without loading design software. The survey is then administered on the design site's server. Some offer tabulation and analysis packages as well. One popular site that offers Web hosting services is Vovici.

ONLINE PANEL PROVIDERS Often researchers use online panel providers for a ready-made sample population. Online panel providers such as Survey Sampling International and e-Rewards pre-recruit people who agree to participate in online market research surveys.

Some online panels are created for specific industries and may have a few thousand panel members, while the large commercial online panels have millions of people waiting to be surveyed. When people join online panels, they answer an extensive profiling questionnaire that enables the panel provider to target research efforts to panel members who meet specific criteria.

ONLINE FOCUS GROUPS A relatively recent development in qualitative research is the online or cyber focus group. A number of organizations are currently offering this new means of conducting focus groups. The process is fairly simple. The research firm builds a database of respondents via a screening questionnaire on its Web site. When a client comes to a firm with a need for a particular focus group, the firm goes to its database and identifies individuals who appear to qualify. It sends an e-mail message to these individuals, asking them to log on to a particular site at a particular time scheduled for the group. The firm pays them an incentive for their participation.

The firm develops a discussion guide similar to the one used for a conventional focus group, and a moderator runs the group by typing in questions online for all to see. The group operates in an environment similar to that of a chat room so that all participants see all questions and all responses. The firm captures the complete text of the focus group and makes it available for review after the group has finished.

Online focus groups also allow respondents to view things such as a concept statement, a mockup of a print ad, or a short product demonstration video. The moderator simply provides a URL reference for the respondents to go to in another browser window. One of the risks of doing this, however, is that once respondents open another browser, they have "left the room" and the moderator may lose their attention; researchers must hope that respondents will return within the specified amount of time.

More advanced virtual focus group software reserves a frame (section) of the screen for stimuli to be shown. Here, the moderator has control over what is shown in the stimulus area. The advantage of this approach is that the respondent does not have to do any work to see the stimuli.

WEB COMMUNITY RESEARCH, TEXT MESSAGE–BASED RESEARCH, AND BLOGGING ASSIGNMENTS A Web community is a carefully selected group

ADVANTAGES OF ONLINE FOCUS GROUPS

Many advantages are claimed for cyber groups:

▸ **BETTER PARTICIPATION RATES:** Typically, online focus groups can be conducted over the course of days; once participants are recruited, they are less likely to pull out due to time conflicts.

▸ **COST-EFFECTIVENESS:** Face-to-face focus groups incur costs for facility rental, airfare, hotel, and food. None of these costs is incurred with online focus groups.

▸ **BROAD GEOGRAPHIC SCOPE:** Time is flexible online; respondents can be gathered from all over the world.

▸ **ACCESSIBILITY:** Online focus groups give you access to individuals who otherwise might be difficult to recruit (e.g., business travelers, senior executives, mothers with infants).

▸ **HONESTY:** From behind their screen names, respondents are anonymous to other respondents and tend to talk more freely about issues that might create inhibitions in a face-to-face group.

consumer-generated media (CGM) media that consumers generate and share among themselves

scanner-based research a system for gathering information from a single group of respondents by continuously monitoring the advertising, promotion, and pricing they are exposed to and the things they buy

BehaviorScan a scanner-based research program that tracks the purchases of 3,000 households through store scanners in each research market

of consumers who agree to participate in an ongoing dialogue with a particular corporation.[12] All community interaction takes place on a custom-designed Web site. During the life of the community—which may last anywhere from six months to a year or more—community members respond to questions posed by the corporation on a regular basis. In addition to responding to the corporation's questions, community members talk to one another about topics that are of interest to them.

The popularity and power of Web communities initially came from several key benefits. They:

» **engage customers in a space where they are comfortable, allowing clients to interact with them on a deeper level,**

» **achieve customer-derived innovations,**

» **establish brand advocates who are emotionally invested in a company's success, and**

» **offer real-time results, enabling clients to explore ideas that normal time constraints prohibit.**

Additionally, Web communities help companies create a customer-focused organization by putting employees into direct contact with consumers from the comfort of their own desks, as well as providing cost-effective, flexible research.

Two other relatively recent developments in Internet marketing research are text message–based research and blogging assignments. Text message–based research allows marketers to text a basic question (What are you drinking with lunch today?) and a follow-up to respondents (On a scale of 1 to 9, how much do you like your drink?). Because mobile phones are so prevalent, this type of research can reach most demographics, and it is very quick, resulting in higher feedback rates. For blogging assignments, which are different from consumer-generated blogs (covered below), marketers assign respondents to write a brief blog entry each time they use the product being reviewed. These blogs can span any amount of time and offer marketers a closer look at how consumers interact with products. Additionally, because the technology is relatively inexpensive, assignments can

be given to larger numbers of respondents. These blogs are not public and are viewable only by the respondent and the marketer.[13]

9-4c The Role of Consumer-Generated Media in Marketing Research

Consumer-generated media (CGM) are media that consumers generate themselves and share among themselves. CGM comes from various sources, such as blogs, message boards, review sites, and podcasts. Because it is consumer based, CGM is trusted more than traditional forms of advertising and promotion.[14]

CGM can be influenced but not controlled by marketers. Nielsen BuzzMetrics is the leading marketing research firm tracking CGM. BrandPulse is BuzzMetrics' most popular product. BrandPulse can tell a company how much "buzz" exists, where online discussion is taking place, the tone of the discussion, and which issues are most important. BrandPulse provides timely understanding of the opinions and trends affecting a company or brand. Depending on the information the customer needs, other BuzzMetrics products can go into further detail, such as detecting who would be a good candidate for relationship marketing programs.[15]

9-5 SCANNER-BASED RESEARCH

Scanner-based research is a system for gathering information from a single group of respondents by continuously monitoring the advertising, promotion, and pricing they are exposed to and the things they buy. The variables measured are advertising campaigns, coupons, displays, and product prices. The result is a huge database of marketing efforts and consumer behavior.

The two major scanner-based suppliers are Symphony-IRI Group Inc. and The Nielsen Company. Each has about half of the market. However, SymphonyIRI is the founder of scanner-based research. SymphonyIRI's first product is called **BehaviorScan**. A household panel (a group of 3,000 long-term participants in the research project) has been recruited and maintained in each BehaviorScan town. Each panel member shops with an ID card, which is presented at

InfoScan a scanner-based sales-tracking service for the consumer packaged-goods industry

neuromarketing a field of marketing that studies the body's responses to marketing stimuli

the checkout in scanner-equipped grocery stores and drugstores, allowing SymphonyIRI to track electronically each household's purchases, item by item, over time. It uses microcomputers to measure television viewing in each panel household and can send special commercials to panel member television sets. With such a measure of household purchasing, it is possible to manipulate marketing variables, such as television advertising or consumer promotions, or to introduce a new product and analyze real changes in consumer buying behavior.

SymphonyIRI's most successful product is **InfoScan,** a scanner-based sales-tracking service for the consumer packaged-goods industry. Retail sales, detailed consumer purchasing information (including measurement of store loyalty and total grocery basket expenditures), and promotional activity by manufacturers and retailers are monitored and evaluated for all bar-coded products. Data are collected weekly from more than 70,000 supermarkets, drugstores, and mass merchandisers.[16]

Some companies have begun studying microscopic changes in skin moisture, heart rate, brain waves, and other biometrics to see how consumers react to things such as package designs and ads. This **neuromarketing** approach is a fresh attempt to better understand consumers' responses to promotion and purchase motivations.

9-6 WHEN SHOULD MARKETING RESEARCH BE CONDUCTED?

When managers have several possible solutions to a problem, they should not instinctively call for marketing research. In fact, the first decision to make is whether to conduct marketing research at all.

Some companies have been conducting research in certain markets for many years. Such firms understand the characteristics of target customers and their likes and dislikes about existing products. Under these circumstances, further research would be repetitive and waste money. Procter & Gamble, for example, has extensive knowledge of the coffee market. After it conducted initial taste tests with Folgers Instant Coffee, P&G went into national distribution without further research. Sara Lee followed the same strategy with its frozen croissants, as did Quaker Oats with Chewy Granola Bars. This tactic, however, can backfire. Marketers may think they understand a particular market thoroughly and so bypass market research for a product, only to have the product fail and be withdrawn from the market.

If information were available and free, managers would rarely refuse more, but because marketing information can require a great deal of time and expense to accumulate, they might decide to forgo additional information. Ultimately, the willingness to acquire additional decision-making information depends on managers' perceptions of its quality, price, and timing. Research should be undertaken only when the expected value of the information is greater than the cost of obtaining it.

9-6a Customer Relationship Management

Recall from the beginning of the chapter that databases play a key role in marketing decision support systems. A key subset of most support systems is a customer relationship management system. CRM was introduced in Chapters 1 and 8. The key to managing relationships with customers is the customer relationship management cycle (Exhibit 9.6).

To initiate the CRM cycle, a company must *identify customer relationships with the*

organization. This may simply entail learning who the customers are or where they are located, or it may require more detailed information about the products and services they are using. Next, the company must *understand the interactions with current customers*. Companies accomplish this by collecting data on all types of communications a customer has with the company.

Using this knowledge of its customers and their interactions, the company then *captures relevant customer data on interactions*. Information technology is used not only to enhance the collection of customer data but also to *store and integrate customer data* throughout the company and, ultimately, to "get to know" customers on a more personal level. Customer data are the firsthand responses that are obtained from customers through investigation or by asking direct questions.

Every customer wants to be a company's main priority. Yet not all customers are equally important in the eyes of a business. Consequently, the company must *identify its profitable and unprofitable customers*. Data mining is an analytical process that compiles actionable data about the purchase habits of a firm's current and potential customers. Essentially, data mining transforms customer data into customer information a company can use to make managerial decisions.

Once customer data are analyzed and transformed into usable information, the information must be *leveraged*. The CRM system sends the customer information to all areas of a business because the customer interacts with all aspects of the business. Essentially, the company is trying to enhance customer relationships by getting the right information to the right person in the right place at the right time.

VCC, an international retail construction company, invested in Smartphones and iPads equipped with CRM tools from IBM for VCC's business managers. These tools, such as Mobile Edge, allow business managers to upload data, identify prospects, and even highlight leads for work that is similar to existing projects, which encourages efficient lead follow-up.[17] In addition to basic demographic information, the types of information gathered include how frequently

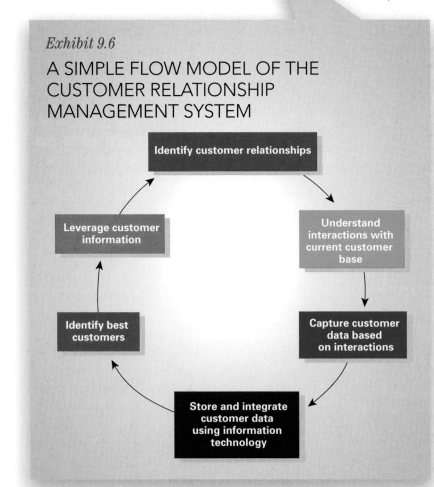

Exhibit 9.6

A SIMPLE FLOW MODEL OF THE CUSTOMER RELATIONSHIP MANAGEMENT SYSTEM

- Identify customer relationships
- Understand interactions with current customer base
- Capture customer data based on interactions
- Store and integrate customer data using information technology
- Identify best customers
- Leverage customer information

© Cengage Learning

consumers purchase goods, how much they purchase, and how far they drive.

IBM's mobile technologies enable field managers to quickly locate and understand all previous interactions with a client without memorizing printouts or guessing in the field. Mobile technology gives VCC managers access to key information that allows them to answer customer queries and take specific courses of action based on previous decisions.

After meeting with a potential or current client, VCC business managers can immediately upload information about the meeting, including decisions reached, proposals made, and data for the project, directly to the construction company's central database. VCC works with IBM to maintain a well-organized CRM app so the business managers in the field have the most relevant information to maintain customer relationships.

After VCC secures a new job, the iExtensions app flags similar opportunities as high priorities. Those flags are relayed to other business managers to pursue as well-qualified leads. VCC has found that getting timely customer information to its business managers has been profitable in several ways: New client business is up 40 percent; employees are working 400 fewer hours each month; and VCC has added clients in government, schools, and hospitals.[18]

HIGH PRIORITY

© iStockphoto.com/Sergey Galushko

competitive intelligence (CI) an intelligence system that helps managers assess their competition and vendors in order to become more efficient and effective competitors

9-7 COMPETITIVE INTELLIGENCE

Derived from military intelligence, competitive intelligence is an important tool for helping a firm overcome a competitor's advantage. Specifically, competitive intelligence can help identify the advantage and play a major role in determining how it was achieved.

Competitive intelligence (CI) helps managers assess their competitors and their vendors in order to become more efficient and effective competitors. Intelligence is analyzed information. It becomes decision-making intelligence when it has implications for the organization. For example, a primary competitor may have plans to introduce a product with performance standards equal to those of the company gathering the information but with a 15 percent cost advantage. The new product will reach the market in eight months. This intelligence has important decision-making and policy consequences for management. CI and environmental scanning (see Chapter 2) combine to create marketing intelligence. Marketing intelligence is then used as input into a marketing decision support system.

The Internet is an important resource for gathering CI, but noncomputer sources can be equally valuable. Some examples include company salespeople, industry experts, CI consultants, government agencies, Uniform Commercial Code filings, suppliers, periodicals, the Yellow Pages, and industry trade shows.

STUDY TOOLS 9

↑ LOCATED AT BACK OF THE TEXTBOOK

☐ Rip out Chapter Review Card

LOCATED AT WWW.CENGAGE.COM/LOGIN

☐ Review Key Terms Flashcards (print or online)

☐ Download audio and visual summaries to review on the go

☐ Complete both Practice Quizzes to prepare for tests

☐ Play "Beat the Clock" and "Quizbowl" to master concepts

☐ Complete "Crossword Puzzle" to review key terms

☐ Watch Video on "The Nederlander Organization" for a real company example

10-1 WHAT IS A PRODUCT?

The product offering, the heart of an organization's marketing program, is usually the starting point in creating a marketing mix. A marketing manager cannot determine a price, design a promotion strategy, or create a distribution channel until the firm has a product to sell. Moreover, an excellent distribution channel, a persuasive promotion campaign, and a fair price have no value when the product offering is poor or inadequate.

⌈The product is the starting point in creating a marketing mix.⌋

product everything, both favorable and unfavorable, that a person receives in an exchange

business product (industrial product) a product used to manufacture other goods or services, to facilitate an organization's operations, or to resell to other customers

consumer product a product bought to satisfy an individual's personal wants

A **product** may be defined as everything, both favorable and unfavorable, that a person receives in an exchange. A product may be a tangible good like a pair of shoes, a service like a haircut, an idea like "don't litter," or any combination of these three. Packaging, style, color, options, and size are some typical product features. Just as important are intangibles such as service, the seller's image, the manufacturer's reputation, and the way consumers believe others will view the product.

To most people, the term *product* means a tangible good. However, services and ideas are also products. (Chapter 12 focuses specifically on the unique aspects of marketing services.) The marketing process identified in Chapter 1 is the same whether the product marketed is a good, a service, an idea, or some combination of these.

10-2 TYPES OF CONSUMER PRODUCTS

Products can be classified as either business (industrial) or consumer products, depending on the buyer's intentions. The key distinction between the two types of products is their intended use. If the intended use is a business purpose, the product is classified as a business or industrial product. As explained in Chapter 7, a **business product**, or **industrial product**, is used to manufacture other goods or services, to facilitate an organization's operations, or to resell to other customers. A **consumer product** is bought to satisfy an individual's personal wants. Sometimes the same item can be classified as either a business or a consumer product, depending on its intended use. Examples include lightbulbs, pencils and paper, and computers.

Chapter *10*
Product Concepts

After you finish this chapter go to
p177 *for* **STUDY TOOLS** ▭ ------→

We need to know about product classifications because business and consumer products are marketed differently. They are marketed to different target markets and tend to use different distribution, promotion, and pricing strategies.

Chapter 7 examined seven categories of business products: major equipment, accessory equipment, component parts, processed materials, raw materials, supplies, and services. This chapter examines an effective way of categorizing consumer products. Although there are several ways to classify them, the most popular approach includes these four types: convenience products, shopping products, specialty products, and unsought products. This approach classifies products according to how much effort is normally used to shop for them.

10-2a Convenience Products

A **convenience product** is a relatively inexpensive item that merits little shopping effort—that is, a consumer is unwilling to shop extensively for such an item. Candy, soft drinks, aspirin, small hardware items, dry cleaning, and car washes fall into the convenience product category.

Consumers buy convenience products regularly, usually without much planning. Nevertheless, consumers do know the brand names of popular convenience products, such as Coca-Cola, Bayer aspirin, and Old Spice deodorant. Convenience products normally require wide distribution in order to sell sufficient quantities to meet profit goals. For example, the gum brand Extra is available everywhere, including Walmart, Walgreens, gas stations, newsstands, and vending machines.

10-2b Shopping Products

A **shopping product** is usually more expensive than a convenience product and is found in fewer stores. Consumers usually buy a shopping product only after comparing several brands or stores on style, practicality, price, and lifestyle compatibility. They are willing to invest some effort into this process to get the desired benefits.

There are two types of shopping products: homogeneous and heterogeneous. Consumers perceive *homogeneous* shopping products as basically similar—for example, washers, dryers, refrigerators, and televisions. With homogeneous shopping products, consumers typically look for the lowest-priced brand that has the desired features. For example, they might compare Kenmore, Whirlpool, and General Electric refrigerators.

In contrast, consumers perceive *heterogeneous* shopping products as essentially different—for example, furniture, clothing, housing, and universities. Consumers often have trouble comparing heterogeneous shopping products because the prices, quality, and features vary so much. The benefit of comparing heterogeneous shopping products is "finding the best product or brand for me"; this decision is often highly individual. For example, it would be difficult to compare a small, private college with a large, public university.

10-2c Specialty Products

When consumers search extensively for a particular item and are very reluctant to accept substitutes, that item is a **specialty product**. Omega watches, Rolls-Royce automobiles, Bose speakers, Ruth's Chris Steak House, and highly specialized forms of medical care are generally considered specialty products.

Marketers of specialty products often use selective, status-conscious advertising to maintain a product's exclusive image. Distribution is often limited to one or a very few outlets in a geographic area. Brand names and quality of service are often very important.

10-2d Unsought Products

A product unknown to the potential buyer or a known product that the buyer does not actively seek is referred to as an **unsought product**. New products fall into this category until advertising and distribution increase consumer awareness of them.

Some goods are always marketed as unsought items, especially needed products we do not like to think about or care to spend money on. Insurance, burial plots, and similar items require aggressive personal selling and highly persuasive advertising. Salespeople actively seek leads to potential buyers. Because consumers usually do not seek out this type of product, the company must go directly to them through a salesperson, direct mail, or direct response advertising.

SEEKING THE UNSOUGHT: GREEN BURIALS

The funeral industry is not known for its innovation. And as burial is not a pleasant event to contemplate, it's not surprising that many funeral homes are not hitting the streets with new, exciting burial ideas. Except, several are. There is a growing demand for eco-friendly **human disposal methods,** and they are increasingly creative. Some are raising legal battles, such as alkaline hydrolysis, which liquefies human remains with only a fraction of the carbon emissions produced by cremation. Other options span from cheesy to ancestral. Design-your-own coffins are made from recycled paper and wood pulp and have themed graphics like sports, music and video games. Cremated remains can also be mixed into cement and thrown into the ocean to start coral reefs. And in a new twist on a family plot, up to fifteen members of a family can be buried at the dip line of a "family tree" to provide nutrients to the tree.

Source: "Eco-Funerals," *Bloomberg Businessweek,* November 7–13, 2011, 102–103.

© Winston Link/Shutterstock.com / © iStockphoto.com/Bill Noll

10-3 PRODUCT ITEMS, LINES, AND MIXES

Rarely does a company sell a single product. More often, it sells a variety of things. A **product item** is a specific version of a product that can be designated as a distinct offering among an organization's products. Campbell's Cream of Chicken soup is an example of a product item (see Exhibit 10.1 on the next page).

A group of closely related product items is called a **product line**. For example, the column in Exhibit 10.1 titled "Soups" represents one of Campbell's product lines. Different container sizes and shapes also distinguish items in a product line. Diet Coke, for example, is available in cans and various plastic containers. Each size and each container are separate product items.

An organization's **product mix** includes all the products it sells. All Campbell's products—soups, sauces, frozen entrées, beverages, and biscuits—constitute its product mix. Each product item in the product mix may require a separate marketing strategy. In some cases, however, product lines and even entire product mixes share some marketing strategy components. UPS promotes its various services by demonstrating its commitment to its line of work with the tagline "We [heart] Logistics." Organizations derive several benefits from organizing related items into product lines:

▸▸ **ADVERTISING ECONOMIES:** Product lines provide economies of scale in advertising. Several products can be advertised under the umbrella of the line. Campbell's can talk about its soup being " M'm, M'm, Good!" and promote the entire line.

▸▸ **PACKAGE UNIFORMITY:** A product line can benefit from package uniformity. All packages in the line may have a common look and still keep their individual identities. Again, Campbell's soup is a good example.

▸▸ **STANDARDIZED COMPONENTS:** Product lines allow firms to standardize components, thus reducing manufacturing and inventory costs. For example, General Motors uses the same parts on many automobile makes and models.

▸▸ **EFFICIENT SALES AND DISTRIBUTION:** A product line enables sales personnel for companies like Procter & Gamble to provide a full range of choices to customers. Distributors and retailers are often more inclined to stock the company's products if it offers a full line. Transportation and warehousing costs are likely to be lower for a product line than for a collection of individual items.

▸▸ **EQUIVALENT QUALITY:** Purchasers usually expect and believe that all products in a line are about equal in quality. Consumers expect that all Campbell's soups and all Gillette razors will be of similar quality.

Product mix width (or breadth) refers to the number of product lines an organization offers. In Exhibit 10.1, for example, the width of Campbell's product mix is five product lines. **Product line depth** is the number of product items in a product line. As shown in Exhibit 10.1, the sauces product line consists of four product items; the frozen entrée product line includes three product items.

Firms increase the *width* of their product mix to diversify risk. To generate sales and boost profits, firms spread risk across many product lines rather than depend on only one or two. Firms also widen their product mix to capitalize on established reputations. Patagonia, a popular outdoor clothing brand and retailer, recently launched a line of Salmon Jerky as the first products in its Patagonia Provisions line. Patagonia is hoping to provide food for climbers and other outdoor enthusiasts based on its reputation for high-quality, sustainable products.[1]

Firms increase the *depth* of their product lines to attract buyers with different preferences, to increase sales and profits by further segmenting the market, to capitalize on economies of scale in production and marketing, and to even out seasonal sales patterns.

10-3a Adjustments to Product Items, Lines, and Mixes

Over time, firms change product items, lines, and mixes to take advantage of new technical or product developments or to respond to changes in the environment. They may adjust by modifying products, repositioning products, or extending or contracting product lines.

PRODUCT MODIFICATION Marketing managers must decide if and when to modify existing products. **Product modification** changes one or more of a product's characteristics:

▸ **QUALITY MODIFICATION: change in a product's dependability or durability. Reducing a product's quality may let the manufacturer lower the price and appeal to target markets unable to afford the original product. Conversely, increasing quality can help the firm compete with rival firms. For example, Barnes & Noble offers a color version of its NOOK that runs Android apps, allowing it to compete with tablet and netbook makers, such as Dell and Asus. Increasing quality can also result in increased brand loyalty, greater ability to raise prices, or new opportunities for market segmentation.**

▸ **FUNCTIONAL MODIFICATION: change in a product's versatility, effectiveness, convenience, or safety. Men's swim trunks have been the target of recent makeovers as men are invited to office**

Exhibit 10.1

CAMPBELL'S PRODUCT LINES AND PRODUCT MIX

	Width of the Product Mix				
DEPTH (Depth of the Product Lines)	**Soups**	**Sauces**	**Frozen Entrées**	**Beverages**	**Biscuits**
	Cream of Chicken	Cheddar Cheese	Macaroni and Cheese	Tomato Juice	Arnott's:
	Cream of Mushroom	Alfredo	Golden Chicken Fricassee	V-Fusion Juices	Water Cracker
	Vegetable Beef	Italian Tomato	Traditional Lasagna	V8 Splash	Butternut Snap
	Chicken Noodle	Hollandaise			Chocolate Ripple
	Tomato				Spicy Fruit Roll
	Bean with Bacon				Chocolate Wheaten
	Minestrone				
	Clam Chowder				
	French Onion				
	and more . . .				

Source: Campbell's Web site: www.campbellsoup.com.

Women's swimming suits are known for coming in wide VARIETIES of styles from functional to poolside lounging

functions or weddings that involve water activities. For business professionals or men uncomfortable in oversized board shorts, companies like Lands' End are making swim trunks a little shorter and with narrower cuts, which cuts down on ballooning when entering the water and transitions more easily from water to lunch because they look more like normal shorts. These changes are not only for style but offer added convenience to men.[2]

▸ **STYLE MODIFICATION:** aesthetic product change rather than a quality or functional change. Clothing and auto manufacturers commonly use style modifications to motivate customers to replace products before they are worn out.

Planned obsolescence is a term commonly used to describe the practice of modifying products so that those that have already been sold become obsolete before they actually need replacement. For example, products such as printers and cell phones become obsolete because technology changes so quickly.

Some argue that planned obsolescence is wasteful; some claim it is unethical. Marketers respond that consumers favor style modifications because they like changes in the appearance of goods such as clothing and cars. Marketers also contend that consumers, not manufacturers and marketers, decide when styles are obsolete.

REPOSITIONING Repositioning, as Chapter 8 explained, involves changing consumers' perceptions of a brand. Laundry detergent Woolite is trying to reposition itself as an everyday laundry detergent that will benefit all fabrics, rather than being just for delicate blacks or handwashing. Its new campaign, directed by horror film director and metal musician Rob Zombie, mimics creepy horror films and shows a deformed man "torturing" clothes by stretching, shrinking, and exposing them to bright lights. The company says the goal is to interest women ages twenty-five to forty by recalling the horror films of their youth. The ads stand out for being dark and bleak in an industry characterized by Snuggle the bear and cheerful women washing bright clothing.[3] Changing demographics, declining sales, or changes in the social environment often motivate firms to reposition established brands. For example, HTC, a Smartphone maker that has lost significant market share to Apple and Samsung over the past year, has recently purchased majority shares in several music and gaming companies, including Beats Electronics, the popular headphone company. Realizing that making Smartphones will be a losing battle for market share, HTC is hoping to expand its brand beyond gadgets and to become a technology icon that offers a suite of services to device owners, a more ubiquitous part of people's entertainment lives.[4]

PRODUCT LINE EXTENSIONS A **product line extension** occurs when a company's management decides to add products to an existing product line in order to compete more broadly in the industry. Hasbro and Mattel have added a series of games using the Scrabble name, some without boards or tiles, such as Scrabble Slam, and a version with proper noun usage called Scrabble Trickster. Hasbro, through a licensing agreement with USAopoly, has also expanded category scrabble boards, such as Book Lovers Scrabble and Gardening Scrabble, where players receive extra points for playing words associated with the theme.[5]

A company can add too many products, or demand can change for the type of products that were introduced over time. When this happens, a

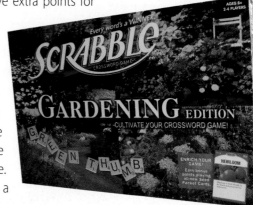

planned obsolescence the practice of modifying products so those that have already been sold become obsolete before they actually need replacement

product line extension adding additional products to an existing product line in order to compete more broadly in the industry

brand a name, term, symbol, design, or combination thereof that identifies a seller's products and differentiates them from competitors' products

brand name that part of a brand that can be spoken, including letters, words, and numbers

brand mark the elements of a brand that cannot be spoken

brand equity the value of company and brand names

global brand a brand that obtains at least a third of its earnings from outside its home country, is recognizable outside its home base of customers, and has publicly available marketing and financial data

brand loyalty consistent preference for one brand over all others

product line is overextended. Product lines can be overextended when:

» **Some products in the line do not contribute to profits because of low sales or cannibalize sales of other items in the line.**

» **Manufacturing or marketing resources are disproportionately allocated to slow-moving products.**

» **Some items in the line are obsolete because of new-product entries in the line or new products offered by competitors.**

PRODUCT LINE CONTRACTION Sometimes, marketers can get carried away with product extensions. (Does the world really need thirty-one varieties of Head & Shoulders shampoo?) Contracting product lines is a strategic way to deal with overextension. For example, when Procter & Gamble's Pantene brand lost 9 percent of sales in 2009, P&G marketing research showed that shoppers were overwhelmed by the wall of white. Pantene had 165 different products grouped into fourteen collections. In an effort to regain the lost sales, P&G cut product offerings to 120 items in four groups.[6]

Three major benefits are likely when a firm contracts overextended product lines. First, resources become concentrated on the most important products. Second, managers no longer waste resources trying to improve the sales and profits of poorly performing products. Third, new-product items have a greater chance of being successful because more financial and human resources are available to manage them.

10-4 BRANDING

The success of any business or consumer product depends in part on the target market's ability to distinguish one product from another. Branding is the main tool marketers use to distinguish their products from those of the competition.

A **brand** is a name, term, symbol, design, or combination thereof that identifies a seller's products and differentiates them from competitors' products. A **brand name** is

that part of a brand that can be spoken, including letters (GM, YMCA), words (Chevrolet), and numbers (WD-40, 7-Eleven). The elements of a brand that cannot be spoken are called the **brand mark**—for example, the well-known Mercedes-Benz and Delta Air Lines symbols.

10-4a Benefits of Branding

Branding has three main purposes: product identification, repeat sales, and new-product sales. The most important purpose is *product identification*. Branding allows marketers to distinguish their products from all others. Many brand names are familiar to consumers and indicate quality.

The term **brand equity** refers to the value of company and brand names. A brand that has high awareness, perceived quality, and brand loyalty among customers has high brand equity. Starbucks, Subaru, and Apple are companies with high brand equity. A brand with strong brand equity is a valuable asset. For example, Oprah Winfrey leverages her personal brand (her name) to sell her magazines; create shows (Dr. Phil owes his celebrity to her); and develop schools, charities, and cable networks.[7]

The term **global brand** refers to a brand that obtains at least a third of its earnings from outside its home country, is recognizable outside its home base of customers, and has publicly available marketing and financial data. Yum! Brands, which owns Pizza Hut, KFC, and Taco Bell, is a good example of a company that has developed strong global brands. Yum! believes that it has to adapt its restaurants to local tastes and different cultural and political climates. In Japan, for instance, KFC sells tempura crispy strips. In northern England, KFC focuses on gravy and potatoes, and in Thailand it offers rice with soy or sweet chili sauce.

The best generator of *repeat sales* is satisfied customers. Branding helps consumers identify products they wish to buy again and avoid those they do not. **Brand loyalty**, a consistent preference for one brand over all others, is quite high in some product categories. More than half the consumers in product categories such as cigarettes, mayonnaise, toothpaste, coffee, headache remedies, bath soap, and ketchup are loyal to one brand. Many students go to college and purchase the same brands they used at home rather than choosing by price. Brand identity is essential to developing brand loyalty.

The third main purpose of branding is to *facilitate new-product sales*. Having a well-known and respected company and brand name is extremely useful when introducing new products.

FAGE TOTAL
STRAWBERRY YOGURT:

$1.00/6 OZ.

VERSUS

SAFEWAY'S
OPEN NATURE
STRAWBERRY YOGURT:

$1.39/6 OZ.

© Mny-Jhee/Shutterstock.com

10-4b Branding Strategies

Firms face complex branding decisions. Firms may choose to follow a policy of using manufacturers' brands, private (distributor) brands, or both. In either case, they must then decide among a policy of individual branding (different brands for different products), family branding (common names for different products), or a combination of individual branding and family branding.

MANUFACTURERS' BRANDS VERSUS PRIVATE BRANDS The brand name of a manufacturer—such as La-Z-Boy or Fruit of the Loom—is called a **manufacturer's brand**. Sometimes "national brand" is used as a synonym for "manufacturer's brand." This term is not always accurate, however, because many manufacturers serve only regional markets. Using "manufacturer's brand" precisely defines the brand's owner.

A **private brand**, also known as a private label or store brand, is a brand name owned by a wholesaler or a retailer. Target's Archer Farms brand is a popular private label. Walgreens sells Walgreens brand products, and this year it is advertising them on television and with several bloggers. The company emphasizes the comparison of its private label brands to brand name quality by offering a satisfaction guarantee.[8] Private labels are increasing in popularity and price as customers develop loyalties to particular stores brands, such as Archer Farms. Today, private label products have a 29 percent market share of the food and beverage market—nearly ten points higher than ten years ago.[9]

Retailers love consumers' greater acceptance of private brands. Because overhead is low and there are no marketing costs, private label products bring 10 percent higher profit margins, on average, than manufacturers' brands. More than that, a trusted store brand can differentiate a chain from its competitors. Exhibit 10.2 illustrates key issues that wholesalers and retailers should consider in deciding whether to sell manufacturers' brands or private brands. Many firms offer a combination of both. Instead of marketing private brands

manufacturer's brand the brand name of a manufacturer

private brand a brand name owned by a wholesaler or a retailer

---

Exhibit 10.2

COMPARISON OF MANUFACTURERS' AND PRIVATE BRANDS FROM THE RESELLER'S PERSPECTIVE

Key Advantages of Carrying Manufacturers' Brands	Key Advantages of Carrying Private Brands
• Heavy advertising to the consumer by manufacturers such as Procter & Gamble helps develop strong consumer loyalties.	• A wholesaler or retailer can usually earn higher profits on its own brand. In addition, because the private brand is exclusive, there is less pressure to mark down the price to meet competition.
• Well-known manufacturers' brands, such as Fisher-Price, can attract new customers and enhance the dealer's (wholesaler's or retailer's) prestige.	• A manufacturer can decide to drop a brand or a reseller at any time or even become a direct competitor to its dealers.
• Many manufacturers offer rapid delivery, enabling the dealer to carry less inventory.	• A private brand ties the customer to the wholesaler or retailer. A person who wants a DieHard battery must go to Sears.
• If a dealer happens to sell a manufacturer's brand of poor quality, the customer may simply switch brands and remain loyal to the dealer.	• Wholesalers and retailers have no control over the intensity of distribution of manufacturers' brands. Walmart store managers don't have to worry about competing with other sellers of Sam's American Choice products or Ol' Roy dog food. They know that these brands are sold only in Walmart and Sam's Club stores.

© Cengage Learning

as cheaper and inferior to manufacturers' brands, many retailers are creating and promoting their own **captive brands**. These brands carry no evidence of the store's affiliation, are manufactured by a third party, and are sold exclusively at the chains. This strategy allows the retailer to ask a price similar or equal to manufacturers' brands, and the captive brands are typically displayed alongside mainstream products. For example, Simple Truth is Kroger's line of natural and organic products designed to meet consumer desire for upscale brands. It currently sells a half gallon of soy milk for twenty cents more than Silk, the popular manufacturer's brand.[10]

INDIVIDUAL BRANDS VERSUS FAMILY BRANDS
Many companies use different brand names for different products, a practice referred to as **individual branding**. Companies use individual brands when their products vary greatly in use or performance. For instance, it would not make sense to use the same brand name for a pair of dress socks and a baseball bat. Procter & Gamble targets different segments of the laundry detergent market with Bold, Cheer, Dash, Dreft, Era, Gain, Ivory Snow, Oxydol, Solo, and Tide.

In contrast, a company that markets several different products under the same brand name is practicing **family branding**. Jack Daniel's family brand includes whiskey, coffee, mustard, playing cards, and clothing lines.

CO-BRANDING Co-branding entails placing two or more brand names on a product or its package. Three common types of co-branding are ingredient branding, cooperative branding, and complementary branding. *Ingredient branding* identifies the brand of a part that makes up the product—for example, Procter & Gamble has developed Mr. Clean Disinfecting Wipes with Febreze (a scent) Freshness. Febreze is also co-branded with Tide, Bounce, and Downy.[11] *Cooperative branding* occurs when two brands receiving equal treatment (in the context of an advertisement) borrow from each other's brand equity. A promotional contest jointly sponsored by Ramada Inn, American Express, and United Airlines used cooperative branding. Guests at Ramada who paid with an American Express card were automatically entered in a contest and

GET BETTER, FASTER.
GET FREE.

NIKE FREE
NIKE.COM/FREE

Image courtesy of The Advertising Archives

This ad promotes Nike + iPod software that allows walkers and runners to keep track of the distance and pace of workouts.

were eligible to win more than a hundred getaways for two at any Ramada in the continental United States and round-trip airfare from United. Finally, with *complementary branding*, products are advertised or marketed together to suggest usage, such as a spirits brand (Seagram's) and a compatible mixer (7-Up).

Co-branding is a useful strategy when a combination of brand names enhances the prestige or perceived value of a product or when it benefits brand owners and users. For example, people perceive a higher value for a Glad trash bag that has Febreze between its two layers of plastic than for a Ruffies trash bag that uses baking soda to block odor.[12] Co-branding may be used to increase a company's presence in markets where it has little or no market share.

10-4c Trademarks

A **trademark** is the exclusive right to use a brand or part of a brand. Others are prohibited from using the brand without permission. A **service mark** performs the same function for services, such as H&R Block and Weight

The Tree design, LITTLE TREES and CAR-FRESHNER are trademarks of Julius Sämann Ltd. and are used with permission. © 2011 Julius Sämann Ltd.

Watchers. Parts of a brand or other product identification may qualify for trademark protection. Some examples are:

- **Sounds, such as the MGM lion's roar.**
- **Shapes, such as the Jeep front grille and the Coca-Cola bottle.**
- **Ornamental colors or designs, such as the decoration on Nike tennis shoes, the black-and-copper color combination of a Duracell battery, Levi's small tag on the left side of the rear pocket of its jeans, or the cutoff black cone on the top of Cross pens.**
- **Catchy phrases, such as Prudential's "Own a piece of the rock," Mountain Dew's "Do the Dew," and Nike's "Just Do It!"**
- **Abbreviations, such as Bud, Coke, or The Met.**

It is important to understand that trademark rights come from use rather than registration. An intent-to-use application is filed with the U.S. Patent and Trademark Office, and a company must have a genuine intention to use the mark when it files and must actually use the mark within three years of the granting of the application. Trademark protection typically lasts for ten years.[13] To renew the trademark, the company must prove it is using the mark. Rights to a trademark last as long as the mark is used. Normally, if the firm does not use it for two years, the trademark is considered abandoned, and a new user can claim exclusive ownership of the mark.

In November 1999, legislation went into effect that explicitly applies trademark law to the online world. This law includes financial penalties for those who violate trademarks or register an otherwise trademarked term as a domain name.[14]

Companies that fail to protect their trademarks face the possibility that their product names will become generic. A **generic product name** identifies a product by class or type and cannot be trademarked. Former brand names that were not sufficiently protected by their owners and were subsequently declared to be generic product names by U.S. courts include aspirin, cellophane, linoleum, thermos, kerosene, monopoly, cola, and shredded wheat.

Companies such as Rolls-Royce, Cross, Xerox, Levi Strauss, Frigidaire, and McDonald's aggressively enforce their trademarks. Rolls-Royce, Coca-Cola, and Xerox even run newspaper and magazine ads stating that their names are trademarks and should not be used as descriptive or generic terms. When Apple introduced its cloud-based storage services, iCloud, a company called iCloud Communications, which offers similar services and has been in business since 2005, filed a trademark infringement lawsuit against Apple. iCloud Communications claims that Apple's iCloud not only is confusing potential customers but is actively detracting from iCloud Communications' business.[15]

To try to stem the number of trademark infringements, violations carry steep penalties. Despite the risk of incurring a penalty, infringement lawsuits are still common. Serious conflict can occur when brand names resemble one another too closely. Bacardi's Havana Club rum won a trademark victory over Pernod Ricard in 2010. Pernod also sells Havana Club rum outside the United States. Bacardi only sells Havana Club rum in the United States and Puerto Rico, where it is distilled, so there is little brand overlap in their respective markets, but the trademark dispute has been going on since 1996. Pernod filed an appeal after the 2010 decision.[16]

Companies must also contend with fake or unauthorized brands. Knockoffs of trademarked clothing lines are

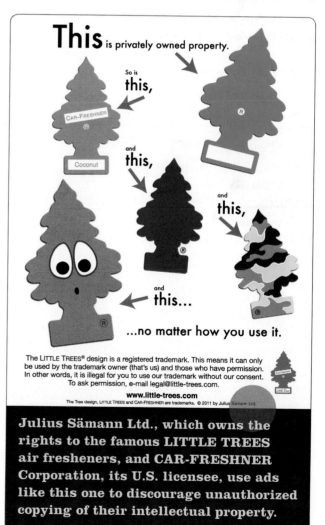

Julius Sämann Ltd., which owns the rights to the famous LITTLE TREES air fresheners, and CAR-FRESHNER Corporation, its U.S. licensee, use ads like this one to discourage unauthorized copying of their intellectual property.

generic product name identifies a product by class or type and cannot be trademarked easy to find in cheap shops all over the world, and loose imitations are found in some reputable department stores as well. Today, whole stores are faked in China. Apple stores selling real iPhones and iPads in stores with sparse décor and bright lighting may seem real but are frequently imitating the real deal. Ikea and Dairy Queen (the imitation store is called Dairy Fairy) are both victims of knockoff stores mimicking their layouts and products.[17]

In Europe, you can sue counterfeiters only if your brand, logo, or trademark is formally registered. Until recently, formal registration was required in each country in which a company sought protection. A company can now register its trademark in all European Union (EU) member countries with one application.

10-5 PACKAGING

Packages have always served a practical function— that is, they hold contents together and protect goods as they move through the distribution channel. Today, however, packaging is also a container for promoting the product and making it easier and safer to use.

10-5a Packaging Functions

The three most important functions of packaging are to contain and protect products; promote products; and facilitate the storage, use, and convenience of products. A fourth function of packaging that is becoming increasingly important is to facilitate recycling and reduce environmental damage.

CONTAINING AND PROTECTING PRODUCTS The most obvious function of packaging is to contain products that are liquid, granular, or otherwise divisible. Packaging also enables manufacturers, wholesalers, and retailers to market products in specific quantities, such as ounces.

Physical protection is another obvious function of packaging. Most products are handled several times between the time they are manufactured, harvested, or otherwise produced and the time they are consumed or used. Many products are also shipped, stored, and inspected several times between production and consumption. Some, like milk, need to be refrigerated. Others, like beer, are sensitive to light. Still others, like medicines and bandages, need to be kept sterile. Packages protect products from breakage, evaporation, spillage, spoilage, light, heat, cold, infestation, and many other conditions.

PROMOTING PRODUCTS Packaging does more than identify the brand, list the ingredients, specify features, and give directions. A package differentiates a product from competing products and may associate a new product with a family of other products from the same manufacturer. However, some products packaging lacks useful information, like lightbulbs. GE is looking to remedy that by adding a lighting facts label to all its lighting packages. The label provides information about the bulb's brightness (lumens), energy cost, life span, light appearance, energy used, and mercury content. The label is one step in simplifying the lightbulb shopping process and will be used by all lighting companies in the future.[18]

© Terri Miller/E-Visual Communications, Inc.

Packages use designs, colors, shapes, and materials to try to influence consumers' perceptions and buying behavior. For example, marketing research shows that health-conscious consumers are likely to think that any food is probably good for them as long as it comes in green packaging. Packaging can also influence consumer perceptions of quality and/or prestige. Safeway has introduced a new line of snack food called Snack Artist, which includes bags of cheese curls and tortilla chips in resealable bags—something the other snack food companies don't have.[19]

FACILITATING STORAGE, USE, AND CONVENIENCE Wholesalers and retailers prefer packages that are easy to ship, store, and stock on shelves. They also like packages that protect products, prevent spoilage or breakage, and extend the product's shelf life.

Consumers' requirements for storage, use, and convenience cover many dimensions. Consumers are constantly seeking items that are easy to handle, open, and reclose, although some consumers want packages that are tamperproof or childproof. Research indicates that hard-to-open packages are among consumers' top complaints—especially when it comes to clamshell electronics packaging. As oil prices force the cost of plastics used in packaging skyward, companies such as Target and Walmart are pushing suppliers to do away with excess packaging. Clamshell packaged items have been the first to experience repackaging—lightbulbs, Swiss Army knives, USB cables, and scissors are being packed with less plastic, making them easier to access and keeping costs down.[20] Such packaging innovations as zipper tear strips, hinged lids, tab slots, screw-on tops, and pour spouts were introduced to solve these and other problems. Easy openings are especially important for kids and aging baby boomers.

Some firms use packaging to segment markets. For example, a C&H sugar carton with an easy-to-pour, reclosable top is targeted to consumers who don't do a lot of baking and are willing to pay at least twenty cents more for the package. Different-sized packages appeal to heavy, moderate, and light users. Campbell's soup is packaged in single-serving cans aimed at the elderly and singles market segments. Packaging convenience can increase a product's utility and, therefore, its market share and profits.

FACILITATING RECYCLING AND REDUCING ENVIRONMENTAL DAMAGE One of the most important packaging issues today is eco-consciousness, a trend that has recently been in and out of consumer and media attention. Studies conflict as to whether consumers will pay more for eco-friendly packaging, though consumers repeatedly iterate the desire to purchase such products. One New Jersey marketing firm released a study revealing that, while customers reported increased interest in buying products made from recycled materials, only 17 percent said that they checked a package to see if it was recyclable before buying it.[21] Some firms use their packaging to target environmentally concerned market segments. Dell has recently begun growing its own packaging. The company seeds agricultural waste such as cotton hulls with mushroom spores, which grow into cushions in five to ten days. The result is a dense cushion that offers enough protection to ship heavy servers and desktop computers. Once the product ships, the packaging is completely compostable.[22]

© B.G. Smith/Shutterstock.com

10-5b Labeling

An integral part of any package is its label. Labeling generally takes one of two forms: persuasive or informational. **Persuasive labeling** focuses on a promotional theme or logo, and consumer information is secondary. Note that the standard promotional claims—such as "new," "improved," and "super"—are no longer very persuasive. Consumers have been saturated with "newness" and thus discount these claims.

Informational labeling, in contrast, is designed to help consumers make proper product selections and lower their cognitive dissonance after the purchase. Most major furniture manufacturers affix labels to their wares that explain the products' construction features, such as type of frame, number of coils, and fabric characteristics. The Nutritional Labeling and Education Act of 1990 mandated detailed nutritional information on most food packages and standards for health claims on food packaging. An important outcome of this legislation has been guidelines from the Food and Drug Administration for using terms such as *low fat*, *light*, *reduced cholesterol*, *low sodium*, *low calorie*, *low carb*, and *fresh*. Getting the right information is very important to consumers, and one company wants to help consumers shop smart. NuVal LLC ranks supermarket products on a scale from 1 to 100 based on nutritional information presented in on-pack labels. A higher score indicates higher nutritional value. The NuVal score is placed on the shelf label next to the price in stores paying a licensing fee. The scores allow consumers to easily compare the nutritional elements of packaged foods.[23]

GREENWASHING There are numerous products in every product category that use *greenwashing* to try and sell products. Greenwashing is when a product or company attempts to give the impression of environmental friendliness whether or not it is environmentally friendly.

As consumer demand for "green" products appeared to escalate, "green" certifications proliferated. Companies could create their own certifications and logos, resulting in more than 300 possible certification labels, ranging in price from free to thousands of dollars. Consumer distrust and confusion caused the Federal Trade Commission to issue new rules. Starting in late 2011, new regulations apply to labeling products with "green" certification logos. If the same company that produced the product performed the certification, that relationship must be clearly marked. This benefits organizations such as Green Seal, which uses unbiased, third-party scientists and experts to verify claims about emissions or biodegradability, and hopes to increase consumer confidence in "green" products.[24]

persuasive labeling a type of package labeling that focuses on a promotional theme or logo, and consumer information is secondary

informational labeling a type of package labeling designed to help consumers make proper product selections and lower their cognitive dissonance after the purchase

universal product codes (UPCs) a series of thick and thin vertical lines (bar codes), readable by computerized optical scanners, that represent numbers used to track products

The labels on Coca-Cola products in China are easily recognizable despite using Chinese characters.

10-5c Universal Product Codes

The **universal product codes (UPCs)** that appear on most items in supermarkets and other high-volume outlets were first introduced in 1974. Because the numerical codes appear as a series of thick and thin vertical lines, they are often called *bar codes*. The lines are read by computerized optical scanners that match codes with brand names, package sizes, and prices. They also print information on cash register tapes and help retailers rapidly and accurately prepare records of customer purchases, control inventories, and track sales. The UPC system and scanners are also used in scanner-based research (see Chapter 9).

10-6 GLOBAL ISSUES IN BRANDING AND PACKAGING

When planning to enter a foreign market with an existing product, a firm has three options for handling the brand name:

▸ **ONE BRAND NAME EVERYWHERE:**
This strategy is useful when the company markets mainly one product and the brand name does not have negative connotations in any local market. The Coca-Cola Company uses a one-brand-name strategy in more than 195 countries around the world. The advantages of a one-brand-name strategy are greater identification of the product from market to market and ease of coordinating promotion from market to market.

▸ **ADAPTATIONS AND MODIFICATIONS:**
A one-brand-name strategy is not possible when the name cannot be pronounced in the local language, when the brand name is owned by someone else, or when the brand name has a negative or vulgar connotation in the local language. The Iranian detergent Barf, for example, might encounter some problems in the U.S. market.

▸ **DIFFERENT BRAND NAMES IN DIFFERENT MARKETS:** Local brand names are often used when translation or pronunciation problems occur, when the marketer wants the brand to appear to be a local brand, or when regulations require localization. Gillette's Silkience hair conditioner is called Soyance in France and Sientel in Italy. Coca-Cola's Sprite brand had to be renamed Kin in Korea to satisfy a government prohibition on the unnecessary use of foreign words.

In addition to global branding decisions, companies must consider global packaging needs. Three aspects of packaging that are especially important in international marketing are labeling, aesthetics, and climate considerations. The major *labeling* concern is properly translating ingredient, promotional, and instructional information on labels. Care must also be employed in meeting all local labeling requirements. Several years ago, an Italian judge ordered that all bottles of Coca-Cola be removed from retail shelves because the ingredients were not properly labeled. Labeling is also harder in countries like Belgium and Finland, which require packaging to be bilingual.

Package *aesthetics* may also require some attention. Even though simple visual elements of the brand, such as a symbol or logo, can be a standardizing element across products and countries, marketers must stay attuned to cultural traits in host countries. For example, colors may have different connotations. Red is associated with witchcraft in some countries, green may be a sign of danger, and white may be symbolic of death. Such cultural differences could necessitate a packaging change if colors are chosen for another country's interpretation. In the United States, green typically symbolizes an eco-friendly product, but that packaging could keep customers away in a country where green indicates danger. Aesthetics also influence package size. Soft drinks are not sold in six-packs in countries that lack refrigeration. In some countries, products such as detergent may be bought only in small quantities because of a lack of storage space. Other products, such as cigarettes, may be bought in small quantities, and even single units, because of the low purchasing power of buyers.

Extreme climates and long-distance shipping necessitate sturdier and more durable packages for goods sold overseas. Spillage, spoilage, and breakage are all more important concerns when products are shipped long distances or frequently handled during shipping and storage. Packages may also have to ensure a longer product life if the time between production and consumption lengthens significantly.

10-7 PRODUCT WARRANTIES

Just as a package is designed to protect the product, a warranty protects the buyer and gives essential information about the product. A warranty confirms the quality or performance of a good or service. An **express warranty** is a written guarantee. Express warranties range from simple statements—such as "100-percent cotton" (a guarantee of quality) and "complete satisfaction guaranteed" (a statement of performance)—to extensive documents written in technical language. In contrast, an **implied warranty** is an unwritten guarantee that the good or service is fit for the purpose for which it was sold. All sales have an implied warranty under the Uniform Commercial Code.

Congress passed the Magnuson-Moss Warranty–Federal Trade Commission Improvement Act in 1975 to help consumers understand warranties and get action from manufacturers and dealers. A manufacturer that promises a full warranty must meet certain minimum standards, including repair "within a reasonable time and without charge" of any defects and replacement of the merchandise or a full refund if the product does not work "after a reasonable number of attempts" at repair. Any warranty that does not live up to this tough prescription must be "conspicuously" promoted as a limited warranty.

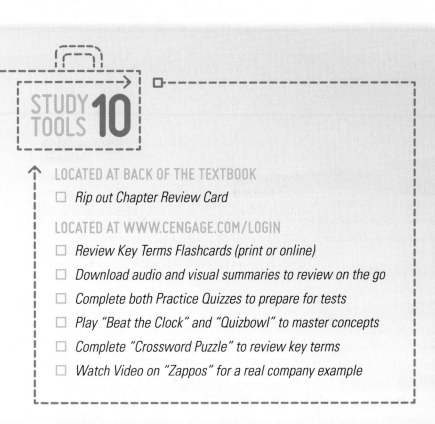

11-1 THE IMPORTANCE OF NEW PRODUCTS

New products are important to sustain growth, increase revenues and profits, and replace obsolete items. Each year *Fast Company* rates and ranks its most innovative companies, based on the ability to buck tradition in the interest of reaching more people, building a better business, and spurring mass-market appeal for unusual or highly technical products or services. In 2011, the top five companies were Apple, Twitter, Facebook, Nissan, and Groupon. It should come as little surprise that each of those companies is well known—their innovations have changed the way people communicate (Twitter, Facebook, Apple), get around (Nissan), and shop (Groupon).[1]

The average fast-moving consumer goods company introduces seventy to eighty new products per year.

new product a product new to the world, the market, the producer, the seller, or some combination of these

11-1a Categories of New Products

The term **new product** is somewhat confusing because its meaning varies widely. Actually, the term has several "correct" definitions. A product can be new to the world, to the market, to the producer or seller, or some combination of these. There are six categories of new products:

▸▸ **NEW-TO-THE-WORLD PRODUCTS** (also called discontinuous innovations): These products create an entirely new market. For example, a new virtual cane uses sonar-like technology and vibrations to give blind and visually impaired users an idea of the spatial layout of a room. The strength of the vibrations indicates the proximity of obstacles. This product is intended to be a technological replacement for traditional canes.[2] New-to-the-world products represent the smallest category of new products.

▸▸ **NEW PRODUCT LINES:** These products, which the firm has not previously offered, allow it to enter an established market. For example, Moleskine's first products were simple black-covered journals. Since then, the company has expanded into pens, travel bags, and even digital creative tools available on the iPhone and iPad.[3]

▸▸ **ADDITIONS TO EXISTING PRODUCT LINES:** This category includes new products that supplement a firm's established line. Frito-Lay frequently adds (or retires) flavors to its Doritos line of chips, such as Mr. Dragon's Fire Chips, which were

Chapter 11

Developing and Managing Products

Learning Outcomes

11–1 *Explain the importance of developing new products and describe the six categories of new products* 178–180

11–2 *Explain the steps in the new-product development process* 180–186

11–3 *Discuss global issues in new-product development* 187

11–4 *Explain the diffusion process through which new products are adopted* 187–189

11–5 *Explain the concept of product life cycles* 189–192

After you finish this chapter go to
p192 *for* **STUDY TOOLS** 📁 ------>

wasabi flavored, or Taco Flavor Doritos, which first appeared in 1967 and were recently brought back to the market.[4]

▸▸ **IMPROVEMENTS OR REVISIONS OF EXISTING PRODUCTS:** The "new and improved" product may be significantly or only slightly changed. For example, Boeing is offering planes with re-designed interiors that give passengers more headroom, a quieter cabin, and better lighting. The mechanics of the planes are the same, making this an aesthetic makeover that airlines hope will appease frustrated travelers.[5]

▸▸ **REPOSITIONED PRODUCTS:** These are existing products targeted at new markets or market segments, or ones repositioned to change the current market's perception of the product or company, which may be done to boost declining sales. Ford is repositioning its long-time favorite, the Mustang, to appeal to a younger group of buyers. Since 2005, the Mustang has had a retro style that appealed to baby boomer nostalgia. Now that boomers are exiting their car-buying years, Ford hopes to position the Mustang for Generation Y as they enter their strongest car-buying years. To do so, the company will restyle the car to create a more modern, sleek look, though it will still have the signature shark-nose grille and round headlights that define the car.[6]

▸▸ **LOWER-PRICED PRODUCTS:** This category refers to products that provide performance similar to competing brands at a lower price. HP LaserJet 3100 is a scanner, copier, printer, and fax machine combined. This new product is priced lower than many conventional color copiers and much lower than the combined price of the four items purchased separately.

11-2 THE NEW-PRODUCT DEVELOPMENT PROCESS

Most companies follow a formal new-product development process, as illustrated in Exhibit 11.1. The management consulting firm Booz Allen Hamilton has studied the new-product development process for more than thirty years. Analyzing five major studies undertaken during this period, the firm has concluded that the companies most likely to succeed in developing and introducing new products are those that take the following actions:

▸▸ Make the long-term commitment needed to support innovation and new-product development.

▸▸ Use a company-specific approach, driven by corporate objectives and strategies, with a well-defined new-product strategy at its core.

▸▸ Capitalize on experience to achieve and maintain competitive advantage.

▸▸ Establish an environment—a management style, organizational structure, and degree of top management support—conducive to achieving company-specific new-product and corporate objectives.

Exhibit 11.1

NEW-PRODUCT DEVELOPMENT PROCESS

1. New-product strategy
2. Idea generation
3. Idea screening
4. Business analysis
5. Development
6. Test marketing
7. Commercialization

New product

Beginning with the new-product strategy, this section will trace the seven-step process for developing new products. Exhibit 11.1 is funnel-shaped to highlight the fact that each stage acts as a screen. The purpose is to filter out unworkable ideas.

11-2a New-Product Strategy

A **new-product strategy** links the new-product development process with the objectives of the marketing department, the business unit, and the corporation. A new-product strategy must be compatible with these objectives, and in turn, all three of the objectives must be consistent with one another.

A new-product strategy is part of the organization's overall marketing strategy. It sharpens the focus and provides general guidelines for generating, screening, and evaluating new-product ideas. The new-product strategy specifies the roles that new products must play in the organization's overall plan and describes the characteristics of products the organization wants to offer and the markets it wants to serve.

In the traditional development process of new products, many versions of a core idea are discussed, tested, winnowed, and retested until a winning product emerges.

Businesses should expect four out of five new products to fail under a strict traditional model.[7] Nevertheless, companies continue to work to innovate. Following a slow year in 2009, leading firms such as Procter & Gamble, Kimberly-Clark, Energizer Holdings, and Unilever committed to increasing new-product activity in 2010.[8]

11-2b Idea Generation

New-product ideas come from many sources, including customers, employees, distributors, competitors, vendors, research and development (R&D), and consultants.

▸ **CUSTOMERS:** The marketing concept suggests that customers' wants and needs should be the springboard for developing new products. Companies can derive insight from listening to Internet chatter or reading blogs, which often indicate early trends or areas consumers are interested in seeing develop or change. Another approach for generating new-product ideas is using what some companies are calling "customer innovation centers." The idea is to provide a forum for meeting with customers and directly involving them in the innovation process. Dr. John Horn, vice president for research and

new-product strategy a plan that links the new-product development process with the objectives of the marketing department, the business unit, and the corporation

ACCESSORIES FOR APPLE AND THE DESIGN DILEMMA

With Apple's popularity soaring, it is no surprise that companies are flocking to manufacture accessories for the iPhone and iPad. So many companies are vying for iPhone case market share that some companies are trying to jump ahead of the pack by risking significant capital. How? Hard Candy Cases speculates as to what the latest design for Apple's next generation of iPhones will be and manufactures the cases to arrive just days after the new product is released to the market. Hard Candy uses leaked specs from Chinese manufacturers in Shenzhen and Guangzhou to approximate any changes Apple makes to its latest gadgets. Using leaked specs, Hard Candy's $30 iPod touch cases achieved a 60 percent gross margin by being early to the market. But the specs aren't always right—when Apple released the iPhone 4S, there were no significant body changes. Unfortunately for Hard Candy, the specs it received from China had indicated several body changes, and the cases based on those faulty specs were already on the way to the United States. That meant lost money and lost time for Hard Candy.

Source: Douglass MacMillan and Adam Satariano, "The Shadowy World of iPhone Cases," *Bloomberg Businessweek*, October 17–23, 2011, 44–46.

product development
a marketing strategy that entails the creation of marketable new products; the process of converting applications for new technologies into marketable products

development in a 3M division, says that the goal is to understand what customers are trying to accomplish instead of what they say they need.[9] Customers might be better at designing products than are elite teams of product designers.

» **EMPLOYEES:** Marketing personnel—advertising and marketing research employees, as well as salespeople—often create new-product ideas because they analyze and are involved in the marketplace. Encouraging employees from different divisions to exchange ideas is also a useful strategy. A developing trend collects employee ideas through innovation-management programs that allow employees to submit and vote on ideas. PricewaterhouseCoopers uses a system called iPlace and has seen 60 percent of its employees participate in the idea-generation process; 140 of the 3,300 ideas have already been implemented.[10]

Some firms reward employees for coming up with creative new ideas. Many companies want to encourage risk-taking through new ideas and have begun implementing rewards for failing after taking a big risk. When trying to land a kitty litter maker for her ad agency, Amanda Zolten took a big risk by putting a used litterbox filled with the company's litter under the table during their meeting. No one noticed until she pointed it out (and also pointed out that no one smelled it). Two of the attendees left the room, and several executives left the table. But more importantly, two laughed. Amanda's boss gave her the first quarterly "Heroic Failure" award for her risk-taking.[11]

» **DISTRIBUTORS:** A well-trained sales force routinely asks distributors about needs that are not being met. Because they are closer to end users, distributors are often more aware of customer needs than are manufacturers. The inspiration for Rubbermaid's Sidekick, a litter-free lunch box, came from a distributor who suggested that the company place some of its plastic containers inside a lunch box and sell the box as an alternative to plastic wrap and paper bags.

» **VENDORS:** 7-Eleven Inc. regularly forges partnerships with vendors to create proprietary products. Coca-Cola invented the flavor Blue Vanilla for a 7-Eleven Slurpee drink, and the matching Laffy Taffy Blue Vanilla Rope candy was developed by Nestlé's Wonka division exclusively for 7-Eleven.

» **COMPETITORS:** No firms rely solely on internally generated ideas for new products. A big part of any organization's marketing intelligence system

should be monitoring the performance of competitors' products. One purpose of competitive monitoring is to determine which, if any, of the competitors' products should be copied. There is plenty of information about competitors on the Internet. For example, AltaVista (www.altavista.com) is a powerful index tool that can be used to locate information about products and companies. Fuld & Company's competitive intelligence guide provides links to a variety of market intelligence sites.

» **RESEARCH AND DEVELOPMENT:** R&D is carried out in four distinct ways. You learned about basic research and applied research in Chapter 4. The other two ways are product development and product modification. Product development goes beyond applied research by converting applications into marketable products. Product modification makes cosmetic or functional changes in existing products. Many new-product breakthroughs come from R&D activities. When Nike asked Olympic marathon competitors what they wanted in a shoe, they said they wanted a sock. At Nike's Innovation Kitchen, engineers and designers went through numerous prototypes and developed entirely new machinery to mimic the snug, smooth fit of a sock while still maintaining the support and look of a tennis shoe. The four years of research and development paid off in the 2012 summer Olympics when the marathon racers wore the shoe, called the Flyknit, and limited editions were sold in New York City, Tokyo, and London.[12]

» **CONSULTANTS:** Outside consultants are always available to examine a business and recommend product ideas. Examples include the Weston Group, Booz Allen Hamilton, and Management Decisions Inc. Traditionally, consultants determine whether a company has a balanced portfolio of products and, if not, what new-product ideas are needed to offset the imbalance. General Mills' Web site at www.generalmills.com/Company/Innovation/G-Win.aspx includes interactive features that let independent inventors and food scientists know what topics the company is interested in pursuing. If General Mills likes an idea it receives, it may pursue a licensing or joint venture arrangement.[13]

Creativity is the wellspring of new-product ideas, regardless of who comes up with them. A variety of approaches and techniques have been developed to stimulate creative thinking. The two considered most useful for generating new-product ideas are brainstorming and focus-group exercises. The goal of **brainstorming** is to get a group to think of unlimited ways to vary a product or solve a problem. Group members avoid criticism of an idea, no matter how ridiculous it may seem. Objective evaluation is postponed. The sheer quantity of ideas is what matters. As noted in Chapter 9, an objective of focus-group interviews is to stimulate insightful comments through group interaction. In the industrial market, machine tools, keyboard designs, aircraft interiors, and backhoe accessories have evolved from focus groups.

11-2c Idea Screening

After new ideas have been generated, they pass through the first filter in the product development process. This stage, called **screening**, eliminates ideas that are inconsistent with the organization's new-product strategy or are obviously inappropriate for some other reason. The new-product committee, the new-product department, or some other formally appointed group performs the screening review. General Motors' Advanced Portfolio Exploration Group (APEx) knows that only one out of every twenty new car concepts developed by the group will ever become a reality. That's not a bad percentage. In the pharmaceutical business, the percentage is much lower. Most new-product ideas are rejected at the screening stage.

Concept tests are often used at the screening stage to rate concept (or product) alternatives. A **concept test** evaluates a new-product idea, usually before any prototype has been created. Typically, researchers get consumer reactions to descriptions and visual representations of a proposed product.

Concept tests are considered fairly good predictors of success for line extensions. They have also been relatively precise predictors of success for new products that are not copycat items, are not easily classified into existing product categories, and do not require major changes in consumer behavior—such as Betty Crocker Tuna Helper. However, concept tests are usually inaccurate in predicting the success of new products that create new consumption patterns and require major changes in consumer behavior—such as microwave ovens, digital music players, and computers.

© Roz Woodward/PhotoDisc/Jupiterimages

11-2d Business Analysis

New-product ideas that survive the initial screening process move to the **business analysis** stage, where preliminary figures for demand, cost, sales, and profitability are calculated. For the first time, costs and revenues are estimated and compared. Depending on the nature of the product and the company, this process may be simple or complex.

The newness of the product, the size of the market, and the nature of the competition all affect the accuracy of revenue projections. In an established market like soft drinks, industry estimates of total market size are available. Forecasting market share for a new entry is a bigger challenge.

Analyzing overall economic trends and their impact on estimated sales is especially important in product categories that are sensitive to fluctuations in the business cycle. If consumers view the economy as uncertain and risky, they will put off buying durable goods such as major home appliances, automobiles, and homes. Likewise, business buyers postpone major equipment purchases if they expect a recession. Understanding the market potential is important because costs increase dramatically once a product idea enters the development stage.

COMMON QUESTIONS IN THE BUSINESS ANALYSIS STAGE

▸▸ **What is the likely demand for the product?**

▸▸ **What impact would the new product probably have on total sales, profits, market share, and return on investment?**

▸▸ **How would the introduction of the product affect existing products? Would the new product cannibalize existing products?**

▸▸ **Would current customers benefit from the product?**

▸▸ **Would the product enhance the image of the company's overall product mix?**

▸▸ **Would the new product affect current employees in any way? Would it lead to increasing or reducing the size of the workforce?**

▸▸ **What new facilities, if any, would be needed?**

▸▸ **How might competitors respond?**

▸▸ **What is the risk of failure? Is the company willing to take the risk?**

brainstorming the process of getting a group to think of unlimited ways to vary a product or solve a problem

screening the first filter in the product development process, which eliminates ideas that are inconsistent with the organization's new-product strategy or are obviously inappropriate for some other reason

concept test a test to evaluate a new-product idea, usually before any prototype has been created

business analysis the second stage of the screening process where preliminary figures for demand, cost, sales, and profitability are calculated

© Mike Flippo/Shutterstock.com

YOUR DESIGN HERE

11-2e Development

In the early stage of **development**, the R&D or engineering department may develop a prototype of the product. During this stage, the firm should start sketching a marketing strategy. The marketing department should decide on the product's packaging, branding, labeling, and so forth. In addition, it should map out preliminary promotion, price, and distribution strategies. The feasibility of manufacturing the product at an acceptable cost should be thoroughly examined. The development stage can last a long time and thus be very expensive. It took ten years to develop Crest toothpaste, fifteen years to develop the Polaroid Colorpack camera and the Xerox copy machine, eighteen years to develop Minute Rice, and fifty-one years to develop the television. Gillette developed three shaving systems over a twenty-seven-year period (Trac II, Atra, and Sensor) before introducing the Mach3 in 1998 and Fusion in 2006.[14]

The development process works best when all the involved areas (R&D, marketing, engineering, production, and even suppliers) work together rather than sequentially, a process called **simultaneous product development**. This approach allows firms to shorten the development process and reduce costs. With simultaneous product development, all relevant functional areas and outside suppliers participate in all stages of the development process. Rather than proceeding through highly structured stages, the cross-functional team operates in unison. Involving key suppliers early in the process capitalizes on their knowledge and enables them to develop critical component parts.

The Internet is a useful tool for implementing simultaneous product development. On the Web, multiple partners from a variety of locations can meet regularly to assess new-product ideas, analyze markets and demographics, and review cost information. Ideas judged to be feasible can quickly be converted into new products. Without the Internet, it would be impossible to conduct simultaneous product development from different parts of the world. Global R&D is important for two reasons. First, large companies have become global and are no longer focused only on one market. Global R&D is necessary to connect with customers in different parts of the world. Second, companies want to tap into the world's best talent—which isn't always found in the United States.[15]

Some firms use online brain trusts to solve technical problems. InnoCentive Inc. is a network of 80,000 self-selected science problem solvers in 173 countries. Its clients include NASA, *Popular Science*, and *The Economist*. When one of InnoCentive's partners selects an idea for development, it no longer tries to develop the idea from the ground up with its own resources and time. Instead, it issues a brief to its network of thinkers, researchers, technology entrepreneurs, and inventors around the world, hoping to generate dialogue, suggestions, and solutions.

Innovative firms are also gathering a variety of R&D input from customers online. Threadless, a T-shirt company, and RYZ, an athletic shoe manufacturer, ask consumers to vote online for their favorites. The companies use these results to determine the products they sell over the Internet.[16]

Laboratory tests are often conducted on prototype models during the development stage. User safety is an important aspect of laboratory testing, which actually subjects products to much more severe treatment than is expected by end users. The Consumer Product Safety Act of 1972 requires manufacturers to conduct a "reasonable testing program" to ensure that their products conform to established safety standards.

Many products that test well in the laboratory are also tried out in homes or businesses. Examples of product categories well suited for such use tests include human and pet food products, household cleaning products, and industrial chemicals and supplies. These products are all relatively inexpensive, and their performance characteristics are apparent to users. For example, Procter & Gamble tests a variety of personal and home-care products in the community around its Cincinnati, Ohio, headquarters.

11-2f Test Marketing

After products and marketing programs have been developed, they are usually tested in the marketplace. **Test marketing** is the limited introduction of a product and a marketing program to determine the reactions of potential customers in a market situation. Test marketing allows management to evaluate alternative strategies and to assess how well the various aspects of the marketing mix fit together. Even established products are test marketed to assess new marketing strategies.

The cities chosen as test sites should reflect market conditions in the new product's projected market area. Yet no "magic city" exists that can universally represent market conditions, and a product's success in one city doesn't guarantee that it will be a nationwide hit. When selecting test market cities, researchers should therefore find locations where the demographics and purchasing habits mirror the overall market. The company should also have good distribution in test cities. Wendy's uses Columbus, Ohio, as a test market for new burgers. Because the city has a nearly perfect cross-section of America's demographic breakdown, it is the perfect testing ground for new products. Most recently, Wendy's has been testing the reception of its Black Label Hamburger.[17] Moreover, test locations should be isolated from the media. If the television stations in a particular market reach a very large area outside that market, the advertising used for the test product may pull in many consumers from outside the market. The product may then appear more successful than it really is.

THE HIGH COSTS OF TEST MARKETING Test marketing frequently takes one year or longer, and costs can exceed $1 million. Some products remain in test markets even longer. In 2010, Google announced a plan to test market an ultra-high-speed broadband network in one or more communities at a competitive price. The search giant planned to test its fiber-to-the-home concept by providing up to 500,000 homes with 1-gigabyte-per-second broadband access. Communities in every state except Delaware requested to be one of the test markets. Topeka, Kansas, even changed its name to Google, Kansas, for a month in an effort to be chosen.[18] Google eventually selected Topeka's neighbors to the east, Kansas City, Kansas, and Kansas City, Missouri, for the expensive test. Despite the cost, many firms believe it is better to fail in a test market than in a national introduction. Because test marketing is so expensive, some companies do not test line extensions of well-known brands.

The high cost of test marketing is not just financial. One unavoidable problem is that test marketing exposes the new product and its marketing mix to competitors before its introduction. Thus, the element of surprise is lost. Competitors can also sabotage or "jam" a testing program by introducing their own sales promotion, pricing, or advertising campaign. The purpose is to hide or distort the normal conditions that the testing firm might expect in the market.

ALTERNATIVES TO TEST MARKETING Many firms are looking for cheaper, faster, safer alternatives to traditional test marketing. In the early 1980s, Information Resources Inc. pioneered one alternative: scanner-based research (discussed in Chapter 9). A typical supermarket scanner test costs about $300,000. Another alternative to traditional test marketing is **simulated (laboratory) market testing**. Advertising and other promotional materials for several

© iStockphoto.com/ansonsaw

test marketing the limited introduction of a product and a marketing program to determine the reactions of potential customers in a market situation

simulated (laboratory) market testing the presentation of advertising and other promotional materials for several products, including a test product, to members of the product's target market products, including the test product, are shown to members of the product's target market. These people are then taken to shop at a mock or real store, where their purchases are recorded. Shopper behavior, including repeat purchasing, is monitored to assess the product's likely performance under true market conditions. Research firms offer simulated market tests for $25,000 to $100,000, compared to $1 million or more for full-scale test marketing.

The Internet offers a fast, cost-effective way to conduct test marketing. Procter & Gamble uses the Internet to assess customer demand for potential new products. Many products that are not available in grocery stores or drugstores can be sampled from P&G's Web site devoted to samples and coupons, www.pgeveryday.com.[19]

Despite these alternatives, most firms still consider test marketing essential for most new products. The high price of failure simply prohibits the widespread introduction of most new products without testing.

11-2g Commercialization

The final stage in the new-product development process is **commercialization**, the decision to market a product. The decision to commercialize the product sets several tasks in motion: ordering production materials and equipment, starting production, building inventories, shipping the product to field distribution points, training the sales force, announcing the new product to the trade, and advertising to potential customers.

The time from the initial commercialization decision to the product's actual introduction varies. It can range from a few weeks for simple products that use existing equipment to several years for technical products that require custom manufacturing equipment. And the total cost of development and initial introduction can be staggering. Gillette spent $750 million developing the Mach3, and the first-year marketing budget for the new three-blade razor was $300 million.

The most important factor in successful new-product introduction is a good match between the product and market needs—as the marketing concept would predict. Successful new products deliver a meaningful and

PUSH THE BUTTON. FEEL THE POWER.

New **M3 POWER NITRO**

M3Power™ is the first battery-powered shaving system from Gillette. It's a real boost in shaving performance. Nitro is M3Power with a bold, sleek look. Feel the power of Gillette's closest, most comfortable shave.

Just push the button to turn it on.

A motor sends micro-pulses to the blades.

With PowerGlide™ blades you can shave closer than ever.

Gillette
The Best a Man Can Get™

www.GilletteM3Power.com

Image courtesy of The Advertising Archives

Product development for Gillette razors can be very expensive, even before the product hits the market!

perceivable benefit to a sizable number of people or organizations and are different in some meaningful way from their intended substitutes. Firms that routinely experience success in new-product introductions tend to share the following characteristics:

- ▸▸ **A history of listening carefully to customers**
- ▸▸ **An obsession with producing the best product possible**
- ▸▸ **A vision of what the market will be like in the future**
- ▸▸ **Strong leadership**
- ▸▸ **A commitment to new-product development**
- ▸▸ **A project-based team approach to new-product development**
- ▸▸ **Getting every aspect of the product development process right**

11-3 GLOBAL ISSUES IN NEW-PRODUCT DEVELOPMENT

Increasing globalization of markets and competition provides a reason for multinational firms to consider new-product development from a worldwide perspective. A firm that starts with a global strategy is better able to develop products that are marketable worldwide. In many multinational corporations, every product is developed for potential worldwide distribution, and unique market requirements are satisfied during development whenever possible.

Some global marketers design their products to meet regulations in their major markets and then, if necessary, meet smaller markets' requirements country by country. Nissan develops lead-country car models that, with minor changes, can be sold in most markets. With this approach, Nissan has been able to reduce the number of its basic models from forty-eight to eighteen. Some products, however, have little potential for global market penetration without modification. In other cases, companies cannot sell their products at affordable prices and still make a profit in many countries.

11-4 THE SPREAD OF NEW PRODUCTS

Managers have a better chance of successfully marketing products if they understand how consumers learn about and adopt products.

11-4a Diffusion of Innovation

An **innovation** is a product perceived as new by a potential adopter. It really doesn't matter whether the product is "new to the world" or some other category of new product. If it is new to a potential adopter, it is an innovation in this context. **Diffusion** is the process by which the adoption of an innovation spreads.

Five categories of adopters participate in the diffusion process:

▸▸ **INNOVATORS:** the first 2.5 percent of all those who adopt the product. Innovators are eager to try new ideas and products, almost as an obsession. In addition to having higher incomes, they are more worldly and more active outside their community than noninnovators. They rely less on group norms and are more self-confident. Because they are well educated, they are more likely to get their information from scientific sources and experts. Innovators are characterized as being venturesome.

▸▸ **EARLY ADOPTERS:** the next 13.5 percent to adopt the product. Although early adopters are not the very first, they do adopt early in the product's life cycle. Compared to innovators, they rely much more on group norms and values. They are also more oriented to the local community, in contrast to the innovators' worldly outlook. Early adopters are more likely than innovators to be opinion leaders because of their closer affiliation with groups. Early adopters are a new product's best friends.[20] The respect of others is a dominant characteristic of early adopters.

▸▸ **EARLY MAJORITY:** the next 34 percent to adopt. The early majority weighs the pros and cons before adopting a new product. They are likely to collect more information and evaluate more brands than early adopters, thereby extending the adoption process. They rely on the group for information but are unlikely to be opinion leaders themselves. Instead, they tend to be opinion leaders' friends and neighbors. The early majority is an important link in the process of diffusing new ideas because they are positioned between earlier and later adopters. A dominant characteristic of the early majority is deliberateness.

▸▸ **LATE MAJORITY:** the next 34 percent to adopt. The late majority adopts a new product because most of their friends have already adopted it. Because they also rely on group norms, their adoption stems from pressure to conform. This group tends to be older and below average in income and education. They depend mainly on word-of-mouth communication rather than on the mass media. The dominant characteristic of the late majority is skepticism.

▸▸ **LAGGARDS:** the final 16 percent to adopt. Like innovators, laggards do not rely on group norms. Their independence is rooted in their ties to tradition. Thus, the past heavily influences their decisions. By the time laggards adopt an innovation, it has probably been outmoded and replaced by something else. For example, they may have bought their first black-and-white television set after color television was already widely diffused. Laggards have the longest adoption time and the lowest socioeconomic status. They tend

innovation a product perceived as new by a potential adopter

diffusion the process by which the adoption of an innovation spreads to be suspicious of new products and alienated from a rapidly advancing society. The dominant value of laggards is tradition. Marketers typically ignore laggards, who do not seem to be motivated by advertising or personal selling and are virtually impossible to reach online.

Note that some product categories may never be adopted by 100 percent of the population. The adopter categories refer to all of those who will eventually adopt a product, not the entire population.

11-4b Product Characteristics and the Rate of Adoption

Five product characteristics can be used to predict and explain the rate of acceptance and diffusion of a new product:

» **COMPLEXITY: the degree of difficulty involved in understanding and using a new product. The more complex the product, the slower is its diffusion.**

» **COMPATIBILITY: the degree to which the new product is consistent with existing values and product knowledge, past experiences, and current needs. Incompatible products diffuse more slowly than compatible products.**

» **RELATIVE ADVANTAGE: the degree to which a product is perceived as superior to existing substitutes. Because it can store and play back thousands of songs, the iPod has a clear relative advantage over the portable CD player.**

» **OBSERVABILITY: the degree to which the benefits or other results of using the product can be observed by others and communicated to target customers. For instance, fashion items and automobiles are highly visible and more observable than personal-care items.**

» **"TRIALABILITY": the degree to which a product can be tried on a limited basis. It is much easier to try a new toothpaste or breakfast cereal than a new automobile or microcomputer.**

11-4c Marketing Implications of the Adoption Process

Two types of communication aid the diffusion process: *word-of-mouth communication* among consumers and communication from marketers to consumers. Word-of-mouth communication within and across groups speeds diffusion. Opinion leaders discuss new products with their

A vacuum with wheels makes you go back and forth.

Vacuums still have wheels that make it hard work to move around objects and unnecessarily difficult to vacuum in corners.

A ball just turns.

dyson ball
No more awkward turns.

www.dyson.com

Dyson vacuums are held in high esteem and are very successful products, in part because of their effective advertising campaigns. This ad demonstrates the innovative structure of the Dyson Ball, which makes the chore of vacuuming more efficient and easier.

followers and with other opinion leaders. Marketers must therefore ensure that opinion leaders have the types of information desired in the media that they use. Suppliers of some products, such as professional and health care services, rely almost solely on word-of-mouth communication for new business.

The second type of communication aiding the diffusion process is *communication directly from the marketer to potential adopters*. Messages directed toward early adopters should normally use different appeals than messages directed toward the early majority, the late majority, or the laggards. Early adopters are more important than innovators because they make up a larger group, are more socially active, and are usually opinion leaders.

As the focus of a promotional campaign shifts from early adopters to the early majority and the late majority, marketers should study the dominant characteristics, buying behavior, and media characteristics of these target markets. Then they should revise messages and media strategy to fit. The diffusion model helps guide marketers in developing and implementing promotion strategy.

11-5 PRODUCT LIFE CYCLES

The product life cycle (PLC) is one of the most familiar concepts in marketing. Few other general concepts have been so widely discussed. Although some researchers and consultants have challenged the theoretical basis and managerial value of the PLC, many believe it is a useful marketing management diagnostic tool and a general guide for marketing planning in various life cycle stages.[21]

The PLC is a biological metaphor that traces the stages of a product's acceptance, from its introduction (birth) to its decline (death). As Exhibit 11.2 shows, a product progresses through four major stages: introduction, growth, maturity, and decline.

The PLC concept can be used to analyze a brand, a product form, or a product category. The PLC for a product form is usually longer than the PLC for any one brand. The exception would be a brand that was the first and last competitor in a product form market. In that situation, the brand and product form life cycles would be equal in length. Product categories have the longest life cycles. A **product category** includes all brands that satisfy a particular type of need such as shaving products, passenger automobiles, or soft drinks.

The time a product spends in any one stage of the life cycle may vary dramatically. Some products, such as fad items, move through the entire cycle in weeks. Fads are typically characterized by a sudden and unpredictable spike in sales followed by a rather abrupt decline. Examples of fad items are Silly Bandz, Beanie Babies, and Crocs. Other products, such as electric clothes washers and dryers, stay in the maturity stage for

decades. Exhibit 11.2 illustrates the typical life cycle for a consumer durable good, such as a washer or dryer. In contrast, Exhibit 11.3 on the next page illustrates typical life cycles for styles (such as formal, business, or casual clothing), fashions (such as miniskirts or baggy jeans), and fads (such as leopard-print clothing). Changes in a product, its uses, its image, or its positioning can extend that product's life cycle.

The PLC concept does not tell managers the length of a product's life cycle or its duration in any stage. It does not dictate marketing strategy. It is simply a tool to help marketers forecast future events and suggest appropriate strategies.

11-5a Introductory Stage

The **introductory stage** of the PLC represents the full-scale launch of a new product into the marketplace. Computer databases for personal use, room-deodorizing air-conditioning filters, and wind-powered home electric generators are all product categories that have recently entered the PLC. A high failure rate, little competition, frequent product modification, and limited distribution typify the introductory stage of the PLC.

product life cycle (PLC) a concept that provides a way to trace the stages of a product's acceptance, from its introduction (birth) to its decline (death)

product category all brands that satisfy a particular type of need

introductory stage the full-scale launch of a new product into the marketplace

© Cengage Learning

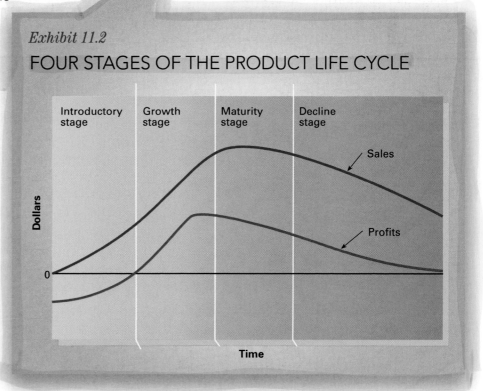

Exhibit 11.2

FOUR STAGES OF THE PRODUCT LIFE CYCLE

Exhibit 11.3

PRODUCT LIFE CYCLES FOR STYLES, FASHIONS, AND FADS

© Cengage Learning

Marketing costs in the introductory stage are normally high for several reasons. High dealer margins are often necessary to obtain adequate distribution, and incentives are needed to get consumers to try the new product. Advertising expenses are high in order to educate consumers about the new product's benefits. Production costs are also often high in this stage, as product and manufacturing flaws are identified and corrected and efforts are undertaken to develop mass production economies.

Sales normally increase slowly during the introductory stage. Moreover, profits are usually negative because of R&D costs, factory tooling, and high introduction costs. The length of the introductory phase is largely determined by product characteristics, such as the product's advantages over substitute products, the educational effort required to make the product known, and management's commitment of resources to the new item. A short introductory period is usually preferred to help reduce the impact of negative earnings and cash flows. As soon as the product gets off the ground, the financial burden should begin to diminish. Also, a short introduction helps dispel some of the uncertainty as to whether the new product will be successful.

Promotion strategy in the introductory stage focuses on developing product awareness and informing consumers about the product category's potential benefits. At this stage, the communication challenge is to stimulate primary demand—demand for the product in general rather than for a specific brand. Intensive personal selling is often required to gain acceptance for the product among wholesalers and retailers. Promotion of convenience products often requires heavy consumer sampling and couponing. Shopping and specialty products demand educational advertising and personal selling to the final consumer.

11-5b Growth Stage

If a product category survives the introductory stage, it then advances to the **growth stage** of the life cycle. In this stage, sales typically grow at an increasing rate, many competitors enter the market, and large companies may start to acquire small pioneering firms. Profits rise rapidly in the growth stage, reach their peak, and begin declining as competition intensifies. Emphasis switches from primary demand promotion (e.g., promoting e-readers) to aggressive brand advertising and communication of the differences between brands (e.g., promoting Kindle versus NOOK).

Distribution becomes a major key to success during the growth stage, as well as in later stages. Manufacturers scramble to sign up dealers and distributors and to build long-term relationships. Without adequate distribution, it is impossible to establish a strong market position.

Madewell, a workwear company founded in 1937, fell out of awareness until 2004, when the brand was purchased by Millard Drexler, who revamped its image into a casual, modern, and youthful collection. Over the past six years, Drexler has worked with J. Crew, leasing the brand to the well-known company for $1 a year to develop the brand conscientiously, creating a solid foundation for growth in luxury denim. In 2011, the company approached $100 million in sales volume, generating profit for the first time. With such success, the plan to increase retail presence by 30 percent and add a marketing campaign should only increase the company's growth.[22]

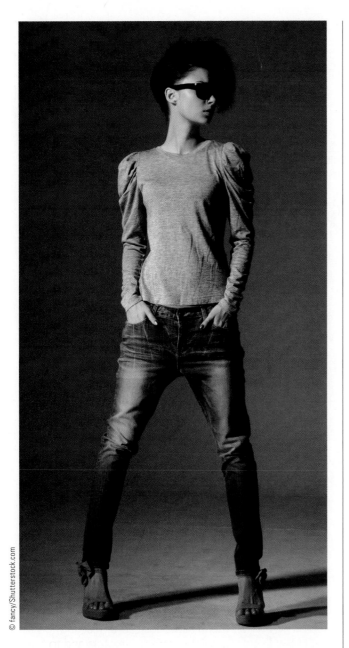

© fancy/Shutterstock.com

11-5c Maturity Stage

A period during which sales increase at a decreasing rate signals the beginning of the **maturity stage** of the life cycle. New users cannot be added indefinitely, and sooner or later the market approaches saturation. Normally, this is the longest stage of the PLC. Many major household appliances are in the maturity stage of their life cycles.

For shopping products such as durable goods and electronics, and many specialty products, annual models begin to appear during the maturity stage. Product lines are lengthened to appeal to additional market segments. Service and repair assume more important roles as manufacturers strive to distinguish their products from others.

Product design changes tend to become stylistic (How can the product be made different?) rather than functional (How can the product be made better?).

As prices and profits continue to fall, marginal competitors start dropping out of the market. Dealer margins also shrink, resulting in less shelf space for mature items, lower dealer inventories, and a general reluctance to promote the product. Thus, promotion to dealers often intensifies during this stage in order to retain loyalty.

Heavy consumer promotion by the manufacturer is also required to maintain market share. Cutthroat competition during this stage can lead to price wars. Another characteristic of the maturity stage is the emergence of "niche marketers" that target narrow, well-defined, underserved segments of a market.

11-5d Decline Stage

A long-run drop in sales signals the beginning of the **decline stage**. The rate of decline is governed by how rapidly consumer tastes change or substitute products are adopted. Many convenience products and fad items lose their market overnight, leaving large inventories of unsold items, such as designer jeans. Others die more slowly. Landline telephone service is an example of a product in the decline stage of the product life cycle. Nearly 32 percent of American homes do not have a landline, which represents a continued steady increase since 2010—and a steady drop in the use of landlines.[23] People abandoning landlines to go wireless and households replacing landlines with Internet phones have both contributed to this long-term decline.

Some firms have developed successful strategies for marketing products in the decline stage of the PLC. They eliminate all nonessential marketing expenses and let sales decline as more and more customers discontinue purchasing the products. Eventually, the product is withdrawn from the market.

Some firms practice what management sage Peter Drucker has called "organized abandonment," which is based upon a periodic audit of all goods and services that a firm markets. One key question is, if we weren't already marketing the product, would we be willing to introduce it now? If the answer is "no," the product should be carefully considered as a candidate for elimination from the product mix.[24]

Exhibit 11.4

RELATIONSHIP BETWEEN THE DIFFUSION PROCESS AND THE PRODUCT LIFE CYCLE

© Cengage Learning

11-5e Implications for Marketing Management

The PLC concept encourages marketing managers to plan so that they can take the initiative instead of reacting to past events. The PLC is especially useful as a predicting or forecasting tool. Because products pass through distinctive stages, it is often possible to estimate a product's location on the curve using historical data. Profits, like sales, tend to follow a predictable path over a product's life cycle.

Exhibit 11.4 shows the relationship between the adopter categories and stages of the PLC. Note that the various categories of adopters first buy products in different stages of the life cycle. Almost all sales in the maturity and decline stages represent repeat purchasing.

STUDY TOOLS 11

LOCATED AT BACK OF THE TEXTBOOK

☐ *Rip out Chapter Review Card*

LOCATED AT WWW.CENGAGE.COM/LOGIN

☐ *Review Key Terms Flashcards (print or online)*

☐ *Download audio and visual summaries to review on the go*

☐ *Complete both Practice Quizzes to prepare for tests*

☐ *Play "Beat the Clock" and "Quizbowl" to master concepts*

☐ *Complete "Crossword Puzzle" to review key terms*

☐ *Watch Video on "GaGa's Inc." for a real company example*

ANATOMY OF A PRODUCT LIFE: VCR

VCR SALES DROPPED RAPIDLY IN THE FACE OF GROWING DVD COMPETITION.

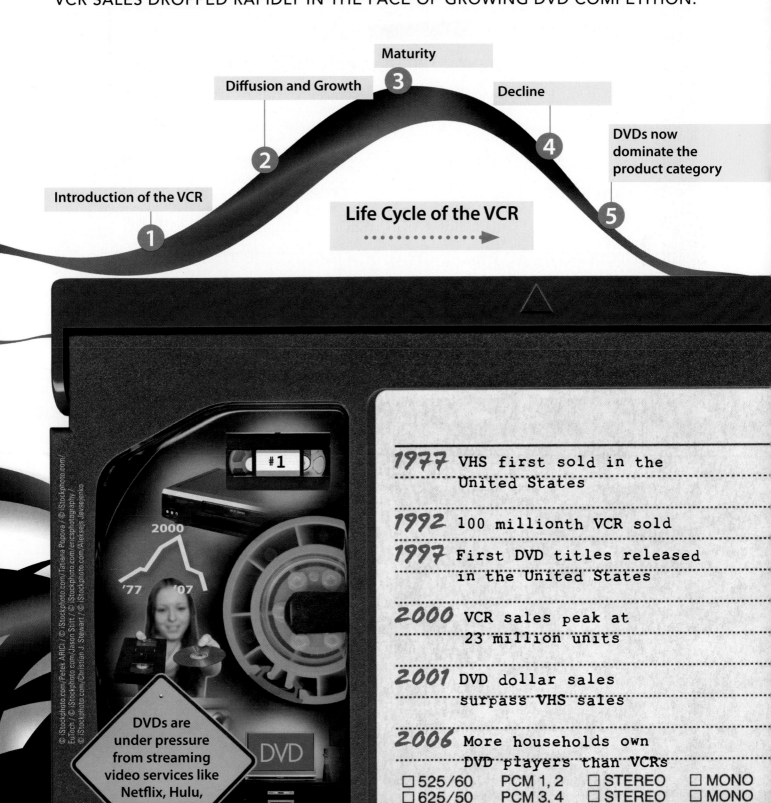

Maturity ③

Diffusion and Growth ②

Decline ④

DVDs now dominate the product category ⑤

Introduction of the VCR ①

Life Cycle of the VCR →

DVDs are under pressure from streaming video services like Netflix, Hulu, and Roku.

1977 VHS first sold in the United States

1992 100 millionth VCR sold

1997 First DVD titles released in the United States

2000 VCR sales peak at 23 million units

2001 DVD dollar sales surpass VHS sales

2006 More households own DVD players than VCRs

☐ 525/60   PCM 1, 2   ☐ STEREO   ☐ MONO
☐ 625/50   PCM 3, 4   ☐ STEREO   ☐ MONO

12-1 THE IMPORTANCE OF SERVICES

A service is the result of applying human or mechanical efforts to people or objects. Services involve a deed, a performance, or an effort that cannot be physically possessed. Today, the service sector substantially influences the U.S. economy. The U.S. Census Bureau completes a yearly Service Survey to review all the revenue and activities in the service sector from the previous year. The 2010 survey covered all service industries and found that they accounted for 55 percent of U.S. GDP. The initial survey results found increased revenue in ten of the eleven service sectors.[1] These numbers are particularly significant because they reflect the growth during the recession. The largest gains came in the information services sector, particularly Internet publishing and broadcasting. The only sector to post a loss was the finance and insurance sector.[2]

⌐In 2010, service industries accounted for 55 percent of U.S. GDP and demonstrated growth in ten of eleven sectors while nonservice sectors saw almost universal decline.⌐

service the result of applying human or mechanical efforts to people or objects

The marketing process described in Chapter 1 is the same for all types of products, whether they are goods or services. In addition, although a comparison of goods and services marketing can be beneficial, in reality it is hard to distinguish clearly between manufacturing and service firms. Indeed, many manufacturing firms can point to service as a major factor in their success. For example, maintenance and repair services offered by the manufacturer are important to buyers of copy machines. Nevertheless, services have some unique characteristics that distinguish them from goods, and marketing strategies need to be adjusted for these characteristics.

12-2 HOW SERVICES DIFFER FROM GOODS

Services have four unique characteristics that distinguish them from goods. Services are intangible, inseparable, heterogeneous, and perishable.

Chapter **12**

Services and Nonprofit Organization Marketing

Learning Outcomes

After you finish this chapter go to
p207 *for* **STUDY TOOLS** �- - - - - →

intangibility the inability of services to be touched, seen, tasted, heard, or felt in the same manner that goods can be sensed

search quality a characteristic that can be easily assessed before purchase

experience quality a characteristic that can be assessed only after use

credence quality a characteristic that consumers may have difficulty assessing even after purchase because they do not have the necessary knowledge or experience

inseparability the inability of the production and consumption of a service to be separated; consumers must be present during the production

heterogeneity the variability of the inputs and outputs of services, which causes services to tend to be less standardized and uniform than goods

12-2a Intangibility

The basic difference between services and goods is that services are intangible performances. Because of their **intangibility**, they cannot be touched, seen, tasted, heard, or felt in the same manner that goods can be sensed.

Evaluating the quality of services before or even after making a purchase is harder than evaluating the quality of goods because, compared to goods, services tend to exhibit fewer search qualities. A **search quality** is a characteristic that can be easily assessed before purchase—for instance, the color of an appliance or automobile. At the same time, services tend to exhibit more experience and credence qualities. An **experience quality** is a characteristic that can be assessed only after use, such as the quality of a meal in a restaurant. A **credence quality** is a characteristic that consumers may have difficulty assessing even after purchase because they do not have the necessary knowledge or experience. Medical and consulting services are examples of services that exhibit credence qualities.

These characteristics also make it harder for marketers to communicate the benefits of an intangible service than to communicate the benefits of tangible goods. Thus, marketers often rely on tangible cues to communicate a service's nature and quality. For example, Travelers Insurance Company uses an umbrella symbol as a tangible reminder of the protection that insurance provides.

The facilities that customers visit, or from which services are delivered, are a critical tangible part of the total service offering. Messages about the organization are communicated to customers through such elements as the décor, the clutter or neatness of service areas, and the staff's manners and dress. Hotels know that guests form opinions quickly and are more willing to tweet them within the first fifteen minutes of their stay than ever before. Some hotels go to great lengths to make their guests feel at home right away. At the Ritz-Carlton, Toronto, the doormen radio guests' names to the front desk and the bellhop so they can give the guests a personalized welcome.[3]

12-2b Inseparability

Goods are produced, sold, and then consumed. In contrast, services are often sold, produced, and consumed at the same time. In other words, their production and consumption are inseparable activities. This **inseparability** means that, because consumers must be present during the production of services like haircuts or surgery, they are actually involved in the production of the services they buy. That type of consumer involvement is rare in goods manufacturing.

Simultaneous production and consumption also means that services normally cannot be produced in a centralized location and consumed in decentralized locations, as goods typically are. Services are also inseparable from the perspective of the service provider. Thus, the quality of service that firms are able to deliver depends on the quality of their employees.

12-2c Heterogeneity

One great strength of McDonald's is consistency. Whether customers order a Big Mac in Chicago or Seattle, they know exactly what they are going to get. This is not the case with many service providers. Because services have greater **heterogeneity,** or variability of inputs and outputs, they tend to be less standardized and uniform than goods. For example, physicians in a group practice or barbers in a barbershop differ within each group in their technical and interpersonal skills. Because

© James Steidl/Shutterstock.com

services tend to be labor intensive and production and consumption are inseparable, consistency and quality control can be hard to achieve.

Standardization and training help increase consistency and reliability. For example, Pret a Manger, a British grab-n-go sandwich shop that is slowly growing in the United States, gives its employees a picture and a recipe card for each sandwich they make. In addition, the company offers myriad rewards and advancements for employees who are cheerful and ensure that customers have the best experience possible in the restaurant.[4]

12-2d Perishability

Perishability is the fourth characteristic of services. **Perishability** refers to the inability of services to be stored, warehoused, or inventoried. An empty hotel room or airplane seat produces no revenue that day. The revenue is lost. Yet service organizations are often forced to turn away full-price customers during peak periods.

One of the most important challenges in many service industries is finding ways to synchronize supply and demand. The philosophy that some revenue is better than none has prompted many hotels to offer deep discounts on weekends and during the off-season.

12-3 SERVICE QUALITY

Because of the four unique characteristics of services, service quality is more difficult to define and measure than is the quality of tangible goods. Business executives rank the improvement of service quality as one of the most critical challenges facing them today.

Research has shown that customers evaluate service quality by the following five components:[5]

▸ **Reliability: the ability to perform the service dependably, accurately, and consistently. Reliability is performing the service right the first time. This component has been found to be the one most important to consumers.**

▸ **Responsiveness: the ability to provide prompt service. Examples of responsiveness include calling the customer back quickly, serving lunch fast to someone who is in a hurry, or mailing a transaction slip immediately. The ultimate in responsiveness is offering service twenty-four hours a day, seven days a week.**

▸ **Assurance: the knowledge and courtesy of employees and their ability to convey trust. Skilled employees**

who treat customers with respect and make customers feel that they can trust the firm exemplify assurance.

▸ **Empathy: caring, individualized attention to customers. Firms whose employees recognize customers and learn their specific requirements are providing empathy.**

▸ **Tangibles: the physical evidence of the service. The tangible parts of a service include the physical facilities, tools, and equipment used to provide the service, as well as the appearance of personnel.**

Overall service quality is measured by combining customers' evaluations for all five components.

12-3a The Gap Model of Service Quality

A model of service quality called the **gap model** identifies five gaps that can cause problems in service delivery and influence customer evaluations of service quality.[6] These gaps are illustrated in Exhibit 12.1 on the next page:

▸ **GAP 1: the gap between what customers want and what management thinks customers want. This gap results from a lack of understanding or a misinterpretation of the customers' needs, wants, or desires. A firm that does little or no customer satisfaction research is likely to experience this gap. To close gap 1, firms must stay attuned to customer wishes by researching customer needs and satisfaction.**

▸ **GAP 2: the gap between what management thinks customers want and the quality specifications that management develops to provide the service. Essentially, this gap is the result of management's inability to translate customers' needs into delivery systems within the firm. For example, KFC used to rate its managers according to "chicken efficiency," or how much chicken they threw away at closing; customers who came in late would either have to wait for chicken to be cooked or settle for chicken several hours old.**

▸ **GAP 3: the gap between the service quality specifications and the service that is actually provided. If**

perishability the inability of services to be stored, warehoused, or inventoried

reliability the ability to perform a service dependably, accurately, and consistently

responsiveness the ability to provide prompt service

assurance the knowledge and courtesy of employees and their ability to convey trust

empathy caring, individualized attention to customers

tangibles the physical evidence of a service, including the physical facilities, tools, and equipment used to provide the service

gap model a model identifying five gaps that can cause problems in service delivery and influence customer evaluations of service quality both gaps 1 and 2 have been closed, then gap 3 is due to the inability of management and employees to do what should be done. Management needs to ensure that employees have the skills and the proper tools to perform their jobs. Other techniques that help to close gap 3 are training employees so they know what management expects and encouraging teamwork. At Pret a Manger, employees are encouraged to work together through a rewards system. When employees are promoted or pass training

milestones, they receive at least $50 in vouchers—not for personal use, but to hand out to colleagues who helped them achieve the promotion. That is just one of the many reasons that employee turnover is low at Pret a Manger—only 60 percent annually. In comparison, McDonald's averages 300 to 400 percent turnover.[7]

Exhibit 12.1

GAP MODEL OF SERVICE QUALITY

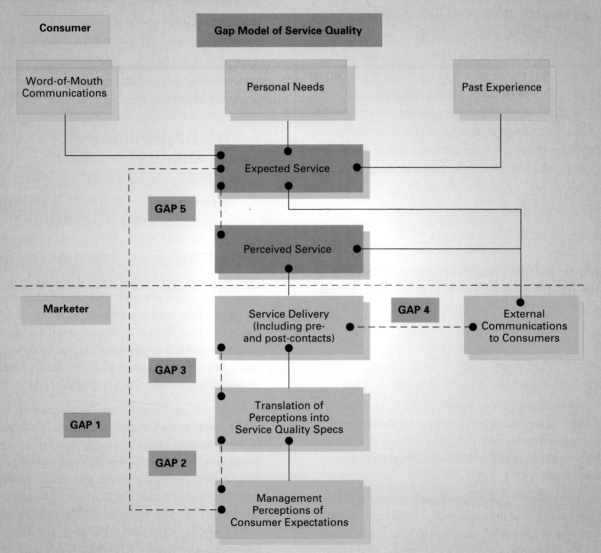

The gap analysis model measures consumer perceptions of service quality. Managers use the model to analyze sources of quality problems and to understand how service quality can be improved.

Source: From Valarie A. Zeithaml, Mary Jo Bitner, and Dwayne Gremler, *Services Marketing*, 6/e, © 2013 (New York: McGraw-Hill, 2012). Used by permission.

▸ **GAP 4:** the gap between what the company provides and what the customer is told it provides. This is clearly a communication gap. It may include misleading or deceptive advertising campaigns promising more than the firm can deliver or doing "whatever it takes" to get the business. To close this gap, companies need to create realistic customer expectations through honest, accurate communication about what the firms can provide.

▸ **GAP 5:** the gap between the service that customers receive and the service they want. This gap can be positive or negative. For example, if a patient expects to wait twenty minutes in the physician's office before seeing the physician but actually waits only ten minutes, the patient's evaluation of service quality will be high. However, a forty-minute wait would result in a lower evaluation.

When one or more of these gaps is large, service quality is perceived as low. As the gaps shrink, service quality perception improves. USAA, a financial-services organization that serves military families, is great at closing gap 1. It knows what its highly mobile customers who face unique financial challenges need. For example, the company was the first bank to allow iPhone deposits, it texts balances to soldiers in the field, and it heavily discounts customers' car insurance while they are deployed overseas.[8]

12-4 MARKETING MIXES FOR SERVICES

Services' unique characteristics—intangibility, inseparability of production and consumption, heterogeneity, and perishability—make marketing more challenging. Elements of the marketing mix (product, place, promotion, and pricing) need to be adjusted to meet the special needs created by these characteristics.

12-4a Product (Service) Strategy

A product, as defined in Chapter 10, is everything a person receives in an exchange. In the case of a service organization, the product offering is intangible and consists in large part of a process or a series of processes. Product strategies for service offerings include decisions on the type of process involved, core and supplementary services, standardization or customization of the service product, and the service mix.

SERVICE AS A PROCESS Two broad categories of things get processed in service organizations: people and objects. In some cases, the process is physical, or tangible, while in others the process is intangible. Based on these characteristics, service processes can be placed into one of four categories:[9]

▸ **People processing** takes place when the service is directed at a customer. Examples are transportation services and health care.

▸ **Possession processing** occurs when the service is directed at customers' physical possessions. Examples are lawn care, dry cleaning, and veterinary services.

▸ **Mental stimulus processing** refers to services directed at people's minds. Examples are theater performances and education.

▸ **Information processing** describes services that use technology or brainpower directed at a customer's assets. Examples are insurance and consulting.

Because customers' experiences and involvement differ for each of these types of services, marketing strategies may also differ. For example, people-processing services require customers to enter the *service factory*, which is a physical location, such as an aircraft, a physician's office, or a hair salon. In contrast, possession-processing services typically do not require the presence of the customer in the service factory. Marketing strategies for the former would therefore focus more on an attractive, comfortable physical environment and employee training on employee–customer interaction issues than would strategies for the latter.

CORE AND SUPPLEMENTARY SERVICE PRODUCTS The service offering can be viewed as a bundle of activities that includes the **core service**, which is the most basic benefit the customer is buying, and a group of **supplementary services** that support or enhance the core service. Exhibit 12.2 illustrates these concepts for an overnight stay at a luxury hotel. The core service is overnight rental of a bedroom, which involves people processing. The supplementary services, some of which involve information processing, include reservations, check-ins and check-outs, room service, and meals.

In many service industries, the core service becomes a commodity as competition increases. Thus, firms usually emphasize supplementary services to create a competitive advantage. On the other hand, some firms are positioning

mass customization
a strategy that uses technology to deliver customized services on a mass basis

themselves in the marketplace by greatly reducing supplementary services.

CUSTOMIZATION/STANDARDIZATION

An important issue in developing the service offering is whether to customize or standardize it. Customized services are more flexible and respond to individual customers' needs. They also usually command a higher price. Standardized services are more efficient and cost less.

Instead of choosing to either standardize or customize a service, a firm may incorporate elements of both by adopting an emerging strategy called **mass customization**. Mass customization uses technology to deliver customized services on a mass basis, which results in giving each customer whatever she or he asks for. For example, Callaway Golf Company released a new driver called the RAZR Fit. What differentiates this driver from Callaway's other clubs is that customers can personalize their club online. Callaway provides options for color, type of shaft, grip style, and wrap length that allow customers to get the exact fit they want.[10]

Personalization services can generate privacy questions and be controversial when implemented without customer approval. Facebook's instant personalization

Exhibit 12.2
CORE AND SUPPLEMENTARY SERVICES FOR A UNIVERSITY

Food Service · Parking · Community learning · Counseling [Career and Degree] · Alumni Services · Housing · Security · Health Care · Entertainment · Janitorial Services · Fitness · Financial Aid

Core Service — Education

Supplementary Services

© Cengage Learning

(IP) service is automatically checked on user profiles and imports profile data onto certain Web sites upon the user's next visit. For example, when a user visits Pandora, the online streaming radio service, it will immediately begin playing music by bands that she has "liked" on her Facebook profile. IP also links real names and other public

A MATCH MADE IN... THE KITCHEN?

Hosting a large party is a huge undertaking, particularly if food is involved. Figuring out what to serve, how much to make, and where to get ingredients is a time-consuming process, particularly for those not in the food industry. However, being a chef doesn't make you a master at marketing yourself or running a business. **Kitchit** is aiming to **matchmake** the two groups. Kitchit is a service that connects diners and party planners with cooks. Hosts are able to choose from a variety of chefs in their area and provide the chosen chefs details such as location, number of guests, and how much they would like to spend. Once the chefs agree, they take care of all the agreed-upon details, including shopping, cooking, and cleaning. Costs range from $25 a person for basic menus to $200 a guest for six-course meals including wine and décor.

Source: Douglas MacMillan, "No, Padma Lakshmi Will Not Come To Your Home," *Bloomberg Businessweek*, December 12–18, 2011, 49–50.

© michaeljung/Shutterstock.com /
© iStockphoto.com/Bill Noll

Facebook information to partner Web sites and other Facebook users. Unless a user turns off Web site–specific settings, he will automatically be publicizing information on his profile (location, name, phone number, etc.) when he uses sites like Pandora, Microsoft's Docs, and Yelp.[11]

THE SERVICE MIX Most service organizations market more than one service. For example, TruGreen offers lawn care, shrub care, carpet cleaning, and industrial lawn services. Each organization's service mix represents a set of opportunities, risks, and challenges. Each part of the service mix should make a different contribution to achieving the firm's goals. To succeed, each service may also need a different level of financial support. Designing a service strategy, therefore, means deciding what new services to introduce to which target market, what existing services to maintain, and what services to eliminate.

Celebrity endorsements can decrease perceived risk in choosing a service. For example, John Travolta endorses Breitling watches for their quality and endurance.

12-4b Place (Distribution) Strategy

Distribution strategies for service organizations must focus on such issues as convenience, number of outlets, direct versus indirect distribution, location, and scheduling. A key factor influencing the selection of a service provider is *convenience*. For example, infirm or elderly patients would probably prefer to use a doctor who makes house calls.

An important distribution objective for many service firms is the number of outlets to use or the number of outlets to open during a certain time. Generally, the intensity of distribution should meet, but not exceed, the target market's needs and preferences. Having too few outlets may inconvenience customers; having too many outlets may boost costs unnecessarily. Intensity of distribution may also depend on the image desired. Having only a few outlets may make the service seem more exclusive or selective.

The next service distribution decision is whether to distribute services to end users *directly* or *indirectly* through other firms. Because of the intangible nature of services,

many service firms have to use direct distribution or franchising. Examples include legal, medical, accounting, and personal-care services. The newest form of direct distribution is the Internet. Most major airlines are now using online services to sell tickets directly to consumers, which results in lower distribution costs for the airlines. Other firms with standardized service packages have developed indirect channels using independent intermediaries. For example, Bank of America offers teller and loan services to customers in small satellite facilities at Albertsons grocery stores in Texas.

The *location* of a service most clearly reveals the relationship between its target market strategy and distribution strategy. For time-dependent service providers such as airlines, physicians, and dentists, *scheduling* is often a more important factor.

12-4c Promotion Strategy

Consumers and business users have more trouble evaluating services than goods because services are less tangible. In turn, marketers have more trouble promoting intangible services than tangible goods. Here are four promotion strategies they can try:

▸ **STRESSING TANGIBLE CUES:** A tangible cue is a concrete symbol of the service offering. To make their intangible services more tangible, hotels turn down the bedcovers and put mints on the pillows. DoubleTree hotels offer their guests a warm chocolate chip cookie as they check in.

▸ **USING PERSONAL INFORMATION SOURCES:** A personal information source is someone consumers are familiar with (such as a celebrity) or someone they admire or can relate to personally. Service firms may seek to simulate positive word-of-mouth communication among present and prospective customers by using real customers in their ads.

▸ **CREATING A STRONG ORGANIZATIONAL IMAGE:** One way to create an image is to manage the evidence, including the physical environment of the service facility, the appearance of the service employees, and the tangible items associated with a service (such as stationery, bills, and business cards). For example, McDonald's golden arches are instantly recognizable. Another way to create an image is through branding.

▸ **ENGAGING IN POSTPURCHASE COMMUNICATION:** Postpurchase communication refers to the follow-up activities that a service firm might engage in after a customer transaction. Postcard surveys, telephone calls, and other types of follow-up show customers that their feedback matters.

12-4d Price Strategy

Considerations in pricing a service are similar to the pricing considerations to be discussed in Chapters 19 and 20. However, the unique characteristics of services present two special pricing challenges.

First, in order to price a service, it is important to define the unit of service consumption. For example, should pricing be based on completing a specific service task (cutting a customer's hair), or should it be time based (how long it takes to cut a customer's hair)? Some services include the consumption of goods, such as food and beverages. Restaurants charge customers for food and drink rather than for the use of a table and chairs.

Second, for services that are composed of multiple elements, the issue is whether pricing should be based on a "bundle" of elements or whether each element should be priced separately. A bundled price may be preferable when consumers dislike having to pay "extra" for every part of the service (e.g., paying extra for baggage or food on an airplane), and it is simpler for the firm to administer. Alternatively, customers may not want to pay for service elements they do not use. Many furniture stores now have "unbundled" delivery charges from the price of the furniture. Customers who wish to can pick up the furniture at the store, saving on the delivery fee.

Marketers should set performance objectives when pricing each service. Three categories of pricing objectives have been suggested:[12]

▸ **Revenue-oriented pricing** focuses on maximizing the surplus of income over costs. A limitation of this approach is that determining costs can be difficult for many services.

▸ **Operations-oriented pricing** seeks to match supply and demand by varying prices. For example, matching hotel demand to the number of available rooms can be achieved by raising prices at peak times and decreasing them during slow times.

▸ **Patronage-oriented pricing** tries to maximize the number of customers using the service. Thus, prices vary with different market segments' ability to pay, and methods of payment (such as credit) are offered that increase the likelihood of a purchase.

A firm may need to use more than one type of pricing objective. In fact, all three objectives probably need to be included to some degree in a pricing strategy, although the importance of each type may vary depending on the type of service provided, the prices that competitors are charging, the differing ability of various customer segments to pay, or the opportunity to negotiate price. For customized services (such as construction services), customers may also have the ability to negotiate a price.

12-5 RELATIONSHIP MARKETING IN SERVICES

Many services involve ongoing interaction between the service organization and the customer. Thus, they can benefit from relationship marketing, the strategy described in Chapter 1, as a means of attracting, developing, and retaining customer relationships. The idea is to develop strong loyalty by creating satisfied customers who will buy additional services from the firm and are unlikely to switch to a competitor. Satisfied customers are also likely to engage in positive word-of-mouth communication, thereby helping to bring in new customers.

Many businesses have found that it is more cost-effective to hang on to the customers they have than to focus only on attracting new ones. A bank executive, for example, found that increasing customer retention by 2 percent can have the same effect on profits as reducing costs by 10 percent.

Services that purchasers receive on a continuing basis (e.g., cable television, banking, insurance) can be considered membership services. This type of service naturally lends itself to relationship marketing. When services involve discrete transactions (e.g., in a movie theater, at a restaurant, or on public transportation), it may be more difficult to build membership-type relationships with customers. Nevertheless, services involving discrete transactions may be transformed into membership relationships using marketing tools. For example, the service could be sold in bulk (e.g., a theater series subscription or a commuter pass on public transportation). Or a service firm could offer special benefits to customers who choose to register with the firm (e.g., loyalty programs for hotels and airlines). The service firm that has a more formalized relationship with its customers has an advantage because it knows who its customers are and how and when they use the services offered.[13]

Relationship marketing can be practiced at three levels:[14]

▸▸ **LEVEL 1:** The firm uses pricing incentives to encourage customers to continue doing business with it. Frequent-flyer programs are an example of level 1 relationship marketing. This level of relationship marketing is the least effective in the long term because its price-based advantage is easily imitated by other firms.

▸▸ **LEVEL 2:** This level of relationship marketing also uses pricing incentives but seeks to build social bonds with customers. The firm stays in touch with customers, learns about their needs, and designs services to meet those needs. Level 2 relationship marketing is often more effective than level 1 relationship marketing.

▸▸ **LEVEL 3:** At this level, the firm again uses financial and social bonds but adds structural bonds to the formula. Structural bonds are developed by offering value-added services that are not readily available from other firms. Many high-end hotels leave treats in repeat-guests' hotel rooms when they celebrate special events, such as a cake for a couple celebrating their anniversary. They also leave treats in rooms where guests have children and boxes of chocolates for returning guests who send positive tweets about the hotel.[15]

Thanks for the tweet

12-6 INTERNAL MARKETING IN SERVICE FIRMS

Services are performances, so the quality of a firm's employees is an important part of building long-term relationships with customers. Employees who like their jobs and are satisfied with the firm they work for are more likely to deliver superior service to customers. In other words, a firm that makes its employees happy has a better chance of retaining customers. Thus, it is critical that service firms practice **internal marketing**, which means treating employees as customers and developing systems and benefits that satisfy their needs. To satisfy employees, companies have designed and instituted a wide variety of programs such as flextime, on-site day care, and concierge services. SAS Institute offers its employees unlimited sick time, free health care, intramural sports leagues, and the option of subsidized Montessori child care.[16]

internal marketing treating employees as customers and developing systems and benefits that satisfy their needs

12-7 GLOBAL ISSUES IN SERVICES MARKETING

The international marketing of services is a major part of global business, and the United States has become the world's largest exporter of services. Competition in international services is increasing rapidly, however. To be successful in the global marketplace, service firms must first determine the nature of their core product. Then the marketing mix elements (additional services, place, promotion, pricing, distribution) should be designed to take into account each country's cultural, technological, and political environment.

Because of their competitive advantages, many U.S. service industries have been able to enter the global marketplace. U.S. banks, for example, have advantages in customer service and collections management.

12-8 NONPROFIT ORGANIZATION MARKETING

A **nonprofit organization** is an organization that exists to achieve some goal other than the usual business goals of profit, market share, or return on investment. Both nonprofit organizations and private-sector service firms market intangible products, and both often require the customer to be present during the production process. Both for-profit and nonprofit services vary greatly from producer to producer and from day to day, even from the same producer.

Few people realize that nonprofit organizations account for more than 20 percent of the economic activity in the United States. The cost of government (i.e., taxes), the predominant form of nonprofit organization, has become the biggest single item in the American family budget—more than housing, food, or health care. Together, federal, state, and local governments collect tax revenues that amount to more than a third of the U.S. gross domestic product. In addition to government entities, nonprofit organizations include hundreds of thousands of private museums, theaters, schools, and churches.

12-8a What Is Nonprofit Organization Marketing?

Nonprofit organization marketing is the effort by nonprofit organizations to bring about mutually satisfying exchanges with target

Taxes have become the single biggest item in the American family budget.

markets. Although these organizations vary substantially in size and purpose and operate in different environments, most perform the following marketing activities:

▶▶ **Identify the customers they wish to serve or attract (although they usually use other terms, such as clients, patients, members, or sponsors)**

▶▶ **Explicitly or implicitly specify objectives**

▶▶ **Develop, manage, and eliminate programs and services**

▶▶ **Decide on prices to charge (although they use other terms, such as fees, donations, tuition, fares, fines, or rates)**

▶▶ **Schedule events or programs, and determine where they will be held or where services will be offered**

▶▶ **Communicate their availability through brochures, signs, public service announcements, or advertisements**

Often, the nonprofit organizations that carry out these functions do not realize they are engaged in marketing.

12-8b Unique Aspects of Nonprofit Organization Marketing Strategies

Like their counterparts in business organizations, nonprofit managers develop marketing strategies to bring about mutually satisfying exchanges with target markets. However, marketing in nonprofit organizations is unique in many ways—including the setting of marketing objectives, the selection of target markets, and the development of appropriate marketing mixes.

OBJECTIVES In the private sector, the profit motive is both an objective for guiding decisions and a criterion for evaluating results. Nonprofit organizations do not seek to make a profit for redistribution to owners or shareholders. Rather, their focus is often on generating enough funds to cover expenses.

Most nonprofit organizations are expected to provide equitable, effective, and efficient services

iStockphoto.com/Valentin Mosichev / © Edyta Pawlowska/Shutterstock.com

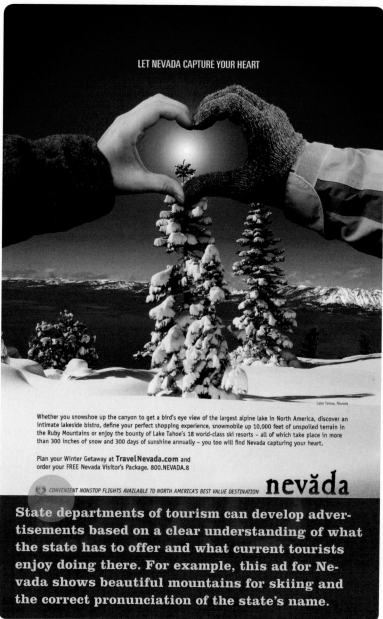

LET NEVADA CAPTURE YOUR HEART

Lake Tahoe, Nevada

Whether you snowshoe up the canyon to get a bird's eye view of the largest alpine lake in North America, discover an intimate lakeside bistro, define your perfect shopping experience, snowmobile up 10,000 feet of unspoiled terrain in the Ruby Mountains or enjoy the bounty of Lake Tahoe's 18 world-class ski resorts – all of which take place in more than 300 inches of snow and 300 days of sunshine annually – you too will find Nevada capturing your heart.

Plan your Winter Getaway at TravelNevada.com and order your FREE Nevada Visitor's Package. 800.NEVADA.8

CONVENIENT NONSTOP FLIGHTS AVAILABLE TO NORTH AMERICA'S BEST VALUE DESTINATION **nevăda**

State departments of tourism can develop advertisements based on a clear understanding of what the state has to offer and what current tourists enjoy doing there. For example, this ad for Nevada shows beautiful mountains for skiing and the correct pronunciation of the state's name.

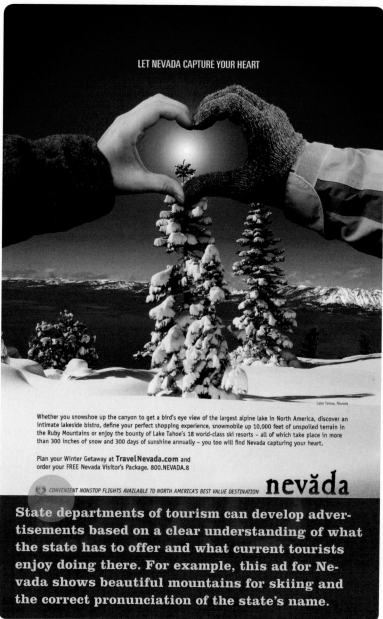

that respond to the wants and preferences of multiple constituencies. These include users, payers, donors, politicians, appointed officials, the media, and the general public. Nonprofit organizations cannot measure their success or failure in strictly financial terms.

The lack of a financial "bottom line" and the existence of multiple, diverse, intangible, and sometimes vague or conflicting objectives make prioritizing objectives, making decisions, and evaluating performance hard for nonprofit managers. They must often use approaches different from the ones commonly used in the private sector.

TARGET MARKETS Three issues relating to target markets are unique to nonprofit organizations:

→ **APATHETIC OR STRONGLY OPPOSED TARGETS:** Private-sector organizations usually give priority to developing those market segments that are most likely to respond to particular offerings. In contrast, nonprofit organizations must often target those who are apathetic about or strongly opposed to receiving their services, such as vaccinations and psychological counseling.

→ **PRESSURE TO ADOPT UNDIFFERENTIATED SEGMENTATION STRATEGIES:** Nonprofit organizations often adopt undifferentiated strategies (see Chapter 8) by default. Sometimes they fail to recognize the advantages of targeting, or an undifferentiated approach may appear to offer economies of scale and low per-capita costs. In other instances, nonprofit organizations are pressured or required to serve the maximum number of people by targeting the average user.

→ **COMPLEMENTARY POSITIONING:** The main role of many nonprofit organizations is to provide services, with available resources, to those who are not adequately served by private-sector organizations. As a result, the nonprofit organization must often complement, rather than compete with, the efforts of others. The positioning task is to identify underserved market segments and to develop marketing programs that match their needs rather than target the niches that may be most profitable. For example, a university library may see itself as complementing the services of the public library rather than as competing with it.

PRODUCT DECISIONS There are three product-related distinctions between business and nonprofit organizations:

→ **BENEFIT COMPLEXITY:** Nonprofit organizations often market complex behaviors or ideas. Examples include the need to exercise or eat right and the need to quit smoking. The benefits that a person receives are complex, long term, and intangible, and therefore are more difficult to communicate to consumers.

→ **BENEFIT STRENGTH:** The benefit strength of many nonprofit offerings is quite weak or indirect. What are the direct, personal benefits to you

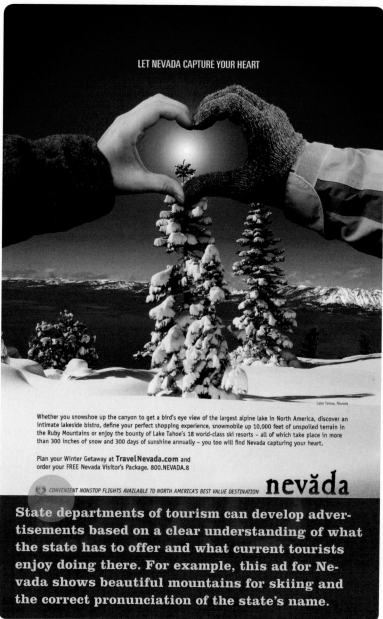

of driving 55 miles per hour or donating blood? In contrast, most private-sector service organizations can offer customers direct, personal benefits in an exchange relationship.

▸ **INVOLVEMENT:** Many nonprofit organizations market products that elicit very low involvement ("Prevent forest fires") or very high involvement ("Stop smoking"). The typical range for private-sector goods is much narrower. Traditional promotional tools may be inadequate to motivate adoption of either low- or high-involvement products.

PLACE (DISTRIBUTION) DECISIONS A nonprofit organization's capacity for distributing its service offerings to potential customer groups when and where they want them is typically a key variable in determining the success of those service offerings. For example, many large universities have one or more satellite campus locations to provide easier access for students in other areas. Some educational institutions also offer classes to students at off-campus locations via interactive video technology or at home via the Internet.

The extent to which a service depends on fixed facilities has important implications for distribution decisions. Services like rail transit and lake fishing can be delivered only at specific points. Many nonprofit services, however, do not depend on special facilities.

PROMOTION DECISIONS Many nonprofit organizations are explicitly or implicitly prohibited from advertising, thus limiting their promotion options. Most federal agencies fall into this category. Other nonprofit organizations simply do not have the resources to retain advertising agencies, promotion consultants, or marketing staff. However, nonprofit organizations have a few special promotion resources to call on:

▸ **PROFESSIONAL VOLUNTEERS:** Nonprofit organizations often seek out marketing, sales, and advertising professionals to help them develop and

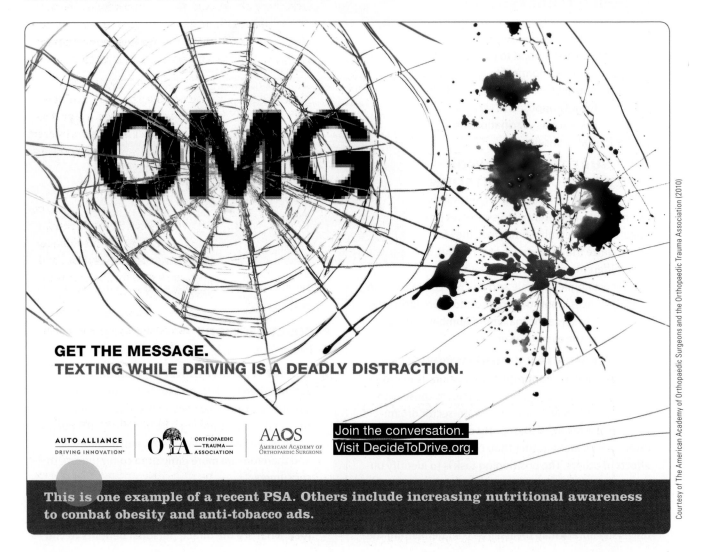

GET THE MESSAGE.
TEXTING WHILE DRIVING IS A DEADLY DISTRACTION.

AUTO ALLIANCE DRIVING INNOVATION® | OTA ORTHOPAEDIC TRAUMA ASSOCIATION | AAOS AMERICAN ACADEMY OF ORTHOPAEDIC SURGEONS

Join the conversation.
Visit DecideToDrive.org.

This is one example of a recent PSA. Others include increasing nutritional awareness to combat obesity and anti-tobacco ads.

Courtesy of The American Academy of Orthopaedic Surgeons and the Orthopaedic Trauma Association (2010)

implement promotion strategies. In some instances, an advertising agency donates its services in exchange for potential long-term benefits. Donated services create goodwill; personal contacts; and general awareness of the donor's organization, reputation, and competency.

» **SALES PROMOTION ACTIVITIES:** Sales promotion activities that make use of existing services or other resources are increasingly being used to draw attention to the offerings of nonprofit organizations. Sometimes nonprofit charities even team up with other companies for promotional activities.

» **PUBLIC SERVICE ADVERTISING:** A public service advertisement (PSA) is an announcement that promotes a program of a federal, state, or local government or of a nonprofit organization. Unlike a commercial advertiser, the sponsor of the PSA does not pay for the time or space. Instead, it is donated by the medium. The Advertising Council's PSAs are some of the most memorable advertisements of all time. For example, Smokey the Bear reminds everyone to be careful not to start wildfires.

PRICING DECISIONS Five key characteristics distinguish the pricing decisions of nonprofit organizations from those of the profit sector:

» **PRICING OBJECTIVES:** The main pricing objective in the profit sector is revenue or, more specifically, profit maximization, sales maximization, or target return on sales or investment. Many nonprofit organizations must also be concerned about revenue. Often, however, nonprofit organizations seek to either partially or fully defray costs rather than to achieve a profit for distribution to stockholders. Nonprofit organizations also seek to redistribute income—for instance, through taxation and sliding-scale fees. Moreover, they strive to allocate resources fairly among individuals or households or across geographic or political boundaries.

» **NONFINANCIAL PRICES:** In many nonprofit situations, consumers are not charged a monetary price but instead must absorb nonmonetary costs. The importance of those costs is illustrated by the large number of eligible citizens who do not take advantage of so-called "free" services for the poor. In many public assistance programs, about half the people who are eligible don't participate. Nonmonetary costs include time, embarrassment, and effort.

» **INDIRECT PAYMENT:** Indirect payment through taxes is common to marketers of "free" services, such as libraries, fire protection, and police protection. Indirect payment is not a common practice in the profit sector.

» **SEPARATION BETWEEN PAYERS AND USERS:** By design, the services of many charitable organizations are provided for those who are relatively poor and are largely paid for by those who are better off financially. Although examples of separation between payers and users can be found in the profit sector (such as insurance claims), the practice is much less prevalent.

» **BELOW-COST PRICING:** An example of below-cost pricing is university tuition. Virtually all private and public colleges and universities price their services below full cost.

public service advertisement (PSA) an announcement that promotes a program of a federal, state, or local government or of a nonprofit organization

STUDY TOOLS 12

↑ LOCATED AT BACK OF THE TEXTBOOK
- ☐ *Rip out Chapter Review Card*

LOCATED AT WWW.CENGAGE.COM/LOGIN
- ☐ *Review Key Terms Flashcards (print or online)*
- ☐ *Download audio and visual summaries to review on the go*
- ☐ *Complete both Practice Quizzes to prepare for tests*
- ☐ *Play "Beat the Clock" and "Quizbowl" to master concepts*
- ☐ *Complete "Crossword Puzzle" to review key terms*
- ☐ *Watch Video on "Pepe's Pizzeria" for a real company example*

13-1 SUPPLY CHAINS AND SUPPLY CHAIN MANAGEMENT

Many modern companies are turning to supply chain management for competitive advantage. A company's **supply chain** includes all of the companies involved in all of the upstream and downstream flows of products, services, finances, and information, from initial suppliers (the point of origin) to the ultimate customer (the point of consumption). The goal of **supply chain management** is to coordinate and integrate all of the activities performed by supply chain members into a seamless process, from the source to the point of consumption, ultimately giving supply chain managers "total visibility" of the supply chain both inside and outside the firm. The philosophy behind supply chain management is that by visualizing the entire supply chain, supply chain managers can maximize strengths and efficiencies at each level of the process to create a highly competitive, customer-driven supply system that is able to respond immediately to changes in supply and demand.

⌐In today's marketplace, products are being driven by customer demand and businesses' need to balance demand with supply.⌐

supply chain the connected chain of all of the business entities, both internal and external to the company, that perform or support the logistics function

supply chain management a management system that coordinates and integrates all of the activities performed by supply chain members into a seamless process, from the source to the point of consumption, resulting in enhanced customer and economic value

Supply chain management reflects a completely customer-driven management philosophy. In the mass production era, manufacturers produced standardized products that were "pushed" down through marketing channels to consumers, who were convinced by salespeople to buy whatever was produced. In today's marketplace, however, demand is being driven by customers who expect to receive product configurations and services matched to their unique needs. The focus of businesses has shifted to determining how products and services are being "pulled" into the marketplace and partnering with members of the supply chain to enhance customer value. For example, strong supply chain relationships between automobile manufacturers and the after-market auto-parts industry make it possible to customize an automobile to a customer's specifications.[1]

Chapter **13**

Supply Chain Management

Learning Outcomes

13-1 *Define the terms* supply chain *and* supply chain management, *and discuss the benefits of supply chain management* 208–210

13-2 *Discuss the concepts of internal and external supply chain integration, and explain why each of these types of integration is important* 210–211

13-3 *Identify the eight key processes of excellent supply chain management, and discuss how each of these processes affects the end customer* 212–215

13-4 *Understand which key functional areas of a business impact supply chain success, and how* 215–220

13-5 *Discuss new technology and emerging trends in supply chain management* 221–223

After you finish this chapter go to **p223** *for* **STUDY TOOLS** 🧳 - - - - - →

supply chain agility an operational strategy focused on inducing inventory velocity and operational flexibility simultaneously in the supply chain

supply chain integration when multiple firms or business functions in a supply chain coordinate their activities and processes so that they are seamlessly linked to one another in an effort to satisfy the customer

demand-supply integration (DSI) a supply chain operational philosophy focused on integrating the supply-management and demand-generating functions of an organization

This reversal of the flow of demand from "push" to "pull" has resulted in a radical reformulation of traditional marketing, production, and distribution functions toward a philosophy of **supply chain agility**. Agile companies synchronize their activities through the sharing of supply and demand information, spend more time than their competitors on activities that create direct customer benefits, partner closely with suppliers and service providers to reduce customer wait times for products, and constantly seek to reduce supply chain complexity through the evaluation and reduction of nonperforming stock-keeping units (SKUs), among other strategies. By managing the product pipeline in this way, companies are able to reduce supply chain costs while at the same time offering better service and therefore can deliver improved products at better prices to customers.

13-1a Benefits of Supply Chain Management

Supply chain management is a key means of differentiation for a firm and a critical component in marketing and corporate strategy. Companies that focus on supply chain management commonly report lower inventory, transportation, warehousing, and packaging costs; greater supply chain flexibility; improved customer service; and higher revenues. Research has shown a clear relationship between supply chain performance and profitability. Additionally, because well-managed supply chains are able to provide better value to customers with only marginal incremental expenditure

In a supply chain, agility, which involves having a nimble quality recognized in many athletes, allows companies to adapt quickly to customer needs while reducing costs and increasing satisfaction.

on company assets, best-in-class supply chain companies such as Con-Agra Foods are becoming significantly more valuable investments for investors.

13-2 SUPPLY CHAIN INTEGRATION AND ITS BENEFITS

A key principle of supply chain management is that multiple firms and their functional areas work together to perform tasks as a single, unified system rather than as several individual companies or business units acting in isolation. Companies in a world-class supply chain combine their resources, capabilities, and innovations across multiple business functions such that they are used for the best interest of the entire supply chain as a whole. The goal is that the overall performance of the supply chain will be greater than the sum of its parts. As firms become increasingly supply chain oriented, they develop management practices that are consistent with this systems approach.

Management practices that are reflective of a highly coordinated effort between supply chain firms or across business functions within the same or different firms are said to be "integrated." In other words, **supply chain integration** occurs when multiple firms or their functional areas in a supply chain coordinate business processes so that they are seamlessly linked to one another. In a world-class supply chain, the customer may not know where the business activities of one firm or business unit end and where those of another begin—all the participating firms and business units appear to be reading from the same script.

In the modern supply chain, integration can be either internal or external to a focal firm, or in an ideal scenario, both. From an internal perspective, the very best companies develop a managerial orientation toward **demand-supply integration (DSI)**. Under the DSI philosophy, those functional areas in the company charged with creating customer demand (such as marketing, sales, or research/development) communicate frequently and are synchronized with the parts of the business charged with fulfilling the created

© ostill/Shutterstock.com

demand (purchasing, manufacturing, and logistics). This type of alignment enhances customer satisfaction by ensuring that, for example, salespeople make promises to customers that can actually be delivered on or that raw materials being purchased actually meet customer specifications before they are placed into the process. Simultaneously, the company gains efficiencies from ordering and using only those materials that lead directly to sales. In short, companies operating under a DSI philosophy are better at their business because all of the different divisions within the company "play from the same sheet of music."[2]

Additionally, the practice of world-class supply chain management requires that different companies act as if they are connected by a single mission and leadership. To accomplish this task across companies that have different ownership and interests, five types of external integration are sought by firms interested in providing top-level service to customers:[3]

Relationally integrated supply chains have a set of rules, policies, and/or procedures that dictate how firms will work together and that specify how conflicts among supply chain partners will be resolved.

▸ **RELATIONSHIP INTEGRATION** is the ability of two or more companies to develop social connections that serve to guide their interactions when working together. More specifically, relationship integration is the capability to develop and maintain a shared mental framework across companies that describes how they will depend on one another when working together. This includes the ways in which they will collaborate on activities or projects so that the customer gains the maximum amount of total value possible from the supply chain.

▸ **MEASUREMENT INTEGRATION** reflects the idea that performance assessments should be transparent and measurable across the borders of different firms, and should also assess the performance of the supply chain as a whole while holding each individual firm or business unit accountable for meeting its own goals.

▸ **TECHNOLOGY AND PLANNING INTEGRATION** refers to the creation and maintenance of information technology systems that connect managers across the firms in the supply chain; it requires information hardware and software systems that can exchange information when needed between customers, suppliers, and internal operational areas of each of the supply chain partners.

▸ **MATERIAL AND SERVICE SUPPLIER INTEGRATION** requires firms to link seamlessly to those outsiders that provide goods and services to them so that they can streamline work processes and thereby provide smooth, high-quality customer experiences. Both sides need to have a common vision of the total value creation process and be willing to share the responsibility for satisfying customer requirements to make supplier integration successful.

▸ **CUSTOMER INTEGRATION** is a competency that enables firms to offer long-lasting, distinctive, value-added offerings to those customers who represent the greatest value to the firm or supply chain. Highly customer-integrated firms assess their own capabilities and then match them to customers whose desires they can meet and who offer large enough sales potential for the linkage to be profitable over the long term.

Organizational success in achieving both the internal and external types of integration is very important. Highly integrated supply chains (those that are successful in achieving many or all of these types of integration) have been shown to be better at satisfying customers, managing costs, delivering high-quality products, enhancing productivity, and utilizing company or business unit assets, all of which translate into greater profitability for the firms and their partners working together in the supply chain.

13-3 THE KEY PROCESSES OF SUPPLY CHAIN MANAGEMENT

When firms practice good supply chain management, their functional departments or areas, such as marketing, research and development, and/or production, are integrated both within and across the linked firms. Integration, then, is "how" excellent supply chain management works. The business processes on which the linked firms work together represent the "what" of supply chain management—they are the objects of focus on which firms, departments, areas, and people work together when seeking to reduce supply chain costs or to generate additional revenues. **Business processes** are composed of bundles of interconnected activities that stretch across firms in the supply chain; they represent key areas that some or all of the involved firms are constantly working on in order to reduce costs and/or generate revenues for everyone throughout supply chain management. There are eight critical business processes on which supply chain managers must focus:

1. Customer relationship management
2. Customer service management
3. Demand management
4. Order fulfillment
5. Manufacturing flow management
6. Supplier relationship management
7. Product development and commercialization
8. Returns management[4]

13-3a Customer Relationship Management

The **customer relationship management (CRM) process** allows companies to prioritize their marketing focus on different customer groups according to each group's long-term value to the company or supply chain. Once higher-value customers are identified, firms should focus more on providing customized products and better service to this group than to others. The CRM process includes customer segmentation by value and subsequent generation of customer loyalty for the most attractive segments. This process provides a set of comprehensive principles for the initiation and maintenance of customer relationships and is often carried out with the assistance of specialized CRM computer software.

13-3b Customer Service Management

Whereas the CRM process is designed to identify and build relationships with good customers, the customer service management process is designed to ensure that those customer relationships remain strong. The **customer service management process** presents a multi-company, unified response system to the customer whenever complaints, concerns, questions, or comments are voiced. When the process is well executed, it can have a strong positive impact on revenues, often as a result of quick positive response to negative customer feedback, and sometimes even in the form of additional sales gained through the additional customer contact. Customers expect service from the moment a product is purchased until it is disposed of, and the customer service management process allows for touch points between the buyer and seller throughout this life cycle. The use of customer care software enables companies to enhance their customer service management process.

13-3c Demand Management

The **demand management process** seeks to align supply and demand throughout the supply chain by anticipating customer requirements at each level and creating demand-related plans of action prior to actual customer purchasing behavior. At the same time, demand management seeks to minimize the costs of serving multiple types of customers who have variable wants and needs. In other words, the demand management process allows companies in the supply chain to satisfy customers in the most efficient and effective ways possible. The activities such as collecting customer data, forecasting future demand, and developing activities that serve to "smooth out" demand help bring available inventory into alignment with customer desires. Though it is very difficult to predict exactly what items and quantities customers will buy prior

order fulfillment process a highly integrated process, often requiring persons from multiple companies and multiple functions to come together and coordinate to create customer satisfaction at a given place and time

manufacturing flow management process concerned with ensuring that firms in the supply chain have the needed resources to manufacture with flexibility and to move products through a multi-stage production process

supplier relationship management process supports manufacturing flow by identifying and maintaining relationships with highly valued suppliers

to purchase, demand management can ease the pressure on the production process and allow companies to satisfy most of their customers through greater flexibility in manufacturing, marketing, and sales programs. Much of the uncertainty in demand planning can be mitigated, however, by conducting collaborative planning, forecasting, and replenishment (CPFR) activities with the company's customers and suppliers. The Porsche assembly line in Leipzig, Germany, deals with any unexpected changes in demand through a flexible system. Parts arrive from all over the world just in time for assembly, and the line can work on two different models simultaneously to fill the exact number of vehicles needed.[5]

13-3d Order Fulfillment

One of the most fundamental processes in supply chain management is the order fulfillment process, which involves generating, filling, delivering, and providing on-the-spot service for customer orders. The **order fulfillment process** is a highly integrated process, often requiring persons from multiple companies and multiple functions to come together and coordinate to create customer satisfaction at a given place and time. The best order fulfillment processes reduce the time between order and customer receipt as much as possible while ensuring that the customer receives exactly what he or she wants. The shorter lead times are beneficial in that they allow firms to carry reduced inventory levels and free up cash that can be used on other projects. Overall, the order fulfillment process involves understanding both internal capabilities and external customer needs, and matching these together so that the supply chain maximizes profits while minimizing costs and waste. Amazon.com now uses Kiva robots to help workers pack three to four times as many orders per hour. The robots bring shelves to the packer based on what is in each customer's order, and the packer picks the correct item, packs it, and sends it off on another robot to be shipped, making the order fulfillment process in Amazon's warehouses go much faster.[6]

13-3e Manufacturing Flow Management

The **manufacturing flow management process** is concerned with ensuring that firms in the supply chain have the needed resources to manufacture with flexibility and to move products through a multi-stage production process. Firms with flexible manufacturing have the ability to create a wide variety of goods and/or services with minimized costs associated with changing production techniques. The manufacturing flow process includes much more than simple production of goods and services—it means creating flexible agreements with suppliers and shippers so that unexpected demand bursts can be accommodated.

The goals of the manufacturing flow management process are centered on leveraging the capabilities held by multiple members of the supply chain to improve overall manufacturing output in terms of quality, delivery speed, and flexibility, all of which tie to profitability.

13-3f Supplier Relationship Management

The **supplier relationship management process** is closely related to the manufacturing flow management process and contains several characteristics that parallel the customer relationship management process. The manufacturing flow management process is highly dependent on supplier relationships for flexibility. Furthermore, in a way similar to that found in the customer relationship management process, supplier relationship management provides structural support for developing and maintaining relationships with suppliers. Thus, by integrating these two ideas, supplier relationship management supports manufacturing flow by identifying and maintaining relationships with highly valued suppliers. Just as firms benefit from developing close-knit, integrated relationships with customers, close-knit, integrated relationships with suppliers provide a means through which performance advantages can be gained.

The management of supplier relationships is a key step toward ensuring that firms' manufacturing resources are available. Thus, the supplier relationship management process has a direct impact on each supply chain member's bottom-line financial performance.

PepsiCo decided it needed more control over major parts of its supply chain and purchased two of its major bottlers. As a result, PepsiCo is able to work more closely with its retailers.[7]

13-3g Product Development and Commercialization

The **product development and commercialization process** (discussed in detail in Chapter 11) includes the group of activities that facilitates the joint development and marketing of new offerings among a group of supply chain partner firms. In many cases, new products and services are not the sole responsibility of a single firm that serves as inventor, engineer, builder, marketer, and sales agent; rather, they are often the product of a multi-company collaboration with multiple firms and business units playing unique roles in new-product development, testing, and launch activities, among others. The capability for developing and introducing new offerings quickly is key for competitive success versus rival firms, so it is often advantageous to involve many supply chain partners in the effort. The process requires the close cooperation of suppliers and customers who provide input throughout the process and serve as advisers and co-producers for the new offering(s).

13-3h Returns Management

The final supply chain management process deals with situations in which customers choose to return a product to the retailer or supplier, thereby creating a reversed flow of goods within the supply chain. The **returns management process** enables firms to manage volumes of returned product efficiently while minimizing returns-related costs and maximizing the value of the returned assets to the firms in the supply chain. Returns have the potential to affect a firm's financial position in a major and negative way if mishandled. In certain industries, such as apparel e-retailing, returns can amount to as much as 40 percent of sales volume.

In addition to the value of managing returns from a pure asset-recovery perspective, many firms are discovering that returns management

Oh man, this is the wrong color…

© PedroVieira/Shutterstock.com / © Jozsef Bagota/Shutterstock.com also creates additional marketing and customer service touch points that can be leveraged for added customer value above and beyond normal sales and promotion-driven encounters. Handling returns gives the company an additional opportunity to please the customer, and customers who have positive experiences with the returns management process can become very confident buyers who are willing to reorder, since they know any problems they encounter with purchases will be quickly and fairly rectified. In addition, the returns management process allows the firm to recognize weaknesses in product design and/or areas for potential improvement through the direct customer feedback that initiates the process.

13-4 HOW BUSINESS LOGISTICS FUNCTIONS IMPACT THE SUPPLY CHAIN

Critical to the success of any supply chain is orchestrating the means by which products move physically through it. This is accomplished via the execution of three interdependent groups of functions within a business organization that are collectively known as logistics. Often described as a sequence of "source, make, and deliver," **logistics** is the process of strategically managing the efficient flow and storage of raw materials, in-process inventory, and finished goods from point of origin to point of consumption. As mentioned earlier, supply chain management coordinates and integrates all of the activities performed by supply chain members into a seamless process. In a world-class supply chain organization, these three groups of functions are supported by a well-developed supply chain information system and are coordinated by a supply chain team. The **supply chain team**, in concert with the supply chain information system, orchestrates the movement of goods, services, and information from the source to the consumer. Supply chain teams typically cut across organizational boundaries, embracing all parties who participate in moving the product to market. The best supply chain teams also move beyond the organization to include the external participants in the chain, such as suppliers, transportation carriers, and third-party logistics suppliers. Members of the supply chain communicate, coordinate, and cooperate extensively.

13-4a Sourcing and Procurement

Beginning with the "source" category of functions, one of the most important links in the supply chain is that between the manufacturer and the supplier. Purchasing professionals are on the front lines of supply chain management. Purchasing, or procurement, departments plan strategies, develop specifications, select suppliers, and negotiate price and service levels.

The goal of most sourcing and procurement activities is to reduce the costs of raw materials and supplies. Purchasing professionals have traditionally relied on tough negotiations to get the lowest price possible from suppliers of raw materials, supplies, and components. Perhaps the biggest contribution purchasing can make to supply chain management, however, is in the area of vendor relations. Companies can use the purchasing function to strategically manage suppliers in order to reduce the total cost of materials and services. Through enhanced vendor relations, buyers and sellers can develop cooperative relationships that reduce costs and improve efficiency with the aim of lowering prices and enhancing profits. By integrating suppliers into their companies' businesses, purchasing managers have become better able to streamline purchasing processes, manage inventory levels, and reduce overall costs of the sourcing and procurement operations.

13-4b Inventory Control

The organization's **inventory control system** develops and maintains an adequate assortment of materials or products to meet a manufacturer's or a customer's demands. Inventory decisions, for both raw materials and finished goods, have a big impact on supply chain costs and the level of service provided. If too many products are kept in inventory, costs increase—as do risks of obsolescence, theft, and damage. If too few products are kept on hand, then the company risks product shortages and angry customers, and ultimately lost sales. The goal of inventory management, therefore, is to keep inventory levels as low as possible while maintaining an adequate supply of goods to meet customer demand.

logistics the process of strategically managing the efficient flow and storage of raw materials, in-process inventory, and finished goods from point of origin to point of consumption

supply chain team an entire group of individuals who orchestrate the movement of goods, services, and information from the source to the consumer

inventory control system a method of developing and maintaining an adequate assortment of materials or products to meet a manufacturer's or a customer's demand

materials requirement planning (MRP; materials management) an inventory control system that manages the replenishment of raw materials, supplies, and components from the supplier to the manufacturer

distribution resource planning (DRP) an inventory control system that manages the replenishment of goods from the manufacturer to the final consumer

automatic replenishment program a real-time inventory system that triggers shipments only when a good is sold to the end user

order processing system a system whereby orders are entered into the supply chain and filled

electronic data interchange (EDI) information technology that replaces the paper documents that usually accompany business transactions, such as purchase orders and invoices, with electronic transmission of the needed information to reduce inventory levels, improve cash flow, streamline operations, and increase the speed and accuracy of information transmission

Managing inventory from the supplier to the manufacturer is called **materials requirement planning (MRP)**, or **materials management**. This system also encompasses the sourcing and procurement operations, signaling when raw materials, supplies, or components will need to be replenished for the production of more goods. The system that manages the finished goods inventory from manufacturer to end user is commonly referred to as **distribution resource planning (DRP)**. Both inventory systems use various inputs, such as sales forecasts, available inventory, outstanding orders, lead times, and mode of transportation to be used, to determine what needs to be done to replenish goods at all points in the supply chain. Marketers identify demand at each level in the supply chain, from the retailer back up the chain to the manufacturer, and use electronic data interchange to transmit important information throughout the channel. This process is discussed in more detail below.

Some inventory replenishment systems use little or no forecasting. These **automatic replenishment programs** trigger shipments only when a good is sold to the end user and use an electronic link connected with bar-code scanners so that the supplier can view inventory in real time. When stock at the customer's location drops below predetermined levels, the supplier takes responsibility for restocking the shelves or the warehouse. This process often results in lower inventory levels.

13-4c Order Processing

Let's now turn to the "make" group of business logistics functions. The manufacturing process begins with a customer order. An **order processing system** processes the requirements of the customer and sends the information into the supply chain via the logistics information system. The order goes to the manufacturer's warehouse.

If the product is in stock, the order is filled, and arrangements are made to ship it. If the product is not in stock, the order triggers a replenishment request that finds its way to the factory floor.

Proper order processing is critical to good service. As an order enters the system, management must monitor two flows: the flow of goods and the flow of information. Good communication among sales representatives, office personnel, and warehouse and shipping personnel is essential to correct order processing. Shipping incorrect merchandise or partially filled orders can create just as much dissatisfaction as stockouts or slow deliveries. The flow of goods and information must be continually monitored so that mistakes can be corrected before an invoice is prepared and the merchandise shipped.

Order processing is becoming more automated through the use of computer technology known as **electronic data interchange (EDI)**. The basic idea of EDI is

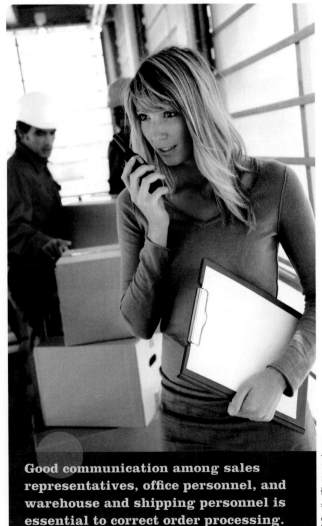

Good communication among sales representatives, office personnel, and warehouse and shipping personnel is essential to correct order processing.

© Goodluz/Shutterstock.com

to replace the paper documents that usually accompany business transactions, such as purchase orders and invoices, with electronic transmission of the needed information. A typical EDI message includes all the information that would traditionally be included on a paper invoice, such as product code, quantity, and transportation details. The information is usually sent via private networks, which are more secure and reliable than the networks used for standard e-mail messages. Most important, the information can be read and processed by computers, significantly reducing costs and increasing efficiency. Companies using EDI can reduce inventory levels, improve cash flow, streamline operations, and increase the speed and accuracy of information transmission. EDI also creates a closer relationship between buyers and sellers.

13-4d Production

Under traditional mass-market **build-to-stock** manufacturing, production begins when forecasts call for additional products to be made or when inventory control systems signal low inventory levels. The firm then makes a product and transports the finished goods to its own warehouses or those of intermediaries, where the goods wait to be ordered by retailers or customers. For example, many types of convenience goods, such as toothpaste, deodorant, and detergent, are manufactured based on past sales and demand and then sent to retailers to resell. Build-to-stock production scheduling, based on forecasts and push selling, obviously has its disadvantages, the most notable being that companies risk making products that may become obsolete or that consumers don't want in the first place.

In the modern "pull" manufacturing environment, production of goods or services is not scheduled until the customer (specifying a desired configuration) places an order. This process, known as **mass customization**, or **build-to-order**, uniquely tailors mass-market goods and services to the needs of the individuals who buy them. Companies as diverse as BMW, Dell, Levi Strauss, Mattel, and a host of Web-based businesses are adopting mass customization to maintain or obtain a competitive edge.

A hybrid strategy that minimizes the risks and maximizes the benefits of both the build-to-stock and build-to-order strategies is **postponement**. With postponement, the product is partially produced based on generic forecasts of aggregate demand and is shipped to distribution locations near where demand is forecasted to occur. Then, once customers place an order, the production process is completed to the customers' specifications. This strategy allows companies to maximize customer satisfaction (by giving them exactly what they want) while at the same time controlling costs (by minimizing the number of basic units needed to do so).

The emergence of these different approaches to production has lead to the development of parallel operational philosophies known as lean, agile, and leagile supply chain management. Based on the Toyota Production System, the lean system emphasizes reduction of waste and maximization of efficiency in a build-to-stock system. Alternatively, an agile system employs a more expensive but more effective "wait-and-see" approach that includes the use of flexible production and quick reaction to customer demand changes. The hybrid leagile system allows for the use of build-to-stock strategies for high volume, stable demand products, and build-to-order strategies for everything else. This strategy was popularly employed for the production of Toyota's Scion brand of cars, with the base model produced in a Japanese factory and a number of customer options added at a small plant near the Port of Long Beach, California.[8]

13-4e Warehousing and Materials Handling

Finally, we consider the functional areas that together make up the "deliver" or distribution functions of logistics. Although some manufacturing processes may eliminate the need to warehouse many raw materials, manufacturers may keep some safety stock on hand in the event of an emergency, such as a strike at a supplier's plant or a catastrophic event that temporarily stops the flow of raw materials to the production line. Likewise, the final user may not need or want the goods at the same time the manufacturer produces and wants to sell them. Products such as grain and corn are produced seasonally, but consumers demand them year-round. Other products such as Christmas ornaments and turkeys are produced year-round, but consumers do not want them until autumn or winter. Therefore, management must have a storage system to hold these products until they are shipped.

build-to-stock a production method whereby products are made in advance of demand based on forecasts and are stored until customer orders arrive

mass customization (build-to-order) a production method whereby products are not made until an order is placed by the customer; products are made according to customer specifications

postponement a hybrid production method whereby basic units of a finished good are manufactured in advance of actual demand and held in strategic form or location until demand occurs, when final customization takes place

Storage helps manufacturers manage supply and demand, or production and consumption. It provides time utility to buyers and sellers, which means that the seller stores the product until the buyer wants or needs it. But storing additional product does have disadvantages, including the costs of insurance on the stored product, taxes, obsolescence or spoilage, theft, and warehouse operating costs. Another drawback is opportunity costs—that is, the opportunities lost because money is tied up in stored product instead of being used for something else.

Because businesses are focusing on cutting supply chain costs, the warehousing industry is investing in services using sophisticated tracking technology such as materials-handling systems. An effective **materials-handling system** moves inventory into, within, and out of the warehouse quickly with minimal handling. With a manual, nonautomated materials-handling system, a product may be handled more than a dozen times. Each time it is handled, the cost and risk of damage increase; each lifting of a product stresses its packaging. Consequently, most manufacturers today have moved to automated systems. Scanners quickly identify goods entering and leaving a warehouse through bar codes affixed to the packaging. Automatic storage and retrieval systems store and pick goods in the warehouse or distribution center. Automated materials-handling systems decrease product handling, ensure accurate placement of product, and improve the accuracy of order picking and the rates of on-time shipment. For example, Dell uses a computer system called OptiPlex to run its factories. The computer software receives orders, sends requests for parts to suppliers, orders components, organizes assembly of the product, and even arranges for the product to be shipped. Instead of hundreds of workers, often fewer than six are working at a Dell factory at one time. An order for a few hundred computers can be filled in less than eight hours using the automated system. With the OptiPlex system, productivity has increased dramatically.

13-4f Transportation

Transportation has traditionally accounted for 5–10 percent of the price of goods, though steadily rising fuel costs have recently elevated this proportion to as much as 17 percent. Supply chain logisticians must decide which mode of transportation to use to move products from supplier to producer and from producer to buyer. These

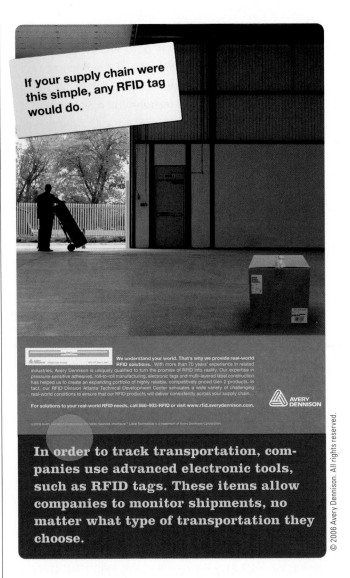

If your supply chain were this simple, any RFID tag would do.

We understand your world. That's why we provide real-world **RFID solutions.** With more than 70 years' experience in related industries, Avery Dennison is uniquely qualified to turn the promise of RFID into reality. Our expertise in pressure-sensitive adhesives, roll-to-roll manufacturing, electronic tags and multi-layered label construction has helped us to create an expanding portfolio of highly reliable, competitively priced Gen 2 products. In fact, our RFID Division Atlanta Technical Development Center simulates a wide variety of challenging real-world conditions to ensure that our RFID products will deliver consistently across your supply chain.

For solutions to your real-world RFID needs, call 866-903-RFID or visit www.rfid.averydennison.com.

AVERY DENNISON

In order to track transportation, companies use advanced electronic tools, such as RFID tags. These items allow companies to monitor shipments, no matter what type of transportation they choose.

decisions are, of course, related to all other logistics decisions. The five major modes of transportation are railroads, motor carriers, pipelines, water transportation, and airways. Maersk, a global container shipping line, has drastically reduced the cost of shipping overseas by manufacturing container ships that can carry 18,000 containers (each one twenty feet long) at once. These ships are the largest ever built. Larger ships have a greater economy of scale (meaning that they can transport so many more items that the price per item decreases drastically), enabling companies to ship a greater variety of items, from wheat and trucks to iPods and powdered milk.[9] Supply chain managers generally choose a mode of transportation on the basis of several criteria:

▸▸ **COST:** The total amount a specific carrier charges to move the product from the point of origin to the destination.

» **TRANSIT TIME:** The total time a carrier has possession of goods, including the time required for pickup and delivery, handling, and movement between the point of origin and the destination.

» **RELIABILITY:** The consistency with which the carrier delivers goods on time and in acceptable condition.

» **CAPABILITY:** The ability of the carrier to provide the appropriate equipment and conditions for moving specific kinds of goods, such as those that must be transported in a controlled environment (e.g., under refrigeration).

» **ACCESSIBILITY:** A carrier's ability to move goods over a specific route or network.

» **TRACEABILITY:** The relative ease with which a shipment can be located and transferred.

The mode of transportation used depends on the needs of the shipper as they relate to these six criteria. Exhibit 13.1 compares the basic modes of transportation based on these criteria.

In many cases, especially in a build-to-order environment, the transportation network replaces the warehouse or eliminates the expense of storing inventories, as goods are timed to arrive the moment they're needed on the assembly line or for shipment to customers.

13-4g Supply Chain Technology

Finally, it is important to note that all of the source, make, and deliver functions must be supported by adequate information systems architecture. The most prominent of these elements, the **logistics information system**, serves as the link connecting all of the operational components of the supply chain. The components of the system include, for example, software for materials acquisition and handling, warehouse-management and enterprise-wide solutions, data storage and integration in data warehouses, mobile communications, electronic data interchange, radio-frequency identification (RFID) chips, and the Internet. Working together, the components of the logistics information system are the fundamental enablers of successful supply chain management.

In addition to the logistics information system, several other technological advances and business trends are affecting the job of the supply chain manager today. Advanced computer technology has boosted the efficiency of logistics dramatically with tools such as automatic identification systems (auto ID) using bar coding and radio frequency technology, communications technology, and supply chain software systems that help synchronize the flow of goods and information with customer demand. Looking again at Amazon.com's state-of-the-art fulfillment centers, warehouse management system technology is used to maximize efficiency. Incoming product is immediately sent to the first available empty shelf space. That means a shipment of golf balls could end up next to *Best American Short Stories 2011*. As online orders come in, Kiva robot pods pull moveable shelves and take them to the employees who pull the order items (indicated with a laser pointer), scan them, pack them, and place them on another Kiva pod to go to shipping.[10]

Smart RFID (radio-frequency identification) tags, which are an inventory handling and tracking system that employs radio-frequency electromagnetic fields to transfer and read product data via an electronic tag, are another type of advanced computer technology that is helping companies manage their supply chains. Walmart requires many of its clothing suppliers to put smart tags on items of clothing so that it can identify if any pieces are missing in stores or in shipments.

logistics information system the link that connects all the logistics functions of the supply chain

smart RFID an inventory handling and tracking system that employs radio-frequency electromagnetic fields to transfer and read product data via an electronic tag

Exhibit 13.1

CRITERIA FOR RANKING MODES OF TRANSPORTATION

	Highest				Lowest
Relative Cost	Air	Truck	Rail	Pipe	Water
Transit Time	Water	Rail	Pipe	Truck	Air
Reliability	Pipe	Truck	Rail	Air	Water
Capability	Water	Rail	Truck	Air	Pipe
Accessibility	Truck	Rail	Air	Water	Pipe
Traceability	Air	Truck	Rail	Water	Pipe

© Cengage Learning

Previously, Walmart tracked pallets or boxes, allowing it to track shipments on an aggregated level but not individual items. The individual tags also allow Walmart to track individual pieces back to the manufacturer; and furthermore, the company hopes to use this itemized technology to reduce shoplifting and employee theft and increase sales.

American Apparel tested similar technology and saw individual store sales rise as much as 14.3 percent over stores without the smart RFID tags. When theft is reduced, merchandise that shoplifters tend to target remains available for sale, increasing a store's likelihood of having better sales figures.[11]

INNOVATIVE USES OF RFID AT THE GAME

When fans take their seats at a Seattle Seahawks football game, they enjoy a different experience than patrons of many other NFL stadiums due to smart RFID. Based on ultra-high-frequency smart tags embedded within their game tickets, each fan gets a customized fan experience based on speed of service. Whereas fans of other teams wait in long lines for concessions and fan gear, fans with a **Seahawks PowerPay smart tag** simply walk up, select the items they want, and return to their seats. The smart tag embedded in their ticket connects simultaneously to a personal profile with their credit card information and a similar tag attached to the product containing pricing information. When the fan leaves the retail area, a reader detects each of these signals and charges the customer's account. With fewer employees needed to complete transactions, the employees can turn their attention to ensuring that shelves are stocked and food is fresh. The Seahawks say this process reduced the typical wait time for an average transaction from 37.5 seconds to as little as 6.5 seconds. Because the lines were short (or nonexistent) and more products were available, fans made multiple purchases per game. Following the Seahawks' PowerPay success, several other teams in multiple sports have adopted similar technology for an array of purposes. The New York Red Bulls, a Major League Soccer Team, use the technology at turnstiles for fan admission as well as for in-stadium purchases, and fans can always print a receipt at several kiosks located within the facility. As an incentive to try the program out, some fans received text messages from star players inviting them to private autograph sessions before or after matches based on their presence at the game being detected.

Source: Jack Bell, "RBNY to Use RFID at Turnstiles," *New York Times*, February 22, 2010, D4.

13-5 TRENDS IN SUPPLY CHAIN MANAGEMENT

Several technological advances and business trends are affecting the job of the supply chain manager today. Some of the business trends that are affecting supply chain management include outsourcing logistics, maintaining a secure supply chain and minimizing supply chain risk, and maintaining a sustainable supply chain. While these trends exert pressure on managers to change the way their supply chains function, electronic distribution is being used and changed frequently to help make supply chain management more integrated and easier to track.

13-5a Outsourcing Logistics Functions

Partnering organizations are becoming increasingly efficient at dividing responsibility for supply chain management. **Outsourcing**, or **contract logistics**, is a rapidly growing initiative in which a manufacturer or supplier turns over an entire logistical function (often buying and managing transportation, warehousing, and/or light postponed manufacturing) to an independent **third-party logistics company (3PL)**. When a firm's order fulfillment process is managed diligently, the amount of time between order placement and receipt of the customer's payment following order shipment (known as the order-to-cash cycle) is minimized as much as possible. Since many firms do not view order fulfillment as a core competency (versus, for example, product development or marketing), they often outsource this function to a 3PL that specializes in the order fulfillment process. The 3PL becomes a semi-permanent part of the firm's supply chain and is assigned to manage one or more specialized functions.[12] Other, more comprehensive partners, often known as **fourth-party logistics**

companies (4PLs) or logistics integrators, create and manage entire solutions for getting products where they need to be, when they need to be there. Many times 3PLs and 4PLs provide a firm's only interaction with the customer, so they need to represent the needs and interests of the entire firm and supply chain. Developing and training these firms' employees to be empowered and to respond to the customer's needs in the best interest of the supply chain is becoming increasingly important.

Outsourcing enables companies to cut inventories, locate stock at fewer plants and distribution centers, and still provide the same level of service or even better. The companies then can refocus investment on their core business. In the hospitality industry, Avendra negotiates with suppliers to obtain virtually everything a hotel might need, from food and beverages to golf course maintenance. For example, by relying on Avendra to manage many aspects of the supply chain, companies like Fairmont Hotels & Resorts and

outsourcing (contract logistics) a manufacturer's or supplier's use of an independent third party to manage an entire function of the logistics system, such as transportation, warehousing, or order processing

third-party logistics company (3PL) a firm that provides functional logistics services to others

fourth-party logistics company (4PL or logistics integrator) a consulting-based organization that assesses another's entire logistical service needs and provides integrated solutions, often drawing on multiple 3PLs for actual service

Hotels that use an outside company to manage the logistics of providing food, beverages, and even landscaping are able to focus more on their core goal of providing service to guests.

© iStockphoto.com/Steve Debenport

offshoring the outsourcing of a business process from one country to another for the purpose of gaining economic advantage

nearshoring the transfer of an offshored activity from a distant to a nearby country

supply chain risk any potential disruption that threatens the supply chain's efficient and effective operations

supply chain security efforts made by companies to protect their in-transit inventory or value-transforming assets from external or internal threats

supply chain resilience the ability of a supply chain to return to its ideal operational state after being disrupted

electronic distribution a distribution technique that includes any kind of product or service that can be distributed electronically, whether over traditional forms such as fiber-optic cable or through satellite transmission of electronic signals

three-dimensional printing (3DP) the creation of three-dimensional objects via an additive manufacturing (printing) technology that layers raw material into desired shapes

InterContinental Hotels Group can concentrate on their core function—providing hospitality. The most progressive companies are engaging in vested outsourcing relationships, whereby both parties collaborate deeply to find mutually beneficial arrangements that allow both parties to "win" by reducing overall costs while achieving better performance.[13]

Because a logistics service provider is focused on logistical functions only, clients receive better service in a timely, efficient manner, thereby increasing their customers' satisfaction and boosting the perception of added value to a company's offerings. In many recent instances, North American companies have been **offshoring**, or outsourcing logistics to service providers located in countries with lower labor costs, such as China or India. However, as fuel costs have risen and security issues become more prominent, many companies have begun to relocate outsourced operations closer to home. **Nearshoring** to locations such as Mexico or the Caribbean nations ensures low costs while reducing supply chain risk.

13-5b Supply Chain Risk, Security, and Resilience

Throughout history, it has been important for organizations to protect their supplies and assets from unexpected disruptions, delays, and damage. It was not until the 9/11 tragedy in the United States, however, that the management of **supply chain risk** became a critical business focus. Modern companies undertake contingency and crisis planning to mitigate the effects of disruptions such as terrorist attacks, disastrous weather events or other acts of God, systems failures such power grid failure or widespread computer viruses, and volatile changes in supply or demand.

Leading supply chain companies are enacting two sets of countermeasures. Proactive **supply chain**

> ## Rising fuel costs and security concerns have driven outsourced operations closer to home in a new practice called *nearshoring*.

© iStockphto.com/Chris Lemmens

security measures seek to protect key inventory and assets from damage, theft, or destruction, while reactive **supply chain resilience** measures ensure that the supply chain is back up and running as soon as possible in the event that a disruption occurs. Many firms are enacting both types of countermeasures simultaneously. To improve its resilience, Toyota is asking its Japanese-based suppliers to spread its production capacity across a broader geographic area in the event another earthquake were to hit the island. Additionally, the company is using multiple distribution centers such that any single disruption would leave it with sufficient finished goods inventory to continue selling cars.[14]

13-5c Electronic Distribution

Electronic distribution is the most recent development in the logistics arena. Broadly defined, **electronic distribution** includes any kind of product or service that can be distributed electronically, whether over traditional forms such as fiber-optic cable or through satellite transmission of electronic signals. Companies like E*TRADE, Apple (iTunes), and Movies.com have built their business models around electronic distribution.

In the near future, however, electronic distribution will not be limited only to products and services that are mostly composed of information that can therefore be easily digitized. Experiments with **three-dimensional printing (3DP)** have been successful in industries such as auto parts, biomedical, and even fast food. Using 3DP technology, objects are built to precise specifications using liquefied raw materials at or near the location where they will be consumed. MakerBot Industries prints customized nylon bicycle frames based on customer specifications in only a few hours, thus reducing the need to transport steel frames around the world before they can be assembled and sold.[15] Shipping liquefied raw material such as nylon is cheaper than shipping finished bicycles because it can be enclosed in a perfectly cubic container, thereby making transportation much more efficient and cost effective.

13-5d Sustainable Supply Chain Management

In response to the need for firms to both gain cost savings and act as leaders in protecting the natural environment, many are adopting sustainable supply chain management principles as a key part of their supply chain strategy. **Sustainable supply chain management** involves the integration of environmentally conscious thinking into all phases of key supply chain management processes. Such activities include green supply chain initiatives like environmentally friendly materials sourcing; the design of products with consideration given to their environmental impact based on packaging, shipment, and use; and end-of-life management for products including easy recycling and/or clean disposal. By enacting sustainable supply chain management principles, firms hope to simultaneously generate cost savings and protect the Earth's natural resources from excess pollution, damage, and/or wastefulness.

> **sustainable supply chain management**
> a supply chain management philosophy that embraces the need for optimizing social and environmental costs in addition to financial costs

UPS is working continuously on developing a more sustainable supply chain. Integrating technology, mechanics, and employees makes delivering packages more fuel- and emissions-efficient—the proof lies in the 3.3 percent reduction in fuel use per package from 2009 to 2010. Additionally, UPS has logged 200 million miles on alternative fuel vehicles and offers carbon-neutral delivery in thirty-six countries.[16]

13-5e Global Logistics and Supply Chain Management

Global markets present their own sets of logistical challenges. It is critical for importers of any size to understand and cope with the legalities of trade in other countries. Shippers and distributors must be aware of the permits, licenses, and registrations they may need to acquire and, depending on the type of product they are importing, the tariffs, quotas, and other regulations that apply in each country. This multitude of different rules is why multinational companies are so committed to working through the World Trade Organization to develop a global set of rules and to encourage countries to participate.

Transportation can also be a major issue for companies dealing with global supply chains. Uncertainty regarding shipping usually tops the list of reasons companies, especially smaller ones, resist international markets. In some instances, poor infrastructure makes transportation dangerous and unreliable. And the process of moving goods across the borders of even the most industrialized nations can still be complicated by government regulations.

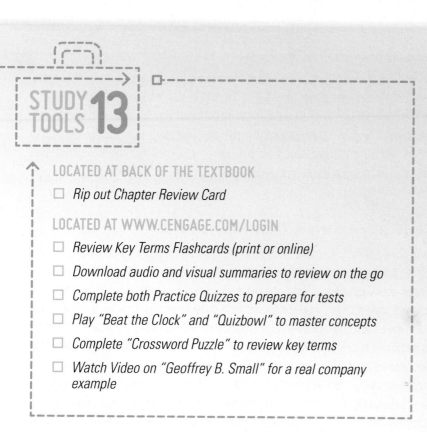

STUDY TOOLS 13

↑ LOCATED AT BACK OF THE TEXTBOOK
☐ *Rip out Chapter Review Card*

LOCATED AT WWW.CENGAGE.COM/LOGIN
☐ *Review Key Terms Flashcards (print or online)*
☐ *Download audio and visual summaries to review on the go*
☐ *Complete both Practice Quizzes to prepare for tests*
☐ *Play "Beat the Clock" and "Quizbowl" to master concepts*
☐ *Complete "Crossword Puzzle" to review key terms*
☐ *Watch Video on "Geoffrey B. Small" for a real company example*

14-1 MARKETING CHANNELS

A marketing channel can be viewed as a canal or pipeline through which products, their ownership, communication, financing and payment, and accompanying risk flow to the consumer. A **marketing channel** (also called a **channel of distribution**) is a business structure of interdependent organizations that reaches from the point of production to the consumer and facilitates the downstream physical movement of goods through the supply chain. Channels represent the "place" or "distribution" element of the marketing mix (product, price, promotion, and place).

> Retailers link the consumer and the supply chain, and are charged with facilitating the eventual purchase of goods manufactured upstream in the channel.

marketing channel (channel of distribution) a set of interdependent organizations that eases the transfer of ownership as products move from producer to business user or consumer

channel members all parties in the marketing channel who negotiate with one another, buy and sell products, and facilitate the change of ownership between buyer and seller in the course of moving the product from the manufacturer into the hands of the final consumer

Many different types of organizations participate in marketing channels. **Channel members** (also called *intermediaries*, *resellers*, and *middlemen*) negotiate with one another, buy and sell products, and facilitate the change of ownership between buyer and seller in the course of moving the product from the manufacturer into the hands of the final consumer. As products move to the final consumer, channel members facilitate the distribution process by providing specialization and division of labor, overcoming discrepancies, and providing contact efficiency.

14-1a How Marketing Channels Work

According to the concept of *specialization and division of labor*, breaking down a complex task into smaller, simpler ones and allocating them to specialists will create greater efficiency and lower average production costs via economies of scale. Marketing channels attain economies of scale through specialization and division of labor by aiding upstream producers (who often lack motivation, financing, or expertise) to market to end users or consumers. In some cases, such as for consumer goods like soft drinks, the cost of marketing directly to millions of consumers—taking and shipping individual orders—is prohibitive. For this reason, producers engage other channel members such as wholesalers and retailers to do what the producers are not well suited to do. Some channel members can accomplish certain tasks more efficiently than others because they have built strategic relationships with key suppliers or customers, or have unique capabilities. Their

Chapter 14

Marketing Channels and Retailing

Learning Outcomes

After you finish this chapter go to
p245 *for* **STUDY TOOLS**

© iStockphoto.com/OSTILL

form utility the elements of the composition and appearance of a product that make it desirable

time utility the increase in customer satisfaction gained by making a good or service available at the appropriate time

place utility the usefulness of a good or service as a function of the location at which it is made available

exchange utility the increased value of a product that is created as its ownership is transferred

retailer a channel intermediary that sells mainly to consumers

merchant wholesaler an institution that buys goods from manufacturers and resells them to businesses, government agencies, and other wholesalers or retailers and that receives and takes title to goods, stores them in its own warehouses, and later ships them

specialized expertise enhances the overall performance of the channel.

Because customers, like businesses, are specialized, they rely on other entities for the fulfillment of most of their needs. Imagine what your life would be like if you had to grow your own food, make your own clothes, produce your own television shows, and assemble your own automobile! Luckily, members of marketing channels are available to undertake these tasks for us. However, not all goods and services produced by channel members exist in exactly the ways we'd like, at least at first. Marketing channels are valuable because they aid producers in creating form, time, place, and exchange utility for customers, such that products become aligned with their needs. Channel members provide **form utility** when they transform oats grown on a distant farm into the Cheerios that we like to eat for breakfast. **Time** and **place utility** are created when a transport company hired by the producer physically moves boxes of cereal to a store near our homes in time for our next scheduled shopping trip. And a retailer, who is willing to swap the desired product for some amount of money we are willing to reasonably give, creates **exchange utility** in doing so.

14-1b Contact Efficiency—The Special Retailer Role

Retailers are those firms in the channel that sell directly to consumers as their primary function. A critical role fulfilled by retailers within the marketing channel is that they provide contact efficiency for consumers. Suppose you had to buy your milk at a dairy and your meat at a stockyard, etc. You would spend a great deal of time, money, and energy just shopping for a few groceries. Retailers simplify distribution by cutting the number of transactions

required by consumers, making an assortment of goods available in one location. Consider the example illustrated in Exhibit 14.1. Four consumers each want to buy a television set. Without a retail intermediary like Best Buy, television manufacturers JVC, Zenith, Sony, Toshiba, and RCA would each have to make four contacts to reach the four consumers who are in the target market, for a total of twenty transactions. However, when Best Buy acts as an intermediary between the producer and consumers, each producer has to make only one contact, reducing the number to nine transactions. This benefit to customers accrues whether the retailer operates in a physical store location or online format.

14-1c Functions and Activities of Intermediaries

Intermediaries in a channel negotiate with one another, facilitate the change of ownership between buyers and sellers, and physically move products from the manufacturer to the final consumer. The most prominent difference separating intermediaries is whether they take title to the product. *Taking title* means they own the merchandise and control the terms of the sale—for example, price and delivery date. Retailers and merchant wholesalers are examples of intermediaries that take title to products in the marketing channel and resell them. **Merchant wholesalers** are organizations that facilitate the movement of products

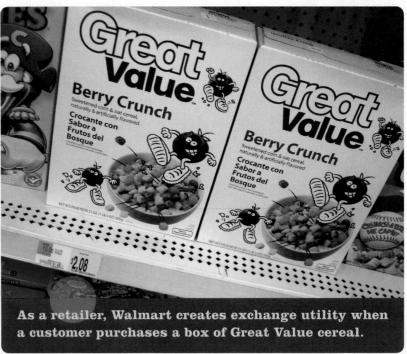

As a retailer, Walmart creates exchange utility when a customer purchases a box of Great Value cereal.

© Terri Miller/E-Visual Communications, Inc.

and services from the manufacturer to producers, resellers, governments, institutions, and retailers. All merchant wholesalers take title to the goods they sell, and most of them operate one or more warehouses where they receive goods, store them, and later reship them to retailers, manufacturers, and institutional clients. Since wholesalers do not typically alter the form of a good or sell it directly to the consumer, their value hinges on their providing time and place utility and contact efficiency to retailers.

Other intermediaries do not take title to goods and services they market but do facilitate the exchange of ownership between sellers and buyers. **Agents and brokers** simply facilitate the sale of a product from producer to end user by representing retailers, wholesalers, or manufacturers. Unlike wholesalers, agents or brokers only facilitate sales and generally have little input into the terms of the sale. They do, however, get a fee or commission based on sales volume. For example, when selling a home, the owner usually hires a real estate agent who then brings potential buyers to see the house. The agent facilitates the sale by bringing the buyer and owner together but never actually takes ownership of the home.

Variations in channel structures are due in large part to variations in the numbers and types of wholesaling intermediaries. Generally, product characteristics, buyer considerations, and market conditions determine the types and number of intermediaries the manufacturer should use.

▸▸ Standardized, customized, or highly complex products such as insurance are usually sold through an agent or broker who may represent one or multiple companies. In contrast, a standardized product such as soda is sold through a merchant wholesaler and retailer channel.

▸▸ Buyer considerations such as purchase frequency or customer wait time influence channel choice. When there is no time pressure, customers may save money on books by ordering online and taking direct distribution from a wholesaler. However, if a book is needed immediately, it will have to be purchased at retail—at the school bookstore—and will include a markup.

agents and brokers wholesaling intermediaries who do not take title to a product but facilitate its sale from producer to end user by representing retailers, wholesalers, or manufacturers

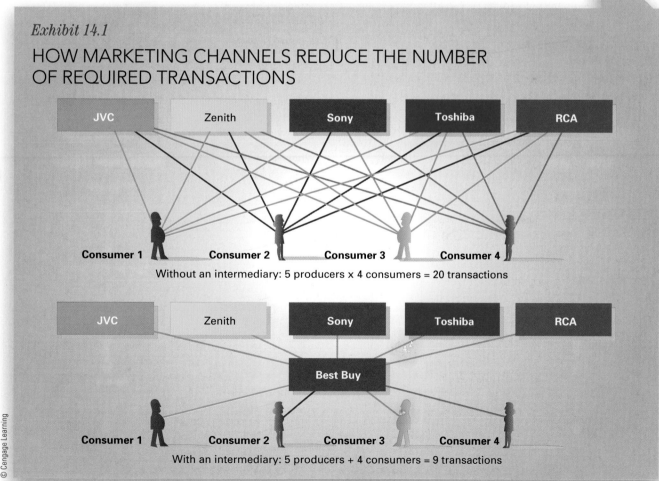

Exhibit 14.1

HOW MARKETING CHANNELS REDUCE THE NUMBER OF REQUIRED TRANSACTIONS

Without an intermediary: 5 producers x 4 consumers = 20 transactions

With an intermediary: 5 producers + 4 consumers = 9 transactions

© Cengage Learning

▸▸ **Market characteristics such as how many buyers are in the market and whether they are concentrated in a general location also influence channel design. In a home sale, the buyer and seller are localized in one area, which facilitates the use of a simple agent/broker relationship, whereas mass-manufactured goods such as automobiles may require parts from all over the world and therefore many intermediaries.**

14-1d Channel Functions Performed by Intermediaries

Retailing and wholesaling intermediaries in marketing channels perform essential functions that enable goods to flow between producer and consumer. *Transactional* functions involve contacting and communicating with prospective buyers to make them aware of existing products and to explain their features, advantages, and benefits. Intermediaries in the channel also provide *logistical* functions. Logistics functions typically include transportation and storage of assets, as well as their sorting, accumulation, consolidation, and/or allocation for the purpose of conforming to customer requirements. These issues are described in detail in Chapter 13. The third basic channel function, *facilitating*, includes research and financing.

Research provides information about channel members and consumers by getting answers to key questions: Who are the buyers? Where are they located? Why do they buy? Financing ensures that channel members have the money to keep products moving through the channel to the ultimate consumer. Although individual members can be added to or deleted from a channel, someone must still perform these essential functions. Producers, end users, or consumers can perform them, as can channel intermediaries such as wholesalers and retailers, and sometimes nonmember channel participants such as service providers.

14-2 CHANNEL STRUCTURES

A product can take many routes to reach its final consumer. Marketers and consumers each search for the most efficient channel from many available alternatives. Marketing a consumer convenience good such as candy differs from marketing a specialty good like a Prada handbag. Exhibit 14.2 illustrates the four ways manufacturers can route products to consumers. When possible, producers use the **direct channel** to sell directly to consumers.

Exhibit 14.2

MARKETING CHANNELS FOR CONSUMER PRODUCTS

Direct channel	Retailer channel	Wholesaler channel	Agent/broker channel
Producer	Producer	Producer	Producer
			Agents or brokers
		Wholesalers	Wholesalers
	Retailers	Retailers	Retailers
Consumers	Consumers	Consumers	Consumers

© Cengage Learning

Direct marketing activities—including telemarketing, mail order and catalog shopping, and forms of electronic retailing such as online shopping and shop-at-home television networks—are a good example of this type of channel structure. There are no intermediaries. Producer-owned stores and factory outlet stores—like Sherwin-Williams, Polo Ralph Lauren, Oneida, and WestPoint Home—are examples of direct channels.

By contrast, when one or more channel members are small companies lacking in marketing power, an *agent/broker channel* may be the best solution. Agents or brokers bring manufacturers and wholesalers together for negotiations, but they do not take title to merchandise. Ownership passes directly to one or more wholesalers and then to retailers, who sell to the ultimate consumer.

Most consumer products are sold through distribution channels similar to the other two alternatives: the retailer channel and the wholesaler channel. A *retailer channel* is most common when the retailer is large and can buy in large quantities directly from the manufacturer. Walmart, Sears, and car dealers are examples of retailers that often bypass a wholesaler. A *wholesaler channel* is commonly used for low-cost items that are frequently purchased, such as candy, cigarettes, and magazines.

14-2a Channels for Business and Industrial Products

As Exhibit 14.3 illustrates, five channel structures are common in business and industrial markets. First, *direct channels* are typical in business and industrial markets. For example, manufacturers buy large quantities of raw materials, major equipment, processed materials, and supplies directly from other manufacturers. Manufacturers that require suppliers to meet detailed technical specifications often prefer direct channels. Apple uses a direct channel to purchase high-resolution retina displays for its innovative third-generation iPad. To ensure supply for iPad construction, Apple takes direct shipments of the screens from Sharp, LG, and Samsung.[1]

Alternatively, companies selling standardized items of moderate or low value often rely on *industrial distributors*. In many ways, an industrial distributor is like a supermarket

Exhibit 14.3

CHANNELS FOR BUSINESS AND INDUSTRIAL PRODUCTS

Direct channel	Direct channel	Industrial distributor channel	Agent/broker channel	Agent/broker–industrial distributor channel
Producer	Producer	Producer	Producer	Producer
			Agents or brokers	Agents or brokers
		Industrial distributors		Industrial distributors
Industrial users	Government buyers	Industrial users	Industrial users	Industrial users

dual distribution (multiple distribution) the use of two or more channels to distribute the same product to target markets

nontraditional channels non-physical (often electronic) channels that facilitate the unique market access of products and services

strategic channel alliance a cooperative agreement between business firms to use the other's already established distribution channel

for organizations. Industrial distributors are wholesalers and channel members that buy and take title to products. Moreover, they usually keep inventories of their products and sell and service them. Often small manufacturers cannot afford to employ their own sales force. Instead, they rely on manufacturers' representatives or selling agents to sell to either industrial distributors or users. Additionally, the Internet has enabled virtual distributors to emerge and has forced traditional industrial distributors to expand their business model. Many manufacturers and consumers are bypassing distributors and going direct, often via the Internet.

14-2b Alternative Channel Arrangements

Rarely does a producer use just one type of channel to move its product. It usually employs several different or alternative channels, which include multiple channels, nontraditional channels, and strategic channel alliances. When a producer selects two or more channels to distribute the same product to target markets, this arrangement is called **dual distribution** (or **multiple distribution**). As more people embrace online shopping, an increasing number of retailers are using multiple distribution channels. Additionally, **nontraditional channels** may help differentiate a firm's product from the competition. Nontraditional channels include the Internet, mail-order channels, or infomercials. Although nontraditional channels may limit a brand's coverage, they can give a producer serving a niche market a way to gain market access and customer attention without having to establish channel intermediaries and can also provide another avenue of sales for larger firms. Furthermore, companies often form **strategic channel alliances** that enable them to use another manufacturer's already-established channel. Alliances are used most often when the creation of marketing channel relationships may be too expensive and time consuming. Whirlpool signed a deal with Chinese retailer Suning Appliance Company to have access to its 1,700 stores in China. This helps Whirlpool reach growing markets in smaller cities and broadens its small market in China.[2]

14-2c Factors Affecting Channel Choice

Managers must answer many questions before choosing a marketing channel. Managers must decide what role distribution will play in the overall marketing strategy. In addition, they must be sure that the channel strategy chosen is consistent with product, promotion, and pricing strategies. In making these decisions, marketing managers must determine what factors will influence the choice of channel and what level of distribution intensity will be appropriate. The final choice depends on the analysis of market factors, product factors, and producer factors.

MARKET FACTORS Among the most important market factors affecting the choice of distribution channel are target customer considerations. Specifically, managers should answer the following questions: Who are the potential customers? What do they buy? Where do they buy? When do they buy? How do they buy? Additionally, the choice of channel depends on whether the producer is selling to consumers or to industrial customers—due to differences in the buying routines of these groups. The geographic location and size of the market are also important to channel selection. As a rule, if the target market is concentrated in one or more specific areas, then direct selling through a sales force is appropriate, whereas intermediaries would be less expensive in broader markets.

PRODUCT FACTORS Complex, customized, and expensive products tend to benefit from shorter and more direct marketing channels. These types of products sell better through a direct sales force. Examples include pharmaceuticals, scientific instruments, airplanes, and mainframe computer systems. On the other hand, the more standardized a product is, the longer its distribution channel can be and the greater the number of intermediaries that can be involved. For example, with the exception of flavor and shape, the formula for chewing gum is about the same from producer to producer. As a result, the distribution channel for gum tends to involve many wholesalers and retailers.

The product's life cycle is also an important factor in choosing a marketing channel. In fact, the choice of channel may change over the life of the product. As products become more common and less intimidating to potential users, producers tend to look for alternative channels. Similarly, perishable products such as vegetables and milk have a relatively short life span, and fragile products like china and crystal require a minimum amount of handling. Therefore, both

Fragile products require
SHORT CHANNELS.

Less delicate products have more
CHANNEL FLEXIBILITY.

intensive distribution a form of distribution aimed at having a product available in every outlet where target customers might want to buy it

selective distribution a form of distribution achieved by screening dealers to eliminate all but a few in any single area

exclusive distribution a form of distribution that establishes one or a few dealers within a given area

require fairly short marketing channels. Online retailers such as eBay facilitate the sale of unusual or difficult-to-find products that benefit from a direct channel.

PRODUCER FACTORS Several factors pertaining to the producer itself are important to the selection of a marketing channel. In general, producers with large financial, managerial, and marketing resources are better able to use more direct channels. These producers have the ability to hire and train their own sales forces, warehouse their own goods, and extend credit to their customers. Smaller or weaker firms, on the other hand, must rely on intermediaries to provide these services for them. Compared to producers with only one or two product lines, producers that sell several products in a related area are able to choose channels that are more direct. Sales expenses then can be spread over more products.

A producer's desire to control pricing, positioning, brand image, and customer support also tends to influence channel selection. For instance, firms that sell products with exclusive brand images, such as designer perfumes and clothing, usually avoid channels in which discount retailers are present. Manufacturers of upscale products, such as Gucci (handbags) and Godiva (chocolates), may sell their wares only in expensive stores in order to maintain an image of exclusivity. Many producers have opted to risk their image, however, and test sales in discount channels. For example, Levi Strauss expanded its distribution to include JCPenney, Sears, and Walmart.

14-2d Levels of Distribution Intensity

Organizations have three options for intensity of distribution: intensive distribution, selective distribution, or

exclusive distribution. **Intensive distribution** is a form of distribution aimed at maximum market coverage. Here, the manufacturer tries to have the product available in every outlet where potential customers might want to buy it. If buyers are unwilling to search for a product, it must be made very accessible to buyers. The next level of distribution, **selective distribution**, is achieved by screening dealers and retailers to eliminate all but a few in any single area. Because only a few are chosen, the consumer must seek out the product. For example, HBO selectively distributes its popular television shows through a series of its own subscription-based channels (HBO, HBO on Demand, and HBO Go for mobile devices) and sells subscriptions or single episodes through Apple, Amazon.com, and Sony's online stores but does not stream them through Netflix or Blockbuster. The most restrictive form of market coverage is **exclusive distribution**, which entails only one or a few dealers within a given area. Because buyers may have to search or travel extensively to buy the product, exclusive distribution is usually confined to consumer specialty goods, a few shopping goods, and major industrial equipment. Products such as Rolls-Royce automobiles, Chris-Craft powerboats, and Pettibone tower cranes are distributed under exclusive arrangements.

14-3 TYPES OF CHANNEL RELATIONSHIPS

A marketing channel is more than a set of institutions linked by economic ties. Social relationships play an important role in building unity among channel members.

Glossary (margin)

arm's-length relationship
a relationship between companies that is loose, characterized by low relational investment and trust, and usually taking the form of a series of discrete transactions with no or low expectation of future interaction or service

cooperative relationship
a relationship between companies that takes the form of informal partnership with moderate levels of trust and information sharing as needed to further each company's goals

integrated relationship
a relationship between companies that is tightly connected, with linked processes across and between firm boundaries and high levels of trust and interfirm commitment

FLASH SALES AS CHANNEL ALTERNATIVES

With the booming popularity of **flash sale sites** like Gilt.com and Ruelala.com, where every day new fashion boutiques are revealed and discounts range from 15 to 80 percent, beauty brands are jumping on board to increase brand awareness. Companies such as Chrysallis are taking advantage of the daily traffic and customer base of flash sales sites to reach their target market. With an average shopper between twenty-five and forty years of age sporting an average income of $100,000 and expressing an interest in fashion and beauty, flash sales would seem to be a great alternative channel to add to the premium beauty channel structure.

Source: Jenny Fine, "Instant Gratification," *Women's Wear Daily*, April 22, 2011, 32–33.

Marketing managers should carefully consider the types of relationships they choose to foster between their company and other companies and in doing so pay close attention to the benefits and hazards associated with each relationship type. Relationships among channel members range from "loose" to "tight," taking the form of a continuum stretching from single transactions to complex interdependent relationships such as partnerships or alliances. The choice of relationship type is important for channel management because each relationship type carries with it different levels of time, financial, and resource investment. There are three basic types of relationships, organized here by degree of closeness:

▸ **Arm's-length relationships** are considered by channel members to be temporary or one-time-only and often arise from a sudden or unique need. These relationships are characterized by the companies' unwillingness or lack of ability to develop a closer type of relationship. Both parties typically retain their independence and pursue only their own interests while attempting to benefit from the goods or services provided by the other. A major weakness of arm's-length relationships is the potential for opportunism. Opportunistic behavior may occur when the members do not have a common goal; when members have not formed a formal relationship; when one company is more dependent on the other than vice versa; or when there is uncertainty within the relationship and the market.

▸ **Cooperative relationships**, generally administered using some kind of formal contract, are used when a company wants less ambiguity but doesn't want the long-term and/or capital investment necessary in an integrated relationship. Cooperative relationships tend to be more flexible than integrated relationships but are more structured than arm's-length relationships, and they include non-equity agreements such as franchising and licensing as well as joint ventures and strategic alliances.

▸ **Integrated relationships** are closely bonded relationships characterized by formal arrangements that explicitly define the relationships of the channel members. These relationships may take two forms. With vertical integration, all the related channel members are owned by a single legal entity, whereas in a supply chain, several companies act as one.

14-3a Global Channel Relationships

Some countries enact economic policies that directly or indirectly regulate channel choices. For example, due to the size of India's market, many companies are interested in operating there. India does not explicitly prohibit foreign retailers from entering its market, but it protects its businesses by levying heavy taxes on foreign retailers. To address this issue, many companies, including Mercedes-Benz, Toyota, and General Motors, have entered joint ventures with local Indian companies. Through these joint ventures, foreign companies are able to compete effectively in India's available distribution channels.[3]

Marketers must also be aware that many countries have "gray" marketing channels in which products are distributed through unauthorized channel intermediaries. It is estimated that sales of counterfeit luxury items like Prada handbags and Big Bertha golf clubs have reached almost

$2 billion a year. The Internet has also proved to be a way for pirates to circumvent authorized distribution channels, especially in the case of popular prescription drugs.

14-3b Social Influences in Channels

In addition to considering the multiple different types of channel relationships and their costs and benefits, managers must also be aware of the social dimensions that are constantly affecting their relationships. The basic social dimensions of channels are power, control, leadership, conflict, and partnering. **Channel power** is a channel member's ability to control or influence the behavior of other channel members. For example, Walmart's size and buying power have allowed it to pressure its Chinese suppliers into becoming more environmentally conscious.[4] **Channel control** occurs when one channel member's power affects another member's behavior. To achieve

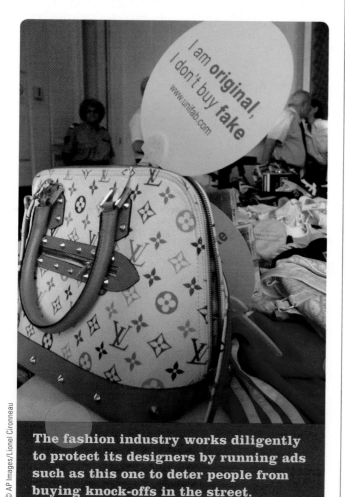

The fashion industry works diligently to protect its designers by running ads such as this one to deter people from buying knock-offs in the street.

control, a channel member assumes channel leadership and exercises authority and power. This member is termed the **channel captain**. In one marketing channel, a manufacturer may be the captain because it controls new-product designs and product availability, while in another, a retailer may be a follower because it lacks relative power and control over the retail price, inventory levels, and postsale service.

Inequitable channel relationships often lead to **channel conflict**, which is a clash of goals and methods among the members of a distribution channel. In a broad context, conflict may not be bad. Often it arises because staid, traditional channel members refuse to keep pace with the times. Removing an outdated intermediary may result in reduced costs for the entire channel. The Internet has forced many intermediaries to offer services such as merchandise tracking and inventory availability online. Conflict within a channel can be either horizontal or vertical. **Horizontal conflict** occurs among channel members on the same level, such as two or more different wholesalers or two or more different retailers that handle the same manufacturer's brands. This type of channel conflict is found most often when manufacturers practice dual or multiple distribution strategies. When Apple changed its distribution strategy and began opening its own stores, it angered its traditional retail partners, some of whom ultimately filed lawsuits against the company. However, much more serious is **vertical conflict**, which occurs between different levels in a marketing channel, most typically between the manufacturer and wholesaler or the manufacturer and retailer. Producer-versus-wholesaler conflict occurs when the producer chooses to bypass the wholesaler and deals directly with the consumer or retailer.

Regardless of who holds power or what conflicts arise, channel members rely heavily on one another. **Channel partnering** is the joint effort of all channel

channel power
the capacity of a particular marketing channel member to control or influence the behavior of other channel members

channel control
a situation that occurs when one marketing channel member intentionally affects another member's behavior

channel captain
a member of a marketing channel that exercises authority and power over the activities of other channel members

channel conflict
a clash of goals and methods between distribution channel members

horizontal conflict
a channel conflict that occurs among channel members on the same level

vertical conflict
a channel conflict that occurs between different levels in a marketing channel, most typically between the manufacturer and wholesaler or between the manufacturer and retailer

channel partnering the joint effort of all channel members to create a channel that serves customers and creates a competitive advantage

retailing all the activities directly related to the sale of goods and services to the ultimate consumer for personal, nonbusiness use

members to create a channel that serves customers and creates a competitive advantage. Channel partnering is vital if each member is to gain something needed from other members.

14-4 THE ROLE OF RETAILING

Retailing represents all the activities directly related to the sale of goods and services to the ultimate consumer for personal, nonbusiness use and has enhanced the quality of our daily lives. When we shop for groceries, hair styling, clothes, books, and many other products and services, we patronize retailers. The millions of goods and services provided by retailers mirror the needs and styles of modern society. The U.S. economy depends heavily on the retail sector. In early 2012, indicators estimated that approximately two-thirds of the U.S. gross domestic product comes from retail activity.[5]

Retailing affects all people directly or indirectly. The retailing industry is one of the largest employers in the United States, with over 1.5 million U.S. retailers employing more than 15 million people—about one in five American workers. And the industry is expected to grow to over 16.5 million by 2018.[6] In addition, retail trade accounts for 10.8 percent of all U.S. employment, and almost 10 percent of all businesses in 2012 were classified as retailers.[7] Yet, retailing is still largely a mom-and-pop business. Almost nine out of ten retail companies employ fewer than twenty employees, and according to the National Retail Federation, over 90 percent of all retailers operate just one store.[8] Though most retailers are quite small, a few giant organizations such as Walmart dominate the industry; Walmart's annual U.S. sales are greater than the sales of the four next largest U.S. retailers combined.

14-5 CLASSES OF RETAIL OPERATIONS

Retail establishments can be classified according to ownership, level of service, product assortment, and price, and retailers use the latter three variables to position themselves in the competitive marketplace. These variables can be combined in several ways to create distinctly different retail operations. Exhibit 14.4 depicts the major types of retail stores and classifies them by level of service, product assortment, price, and gross margin.

14-5a Ownership

Depending on the type of ownership arrangement, a retailer can also gain advantages from broad brand identity or freedom to take risks and innovate. Retail ownership takes one of three forms: independent, part of a chain, or

Exhibit 14.4

TYPES OF STORES AND THEIR CHARACTERISTICS

Type of Retailer	Level of Service	Product Assortment	Price	Gross Margin
Department store	Moderately high to high	Broad	Moderate to high	Moderately high
Specialty store	High	Narrow	Moderate to high	High
Supermarket	Low	Broad	Moderate	Low
Drugstore	Low to moderate	Medium	Moderate	Low
Convenience store	Low	Medium to narrow	Moderately high	Moderately high
Full-line discount store	Moderate to low	Medium to broad	Moderately low	Moderately low
Specialty discount store	Moderate to low	Medium to broad	Moderately low to low	Moderately low
Warehouse club	Low	Broad	Low to very low	Low
Off-price retailer	Low	Medium to narrow	Low	Low
Restaurant	Low to high	Narrow	Low to high	Low to high

© Cengage Learning

a franchise outlet. An **independent retailer** is a retailer owned by a single person or group and is not operated as part of a larger network. Around the world, most retailers are independent, operating singular stores within a local community. Local florists and ethnic food markets typically fit this classification. Alternatively, a **chain store** is part of a group of the same stores owned and operated by a single organization. Under this form of ownership, a home office for the entire chain handles many administrative tasks. The home office also buys most of the merchandise sold in the stores. Gap and Starbucks are retail chains. A **franchise** is a business where the operator is granted a license to operate and sell a product under a larger supporting organization, such as Subway and Quiznos. Franchising is covered in greater detail below.

14-5b Level of Service

The level of service that retailers provide can be classified along a continuum, from full-service to self-service. Some retailers, such as exclusive clothing stores, offer high levels of service. They provide alterations, credit, delivery, consulting, liberal return policies, layaway, gift wrapping, and personal shopping. Retailers like factory outlets and warehouse clubs offer virtually no services.

14-5c Product Assortment

The third basis for positioning or classifying retailers is by the breadth and depth of their product line. Specialty stores such as Best Buy, Toys"R"Us, or GameStop have the most concentrated product assortments, usually carrying single or narrow product lines but with considerable depth. For example, a specialty pet store like PetSmart may carry as many as twenty brands of dog food in a large variety of flavors, shapes, and sizes. On the other end of the spectrum, full-line discounters typically carry broad assortments of merchandise with limited depth.

Stores often modify their product assortment in order to accommodate environmental factors. During the recent recession, Saks broadened its product assortment to include entry-level-priced items, which are less expensive than the company's traditional luxury offerings. Over the last year, however, Saks has seen sales increase dramatically, so it is expanding its offerings to include a new line of private label women's shoes to take advantage of increased spending.[9] Other retailers, such as Nike factory outlet stores, may carry only part of a single line.

independent retailer a retailer owned by a single person or partnership and not operated as part of a larger retail institution

chain store a store that is part of a group of the same stores owned and operated by a single organization

franchise a relationship in which the business rights to operate and sell a product are granted by the franchisor to the franchisee.

gross margin the amount of money the retailer makes as a percentage of sales after the cost of goods sold is subtracted

14-5d Price

Price is the fourth way to position retail stores. Traditional department stores and specialty stores typically charge the full "suggested retail price." In contrast, discounters, factory outlets, and off-price retailers use low prices to lure shoppers. The last column in Exhibit 14.4 shows the typical **gross margin**—how much the retailer makes as a percentage of sales after the cost of the goods sold is subtracted.

14-5e Types of Retail Operations

Traditionally, there have been several distinct types of retail stores, each offering a different product assortment, type of service, and price level according to its customers' shopping preferences. Recently, however, retailers are experimenting with alternative formats that make it harder to classify them. For instance, supermarkets are expanding their nonfood items and services, discounters are adding groceries, drugstores are becoming more like convenience stores, and department stores are experimenting with smaller stores. Nevertheless, many stores still fall into the basic types:

▸ **DEPARTMENT STORES:** This category of retailer carries a wide variety of shopping and specialty goods, including apparel, cosmetics, housewares, electronics, and sometimes furniture. Each department is treated as a separate buying center, and central management sets broad policies about the types of merchandise carried and prices. Macy's, JCPenney, Sears, Dillard's, and Nordstrom are some of the largest U.S. department store chains.

▸ **SPECIALTY STORES:** This category is not only a type of store but also a method of retail operations—namely, specializing in a given type of merchandise. A typical specialty store carries a deeper but narrower assortment of specialty merchandise, and its knowledgeable salesclerks offer more attentive customer service. The Children's Place, Williams-Sonoma, and Foot Locker are examples of successful chain specialty retailers. Consumers usually consider price to be secondary in specialty outlets.

▸▸ **SUPERMARKETS:** These retailers are large, departmentalized, self-service retailers that specialize in food and some nonfood items. Some conventional supermarkets are being replaced by bigger *superstores*, which are often twice their size. Superstores meet the needs of today's customers for convenience, variety, and service by offering one-stop shopping for many food and nonfood needs, as well as many services—including pharmacies, flower shops, salad bars, photo processing, banking, etc. Their tendency to offer a wide variety of nontraditional goods and services under one roof is called scrambled merchandising.

▸▸ **DRUGSTORES:** This type of retailer stocks pharmacy-related products and services as its main draw, but drugstores also carry an extensive selection of cosmetics, health and beauty aids, seasonal merchandise, greeting cards, toys, and some non-refrigerated convenience foods. As competition has increased from mass merchandisers and supermarkets with their own pharmacies, as well as from direct mail prescription services, drugstores have added services such as twenty-four-hour drive-through pharmacies and low-cost health clinics staffed by nurse practitioners.

▸▸ **CONVENIENCE STORES:** These retailers can be defined as miniature supermarkets, carrying only a limited line of high-turnover convenience goods. These self-service stores are typically located near residential areas and are often open twenty-four hours a day, seven days a week. Convenience stores offer exactly what their name implies: convenient location, long hours, and fast service. The customer pays a surcharge for convenience, so prices are almost always higher at a convenience store than at a supermarket.

▸▸ **DISCOUNT STORES:** This category of retailer competes on the basis of low prices, high turnover, and high volume. Discounters can be classified into several major categories.

▸▸ *Full-line discount stores* offer consumers very limited service and carry a much broader assortment of well-known, nationally branded "hard goods," including housewares, toys, automotive parts, hardware, sporting goods, garden items,

T.J.Maxx offers few services, in keeping with its classification as an off-price retailer.

and clothing. As with department stores, national chains dominate the discounters; Walmart is the largest full-line discount store in terms of sales.

▸▸ *Supercenters* combine a full line of groceries and general merchandise with a wide range of services, including pharmacy, dry cleaning, portrait studios, photo finishing, hair salons, optical shops, and restaurants—all in one location. For supercenter operators such as Target, food is a customer magnet that sharply increases the store's overall volume while taking customers away from traditional supermarkets.

▸▸ *Specialty discount stores* are another type of discount store that carry a single line—for example, stores selling sporting goods, electronics, auto parts, office supplies, housewares, or toys. These stores offer a nearly complete selection of single-line merchandise and use self-service, discount prices, high volume, and high turnover to their advantage. A *category killer* is a specialty discount store that heavily dominates its narrow merchandise segment. Examples include Best Buy in electronics, Staples and Office Depot in office supplies, and IKEA in home furnishings.

▸▸ A *warehouse membership club* is a limited-service merchant wholesaler that sells a limited selection of brand name appliances, household items, and groceries. These are usually sold in bulk from warehouse outlets on a cash-and-carry basis to members only. Currently, the leading stores in this category are Walmart's Sam's Club, Costco, and BJ's Wholesale Club.

▸▸ **OFF-PRICE RETAILERS:** This type of retailer sells at prices 25 percent or more below traditional department store prices because it pays cash for its stock and usually doesn't ask for return privileges. Off-price retailers buy manufacturers' overruns at cost or for even less. They also absorb goods from bankrupt stores, irregular merchandise, and unsold end-of-season output. Today there are hundreds of off-price retailers; among the best known are T.J.Maxx, Ross Stores, Marshalls, and Tuesday Morning. **Factory outlets** are an interesting variation on the off-price concept. A *factory outlet* is an off-price retailer that is owned and operated by a manufacturer. Thus, it carries one line of merchandise—its own. With factory outlets, manufacturers can regulate where their surplus is sold, and they can realize higher profit margins than they would by disposing of the goods through independent wholesalers and retailers.

▸▸ **RESTAURANTS:** Not quite retailers, restaurants straddle the line between retailing establishments and service establishments. Restaurants do sell tangible products—food and drink—but they also provide a valuable service for consumers in the form of food preparation and food service. Most restaurants could even fall into the definition of a specialty retailer given that most concentrate their menu offerings on a distinctive type of cuisine—for example, Olive Garden Italian restaurants and Starbucks coffeehouses.

14-5f Nonstore Retailing

The retailing formats discussed so far have been in-store methods, in which customers must physically shop at stores. In contrast, **nonstore retailing** is shopping without visiting a store. Because consumers demand convenience, nonstore retailing is currently growing faster than in-store retailing. The major forms of nonstore retailing are automatic vending, direct retailing, direct marketing, and electronic retailing.

Automatic vending implies the use of machines to offer goods for sale—for example, the soft drink, candy, or snack vending machines found in college cafeterias and office buildings. Vending is the most pervasive retail business in the United States, and retailers are constantly seeking new opportunities to sell via vending. Many vending machines today sell nontraditional kinds of merchandise such as DVDs, digital cameras, perfumes, and even ice cream.

In **direct retailing**, representatives sell products door-to-door, office-to-office, or at home sales parties. Companies like Avon and The Pampered Chef have used this approach for years, though Avon has failed to keep up with the popularity of social media. Its sales representatives struggle to make sure their online clients can make a purchase that reflects the correct salesperson, which causes frustration and lost sales for everyone.[10]

Direct marketing, sometimes called **direct response marketing**, refers to the techniques used to get consumers to make a purchase from their home, office, or other nonretail setting. Those techniques include telemarketing, direct mail, catalogs and mail order, and electronic retailing. Shoppers using these methods are less bound by traditional shopping situations. Time-strapped consumers and those who live in rural or suburban areas

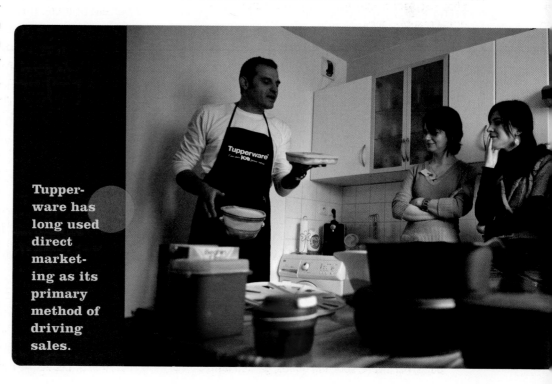

Tupperware has long used direct marketing as its primary method of driving sales.

© Jean-Phillipe Ksiazek/AFP/Getty Images

are most likely to be direct response shoppers because they value the convenience and flexibility that direct marketing provides.

Telemarketing is the use of the telephone to sell directly to consumers. It consists of outbound sales calls, usually unsolicited, and inbound calls—that is, orders through toll-free 800 numbers or fee-based 900 numbers. The use of telemarketing is not at all insignificant in modern marketing; recent estimates indicate that U.S. companies will spend over $15 billion on inbound and outbound calls by 2015.[11]

Direct mail can be the most efficient or the least efficient retailing method, depending on the quality of the mailing list and the effectiveness of the mailing piece. With direct mail, marketers can precisely target their customers according to demographics, geographics, and even psychographics. Direct mailers are becoming more sophisticated in targeting the "right" customers. Using statistical methods to analyze census data, lifestyle and financial information, and past purchase and credit history, direct mailers can pick out those most likely to buy their products. According to the Direct Marketing Association, every year U.S companies spend more than $150 billion on direct marketing, representing over 50 percent of their advertising expenditures and generating about $1.79 trillion in sales.[12]

Shop-at-home television networks are specialized forms of direct response marketing. These shows display merchandise, with the retail price, to home viewers. Viewers can phone in their orders directly on a toll-free line and shop with a credit card. The shop-at-home industry has quickly grown into a multi-billion-dollar business with a loyal customer following. Shop-at-home networks can reach nearly every home with a television set. The best-known shop-at-home networks are HSN (formerly the Home Shopping Network) and the QVC (Quality, Value, Convenience) Network.

Online retailing, or **e-tailing**, is a type of shopping available to consumers with personal computers and access to the Internet. Online sales accounted for $165.4 billion in sales in 2012, an increase of more than 14 percent over the previous year, and are expected to continue to grow by at least 10 percent annually through 2015.[13] Online retailing has exploded in the last several years as consumers have found this type of shopping convenient and, in many instances, less costly. Consumers can shop without leaving home, choose from a wide selection of merchants, use shopping comparison services to search the Web for the best price, and then have the items delivered to their doorsteps.

14-5g Franchising

As you read at the beginning of this section, a franchise is a continuing relationship in which a franchisor grants to a franchisee the business rights to operate or sell a product. The **franchisor** originates the trade name, product, methods of operation, and so on. The **franchisee**, in return, pays the franchisor for the right to use its name, product, or business methods. A franchise agreement between the two parties usually lasts for ten to twenty years, at which time the agreement can be renewed if both parties are agreeable.

To be granted the rights to a franchise, a franchisee usually pays an initial, one-time franchise fee. The amount of this fee depends solely on the individual franchisor, but it generally ranges from $50,000 to $250,000 or higher. In addition to this initial franchise fee, the franchisee is expected to pay royalty fees, usually in the range of 3 to 7 percent of gross revenues but occasionally as high as 12 percent or more. The franchisee may also be expected to pay advertising fees, which usually cover the cost of promotional materials and, if the franchise organization is large enough, regional or national advertising. A small mobile franchise called The Game Dudes, which sends video game–equipped vans to kids' parties, has an initial investment of $115,000 to $140,000, which includes a twenty-four-foot Mercedes-Benz van and training and marketing support.[14] Fees such as these are typical for all major franchisors, including Burger King and Subway.

Two basic forms of franchises are used today: product and trade name franchising and business format franchising. In *product and trade name franchising*, a dealer agrees to sell certain products provided by a manufacturer or a wholesaler. This approach has been used most widely in the auto and truck, soft drink bottling, tire, and gasoline service industries. For example, a local tire retailer may hold a franchise to sell Michelin tires. *Business format franchising* is an ongoing business relationship between a franchisor and a franchisee. Typically, a franchisor "sells" a franchisee the rights to use the franchisor's format or approach to doing business. This form of franchising has rapidly expanded through retailing, restaurant, food service, hotel and motel, printing, and real estate franchises. Exhibit 14.5 depicts the world's top franchising companies.

14-6 RETAIL MARKETING STRATEGY

Retailers must develop marketing strategies based on their periodic goals and overall strategic plans. Periodic retailing goals might include more traffic, higher sales of a specific item, developing a more upscale image, or creating heightened public awareness of the retail operation. The strategies that retailers use to obtain their goals might include a sale, updated décor, or a new advertisement. The key tasks in strategic retailing are defining and selecting a target market and developing the retailing mix to successfully meet the needs of the chosen target market.

14-6a Defining a Target Market

The first and foremost task in developing a retail strategy is to define the target market. This process begins with market segmentation, the topic of Chapter 8. Successful retailing has always been based on knowing the customer. Sometimes retailing chains flounder when management loses sight of the customers the stores should be serving.

Target markets in retailing are often defined by demographics, geographics, and psychographics. For example, high-end hotels such as W, Westin, and Marriott are tailoring their in-hotel shopping boutiques to meet the needs and wants of their customers. This includes stocking carry-on friendly merchandise, bedding, and geographically appropriate merchandise. Miami hotels have bathing suits, and New York hotels get ritzy shoes and skirts. By making sure that products meet the hotels' clientele, the boutiques ensure purchases will be made.[15] Determining a target market is a prerequisite to creating the retailing mix. For example, Target's merchandising approach for sporting goods is to match its product assortment to the demographics of the local store and region.

14-6b Choosing the Retailing Mix

Retailers combine the elements of the retailing mix to come up with a single retailing method to attract the target market. The **retailing mix** consists of six Ps: the four Ps of the marketing mix (product, place, promotion, and price) plus presentation and personnel (see Exhibit 14.6 on the next page). The combination of the six Ps projects a store's image, which influences consumers' perceptions. Using these impressions of stores, shoppers position one store against another. A retail manager must make sure that the store's positioning is aligned with target customers' expectations.

PRODUCT The first element in the retailing mix is the *product offering*, also called the *product assortment* or *merchandise mix*. Developing a product offering is essentially a question of the width and depth of the product assortment. *Width* refers to the assortment of products offered; *depth* refers to the number of different brands offered within each assortment. Price, store design, displays, and service are important to consumers in determining where to shop, but the most critical factor is merchandise selection. This reasoning also holds true for online retailers. Amazon.com, for instance, offers considerable width in its product assortment with millions of different items, including books, music, toys, videos, tools and hardware, health and beauty aids, electronics, and software. Conversely, online specialty retailers, such as 1-800-Flowers.com and Polo.com, focus on a single category of merchandise, hoping to attract loyal customers with a larger depth of products at lower prices and excellent customer service. Many online retailers purposely focus on single product line niches that could never garner enough foot traffic to support a traditional brick-and-mortar store. For instance, Web

retailing mix
a combination of the six Ps— product, place, promotion, price, presentation, and personnel— to sell goods and services to the ultimate consumer

Exhibit 14.5
TOP TEN FRANCHISORS

1. Hampton Hotels	6. McDonald's
2. Subway	7. Denny's
3. 7-Eleven	8. H&R Block
4. ServPro	9. Pizza Hut
5. Days Inn	10. Dunkin' Donuts

Source: Jason Daley, "The Top Ten Franchises for 2012," *Entrepreneur*, December 4, 2011, www.entrepreneur.com/slideshow/222422 (Accessed July 23, 2012).

Exhibit 14.6

THE RETAILING MIX

Product
Width and depth of product assortment

Personnel
Customer service and personal selling

Place (distribution)
Location and hours

Presentation
Layout and atmosphere

Promotion
Advertising, publicity, and public relations

Price

Target market

sites such as bugbitingplants.com and petflytrap.com sell and ship live carnivorous plants in the United States. After determining what products will satisfy target customers' desires, retailers must find sources of supply and evaluate the products. When the right products are found, the retail buyer negotiates a purchase contract.

PROMOTION Retail promotion strategy includes advertising, public relations and publicity, and sales promotion. The goal is to help position the store in consumers' minds. Retailers design intriguing ads, stage special events, and develop promotions aimed at their target markets. Today's grand openings are a carefully orchestrated blend of advertising, merchandising, goodwill, and glitter. All the elements of an opening—press coverage, special events, media advertising, and store displays—are carefully planned.

Retailers' advertising is carried out mostly at the local level. Local advertising by retailers usually provides specific information about their stores, such as location, merchandise, hours, prices, and special sales. In contrast, national retail advertising generally focuses on image. For example, Target uses advertisements similar to designer fashion advertisements to depict high-quality goods. Paired with the ubiquitous red target and tag line "Expect more. Pay less," Target is demonstrating that it sells products that

consumers normally aspire to own at prices they can afford.

Target's advertising campaign also takes advantage of cooperative advertising, another popular retail advertising practice. Traditionally, marketers would pay retailers to feature their products in store mailers, or a marketer would develop a television campaign for the product and simply tack on several retailers' names at the end. But Target's advertising makes use of a more collaborative trend by integrating products such as Tide laundry detergent or Coca-Cola into the actual campaign. Another common form of cooperative advertising involves promotion of exclusive products. For example, Target hires famous trendy designers for temporary partnerships, during which they develop reasonably priced product lines available exclusively at Target stores.

PLACE The retailing axiom "location, location, location" has long emphasized the importance of place to the retail mix. The *location* decision is important first because the retailer is making a large, semi-permanent commitment of resources that can reduce its future flexibility. Second, the location will affect the store's future growth and profitability.

Site location begins by choosing a community. Important factors to consider are the area's economic growth potential, the amount of competition, and geography. For instance, retailers like T.J.Maxx and Walmart often build stores in new communities that are still under development. Fast-food restaurants tend to place a priority on locations with other fast-food restaurants because being located in clusters helps to draw customers for each restaurant. However, even after careful research, the perfect position can be elusive in the face of changing markets. For example, Wendy's found, when attempting to enter the competitive breakfast business, that its locations weren't positioned on the right side of the road to attract the bulk of commuters looking for breakfast.[16] After settling on a geographic region or community, retailers must choose a specific site. In addition to growth potential, the important

destination store
a store that consumers
purposely plan to visit

factors to consider are neighborhood socioeconomic characteristics, traffic flows, land costs, zoning regulations, and public transportation. A particular site's visibility, parking, entrance and exit locations, accessibility, and safety and security issues are also important considerations.

Additionally, a retailer should consider how its store will fit into the surrounding environment. Retail decision makers probably would not locate a Dollar General store next door to a Neiman Marcus department store. Furthermore, retailers face decisions related to whether to have a freestanding unit or to become a tenant in a shopping center or mall. Large retailers like Walmart or Target and sellers of shopping goods like furniture and cars can use an isolated, freestanding location because they are "destination stores." A **destination store** is a store consumers seek out and purposely plan to visit. An isolated store location may have the advantages of low site cost or rent and no nearby competitors. On the other hand, it may be hard to attract customers to a freestanding location, and no other retailers are around to share costs.

Freestanding units are increasing in popularity as retailers strive to make their stores more convenient to access, more enticing to shop, and more profitable. Freestanding sites now account for more than half of all retail construction starts in the United States as more and more retailers are deciding not to locate in pedestrian malls. Perhaps the greatest reason for developing a freestanding site is greater visibility. Retailers often feel they get lost in huge centers and malls, but freestanding units can help stores develop an identity with shoppers. Also, an aggressive expansion plan may not allow time to wait for shopping centers to be built. Drugstore chains like Walgreens have been purposefully relocating their existing shopping center stores to freestanding sites, especially street corner sites for drive-through accessibility.

Shopping centers first appeared in the 1950s when the U.S. population started migrating to the suburbs. The first shopping centers were *strip centers*, typically located along busy streets. They usually included a supermarket, a variety store, and perhaps a few specialty stores. Then *community shopping centers* emerged, with one or two small department stores, more specialty stores, a couple of restaurants, and several apparel stores. These community shopping centers provided off-street parking and a broader variety of merchandise. *Regional malls* offering a much wider variety of merchandise started appearing in the mid-1970s. Regional malls are either entirely enclosed or roofed to allow shopping in any weather. Most are landscaped with trees, fountains, sculptures, and the like to enhance the shopping environment. They have acres of free parking. The *anchor stores* or *generator stores* (often major department stores) are usually located at opposite ends of the mall to create heavy foot traffic.

According to shopping center developers, *lifestyle centers* are emerging as the newest generation of shopping centers. Lifestyle centers typically combine outdoor shopping areas composed of upscale retailers and restaurants, with plazas, fountains, and pedestrian streets. They appeal to retail developers looking for an alternative to the traditional shopping mall, a concept rapidly losing favor among shoppers.

Many smaller specialty lines are opening shops inside larger stores to expand their retail opportunities without risking investment

Heidi Klum and other Victoria's Secret models celebrate at an opening ceremony for a New York store. The women are part of the Victoria's Secret promotion strategy.

© ny1/ny1/ZUMA Press/Newscom

in a separate store. Popular publisher Penguin teamed up with Barnes & Noble to open store-within-a-store boutiques. The boutiques are 220-square feet and have Penguin books as well as Penguin merchandise like tote-bags and stationery.[17] The Penguin boutiques reflect a popular trend of pop-up shops—tiny, temporary stores that stay in one location only for a few months. They help retailers reach a wide market while avoiding high rent at retail locations. Pop-up shops have become the marketing tool du jour for large companies.

PRICE Another important element in the retailing mix is price. Retailing's ultimate goal is to sell products to consumers, and the right price is critical in ensuring sales. Because retail prices are usually based on the cost of the merchandise, an essential part of pricing is efficient and timely buying. Price is also a key element in a retail store's positioning strategy. Higher prices often indicate a level of quality and help reinforce the prestigious image of retailers, as they do for Lord & Taylor and Neiman Marcus. On the other hand, discounters and off-price retailers, such as Target and T.J.Maxx, offer a good value for the money.

PRESENTATION The presentation of a retail store helps determine the store's image and positions the retail store in consumers' minds. For instance, a retailer that wants to position itself as an upscale store would use a lavish or sophisticated presentation. The main element of a store's presentation is its **atmosphere**, the overall impression conveyed by a store's physical layout, décor, and surroundings. The atmosphere might create a relaxed or busy feeling, a sense of luxury or efficiency, a friendly or cold attitude, a sense of organization or clutter, or a fun or serious mood. Urban Outfitters stores, targeted to Generation Y consumers, use raw concrete, original brick,

ANATOMY OF A
FITTING ROOM

A screen or closet offers a place to store unwanted items so they won't clutter the fitting room.

Assisted shoppers are twice as likely to make a purchase.

The changing room is private, well lit, spacious, and clean. Some stores use whiteboards to write shoppers' names on the door of the fitting room, offering a personalized touch.

Mirrors with movable panels encourage shoppers to step into the shared space, where assistants can make add-on sales and further interact with the customer.

Rugs break up a room and make it more colorful and inviting, which encourages customers to stay longer in the store.

Comfortable couches or chairs offer shoppers a place to rest.

layout the internal design and configuration of a store's fixtures and products

rusted steel, and unfinished wood to convey an urban feel. These are the most influential factors in creating a store's atmosphere:

→ **EMPLOYEE TYPE AND DENSITY:** Employee type refers to an employee's general characteristics— for instance, neat, friendly, knowledgeable, or service oriented. Density is the number of employees per thousand square feet of selling space. Whereas low employee density creates a "do-it-yourself," casual atmosphere, high employee density denotes readiness to serve the customer's every whim.

→ **MERCHANDISE TYPE AND DENSITY:** A prestigious retailer like Nordstrom or Neiman Marcus carries the best brand names and displays them in a neat, uncluttered arrangement. Discounters and off-price retailers often carry seconds or out-of-season goods crowded into small spaces and hung on long racks by category—tops, pants, skirts, etc.—creating the impression that "We've got so much stuff, we're practically giving it away."

→ **FIXTURE TYPE AND DENSITY:** Fixtures can be elegant (rich woods) or trendy (chrome and smoked glass); they can even consist of old, beat-up tables, as in an antiques store. The fixtures should be consistent with the general atmosphere the store is trying to create.

→ **SOUND:** Sound can be pleasant or unpleasant for a customer. Music can entice customers to stay in the store longer and buy more or to eat quickly and leave a table for others. It can also control the pace of the store traffic, create an image, and attract or direct the shopper's attention.

→ **ODORS:** Smell can either stimulate or detract from sales. Research suggests that people evaluate merchandise more positively, spend more time shopping, and are generally in a better mood when an agreeable odor is present. Retailers use fragrances as an extension of their retail strategy.

→ **VISUAL FACTORS:** Colors can create a mood or focus attention and therefore are an important factor in atmosphere. Red, yellow, and orange are considered warm colors and are used when a feeling of warmth and closeness is desired. Cool colors like blue, green, and violet are used to open up closed-in places and create an air of elegance and cleanliness. Many retailers have found that natural lighting, either from windows or skylights, can lead to increased sales. Outdoor lighting can also affect consumer patronage.

The **layout** of retail stores is also a key factor in their success. The goal is to use all of the store's space effectively, including aisles, fixtures, merchandise displays, and non-selling areas. In addition to making shopping easy and convenient for the customer, an effective layout has a powerful influence on traffic patterns and purchasing behavior. Layout also includes where products are placed in the store. Many technologically advanced retailers are using a technique called *market-basket analysis* to sift through the data collected by their point-of-purchase scanning equipment. The analysis looks for products that are commonly purchased together to help retailers find ideal locations for each product. Walmart uses market-basket analysis to determine where in the store to stock products for customer convenience. Kleenex tissues, for example, are in the paper-goods aisle and beside the cold medicines.

PERSONNEL People are a unique aspect of retailing. Most retail sales involve a customer–salesperson relationship, if only briefly. Sales personnel provide their customers with the amount of service prescribed by the retail strategy of the store.

Retail salespeople serve another important selling function: They persuade shoppers to buy. They must therefore be able to persuade customers that what they are selling is what the customer needs. Salespeople are trained in two common selling techniques: trading up and suggestion selling. *Trading up* means persuading customers to buy a higher-priced item than they originally intended to purchase. To avoid selling customers something they do not need or want, however, salespeople should take care when practicing trading-up techniques. *Suggestion selling*, a common practice among most retailers, seeks to broaden customers' original purchases with related items. For example, if you buy a new printer at Office Depot, the sales representative will ask if you would like to purchase paper, a USB cable, and/or extra ink cartridges. Suggestion selling by sales or service associates should always help shoppers recognize true needs rather than sell them unwanted merchandise.

Providing great customer service is one of the most challenging elements in the retail mix because customer expectations for service vary greatly. What customers expect in a department store is very different from what they expect in a discount store. Customer expectations also change. Ten years ago, shoppers wanted personal one-on-one attention. Today, most customers are happy to help themselves as long as they can easily find what they need.

14-6c Channels and Retailing Decisions for Services

The fastest-growing part of our economy is the service sector. Although distribution in the service sector is difficult to visualize, the same skills, techniques, and strategies used to manage inventory can also be used to manage service inventory, such as hospital beds, bank accounts, or airline seats. The quality of the planning and execution of distribution can have a major impact on costs and customer satisfaction.

Because service industries are so customer oriented, customer service is a priority. To manage customer relationships, many service providers, such as insurance carriers, physicians, hair salons, and financial services, use technology to schedule appointments, manage accounts, and disburse information. Service distribution focuses on four main areas:

➤ **MINIMIZING WAIT TIMES:** Minimizing the amount of time customers wait in line is a key factor in maintaining the quality of service.

➤ **MANAGING SERVICE CAPACITY:** If service firms don't have the capacity to meet demand, they must either turn down some prospective customers, let service levels slip, or expand capacity.

➤ **IMPROVING SERVICE DELIVERY:** Service firms are now experimenting with different distribution channels for their services. Choosing the right distribution channel can increase the times that services are available or add to customer convenience.

➤ **ESTABLISHING CHANNEL-WIDE NETWORK COHERENCE:** Because services are to some degree intangible, service firms also find it necessary to standardize their service quality across different geographic regions in order to maintain their brand image.

14-7 THE RELATIONSHIP BETWEEN RETAILER DECISION MAKING AND CUSTOMER DATA

Retailers decide what to sell on the basis of what their target market wants to buy. They can base their decision on market research, past sales, fashion trends, customer requests, and other sources. **Data mining** uses complex mathematical models to help retailers make better product mix decisions. Dillard's, Target, and Walmart use data mining to determine which products to stock at what price, how to manage markdowns, and how to advertise to draw target customers. The data they collect in CRM (customer relationship management) databases allows manufacturers and retailers to gain better insight into who is buying their products. Instead of simply unloading products into the distribution channel and leaving marketing and relationship building to dealers, auto manufacturers today are using Web sites to keep in touch with customers and prospects, learn about

QUALITY OF SERVICE IS DIRECTLY TIED TO HOW LONG PEOPLE HAVE TO WAIT IN LINE.

© fStop/Alamy

their lifestyles and hobbies, understand their vehicle needs, and develop relationships in the hope that these consumers will reward them with brand loyalty in the future. BMW and other vehicle manufacturers have databases with names of millions of consumers who have expressed an interest in their products.

14-8 NEW DEVELOPMENTS IN RETAIL AND CHANNEL MANAGEMENT

With online shopping increasing but customers not always able to be home to sign for packages, there have been new developments in package delivery. Amazon.com has developed a new delivery option for its customers. In large cities, Amazon Lockers sit in banks at some drugstores and department stores. Customers can have small packages dropped at a nearby set of lockers, enter their information, and retrieve the package at their convenience.[18]

With technology changing rapidly, there are always new trends developing both in retail and in channel management. Mobile commerce is continuing to be the avenue with the largest growth in both retail and channel decision making, in part because of its more than $5 billion in yearly revenue. For example, eBay added to its virtual auction empire during the holiday season by opening up pop-up shops where shoppers scanned QR codes (quick response codes that act like a customer bar code for a programmed URL) on each item. The QR code directed shoppers to eBay's payment screen. The auction giant also handed out shopping guides with QR codes next to popular gifts to encourage customers to shop with eBay.[19]

M-commerce (mobile e-commerce) enables consumers using wireless mobile devices to connect to the Internet and shop. Essentially, m-commerce goes beyond text message advertisements to allow consumers to purchase goods and services using wireless mobile devices, such as mobile telephones, Smartphones, and tablet computers. M-commerce users adopt the new technology because it saves time and offers more convenience in a greater number of locations.

Many major companies, ranging from Polo Ralph Lauren to Sears, already offer shopping on mobile phones, and the growth potential is huge. Currently, 3.5 percent of North American mobile phone users have made online purchases via their phones.[20] Nearly 300 million data-capable mobile devices are in use in the United States, more than 80 million of which are fully Web-enabled Smartphones or 3G-enabled laptops.[21] The gap between the number of Smartphones owned and Smartphones used for purchases is closing rapidly. Several surveys conducted over the 2011 holiday season discovered that more than half of Smartphone owners planned to check prices using some kind of price comparison app and to read reviews. More than 40 percent of the thousands surveyed used their mobile devices to make purchases.[22]

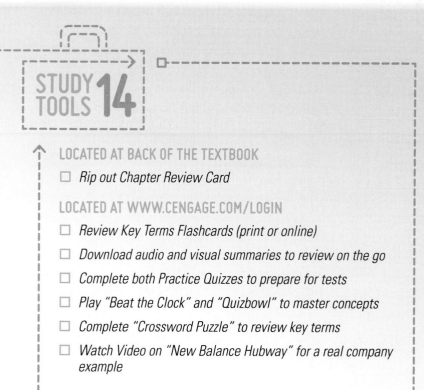

STUDY TOOLS 14

LOCATED AT BACK OF THE TEXTBOOK

☐ *Rip out Chapter Review Card*

LOCATED AT WWW.CENGAGE.COM/LOGIN

☐ *Review Key Terms Flashcards (print or online)*

☐ *Download audio and visual summaries to review on the go*

☐ *Complete both Practice Quizzes to prepare for tests*

☐ *Play "Beat the Clock" and "Quizbowl" to master concepts*

☐ *Complete "Crossword Puzzle" to review key terms*

☐ *Watch Video on "New Balance Hubway" for a real company example*

15-1 THE ROLE OF PROMOTION IN THE MARKETING MIX

Few goods or services, no matter how well developed, priced, or distributed, can survive in the marketplace without effective promotion—communication by marketers that informs, persuades, and reminds potential buyers of a product in order to influence an opinion or elicit a response.

⌐Few goods or services can survive in the marketplace without effective promotion.⌐

promotion communication by marketers that informs, persuades, and reminds potential buyers of a product in order to influence an opinion or elicit a response

promotional strategy a plan for the optimal use of the elements of promotion: advertising, public relations, personal selling, sales promotion, and social media

competitive advantage one or more unique aspects of an organization that cause target consumers to patronize that firm rather than competitors

communication the process by which we exchange or share meaning through a common set of symbols

Promotional strategy is a plan for the optimal use of the elements of promotion: advertising, public relations, personal selling, sales promotion, and social media. As Exhibit 15.1 on page 248 shows, the marketing manager determines the goals of the company's promotional strategy in light of the firm's overall goals for the marketing mix—product, place (distribution), promotion, and price. Using these overall goals, marketers combine the elements of the promotional strategy (the promotional mix) into a coordinated plan. The promotion plan then becomes an integral part of the marketing strategy for reaching the target market.

The main function of a marketer's promotional strategy is to convince target customers that the goods and services offered provide a competitive advantage over the competition. A **competitive advantage** is the set of unique features of a company and its products that are perceived by the target market as significant and superior to those of the competition. Such features can include high product quality, rapid delivery, low prices, excellent service, or a feature not offered by the competition. For example, Toyota's Lexus line resonates with customers because it offers Mercedes-quality cars at a lower price. The luxury line implies that the driver is successful enough to buy what she wants and sensible enough to get a great price on it. The savvy, affluent customer position has given Lexus a competitive advantage in the luxury car market.[1] Thus, promotion is a vital part of the marketing mix, informing consumers of a product's benefits and thereby positioning the product in the marketplace.

15-2 MARKETING COMMUNICATION

Promotional strategy is closely related to the process of communication. As humans, we assign meaning to feelings, ideas, facts, attitudes, and emotions. **Communication** is the process by which meanings are exchanged or shared through

Marketing Communications

After you finish this chapter go to
p265 *for* **STUDY TOOLS** ⌸ - - - - - - >

interpersonal communication
direct, face-to-face communication between two or more people

mass communication
the communication of a concept or message to large audiences

a common set of symbols. When a company develops a new product, changes an old one, or simply tries to increase sales of an existing good or service, it must communicate its selling message to potential customers. Marketers communicate information about the firm and its products to the target market and various publics through its promotion programs.

Domino's Pizza recently had a serious communications problem. After customer complaints about the quality of its product (and a disturbing video featuring one of its employees doing things to the pizza that was posted on YouTube and went viral), the company decided to do something that no other company had done—it promoted the complaints in advertising and social media. Domino's embraced the research—coming from social media as well as from focus groups—that talked about the problems with the product (from the quality of the ingredients to the quality of the pizza crust). Working with ad agency Crispin Porter + Bogusky, Domino's embraced authenticity by announcing that its pizza photos would not have "fancy touch ups" and encouraged consumers to take photos of their pizza and post them to a new Web site. Dubbed the "Pizza Turnaround," the campaign featured the CEO reacting (and apologizing) to consumer complaints about the "crust tasting like cardboard" and the "sauce tasting like ketchup." Domino's changed its recipe and positioned the brand as "real" and "authentic," an

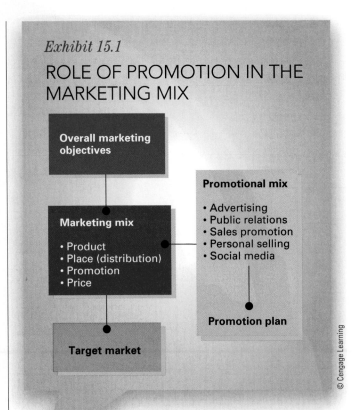

Exhibit 15.1

ROLE OF PROMOTION IN THE MARKETING MIX

© Cengage Learning

old positioning base to be sure, but one that was particularly relevant given consumer mistrust of advertising and corporations in general. And it worked. Sales increased 14 percent from one quarter to the next, and research showed the ads were some of the most effective in years.[2] Not only that, but Domino's Pizza increased its level of authenticity. Since it listened to customers and embraced the transparency, the company strengthened its relationships with its customers.

Communication can be divided into two major categories: interpersonal communication and mass communication. **Interpersonal communication** is direct, face-to-face communication between two or more people. When communicating face-to-face, people see the other person's reaction and can respond almost immediately. A salesperson speaking directly with a client is an example of an interpersonal marketing communication.

Mass communication involves communicating a concept or message to large audiences. A great deal of marketing communication is directed to consumers as a whole, usually through a mass medium such as television or newspapers. When a company advertises, it generally does not personally know the people with whom it is trying

© AP Images/PRNewsFoto/Domino's Pizza

to communicate. Furthermore, the company often cannot respond immediately to consumers' reactions to its messages (unless they are using social media or other Internet-based marketing tools). Instead, the marketing manager must wait to see whether people are reacting positively or negatively to the mass-communicated promotion. Any clutter from competitors' messages or other distractions in the environment can reduce the effectiveness of the mass-communication effort.

15-2a The Communication Process

Marketers are both senders and receivers of messages. As *senders*, marketers attempt to inform, persuade, and remind the target market to adopt courses of action compatible with the need to promote the purchase of goods and services. As *receivers*, marketers attune themselves to the target market in order to develop the appropriate messages, adapt existing messages, and spot new communication opportunities. In this way, most marketing communication is a two-way, rather than one-way, process. The two-way nature of the communication process is shown in Exhibit 15.2.

THE SENDER AND ENCODING

sender the originator of the message in the communication process

The **sender** is the originator of the message in the communication process. In an interpersonal conversation, the sender may be a parent, a friend, or a salesperson. For an advertisement, press release, or social media campaign, the sender is the company or organization itself. For example, to take advantage of the World Cup and gain market share in Africa against Pepsi, Coca-Cola launched a huge marketing campaign called "What's Your Celebration?" inspired by Roger Milla, a former Cameroon soccer player, and the famous, impromptu celebration dance that he did after scoring a goal in the 1990 World Cup. Coca-Cola used Milla's dance to encourage everyone to loosen up with Coke and embrace the joys of the World Cup. In addition to asking people "what's your celebration?" Coca-Cola worked with Somalian-born singer K'Naan to create a catchy, inspiring song to play at the soccer games that incorporated Coke's iconic five-note melody. The song, "Wavin' Flag," became the top download on iTunes and the unofficial anthem of the 2010 World Cup, as well as a key part of Coca-Cola's message of celebration.[3] Additionally, the sender can also share the message with friends and followers on social media, which allows those people to share it as well.

Exhibit 15.2
COMMUNICATION PROCESS

Noise
- Other advertisements
- News articles
- Other store displays

Sender
- Marketing manager
- Advertising manager
- Advertising agency
- Other consumers

Encoding the message
- Advertisement
- Sales presentation
- Store display
- Coupon
- Press release
- Social media

Message channel
- Media
- Salesperson
- Retail store
- Local news show

Decoding the message
- Receiver interpretation of message

Receiver
- Customers
- Viewers/ listeners
- News media
- Clients

Feedback channel
- Market research
- Sales results
- Change in market share
- Social media

© Cengage Learning

Encoding is the conversion of the sender's ideas and thoughts into a message, usually in the form of words or signs. Coca-Cola encoded the "What's Your Celebration?" message into the song "Wavin' Flag" and into ads showing various teams and their goal celebrations, from backflips to coordinated slides, and fans dancing and waving flags. Fans were then encouraged to upload their own celebration videos on Coca-Cola's World Cup Web site. On the Web site, in the commercials, and during games, the drum beats and catchy rhythms of "Wavin' Flag" encouraged celebration with Coke.[4]

A basic principle of encoding is that what matters is not what the source says but what the receiver hears. One way of conveying a message that the receiver will hear properly is to use concrete words and pictures.

MESSAGE TRANSMISSION Transmission of a message requires a **channel**—a voice, radio, newspaper, computer, Smartphone, or other communication medium. A facial expression or gesture can also serve as a channel. Coca-Cola used South African restaurants as one of its channels to get the "What's Your Celebration?" campaign to the African people. The company donated televisions encased in red plastic and Coke-themed tables to more than 1,000 South African restaurants so they could show the games and bring people together. Coca-Cola also sponsored the World Cup Trophy Tour, which allowed soccer fans in eighty-four countries (fifty in Africa) to take pictures with the cup, attend concerts, play games, and watch 3D soccer highlights celebrating the history of the game.

Reception occurs when the message is detected by the receiver and enters his or her frame of reference. In a two-way conversation such as a sales pitch given by a sales representative to a potential client, reception is normally high. Similarly, when the message is a recommendation from a friend, the reception is high as well. In contrast, the desired receivers may or may not detect the message when it is mass communicated because most media are cluttered by **noise**—anything that interferes with, distorts, or slows down the transmission of information. In some media overcrowded with advertisers, such as newspapers and television, the noise level is high and the reception level is low. For example, competing network advertisements, other entertainment option advertisements, or

lemonade's **new sweetie**

new frozen **strawberry** lemonade

If this ad for frozen lemonade is on a downtown billboard in the summer, it will be seen by the target audience—thirsty, hot people. But the same location in the winter is going to have a negative effect—cold, hurried commuters aren't going to be interested in a frosty beverage.

© Terri Miller/E-Visual Communications, Inc.

other programming on the network itself might hamper reception of Coca-Cola's advertising campaign message. Transmission can also be hindered by situational factors such as physical surroundings like light, sound, location, and weather; the presence of other people; consumer multitasking, or the temporary moods consumers might bring to the situation. Mass communication may not even reach all the right consumers. Because Coca-Cola was targeting an event with a dedicated audience of soccer fans, it was more likely that the target audience experienced the "What's Your Celebration?" campaign, particularly the "Wavin' Flag" song with Coke's jingle in it. However, other Coke ads may run when the target audience of soccer viewers is not watching.

THE RECEIVER AND DECODING Marketers communicate their message through a channel to customers, or **receivers**, who will decode the message. It is important to note that there can be multiple receivers as consumers

decoding interpretation of the language and symbols sent by the source through a channel

feedback the receiver's response to a message

share their experiences and their recommendations online through social networks and other types of social media. These conversations online are becoming an increasingly influential way to promote products and services. Indeed, this new empowerment of the receiver has transformed marketing and advertising. Receivers can easily share new information with their friends and followers on social media, and those new receivers can then share that information as well. This leads to a more diverse interrelationship between senders and receivers of social media messages. **Decoding** is the interpretation of the language and symbols sent by the source through a channel. Common understanding between two communicators, or a common frame of reference, is required for effective communication. Therefore, marketing managers must ensure a proper match between the message to be conveyed and the target market's attitudes and ideas.

Even though a message has been received, it will not necessarily be properly decoded—or even seen, viewed, or heard—because of selective exposure, distortion, and retention. Even when people receive a message, they tend to manipulate, alter, and modify it to reflect their own biases, needs, knowledge, and culture. Differences in age, social class, education, culture, and ethnicity can lead to miscommunication. Further, because people don't always listen or read carefully, they can easily misinterpret what is said or written. In fact, researchers have found that consumers misunderstand a large proportion of both printed and televised communications. Bright colors and bold graphics have been shown to increase consumers' comprehension of marketing communication. Even these techniques are not foolproof, however.

Marketers targeting consumers in foreign countries must also worry about the translation and possible miscommunication of their promotional messages by other cultures. Global marketers must decide whether to standardize or customize the message for each global market in which they sell. Coke's "What's Your Celebration?" campaign was very similar all over the world, though the company released the Roger Milla ads at different times of the year before the World Cup

began. Coca-Cola also promoted its POWERade brand through the World Cup, targeting individual countries by featuring individual members of each country's team in POWERade print ads. For Coca-Cola, being highly visible before and during one of the world's most watched events paid off with 5 percent worldwide growth for the period including the World Cup.[5]

FEEDBACK In interpersonal communication, the receiver's response to a message is direct **feedback** to the source. Feedback may be verbal, as in saying "I agree," or nonverbal, as in nodding, smiling, frowning, or gesturing.

Because mass communicators like Coca-Cola are often cut off from direct feedback, they must rely on market research, social media, or analysis of viewer responses for indirect feedback. Coca-Cola might use such measurements

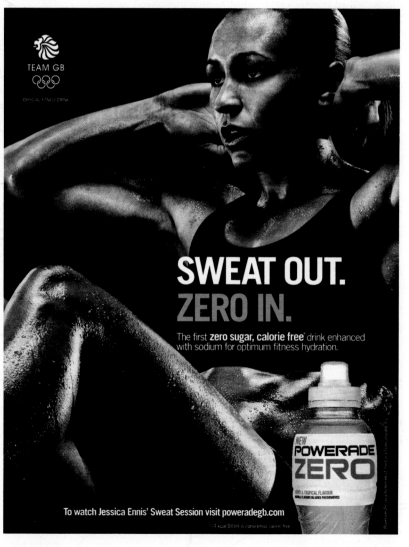

as the percentage of television viewers who recognized, recalled, or stated that they were exposed to the company's messages. Indirect feedback enables mass communicators to decide whether to continue, modify, or drop a message. Web sites also facilitate feedback. Coca-Cola used its World Cup Web site as a place where people could upload their celebrations. Each video suggested a person who responded positively to the "What's Your Celebration?" campaign.

With the increase in online advertising, marketers are able to get more feedback than before the Internet became such a driving social force. Using analytics, marketers can see how long a consumer stays on a Web site or which pages they view. Moreover, social media enable instant feedback by allowing companies, such as JCPenney and Comcast, to respond to consumers' posts on Facebook and to complaints posted on Twitter.

As the preceding paragraph implies, the Internet and social media have had an impact on the communication model. That model shows the feedback channel as primarily impersonal and numbers driven. In the traditional communication process, marketers can see the results of consumer behavior (e.g., a drop or rise in sales) but are able to explain those changes only by using their judgment. When marketers launch a social media campaign, they create an unfiltered feedback channel. Social media campaigns enable marketers to personalize the feedback channel by opening the door for direct conversation with consumers. However, because social media are in real time and are public, any negative posts or complaints are highly visible. Thus, many companies have a crisis communication strategy to deal with negative information.

15-3 THE GOALS OF PROMOTION

People communicate with one another for many reasons. They seek amusement, ask for help, give assistance or instructions, provide information, and express ideas and thoughts. Promotion, on the other hand, seeks to modify behavior and thoughts in some way. For example, promoters may try to persuade consumers to eat at Burger King rather than at McDonald's. Promotion also strives to reinforce existing behavior—for instance, getting consumers to continue dining at Burger King once they have switched. The source (the seller) hopes to project a favorable image or to motivate purchase of the company's goods and services.

Promotion can perform one or more of four tasks: *inform* the target audience, *persuade* the target audience, *remind* the target audience, or *connect* with the audience. The ability to *connect* to consumers is one task that can be facilitated through social media. Often a marketer will try to accomplish two or more of these tasks at the same time.

15-3a Informing

Informative promotion seeks to convert an existing need into a want or to stimulate interest in a new product. It is generally more prevalent during the early stages of the product life cycle. People typically will not buy a product or service or support a nonprofit organization until they know its purpose and its benefits to them. Informative messages are important for promoting complex and technical products such as automobiles, computers, and investment services. For example, when Apple released the iPhone, its touch screen functions were new to the Smartphone category. To inform consumers of the phone's features and how it worked, Apple ran a series of commercials showing a hand manipulating the phone. The voiceover provided information about the benefits of the phone by telling a story around how the iPhone makes life easier. Similar commercials have run for the iPad to inform consumers about the benefits of a larger touch screen. Informative promotion is also important for a "new" brand being introduced into an "old" product class. The new product cannot establish itself against more mature products unless potential buyers are aware of it, value its benefits, and understand its positioning in the marketplace.

15-3b Persuading

Persuasive promotion is designed to stimulate a purchase or an action. Persuasion normally becomes the main promotion goal when the product enters the growth stage of its life cycle. By this time, the target market should have general product awareness and some knowledge of how the product can fulfill its wants. Therefore, the promotional task switches from informing consumers about the product category to persuading them to buy the company's brand rather than that of the competitor. At this time, the promotional message emphasizes the product's real and perceived competitive advantages, often appealing to emotional needs such as love, belonging, self-esteem, and ego satisfaction. For example, advertisers of phones using the Android operating system are trying to persuade users to purchase their phone instead of an iPhone (or even instead of another brand of Android phone). Advertising messages, therefore, are highlighting the unique technological benefits of Android phones, such as a faster processor or larger screen.

Persuasion can also be an important goal for very competitive mature product categories such as many household items and soft drinks. In a marketplace characterized by many competitors, the promotional message often encourages brand switching and aims to convert some buyers into loyal users. Critics believe that some promotional messages and techniques can be too persuasive, causing consumers to buy products and services they don't really need.

15-3c Reminding

Reminder promotion is used to keep the product and brand name in the public's mind. This type of promotion prevails during the maturity stage of the life cycle. It assumes that the target market has already been persuaded of the merits of the good or service. Its purpose is simply to trigger a memory. Crest toothpaste and other consumer products often use reminder promotion.

15-3d Connecting

The idea behind social media is to form relationships with customers and potential customers through technological ties such as Facebook, Twitter, YouTube, or other social media platforms. Indeed, some companies, such as Starbucks, have their own social networks that allow customers to share ideas, information, and feedback. By facilitating this exchange of information through a transparent process, brands are increasingly connecting with their customers in hopes they become brand advocates that promote the brand through their own social networks. Tools for connection include social networks, social games, social publishing tools, as well as social commerce.

15-4 THE PROMOTIONAL MIX

Most promotional strategies use several tools— which may include advertising, public relations, sales promotion, personal selling, and social media—to reach a target market. That combination is called the **promotional mix**. The proper promotional mix is the one that management believes will meet the needs of the target market and fulfill the organization's overall goals. The more funds allocated to each promotional ingredient and the more managerial emphasis placed on each technique, the more important that element is thought to be in the overall mix.

15-4a Advertising

Almost all companies selling a good or a service use advertising, whether in the form of a multi-million-dollar campaign or a simple classified ad in a newspaper. **Advertising** is any form of impersonal paid communication in which the sponsor or company is identified. Traditional media—such as television, radio, newspapers, magazines, pay-per-click online advertising, banner advertising, direct mail, billboards, and transit

promotional mix
the combination of promotional tools—including advertising, public relations, personal selling, sales promotion, and social media—used to reach the target market and fulfill the organization's overall goals

advertising
impersonal, one-way mass communication about a product or organization that is paid for by a marketer

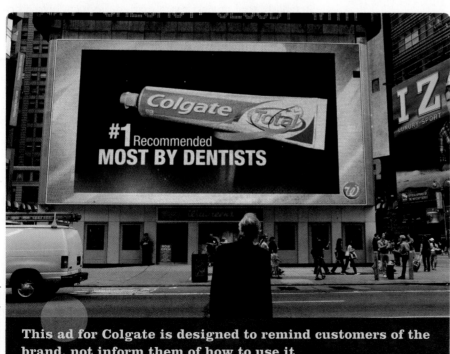
© Richard Levine/Alamy

This ad for Colgate is designed to remind customers of the brand, not inform them of how to use it

advertising (such as on buses and taxis and at bus stops)—are most commonly used to transmit advertisements to consumers. With the increasing fragmentation of traditional media choices, marketers are using new methods, such as Web sites, e-mail, blogs, and interactive video kiosks to send their advertisements to consumers. However, as the Internet becomes a more vital component of many companies' promotion and marketing mixes, consumers and lawmakers are increasingly concerned about possible violations of consumers' privacy. Social networking sites like Facebook are having to re-examine their privacy policies.

One of the primary benefits of advertising is its ability to communicate to a large number of people at one time. Cost per contact, therefore, is typically very low. Advertising has the advantage of being able to reach the masses (e.g., through national television networks), but it can also be microtargeted to small groups of potential customers, such as television ads on a targeted cable network. Although the *cost per contact* in advertising is very low, the *total cost* to advertise is typically very high. This hurdle tends to restrict advertising on a national basis. Chapter 16 examines advertising in greater detail.

15-4b Public Relations

Concerned about how they are perceived by their target markets, organizations often spend large sums to build a positive public image. **Public relations** is the marketing function that evaluates public attitudes, identifies areas within the organization the public may be interested in, and executes a program of action to earn public understanding and acceptance. Public relations helps an organization communicate with its customers, suppliers, stockholders, government officials, employees, and the community in which it operates. Marketers use public relations not only to maintain a positive image but also to educate the public about the company's goals and objectives, introduce new products, and help support the sales effort.

A public relations program can generate favorable **publicity**—public information about a company, product, service, or issue appearing in the mass media

as a news item. Organizations generally do not pay for the publicity and are not identified as the source of the information, but they can benefit tremendously from it. Social media sites like Twitter can provide large amounts of publicity quickly. For example, in 2011 John Green, a young-adult fiction author, shared the name of his next book, *The Fault in Our Stars*, on Twitter, Tumblr, and YourPants.org; promised to sign all pre-orders; and read an excerpt on a live YouTube show. Almost immediately, fans began discussing pre-ordering on Twitter and designing dust jackets for the book. The same day, *The Fault in Our Stars* became the number one seller on Amazon.com and BarnesandNoble.com.[6]

Although organizations do not directly pay for publicity, it should not be viewed as free. Preparing news releases, staging special events, and persuading media personnel to broadcast or print publicity messages costs money. Public relations and publicity are examined further in Chapter 16.

15-4c Sales Promotion

Sales promotion consists of all marketing activities—other than personal selling, advertising, and public relations—that stimulate consumer purchasing and dealer effectiveness. Sales promotion is generally a short-run tool used to stimulate immediate increases in demand. Sales promotion can be aimed at end consumers, trade customers, or a company's employees. Sales promotions include free samples, contests, premiums, trade shows, vacation giveaways, and coupons. Increasingly, companies such as LivingSocial and Groupon have combined social networks and sales promotions. Facebook is a growing platform through which companies run sweepstakes. For example, JPMorgan Chase ran a sweepstakes where Facebook users entered a drawing for a $1,000 grocery store gift card by "liking" the Chase Freedom Facebook page. In the past, Chase Freedom has run other Facebook sweepstakes where players could "like" the page to win $1 million. In addition to being entered into the large drawing, players were entered for a chance to win $500 every hour. The company runs this type of sweepstakes to educate potential customers about its cash-back rewards program available through the Chase Freedom credit card.[7]

Marketers often use sales promotion to improve the effectiveness of other ingredients in the promotional mix, especially advertising and personal selling. Research shows that sales promotion complements advertising by yielding faster sales responses.

facebook

Chase Freedom $1,000 Sweepstakes ▼   👍 Like

"Like" us for a chance to win a **$1,000** Grocery Store Gift Card.

$1,000 GROCERY GIFT CARD SWEEPSTAKES

CHASE ○ *freedom*

Then simply complete the entry form for a chance to win.
See official rules >

Many companies are using Facebook as a platform to run sweepstakes or contests. For sweepstakes such as those run by JPMorgan Chase for its Chase Freedom credit card, consumers can enter to win by "liking" the Facebook page and filling out a brief form.

personal selling
a purchase situation involving a personal, paid-for communication between two people in an attempt to influence each other

15-4d Personal Selling

Personal selling is a purchase situation involving a personal, paid-for communication between two people in an attempt to influence each other. In this dyad, both the buyer and the seller have specific objectives they wish to accomplish. The buyer may need to minimize cost or assure a quality product, for instance, while the salesperson may need to maximize revenue and profits.

Traditional methods of personal selling include a planned presentation to one or more prospective buyers for the purpose of making a sale. Whether it takes place face-to-face or over the phone, personal selling attempts to persuade the buyer to accept a point of view. For example, a car salesperson may try to persuade a car buyer that a particular model is superior to a competing model in certain features, such as gas mileage. Once the buyer is somewhat convinced, the salesperson may attempt to elicit some action from the buyer, such as a test-drive or a purchase. Frequently, in this traditional view of personal selling, the objectives of the salesperson are at the expense of the buyer, creating a win-lose outcome.

More current notions on personal selling emphasize the relationship that develops between a salesperson and a buyer. Initially, this concept was more typical in business-to-business selling situations, involving the sale of products like heavy machinery or computer systems. More recently, both business-to-business and business-to-consumer selling focus on building long-term relationships rather than on making a one-time sale.

Relationship selling emphasizes a win-win outcome and the accomplishment of mutual objectives that benefit both buyer and salesperson in the long term. Rather than focusing on a quick sale, relationship selling attempts to create a long-term, committed relationship based on trust, increased customer loyalty, and a continuation of the relationship between the salesperson and the customer. Personal selling, like other promotional mix elements, is increasingly dependent on the Internet. Most companies use their Web sites to attract potential buyers seeking information on products and services and to drive customers to their physical locations where personal selling can close the sale. Personal selling is discussed further in Chapter 17.

15-4e Social Media

Social media are promotion tools used to facilitate conversations among people online. When used by marketers, these tools facilitate consumer empowerment. For the first time, consumers are able to speak directly to other consumers, the company, and Web communities. Social media include blogs (online journals), microblogs (Twitter), podcasting (online audio shows), vodcasts (online videos and newscasts, especially on YouTube), and social networks such as Facebook and LinkedIn. Initially, these tools were used primarily by individuals for self-expression. For example, a lawyer might develop a blog to talk about politics because that is her hobby. Or a college freshman might develop a profile on Facebook to stay in touch with his high school friends. But soon, businesses saw that these tools could be used to engage with consumers as well. Indeed, social media have become a "layer" in promotional strategy. Social media are ubiquitous—it just depends on how deep that layer goes for each brand. The rise of blogging, for example, has created a completely new way for marketers to manage their image, connect with consumers, and generate interest in and desire for their companies' products. Now marketers are using social media as integral aspects of their campaigns and as a way to extend the benefits of their traditional media. Social media are discussed in more detail in Chapter 18.

15-4f The Communication Process and the Promotional Mix

The Internet has changed how businesses promote their brands. Traditionally marketing managers have been in charge of defining the essence of the brand. This included complete brand control and mostly one-way communication between the brand and customers. All of the content and messages were focused on defining and communicating the brand value. The focus for many campaigns was pure entertainment, and the brand created all of the content for campaigns—from the Web site to television spots to print ads.

That approach has now changed. The consumer has much more control (which makes some brands quite nervous!). The communication space is increasingly controlled by the consumer, as is the brand message. Perception is reality as consumers have more control to adapt the brand message to fit their ideas. Instead of repetition, social media rely on the idea of customization and adaption of the message. Information is positioned as more valuable as opposed to being strictly entertaining. Probably the most important aspect is the idea of consumer-generated

THE COST OF NOT HARNESSING SOCIAL MEDIA

Avon has long been one of the top direct sales companies. Its salespeople go door to door supplying their friends and family with all of their makeup needs. However, in recent years, as customers are more and more pressed for time, Avon and its representatives have seen sales drop. Customers are shopping online for their makeup, and Avon hasn't made the transition. Its current system requires shoppers to select their representative from a drop-down list, and if they get the name wrong, the sale gets credited elsewhere. This is frustrating not only for the representatives but also for the consumer, who can easily shop at other large beauty retail Web sites. Avon's Mark brand has an app that allows representatives to show products and videos, but it is limited to the Mark brand. Mary Kay, one of Avon's main competitors, gives each rep her own site and is developing tracking tools and training to facilitate smart use of the site. If Avon doesn't get into the social media and mobile marketing game, its $1.7 billion in U.S. sales won't be growing and is likely to drop as customers seek more savvy brands.

Source: Emily Glazer, "Avon Is Late to Social Media's Party," *Wall Street Journal*, April 23, 2012, B1–2.

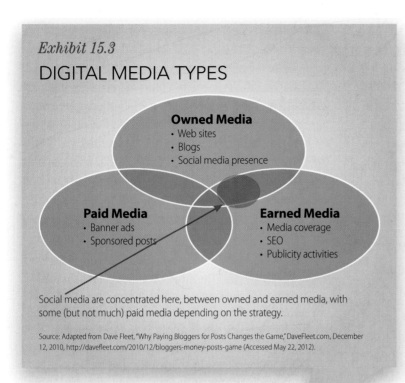

Exhibit 15.3
DIGITAL MEDIA TYPES

Owned Media
- Web sites
- Blogs
- Social media presence

Paid Media
- Banner ads
- Sponsored posts

Earned Media
- Media coverage
- SEO
- Publicity activities

Social media are concentrated here, between owned and earned media, with some (but not much) paid media depending on the strategy.

Source: Adapted from Dave Fleet, "Why Paying Bloggers for Posts Changes the Game," DaveFleet.com, December 12, 2010, http://davefleet.com/2010/12/bloggers-money-posts-game (Accessed May 22, 2012).

Owned media are a new form of promotional tactic where brands are becoming publishers of their own content in order to maximize the brand's value to customers as well as increase its search rank in Google. Owned media include the company's Web sites as well as its official presence on Facebook, Twitter, YouTube channels, blogs, and other platforms. These media are controlled by the brand but continuously keep the customer and his or her needs in mind as videos, blog posts, contests, photos, and other pieces of content are created.

The elements of the promotional mix differ in their ability to affect the target audience. For instance, promotional mix elements may communicate with the consumer directly or indirectly. The message may flow one way or two ways. Feedback may be fast or slow, a little or a lot. Likewise, the communicator may have varying degrees of control over message delivery, content, and flexibility. Exhibit 15.4 on the next page outlines characteristics among the promotional mix elements with respect to mode of communication, marketer's control over the communication process, amount and speed of feedback, direction of message flow, marketer's control over the message, identification of the sender, speed in reaching large audiences, and message flexibility.

From Exhibit 15.4, you can see that most elements of the promotional mix are indirect and impersonal when used to communicate with a target market, providing only one direction of message flow. For example, advertising, public relations, and sales promotion are generally impersonal, one-way means of mass communication. Because they provide no opportunity for direct feedback, it is more difficult to adapt these promotional elements to changing consumer preferences, individual differences, and personal goals.

Personal selling, on the other hand, is personal, two-way communication. The salesperson receives immediate feedback from the consumer and can adjust the message in response. Personal selling, however, is very slow in dispersing the marketer's message to large audiences. Because a salesperson can communicate to only one person or a small group of persons at one time, it is a poor

content, whereby consumers are able to both take existing content and modify it or to create completely new content for a brand. For example, Doritos has the "Crash the Super Bowl" promotion, where ordinary people are invited to create television commercials for Doritos that are then uploaded to www.crashthesuperbowl.com and voted on by millions of Doritos fans. The winning spots then run during the Super Bowl.

As a result of the impact of social media as well as the proliferation of new platforms, tools, and ideas, promotional tactics can also be categorized according to media type—paid, earned, or owned, as shown in Exhibit 15.3. **Paid media** are based on the traditional advertising model, whereby a brand pays for media space. Traditionally, paid media have included television, magazine, outdoor, radio, or newspaper advertising. Increasingly, paid media come in the form of display advertising on Web sites or pay-per-click advertising on search engines such as Google. Paid media are quite important, especially as they migrate to the Web. **Earned media** are based on a public relations or publicity model. The idea is to get people talking about the brand—whether through media coverage (as in traditional public relations) or through word of mouth (through sharing on social media sites). Search engine optimization (SEO), where companies embed key words into content in order to increase their positioning on search engine results pages (SERPs), can also be considered earned media.

paid media a category of promotional tactic based on the traditional advertising model, whereby a brand pays for media space

earned media a category of promotional tactic based on a public relations or publicity model that gets customers talking about products or services

owned media a new category of promotional tactic based on brands becoming publishers of their own content in order to maximize the brands' value to customers

AIDA concept a model that outlines the process for achieving promotional goals in terms of stages of consumer involvement with the message; the acronym stands for attention, interest, desire, and action

choice if the marketer wants to send a message to many potential buyers. Social media are also considered two-way communication, though not quite as immediate as personal selling. Social media can disperse messages to a wide audience and allow for engagement and feedback from customers through Twitter, Facebook, and blog posts.

15-5 PROMOTIONAL GOALS AND THE AIDA CONCEPT

The ultimate goal of any promotion is to get someone to buy a good or service or, in the case of nonprofit organizations, to take some action (e.g., donate blood). A classic model for reaching promotional goals is called the **AIDA concept**.[8] The acronym stands for *attention*, *interest*, *desire*, and *action*—the stages of consumer involvement with a promotional message.

This model proposes that consumers respond to marketing messages in a cognitive (thinking), affective (feeling), and conative (doing) sequence.

First, a promotion manager may focus on attracting a consumer's *attention* by training a salesperson to use a friendly greeting and approach or by using loud volume, bold headlines, movement, bright colors, and the like in an advertisement. Next, a good sales presentation, demonstration, or advertisement creates *interest* in the product and then, by illustrating how the product's features will satisfy the consumer's needs, arouses *desire*. Finally, a special offer or a strong closing sales pitch may be used to obtain purchase *action*.

The AIDA concept assumes that promotion propels consumers along the following four steps in the purchase-decision process:

1. **ATTENTION:** The advertiser must first gain the attention of the target market. A firm cannot sell something if the market does not know that the good or service exists. When Apple introduced the iPad, it quickly became one of the largest electronics product launches in history. To create awareness and gain attention for its revolutionary tablet computer, Apple not only used traditional media advertising but also contacted influential bloggers and journalists so that they would write about the product in blogs, newspapers, and magazines. Because the iPad was a brand extension of the Apple computer, it required less effort than an entirely new brand would have. At the same

Exhibit 15.4

CHARACTERISTICS OF THE ELEMENTS IN THE PROMOTIONAL MIX

	Advertising	Public Relations	Sales Promotion	Personal Selling	Social Media
Mode of Communication	Indirect and impersonal	Usually indirect and impersonal	Usually indirect and impersonal	Direct and face-to-face	Indirect but instant
Communicator Control over Situation	Low	Moderate to low	Moderate to low	High	Moderate
Amount of Feedback	Little	Little	Little to moderate	Much	Much
Speed of Feedback	Delayed	Delayed	Varies	Immediate	Intermediate
Direction of Message	One-way	One-way	Mostly one-way	Two-way	Two-way, multiple ways
Control over Message Content	Yes	No	Yes	Yes	Varies, generally no
Identification of Sponsor	Yes	No	Yes	Yes	Yes
Speed in Reaching Large Audience	Fast	Usually fast	Fast	Slow	Fast
Message Flexibility	Same message to all audiences	Usually no direct control over message audiences	Same message to varied targets	Tailored to prospective buyer	Some of the most targeted opportunities

© Cengage Learning

time, because the iPad was an innovative new product line, the promotion had to get customers' attention and create awareness of a new idea from an established company.

2. **INTEREST:** Simple awareness of a brand seldom leads to a sale. The next step is to create interest in the product. A print ad cannot tell potential customers all the features of the iPad. Therefore, Apple had to arrange iPad demonstrations and target messages to innovators and early adopters to create interest in the new tablet computer. To do this, Apple used both online videos on YouTube and personal demonstrations in Apple Stores. The iPad also received extensive media coverage from both online and traditional media outlets.

3. **DESIRE:** Potential customers for the Apple iPad may like the concept of a portable tablet computer, but they may not necessarily think that it is better than a laptop or Smartphone. Therefore, Apple had to create brand preference with the iTunes Music Store, apps, multiple functionality, power, light weight, and other features of the iPad. Specifically, Apple had to convince potential customers that the iPad was the best solution to their desire for a tablet computer with Smartphone accessibility.

4. **ACTION:** Some potential target market customers may have been persuaded to buy an iPad but had yet to make the actual purchase. To motivate them to take action, Apple continued advertising to communicate the features and benefits more effectively. And the strategy worked. In less than three months, the iPad sold more than 3 million units; more than half a million of these sales came during launch week despite the average $429 price tag.[9]

Most buyers involved in high-involvement purchase situations pass through the four stages of the AIDA model on the way to making a purchase. The promoter's task is to determine where on the purchase ladder most of the target consumers are located and design a promotion plan to meet their needs. For example, if Apple learned from its market research that many potential customers were in the desire stage but had not yet bought an iPad for some reason, then

Apple could place advertising on Google and perhaps in video games to target younger individuals, who are the primary target market, with messages to motivate them to buy an iPad.

The AIDA concept does not explain how all promotions influence purchase decisions. The model suggests that promotional effectiveness can be measured in terms of consumers progressing from one stage to the next. However, the order of stages in the model, as well as whether consumers go through all steps, has been much debated. A purchase can occur without interest or desire, perhaps when a low-involvement product is bought on impulse. Regardless of the order of the stages or consumers' progression through these stages, the AIDA concept helps marketers by suggesting which promotional strategy will be most effective.[10]

15-5a AIDA and the Promotional Mix

Exhibit 15.5 depicts the relationship between the promotional mix and the AIDA model. It shows that although advertising does have an impact in the later stages, it is most useful in gaining attention for goods or services. In contrast, personal selling reaches fewer people at first. Salespeople are more effective at creating customer interest for merchandise or a service and at creating desire. For example, advertising may help a potential computer purchaser gain knowledge about competing brands, but the salesperson may be the one who actually encourages the buyer to decide a

Exhibit 15.5

THE PROMOTIONAL MIX AND AIDA

	Attention	Interest	Desire	Action
Advertising	●	●	○	●
Public Relations	●	●	○	●
Sales Promotion	○	○	●	○
Personal Selling	○	●	●	●
Social Media	●	●	○	○

● Very effective　○ Somewhat effective　● Not effective

particular brand is the best choice. The salesperson also has the advantage of having the computer physically there to demonstrate its capabilities to the buyer.

Public relations has its greatest impact in gaining attention for a company, good, or service. Many companies can attract attention and build goodwill by sponsoring community events that benefit a worthy cause such as antidrug and antigang programs. Such sponsorships project a positive image of the firm and its products into the minds of consumers and potential consumers. Book publishers push to get their titles on the best-seller lists of major publications, such as *Publishers Weekly* or the *New York Times*. Book authors also make appearances on talk shows and at bookstores to personally sign books and speak to fans.

Sales promotion's greatest strength is in creating strong desire and purchase intent. Coupons and other price-off promotions are techniques used to persuade customers to buy new products. Frequent buyer sales promotion programs, popular among retailers, allow consumers to accumulate points or dollars that can later be redeemed for goods. Frequent buyer programs tend to increase purchase intent and loyalty and encourage repeat purchases.

Social media are a strong way to gain attention and interest in a brand, particularly if content goes viral. It can then reach a massive audience. Social media are also effective at engaging with customers and enabling companies to maintain interest in the brand if properly managed.

15-6 INTEGRATED MARKETING COMMUNICATIONS

Ideally, marketing communications from each promotional mix element (personal selling, advertising, sales promotion, social media, and public relations) should be integrated—that is, the message reaching the consumer should be the same regardless of whether it is from an advertisement, a salesperson in the field, a magazine article, a Facebook fan page, or a coupon in a newspaper insert.

From the consumer's standpoint, a company's communications are already integrated. Consumers do not think in terms of the five elements of promotion: personal selling, advertising, sales promotion, public relations, and social media. Instead, everything is an "ad." The only people who recognize the distinctions among these communications elements are the marketers themselves. Unfortunately, many marketers neglect this fact when planning promotional messages and fail to integrate their communication efforts from one element to the next. The most common rift typically occurs between personal selling and the other elements of the promotional mix.

This unintegrated, disjointed approach to promotion has propelled many companies to adopt the concept of **integrated marketing communications (IMC)**. IMC is the careful coordination of all promotional messages—traditional advertising, direct marketing, social media, interactive, public relations, sales promotion, personal selling, event marketing, and other communications—for a product or service to assure the consistency of messages at every contact point where a company meets the consumer. Following the concept of IMC, marketing managers carefully work out the roles that various promotional elements will play in the marketing mix. Timing of promotional activities is coordinated, and the results of each campaign are carefully monitored to improve future use of the promotional mix tools. Typically, a marketing communications director is appointed who has overall responsibility for integrating the company's marketing communications.

Procter & Gamble's Old Spice was competing in a very mature and competitive market of men's products (like deodorant and body wash). Sales had been declining until ad agency Wieden + Kennedy (of Nike fame) developed a television spot called "The man your man could smell like" with former football player Isaiah Mustafa. The television spot aired online during the Super Bowl and was viewed by millions of people. Soon it became not only a pop culture phenomenon but also a viral blockbuster. The overall campaign included coupons; public relations; coverage on blogs, Facebook, and Twitter; as well as print and television advertising. However, what sent this campaign over the top was pure genius. Old Spice solicited questions for the "Old Spice Guy" via Twitter and Facebook and then had Mustafa "answer" the questions using short video clips online—186 clips to be exact. The videos have been viewed hundreds of millions of times on YouTube, making the Old Spice YouTube channel one of the most popular channels. The results? Sales increased 107 percent, and Old Spice now has more than a million fans on Facebook, thousands of Twitter followers, higher Web site traffic, and press coverage valued at close to one billion impressions.

Crisp Breeze, Majestic Icicles, Matterhorn Old Spice, Fabio, You Can.

NewOldSpiceGuyFabio.Com   Old Spices

Fabio is part of recent Old Spice commercials. The campaign is capitalizing on Fabio's cultural currency of manliness in conjunction with the irreverence of the Old Spice campaign using Isaiah Mustafa.

Image courtesy of The Advertising Archives

This campaign leveraged a television spot by extending its life online and by engaging consumers online.[11]

The IMC concept has been growing in popularity for several reasons. First, the proliferation of thousands of media choices beyond traditional television has made promotion a more complicated task. Instead of promoting a product just through mass-media options, like television and magazines, promotional messages today can appear in many varied sources. Further, the mass market has also fragmented—more selectively segmented markets and an increase in niche marketing have replaced the traditional broad market groups that marketers promoted to in years past. Finally, marketers have slashed their advertising spending in favor of promotional techniques that generate immediate sales responses and those that are more easily measured, such as direct marketing. Online advertising has earned a bigger share of the budget as well due to its measurability. Thus, the interest in IMC is largely a reaction to the scrutiny that marketing communications have

come under and, particularly, to suggestions that uncoordinated promotional activity leads to a strategy that is wasteful and inefficient.

15-7 FACTORS AFFECTING THE PROMOTIONAL MIX

Promotional mixes vary a great deal from one product and one industry to the next. Normally, advertising and personal selling are used to promote goods and services, supported and supplemented by sales promotion. Public relations helps develop a positive image for the organization and the product line. Social media have been used more for consumer goods, but business-to-business marketers are increasingly using these media. A firm may choose not to use all five promotional elements in its promotional mix, or it may choose to use them in varying degrees. The particular promotional mix chosen by a firm for a product or service depends on several factors: the nature of the product, the stage in the product life cycle, target market characteristics, the type of buying decision, funds available for promotion, and whether a push or a pull strategy will be used.

15-7a Nature of the Product

Characteristics of the product itself can influence the promotional mix. For instance, a product can be classified as either a business product or a consumer product. (Refer to Chapters 7 and 10.) As business products are often custom-tailored to the buyer's exact specifications, they are often not well suited to mass promotion. Therefore, producers of most business goods, such as computer systems or industrial machinery, rely more heavily on personal selling than on advertising. Advertising, however, still serves a purpose in promoting business goods. Advertising in trade media can help locate potential customers for the sales force. For example, print media advertising often includes coupons soliciting the potential customer to "fill this out for more detailed information."

In contrast, because consumer products generally are not custom-made, they do not require the selling efforts of a company representative who can tailor them to the user's needs. Thus, consumer goods are promoted mainly through advertising or social media to create brand familiarity. Television and radio advertising, consumer-oriented magazines, and increasingly the Internet and other highly targeted media are used to promote consumer goods, especially nondurables. Sales promotion, the brand name, and the product's packaging are about twice as important for consumer goods as for business products. Persuasive personal selling is important at the retail level for goods such as automobiles and appliances.

The costs and risks associated with a product also influence the promotional mix. As a general rule, when the costs or risks of buying and using a product increase, personal selling becomes more important. In fact, inexpensive items cannot support the cost of a salesperson's time and effort unless the potential volume is high. On the other hand, expensive and complex machinery, cars, and new homes represent a considerable investment. A salesperson must assure buyers that they are spending their money wisely and not taking an undue financial risk.

Social risk is an issue as well. Many consumer goods are not products of great social

importance because they do not reflect social position. People do not experience much social risk in buying a loaf of bread. However, buying many specialty products such as jewelry and clothing involves a social risk. Many consumers depend on sales personnel for guidance in making the "proper" choice.

15-7b Stages in the Product Life Cycle

The product's stage in its life cycle is a big factor in designing a promotional mix (see Exhibit 15.6). During the *introduction stage*, the basic goal of promotion is to inform the target audience that the product is available. Initially, the emphasis is on the general product class—for example, Smartphones. This emphasis gradually changes to gaining attention for a particular brand, such as Apple, Nokia, Samsung, Sony Ericsson, or Motorola. Typically, both extensive advertising and public relations inform the target audience of the product class or brand and heighten awareness levels. Sales promotion encourages early trial of the product, and personal selling gets retailers to carry the product.

Exhibit 15.6

PRODUCT LIFE CYCLE AND THE PROMOTIONAL MIX

© Cengage Learning

When the product reaches the *growth stage* of the life cycle, the promotion blend may shift. Often a change is necessary because different types of potential buyers are targeted. Although advertising and public relations continue to be major elements of the promotional mix, sales promotion can be reduced because consumers need fewer incentives to purchase. The promotional strategy is to emphasize the product's differential advantage over the competition. Persuasive promotion is used to build and maintain brand loyalty during the growth stage. By this stage, personal selling has usually succeeded in getting adequate distribution for the product.

As the product reaches the *maturity stage* of its life cycle, competition becomes fiercer, and thus persuasive and reminder advertising are more strongly emphasized. Sales promotion comes back into focus as product sellers try to increase their market share.

All promotion, especially advertising, is reduced as the product enters the *decline stage*. Nevertheless, personal selling and sales promotion efforts may be maintained, particularly at the retail level.

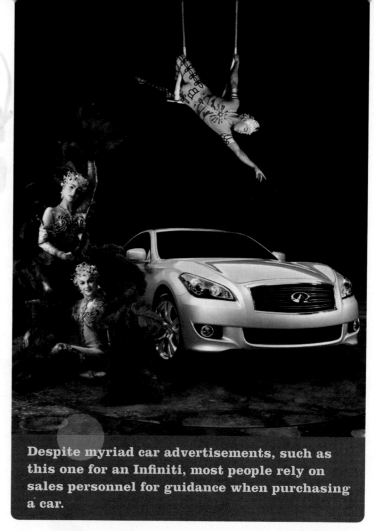

Despite myriad car advertisements, such as this one for an Infiniti, most people rely on sales personnel for guidance when purchasing a car.

© AP Images/PRNewsFoto/Infiniti

15-7c Target Market Characteristics

A target market characterized by widely scattered potential customers, highly informed buyers, and brand-loyal repeat purchasers generally requires a promotional mix with more advertising and sales promotion and less personal selling. Sometimes, however, personal selling is required even when buyers are well informed and geographically dispersed. Although industrial installations may be sold to well-educated people with extensive work experience, salespeople must be present to explain the product and work out the details of the purchase agreement.

Often firms sell goods and services in markets where potential customers are hard to locate. Print advertising can be used to find them. The reader is invited to go online, call, or mail in a reply card for more information. As the online queries, calls, or cards are received, salespeople are sent to visit the potential customers.

15-7d Type of Buying Decision

The promotional mix also depends on the type of buying decision—for example, a routine decision or a complex decision. For routine consumer decisions like buying toothpaste, the most effective promotion calls attention to the brand or reminds the consumer about the brand. Advertising and, especially, sales promotion are the most productive promotion tools to use for routine decisions.

If the decision is neither routine nor complex, advertising and public relations help establish awareness for the good or service. Suppose a man is looking for a bottle of wine to serve to his dinner guests. As a beer drinker, he is not familiar with wines, yet he has read an article in a popular magazine about the Robert Mondavi Winery and has seen an advertisement for the wine. He may be more likely to buy this brand because he is already aware of it. Online reviews are often important in this type of buying decision as well because the consumer has any number of other consumers' reviews easily accessible.

In contrast, consumers making complex buying decisions are more extensively involved. They rely on large amounts of information to help them reach a purchase decision. Personal selling is most effective in helping these consumers decide. For example, consumers thinking about buying a car typically research the car online using corporate and third-party Web sites. However, few people

push strategy a marketing strategy that uses aggressive personal selling and trade advertising to convince a wholesaler or a retailer to carry and sell particular merchandise

buy a car without visiting the dealership. They depend on a salesperson to provide the information they need to reach a decision. In addition to online resources, print advertising may also be used for high-involvement purchase decisions because it can often provide a large amount of information to the consumer.

15-7e Available Funds

Money, or the lack of it, may easily be the most important factor in determining the promotional mix. A small, undercapitalized manufacturer may rely heavily on free publicity if its product is unique. If the situation warrants a sales force, a financially strained firm may turn to manufacturers' agents, who work on a commission basis with no advances or expense accounts. Even well-capitalized organizations may not be able to afford the advertising rates of publications like *Time Magazine*, *Reader's Digest*, and the *Wall Street Journal*, or the cost of running television commercials during *The Big Bang Theory*, *American Idol*, or the Super Bowl. The price of a high-profile advertisement in these media could support several salespeople for an entire year.

When funds are available to permit a mix of promotional elements, a firm will generally try to optimize its return on promotion dollars while minimizing the *cost per contact*, or the cost of reaching one member of the target market. In general, the cost per contact is very high for personal selling, public relations, and sales promotions like sampling and demonstrations. On the other hand, given the number of people national advertising and social media reach, they have a very low cost per contact. Usually, there is a trade-off among the funds available, the number of people in the target market, the quality of communication needed, and the relative costs of the promotional elements. There are plenty of low-cost options available to companies without a huge budget. Many of these include online strategies and public relations efforts, in which the company relies on free publicity.

15-7f Push and Pull Strategies

The last factor that affects the promotional mix is whether a push or a pull promotional strategy will be used. Manufacturers may use aggressive personal selling and trade advertising to convince a wholesaler or a retailer to carry and sell their merchandise. This approach is known as a **push strategy** (see Exhibit 15.7). The wholesaler, in turn, must often push the merchandise forward by persuading the retailer to handle the goods. The retailer then uses advertising, displays, and other forms of promotion to convince the consumer to buy the "pushed" products.

Exhibit 15.7

PUSH STRATEGY VERSUS PULL STRATEGY

Push strategy

Manufacturer promotes to wholesaler → Wholesaler promotes to retailer → Retailer promotes to consumer → Consumer buys from retailer

Orders to manufacturer

Pull strategy

Manufacturer promotes to consumer → Consumer demands product from retailer → Retailer demands product from wholesaler → Wholesaler demands product from manufacturer

Orders to manufacturer

© Cengage Learning

pull strategy
a marketing strategy that stimulates consumer demand to obtain product distribution

Walmart uses aggressive discounts to consumers to push product out of its stores, such as selling 40-ounce bottles of Heinz ketchup for one dollar, or offering specials on holidays, like discounting sodas or meat for Labor Day barbeques.[12] This concept also applies to services.

At the other extreme is a **pull strategy**, which stimulates consumer demand to obtain product distribution. Rather than trying to sell to the wholesaler, the manufacturer using a pull strategy focuses its promotional efforts on end consumers or opinion leaders. Social media and content marketing (e.g., ensuring there is valuable, quality content on Web sites and social media) are the most recent (and best) example of a pull strategy. The idea is that social media content does not interrupt a consumer's experience with media (like a commercial interrupts your favorite television program). Instead the content invites customers to experience it on social media or a Web site.

When does **nature surprise** you with unexpected flavor?

When you use **all natural** ingredients from start to finish.

Lay's calls attention to its commitment to natural ingredients as a distinguishing attribute in order to help customers make a routine buying decision—purchasing Lay's snack food.

The campaign for Old Spice and the Doritos "Crash the Super Bowl" campaign (discussed earlier) are good examples of enticing consumers to the content. Consumer demand pulls the product through the channel of distribution (see Exhibit 15.7). Heavy sampling, introductory consumer advertising, cents-off campaigns, and couponing are part of a pull strategy.

Rarely does a company use a pull or a push strategy exclusively. Instead, the mix will emphasize one of these strategies. For example, pharmaceutical companies generally use a push strategy, through personal selling and trade advertising, to promote their drugs and therapies to physicians. Sales presentations and advertisements in medical journals give physicians the detailed information they need to prescribe medication to their patients. Most pharmaceutical companies supplement their push promotional strategy with a pull strategy targeted directly to potential patients through advertisements in consumer magazines and on television.

STUDY TOOLS 15

↑ **LOCATED AT BACK OF THE TEXTBOOK**
☐ Rip out Chapter Review Card

LOCATED AT WWW.CENGAGE.COM/LOGIN
☐ Review Key Terms Flashcards (print or online)
☐ Download audio and visual summaries to review on the go
☐ Complete both Practice Quizzes to prepare for tests
☐ Play "Beat the Clock" and "Quizbowl" to master concepts
☐ Complete "Crossword Puzzle" to review key terms
☐ Watch Video on "Pepe's Pizzeria" for a real company example

16-1 THE EFFECTS OF ADVERTISING

Advertising was defined in Chapter 15 as impersonal, one-way mass communication about a product or organization that is paid for by a marketer. It is a popular form of promotion, especially for consumer packaged goods and services. Advertising expenditures typically increase annually. Advertising expenditures by the top 100 U.S. advertisers grew almost 9 percent in 2010, rebounding fiercely in the automotive and financial sectors. Expenditures increased again in 2011 and were expected to grow by about 5.5 percent globally in 2012. Leading the growth in expenditures were American Express, which increased its advertising by nearly 60 percent to $3.1 billion, and Chrysler, which increased spending by 63 percent.[1] With the economic recovery, firms are spending staggeringly large amounts of money to convince people to spend their own money.

The top 100 global marketers spend more than $125.3 billion on measured media.

Advertising and marketing services, agencies, and other firms that provide marketing and communications services to marketers employ an estimated 1.4 million people, including those working in media advertising, such as newspapers, broadcast and cable television, radio, magazines, and Internet media companies.[2] One area that has continued to see rapid growth is the data side of marketing. Companies are collecting huge amounts of information and need skilled, creative, and Web-savvy people to interpret the data coming in from Web, mobile, and other digital ad campaigns. The CEO of MediaMath, an ad company in New York, says, "The demand [for digital ad techs] has far outstripped the supply. The number of things you need to know is high and the number of people that [know them] is low."[3]

Chapter 16

Advertising, Public Relations, and Sales Promotion

Learning Outcomes

16-1 *Discuss the effects of advertising on market share and consumers* 266–269

16-2 *Identify the major types of advertising* 269–270

16-3 *Discuss the creative decisions in developing an advertising campaign* 270–273

16-4 *Describe media evaluation and selection techniques* 273–280

16-5 *Discuss the role of public relations in the promotional mix* 280–282

16-6 *Define and state the objectives of sales promotion and the tools used to achieve them* 282–287

After you finish this chapter go to
p287 *for* **STUDY TOOLS**

16-1a
Advertising and Market Share

The most successful consumer brands, like Ivory soap and Coca-Cola, were built over many years by heavy advertising and marketing investments long ago. Today's advertising dollars for successful consumer brands are spent on maintaining brand awareness and market share.

New brands with a small market share tend to spend proportionately more for advertising and sales promotion than those with a large market share, typically for two reasons. First, beyond a certain level of spending for advertising and sales promotion, diminishing returns set in. That is, sales and market share improvements slow down and eventually decrease no matter how much is spent on advertising and sales promotion. This phenomenon is called the **advertising response function**. Understanding the advertising response function helps marketers use budgets wisely. A market leader like Johnson & Johnson's Neutrogena typically spends proportionately less on advertising than a newer line such as Jergens's Natural Glow moisturizer brand. Neutrogena has already captured the attention of the majority of its target market. It only needs to remind customers of its product.

The second reason new brands tend to require higher spending for advertising and sales promotion is that a certain minimum level of exposure is needed to measurably affect purchase habits. If Jergens advertised its Natural Glow moisturizers in only one or two publications and bought only one or two television spots, it would not achieve the exposure needed to penetrate consumers' perceptual defenses and affect purchase intentions.

16-1b The Effects of Advertising on Consumers

Advertising affects consumers' daily lives, informing them about products and services and influencing their attitudes, beliefs, and ultimately their purchases. Advertising affects the television programs people watch, the content of the newspapers they read, the politicians they elect, the medicines they take, and the toys their children play with.

BECOME ONE OF THE FRESHEST SMELLING PLACES ON EARTH.
Old Spice

Old Spice uses irreverence and humor to appeal to customers. Such personality has won the company a huge fan base.

Image courtesy of The Advertising Archives

Consequently, the influence of advertising on the U.S. socioeconomic system has been the subject of extensive debate in nearly all corners of society.

Though advertising cannot change consumers' deeply rooted values and attitudes, advertising may succeed in transforming a person's negative attitude toward a product into a positive one. For instance, serious or dramatic advertisements are more effective at changing consumers' negative attitudes. Humorous ads, on the other hand, have been shown to be more effective at shaping attitudes when consumers already have a positive image of an advertised brand.[4]

Advertising also reinforces positive attitudes toward brands. Brands with distinct personalities are more likely to have a larger base of loyal customers and market share. The more consistent a brand's personality, the more likely a customer will build a relationship with that brand over his or her lifetime.[5] This is why market leaders spend billions of dollars annually to reinforce and remind their loyal customers about the benefits of their products. For example, Walgreens received $197 million from its vendors (such as Maybelline or Nature's Way vitamins) to advertise those brands in addition to advertising the store itself.[6]

Advertising can also affect the way consumers rank a brand's attributes. For example, in years past, car ads emphasized such brand attributes as roominess, speed, and low maintenance. Today, however, car marketers have added safety, versatility, customization, and fuel efficiency to the list.

16-2 MAJOR TYPES OF ADVERTISING

A firm's promotional objectives determine the type of advertising it uses. If the goal of the promotion plan is to improve the image of the company or the industry, **institutional advertising** may be used. In contrast, if the advertiser wants to enhance the sales of a specific good or service, **product advertising** is used.

16-2a Institutional Advertising

Historically, advertising in the United States has been product oriented. Today, however, companies market multiple products and need a different type of advertising. Institutional advertising, or corporate advertising, promotes the corporation as a whole and is designed to establish, change, or maintain the corporation's identity. It usually does not ask the audience to do anything but maintain a favorable attitude toward the advertiser and its goods and services.

A form of institutional advertising called **advocacy advertising** is typically used to safeguard against negative consumer attitudes and to enhance the company's credibility among consumers who already favor its position. Corporations often use advocacy advertising to express their views on controversial issues. For example, the clothing company United Colors of Benetton has been known for its controversial advertising campaigns that mix selling clothing and political stances. The latest, promoting the UNHATE Foundation, an organization that strives to encourage acceptance of racial diversity around the world, shows prominent leaders kissing each other. The images include one of Pope Benedict XVI kissing Egyptian Imam

Ahmed Mohamed el-Tayeb, and one of President Obama and Chinese leader Hu Jintao. The images were highly controversial because, despite the company's wish to "combat the culture of hatred in all forms," none of the people pictured agreed to the campaign, and it, arguably, portrayed the leaders in an undignified manner.[7] Alternatively, firms' advocacy campaigns react to criticism or blame, or try to ward off increases in regulation, damaging legislation, or the unfavorable outcome of a lawsuit.

16-2b Product Advertising

Unlike institutional advertising, product advertising promotes the benefits of a specific good or service. The product's stage in its life cycle often determines which type of product advertising is used: pioneering advertising, competitive advertising, or comparative advertising.

PIONEERING ADVERTISING Pioneering advertising is intended to stimulate primary demand for a new product or product category. Heavily used during the introductory stage of the product life cycle, pioneering advertising offers consumers in-depth information about the benefits of the product class. Pioneering advertising also seeks to create interest. For example, Samsung recently released a line of televisions that not only have Internet access and connect to DIRECTV without a set-top box, but also include face recognition, voice control, and gesture control. To increase demand for these premium features, Samsung released several ads that show every member of the family—even a toddler—using the voice recognition and gesture control on the television.[8]

COMPETITIVE ADVERTISING Firms use competitive or brand advertising when a product enters the growth phase of the product life cycle and other companies begin to enter the marketplace. Instead of building demand for the product category, the goal of **competitive advertising** is to influence demand for a specific brand. Often, promotion becomes less informative and appeals more to emotions during this phase. Generally,

institutional advertising a form of advertising designed to enhance a company's image rather than promote a particular product

product advertising a form of advertising that touts the benefits of a specific good or service

advocacy advertising a form of advertising in which an organization expresses its views on controversial issues or responds to media attacks

pioneering advertising a form of advertising designed to stimulate primary demand for a new product or product category

competitive advertising a form of advertising designed to influence demand for a specific brand this is where an emphasis on branding begins. Advertisements focus on showing subtle differences between brands, building recall of a brand name, and creating a favorable attitude toward the brand. GEICO uses competitive advertising that discusses the attributes of the brand, how little time it takes to get a quote, how much customers can save, and the ease of submitting a claim. All of its campaigns use humor to promote the brand above others in the industry but without actively comparing GEICO with other insurance companies.

COMPARATIVE ADVERTISING Comparative advertising directly or indirectly compares two or more

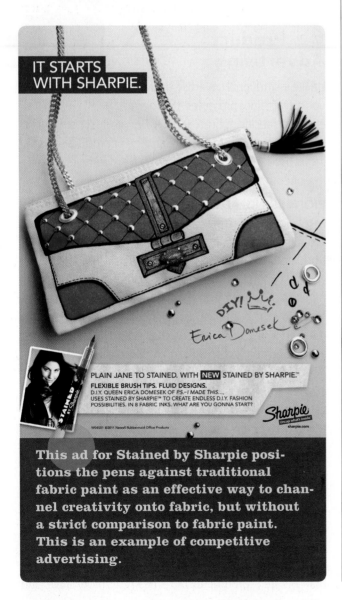

IT STARTS WITH SHARPIE.

DIY!
Erica Domesek

PLAIN JANE TO STAINED. WITH **NEW** STAINED BY SHARPIE.™
FLEXIBLE BRUSH TIPS. FLUID DESIGNS.
D.I.Y. QUEEN ERICA DOMESEK OF P.S.–I MADE THIS...,
USES STAINED BY SHARPIE™ TO CREATE ENDLESS D.I.Y. FASHION
POSSIBILITIES. IN 8 FABRIC INKS. WHAT ARE YOU GONNA START?

Sharpie
Uncap what's inside.™
sharpie.com

W04501 ©2011 Newell Rubbermaid Office Products

This ad for Stained by Sharpie positions the pens against traditional fabric paint as an effective way to channel creativity onto fabric, but without a strict comparison to fabric paint. This is an example of competitive advertising.

competing brands on one or more specific attributes. Some advertisers even use comparative advertising against their own brands. Products experiencing slow growth or those entering the marketplace against strong competitors are more likely to employ comparative claims in their advertising. In contrast to GEICO's "Fifteen minutes can save you 15 percent or more on car insurance" tagline that doesn't explicitly mention any other insurance company, 21st Century Insurance takes on its major competitors directly in its "Door Dings" television ad campaign. The ad features two cars, one labeled GEICO, the other 21st Century. A man wielding a huge mallet puts dings in the doors of both cars, and "since both cars are covered, both get the same repairs."[9] Then the commercial goes on to explain that 21st Century Insurance customers who switch from GEICO save an average of $480 a year, and those switching from Progressive and Allstate save an average of $528 a year.[10] 21st Century is explicitly comparing its insurance rates with those of its main competitors and capitalizing on customers' desire for great coverage at the lowest prices.

Before the 1970s, comparative advertising was allowed only if the competing brand was veiled and unidentified. In 1971, however, the Federal Trade Commission (FTC) fostered the growth of comparative advertising by saying that the advertising provided information to the customer and that advertisers were more skillful than the government in communicating this information. Federal rulings prohibit advertisers from falsely describing competitors' products and allow competitors to sue if ads show their products or mention their brand names in an incorrect or false manner. FTC rules also apply to advertisers making false claims about their own products.

16-3 CREATIVE DECISIONS IN ADVERTISING

Advertising strategies are typically organized around an advertising campaign. An **advertising campaign** is a series of related advertisements focusing on a common theme, slogan, and set of advertising appeals. It is a specific advertising effort for a particular product that extends for a defined period of time.

Before any creative work can begin on an advertising campaign, it is important to determine what goals or objectives the advertising should achieve. An **advertising objective** identifies the specific communication task that a campaign should accomplish for a specified target audience during a specified period. The objectives of a specific advertising campaign often depend on the overall corporate objectives and the product being advertised.

The DAGMAR approach (Defining Advertising Goals for Measured Advertising Results) is one method of setting objectives. According to this method, all advertising objectives should precisely define the target audience, the desired percentage change in some specified measure of effectiveness, and the time frame in which that change is to occur.

Once objectives are defined, creative work can begin on the advertising campaign. Advertising campaigns often follow the AIDA model, which was discussed in Chapter 15. Depending on where consumers are in the AIDA process, the creative development of an advertising campaign might focus on creating attention, arousing interest, stimulating desire, or ultimately leading to the action of buying the product. Specifically, creative decisions include identifying product benefits, developing and evaluating advertising appeals, executing the message, and evaluating the effectiveness of the campaign.

16-3a Identifying Product Benefits

A well-known rule of thumb in the advertising industry is "Sell the sizzle, not the steak"—that is, in advertising, the goal is to sell the benefits of the product, not its attributes. Consumers don't buy attributes, they buy benefits. An attribute is simply a feature of the product such as its easy-open package, special formulation, or new lower price. A benefit is what consumers will receive or achieve by using the product, such as convenience or ease of use. A benefit should answer the consumer's question "What's in it for me?" Benefits might be such things as pleasure, improved health, savings, or relief. A quick test to determine whether you are offering attributes or benefits in your advertising is to ask "So?" Consider this example:

» **ATTRIBUTE:** "DogsBestFriend is an all-natural skin care lotion for dogs that combines traditional medicines and Nigella

sativa seed oils with the newest extraction technology." "So . . . ?"

» **BENEFIT:** "So . . . DogsBestFriend acts as a natural replacement for hydrocortisone, antihistamines, and topical antibiotics that is powerful enough to combat inflammation, itching, and pain, yet safe enough to use on dogs of all ages."[11]

16-3b Developing and Evaluating Advertising Appeals

An **advertising appeal** identifies a reason for a person to buy a product. Developing advertising appeals, a challenging task, is typically the responsibility of the creative team (e.g., art directors and copywriters) in the advertising agency. Advertising appeals typically play off consumers' emotions or address some need or want the consumer has.

Advertising campaigns can focus on one or more advertising appeals. Often the appeals are quite general, thus allowing the firm to develop a number of subthemes or mini campaigns using both advertising and sales promotion. Several possible advertising appeals are listed in Exhibit 16.1.

© Cengage Learning

advertising **objective** a specific communication task that a campaign should accomplish for a specified target audience during a specified period

advertising **appeal** a reason for a person to buy a product

Exhibit 16.1
COMMON ADVERTISING APPEALS

Appeal	Goal
Profit	Lets consumers know whether the product will save them money, make them money, or keep them from losing money.
Health	Appeals to those who are body conscious or who want to be healthy; love or romance is used often in selling cosmetics and perfumes.
Fear	Can center around social embarrassment, growing old, or losing one's health; because of its power, requires advertiser to exercise care in execution.
Admiration	Frequently highlights celebrity spokespeople.
Convenience	Is often used for fast-food restaurants and microwave foods.
Fun and Pleasure	Are the keys to advertising vacations, beer, amusement parks, and more.
Vanity and Egotism	Are used most often for expensive or conspicuous items such as cars and clothing.
Environmental Consciousness	Centers around protecting the environment and being considerate of others in the community.

Choosing the best appeal from those developed usually requires market research. Criteria for evaluation include desirability, exclusiveness, and believability. The appeal first must make a positive impression on and be desirable to the target market. It must also be exclusive or unique. Consumers must be able to distinguish the advertiser's message from competitors' messages. Most important, the appeal should be believable. An appeal that makes extravagant claims not only wastes promotional dollars but also creates ill will for the advertiser.

The advertising appeal selected for the campaign becomes what advertisers call its **unique selling proposition**. The unique selling proposition often becomes all or part of the campaign's slogan. For example, K-Swiss's new Tube line of workout shoes has teamed with HBO's *Eastbound & Down* to create an ad campaign starring the main character of the show, Kenny Powers, a washed-up pitcher with a foul mouth and an overblown confidence in his awesomeness. The campaign

features Powers as the CEO of K-Swiss and his marketing decisions on how to make the brand relevant (or in his words, "making marketing that touches my audience deep inside").[12] K-Swiss is using humor to appeal to its target audience of young males, and the unique selling position for Tubes is that they will help you perform like Powers's all-star athlete employees. The campaign sparked a 250 percent sales increase for K-Swiss and helped bring *Eastbound & Down* into a more mainstream consciousness.[13]

16-3c Executing the Message

Message execution is the way an advertisement portrays its information. In general, the AIDA plan (see Chapter 15) is a good blueprint for executing an advertising message. Any ad should immediately draw the reader's, viewer's, or listener's attention. The advertiser must then use the message to hold interest, create desire for the good or service, and ultimately motivate a purchase.

The style in which the message is executed is one of the most creative elements of an advertisement. Exhibit 16.2

Exhibit 16.2

ELEVEN COMMON EXECUTIONAL STYLES FOR ADVERTISING

Executional Style	Description
Slice-of-Life	Depicts people in normal settings, such as at the dinner table or in their car. McDonald's often uses slice-of-life styles showing youngsters munching on french fries from Happy Meals on family outings.
Lifestyle	Shows how well the product will fit in with the consumer's lifestyle. As his Volkswagen Jetta moves through the streets of the French Quarter, a Gen X driver inserts a techno music CD and marvels at how the rhythms of the world mimic the ambient vibe inside his vehicle.
Spokesperson/ Testimonial	Can feature a celebrity, company official, or typical consumer making a testimonial or endorsing a product. Sheryl Crow represented Revlon's Colorist hair coloring, while Beyoncé Knowles was named the new face of American Express. Dell Inc. founder Michael Dell touts his vision of the customer experience via Dell in television ads.
Fantasy	Creates a fantasy for the viewer built around use of the product. Carmakers often use this style to let viewers fantasize about how they would feel speeding around tight corners or down long country roads in their cars.
Humorous	Advertisers often use humor in their ads, such as Snickers' "Not Going Anywhere for a While" campaign featuring hundreds of souls waiting, sometimes impatiently, to get into heaven.
Real/Animated Product Symbols	Creates a character that represents the product in advertisements, such as the Energizer Bunny or Starkist's Charlie the Tuna. GEICO's suave gecko and disgruntled cavemen became cult classics for the insurance company.
Mood or Image	Builds a mood or image around the product, such as peace, love, or beauty. De Beers ads depicting shadowy silhouettes wearing diamond engagement rings and diamond necklaces portrayed passion and intimacy while extolling that "a diamond is forever."
Demonstration	Shows consumers the expected benefit. Many consumer products use this technique. Laundry detergent spots are famous for demonstrating how their product will clean clothes whiter and brighter. Fort James Corporation demonstrated in television commercials how its Dixie Rinse & ReUse disposable stoneware product line can stand up to the heat of a blowtorch and survive a cycle in a clothes washer.
Musical	Conveys the message of the advertisement through song. For example, Nike's ads depicted a marathoner's tortured feet and a surfer's thigh scarred by a shark attack while strains of Joe Cocker's "You Are So Beautiful" could be heard in the background.
Scientific	Uses research or scientific evidence to give a brand superiority over competitors. Pain relievers like Advil, Bayer, and Excedrin use scientific evidence in their ads.

© Cengage Learning

lists some examples of executional styles used by advertisers. Executional styles often dictate what type of media is to be employed to convey the message. For example, scientific executional styles lend themselves well to print advertising, where more information can be conveyed. Testimonials by athletes are one of the more popular executional styles.

Injecting humor into an advertisement is a popular and effective executional style. Humorous executional styles are more often used in radio and television advertising than in print or magazine advertising, where humor is less easily communicated. Humorous ads are typically used for lower-risk, low-involvement, routine purchases such as candy, cigarettes, and casual jeans than for higher-risk purchases or those that are expensive, durable, or flamboyant.[14]

Sometimes a company will modify its executional styles to make its advertising more effective. Each year, more and more car companies are advertising based on price. But Chrysler, saved from failure by two government bailouts and purchase by Italian carmaker Fiat, has bucked that trend. The new Chief Marketing Officer, Olivier Francois, is bringing customers back into the fold with rappers, pop stars, and freedom. The latest campaigns involve rapper Eminem talking about Detroit's rebirth; Jennifer Lopez driving, singing, and performing a dance routine; and George Washington chasing off the British in a Dodge Challenger. The stylish and evocative imagery rarely focuses on the cars (Eminem's commercial hardly shows the car at all), but it has increased sales dramatically. Sales of the 200 doubled, and Jeep sales were up 44 percent.[15]

16-3d Post-Campaign Evaluation

Evaluating an advertising campaign can be the most demanding task facing advertisers. How can an advertiser assess if the campaign led to an increase in sales or market share or elevated awareness of the product? Many advertising campaigns aim to create an image for the good or service instead of asking for action, so their real effect is unknown. So many

variables shape the effectiveness of an ad that advertisers often must guess whether their money has been well spent. Nonetheless, marketers spend considerable time studying advertising effectiveness and its probable impact on sales, market share, or awareness.

Testing ad effectiveness can be done before and/or after the campaign. Before a campaign is released, marketing managers use pretests to determine the best advertising appeal, layout, and media vehicle. After advertisers implement a campaign, they use several monitoring techniques to determine whether the campaign has met its original goals. Even if a campaign has been highly successful, advertisers still typically do a post-campaign analysis to identify how the campaign might have been more efficient and what factors contributed to its success.

16-4 MEDIA DECISIONS IN ADVERTISING

A major decision for advertisers is the choice of medium—the channel used to convey a message to a target market. Media planning, therefore, is the series of decisions advertisers make regarding the selection and

medium the channel used to convey a message to a target market

media planning the series of decisions advertisers make regarding the selection and use of media, allowing the marketer to optimally and cost-effectively communicate the message to the target audience

Jennifer Lopez drives a Fiat for a commercial, which is part music video, and uses her celebrity to sell the car more than the car itself.

© Icono, PacificCoastNews/Newscom

use of media, enabling the marketer to optimally and cost-effectively communicate the message to the target audience. Specifically, advertisers must determine which types of media will best communicate the benefits of their product or service to the target audience and when and for how long the advertisement will run.

Promotional objectives and the appeal and executional style of the advertising strongly affect the selection of media. Both creative and media decisions are made at the same time: Creative work cannot be completed without knowing which medium will be used to convey the message to the target market. In many cases, the advertising objectives dictate the medium and the creative approach to be used. For example, if the objective is to demonstrate how fast a product operates, a television commercial that shows this action may be the best choice.

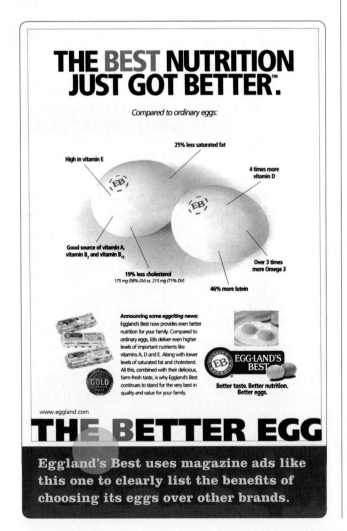

Eggland's Best uses magazine ads like this one to clearly list the benefits of choosing its eggs over other brands.

U.S. advertisers spend roughly $300 billion annually on media monitored by national reporting services—newspapers, magazines, radio, television, the Internet, and outdoor. The remainder is spent on unmonitored media, such as direct mail, trade exhibits, cooperative advertising, brochures, coupons, catalogs, and special events. In 2008, about 48 percent of every media dollar went toward television ads (cable, syndicated, spot, and network), 19 percent to magazines, 2.7 percent to outdoor advertising, and about 16.5 percent for newspaper ads.[16] But these traditional mass-market media are declining in usage as more targeted media are growing. Between 2008 and 2010, spending on magazine advertising declined and Internet advertising rose to 12.6 percent of global ad spending.[17]

16-4a Media Types

Advertising media are channels that advertisers use in mass communication. The six major advertising media are newspapers, magazines, radio, television, the Internet, and outdoor media. Exhibit 16.3 summarizes the advantages and disadvantages of some of these major channels. In recent years, however, alternative media channels have emerged that give advertisers innovative ways to reach their target audience and avoid advertising clutter.

NEWSPAPERS Newspapers are one of the oldest forms of media. The advantages of newspaper advertising include geographic flexibility and timeliness. Although there has been a decline in circulation as well as in the number of newspapers nationally, there are still several major newspapers including the *Wall Street Journal*, *USA Today*, the *New York Times*, the *Los Angeles Times* and the *Washington Post*. But most newspapers are local. Because newspapers are generally a mass-market medium, however, they may not be the best vehicle for marketers trying to reach a very narrow market. Newspaper advertising also encounters a lot of distractions from competing ads and news stories. Therefore, one company's ad may not be particularly visible.

The main sources of newspaper ad revenue are local retailers, classified ads, and cooperative advertising. In **cooperative advertising**, the manufacturer and the retailer split the costs of advertising the manufacturer's brand. For example, Estée Lauder may split the cost of an advertisement with Macy's department store provided that the ad focuses on Estée Lauder's products. One reason manufacturers use cooperative advertising is the impracticality of listing all their dealers in national

Exhibit 16.3

ADVANTAGES AND DISADVANTAGES OF MAJOR ADVERTISING MEDIA

Medium	Advantages	Disadvantages
Newspapers	Geographic selectivity and flexibility; short-term advertiser commitments; news value and immediacy; year-round readership; high individual market coverage; co-op and local tie-in availability; short lead time	Little demographic selectivity; limited color capabilities; low pass-along rate; may be expensive
Magazines	Good reproduction, especially for color; demographic selectivity; regional selectivity; local market selectivity; relatively long advertising life; high pass-along rate	Long-term advertiser commitments; slow audience buildup; limited demonstration capabilities; lack of urgency; long lead time
Radio	Low cost; immediacy of message; can be scheduled on short notice; relatively no seasonal change in audience; highly portable; short-term advertiser commitments; entertainment carryover	No visual treatment; short advertising life of message; high frequency required to generate comprehension and retention; distractions from background sound; commercial clutter
Television	Ability to reach a wide, diverse audience; low cost per thousand; creative opportunities for demonstration; immediacy of messages; entertainment carryover; demographic selectivity with cable stations	Short life of message; some consumer skepticism about claims; high campaign cost; little demographic selectivity with network stations; long-term advertiser commitments; long lead times required for production; commercial clutter
Internet	Fastest-growing medium; ability to reach a narrow target audience; relatively short lead time required for creating Web-based advertising; moderate cost; ability to measure ad effectiveness; ability to engage consumers through search engine marketing, social media, display advertising, and mobile marketing	Most ad exposure relies on "click-through" from display ads; measurement for social media needs much improvement; not all consumers have access to the Internet, and many consumers are not using social media
Outdoor Media	Repetition; moderate cost; flexibility; geographic selectivity	Short message; lack of demographic selectivity; high "noise" level distracting audience

© Cengage Learning

advertising. Also, cooperative advertising encourages retailers to devote more effort to the manufacturer's lines.

MAGAZINES Magazines are another traditional medium that has been successful. Some of the top magazines according to circulation include *AARP*, *Better Homes and Gardens*, *Reader's Digest*, *National Geographic*, and *Good Housekeeping*. However, compared to the cost of other media, the cost per contact in magazine advertising is usually high. The cost per potential customer may be much lower, however, because magazines are often targeted to specialized audiences and thus reach more potential customers.

RADIO Radio has several strengths as an advertising medium: selectivity and audience segmentation, a large out-of-home audience, low unit and production costs, timeliness, and geographic flexibility. Local advertisers are the most frequent users of radio advertising, contributing over 75 percent of all radio ad revenue. Like newspapers, radio also lends itself well to cooperative advertising.

TELEVISION Television broadcasters include network television, independent stations, cable television, and direct broadcast satellite television. Network television reaches a wide and diverse market, and cable television and direct broadcast satellite systems, such as DIRECTV and DISH Network, broadcast a multitude of channels devoted to highly segmented markets. Because of its targeted channels, cable television is often characterized as "narrowcasting" by media buyers.

Advertising time on television can be very expensive, especially for network and popular cable channels. Special events and first-run prime-time shows for top-ranked television programs command the highest rates for a typical thirty-second spot, with the least expensive ads costing about $300,000 and the more expensive ones $500,000. A thirty-second spot during the Super Bowl runs between $2.8 and $3.5 million, which companies are willing to pay. Chrysler's two-minute spot during the 2011 Super Bowl cost $9 million and featured rapper Eminem.[18] An alternative to a commercial spot is the **infomercial**,

advergaming placing advertising messages in Web-based or video games to advertise or promote a product, service, organization, or issue

a thirty-minute or longer advertisement, which is relatively inexpensive to produce and air. Advertisers say the infomercial is an ideal way to present complicated information to potential customers, which other advertising vehicles typically don't allow time to do. Beachbody's P90X or Insanity exercise DVDs are advertised through infomercials.

Probably the most significant trend to affect television advertising is the rise in popularity of digital video recorders (DVRs). For every hour of television programming, an average of fifteen minutes is dedicated to nonprogram material (ads, public service announcements, and network promotions), so the popularity of DVRs among ad-weary viewers is hardly surprising. Like marketers and advertisers, networks are also highly concerned about ad skipping. If consumers are not watching advertisements, then marketers will spend a greater proportion of their advertising budgets on alternative media, and a critical revenue stream for networks will disappear.

THE INTERNET With ad revenues almost $50 billion annually, the Internet has become a versatile advertising medium able to target specific groups. Spending on online advertising is expected to be more than $76 billion by 2016 and represent 35 percent of all advertising expenditures.[19] Online advertising includes search engine marketing (e.g., pay-per-click ads like Google AdWords), display advertising (e.g., banner ads, video ads), social media advertising (e.g., Facebook ads), e-mail marketing, and mobile marketing (including mobile advertising and SMS). Google offers the ability to audience buy; advertisers can purchase ad space targeted to a highly specific group, such as women ages eighteen to thirty-four who like basketball.[20]

Popular Internet sites and search engines generally sell advertising space to marketers to promote their goods and services. Internet surfers click on these ads to be linked to more information about the advertised product or

Outdoor advertising is very diverse. This clever ad for Mondo Pasta is strategically placed on the side of a boat to make it look like the rope is pasta!

service. Both leading advertisers and companies whose ad budgets are not as large have become big Internet advertisers. Because of the relative low cost and high targetability, search engines generate nearly half of all Internet ad revenue. Display and banner ads are the next largest source of Internet revenue.[21]

Another popular Internet advertising format is **advergaming**, in which companies put ad messages in Web-based or video games (on PlayStation or Wii) to advertise or promote a product, service, organization, or issue. Indeed, the issue of gamification is fast becoming one that is important for marketers whether in video games or social media. *Gamification* is the process of using game thinking and mechanics to engage an audience and solve problems. Thus, rewards, incentives, and competition are all important aspects in social media games like FarmVille or Mafia Wars.[22] Sometimes the entire game amounts to a virtual commercial; other times advertisers sponsor games or buy ad space for a product placement in them. Many of these are social games, played on Facebook or similar sites, where players can interact with one another. Social gaming has an audience of more than 300 million, and the players will spend $4.9 billion inside games this year.[23]

More than three-fourths of Americans have mobile phones, and over one-third of those are Smartphones (e.g., iPhone, Android). As a result, more people are accessing the Web on their phones, making mobile Web sites and apps more important.[24] Mobile advertising has substantial upside potential given that there are more than 4 billion cell phone users in the world, and an increasing number of those users have Smartphones or tablets with Internet access. As devices such as the iPad continue to grow in popularity, mobile advertising spending will continue to grow worldwide.

OUTDOOR MEDIA Outdoor or out-of-home advertising is a flexible, low-cost medium that may take a variety of forms. Examples include billboards, skywriting, giant inflatables, mini billboards in malls and media mix the combination of media to be used for a promotional campaign

GOOGLE GOGGLES— LITERALLY

Google currently plays a huge role in online advertising in large part because its ads appear on many Web sites and the search engine is one of the most popular. In addition, Google has become a mobile giant with its android operating system. But now Google is hoping to become even more ubiquitous with its new product—Google glasses. The specs are designed to unify Google's myriad offerings by streaming real-time information right to the viewer's eyes. Wearers can look at a poster for a movie, and ticket sales will pop up. Voice interaction enables users to ask for directions and have a course plotted on Google Maps. A small camera allows users to share what they are looking at and take photos. Calls can be made, e-mails and texts sent, locations shared, and places checked-in to, all through a streamlined, wraparound frame with one small, clear lens. What does this mean for marketers? It means a whole new level of contact. While Google says the glasses are not meant to be worn constantly, being able to display ads for a search, on a map, or even through Facebook or Twitter to a user's eye might be the ultimate in alternative media marketing.

Source: Nick Bilton, "Google Begins Testing Its Augmented-Reality Glasses," *New York Times*, April 4, 2012, http://bits.blogs.nytimes.com/2012/04/04/google-begins-testing-its-augmented-reality-glasses (Accessed April 20, 2012).

© tammy allen/Shutterstock.com / © iStockphoto.com/Bill Noll

on bus stop shelters, signs in sports arenas, and lighted moving signs in bus terminals and airports, as well as ads painted on cars, trucks, buses, water towers, manhole covers, drinking glass coasters, and even people, called "living advertising." The plywood scaffolding surrounding downtown construction sites often holds ads, which in places like Manhattan's Times Square, can reach over a million viewers a day.

Outdoor advertising reaches a broad and diverse market and is therefore ideal for promoting convenience products and services as well as directing consumers to local businesses. One of outdoor advertising's main advantages over other media is that its exposure frequency is very high, yet the amount of clutter from competing ads is very low. Outdoor advertising also can be customized to local marketing needs, which is why local businesses are the leading outdoor advertisers in any given region.

ALTERNATIVE MEDIA To cut through the clutter of traditional advertising media, advertisers are developing new media vehicles, like shopping carts in grocery stores, computer screen savers, DVDs, CDs, interactive kiosks in department stores, advertisements run before movies at the cinema, posters on bathroom stalls, and "advertainments"—mini movies that promote a product and are shown via the Internet.

Marketers are looking for more innovative ways to reach captive and often bored commuters. For instance, subway systems are now showing ads via lighted boxes installed along tunnel walls. Other advertisers seek consumers at home. Some marketers have begun replacing hold music on customer service lines with advertisements and movie trailers. This strategy generates revenue for the company being called and catches undistracted consumers for advertisers. The trick is to amuse and interest this captive audience without annoying them during their ten- to fifteen-minute wait.[25]

16-4b Media Selection Considerations

An important element in any advertising campaign is the **media mix**, the combination of media to be used. Media

cost per contact (cost per thousand or CPM) the cost of reaching one member of the target market

cost per click the cost associated with a consumer clicking on a display or banner ad

reach the number of target consumers exposed to a commercial at least once during a specific period, usually four weeks

frequency the number of times an individual is exposed to a given message during a specific period

audience selectivity the ability of an advertising medium to reach a precisely defined market

mix decisions are typically based on several factors: cost per contact, cost per click, reach, frequency, target audience considerations, flexibility of the medium, noise level, and the life span of the medium.

Cost per contact, also referred to as **cost per thousand (CPM)**, is the cost of reaching one member of the target market. Naturally, as the size of the audience increases, so does the total cost. Cost per contact enables an advertiser to compare the relative costs of specific media vehicles (such as television versus radio or magazine versus newspaper), or more specifically within a media category (such as *Newsweek* versus *Time)*. Thus, an advertiser debating whether to spend local advertising dollars for television spots or radio spots could consider the cost per contact of each. Alternatively, if the question is which magazine to advertise in, she might choose the one with the greater reach. In either case, the advertiser can pick the vehicle with the lowest cost per contact to maximize advertising punch for the money spent. **Cost per click** is the cost associated with a consumer clicking on a display or banner ad. Although there are several variations, this option enables the marketer to pay only for "engaged" consumers—those who opted to click on an ad.

Reach is the number of target customers who are exposed to a commercial at least once during a specific period, usually four weeks. Media plans for product introductions and attempts at increasing brand awareness usually emphasize reach. For example, an advertiser might try to reach 70 percent of the target audience during the first three months of the campaign. Reach is related to a medium's ratings, generally referred to in the industry as *gross ratings points*, or *GRP*. A television program with a higher GRP means that more people are tuning in to the show and the reach is higher. Accordingly, as GRP increases for a particular medium, so does cost per contact.

Because the typical ad is short-lived and because often only a small portion of an ad may be perceived at one time, advertisers repeat their ads so that potential customers will remember the message. **Frequency** is the number of times an individual is exposed to a given message during a specific period. Advertisers use average

frequency to measure the intensity of a specific medium's coverage. For example, Coca-Cola might want an average exposure frequency of five for its POWERade television ads. That means that each of the television viewers who saw the ad saw it an average of five times.

Media selection is also a matter of matching the advertising medium with the product's target market. If marketers are trying to reach teenage females, they might select *Seventeen* magazine. A medium's ability to reach a precisely defined market is its **audience selectivity**. Some media vehicles, like general newspapers and network television, appeal to a wide cross section of the population. Others—such as *Brides*, *Popular Mechanics*, *Architectural Digest*, *Lucky*, MTV, ESPN, and Christian radio stations—appeal to very specific groups.

The *flexibility* of a medium can be extremely important to an advertiser. For example, because of layouts and design, the lead time for magazine advertising is considerably longer than for other media types and so is less flexible. By contrast, radio and Internet advertising provide maximum flexibility. If necessary, an advertiser can change a radio ad on the day it is aired.

Noise level is the level of distraction experienced by the target audience in a medium. Noise can be created by competing ads, as when a street is lined with billboards or when a television program is cluttered with competing ads. Whereas newspapers and magazines have a high noise level, direct mail is a private medium with a low noise level. Typically, no other advertising media or news stories compete for direct mail readers' attention.

Media have either a short or a long *life span*, which means that messages can either quickly fade or persist as tangible copy to be carefully studied. A radio commercial may last less than a minute, but advertisers can overcome this short life span by repeating radio ads often. In contrast, a magazine has a relatively long life span, which is further increased by a high pass-along rate.

Media planners have traditionally relied on the above factors in selecting an effective media mix, with reach, frequency, and cost often the overriding criteria. Well-established brands with familiar messages, however, probably need fewer exposures to be effective, while newer or unfamiliar brands likely need more exposures to become familiar. In addition, today's media planners have more media options than ever before. (Today, there are over 1,600 television stations across the country, whereas forty years ago there were only three.)

The proliferation of media channels is causing *media fragmentation* and forcing media planners to pay as much attention to where they place their advertising as to how often the advertisement is repeated. That is, marketers should evaluate reach *and* frequency in assessing the effectiveness of advertising. In certain situations, it may be important to reach potential consumers through as many media vehicles as possible. When this approach is considered, however, the budget must be large enough to achieve sufficient levels of frequency to have an impact. In evaluating reach versus frequency, therefore, the media planner ultimately must select an approach that is most likely to result in the ad being understood and remembered when a purchase decision is being made.

Advertisers also evaluate the qualitative factors involved in media selection. These include such things as attention to the commercial and the program, involvement, program liking, lack of distractions, and other audience behaviors that affect the likelihood that a commercial

WITH SO MANY WAYS TO AVOID COMMERCIALS (SUCH AS USING A DVR), COMPANIES ARE USING SEVERAL DIFFERENT MEDIUMS TO REACH CONSUMERS ACROSS MULTIPLE PLATFORMS.

message is being seen and, hopefully, absorbed. While advertisers can advertise their product in as many media as possible and repeat the ad as many times as they like, the ad still may not be effective if the audience is not paying attention. Additional research highlights the benefits of cross-media advertising campaigns. Viewers who encounter ads both on television and online are most likely to remember and respond to them. Listerine ran a recent campaign on ABC and ABC.com and found that its mouthwash sales increased 33 percent more among viewers who saw the ad in both places.[26]

16-4c Media Scheduling

After choosing the media for the advertising campaign, advertisers must schedule the ads. A **media schedule** designates the medium or media to be used (such as magazines, television, or radio), the specific vehicles (such as *People* magazine, the show *Mad Men* on television, or Rush Limbaugh's national radio program), and the insertion dates of the advertising.

There are four basic types of media schedules:

▸▸ **Products in the later stages of the product life cycle, which are advertised on a reminder basis, use a continuous media schedule.** A continuous schedule allows the advertising to run steadily throughout the advertising period. Examples include Ivory soap and Charmin toilet tissue, which may have an ad in the newspaper every Sunday and a television commercial on NBC every Wednesday at 7:30 p.m. over a three-month time period.

▸▸ **With a flighted media schedule, the advertiser may schedule the ads heavily every other month or every two weeks to achieve a greater impact with an increased frequency and reach at those times.** Movie studios might schedule television advertising on Wednesday and Thursday nights, when moviegoers are deciding which films to see that weekend.

▸▸ **A pulsing media schedule combines continuous scheduling with flighting. Continuous advertising is simply heavier during the best sale periods. A retail**

media schedule designation of the media, the specific publications or programs, and the insertion dates of advertising

continuous media schedule a media scheduling strategy in which advertising is run steadily throughout the advertising period; used for products in the later stages of the product life cycle

flighted media schedule a media scheduling strategy in which ads are run heavily every other month or every two weeks to achieve a greater impact with an increased frequency and reach at those times

pulsing media schedule a media scheduling strategy that uses continuous scheduling throughout the year coupled with a flighted schedule during the best sales periods

© Artpose Adam Borkowski/Shutterstock.com

seasonal media schedule a media scheduling strategy that runs advertising only during times of the year when the product is most likely to be used

public relations the element in the promotional mix that evaluates public attitudes, identifies issues that may elicit public concern, and executes programs to gain public understanding and acceptance

publicity an effort to capture media attention, often initiated through press releases that further a corporation's public relations plans

department store may advertise on a year-round basis but place more advertising during certain sale periods such as Thanksgiving, Christmas, and back-to-school. For example, beer may be advertised more heavily during the summer months and football season given the higher consumption levels.

▸▸ Certain times of the year call for a **seasonal media schedule**. Products like Sudafed cold tablets and Coppertone sunscreen, which are used more during certain times of the year, tend to follow a seasonal strategy.

New research comparing continuous media schedules versus flighted ones finds that continuous schedules for television advertisements are more effective than flighting in driving sales. The research suggests that it may be more important to get exposure as close as possible to the time when someone is going to make a purchase. Therefore, the advertiser should maintain a continuous schedule over as long a period of time as possible. Often called *recency planning*, this theory of scheduling is now commonly used for scheduling television advertising for frequently purchased products, such as Coca-Cola or Tide detergent. Recency planning's main premise is that advertising works by influencing the brand choice of people who are ready to buy. Mobile advertising may be one of the most promising tactics for contacting consumers when they are thinking about a specific product. For example, a GPS-enabled mobile phone can get text messages for area restaurants around lunchtime to advertise specials to professionals working in a big city.

16-5 PUBLIC RELATIONS

Public relations is the element in the promotional mix that evaluates public attitudes, identifies issues that may elicit public concern, and executes programs to gain public understanding and acceptance. Public relations is a vital link in a progressive company's marketing communication mix. Marketing managers plan solid public relations campaigns that fit into overall marketing plans and focus on targeted audiences. These campaigns strive to maintain a positive image of the corporation in the eyes of the public. As such, they should capitalize on the factors that enhance the firm's image and minimize the factors that could generate a negative image. The concept of earned media is based on public relations and publicity.

Publicity is the effort to capture media attention—for example, through articles or editorials in publications or through human-interest stories on radio or television programs. Corporations usually initiate publicity through press releases that further their public relations plans. A company about to introduce a new product or open a new store may send press releases to the media in the hope that the story will be published or broadcast. Savvy publicity can often create overnight sensations or build up a reserve of goodwill with consumers. Corporate donations and sponsorships can also create favorable publicity.

© Roz Woodward/PhotoDisc/Jupiterimages

PUBLIC RELATIONS DEPARTMENTS

Public relations departments may perform any or all of the following functions:

▸▸ **PRESS RELATIONS:** Placing positive, newsworthy information in the news media or in the hands of influential bloggers to attract attention to a product, a service, or a person associated with the firm or institution

▸▸ **PRODUCT PUBLICITY:** Publicizing specific products or services through a variety of traditional and online channels

▸▸ **CORPORATE COMMUNICATION:** Creating internal and external messages to promote a positive image of the firm or institution

▸▸ **PUBLIC AFFAIRS:** Building and maintaining local, national, or global community relations

▸▸ **LOBBYING:** Influencing legislators and government officials to promote or defeat legislation and regulation

▸▸ **EMPLOYEE AND INVESTOR RELATIONS:** Maintaining positive relationships with employees, shareholders, and others in the financial community

▸▸ **CRISIS MANAGEMENT:** Responding to unfavorable publicity or a negative event

16-5a Major Public Relations Tools

Public relations professionals commonly use several tools, many of which require an active role on the part of the public relations professional, such as writing press releases and engaging in proactive media relations. Sometimes, however, these techniques create their own publicity.

NEW-PRODUCT PUBLICITY Publicity is instrumental in introducing new products and services. Publicity can help advertisers explain what's different about their new product by prompting free news stories or positive word of mouth about it. During the introductory period, an especially innovative new product often needs more exposure than conventional, paid advertising affords. Public relations professionals write press releases or develop videos in an effort to generate news about their new product. They also jockey for exposure of their product or service at major events, on popular television and news shows, or in the hands of influential people. Consider the publicity Apple generated for the release of the iPad, which included press coverage in traditional media as well as online blogs and forums. That was a small aspect of the entire marketing campaign.

PRODUCT PLACEMENT Marketers are increasingly using **product placement** to reinforce brand awareness and create favorable attitudes. Product placement is a strategy that involves getting one's product, service, or name to appear in a movie, television show, radio program, magazine, newspaper, video game, video or audio clip, book, or commercial for another product; on the Internet; or at special events. Indeed, a product mention on the Oprah Winfrey show was linked to increased sales for many products, especially books. Including an actual product, such as a can of Pepsi, adds a sense of realism to a movie, television show, video game, book, or similar vehicle that cannot be created by a can simply marked "soda." Product placements are arranged through barter (trade of product for placement), through paid placements, or at no charge when the product is viewed as enhancing the vehicle it is placed in.

Product placement expenditures total about $5 billion annually.[27] More than two-thirds of product placements are in movies and television shows, but placements in other alternative media are growing, particularly on the Internet and in video games. Digital technology now enables companies to "virtually" place their products in any audio or video production. Virtual placement not only reduces the cost of product placement for new productions but also enables companies to place their products in previously produced programs, such as reruns of television shows. Overall, companies obtain valuable product exposure, brand reinforcement, and increased sales through product placement, often at a much lower cost than in mass media like television ads.

CONSUMER EDUCATION Some major firms believe that educated consumers are more loyal customers. Financial planning firms often sponsor free educational seminars on money management, retirement planning, and investing in the hope that the seminar participants will choose the sponsoring organization for their future financial needs.

SPONSORSHIP Sponsorships are increasing both in number and as a proportion of companies' marketing budgets, with spending reaching $17.9 billion during 2010 in the United States.[28] Probably the biggest reason for the increasing use of sponsorships is the difficulty of reaching audiences and differentiating a product from competing brands through the mass media.

With **sponsorship**, a company spends money to support an issue, cause, or event that is consistent with corporate objectives, such as improving brand awareness or enhancing corporate image. The biggest category is sports, which accounts for almost 70 percent of spending in sponsorships and has seen steady growth despite the recession.[29] Nonsports categories include entertainment tours and attractions, causes, arts, festivals, fairs and annual events, and association and membership organizations.

Although the most popular sponsorship events are still those involving sports, music, or the arts, companies have recently been turning to more specialized events such as tie-ins with schools, charities, and other community service organizations. Marketers sometimes even create their own events tied around their products. Eating competitions often do this—in this formerly trophy-only sport, prize money for the winners can now approach $500,000. P&G paid Joey Chestnut, a star hot dog eater, $100,000 to do a six-stop publicity tour and endorse Pepto-Bismol.[30]

Corporations sponsor issues as well as events. Sponsorship issues are quite diverse, but the three most

product placement a public relations strategy that involves getting a product, service, or company name to appear in a movie, television show, radio program, magazine, newspaper, video game, video or audio clip, book, or commercial for another product; on the Internet; or at special events

sponsorship a public relations strategy in which a company spends money to support an issue, cause, or event that is consistent with corporate objectives, such as improving brand awareness or enhancing corporate image popular are education, health care, and social programs. Firms often donate a percentage of sales or profits to a worthy cause favored by their target market.

COMPANY WEB SITES Companies increasingly are using the Internet in their public relations strategies. Company Web sites are used to introduce new products, provide information to the media including social media news releases, promote existing products, obtain consumer

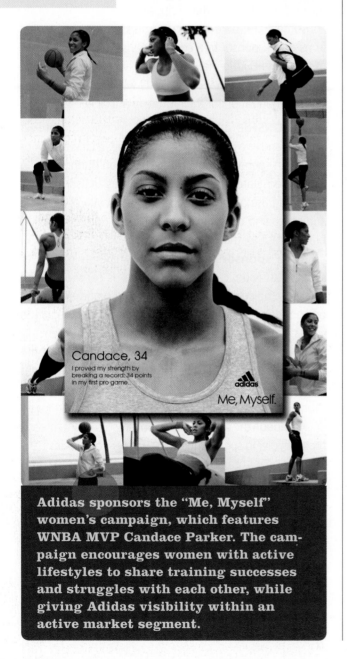

Adidas sponsors the "Me, Myself" women's campaign, which features WNBA MVP Candace Parker. The campaign encourages women with active lifestyles to share training successes and struggles with each other, while giving Adidas visibility within an active market segment.

feedback, communicate legislative and regulatory information, showcase upcoming events, provide links to related sites (including corporate and non-corporate blogs, Facebook, and Twitter), release financial information, interact with customers and potential customers, and perform many more marketing activities. In addition, social media are playing a larger role in how companies interact with customers online, particularly through sites like Facebook, Yelp, or Twitter. Indeed, online reviews (good and bad) from opinion leaders and other consumers help marketers sway purchasing decisions in their favor.

16-5b Managing Unfavorable Publicity

Although marketers try to avoid unpleasant situations, crises do happen. In our free-press environment, publicity is not easily controlled, especially in a crisis. **Crisis management** is the coordinated effort to handle the effects of unfavorable publicity, ensuring fast and accurate communication in times of emergency.

When users found that holding the iPhone 4 a certain way caused poor reception and dropped calls, the media ran a slew of negative stories questioning the iPhone 4's design and usability. In his intial response to the negative publicity, Steve Jobs tried to deflect attacks on the design of the iPhone's antenna by attacking phones by Apple's competitors. Ultimately, however, Jobs and the Apple team offered full refunds on the iPhone 4 for unsatisfied customers or a free cover that helped alleviate the problems caused by the poorly designed antenna. The offers deflated the negative press, and by showing good faith to customers who purchased the phone, Apple may have increased loyalty for its products and its brand.[31]

16-6 SALES PROMOTION

In addition to using advertising and public relations, marketing managers can use sales promotion to increase the effectiveness of their promotional efforts. **Sales promotion** consists of marketing communication activities, other than advertising, personal selling, and public relations, in which a short-term incentive motivates consumers or members of the distribution channel to purchase a good or service immediately, either by lowering the price or by adding value.

© AP Images/PRNewsFoto/adidas

Sales promotion is usually cheaper than advertising and easier to measure. A major national television advertising campaign often costs $5 million or more to create, produce, and place. In contrast, promotional campaigns using the Internet or direct marketing methods can cost less than half that amount. It is also very difficult to determine how many people buy a product or service as a result of radio or television ads. With sales promotion, marketers know the precise number of coupons redeemed or the number of contest entries.

Sales promotion usually has more effect on behavior than on attitudes. Giving the consumer an incentive to make an immediate purchase is the goal of sales promotion, regardless of the form it takes. Sales promotion is usually targeted toward either of two distinctly different markets. **Trade sales promotion** is directed to members of the marketing channel, such as wholesalers and retailers. **Consumer sales promotion** is targeted to the ultimate consumer market. The objectives of a promotion depend on the general behavior of targeted customers (see Exhibit 16.4). For example, marketers who are targeting loyal users of their product need to reinforce existing behavior or increase product usage. An effective tool for strengthening brand loyalty is the *frequent buyer program*, which rewards consumers for repeat purchases. Other types of promotions are more effective with customers prone to brand switching or with those who are loyal to a competitor's product.

A cents-off coupon, free sample, or eye-catching display in a store will often entice shoppers to try a different brand.

Once marketers understand the dynamics occurring within their product category and have determined the particular customers and behaviors they want to influence, they can then go about selecting promotional tools to achieve these goals.

16-6a Tools for Trade Sales Promotion

As we'll discuss in section 16-6b, consumer promotions pull a product through the channel by creating demand. However, trade promotions *push* a product through the distribution channel (see Chapter 14). When selling to members of the distribution channel, manufacturers use many of the same sales promotion tools used in consumer promotions—such as sales contests and premiums. Several tools, however, are unique to manufacturers and intermediaries:

▸▸ **TRADE ALLOWANCES:** A trade allowance is a price reduction offered by manufacturers to intermediaries such as wholesalers and retailers. The price reduction or rebate is given in exchange for doing

trade sales promotion promotion activities directed to members of the marketing channel, such as wholesalers and retailers

consumer sales promotion promotion activities targeted to the ultimate consumer market

trade allowance a price reduction offered by manufacturers to intermediaries such as wholesalers and retailers

Exhibit 16.4

TYPES OF CONSUMERS AND SALES PROMOTION GOALS

Type of Buyer	Desired Results	Sales Promotion Examples
Loyal customers People who buy your product most or all of the time	Reinforce behavior, increase consumption, change purchase timing	• Loyalty marketing programs, such as frequent buyer cards or frequent shopper clubs • Bonus packs that give loyal consumers an incentive to stock up or premiums offered in return for proofs of purchase
Competitor's customers People who buy a competitor's product most or all of the time	Break loyalty, persuade to switch to your brand	• Sampling to introduce your product's superior qualities compared to their brand • Sweepstakes, contests, or premiums that create interest in the product
Brand switchers People who buy a variety of products in the category	Persuade to buy your brand more often	• Any promotion that lowers the price of the product, such as coupons, price-off packages, and bonus packs • Trade deals that help make the product more readily available than competing products
Price buyers People who consistently buy the least expensive brand	Appeal with low prices or supply added value that makes price less important	• Coupons, price-off packages, refunds, or trade deals that reduce the price of the brand to match that of the brand that would have been purchased

Source: From *Sales Promotion Essentials*, 2nd ed., by Don E. Schultz, William A. Robinson, and Lisa A. Petrison. Reprinted by permission of McGraw-Hill Education.

WHEN SELLING TO CHANNEL MEMBERS, MANUFACTURERS USE MANY OF THE SAME SALES PROMOTION TOOLS USED IN CONSUMER PROMOTIONS.

something specific, such as allocating space for a new product or buying something during special periods. For example, a local Best Buy outlet could receive a special discount for running its own promotion on Sony surround sound systems.

▸▸ **PUSH MONEY:** Intermediaries receive push money as a bonus for pushing the manufacturer's brand through the distribution channel. Often the push money is directed toward a retailer's salespeople. LinoColor, the leading high-end scanner company, produces a Picture Perfect Rewards catalog filled with merchandise retailers can purchase with points accrued for every LinoColor scanner they sell.

▸▸ **TRAINING:** Sometimes a manufacturer will train an intermediary's personnel if the product is rather complex—as frequently occurs in the computer and telecommunications industries. For example, representatives of a speaker manufacturer like Bang & Olufsen may train salespeople in how to demonstrate the new features of the latest models of sound systems to consumers.

▸▸ **FREE MERCHANDISE:** Often a manufacturer offers retailers free merchandise in lieu of quantity discounts. Occasionally, free merchandise is used as payment for trade allowances normally provided through other sales promotions. Instead of giving a retailer a price reduction for buying a certain quantity of merchandise, the manufacturer may throw in extra merchandise "free" (i.e., at a cost that would equal the price reduction).

▸▸ **STORE DEMONSTRATIONS:** Manufacturers can also arrange with retailers to perform an in-store demonstration. Food manufacturers often send representatives to grocery stores and supermarkets to let customers sample a product while shopping.

▸▸ **BUSINESS MEETINGS, CONVENTIONS, AND TRADE SHOWS:** Trade association meetings, conferences, and conventions are an important aspect of sales promotion and a growing, multi-billion-dollar market. At these shows, manufacturers, distributors, and other vendors have the chance to display their goods or describe their services to potential customers. Companies participate in trade shows to attract and identify new prospects, serve current customers, introduce new products, enhance corporate image, test the market response to new products, enhance corporate morale, and gather competitive product information.

Trade promotions are popular among manufacturers for many reasons. Trade sales promotion tools help manufacturers gain new distributors for their products, obtain wholesaler and retailer support for consumer sales promotions, build or reduce dealer inventories, and improve trade relations. Car manufacturers annually sponsor dozens of auto shows for consumers. The shows attract millions of consumers, providing dealers with increased store traffic as well as good leads.

16-6b Tools for Consumer Sales Promotion

Marketing managers must decide which consumer sales promotion devices to use in a specific campaign. The methods chosen must suit the objectives to ensure success of the overall promotion plan. The popular tools for consumer sales promotion discussed in the following pages have also been easily transferred to online versions to entice Internet users to visit sites, purchase products, or use services on the Web.

COUPONS AND REBATES A **coupon** is a certificate that entitles consumers to an immediate price reduction when the product is purchased. Coupons are a particularly good way to encourage product trial and repurchase. They are also likely to increase the amount of a product bought. Coupons can be distributed in stores as instant coupons on packaging, on shelf displays with pull-off coupon dispensers, and at cash registers, printed based on what the customer purchased; through freestanding inserts (FSIs); and through various Internet daily deal sites.

Freestanding inserts (FSIs), the promotional coupons inserts found in newspapers, are the traditional way of

American Express is experimenting with Twitter to offer cardholders *great deals* at participating businesses.

circulating printed coupons. FSIs are used to distribute almost 90 percent of coupons. Such traditional types of coupon distribution, which also include direct mail and magazines, had been declining for several years, as consumers used fewer coupons. Recently, however, with the recession tightening consumer spending, coupons experienced the largest increase in usage in seventeen years. In 2011, consumers redeemed 3.5 billion coupons, a 6.1 percent increase from 2010.[32]

The Internet is changing the face of coupons. In addition to Internet coupon sites such as Valpak.com and Coolsavings.com, and social coupon sites such as Groupon and LivingSocial, there are also deal sites like DealSurf.com that aggregate offers from different sites for convenience. While daily deal sites have been quite popular with consumers, sites like Groupon and LivingSocial are coming under some fire as many small businesses claim they lose money or drown under the flood of coupon redemptions. American Express is using Twitter hashtags to drive card use. Customers first sync their credit cards to their Twitter accounts and then send a tweet using an approved hashtag. The cardholder receives automatic discounts from partner businesses when she makes a purchase with her American Express Card.[33]

A **rebate** is similar to a coupon in that a rebate offers the purchaser a price reduction; however, because the purchaser must mail in a rebate form and usually some proof of purchase, the reward is not as immediate. Manufacturers prefer rebates for several reasons. Rebates allow manufacturers to offer price cuts to consumers directly. Manufacturers have more control over rebate promotions because they can be rolled out and shut off quickly. Further, because buyers must fill out forms with their names, addresses, and other data, manufacturers use rebate programs to build customer databases. Perhaps the best reason of all to offer rebates is that although rebates are particularly good at enticing purchase, most consumers never bother to redeem them. The Federal Trade Commission estimates that only half of consumers eligible for rebates collect them.[34]

PREMIUMS A **premium** is an extra item offered to the consumer, usually in exchange for some proof that the promoted product has been purchased. Premiums reinforce the consumer's purchase decision, increase consumption, and persuade nonusers to switch brands. The best example of the use of premiums is the McDonald's Happy Meal, which rewards children with a small toy. Premiums can also include more product for the regular price, such as two-for-the-price-of-one bonus packs or packages that include more of the product. Some companies attach a premium to the product's package, such as a small sample of a complementary hair product attached to a shampoo bottle.

LOYALTY MARKETING PROGRAMS A **loyalty marketing program**, or **frequent buyer program**, rewards loyal consumers for making multiple purchases. The objective of loyalty marketing programs is to build long-term, mutually beneficial relationships between a company and its key customers.

There are more than 2.1 billion loyalty program memberships in the United States; the average household has signed up for eighteen programs.[35] Popularized by the airline industry through frequent-flyer programs, loyalty marketing enables companies to strategically invest sales promotion

rebate a cash refund given for the purchase of a product during a specific period

premium an extra item offered to the consumer, usually in exchange for some proof of purchase of the promoted product

loyalty marketing program a promotional program designed to build long-term, mutually beneficial relationships between a company and its key customers

frequent buyer program a loyalty program in which loyal consumers are rewarded for making multiple purchases of a particular good or service dollars in activities designed to capture greater profits from customers already loyal to the product or company. Co-branded credit cards are an increasingly popular loyalty marketing tool. Most department stores only offer loyalty programs if a customer opens their branded credit card. However, high-end chain Bloomingdale's recently changed its rewards program to include anyone who will sign up. Members of the new Loyalist program receive one point for each dollar they spend and receive a $25 gift card after earning 5,000 points. While Bloomingdale's credit card holders receive more points per dollar spent, the company is hoping to monitor a greater number of its shoppers' spending habits by enabling non-cardholders to join Loyalist.[36]

Through loyalty programs, shoppers receive discounts, alerts on new products, and other types of enticing offers. In exchange, retailers are able to build customer databases that help them better understand customer preference.

CONTESTS AND SWEEPSTAKES Contests and sweepstakes are generally designed to create interest in a good or service, often to encourage brand switching. *Contests* are promotions in which participants use some skill or ability to compete for prizes. A consumer contest usually requires entrants to answer questions, complete sentences, or write a paragraph about the product and submit proof of purchase. Winning a *sweepstakes*, on the other hand, depends on chance, and participation is free. Sweepstakes usually draw about ten times more entries than contests do.

While contests and sweepstakes may draw considerable interest and publicity, generally they are not effective tools for generating long-term sales. To increase their effectiveness, sales promotion managers must make certain the award will appeal to the target market. Offering several smaller prizes to many winners instead of one huge prize to just one person often will increase the effectiveness of the promotion, but there's no denying the attractiveness of a jackpot-type prize.

SAMPLING Sampling allows the customer to try a product risk-free. In a recent study of sampling in Costco, researchers found that sampling increased sales by an average of 88 percent. Expensive items benefited most from sampling, and items under $10, particularly beverages, benefited least from sampling.[37]

Samples can be directly mailed to the customer, delivered door-to-door, packaged with another product, or demonstrated or distributed at a retail store

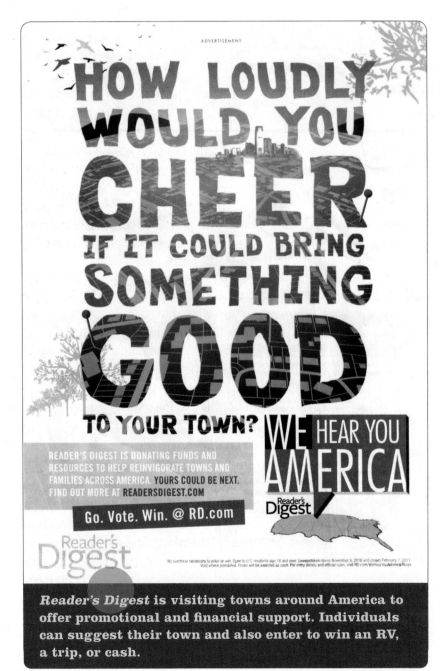

Courtesy of Reader's Digest

or service outlet. Sampling at special events is a popular, effective, and high-profile distribution method that permits marketers to piggyback onto fun-based consumer activities—including sporting events, college fests, fairs and festivals, beach events, and chili cook-offs. Distributing samples to specific location types, such as health clubs, churches, or doctors' offices, is also one of the most efficient methods of sampling. Online sampling is catching up in popularity, however, with the growth of social media. Brands not only run contests through Facebook but also connect with fans, show commercials, and offer samples of new products in exchange for "liking" the brand.

POINT-OF-PURCHASE PROMOTION A **point-of-purchase (P-O-P) display** includes any promotional display set up at the retailer's location to build traffic, advertise the product, or induce impulse buying. P-O-P displays include shelf "talkers" (signs attached to store shelves), shelf extenders (attachments that extend shelves so products stand out), ads on grocery carts and bags, end-aisle and floor-stand displays, television monitors at supermarket checkout counters, in-store audio messages, and audiovisual displays. One big advantage of the P-O-P display is that it offers manufacturers a captive audience in retail stores. Another advantage is that between 70 and 80 percent of all retail purchase decisions are made in-store, so P-O-P displays can be very effective, increasing sales by as much as 65 percent. Other strategies to increase sales include adding cards to the tops of displays, changing messages on signs on the sides or bottoms of displays, adding inflatable or mobile displays, and using signs that advertise the brand's sports, movie, or charity tie-in.[38]

point of purchase (P-O-P) display
a promotional display set up at the retailer's location to build traffic, advertise the product, or induce impulse buying

16-6c Trends in Sales Promotion

The biggest trend in sales promotion on both the trade and consumer side has been the increased use of the Internet. Social media–, e-mail–, and Web site–based promotions have expanded dramatically in recent years. Marketers are now spending billions of dollars annually on such promotions. Sales promotions online have proved effective and cost-efficient, generating response rates three to five times higher than off-line promotions. The most effective types of online sales promotions are free merchandise, sweepstakes, free shipping with purchases, and coupons. One major goal of retailers is to add potential customers to their databases and expand marketing touch points.

Marketers have discovered that online coupon distribution provides another vehicle for promoting their products. In addition, e-coupons can help marketers lure new customers. Online coupons often have a redemption rate of more than 20 percent, as much as ten times higher than for traditional coupons.[39] In fact, nearly 50 percent of consumers who make purchases online use coupons or discount promotional codes. With the speed of compiling data online, marketers can conduct tests in real time and measure the results in time to offer last-minute promotions and react to changing market conditions.[40]

Online versions of loyalty programs are also popping up, and although many types of companies have these programs, the most successful are those run by hotel and airline companies.

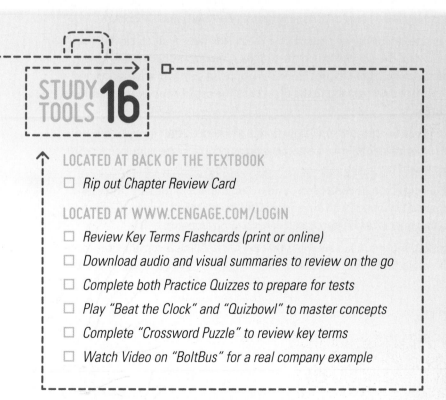

STUDY TOOLS 16

LOCATED AT BACK OF THE TEXTBOOK
☐ *Rip out Chapter Review Card*

LOCATED AT WWW.CENGAGE.COM/LOGIN
☐ *Review Key Terms Flashcards (print or online)*
☐ *Download audio and visual summaries to review on the go*
☐ *Complete both Practice Quizzes to prepare for tests*
☐ *Play "Beat the Clock" and "Quizbowl" to master concepts*
☐ *Complete "Crossword Puzzle" to review key terms*
☐ *Watch Video on "BoltBus" for a real company example*

17-1 PERSONAL SELLING

As mentioned in Chapter 15, *personal selling* is a purchase situation involving a personal, paid-for communication between two people in an attempt to influence each other. In a sense, all businesspeople are salespeople. An individual may become a plant manager, a chemist, an engineer, or a member of any profession and yet still have to sell. During a job search, applicants must "sell" themselves to prospective employers in an interview.

> Advertising offers the consumer a reason to buy; sales promotion offers an incentive to buy.

Personal selling offers several advantages over other forms of promotion:

▶▶ Personal selling provides a detailed explanation or demonstration of the product. This capability is especially needed for complex or new goods and services.

▶▶ The sales message can be varied according to the motivations and interests of each prospective customer. Moreover, when the prospect has questions or raises objections, the salesperson is there to provide explanations. In contrast, advertising and sales promotion can only respond to the objections the copywriter thinks are important to customers.

▶▶ Personal selling can be directed only to qualified prospects. Other forms of promotion include some unavoidable waste because many people in the audience are not prospective customers.

▶▶ Personal selling costs can be controlled by adjusting the size of the sales force (and resulting expenses) in one-person increments. On the other hand, advertising and sales promotion must often be purchased in fairly large amounts.

▶▶ Perhaps the most important advantage is that personal selling is considerably more effective than other forms of promotion in obtaining a sale and gaining a satisfied customer.

Personal selling may also work better than other forms of promotion given certain customer and product characteristics. Generally speaking, personal selling becomes more important as the number of potential customers decreases, as the complexity of the product increases, and as the value of the product grows (see Exhibit 17.1 on page 290). For highly complex goods, such as business jets or private communication systems, a salesperson is needed to determine the prospective customer's needs, explain the product's basic advantages, and propose the exact features and accessories that will meet

Chapter 17

Personal Selling and Sales Management

Learning Outcomes

17-1 *Describe personal selling* 288–290

17-2 *Discuss the key differences between relationship selling and traditional selling* 290–291

17-3 *Describe customer relationship management* 291–296

17-4 *List the steps in the selling process* 296–302

17-5 *Describe the functions of sales management* 302–305

After you finish this chapter go to
p305 *for* **STUDY TOOLS**

Exhibit 17.1

COMPARISON OF PERSONAL SELLING AND ADVERTISING/SALES PROMOTION

Personal selling is more important if . . .	Advertising and sales promotion are more important if . . .
The product has a high value.	The product has a low value.
It is a custom-made product.	It is a standardized product.
There are few customers.	There are many customers.
The product is technically complex.	The product is easy to understand.
Customers are concentrated.	Customers are geographically dispersed.
Examples: Insurance policies, custom windows, airplane engines	**Examples:** Soap, magazine subscriptions, cotton T-shirts

© Cengage Learning

the client's needs. Macy's, Nordstrom, Saks Fifth Avenue, and Barneys New York offer free personal shopping, whereby consultants pull clothing they feel will fit the customer's style and specified need. This free service encourages customers to continue using personal shoppers and develop a relationship with the store.[1] Technology now plays an important role in personal selling through the use of social media like LinkedIn and Facebook, as well as through the use of blogs and Twitter to establish expertise within a field.

17-2 RELATIONSHIP SELLING

Until recently, marketing theory and practice concerning personal selling focused almost entirely on a planned presentation to prospective customers for the sole purpose of making the sale. Marketers were most concerned with making a one-time sale and then moving on to the next prospect.

SELLING IN THE TECHNOLOGY AGE

Personal selling has taken a technological turn in the last decade. Younger shoppers tend to research styles and prices before setting foot in a store. Some even browse other stores' Web sites while trying on clothes in competitors' stores. This type of shopper pushes salespeople away, but stores that embrace their love of technology and independence can gain loyal customers. Stores carrying Bobbi Brown cosmetics use touch-screen televisions that allow customers to see how to apply a smoky eye—without talking to a makeup artist. At Unknwn, the shoe store owned by LeBron James, there are fifty iPads displayed next to the shoes to tell customers about the merchandise. Some stores even have touchpads to customize lighting and music in dressing rooms. Even grocery stores with self-checkout registers appeal to this group. By allowing customers to minimize sales contact when they want to but still having a dedicated sales team ready, these stores give customers what they want and build their loyalty.

Source: Stephanie Clifford, "Browsing While Browsing," *New York Times*, March 9, 2012, B1.

© Tyler Olson/Shutterstock.com / © iStockphoto.com/Bill Noll

Traditional personal selling methods attempted to persuade the buyer to accept a point of view or convince the buyer to take some action. Frequently, the objectives of the salesperson were at the expense of the buyer, creating a win–lose outcome. Although this type of sales approach has not disappeared entirely, it is being used less and less often by professional salespeople.

In contrast, modern views of personal selling emphasize the relationship that develops between a salesperson and a buyer. **Relationship selling**, or **consultative selling**, is a multistage process that emphasizes personalization and empathy as key ingredients in identifying prospects and developing them as long-term, satisfied customers. With relationship selling, the objective is to build long-term branded relationships with consumers and buyers, so the focus is on building mutual trust between the buyer and seller through the delivery of anticipated, long-term, value-added benefits to the buyer.

Relationship or consultative salespeople, therefore, become consultants, partners, and problem solvers for their customers. They strive to build long-term relationships with key accounts by developing trust over time. The emphasis shifts from a one-time sale to a long-term relationship in which the salesperson works with the customer to develop solutions for enhancing the customer's bottom line. Research has shown that positive customer–salesperson relationships contribute to trust, increased customer loyalty, and the intent to

continue the relationship with the salesperson.[2] Thus, relationship selling promotes a win–win situation for both buyer and seller.

The end result of relationship selling tends to be loyal customers who purchase from the company time after time. A relationship selling strategy focused on retaining customers costs a company less than constantly prospecting and selling to new customers.

Relationship selling is more typically used in selling situations for industrial-type goods, such as heavy machinery or computer systems, and services, such as airlines and insurance, than for consumer goods. Exhibit 17.2 lists the key differences between traditional personal selling and relationship or consultative selling. These differences will become more apparent as we explore the personal selling process later in the chapter.

relationship selling (consultative selling) a sales practice that involves building, maintaining, and enhancing interactions with customers in order to develop long-term satisfaction through mutually beneficial partnerships

17-3 CUSTOMER RELATIONSHIP MANAGEMENT AND PERSONAL SELLING

As we have discussed throughout the text, customer relationship management is the ultimate goal of a new trend in marketing that focuses on

Exhibit 17.2

KEY DIFFERENCES BETWEEN TRADITIONAL SELLING AND RELATIONSHIP SELLING

Traditional Personal Selling	Relationship or Consultative Selling
Sell products (goods and services)	Sell advice, assistance, and counsel
Focus on closing sales	Focus on improving the customer's bottom line
Limited sales planning	Consider sales planning as top priority
Spend most contact time telling customers about product	Spend most contact time attempting to build a problem-solving environment with the customer
Conduct "product-specific" needs assessment	Conduct discovery in the full scope of the customer's operations
"Lone wolf" approach to the account	Team approach to the account
Proposals and presentations based on pricing and product features	Proposals and presentations based on profit impact and strategic benefits to the customer
Sales follow-up is short term, focused on product delivery	Sales follow-up is long term, focused on long-term relationship enhancement

Source: Robert M. Peterson, Patrick Schul, and George H. Lucas Jr., "Consultative Selling: Walking the Walk in the New Selling Environment," *National Conference on Sales Management Proceedings*, March 1996.

customer-centric a philosophy under which the company customizes its product and service offering based on data generated through interactions between the customer and the company

learning an informal process of collecting customer data through customer comments and feedback on product or service performance

knowledge management the process by which customer information is centralized and shared in order to enhance the relationship between customers and the organization

interaction the point at which a customer and a company representative exchange information and develop learning relationships

understanding customers as individuals instead of as part of a group. To do so, marketers are making their communications more customer specific using the CRM cycle, covered in Chapter 9, and by developing relationships with their customers through touch points and data mining. Customer relationship management initially was popularized as one-to-one marketing. But CRM is a much broader approach to understanding and serving customer needs than is one-to-one marketing.

Throughout the text, our discussion of a CRM system has assumed two key points. First, customers take center stage in any organization. Second, the business must manage the customer relationship across all points of customer contact throughout the entire organization. By identifying customer relationships, understanding the customer base, and capturing customer data, marketers and salespeople can leverage the information not only to develop deeper relationships but also to close more sales with loyal customers.

17-3a Identify Customer Relationships

Companies that have a CRM system follow a customer-centric focus or model. **Customer-centric** is an internal management philosophy similar to the marketing concept discussed in Chapter 1. Under this philosophy, the company customizes its product and service offering based on data generated through interactions between the customer and the company. This philosophy transcends all functional areas of the business, producing an internal system where all of the company's decisions and actions are a direct result of customer information.

Customer-centric companies continually learn ways to enhance their product and service offerings. **Learning** in a CRM environment involves collecting customer information through comments and feedback on product and service performance.

Each unit of a business typically has its own way of recording what it learns and perhaps even has its own customer information system. The departments' different interests make it difficult to pull all of the customer information together in one place using a common format. To overcome this problem, companies using CRM rely on knowledge management. **Knowledge management** is a process by which customer information is centralized and shared in order to enhance the relationship between customers and the organization. Information collected includes experiential observations, comments, customer actions, and qualitative facts about the customer.

As Chapter 1 explained, empowerment involves delegating authority to solve customers' problems. Usually, organizational representatives are able to make changes during interactions with customers through phone, fax, e-mail, social media, or face-to-face.

An **interaction** occurs when a customer and a company representative exchange information and develop learning relationships. With CRM, the customer—not the organization—defines the terms of the interaction, often by stating his or her preferences. The organization responds by designing products and services around customers' desired experiences. Social media have created numerous new ways for companies to have interactions with customers. Starwood Hotels is using Facebook to have conversations with its customers, finding out what pillows they prefer or drinks they would like in the minibar. Customers can also book a stay through Facebook. The goal is to offer convenience and personalized service that justifies booking through the hotel and not through travel services, which focus on the lowest price and not the amenities.[3]

The success of CRM—building lasting and profitable relationships—can be directly measured by the effectiveness of the interaction between the customer and the organization. In fact, what further differentiates CRM from other strategic initiatives is the organization's ability to establish and manage interactions with its current customer base. The more latitude (empowerment) a company gives its representatives, the more likely the interaction will conclude in a way that satisfies the customer.

17-3b Understand Interactions of the Current Customer Base

The interaction between the customer and the organization is the foundation on which a CRM system is built. Only through effective interactions can organizations learn about the expectations of their customers, generate and manage knowledge about them, negotiate mutually satisfying commitments, and build long-term relationships.

Exhibit 17.3 illustrates the customer-centric approach for managing customer interactions. Following a customer-centric approach, an interaction can occur through a formal or direct communication channel, such as a phone, the Internet, or a salesperson. Any activity or touch point a customer has with an organization, either directly or indirectly, constitutes an interaction.

Companies that effectively manage customer interactions recognize that data provided by customers affect a wide variety of **touch points**. In a CRM system, touch points are all areas of a business where customers have contact with the company and data might be gathered. Touch points might include a customer registering for a particular service; a customer communicating with customer service for product information; a customer completing and returning the warranty information card for a product; or a customer talking with salespeople, delivery personnel, and product installers. Data gathered at these touch points, once interpreted, provide information that affects touch points inside the company. Interpreted information may be redirected to marketing research to develop profiles of extended warranty purchasers, to production to analyze recurring problems and repair components, and

Exhibit 17.3

CUSTOMER-CENTRIC APPROACH FOR MANAGING CUSTOMER INTERACTIONS

Current transaction

Channel

Customer

Past relationship

Requested service

to accounting to establish cost-control models for repair service calls.

Web-based interactions are an increasingly popular touch point for customers to communicate with companies on their own terms. Web users can evaluate and purchase products, make reservations, input preferential data, and provide customer feedback on services and products. Data from these Web-based interactions are then captured, compiled, and used to segment customers, refine marketing efforts, develop new products, and deliver a degree of individual customization to improve customer relationships.

As social media have become more popular, many companies have begun to use these media for "social" CRM.[4] Essentially, social CRM takes the most successful aspects of traditional CRM, such as behavioral targeting, and expands

Social CRM requires understanding where CUSTOMERS INTERACT ONLINE *and finding who the major influencers are.*

them to include ways to engage customers through social media. This new paradigm includes a new customer recommendation value called the net promoter score. The net promoter score measures how much a customer influences the behavior of other customers through recommendations on social media. Social CRM also enables marketers to focus more on the relationship aspect of CRM. For example, REI empowers customers to "carve your own adventure" through its YouTube channel. JetBlue uses Facebook and Twitter to provide advice and updates to travelers. To use social CRM effectively, companies must understand what sites customers use, whether they post opinions, and the major influencers in the category.

Another touch point is through **point-of-sale interactions** in stores or at information kiosks. Many point-of-sale software programs enable customers to easily provide information about themselves without feeling violated. The information is then used for marketing and merchandising activities and to accurately identify the store's best customers and the types of products they buy. Data collected at point-of-sale interactions are also used to increase customer satisfaction through the development of in-store services and customer recognition promotions.

17-3c Capture Customer Data

Vast amounts of data can be obtained from the interactions between an organization and its customers. Therefore, in a CRM system, the issue is not how much data can be obtained but rather what types of data should be acquired and how the data can effectively be used for relationship enhancement.

The traditional approach for acquiring data from customers is through channel interactions. Channel interactions include store visits, conversations with salespeople, interactions via the Web, traditional phone conversations, and wireless communications. In a CRM system, channel interactions are viewed as prime information sources based on the channel selected to initiate the interaction rather than on the data acquired. In some cases, companies use online chat to answer questions customers have about products they are looking for. For example, 24 Hour Fitness has an online chat window that opens when a potential customer begins to review the Web site. If the visitor remains on the site, the online chat window asks if he or she needs help finding something specific.

Interactions between the company and the customer facilitate the collection of large amounts of data. Companies can obtain not only simple contact information (name, address, phone number) but also data pertaining to the customer's current relationship with the organization—past purchase history, quantity and frequency of purchases, average amount spent on purchases, sensitivity to promotional activities, and so forth.

In this manner, a lot of information can be captured from one individual customer across several touch points. Multiply this by the thousands of customers across all of the touch points with an organization, and the volume of data can rapidly become unmanageable for company personnel. The large volume of data resulting from a CRM initiative can be managed effectively only through technology. Once customer data are collected, the question of who owns those data becomes extremely salient. In its privacy statement, Toysmart.com declared that it would never sell information registered at its Web site, including children's names and birth dates, to a third party. When the company filed for bankruptcy protection, it said the information collected constituted a company asset that needed to be sold off to pay creditors. Despite the outrage at this announcement, many dot-com companies closing their doors found they had little in the way of assets and followed Toysmart's lead.

17-3d Leverage Customer Information

Data mining identifies the most profitable customers and prospects. Managers can then design tailored marketing strategies to best appeal to the identified segments. In CRM, this is commonly referred to as leveraging customer information to facilitate enhanced relationships with customers. Exhibit 17.4 shows some common CRM marketing database applications.

CAMPAIGN MANAGEMENT Through campaign management, all areas of the company participate in the development of programs targeted to customers. **Campaign management** involves monitoring and leveraging customer interactions to sell a company's products and to increase customer service. Campaigns are based directly on data obtained from customers through various interactions. Campaign management includes monitoring the

Exhibit 17.4

COMMON CRM MARKETING DATABASE APPLICATIONS

CRM Marketing Database

- Campaign management
- Retaining loyal customers
- Cross-selling other products or services
- Designing targeted marketing communications
- Reinforcing customer purchase decisions
- Inducing product trial by new customers
- Increasing effectiveness of distribution channel marketing
- Improving customer service

customers, as well as giving priority to those products and services that are viewed as most desirable for a specifically designated customer. Even within a highly defined market segment, individual customer differences will emerge. Therefore, interactions among customers must focus on individual experiences, expectations, and desires.

RETAINING LOYAL CUSTOMERS If a company has identified its best customers, then it should make every effort to maintain and increase their loyalty. When a company retains an additional 5 percent of its customers each year, profits will increase by as much as 25 percent. What's more, improving customer retention by a mere 2 percent can decrease costs by as much as 10 percent.[5]

Loyalty programs reward loyal customers for making multiple purchases. The objective is to build long-term mutually beneficial relationships between a company and its key customers. Small- and medium-sized businesses can team up with Belly to develop very individual rewards programs, such as throwing eggs at food trucks after a specified number of purchases or having the owner of your favorite bagel store sing to you after buying 100 bagels. The unique rewards reflect each business's personality, and (ideally) those of its customers, making the rewards programs highly incentive.[6] In addition to rewarding good customers, loyalty programs provide businesses with a wealth of information about their customers and shopping trends, which can be used to make future business decisions.

Redbox, whose movie rental kiosks are found in supermarkets and McDonald's, sends its customers a birthday e-mail with a special promotion code for a free movie rental. Personal touches like this may give Redbox an edge over Netflix for movie rental services.[7]

CROSS-SELLING OTHER PRODUCTS AND SERVICES CRM provides many opportunities to cross-sell related products. Marketers can use the database to match product profiles and consumer profiles so that they can cross-sell customers products that match their demographic, lifestyle, or behavioral characteristics. DesignWorks NY, a graphic design and marketing communications firm, sends a letter to each of its customers. That letter has a checklist of all the services offered by DesignWorks, with the services already used by the customer checked off. The letter helps develop relationships, reminds customers of their experience with DesignWorks, and cross-sells other services to an established customer. Clients respond positively and often sign on for additional services.[8]

success of the communications based on customer reactions through sales, orders, callbacks to the company, and the like. If a campaign appears unsuccessful, it is evaluated and changed to better achieve the company's desired objective.

Campaign management involves developing customized product and service offerings for the appropriate customer segment, pricing these offerings attractively, and communicating these offers in a manner that enhances customer relationships. Customizing product and service offerings requires managing multiple interactions with

sales process (sales cycle) the set of steps a salesperson goes through in a particular organization to sell a particular product or service

A small company, such as this Gorilla Cheese food truck, may use the services of Belly to reward customers for their loyalty.

Internet companies use product and customer profiling to reveal cross-selling opportunities while a customer is surfing their site. Past purchases on a particular Web site and the site a surfer comes from give online marketers clues about the surfer's interests and what items to cross-sell.

DESIGNING TARGETED MARKETING COMMUNICATIONS Using transaction and purchase data, a database allows marketers to track customers' relationships to the company's products and services and modify the marketing message accordingly.

Customers can also be segmented into infrequent users, moderate users, and heavy users. A segmented communications strategy can then be developed based on which group the customer falls into. Communications to infrequent users might encourage repeat purchases through a direct incentive such as a limited-time price discount for ordering again. Web sites such as GNC.com send out periodic e-mails with discounts to customers who purchased once. Communications to moderate users may use fewer incentives and more reinforcement of past purchase decisions. Communications to heavy users would be designed around loyalty and reinforcement of the purchase rather than around price promotions.

17-4 STEPS IN THE SELLING PROCESS

Completing a sale requires several steps. The **sales process**, or **sales cycle**, is simply the set of steps a salesperson goes through to sell a particular product or service. The sales process or cycle can be unique for each product or service, depending on the features of the product or service, characteristics of customer segments, and internal processes in place within the firm such as how leads are gathered.

Some sales take only a few minutes, but others may take much longer to complete. Sales of technical products like a Boeing or Airbus airplane and customized goods and services typically take many months, perhaps even years, to complete. On the other end of the spectrum, sales of less technical products like stationery are generally more routine and may take only a few days. Whether a salesperson spends a few minutes or a few years on a sale, there are seven basic steps in the personal selling process, outlined further in the following sections.

THE SEVEN STEPS IN THE PERSONAL SELLING PROCESS:

1. **Generating leads**
2. **Qualifying leads**
3. **Approaching the customers and probing needs**
4. **Developing and proposing solutions**
5. **Handling objections**
6. **Closing the sale**
7. **Following up**

Like other forms of promotion, these steps of selling follow the AIDA concept discussed in Chapter 15. Once a salesperson has located a prospect with the authority to buy, he or she tries to get the prospect's attention. A thorough needs assessment turned into an effective sales proposal and presentation should generate interest. After developing the customer's initial desire (preferably during the presentation of the sales proposal), the salesperson seeks action in the close by trying to get an agreement to buy. Follow-up after the sale, the final step in the selling process, not only lowers cognitive dissonance (refer to Chapter 6) but also may open up opportunities to discuss future sales. Effective follow-up will also lead to repeat business in which the process may start all over again at the needs assessment step.

Traditional selling and relationship selling follow the same basic steps. They differ in the relative importance placed on key steps in the process. Traditional selling efforts are transaction oriented, focusing on generating as many leads as possible, making as many presentations as possible, and closing as many sales as possible. Minimal effort is placed on asking questions to identify customer needs and wants or matching these needs and wants to the benefits of the product or service. In contrast, salespeople practicing relationship selling emphasize an upfront investment in the time and effort needed to uncover each customer's specific needs and wants and meet them with the product or service offering. By doing their homework up front, salespeople create the conditions necessary for a relatively straightforward close. Look at each step of the selling process individually.

17-4a **Step 1: Generating Leads**

Initial groundwork must precede communication between the potential buyer and the salesperson. **Lead generation**, or **prospecting**, is the identification of those firms and people most likely to buy the seller's offerings. These firms or people become "sales leads" or "prospects."

Sales leads can be obtained in several different ways, most notably through advertising, trade shows and conventions, social media, webinars, or direct mail and telemarketing programs. Favorable publicity also helps to create leads. Company records of past client purchases are another excellent source of leads. Many sales professionals are also securing valuable leads from their firm's Web site.

Another way to gather a lead is through a **referral**—a recommendation from a customer or business associate. The advantages of referrals over other forms of prospecting include highly qualified leads, higher closing rates, larger initial transactions, and shorter

sales cycles. Referrals typically are as much as ten times more productive in generating sales than are cold calls. Unfortunately, although most clients are willing to give referrals, many salespeople do not ask for them. Effective sales training can help to overcome this reluctance to ask for referrals. To increase the number of referrals, some companies even pay or send small gifts to customers or suppliers that provide referrals. Generating referrals is one area that social media and technology can usually make much more efficient.

Networking is using friends, business contacts, coworkers, acquaintances, and fellow members in professional and civic organizations to identify potential clients. Indeed, a number of national networking clubs have been started for the sole purpose of generating leads and providing valuable business advice. Increasingly, sales professionals are also using online networking sites such as LinkedIn to connect with targeted leads and clients around the world, twenty-four hours a day. Some of LinkedIn's estimated 30 million users have reported response rates between 50 and 60 percent, versus 3 percent from direct marketing efforts.[9]

Before the advent of more sophisticated methods of lead generation, such as direct mail and telemarketing,

lead generation (prospecting)
identification of those firms and people most likely to buy the seller's offerings

referral
a recommendation to a salesperson from a customer or business associate

networking
a process of finding out about potential clients from friends, business contacts, coworkers, acquaintances, and fellow members in professional and civic organizations

Advances such as LinkedIn can provide more quality leads than cold calling, but cold calling is still used by some organizations.

most prospecting was done through **cold calling**—a form of lead generation in which the salesperson approaches potential buyers without any prior knowledge of the prospects' needs or financial status. Although cold calling is still used in generating leads, many sales managers have realized the inefficiencies of having their top salespeople use their valuable selling time searching for the proverbial "needle in a haystack." Passing the job of cold calling to a lower-cost employee, typically an internal sales support person, allows salespeople to spend more time and use their relationship-building skills on prospects who have already been identified.

17-4b Step 2: Qualifying Leads

When a prospect shows interest in learning more about a product, the salesperson has the opportunity to follow up, or qualify, the lead. **Lead qualification** is the determination of a sales prospect's recognized need, buying power, receptivity, and accessibility. These qualities are discussed in the box on this page. Personally visiting unqualified prospects wastes valuable salesperson time and company resources. Many leads often go unanswered because salespeople are given no indication as to how qualified the leads are in terms of interest and ability to purchase. Unqualified prospects give vague or incomplete answers to a salesperson's specific questions, try to evade questions on budgets, and request changes in standard procedures like prices or terms of sale. In contrast, qualified leads are real prospects who answer questions, value your time, and are realistic about money and when they are prepared to buy. Salespeople who are given accurate information on qualified leads are more than twice as likely to follow up.[10]

Often the task of lead qualification is handled by a telemarketing group or a sales support person who *prequalifies* the lead for the salesperson. Prequalification systems free sales representatives from the time-consuming task of following up on leads to determine need, buying power, and receptiveness. Prequalification systems may even set up initial appointments with the prospect for the salesperson. The result is more time for the sales force to spend in front of interested customers. Software is increasingly being utilized in lead qualification.

FEATURES OF A QUALIFIED LEAD

▸▸ **A RECOGNIZED NEED:** The most basic criterion for determining whether someone is a prospect for a product is a need that is not being satisfied. The salesperson should first consider prospects who are aware of a need but should not disregard prospects who have not yet recognized that they have one. With a little more information about the product, they may decide they do have a need for it. Preliminary interviews and questioning can often provide the salesperson with enough information to determine whether there is a need.

▸▸ **BUYING POWER:** Buying power involves both authority to make the purchase decision and access to funds to pay for it. To avoid wasting time and money, the salesperson needs to identify the purchasing authority and his or her ability to pay before making a presentation. Organizational charts and information about a firm's credit standing can provide valuable clues.

▸▸ **RECEPTIVITY AND ACCESSIBILITY:** The prospect must be willing to see the salesperson and be accessible to the salesperson. Some prospects simply refuse to see salespeople. Others, because of their stature in their organization, will see only a salesperson or sales manager with similar stature.

Companies are increasingly using their Web sites to qualify leads. When qualifying leads online, companies want visitors to register, indicate the products and services they are interested in, and provide information on their time frame and resources. Leads from the Internet can then be prioritized (those indicating a short time frame, for instance, are given a higher priority) and then transferred to salespeople. Enticing visitors to register also enables companies to customize future electronic interactions.

17-4c Step 3: Approaching the Customer and Probing Needs

Before approaching customers, the salesperson should learn as much as possible about the prospect's organization and its buyers. This process, called the **preapproach**, describes the "homework" that must be done by the salesperson before contacting the prospect. This may include visiting company Web sites; consulting standard reference

© iStockphoto.com/Bill Noll

needs assessment
a determination of the customer's specific needs and wants and the range of options the customer has for satisfying them

sources such as Moody's, Standard & Poor's, or Dun & Bradstreet; or contacting acquaintances or others who may have information about the prospect. Reading the prospect's social media sites (following the company's Twitter feed and reading its Facebook page or blogs) is a great way to get to know the company culture and learn more about daily activities.[11] Another preapproach task is to determine whether the actual approach should be a personal visit, a phone call, a letter, or some other form of communication.

During the sales approach, the salesperson either talks to the prospect or secures an appointment for a future time in which to probe the prospect further as to his or her needs. Relationship selling theorists suggest that salespeople should begin developing mutual trust with their prospect during the approach. Salespeople must sell themselves before they can sell the product. Small talk that projects sincerity and some suggestion of friendship is encouraged to build rapport with the prospect, but remarks that could be construed as insincere should be avoided.

The salesperson's ultimate goal during the approach is to conduct a **needs assessment** to find out as much as possible about the prospect's situation. The salesperson should be determining how to maximize the fit between what he or she can offer and what the prospective customer wants. As part of the needs assessment, the consultative salesperson must know everything there is to know about the following:

▸ **THE PRODUCT OR SERVICE:** Product knowledge is the cornerstone for conducting a successful needs analysis. The consultative salesperson must be an expert on his or her product or service, including technical specifications, the product's features and benefits, pricing and billing procedures, warranty and service support, performance comparisons with the competition, other customers' experiences with the product, and current advertising and promotional campaign messages. For example, a salesperson who is attempting to sell a Xerox copier to a doctor's office should be very knowledgeable about Xerox's selection of copiers, their attributes, capabilities, technological specifications, and postpurchase servicing.

▸ **CUSTOMERS AND THEIR NEEDS:** The salesperson should know more about customers than they know about themselves. That's the secret to relationship and consultative selling, where the salesperson acts not only as a supplier of products and services but also as a trusted consultant and adviser. The professional salesperson brings each client business-building ideas and solutions to problems.

For example, if the Xerox salesperson is asking the "right" questions, then he or she should be able to identify copy-related areas where the doctor's office is losing or wasting money. Rather than just selling a copier, the Xerox salesperson can act as a consultant on how the doctor's office can save money and time.

▸ **THE COMPETITION:** The salesperson must know as much about the competitor's company and products as he or she knows about his or her own company. Competitive intelligence includes many factors: who the competitors are and what is known about them, how their products and services compare, advantages and disadvantages, and strengths and weaknesses. For example, if the Canon copy machine is less expensive than the Xerox copier, the doctor's office may be leaning toward purchasing the Canon. But if the Xerox salesperson can point out that the cost of long-term maintenance and toner cartridges is lower for the Xerox copier, offsetting its higher initial cost, the salesperson may be able to persuade the doctor's office to purchase the Xerox copier.

▸ **THE INDUSTRY:** Knowing the industry requires active research by the salesperson. This means attending industry and trade association meetings, reading articles published in industry and trade journals, keeping track of legislation and regulation that affect the industry, being aware of product alternatives and innovations from domestic and foreign competition, and having a feel for economic and financial conditions that may affect the industry. It is also important to be aware of economic downturns, as businesses may be looking for less expensive financing options.

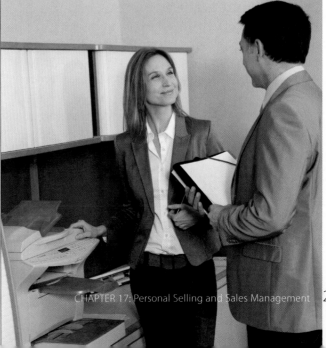

© Goodluz/Shutterstock.com

Creating a *customer profile* during the approach helps salespeople optimize their time and resources. This profile is then used to help develop an intelligent analysis of the prospect's needs in preparation for the next step, developing and proposing solutions. Customer profile information is typically stored and manipulated using sales force automation software packages designed for use on laptop computers. Sales force automation software provides sales reps with a computerized and efficient method of collecting customer information for use during the entire sales process. Further, customer and sales data stored in a computer database can be easily shared among sales team members. The information can also be appended with industry statistics, sales or meeting notes, billing data, and other information that may be pertinent to the prospect or the prospect's company. The more salespeople know about their prospects, the better they can meet their needs.

A salesperson should wrap up the sales approach and need-probing mission by summarizing the prospect's need, problem, and interest. The salesperson should also get a commitment from the customer to some kind of action, whether it's reading promotional material or agreeing to a demonstration. This commitment helps qualify the prospect further and justify additional time invested by the salesperson. The salesperson should reiterate the action he or she promises to take, such as sending information or calling back to provide answers to questions. The date and time of the next call should be set at the conclusion of the sales approach as well as an agenda for the next call in terms of what the salesperson hopes to accomplish, such as providing a demonstration or presenting a solution.

17-4d Step 4: Developing and Proposing Solutions

Once the salesperson has gathered the appropriate information about the client's needs and wants, the next step is to determine whether his or her company's products or services match the needs of the prospective customer. The salesperson then develops a solution, or possibly several solutions, in which the salesperson's product or service solves the client's problems or meets a specific need.

These solutions are typically presented to the client in the form of a sales proposal presented at a sales presentation. A **sales proposal** is a written document or professional presentation that outlines how the company's product or service will meet or exceed the client's needs. The **sales presentation** is the formal meeting in which the salesperson has the opportunity to present the sales proposal. The presentation should be explicitly tied to the prospect's expressed needs. Further, the prospect should be involved in the presentation by being encouraged to participate in demonstrations or by exposure to computer exercises, slides, video or audio, flip charts, photographs, and the like. Technology has become an important part of presenting solutions for many salespeople.

Because the salesperson often has only one opportunity to present solutions, the quality of both the sales proposal and the presentation can make or break the sale. Salespeople must be able to present the proposal and handle any customer objections confidently and professionally. For a powerful presentation, salespeople must be well prepared, use direct eye contact, ask open-ended questions, be poised, use hand gestures and voice

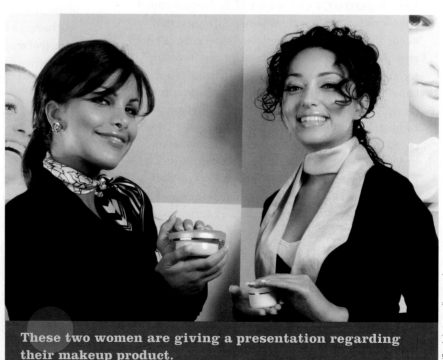

These two women are giving a presentation regarding their makeup product.

© iStockphoto.com/iconogenic

inflection, focus on the customer's needs, incorporate visual elements that impart valuable information, know how to operate the audio/visual or computer equipment being used for the presentation, and make sure the equipment works.[12] Nothing dies faster than a boring presentation. Often customers are more likely to remember how salespeople present themselves than what they say.

17-4e Step 5: Handling Objections

Rarely does a prospect say "I'll buy it" right after a presentation. Instead, the prospect often raises objections or asks questions about the proposal and the product. The potential buyer may insist that the price is too high or that the good or service will not satisfy the present need.

One of the first lessons every salesperson learns is that objections to the product should not be taken personally as confrontations or insults. A good salesperson considers objections a legitimate part of the purchase decision. To handle objections effectively, the salesperson should anticipate specific objections such as concerns about price, fully investigate the objection with the customer, be aware of what the competition is offering, and, above all, stay calm.

Often salespeople can use objections to close the sale. If the customer tries to pit suppliers against each other to drive down the price, the salesperson should be prepared to point out weaknesses in the competitor's offer and stand by the quality in his or her own proposal.

17-4f Step 6: Closing the Sale

At the end of the presentation, the salesperson should ask the customer how he or she would like to proceed. If the customer exhibits signs that he or she is ready to purchase and all questions have been answered and objections have been met, then the salesperson can try to close the sale. Customers often give signals during or after the presentation that they are ready to buy or are not interested. Examples include changes in facial expressions, gestures, and questions asked. The salesperson should look for these signals and respond appropriately.

Closing requires courage and skill. A salesperson should keep an open mind when asking for the sale and be prepared for both a yes and a no. The typical salesperson makes several hundred sales calls a year, many of which are repeat calls to the same client in an attempt to make a sale. Building a good relationship with the customer is very important. Often, if the salesperson has developed a strong relationship with the customer, only minimal efforts are needed to close a sale.

Negotiation often plays a key role in the closing of the sale. **Negotiation** is the process during which both the salesperson and the prospect offer special concessions in an attempt to arrive at a sales agreement. For example, the salesperson may offer a price cut, free installation, or a trial order. Effective negotiators, however, avoid using price as a negotiation tool. Because companies spend millions on advertising and product development to create value, when salespeople give in to price negotiations too quickly, it decreases the value of the product. Instead, effective salespeople should emphasize value to the customer, rendering price a nonissue. Salespeople should also be prepared to ask for trade-offs and try to avoid giving unilateral concessions. Moreover, if the customer asks for a 5 percent discount, the salesperson should ask for something in return, such as higher volume or more flexibility in delivery schedules.

More and more U.S. companies are expanding their marketing and selling efforts into global markets. Salespeople selling in foreign markets should tailor their presentation and closing styles to each market. Different personalities and skills will be successful in some countries and absolute failures in others. For instance, if a salesperson is an excellent closer and always focuses on the next sale, doing business in Latin America might be difficult because people there want to take a long time building a personal relationship with their suppliers.

17-4g Step 7: Following Up

Salespeople's responsibilities do not end with making the sales and placing the orders. One of the most important aspects of their jobs is **follow-up**—the final step in the selling process, in which they must ensure delivery schedules are met, goods or services perform as promised, and buyers' employees are properly trained to use the products.

In the traditional sales approach, follow-up with the customer is generally limited to successful product delivery and performance. A basic goal of relationship selling is to motivate customers to come back, again and again, by developing and nurturing long-term relationships. Exhibit 17.5 depicts the time involved in the sales process

negotiation the process during which both the salesperson and the prospect offer special concessions in an attempt to arrive at a sales agreement

follow-up the final step of the selling process, in which the salesperson ensures delivery schedules are met, goods or services perform as promised, and the buyers' employees are properly trained to use the products

Exhibit 17.5

RELATIVE AMOUNT OF TIME SPENT IN THE KEY STEPS OF THE SELLING PROCESS

	Generating leads	Qualifying leads	Approaching the customer and probing needs	Developing and proposing solutions	Handling objections	Closing the sale	Following up	
High	●	●			●		●	Relationship/Consultative selling
Low	●	●	●	●	●	●	●	Traditional selling

Source: Robert Peterson, Patrick Schul, and George H. Lucas Jr., "Consultative Selling: Walking the Walk in the New Selling Enviroment," *National Conference on Sales Management Proceedings*, March 1996.

and how those elements relate to the traditional and relationship selling approaches.

Most businesses depend on repeat sales, and repeat sales depend on thorough and continued follow-up by the salesperson. When customers feel abandoned, cognitive dissonance arises and repeat sales decline. Today, this issue is more pertinent than ever because customers are far less loyal to brands and vendors. Buyers are more inclined to look for the best deal, especially when they experience poor postsale follow-up. Automated e-mail follow-up marketing—a combination of sales automation and Internet technology—is enhancing customer satisfaction as well as bringing in more business for some marketers. After the initial contact with a prospect, a software program automatically sends a series of personalized e-mail messages over a period of time.

17-5 SALES MANAGEMENT

There is an old adage in business that nothing happens until a sale is made. Without sales there is no need for accountants, production workers, or even a company president. Sales provide the fuel that keeps the corporate engines humming. Companies such as Cisco

Systems, International Paper, Johnson Controls, and several thousand other manufacturers would cease to exist without successful salespeople. Even companies such as Procter & Gamble and Kraft Foods that mainly sell consumer goods and use extensive advertising campaigns still rely on salespeople to move products through the channel of distribution. Thus, sales management is one of marketing's most critical specialties. Effective sales management stems from a success-oriented sales force that accomplishes its mission economically and efficiently. Poor sales management can lead to unmet sales and profit objectives or even to the downfall of the corporation.

Just as selling is a personal relationship, so is sales management. Although the sales manager's basic job is to maximize sales at a reasonable cost while also maximizing profits, he or she also has many other important responsibilities and decisions:

1. **Defining sales goals and the sales process**
2. **Determining the sales force structure**
3. **Recruiting and training the sales force**
4. **Compensating and motivating the sales force**
5. **Evaluating the sales force**

PART OF SALES MANAGEMENT IS DEFINING SALES GOALS FOR THE SALES FORCE.

quota a statement of the salesperson's sales goals, usually based on sales volume

17-5a Defining Sales Goals and the Sales Process

Effective sales management begins with a determination of sales goals. Without goals to achieve, salesperson performance would be mediocre at best, and the company would likely fail. Like any marketing objective, sales goals should be stated in clear, precise, and measurable terms and should always specify a time frame for their completion. Overall sales force goals are usually stated in terms of desired dollar sales volume, market share, or profit level. For example, a life insurance company may have a goal to sell $50 million in life insurance policies annually, to attain a 12 percent market share, or to achieve $1 million in profits. Individual salespeople are also assigned goals in the form of quotas. A **quota** is a statement of the salesperson's sales goals, usually based on sales volume alone but sometimes including key accounts (those with greatest potential), new accounts, repeat sales, and specific products.

17-5b Determining the Sales Force Structure

Because personal selling is so costly, no sales department can afford to be disorganized. Proper design helps the sales manager organize and delegate sales duties and provides direction for salespeople. Sales departments are most commonly organized by geographic regions, by product line, by marketing function performed (such as account development or account maintenance), by market or industry, or by individual client or account. The sales force for Hewlett-Packard could be organized into sales territories covering New England, the Midwest, the South, and the West Coast or into distinct groups selling different product lines. HP salespeople might also be assigned to a specific industry or market, for example, the telecommunications industry, or to key clients such as AT&T, Virgin Mobile, and Verizon.

Market- or industry-based structures and key account structures are gaining popularity in today's competitive selling environment, especially with the emphasis on relationship selling. Being familiar with one industry or market allows sales reps to become experts in their fields and thereby offer better solutions and service. Further, by organizing the sales force around specific customers, many companies hope to improve customer service, encourage collaboration with other arms of the company, and unite salespeople in customer-focused sales teams.

17-5c Recruiting and Training the Sales Force

Sales force recruitment should be based on an accurate, detailed description of the sales task as defined by the sales manager. For example, General Electric uses its Web site to provide prospective salespeople with explanations of different career entry paths and video accounts of what it is like to have a career at GE. Aside from the usual characteristics such as level of experience or education, what traits should sales managers look for in applicants?

▸▸ **EGO STRENGTH:** Great salespeople should have a strong, healthy self-esteem and the ability to bounce back from rejection.

▸▸ **SENSE OF URGENCY AND COMPETITIVENESS:** These traits enable salespeople to push their sales to completion as well as help them persuade people.

▸▸ **ASSERTIVENESS:** Effective salespeople have the ability to be firm in one-to-one negotiations, to lead the sales process, and to get their point across confidently, without being overbearing or aggressive.

▸▸ **SOCIABLE:** Wanting to interact with others is a necessary trait for great salespeople.

▸▸ **RISK TAKERS:** Great salespeople are willing to put themselves in less-than-assured situations, and in doing so, often are able to close unlikely sales.

▸▸ **CAPABLE OF UNDERSTANDING COMPLEX CONCEPTS AND IDEAS:** Quick thinking and comprehension allows salespeople to quickly grasp and sell new products or enter new sales areas.

▸▸ **CREATIVITY:** Great salespeople develop client solutions in creative ways.

▸▸ **EMPATHETIC:** Empathy—the ability to place oneself in someone else's shoes—enables salespeople to understand the client.

In addition to the above traits, almost all successful salespeople say their sales style is relationship oriented rather than transaction oriented.[13]

After the sales recruit has been hired and given a brief orientation, training begins. A new salesperson generally receives instruction in company policies and practices, selling techniques, product knowledge, industry and customer characteristics, and nonselling duties such as filling out sales and market information reports or using a sales automation computer program.

17-5d Compensating and Motivating the Sales Force

Compensation planning is one of the sales manager's toughest jobs. Only good planning will ensure that compensation attracts, motivates, and retains good salespeople. Generally, companies and industries with lower levels of compensation suffer higher turnover

rates, which increase costs and decrease effectiveness. Therefore, compensation needs to be competitive enough to attract and motivate the best salespeople. Firms sometimes take profit into account when developing their compensation plans. Instead of paying salespeople on overall volume, they pay according to the profitability achieved from selling each product. Still other companies tie a part of the salesperson's total compensation to customer satisfaction assessed through periodic customer surveys.

As the emphasis on relationship selling increases, many sales managers feel that tying a portion of a salesperson's compensation to a client's satisfaction with the salesperson and the company encourages relationship building. To determine this, sales managers can survey clients on a salesperson's ability to create realistic expectations and his or her responsiveness to customer needs. At PeopleSoft, which was once one of the world's largest applications software companies, structure, culture, and strategies were built around customer satisfaction. Sales force compensation was tied to both sales quotas and a satisfaction metric that allows clients to voice their opinions on the service provided.[14]

Although the compensation plan motivates a salesperson to sell, sometimes it is not enough to produce the volume of sales or the profit margin required by sales management. Sales managers, therefore, often offer rewards or incentives, such as recognition at ceremonies, plaques, vacations, merchandise, and pay raises or cash bonuses. Cash awards are the most popular sales incentive and are used by virtually all companies. Another possibility is to reward salespeople with a Visa gift card, available from Visa in any amount between $25 and $600. The gift card, which functions like a credit card, can be personalized with a message about the salesperson's performance. It can then be reloaded at the employer's discretion. To recognize and further motivate employees, General Electric uses various rewards including stock options, recognition programs unique to each department, tuition assistance, and product discounts.[15] Rewards may help increase overall sales volume, add new accounts, improve morale and goodwill, move slow items, and bolster slow sales. They can also

© iStockphoto.com/Valentin Mosichev

be used to achieve long-term or short-term objectives, such as unloading overstocked inventory and meeting a monthly or quarterly sales goal. In motivating their sales force, sales managers must be careful not to encourage unethical behavior.

17-5e Evaluating the Sales Force

The final task of sales managers is evaluating the effectiveness and performance of the sales force. To evaluate the sales force, the sales manager needs feedback—that is, regular information from salespeople. Typical performance measures include sales volume, contribution to profit, calls per order, sales or profits per call, or percentage of calls achieving specific goals such as sales of products that the firm is heavily promoting.

Performance information helps the sales manager monitor a salesperson's progress through the sales cycle and pinpoint where breakdowns might be occurring. For example, by learning the number of prospects an individual salesperson has in each step of the sales cycle process and determining where prospects are falling out of the sales cycle, a manager can determine how effective a salesperson might be at lead generation, needs assessment, proposal generation, presenting, closing, and follow-up stages. This information can then tell a manager what sales skills might need to be reassessed or retrained. For example, if a sales manager notices that a sales rep seems to be letting too many prospects slip away after presenting proposals, it might mean he or she needs help with developing proposals, handling objections, or closing sales.

17-5f The Impact of Technology on Personal Selling and Sales Management

Will the increasingly sophisticated technology now available at marketers' fingertips eliminate the need for salespeople? Experts agree that a relationship between the salesperson and customer will always be necessary. Technology, however, can certainly help to improve that relationship. Cell phones, laptops, pagers, e-mail, and electronic organizers allow salespeople to be more accessible to both clients and the company. Moreover, the Internet provides salespeople with vast resources of information on clients, competitors, and the industry.

E-business—buying, selling, marketing, collaborating with partners, and servicing customers electronically using the Internet—has had a significant impact on personal selling. Virtually all large companies and most medium and small companies are involved in e-commerce and consider it to be necessary to compete in today's marketplace. For customers, the Web has become a powerful tool, providing accurate and up-to-date information on products, pricing, and order status. The Internet also cost-effectively processes orders and service requests. Although on the surface the Internet might appear to be a threat to the job security of salespeople, the Web is actually freeing sales reps from tedious administrative tasks like shipping catalogs, placing routine orders, or tracking orders. This leaves them more time to focus on the needs of their clients.

STUDY TOOLS 17

↑ LOCATED AT BACK OF THE TEXTBOOK
☐ *Rip out Chapter Review Card*

LOCATED AT WWW.CENGAGE.COM/LOGIN
☐ *Review Key Terms Flashcards (print or online)*
☐ *Download audio and visual summaries to review on the go*
☐ *Complete both Practice Quizzes to prepare for tests*
☐ *Play "Beat the Clock" and "Quizbowl" to master concepts*
☐ *Complete "Crossword Puzzle" to review key terms*
☐ *Watch Video on "New Balance Hubway" for a real company example*

18-1 WHAT ARE SOCIAL MEDIA?

The most exciting thing to happen to marketing and promotion is the increasing use of online technology to promote brands, particularly using social media. Social media have changed the way that marketers can communicate with their brands—from mass messages to intimate conversations. As marketing moves into social media, marketers must remember that for most people, social media are meant to be a social experience, not a marketing experience. In fact, the term *social media* means different things to different people, though most people think it refers to digital technology. Brian Solis, of FutureWorks, defines **social media** as "any tool or service that uses the Internet to facilitate conversations."[1] However, social media can also be defined relative to traditional advertising like television and magazines: Whereas traditional marketing media offer a mass-media method of interacting with consumers, social media offer more one-to-one ways to meet consumers.

"Interaction and engagement [on social media] is something that you don't necessarily see in traditional media. That's why we [at Ford] continue to accelerate our digital advertising investment to more than 25% of our media dollars." Jim Farley, Ford Global Sales and Marketing Vice President[2]

social media any tool or service that uses the Internet to facilitate conversations

Social media have several implications for marketers and how they can interact with their customers. First, marketers must realize that they often do not control the content on social media sites. Consumers are sharing their thoughts, wishes, and experiences about brands with the world through social media. Because of this level of visibility and discussion, marketers must realize that having a great ad campaign is not enough—the product or service must be great, too.

Chapter 18

Social Media and Marketing

Learning Outcomes

After you finish this chapter go to
p323 *for* **STUDY TOOLS**

© iStockphoto.com/OSTILL

Second, the ability to share experiences quickly and with such large numbers of people amplifies the impact of word of mouth in a way that can eventually affect a company's bottom line. Many companies are developing mascots to drive their marketing message on social media. For example, Progressive auto insurance's perky saleswoman Flo has more than 3.5 million Facebook fans that read her posts about Progressive products. According to the company, since Flo began appearing in ads, the company has seen yearly gains in the number of policies taken out. Kraft is hoping to catch similar success with Mel the MilkBite granola bar. His conflicted personality has drawn more than 160,000 "likes" and much sympathy for the part milk, part granola bar mascot.[3]

Third, social media allow marketers to listen. Domino's Pizza listened to much of what was being posted about its product (and it was not nice) and then decided to take that information and change its product. Social media, along with traditional marketing research, allowed Domino's to gain the insight needed to completely reinvent its pizza. And Domino's then used the simple act of transparency to launch an award-winning promotional campaign. Dell and Gatorade have taken social media monitoring to a whole new level as they literally put social media at the center of their marketing efforts.

Fourth, social media also provide more sophisticated methods of measuring how marketers meet and interact with consumers than traditional advertising does. Currently, social media include tools and platforms like social networks, blogs, microblogs, and media sharing sites, which can be accessed through a growing number of devices such as computers, laptops, Smartphones, e-readers, tablets, and netbooks. This technology changes daily, offering consumers new ways to experience social media platforms, which must constantly innovate to keep up with consumer demands.

Finally, social media allow marketers to have much more direct and meaningful conversations with customers. Social media offer a form of relationship building that will ultimately bring the customer and brand closer. Indeed, the culture of participation that social media invite may well prove to be a fifth "P" for marketing.

At the basic level, consumers of social media want to exchange information, collaborate with others, and have conversations. Social media are designed for people to socialize with each other, and they have changed how and where conversations take place, making human interaction global through popular technology. Research shows that more than 73 percent of active online users have read a blog, and more than half belong to at least one social network. Marketing consultant John Haydon says, "The real value of social media is that it exponentially leverages word-of-mouth."[4] Clearly, conversations are happening online; it is up to the marketer to decide if engaging in those conversations will be profitable and to find the most effective method of entering the conversation.

Marketers are interested in online communication because it is wildly popular: brands, companies, individuals, and celebrities promote their messages online. In fact, some social media are becoming so important that celebrities, sports stars, and even hotels are hiring coaches to help them strike the correct tone. One such coach focuses on Twitter and got her start giving Shaq a helping hand when he played for the Suns in Phoenix. Today Amy Jo Martin, owner of Digital Royalty, still works with Shaq but has added Dana White (UFC president), golfer Bubba Watson, and a host of other sports stars to her client list. Martin keeps the stars in the spotlight by using Twitter to coordinate real-life events and play non-virtual games. For example, she advised Shaq to play hide-and-tweet with his followers, as well as to respond to them personally. White tweeted his phone number to answer calls regarding upcoming fights. Martin's publicity know-how has sparked such massive followings that DoubleTree hotels and Discount Tire Centers have hired her to help them develop their social media strategy and give them a leg up in their industries.[5]

Check out "Shaqtin' A Fool" with @Shaq

11:25 AM

How important is tweeting in the sports world? The UFC puts its fighters through five days of **social media training** every year. Fighters who take the training to heart and get large numbers of positive responses receive money from the $240,000 bonus pool reserved for social media excellence.[6]

© Jojie/Shutterstock.com

social commerce
a subset of e-commerce that involves the interaction and user contribution aspects of social online media to assist online buying and selling of products and services

18-1a How Consumers Use Social Media

Before beginning to understand how to leverage social media for brand building, it is important to understand what consumers are using and how they are using it. Many marketers are looking to get their message on the fastest-growing social media platform—Facebook. Facebook originated as a community for college students that opened to the general public as its popularity grew. It now has hundreds of millions of users: If Facebook were a country, it would be the third largest in the world. Growth in new profiles is highest among baby boomers, who use Facebook as a way to connect with old friends and keep up with family. Other social networks, like hi5 and Bebo, offer an alternative for other demographics. hi5 offers a wide variety of social games (covered later in this chapter), adding two or three each week. Bebo is popular with tweens and teens, though that age group is increasingly moving to Facebook.

Videos are one of the most popular tools by which marketers reach consumers, and YouTube is by far the largest online video repository—it has more content than any major television network. Due to its connection with Google, YouTube offers a powerful search tool as well.[7] Flickr is a popular photo sharing site where millions of people upload new photos daily. Twitter boasts hundreds of millions of registered users who together post a daily average of billions of tweets. Technorati tracks hundreds of millions of blogs and indexes an estimated 2 million new blog posts per day.[8] More than half of Technorati's active users have uploaded photos, and almost a quarter have uploaded videos. The bottom line, according to Universal McCann's Comparative Study on Social Media Trends, is that "if you are online, you are using social media."[9]

Increased usage of alternative platforms like Smartphones and tablet computers has further contributed to the proliferation of social media usage. In the United States, 90 percent of eighteen- to twenty-nine-year-olds own mobile phones. Among this group, 95 percent have sent a text message, 65 percent have accessed the Internet, and at least 23 percent have accessed a social networking site using their phones.[10] In addition, 63 percent of U.S. adults access the Internet through mobile devices—including a growing number of baby boomers.[11] When Apple released the iPad3, the company sold 3 million of the new tablets in three days. Some analysts project that Apple will sell 66 million iPads in 2012.[12] The overall impact of tablet computing on social media (and thus the discipline of marketing) is yet to be seen, but given the incredible impact that the Smartphone has had in its short life span, tablets could prove to be game changing.

SOCIAL COMMERCE A new area of growth in social media is **social commerce**, which combines social media with the basics of e-commerce. Social commerce is a subset of e-commerce that involves the interaction and user contribution aspects of social online media to assist online buying and selling of products and services.[13] Basically, social commerce relies on user-generated content on Web sites to assist consumers with purchases. The current social commerce darling is Pinterest. Pinterest lets users collect ideas and products from all over the Web and "pin" favorite items to individually curated pinboards. Other users browse boards by theme, keyword, or product, click on what they like, and are either taken to the original site, or are able to re-pin the item on their own pinboard. Social commerce sites often include ratings and recommendations (like Amazon.com) and social shopping tools (like Groupon). In general, social commerce sites are designed to help consumers make more informed decisions on purchases or services.

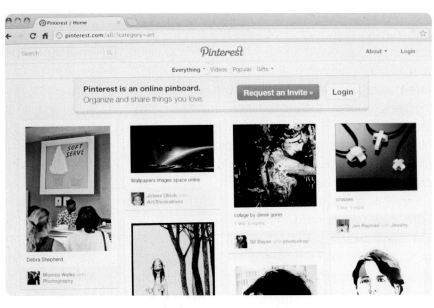

© iStockphoto.com/Alberto Bogo

As companies move into social commerce sites, such as Pinterest, consumer interaction with the sites may change. One way that companies are leveraging social commerce traffic is by running promotions. For example, Lands' End ran a promotion called "Lands' End Canvas Pin It to Win It," and fans who pinned certain items to designated Lands' End Canvas pinboards were eligible to win that item.[14] This type of promotion can undermine the authenticity that many consumers rely on when using social commerce sites. However, some companies hope to cultivate authentic relationships by staying away from promotions. Whole Foods pins items that relate to the company's values but are not promotional or linked back to the Whole Foods site. Customers have built a relationship with Whole Foods based on upcycled products and recipes, rather than free products.[15]

18-1b Social Media and Integrated Marketing Communications

While marketers typically employ a social media strategy alongside traditional channels like print and broadcast, many budget pendulums are swinging toward social media. In the U.S. Interactive Marketing Forecast, 2009–2014, Forrester Research predicted that mobile marketing, social media, e-mail marketing, display advertising, and search marketing would grow from 13 percent of advertising spending in 2010 to more than 21 percent of spending by 2014. The bulk of this budget will still go to search marketing (almost doubling by 2014), but substantial investments will also be made in mobile marketing and social media.[16]

A unique consequence of social media is the widespread shift from one-to-many communication to many-to-many communication. Instead of simply putting a brand advertisement on television with no means for feedback, marketers can use social media to have conversations with consumers, forge deeper relationships, and build brand loyalty. Social media also allow consumers to connect with each other, share opinions, and collaborate on new ideas according to their interests.

With social media, the audience is often in control of the message, the medium, the response, or all three. This distribution of control is often difficult for companies to adjust to, but the focus of social marketing is unavoidably on the audience, and the brand must adapt to succeed. The interaction between producer and consumer becomes less about entertaining and more about listening, influencing, and engaging.

Using consumers to develop and market products is called **crowdsourcing**. Crowdsourcing describes how the input of many people can be leveraged to make decisions that used to be based on the input of only a few people.[17] Companies get feedback on marketing campaigns, new-product ideas, and other marketing decisions by asking customers to weigh in. One company called Talenthouse is offering up the crowd to help musicians fulfill all sorts of needs—for example, someone to photograph a tour or to design a dress for a lead singer. Talenthouse has users submit work to be voted on by Facebook peers. The winner gets the job (though the musician has the final say in who wins). Some musicians see Talenthouse as a way to gain publicity or to help young artists: Paul McCartney set up a contest for Talenthouse competitors to design a piece of art inspired by his music. The winner received $1,000 and various merchandise, and the work was displayed in the London art gallery Idea Generation.[18] Crowdsourcing offers a way for companies to engage heavy users of a brand and receive input, which in turn increases those users' brand advocacy and lessens the likelihood that a change will be disliked enough to drive away loyal customers.

18-2 CREATING AND LEVERAGING A SOCIAL MEDIA CAMPAIGN

Social media is an exciting new field, and its potential for expanding a brand's impact is enormous. Because the costs are often minimal and the learning curve is relatively low, some organizations are tempted to dive headfirst into social media. However, as with any marketing campaign, it is always important to start with a strategy. For most organizations, this means starting with a marketing or communications plan, as covered in Chapter 2. Important evaluative areas such as situation analysis, objectives, and evaluation are still key. It is important to link communication objectives (for example, improving customer service) to the most effective social media tools (for example, Twitter) and to be able to measure the results to determine if the objectives were met. It is also important to understand the various types of media involved.

The new communication paradigm created by a shift to social media marketing raises questions about categorization. In light of the convergence of traditional and digital media, researchers have explored different ways that interactive marketers can categorize media types. One such researcher, Sean Corcoran of Forrester Research, devised a distinction among owned, earned, and paid media. **Owned media** are online content that an organization creates and controls. A brand's Facebook presence, YouTube channel, Twitter presence, Pinterest presence, and presence on other social platforms constitute owned media. Additionally content such as videos, webinars, recommendations, ratings, and blog posts are also considered owned media since they are sharable on social media platforms. The purpose of owned media is to develop deeper relationships with customers. **Earned media** is a PR term connoting free media such as mainstream media coverage. In an interactive space, media are earned through word of mouth or online buzz about something the brand is doing. Earned media include viral videos, retweets, comments on blogs, and other forms of customer feedback resulting from a social media presence. When consumers pass along brand information in the form of retweets, blog comments, or ratings and recommendations, this is an example of earned media. In other words, the word of mouth is spread online rather than face-to-face. **Paid media** are content paid for by the company to be placed online. Paid media are similar to marketing efforts that utilize traditional media, like newspaper, magazine, and television advertisements. In an interactive space, paid media include display advertising, paid search words, and other types of direct online advertising.[19] Ads purchased on Facebook, for example, are considered paid media since the brand is paying for the text-based or visual ad that shows up on the right-hand side of Facebook profiles.

As a result, social media can really be thought of as an additional "layer" that many brands decide to develop. Some layers are quite deep—Doritos, Old Spice, and Nike—can be said to have deeper layers of social media since these are brands that people talk about. Other brands, for example, many B-to-B brands, may have a more shallow social media layer and provide access on only one or two social media platforms. At the end of the day, it really depends on the type of product being sold and the customer's propensity to participate in social media.

To leverage all three types of media, marketers must follow a few key guidelines. First, they must maximize owned media by reaching out beyond their existing Web sites to create portfolios of digital touch points. This is especially true for brands with tight budgets, as the organization may not be able to afford much paid media. Second, marketers must recognize that aptitude at public and media relations no longer translates into earned media. Instead, marketers must learn how to listen and respond to stakeholders. This will stimulate word of mouth. Finally, marketers must understand that paid media are not dead but should serve as a catalyst to drive customer engagement.[20] If balanced correctly, all three types of media can be powerful tools for interactive marketers.

18-2a The Listening System

The first action a marketing team should take when initiating a social media campaign is simple—it should just listen. Customers are on social media and assume that

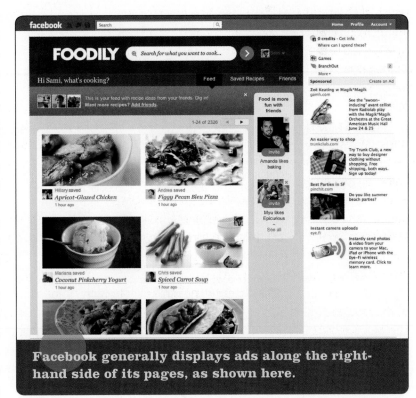

Facebook generally displays ads along the right-hand side of its pages, as shown here.

© AP Images/PRNewsFoto/Foodily

social media monitoring the process of identifying and assessing what is being said about a company, individual, product, or brand

the brand is there as well. They expect a new level of engagement with brands. Developing an effective listening system is necessary to both understanding and engaging an online audience. Marketers must not only hear what is being said about the brand, the industry, the competition, and the customer, but they must also pay attention to who is saying what and act upon that information. The specific ways that customers and noncustomers rate, rank, critique, praise, deride, recommend, snub, and generally discuss brands are all important. Thus, social media have created a new method of market research: These are customers telling marketers what they want and need (and don't want and need).

Once a company has started listening, it typically wants to develop a more formalized approach. **Social media monitoring** is the process of identifying and assessing what is being said about a company,

individual, product, or brand. It can involve *text mining* specific key words on social networking Web sites, blogs, discussion forums, and other social media. Negative comments and complaints are of particular importance, both because they can illuminate unknown brand flaws and because they are the comments that tend to go viral. Listening is important because consumers believe that if negative comments about a brand go unanswered, that brand is insincere, and consumers will take their business elsewhere. Online tools such as Google Alerts, Google Blog Search, Twitter Search, Social Mention, and Socialcast are extremely helpful in monitoring social media. Larger companies typically use an enterprise system such as Radian6 to monitor social media.

In Exhibit 18.1, social media strategists Jeremiah Owyang and Jim Sterne outline eight stages of effective listening. Listening to customers communicate about one's own brand can be very revealing, but social media are also a great way to monitor competitors'

Exhibit 18.1

EIGHT STAGES OF EFFECTIVE LISTENING

Stage	Description	Resources Required	Purpose
Stage 1: Without objective	The organization has established a listening system but has no goals.	Social media notification tools (Google Alerts)	Keep up with brand and competitor information.
Stage 2: Tracking brand mentions	The organization tracks mentions in social space but has no guidance on next steps.	A listening platform with key word report capabilities (Radian6)	Track discussions, understand sentiment, and identify influencers to improve overall marketing strategy.
Stage 3: Identifying market risks and opportunities	The organization seeks discussions online that may result in identification of problems and opportunities.	A listening platform with a large staff dedicated to the client (Converseon)	Staff seeks out discussions and reports to other teams, like product development and sales. These teams then engage the customers directly or conduct further research.
Stage 4: Improving campaign efficiency	The organization uses tools to get real-time data on marketing efficiency.	Web analytics software (Google Analytics)	See a wealth of information about consumers' behavior on their Web sites (and social media).
Stage 5: Measuring customer satisfaction	The organization collects information about satisfaction, including measures of sentiment.	Insight platforms that offer online focus-group solutions	Measure impact of satisfaction or frustration during interaction.
Stage 6: Responding to customer inquiry	The organization identifies customers where they are (e.g., Twitter).	A customer service team is allowed to make real-time responses.	Generate high sense of satisfaction for customer but generates public complaints.
Stage 7: Better understanding of customers	The organization adds social information to demographics and psychographics to gain a better profile.	Social customer relationship management (CRM) systems to sync data	Social CRM marries database and social media to create a powerful analytical tool. (See Chapters 9 and 17 for more on CRM.)
Stage 8: Being proactive and anticipating customer demands	The organization examines previous patterns of data and social behavior to anticipate needs.	Advanced customer database with predictive application (yet to be created)	Modify social media strategy to preempt consumer behavior modifications based on trends.

Sources: Jeremiah Owyang, "Web Strategy Matrix: The Eight Stages of Listening," *Web Strategy*, November 10, 2009, www.web-strategist.com/blog/2009/11/10/evolution-the-eight-stages-of-listening/; Jim Sterne, *Social Media Metrics* (Hoboken, NJ: John Wiley & Sons, 2010).

online presences, fans, and followers. Paying attention to the ways that competing brands attract and engage with their customers can be particularly enlightening for both small businesses and global brands.

18-2b Social Media Objectives

After establishing a listening platform, the organization should develop a list of objectives for its social media team to accomplish. These objectives must be developed with a clear understanding of how social media change the communication dynamic with and for customers. Remember—attempting to reach a mass audience with a static message will never be as successful as influencing people through conversation. Marketing managers must set objectives that reflect this reality. Here are some practical ideas that marketing managers should consider when setting social media objectives:

‣ **LISTEN AND LEARN:** Monitor what is being said about the brand and competitors, and glean insights about audiences. Use online tools and do research to implement the best social media practices. If you have established a listening strategy, this objective should already be accomplished.

‣ **BUILD RELATIONSHIPS AND AWARENESS:** Open dialogues with stakeholders by giving them compelling content across a variety of media. Engage in conversations, and answer customers' questions candidly. This will both increase Web traffic and boost your search engine ranking. This is where crowdsourcing can be useful for product development and communication campaign feedback.

‣ **PROMOTE PRODUCTS AND SERVICES:** The clearest path to increasing the bottom line using social media is to get customers talking about products and services, which ultimately translates into sales.

‣ **MANAGE YOUR REPUTATION:** Develop and improve the brand's reputation by responding to comments and criticism that appear on blogs and forums. Additionally, organizations can position themselves as helpful and benevolent by participating in other forums and discussions. Social media make it much easier to establish and communicate expertise.

‣ **IMPROVE CUSTOMER SERVICE:** Customer comments about products and services will not always be positive. Use social media to search out displeased customers and engage them directly in order to solve their service issues.

18-3 EVALUATION AND MEASUREMENT OF SOCIAL MEDIA

Social media have the potential to revolutionize the way organizations communicate with stakeholders. Given the relative ease and efficiency with which organizations can use social media, a positive return on investment (ROI) is likely for many—if not most—organizations. A Forrester Research report found that 95 percent of marketers planned to increase or maintain their investments in social media. However, though they understand that it is a worthwhile investment, most marketers have not been able to figure out how to measure the benefits of social media. As social media evolve, so do the measurements and metrics that track them.[21] Yet, as with traditional advertising, marketers lack hard evidence as to the relative effectiveness of these tools. Some marketers accept this unknown variable and focus on the fact that social media are less about ROI than about deepening relationships with customers; others work tirelessly to better understand the measurement of social media's effectiveness.

While literally hundreds of metrics have been developed to measure social media's value, these metrics are meaningless unless they are tied to key performance indicators.[22] For example, a local coffee shop manager may measure the success of her social media presence by the raw number of friends on Facebook and followers on Twitter she has accumulated. But these numbers depend entirely on context. The rate of accumulation, investment per fan and follower, and comparison to similarly sized coffee shops are all important variables to consider. Without context, measurements are meaningless.

Some social media metrics to consider include:

1. **BUZZ:** Volume of consumer-created buzz for a brand based on posts and impressions, by social channel, by stage in the purchase channel, by season, and by time of day.

2. **INTEREST:** Number of "likes," fans, followers, and friends; growth rates; rate of virality or pass along; and change in pass along over time.

3. **PARTICIPATION:** Number of comments, ratings, social bookmarks, subscriptions, page views, uploads, downloads, embeds, retweets, Facebook posts, pins, and time spent with social media platform.

4. **SEARCH ENGINE RANKS AND RESULTS:** Increases and decreases on searches and changes in key words.

5. **INFLUENCE:** Media mentions, influences of bloggers reached, influences of customers reached, and second-degree reach based on social graphs.

6. **SENTIMENT ANALYSIS:** Positive, neutral, and negative sentiment; trends of sentiment; and volume of sentiment.

7. **WEB SITE METRICS:** Clicks, click through rates, and percentage of traffic.

And the list goes on. The main issue is to start with good measurable objectives, determine what needs to be measured, and figure it out. This is a hot topic and several marketing blogs cover the areas of social media measurement. Jim Sterne's book *Social Media Metrics* is one of the best sources of information on monitoring and using social media metrics.

18-4 SOCIAL BEHAVIOR OF CONSUMERS

Social media have changed the way that people interact in their everyday lives. Some say that social media have made people smarter by giving people (especially children) access to so much information and interactivity. Social media allow people to stay in touch in ways never before experienced. Social media have also reinvented politics and civic engagement (the Occupy Wall Street movement grew worldwide through social media like Twitter). Social media have drastically changed the advertising business from an industry based on mass-media models (e.g., television) to an industry based on relationships and conversations. This all has implications for how consumers use social media and the purposes for which they use those media.[23]

Once objectives have been determined and measurement tools have been implemented, it is important to identify the consumer the marketer is trying to reach. Who is using social media? What types of social media do they use? How do they use social media? Are they just reading content, or do they actually create it? Does Facebook attract younger users? Do Twitter users retweet viral videos? These types of questions must be considered because they determine not only which tools will be most effective but

also, more importantly, whether launching a social media campaign even makes sense for a particular organization.

Understanding an audience necessitates understanding how that audience uses social media. In *Groundswell*, Charlene Li and Josh Bernoff of Forrester Research identify six categories of social media users:

1. **CREATORS:** Those who produce and share online content like blogs, Web sites, articles, and videos.

2. **CRITICS:** Those who post comments, ratings, and reviews of products and services on blogs and forums.

3. **COLLECTORS:** Those who use RSS feeds to collect information and vote for Web sites online.

4. **JOINERS:** Those who maintain a social networking profile and visit other sites.

5. **SPECTATORS:** Those who read blogs, listen to podcasts, watch videos, and generally consume media.

6. **INACTIVES:** Those who do none of these things.[24]

A 2009 study determined that 24 percent of social media users functioned as creators, 37 percent functioned as critics, 21 percent functioned as collectors, 51 percent functioned as joiners, and 73 percent functioned as spectators. While participation in each of these categories had trended upward, inactives had decreased from 44 percent in 2007 to only 18 percent in 2009.[25] However, recent Forrester research shows that the number of people who contribute content is slowing down. Participation in most categories has fallen slightly, prompting analysts to recommend that marketers re-examine how they are engaging with their customers online.

Despite the apparent slowdown, research also shows that more social networking "rookies" are classified as joiners. Another bright spot is a new category, "conversationalists," or people who post status updates on social networking sites and microblogging services such as Twitter. Conversationalists represent 31 percent of users.[26] This type of classification gives marketers a general idea of who is using social media and how to engage them. It is similar to any type of market segmentation—especially the 80/20 rule. Those who are creating content and active on social media could be those consumers most likely to actively engage with a brand as well as actively post negative comments on social media. The critics and collectors make up most of this group. However, it is important not to miss the joiners and spectators, because they are eager to follow and act on the comments of their fellow customers.

18-5 SOCIAL MEDIA TOOLS: CONSUMER- AND CORPORATE-GENERATED CONTENT

Given that it is important for marketers to engage with customers on social media for the reasons mentioned earlier, there are a number of tools and platforms that can be employed as part of an organization's social media strategy. Blogs, microblogs, social networks, media creation and sharing sites, social news sites, location-based social networking sites, review sites, and virtual worlds and online gaming all have their place in a company's social marketing plan. These are all tools in a marketing manager's toolbox, available when applicable to the marketing plan but not necessarily to be used all at once. Because of the breakneck pace at which technology changes, this list of resources will surely look markedly different five years from now. More tools emerge every day, and branding strategies must keep up with the ever-changing world of technology. For now, the resources highlighted in this section remain a marketer's strongest set of platforms for conversing and strengthening relationships with customers.

18-5a Blogs

Blogs have become staples in many social media strategies and are often a brand's social media centerpiece. A **blog** is a publicly accessible Web page that functions as an interactive journal, whereby readers can post comments on the author's entries. Some experts believe that every company should have a blog that speaks to current and potential customers, not as consumers, but as people.[27] Blogs allow marketers to create content in the form of posts, which ideally build trust and a sense of authenticity in customers. Once posts are made, audience members can provide feedback through comments. Because it opens a dialogue and gives customers a voice, the comments section of a blog post is one of the most important avenues of conversation between brands and consumers.

Blogs can be divided into two broad categories: corporate and professional blogs, and noncorporate blogs such as personal blogs. **Corporate blogs** are sponsored by a company or one of its brands and are maintained by one or more of the company's employees. They disseminate marketing-controlled information and are effective platforms for developing thought leadership, fostering better relationships with stakeholders, maximizing search engine optimization, attracting new customers, endearing the organization with anecdotes and stories about brands, and providing an active forum for testing new ideas. Many companies, however, have moved away

© iStockphoto.com/sad444

JOINER   CREATOR   CONVERSATIONALIST

blog a publicly accessible Web page that functions as an interactive journal, whereby readers can post comments on the author's entries

corporate blogs blogs that are sponsored by a company or one of its brands and maintained by one or more of the company's employees from corporate blogs, replacing the in-depth writing and comment monitoring that come with blog maintenance with the quick, easy, and more social Facebook, Twitter, or Tumblr. In 2010, 50 percent of companies used corporate blogs. In 2011, only 37 percent of companies maintained a blog. Bank of America stopped using its corporate blog in order to focus solely on Facebook and Twitter, where its customers are.[28]

On the other hand, **noncorporate blogs** are independent and not associated with the marketing efforts of any particular company or brand. Because these blogs contain information not controlled by marketers, they are perceived to be more authentic than corporate blogs. Mommy bloggers, women who review children's products and discuss family-related topics on their personal blogs, use noncorporate blogs. The goal of mommy blogs is to share parenting tips and experiences and become part of a community. Food blogs are especially popular, particularly those posting restaurant reviews, diet and exercise tips, and recipes.

Because of the popularity of these and other types of blogs, many bloggers receive products and/or money from companies in exchange for a review. Many bloggers disclose how they obtained the product or if they were paid, but an affiliation is not always clear. Because of this, bloggers must disclose any financial relationship with a company per Federal Trade Commission rules. Marketing managers need to understand the rules behind offering complimentary products to bloggers before using them as a way to capitalize on the high potential for social buzz; four out of five noncorporate bloggers post brand or product reviews. Even if a company does not have a formal social media strategy, chances are the brand is still out in the blogosphere, whether or not a marketing manager approached a blogger.

18-5b Microblogs

Microblogs are blogs that exchange smaller posts than traditional blogs. Twitter, the most popular micro-blogging platform, requires that posts be no more than 140 characters in length. However, there are several other platforms, including Tumblr, Plurk, and, of course, Facebook's status updates. These platforms allow users to post longer content, videos, images, and links. The content posted on microblogs ranges from five-paragraph news stories to scans of sandwiches with the ingredients as captions (scanwiches.com). While Tumblr is growing rapidly, Twitter, originally designed as a short messaging system used for internal communication, is wildly popular and is used as a communication and research tool by individuals and brands around the world. Twitter is effective for disseminating breaking news, promoting longer blog posts and campaigns, sharing links, announcing events, and promoting sales. By following, retweeting, responding to potential customers' tweets, and tweeting content that inspires customers to engage the brand, corporate Twitter users can lay a foundation for meaningful two-way conversation quickly and effectively. Celebrities also flock to Twitter to interact with fans, discuss tour dates, and efficiently promote themselves directly to fans. Research has found that when operated correctly, corporate Twitter accounts are well respected and well received. Twitter can be used to build communities, aid in customer service, gain prospects, increase awareness, and, in the case of nonprofits, raise funds.

The ways a business can use microblogs to successfully engage with customers are almost limitless. A wide variety of companies find Tumblr's easy and customizable format a great way to promote an individual brand. Mashable.com uses its Tumblr to give a glimpse inside the offices and share the company's sense of humor. Ace Hotel, located in New York, Portland, Seattle, and Palm Springs, shows off its properties and local art exhibits on a spare, gallery-like Tumblr. Lure Fishbar shows off its delectable food on its Tumblr.[29]

18-5c Social Networks

Social networking sites allow individuals to connect—or network—with friends, peers, and business associates. Connections may be made around shared interests, shared environments, or personal relationships. Depending on the site, connected individuals may be able to send each other messages, track each other's activity, see each other's personal information, share multimedia, or comment on each other's blog and microblog posts. Depending on a marketing team's goals, there are several social networks that might be engaged as part of a social media strategy: Facebook is the largest and fastest-growing network; hi5 caters to younger audiences; LinkedIn is geared toward professionals and businesses who use it to recruit professionals; and niche networks like Bebo, Last.fm, We Are Teachers, BlackPlanet, and Match.com cater to specialized markets. There is a niche social network for just about every demographic and interest. Beyond those already established, an organization may decide to develop a brand-specific social network or community. Although each social networking site is different, some marketing goals can be accomplished on any such site. Given the right strategy, increasing awareness, targeting audiences, promoting products, forging relationships, highlighting expertise and leadership, attracting event participants, performing research, and generating new business are attainable marketing goals on any social network.

Facebook is by far the largest social networking site and is popular with both individuals and groups. How an individual uses Facebook differs from the way a group or company uses Facebook, as you can see in Exhibit 18.2. Individual Facebook users create profiles, while brands, organizations, and nonprofit causes operate as pages. As opposed to individual profiles, all pages are public and are thus subject to search engine indexing. By maintaining a popular Facebook page, a brand not only increases its social media presence, it also helps to optimize search engine results. Pages often include photo and video albums, brand information, and links to external sites. The most useful page feature, however, is the Wall. The Wall allows a brand to communicate directly with fans via status updates, which enables marketers to build databases of interested stakeholders. When an individual becomes a fan of your organization or posts on your Wall, that information is shared with the individual's friends, creating a mini viral marketing campaign. Other Facebook marketing tools include groups, applications, and ads. Facebook is an extremely important platform for social marketers.

Facebook has proved to be fertile ground for new marketing ideas and campaigns. Many companies use Facebook as a way to share photos of the business they are doing, whether that is images of the plant where the product is made or finished construction on a new project. Offering guides relevant to a company's product as a way to educate interested customers has worked well for Kitchen Cabinet

Exhibit 18.2
FACEBOOK LINGO

Non-Individual (Usually Corporate)	Individual
Page	Profile
Fan of a page, tells fan's friends that the user is a fan, creates mini viral campaign	Friend a person, send private messages, write on the Wall, see friend-only content
Public, searchable	Privacy options, not searchable unless user enabled

© Cengage Learning

Kings, who found that educated customers make more purchases. Modify Watches allows fans to vote on new designs and alerts them to limited stock sales and other promotions, rewarding its followers.[30]

LinkedIn features many of the same services as Facebook (profiles, status updates, private messages, company pages, and groups) but is oriented around business and professional connections. Unlike Facebook, LinkedIn features a question-and-answer forum, where users can ask for advice and share expertise in specific fields, and a file hosting service, where users can upload intellectual property like slides, presentations, and other shared documents.[31] LinkedIn is used primarily by professionals who wish to build their personal brands online and businesses that are recruiting employees and freelancers.

18-5d Media Sharing Sites

Media sharing sites allow users to upload and distribute multimedia content like videos and photos. Sites such as YouTube and Flickr are particularly useful to brands' social marketing strategies because they add a vibrant interactive channel on which to disseminate content. The distribution of user-generated content has changed markedly over the past few years. Today, organizations can tell compelling brand stories through videos, photos, and audio.

Photo sharing sites allow users to archive and share photos. Flickr, Picasa, Twitpic, Photobucket, Facebook, and Imgur all offer free photo hosting services that can be utilized by individuals and businesses alike.

Video creation and distribution have also gained popularity among marketers because of video's rich ability to tell stories. YouTube, the highest-trafficked video-based Web site and the sixth-highest-trafficked site overall, allows users to upload and stream their videos to an enthusiastic and active community.[32] YouTube is not only large (in terms of visitors), but it also attracts a diverse base of users: Age and gender demographics are remarkably balanced.

Many entertainment companies and movie marketers have used YouTube as a showcase for new products, specials, and movie trailers. For example, Lionsgate purchased ad space on the YouTube home page in fifteen countries to promote the *Avatar* movie trailer. Some teen clothing retailers like Forever 21 and JCPenney build followings on YouTube by posting hauls—videos made by teens that focus on fashion. Clearly, user-generated content can be a powerful tool for brands that can use it effectively.

A podcast, another type of user-generated media, is a digital audio or video file that is distributed serially for other people to listen to or watch. Podcasts can be streamed online, played on a computer, uploaded to a portable media player (like an iPod), or downloaded onto a Smartphone. Podcasts are like radio shows that are distributed through various means and not linked to a scheduled time slot. While they have not experienced the exponential growth rates of other digital platforms, podcasts have amassed a steadily growing number of loyal devotees. For example, Etsy, an online marketplace for handmade and vintage wares, offers a podcast series introducing favorite craftspeople to the world—driving business for those individuals.

18-5e Social News Sites

Social news sites allow users to decide which content is promoted on a given Web site by voting that content up or down. Users post news stories and multimedia on

THE FICKLE NATURE OF SOCIAL MEDIA CONSUMPTION

Myspace was the virtual hub for the social media generation until Facebook usurped its title and wooed away its youthful contingent with a cleaner interface. Myspace reached its peak in December 2008, when it was attracting nearly 76 million unique visitors each month. Since late 2009, however, Myspace has lost more than 1 million U.S. users a month. What happened? In part, Myspace grew too quickly without understanding what consumers wanted. Parents came to mistrust it and perceived it as "seedy." Mostly, though, users wanted what Facebook offered: a safe, uncluttered, ad-free (at the time) place where they could interact with the people they wanted to interact with. What initially attracted users to Myspace (the freedom to code your own page, play with widgets and music, freely explore other people's pages) became too much and drove users away—and when they left, the advertisers left, too. In 2009, Myspace generated $470 million in advertising; the projection for 2011 was only $184 million. In 2011, Myspace was sold to Specific Media for $35 million, a far cry from the 2005 sale to News Corporation for $580 million. Specific Media hopes to continue the site as a music- and band-focused hub, but as other come-and-gone social media sites can attest, bringing back users is a difficult task. A social media site grows quickly, as influencers pull in all their peers, but they also pull them away at the first sign of trouble or something new on the horizon—a trend that current social media darlings such as Twitter and LinkedIn should notice. It took only one year for Facebook to eclipse Myspace, and it has taken less than two years for Myspace to lose hundreds of millions of dollars and users.

Sources: Felix Gillette, "The Rise and Inglorious Fall of Myspace," *Bloomberg Businessweek*, June 27–July 3, 2011, 54–59; Brian Stelter, "News Corporation Sells Myspace for $35 Million," *New York Times*, June 29, 2011, http://mediadecoder.blogs.nytimes.com/2011/06/29/news-corp-sells-myspace-to-specific-media-for-35-million (Accessed April 30, 2012).

crowdsourced sites such as Reddit and Digg for the community to vote on. The more interest from readers, the higher the story or video is ranked. Marketers have found that these sites are useful for promoting campaigns, creating conversations around related issues, and building Web site traffic.[33] If content posted to a crowdsourced site is voted up, discussed, and shared enough to be listed among the most popular topics of the day, it can go viral across other sites and, eventually, the entire Web. Social bookmarking sites such as Delicious and StumbleUpon are similar to social news sites, but the objective of their users is to collect, save, and share interesting and valuable links. On these sites, users categorize links with short, descriptive tags. Users can search the site's database of links by specific tags or can add their own tags to others' links. In this way, tags serve as the foundation for information gathering and sharing on social bookmarking sites.[34]

18-5f Location-Based Social Networking Sites

Considered by many to be the next big thing in social marketing, location sites like Foursquare and Loopt should be on every marketer's radar. Essentially, **location-based social networking sites** combine the fun of social networking with the utility of location-based GPS technology. Foursquare, one of the most popular location sites, treats location-based micronetworking as a game: Users earn badges and special statuses based on their number of visits to particular locations. Users can write and read short reviews and tips about businesses, organize meet-ups, and see which Foursquare-using friends are nearby. Foursquare updates can also be posted to linked Twitter and Facebook accounts for followers and friends to see. Location sites such as Foursquare are particularly useful social marketing tools for local businesses, especially when combined with sales promotions like coupons, special offers, contests, and events. Location sites can be harnessed to forge lasting relationships with and deeply engrained loyalty in customers.[35] For example, a local restaurant can allow consumers to check in on Foursquare using their Smartphones and receive coupons for that day's purchases. Since the location site technology is relatively new, many brands are still figuring out how best to utilize Foursquare. Facebook added Places to capitalize on this location-based technology, which allows

people to "check in" and share their location with their online friends. It will be interesting to see how use of this technology grows over time.

18-5g Review Sites

Individuals tend to trust other people's opinions when it comes to purchasing. According to Nielsen Media Research, more than 70 percent of consumers said that they trusted online consumer opinions. This percentage is much higher than that of consumers who trust traditional advertising. Based on the early work of Amazon.com and eBay to integrate user opinions into product and seller pages, countless Web sites allowing users to voice their opinions have sprung up across every segment of the Internet market. **Review sites** allow consumers to post, read, rate, and comment on opinions regarding all kinds of products and services. For example, Yelp, the most active local review directory on the Web, combines customer critiques of local businesses with business information and elements of social networking to create an engaging, informative experience. On Yelp, users scrutinize local restaurants, fitness centers, tattoo parlors, and other businesses, each of which has a detailed profile page. Business owners and representatives can edit their organizations' pages and respond to Yelp reviews both privately and publicly. Yelp even rewards its most popular (and prolific) reviewers by awarding them

© Handout/MCT/Newscom

Elite status. Businesses will throw Elite-only parties to allow these esteemed Yelpers to try out their restaurant, hoping to receive a favorable review.[36] By giving marketers the opportunity to respond to their customers directly and put their businesses in a positive light, review sites certainly serve as useful tools for local and national businesses.

18-5h Virtual Worlds and Online Gaming

Virtual worlds and online gaming present additional opportunities for marketers to engage with consumers. These include massive multiplayer online games (MMOGs) such as *World of Warcraft* and *The Sims Online* as well as online communities (or virtual worlds) such as Second Life, Poptropica, and Habbo Hotel. Consultancy firm KZero Worldwide reported that almost 800 million people participate in some sort of virtual world experience, and the sector's annual revenue approaches $1 billion. Some of the most popular games are on Facebook—such as Mafia Wars and FarmVille. Angry Birds was another popular addition to gaming as was Words with Friends. Much of this revenue has come from in-game advertising—virtual world environments are often fertile grounds for branded content. Several businesses have developed profitable trade presences in Second Life. IBM has used its Second Life space to hold virtual conferences with more than 200 participants.[37] Other organizations, such as the Centers for Disease Control and Prevention and the American Cancer Society, have held their own virtual events in Second Life. Although virtual worlds are unfamiliar to and even intimidating for many traditional marketers, the field is an important, viable, and growing consideration for social media marketing.

One area of growth is social gaming. Nearly 25 percent of people play games within social networking sites like Facebook or on mobile devices like the iPhone. Interestingly, the typical player is a forty-three-year-old woman with a full-time job and college education. Women are most likely to play with real-world friends or relatives as opposed to strangers. Most play multiple times per week, and more than 30 percent play daily. Facebook is by far the largest social network for gaming, though hi5 is hoping to win over more users with its large variety of games. The top five games on Facebook are FarmVille, Bejeweled Blitz, Texas HoldEm Poker, Café World, and Mafia Wars. Many play on mobile devices (and the demographic usually

© Gustavo Arias R./La Nacion de Costa Rica/Newscom

skews younger). Angry Birds sucks in users for 200 million minutes per day, and Zynga's CityVille entices more than 100 million people a month. These games are attractive because they can be played in just five minutes, perhaps while waiting for the train.[38] A growing trend among mobile games is to use mobile ads to generate revenue for the game-makers. As long as the ads are not overly intrusive, most users opt to play the free game with ads over the paid version that doesn't have ads. For example, Angry Birds earns an estimated $1 million a month from in-game ads.[39]

Another popular type of online gaming targets a different group—MMOGs target eighteen- to thirty-four-year-old males. In these environments, thousands of people play simultaneously, and the games have revenues of more than $400 billion annually. Regardless of the type of experience, brands must be creative in how they integrate into games. Social and real-world-like titles are the most appropriate for marketing and advertising (as opposed to fantasy games), and promotions typically include special events, competitions, and sweepstakes. In some games (like *The Sims*), having ads increases the authenticity. For example, Nike offers shoes in *The Sims Online* that allow the player to run faster.

18-6 SOCIAL MEDIA AND MOBILE TECHNOLOGY

While much of the excitement in social media has been based on Web sites and new technology uses, much of the growth lies in new platforms. These platforms include the multitude of Smartphones like iPhones and BlackBerry devices as well as netbooks and iPads. The major implication of this development is that consumers now can access popular Web sites like Facebook, Mashable, Twitter, and Foursquare from all their various platforms.

18-6a Mobile and Smartphone Technology

Worldwide, there are almost 5 billion mobile phones in use, more than 25 percent of which are Smartphones and 75 percent of which can receive text messages.[40] It is no surprise then that the mobile platform is such an effective marketing tool—especially when targeting a younger audience. Smartphones up the ante by allowing individuals to do nearly everything they can do with a computer—from anywhere. With a Smartphone in hand, reading a blog, writing an e-mail, scheduling a meeting, posting to Facebook, playing a multiplayer game, watching a video, taking a picture, using GPS, and surfing the Internet might all occur during one ten-minute car ride. Smartphone technology, often considered the crowning achievement in digital convergence and social media integration, has opened the door to modern mobile advertising as a viable marketing strategy.

According to an eMarketer survey, U.S. mobile marketing spending reached nearly $593 million in 2010 and is expected to grow. There are several reasons for the recent popularity of mobile marketing. First, an effort to standardize mobile platforms has resulted in a low barrier to entry. Second, especially given mobile marketing's younger audiences, there are more consumers than ever acclimating to once-worrisome privacy and pricing policies. Third, because most consumers carry their Smartphones with them at all times, mobile marketing is uniquely effective at garnering consumer attention in real time. Fourth, mobile marketing is measurable: Metrics and usage statistics make it an effective tool for gaining insight into consumer behavior. Finally, mobile marketing's response rate is higher than that of traditional media types like print and broadcast advertisement. Some common mobile marketing tools include:

▶ **SMS (SHORT MESSAGE SERVICE):** 160-character text messages sent to and from cell phones. SMS is typically integrated with other tools.

▶ **MMS (MULTIMEDIA MESSAGING SERVICE):** Similar to SMS but allows the attachment of images, videos, ringtones, and other multimedia to text messages.

▶ **MOBILE WEB SITES (MOBI AND WAP WEB SITES):** Web sites designed specifically for viewing and navigation on mobile devices.

▶ **MOBILE ADS:** Visual advertisements integrated into text messages, applications, and mobile Web sites. Mobile ads are often sold on a cost-per-click basis.

▶ **BLUETOOTH MARKETING:** A signal is sent to Bluetooth-enabled devices, which allows marketers to send targeted messages to users based on their geographic locations.

▶ **SMARTPHONE APPLICATIONS (APPS):** Software designed specifically for mobile and tablet devices. These apps include software to turn phones into scanners for various types of bar codes.

Mobile marketing is also powerful when combined with geo-location platforms such as Foursquare where people can "check in" to places and receive benefits and special offers. A popular application of Smartphone convenience and technology is a "quick response" (QR) code. When scanned by a Smartphone's QR reader, a QR code takes the user to a specific site with content about or a discount for products or services. Uses range from donating to a charity by scanning the code to simply checking out the company's Web site for more information. For example, Modify Watches offers a watch face with no hands. Instead it has a QR code that, when scanned, shows the correct time.[41] Another Smartphone trend is called "near field communication" (NFC), which uses small chips hidden in or behind products that, when touched by compatible devices, will transfer the information on the chip to the device. Barnes & Noble is hoping to work with publishers to ship hardcover books containing NFC chips to Barnes & Noble stores. The chips will be embedded with editorial reviews about that book from BN.com. When a NOOK user touches the hardcover with her NOOK, the book reviews will display on her tablet, helping her make a purchase decision.[42]

18-6b Applications and Widgets

Given the widespread adoption of Apple's iPhone, RIM's BlackBerry line, Android-based phones, and other Smartphones, it's no surprise that millions of applications have been developed for the mobile market. Dozens of new and unique apps that harness mobile technology are added to mobile marketplaces every day. While many apps perform platform-specific tasks, others convert existing content into a mobile-ready format. Whether offering new or existing content, when an app is well branded and integrated into a company's overall marketing strategy, it can create buzz and generate customer engagement.

Web widgets, also known as gadgets and badges, are software applications that run entirely within existing online platforms. Essentially, a Web widget allows a developer to embed a simple application such as a weather forecast, horoscope, or stock market ticker into a Web site, even if the developer did not write (or does not understand) the application's source code. From a marketing perspective, widgets allow customers to display company information (such as current promotions, coupons, or news) on their own Web sites. Widgets are often cheaper than apps to develop, can extend an organization's reach beyond existing platforms, will broaden the listening system, and can make an organization easier to find.[43]

Allowing customers to promote up-to-date marketing material on their own blogs and Web sites is very appealing, but before investing in a marketing-oriented widget, a number of questions should be considered:

» **Does my organization regularly publish compelling content, such as news, daily specials, or coupons, on its Web site or blog?**

» **Does my content engage individuals or appeal to their needs as customers?**

» **Is my content likely to inspire conversations with the company or with other customers? Will customers want to share my content with others?**

If you can answer yes to these questions, a widget may be an effective tool for your organization.

18-7 THE SOCIAL MEDIA PLAN

In order to effectively use the tools in the social media toolbox it is important to have a clearly outlined social media plan. The social media plan is linked to larger plans such as a promotional plan or marketing plan and should fit appropriately into the objectives and steps in those plans (for more information, review Chapters 2 and 16). It is important to research throughout the development of the social media plan in order to keep abreast of the rapidly changing social media world. There are six stages involved in creating an effective social media plan:

1. **THE LISTENING STAGE:** This is covered in more detail in section 18-2a.

2. **SET SOCIAL MEDIA OBJECTIVES:** Set objectives that can be specifically accomplished through social media, with special attention to how to measure the results. There are numerous metrics available, some of which are mentioned throughout the chapter.

3. **DEFINE STRATEGIES:** This includes examining trends and best practices in the industry.

4. **IDENTIFY THE TARGET AUDIENCE:** This should line up with the target market defined in the marketing plan, but in the social media plan, pay special attention to how that audience participates and behaves online.

5. **SELECT THE TOOLS AND PLATFORMS:** Based on the result of step 4, choose the social media tools and platforms that will be most relevant. These choices are based on the knowledge of where the target audience participates on social media.

6. **IMPLEMENT AND MONITOR THE STRATEGY:** Social media campaigns can be fluid, so it is important to keep a close eye on what is successful and what isn't. Based on the observations, make changes as needed. It becomes important, therefore, to go back to the listening stage to interpret how consumers are perceiving the social media campaign.

Listening to customers and industry trends, as well as continually revising the social media plan to meet the needs of the changing social media market are keys to successful social media marketing. There are numerous industry leaders sharing some of their best practices, and sources such as *Fast Company* and the *Wall Street Journal* report regularly on how

Exhibit 18.3

SOCIAL MEDIA TRENDS

Trend	Change	Where Is It Now?
Facebook	Threaded commenting, up/down voting comments.	
Twitter	Promoted tweets.	
Facebook/Bing	Facebook-linked searching in Bing. Search pulls information from your profile to find more accurate information.	
Foursquare/Facebook Places/location-based applications	Facebook Places, Foursquare gaining popularity away from major cities.	
Google+	Just released, claimed by some to be a Facebook killer.	
Key Ring, CardStar, Google Wallet	Eliminate plastic loyalty cards and use Smartphones as a single digital repository for loyalty cards, credit cards, and other scannable or swipeable cards typically found in a wallet.	
Stickybits, Bakodo	Ability to use barcode scanner on a Smartphone and QR code check-ins.	
Groupon, LivingSocial, Woot, and programs by Yelp, Zagat, and Open Table	Mainstream of the deal-a-day, social coupon trend.	

large and small companies are successfully using social media to gain market share and sales. A good example of using social media strategies is Hubspot, which is a company that practices what it preaches. It preaches the benefits of building valuable content online and then using social media to pull customers to its Web site. Social engine profiles have increased HubSpot's Web site traffic, which has made its lead generation program much more effective.

18-7a The Changing World of Social Media

As you read through the chapter, some of the trends that are noted may already seem ancient to you. The rate of change in social media is astounding—usage statistics change daily for sites like Facebook and Twitter. Some things that are in the rumor mill as we write this may have exploded in popularity; others may have fizzled out without even appearing on your radar. In Exhibit 18.3, we've listed some of the items that seem to be on the brink of exploding on to the social media scene. Take a moment to fill in the current state of each in the third column. Have you heard of it? Has it come and gone? Maybe it is still rumored, or maybe it has petered out. This exercise highlights not only the speed with which social media change but also the importance of keeping tabs on rumors. Doing so may result in a competitive advantage by being able to understand and invest in the next big social media site.

STUDY TOOLS **18**

↑ LOCATED AT BACK OF THE TEXTBOOK

☐ *Rip out Chapter Review Card*

LOCATED AT WWW.CENGAGE.COM/LOGIN

☐ *Review Key Terms Flashcards (print or online)*

☐ *Download audio and visual summaries to review on the go*

☐ *Complete both Practice Quizzes to prepare for tests*

☐ *Play "Beat the Clock" and "Quizbowl" to master concepts*

☐ *Complete "Crossword Puzzle" to review key terms*

☐ *Watch Video on "Zappos" for a real company example*

19-1 THE IMPORTANCE OF PRICE

Price means one thing to the consumer and something else to the seller. To the consumer, it is the cost of something. To the seller, price is revenue—the primary source of profits. In the broadest sense, price allocates resources in a free-market economy. Marketing managers are frequently challenged by the task of price setting. Yet over the past two decades, managers have learned that meeting the challenge of setting the right price can have a significant impact on the firm's bottom line. Large organizations that successfully manage prices do so by creating a pricing infrastructure within the company. This means defining pricing goals, searching for ways to create greater customer value, assigning authority and responsibility for pricing decisions, and creating tools and systems to continually improve pricing decisions. Obtaining pricing excellence is a very worthwhile activity: a 1 percent improvement in the average price of goods and services leads to an 8.7 percent increase in net profits for the typical Global 1200 company.[1] The Global 1200 are the world's 1,200 largest public companies.

> Trying to set the right price is one of the most stressful and pressure-filled tasks of the marketing manager.

price that which is given up in an exchange to acquire a good or service

19-1a What Is Price?

Price is that which is given up in an exchange to acquire a good or service. Price plays two roles in the evaluation of product alternatives: as a measure of sacrifice and as an information cue. To some degree, these are two opposing effects.[2]

THE SACRIFICE EFFECT OF PRICE Price is, again, "that which is given up," which means what is sacrificed to get a good or service. In the United States, the sacrifice is usually money, but it can be other things as well. It may also be time lost while waiting

Pricing Concepts

After you finish this chapter go to
p341 *for* **STUDY TOOLS** ⬚- - - - - →

© iStockphoto.com/Chris Pecoraro

revenue the price charged to customers multiplied by the number of units sold

profit revenue minus expenses

to acquire the good or service. Price might also include "lost dignity" for individuals who lose their jobs and must rely on charity.

THE INFORMATION EFFECT OF PRICE Consumers do not always choose the lowest-priced product in a category, such as shoes, cars, or wine, even when the products are otherwise similar. One explanation of this behavior, based upon research, is that we infer quality information from price.[3] That is, higher quality equals higher price. The information effect of price may also extend to favorable price perceptions by others because higher prices can convey the prominence and status of the purchaser to other people. Thus, both a Swatch and a Rolex can tell time accurately, but they convey different meanings. The price–quality relationship will be discussed later in the chapter.

VALUE IS BASED UPON PERCEIVED SATISFACTION

Consumers are interested in obtaining a "reasonable price." "Reasonable price" really means "perceived reasonable value" at the time of the transaction. The price paid is based on the satisfaction consumers *expect* to receive from a product and not necessarily the satisfaction they *actually* receive. Price can relate to anything with perceived value, not just money. When goods and services are exchanged, the trade is called *barter*.

19-1b The Importance of Price to Marketing Managers

As noted in the chapter introduction, prices are the key to revenues, which in turn are the key to profits for an organization. **Revenue** is the price charged to customers multiplied by the number of units sold. Revenue is what pays for every activity of the company: production, finance, sales, distribution, and so on. What's left over (if anything)

is **profit**. Managers usually strive to charge a price that will earn a fair profit.

Price × Units = Revenue

To earn a profit, managers must choose a price that is not too high or too low—a price that equals the perceived value to target consumers. If, in consumers' minds, a price is set too high, the perceived value will be less than the cost, and sale opportunities will be lost. Conversely, if a price is too low, the consumer may perceive it as a great value, but the firm loses revenue it could have earned.

Trying to set the right price is one of the most stressful and pressure-filled tasks of the marketing manager, as trends in the consumer market attest:

▸▸ **Confronting a flood of new products, potential buyers carefully evaluate the price of each one against the value of existing products.**

▸▸ **The increased availability of bargain-priced private and generic brands has put downward pressure on overall prices.**

▸▸ **Many firms are trying to maintain or regain their market share by cutting prices.**

▸▸ **The Internet has made comparison shopping easier.**

▸▸ **The United States was in a recession from late 2007 until 2009 and was still recovering very slowly in 2012.**

In the business market, buyers are also becoming more price sensitive and better informed. Computerized information systems enable organizational buyers to compare price and performance with great ease and accuracy. Improved communication and the increased use of direct marketing and computer-aided selling have also opened up many markets to new competitors. Finally, competition in general is increasing, so some installations, accessories, and component parts are being marketed like indistinguishable commodities.

© DuleS/Shutterstock.com

19-2 PRICING OBJECTIVES

To survive in today's highly competitive marketplace, companies need pricing objectives that are specific, attainable, and measurable. Realistic pricing goals then require periodic monitoring to determine the effectiveness of the company's strategy. For convenience, pricing objectives can be divided into three categories: profit oriented, sales oriented, and status quo.

19-2a Profit-Oriented Pricing Objectives

Profit-oriented objectives include profit maximization, satisfactory profits, and target return on investment.

PROFIT MAXIMIZATION *Profit maximization* means setting prices so that total revenue is as large as possible relative to total costs. Profit maximization does not always signify unreasonably high prices, however. Both price and profits depend on the type of competitive environment a firm faces, such as whether it is in a monopoly position (being the only seller) or in a much more competitive situation. Also, remember that a firm cannot charge a price higher than the product's perceived value. Many firms do not have the accounting data they need for maximizing profits.

Sometimes managers say that their company is trying to maximize profits—in other words, trying to make as much money as possible. Although this goal may sound impressive to stockholders, it is not good enough for planning.

In attempting to maximize profits, managers can try to expand revenue by increasing customer satisfaction, or they can attempt to reduce costs by operating more efficiently. A third possibility is to attempt to do both. Some companies may focus too much on cost reduction at the expense of the customer, or rely so heavily on customer satisfaction to increase revenue that costs creep up unnecessarily. However, a company can maintain or slightly cut costs while increasing customer loyalty through customer service initiatives, loyalty programs, and customer relationship management programs and allocating fewer resources to programs that are designed to improve efficiency and reduce costs. Both types of programs, of course, are critical to the success of the firm.

SATISFACTORY PROFITS Satisfactory profits are a reasonable level of profits. Rather than maximizing profits, many organizations strive for profits that are satisfactory to the stockholders and management—in other words, a level of profits consistent with the level of risk an organization faces. In a risky industry, a satisfactory profit may be 35 percent. In a low-risk industry, it might be 7 percent.

TARGET RETURN ON INVESTMENT The most common profit objective is a target **return on investment (ROI)**, sometimes called the firm's return on total assets. ROI measures management's overall effectiveness in generating profits with the available assets. The higher the

firm's ROI, the better off the firm is. Many companies use a target ROI as their main pricing goal. In summary, ROI is a percentage that puts a firm's profits into perspective by showing profits relative to investment.

Return on investment is calculated as follows:

$$\text{Return on investment} = \frac{\text{Net profits after taxes}}{\text{Total assets}}$$

Assume that in 2012 Johnson Controls had assets of $4.5 million, net profits of $550,000, and a target ROI of 10 percent. This was the actual ROI:

$$\text{ROI} = \frac{\$550,000}{\$4,500,000} = 12.2 \text{ percent}$$

As you can see, the ROI for Johnson Controls exceeded its target, which indicates that the company prospered in 2012.

Comparing the 12.2 percent ROI with the industry average provides a more meaningful picture, however. Any ROI needs to be evaluated in terms of the competitive environment, risks in the industry, and economic conditions. Generally speaking, firms seek ROIs in the 10 to 30 percent range. In some industries, such as the grocery industry, however, a return of under 5 percent is common and acceptable.

A company with a target ROI can predetermine its desired level of profitability. The marketing manager can use the standard, such as 10 percent ROI, to determine whether a particular price and marketing mix are feasible. In addition, however, the manager must weigh the risk of a given strategy even if the return is in the acceptable range.

19-2b Sales-Oriented Pricing Objectives

Sales-oriented pricing objectives are based either on market share or on dollar or unit sales.

return on investment (ROI) net profit after taxes divided by total assets

MARKET SHARE Market share is a company's product sales as a percentage of total sales for that industry. Sales can be reported in dollars or in units of product. It is very important to know whether market share is expressed in revenue or units because the results may be different. Consider four companies competing in an industry with 2,000 total unit sales and total industry revenue of $4,000 (see Exhibit 19.1). Company A has the largest unit market share at 50 percent, but it has only 25 percent of the revenue market share. In contrast, company D has only a 15 percent unit share but the largest revenue share: 30 percent. Usually, market share is expressed in terms of revenue and not units.

Many companies believe that maintaining or increasing market share is an indicator of the effectiveness of their marketing mix. Larger market shares have indeed often meant higher profits, thanks to greater economies of scale, market power, and ability to compensate top-quality management. Conventional wisdom also says that market share and ROI are strongly related. For the most part they are; however, many companies with low market share survive and even prosper. To succeed with a low market share, companies need to compete in industries with slow growth and few product changes—for instance, industrial supplies. Otherwise, they must vie in an industry that makes frequently bought items, such as consumer convenience goods.

The conventional wisdom about market share and profitability isn't always reliable, however. Because of extreme competition in some industries, many market share leaders either do not reach their target ROI or actually lose money. Procter & Gamble switched from market share to ROI objectives after realizing that profits don't automatically follow from a large market share.

Still, the struggle for market share can be all-consuming in certain industries. For example, competition in the laptop market forces companies to lower prices by working with manufacturers to cut costs and protect the decreasing profit margin. On the other hand, the more recent and growing tablet market allows companies to operate with less pressure on their profit margins, making it a more attractive market to enter.[4]

SALES MAXIMIZATION Rather than strive for market share, sometimes companies try to maximize sales. A firm with the objective of maximizing sales ignores profits, competition, and the marketing environment as long as sales are rising.

If a company is strapped for funds or faces an uncertain future, it may try to generate a maximum amount of cash in the short run. Management's task when using this objective is to calculate which price–quantity relationship generates the greatest cash revenue. Sales maximization can also be effectively used on a temporary basis to sell off excess inventory.

Maximization of cash should never be a long-run objective because cash maximization may mean little or no profitability.

19-2c Status Quo Pricing Objectives

Status quo pricing seeks to maintain existing prices or to meet the competition's prices. This third category of pricing objectives has the major advantage of requiring little planning. It is essentially a passive policy.

Often firms competing in an industry with an established price leader simply meet the competition's prices. These industries typically have fewer price wars than those with direct price competition. In other cases, managers regularly shop competitors' stores to ensure that their prices are comparable.

Status quo pricing often leads to suboptimal pricing. This occurs because the strategy ignores customers' perceived value of both the

Exhibit 19.1
TWO WAYS TO MEASURE MARKET SHARE (UNITS AND REVENUE)

Company	Units Sold	Unit Price	Total Revenue	Unit Market Share	Revenue Market Share
A	1,000	$1.00	$1,000	50	25
B	200	4.00	800	10	20
C	500	2.00	1,000	25	25
D	300	4.00	1,200	15	30
Total	2,000		$4,000		

© Cengage Learning

firm's goods or services and those offered by its competitors. Status quo pricing also ignores demand and costs. Although the policy is simple to implement, it can lead to a pricing disaster.

19-3 THE DEMAND DETERMINANT OF PRICE

After marketing managers establish pricing goals, they must set specific prices to reach those goals. The price they set for each product depends mostly on two factors: the demand for the good or service and the cost to the seller for that good or service. When pricing goals are mainly sales oriented, demand considerations usually dominate. Other factors, such as distribution and promotion strategies, perceived quality, needs of large customers, the Internet, and the stage of the product life cycle, can also influence price.

19-3a The Nature of Demand

Demand is the quantity of a product that will be sold in the market at various prices for a specified period. The quantity of a product that people will buy depends on its price. The higher the price, the fewer goods or services consumers will demand. Conversely, the lower the price, the more goods or services they will demand.

This trend is illustrated in the graph in Exhibit 19.2a, which shows the demand per week for gourmet cookies at a local retailer at various prices. This graph is called a *demand curve*. The vertical axis of the graph shows different prices of gourmet cookies, measured in dollars per package. The horizontal axis measures the quantity of gourmet cookies that will be demanded per week at each price. For example, at a price of $2.50, 50 packages will be sold per week; at $1.00, consumers will demand 120 packages—as the *demand schedule* (Exhibit 19.2b) shows.

Notice how the demand curve slopes downward and to the right, which indicates that more gourmet cookies are demanded as the price is lowered. In other words, if cookie manufacturers put a greater quantity on the market, then their hope of selling all of it will be realized only by selling it at a lower price. One reason more is sold at lower prices than at higher prices is that lower prices bring in new buyers. With each reduction in price, existing customers may also buy more.

Supply is the quantity of a product that will be offered to the market by a supplier or suppliers at various prices for a specified period. The graph in Exhibit 19.3a on the next page illustrates the

Exhibit 19.2

DEMAND CURVE AND DEMAND SCHEDULE FOR GOURMET COOKIES

(a) Demand curve

(b) Demand schedule

Price per package of gourmet cookies ($)	Packages of gourmet cookies demanded per week
3.00	35
2.50	50
2.00	65
1.50	85
1.00	120

© Miguel Angel Salinas Salinas/Shutterstock.com / © iStockphoto.com/AndyL

© Cengage Learning

price equilibrium
the price at which demand and
supply are equal

resulting *supply curve* for gourmet cookies. Unlike the falling demand curve, the supply curve for gourmet cookies slopes upward and to the right. At higher prices, gourmet cookie manufacturers will obtain more resources (flour, eggs, chocolate) and produce more gourmet cookies. If the price consumers are willing to pay for gourmet cookies increases, producers can afford to buy more ingredients.

Output tends to increase at higher prices because manufacturers can sell more cookies and earn greater profits. The *supply schedule* in Exhibit 19.3b shows that at $2, suppliers are willing to place 110 packages of gourmet cookies on the market, but they will offer 140 packages at a price of $3.

19-3b How Demand and Supply Establish Prices

At this point, combine the concepts of demand and supply to see how competitive market prices are determined. So far, the premise is that if the price is X, then consumers will purchase Y amount of gourmet cookies. The demand curve cannot predict consumption, nor can the supply curve alone forecast production. Instead, we need to look at what happens when supply and demand interact—as shown in Exhibit 19.4.

At a price of $3, the public would demand only 35 packages of gourmet cookies. However, suppliers stand ready to place 140 packages on the market at this price (data from the demand and supply schedules). If they do, they would create a surplus of 105 packages of gourmet cookies. How does a merchant eliminate a surplus? She lowers the price.

At a price of $1.00, 120 packages would be demanded, but only 25 would be placed on the market. A shortage of 95 units would be created. If a product is in short supply and consumers want it, how do they entice the dealer to part with one unit? They offer more money—that is, pay a higher price.

Now let's examine a price of $1.50. At this price, 85 packages are demanded and 85 are supplied. When

Exhibit 19.3

SUPPLY CURVE AND SUPPLY SCHEDULE FOR GOURMET COOKIES

(a) Supply curve

(b) Supply schedule

Price per package of gourmet cookies ($)	Packages of gourmet cookies supplied per week
3.00	140
2.50	130
2.00	110
1.50	85
1.00	25

© Cengage Learning

Exhibit 19.4

EQUILIBRIUM PRICE FOR GOURMET COOKIES

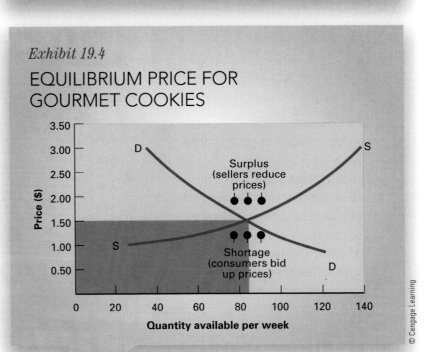

© Cengage Learning

demand and supply are equal, a state called **price equilibrium** is achieved. A temporary price below equilibrium—say, $1.00—results in a shortage because at that price the demand for gourmet cookies is greater than the available supply. Shortages put upward pressure on price. As long as demand and supply remain the same, however, temporary price increases or decreases tend to return to equilibrium. At equilibrium, there is no inclination for prices to rise or fall.

Prices may fluctuate during a trial-and-error period as the market for a good or service moves toward equilibrium. Sooner or later, however, demand and supply will settle into proper balance.

19-3c Elasticity of Demand

To appreciate demand analysis, you should understand the concept of elasticity. **Elasticity of demand** refers to consumers' responsiveness or sensitivity to changes in price. **Elastic demand** is a situation in which consumer demand is sensitive to price changes. Conversely, **inelastic demand** means that an increase or a decrease in price will not significantly affect demand for the product.

Elasticity over the range of a demand curve can be measured by using this formula:

$$\text{Elasticity } (E) = \frac{\text{Percentage change in quantity demanded of good A}}{\text{Percentage change in price of good A}}$$

If E is greater than 1, demand is elastic.

If E is less than 1, demand is inelastic.

If E is equal to 1, demand is unitary.

Unitary elasticity means that an increase in sales exactly offsets a decrease in prices, so total revenue remains the same.

Elasticity can be measured by observing these changes in total revenue:

▸▸ **If price goes down and revenue goes up, demand is elastic.**

▸▸ **If price goes down and revenue goes down, demand is inelastic.**

▸▸ **If price goes up and revenue goes up, demand is inelastic.**

▸▸ **If price goes up and revenue goes down, demand is elastic.**

▸▸ **If price goes up or down and revenue stays the same, elasticity is unitary.**

> **elasticity of demand** consumers' responsiveness or sensitivity to changes in price
>
> **elastic demand** a situation in which consumer demand is sensitive to changes in price
>
> **inelastic demand** a situation in which an increase or a decrease in price will not significantly affect demand for the product
>
> **unitary elasticity** a situation in which total revenue remains the same when prices change

SUPPLY AND DEMAND— THE MILK MARKET

Milk graces many tables in many households across America. But the 5 percent of milk buyers who purchase organic milk are struggling with increased milk prices. Organic milk has increased up to 50 cents a half-gallon due to grain shortages. As farmers battle to buy the ever-more-expensive grain to feed their cattle, the cost increase transfers to the final milk product. Non-organic milk went through a similar price surge in 2011, but those prices adjust more quickly due to federal pricing rules. The organic milk industry is not tied to the same rules, so costs change more slowly based on feed prices, demand, and supplier contracts. The largest organic milk companies, Organic Valley and Dean's Horizon Organic, are combating the rising feed costs by rationing milk to grocery stores. Prices increase further—an additional 26 cents per gallon—as the supply begins to drop below demand. Some farmers, however, are worried that the price hikes will slow demand and force prices to drop further as grain continues to rise in price. Regardless, the complex ecosystem of both customer and supplier demand has worked to pull organic milk prices near $5 for a half-gallon in New York City, a price that Horizon Organic Milk executives say is not dropping anytime soon.

Source: Scott Killman, "Organic Milk Prices Are Pulled Higher on Tug of Supply-Demand Fundamentals," *Wall Street Journal*, February 18–19, 2012, B4.

© smit/Shutterstock.com / © iStockphoto.com/Bill Noll

The demand curve for Sony DVD players is very elastic. Decreasing the price of one of these players from $300 to $200 increases sales from 18,000 units to 59,000 units. Revenue increases from $5.4 million ($300 x 18,000) to $11.8 million ($200 x 59,000). The price decrease results in a large increase in sales and revenue.

INELASTIC DEMAND When price and total revenue fall, demand is inelastic. When demand is inelastic, sellers can raise prices and increase total revenue. Often, items that are relatively inexpensive but convenient tend to have inelastic demand. Crops such as wheat, soybeans, and corn have inelastic demand. When there is a particularly productive year (as 2010 was in the United States), excess or bumper crops cause the prices of these crops to fall. But unless there is a drastic change in consumption rates, consumers won't readily buy greater amounts of grain, so revenue decreases with the price of the crops. If there is a crop shortage, prices escalate, but consumers still maintain the same level of demand because food is a necessity, and they will continue to purchase the more expensive crop.[5]

ELASTIC DEMAND In the previous example of Sony DVD players, when the price is dropped from $300 to $200, total revenue increases by $6.4 million ($11.8 million minus $5.4 million). An increase in total revenue when price falls indicates that demand is elastic. Let's measure Sony's elasticity of demand when the price drops from $300 to $200 by applying the formula presented earlier:

$$E = \frac{\text{Change in quantity/(Sum of quantities/2)}}{\text{Change in price/(Sum of prices/2)}}$$

$$E = \frac{(59,000 - 18,000)/[(59,000 + 18,000)/2]}{(\$300 - \$200)/[(\$300 + \$200)/2]}$$

$$E = \frac{41,000/38,500}{\$100/\$250}$$

$$E = \frac{1.065}{.4} = 2.66$$

Because E is greater than 1, demand is elastic.

FACTORS THAT AFFECT ELASTICITY Several factors affect elasticity of demand, including the following:

▸▸ **AVAILABILITY OF SUBSTITUTES:** When many substitute products are available, the consumer can easily switch from one product to another, making demand elastic. The same

is true in reverse: A person with complete renal failure will pay whatever is charged for a kidney transplant because there is no substitute.

▸▸ **PRICE RELATIVE TO PURCHASING POWER:** If a price is so low that it is an inconsequential part of an individual's budget, demand will be inelastic.

▸▸ **PRODUCT DURABILITY:** Consumers often have the option of repairing durable products rather than replacing them, thus prolonging their useful life. In other words, people are sensitive to the price increase, and demand is elastic.

▸▸ **A PRODUCT'S OTHER USES:** The greater the number of different uses for a product, the more elastic demand tends to be. If a product has only one use, as may be true of a new medicine, the quantity purchased probably will not vary as price varies. A person will consume only the prescribed quantity, regardless of price. On the other hand, a product like steel has many possible applications. As its price falls, steel becomes more economically feasible in a wider variety of applications, thereby making demand relatively elastic.

▸▸ **RATE OF INFLATION:** Recent research has found that when a country's inflation rate (the rate at which the price level is rising) is high, demand becomes more elastic. In other words, rising price levels make consumers more price sensitive. During inflationary periods, consumers base their timing (when to buy) and quantity decisions on price promotions. This suggests that a brand gains additional sales or market share if the product is effectively promoted or if the marketing manager keeps the brand's price increases low relative to the inflation rate.[6]

Examples of both elastic and inelastic demand abound in everyday life. Recently, fans balked at high prices for concerts. Promoters lost money and some shows, including some by artists Christina Aguilera and Marc Anthony, were canceled. This is price elasticity in action. On the other hand, demand for some tickets was highly inelastic. The Rolling Stones are still selling out concerts with tickets priced at up to $400.[7]

19-4 THE POWER OF YIELD MANAGEMENT SYSTEMS

When competitive pressures are high, a company must know when it can raise prices to maximize its revenues. More and more companies are turning to yield management systems, also known as revenue management systems, to help adjust prices. First developed in the airline industry, **yield management systems (YMS)** use complex mathematical software to profitably fill unused capacity. The software employs techniques such as discounting early purchases, limiting early sales at these discounted prices, and overbooking capacity. One of the key inputs in airlines' yield management systems is what has been the historical pattern of demand for a specific flight. Other service industries are now using YMS as well. Royal Caribbean Cruises, for example, uses its yield management system to adjust hundreds of prices through the course of a day.

Now YMS are spreading beyond service industries as their popularity increases. The lessons of airlines and hotels aren't entirely applicable to other industries, however, because plane seats and hotel beds are perishable—if they go empty, the revenue opportunity is lost forever. So it makes sense to slash prices to move toward capacity if it's possible to do so without reducing the prices that other customers pay. Cars and steel aren't so perishable, but the capacity to make them is. An underused factory is a lost revenue opportunity. So it makes sense to cut prices to use up capacity if it's possible to do so while getting other customers to pay full price.

Pharmacy chain Duane Reade uses DemandTec's algorithms to determine prices for two-thirds of the items it sells. For example, the software analyzed historical data and suggested a new system for pricing diapers. Now the price is related to the wearer's age. Diapers for infants are more expensive than those for toddlers. Since the system was instituted, diaper sales have increased so much that baby care revenues are up by 27 percent.[8]

19-5 THE COST DETERMINANT OF PRICE

Sometimes companies minimize or ignore the importance of demand and decide to price their products largely or solely on the basis of costs. Prices determined strictly on the basis of costs may be too high for the target market, thereby reducing or eliminating sales. On the other hand, cost-based prices may be too low, causing the firm to earn a lower return than it should. Nevertheless, costs should generally be part of any price determination, if only as a floor below which a good or service must not be priced in the long run.

The idea of cost may seem simple, but it is actually a multifaceted concept, especially for producers of goods and services. A **variable cost** is a cost that varies with changes in the level of output; an example of a variable cost is the cost of materials. In contrast, a **fixed cost** does not change as output is increased or decreased. Examples include rent and executives' salaries.

To compare the cost of production to the selling price of a product, it is helpful to calculate costs per unit, or average costs. **Average variable cost (AVC)** equals total variable costs divided by quantity of output. **Average total cost (ATC)** equals total costs divided by output. As the graph in Exhibit 19.5a on the next page shows, AVC and ATC are basically U-shaped curves. In contrast, average fixed cost (AFC) declines continually as output increases because total fixed costs are constant.

Marginal cost (MC) is the change in total costs associated with a one-unit change in output. Exhibit 19.5b shows that when output rises from seven to eight units, the change in total cost is from $640 to $750; therefore, MC is $110.

yield management systems (YMS) a technique for adjusting prices that uses complex mathematical software to profitably fill unused capacity by discounting early purchases, limiting early sales at these discounted prices, and overbooking capacity

variable cost a cost that varies with changes in the level of output

fixed cost a cost that does not change as output is increased or decreased

average variable cost (AVC) total variable costs divided by quantity of output

average total cost (ATC) total costs divided by quantity of output

marginal cost (MC) the change in total costs associated with a one-unit change in output

All the curves illustrated in Exhibit 19.5a have definite relationships:

▸▸ **AVC plus AFC equals ATC.**

▸▸ **MC falls for a while and then turns upward, in this case with the fourth unit. At that point, diminishing returns set in, meaning that less output is produced for every additional dollar spent on variable input.**

▸▸ **MC intersects both AVC and ATC at their lowest possible points.**

▸▸ **When MC is less than AVC or ATC, the incremental cost will continue to pull the averages down. Conversely, when MC is greater than AVC or ATC, it pulls the averages up, and ATC and AVC begin to rise.**

▸▸ **The minimum point on the ATC curve is the least cost point for a fixed-capacity firm, although it is not necessarily the most profitable point.**

Costs can be used to set prices in a variety of ways. Markup pricing

Exhibit 19.5

HYPOTHETICAL SET OF COST CURVES AND A COST SCHEDULE

(a) Cost curves

(b) Cost schedule

	Total-cost data, per week			Average-cost data, per week			
(1) Total product (Q)	**(2)** Total fixed cost (TFC)	**(3)** Total variable cost (TVC)	**(4)** Total cost (TC)	**(5)** Average fixed cost (AFC)	**(6)** Average variable cost (AVC)	**(7)** Average total cost (ATC)	**(8)** Marginal cost (MC)
			$TC = TFC + TVC$	$AFC = \dfrac{TFC}{Q}$	$AVC = \dfrac{TVC}{Q}$	$ATC = \dfrac{TC}{Q}$	$MC = \dfrac{\text{change in TC}}{\text{change in Q}}$
0	$100	$ 0	$ 100	—	—	—	—
1	100	90	190	$100.00	$90.00	$190.00	$ 90
2	100	170	270	50.00	85.00	135.00	80
3	100	240	340	33.33	80.00	113.33	70
4	100	300	400	25.00	75.00	100.00	60
5	100	370	470	20.00	74.00	94.00	70
6	100	450	550	16.67	75.00	91.67	80
7	100	540	640	14.29	77.14	91.43	90
8	100	650	750	12.50	81.25	93.75	110
9	100	780	880	11.11	86.67	97.78	130
10	100	930	1,030	10.00	93.00	103.00	150

is relatively simple. Profit maximization pricing and break-even pricing make use of the more complicated concepts of cost.

19-5a Markup Pricing

Markup pricing, the most popular method used by wholesalers and retailers to establish a selling price, does not directly analyze the costs of production. Instead, **markup pricing** uses the cost of buying the product from the producer, plus amounts for profit and for expenses not otherwise accounted for. The total determines the selling price.

A retailer, for example, adds a certain percentage to the cost of the merchandise received to arrive at the retail price. An item that costs the retailer $1.80 and is sold for $2.20 carries a markup of 40 cents, which is a markup of 22 percent of the cost ($0.40 ÷ $1.80). Retailers tend to discuss markup in terms of its percentage of the retail price—in this example, 18 percent ($0.40 ÷ $2.20). The difference between the retailer's cost and the selling price (40 cents) is the gross margin.

The formula for calculating the retail price given a certain desired markup is as follows:

$$\text{Retail price} = \frac{\text{Cost}}{1 - \text{Desired return on sales}}$$

$$= \frac{\$1.80}{1.00 - 0.18}$$

$$= \$2.20$$

If the retailer wants a 30 percent return, then:

$$\text{Retail price} = \frac{\$1.80}{1.00 - 0.30}$$

$$= \$2.57$$

The reason that retailers and others speak of markups on selling price is that many important figures in financial reports, such as gross sales and revenues, are sales figures, not cost figures.

To use markup based on cost or selling price effectively, the marketing manager must calculate an adequate gross margin—the amount added to cost to determine price. The margin must ultimately provide adequate funds to cover selling expenses and profit. Once an appropriate margin has been determined, the markup technique has the major advantage of being easy to employ.

Markups are often based on experience. For example, many small retailers mark up merchandise 100 percent over cost. (In other words, they double the cost.) This tactic is called **keystoning**. Some other factors that influence markups are the merchandise's appeal to customers, past response to the markup (an implicit demand consideration), the item's promotional value, the seasonality of the goods, their fashion appeal, the product's traditional selling price, and competition. Most retailers avoid any set markup because of such considerations as promotional value and seasonality.

19-5b Profit Maximization Pricing

Producers tend to use more complicated methods of setting prices than distributors use. One is **profit maximization**, which occurs when marginal revenue equals MC. You learned earlier that MC is the change in total costs associated with a one-unit change in output. Similarly, **marginal revenue (MR)** is the extra revenue associated with selling an extra unit of output. As long as the revenue of the last unit produced and sold is greater than the cost of the last unit produced and sold, the firm should continue manufacturing and selling the product.

Exhibit 19.6 on the next page shows the MRs and MCs for a hypothetical firm, using the cost data from Exhibit 19.5b. The profit-maximizing quantity, where MR = MC, is six units. You might say, "If profit is zero, why produce the sixth unit? Why not stop at five?" In fact, you would be right. The firm, however, would not know that the fifth unit would produce zero profits until it determined that profits were no longer increasing. Economists suggest producing up to the point where MR = MC. If MR is just one penny greater than MC, it will still increase total profits.

19-5c Break-Even Pricing

Now let's take a closer look at the relationship between sales and cost. **Break-even analysis** determines what sales volume must be reached before the company breaks even (its total costs equal total revenue) and no profits are earned.

Exhibit 19.6

POINT OF PROFIT MAXIMIZATION

Quantity	Marginal Revenue	Marginal Cost	Cumulative Total Profit
0	—	—	—
1	$140	$ 90	$ 50
2	130	80	100
3	105	70	135
4	95	60	170
5	85	70	185
*6	80	80	185
7	75	90	170
8	60	110	120
9	50	130	40
10	40	150	(70)

*Profit maximization.

© Cengage Learning

The typical break-even model assumes a given fixed cost and a constant AVC. Suppose that Universal Sportswear, a hypothetical firm, has fixed costs of $2,000 and that the cost of labor and materials for each unit produced is 50 cents. Assume that it can sell up to 6,000 units of its product at $1 without having to lower its price.

Exhibit 19.7a illustrates Universal Sportswear's break-even point. As Exhibit 19.7b indicates, Universal Sportswear's total variable costs increase by 50 cents every time a new unit is produced, and total fixed costs remain constant at $2,000 regardless of the level of output. Therefore, for 4,000 units of output, Universal Sportswear has $2,000 in fixed costs and $2,000 in total variable costs (4,000 units x $0.50), or $4,000 in total costs.

Revenue is also $4,000 (4,000 units x $1), giving a net profit of zero dollars at the break-even point of 4,000 units. Notice that once the firm gets past the break-even point, the gap between total revenue and total costs gets wider and wider because both functions are assumed to be linear.

The formula for calculating break-even quantities is simple:

$$\text{Break-even quantity} = \frac{\text{Total fixed costs}}{\text{Fixed cost contribution}}$$

Fixed cost contribution is the price minus the AVC. Therefore, for Universal Sportswear,

$$\text{Break-even quantity} = \frac{\$2,000}{(\$1.00 - \$0.50)} = \frac{\$2,000}{\$0.50}$$

$$= 4,000 \text{ units}$$

The advantage of break-even analysis is that it provides a quick estimate of how much the firm must sell to break even and how much profit can be earned if a higher sales volume is obtained. If a firm is operating close to the break-even point, it may want to see what can be done to reduce costs or increase sales. Moreover, in a simple break-even analysis, it is not necessary to compute MCs and MRs because price and average cost per unit are assumed to be constant. Also, because accounting data for marginal cost and revenue are frequently unavailable, it is convenient not to have to depend on that information.

Break-even analysis is not without several important limitations. Sometimes it is hard to know whether a cost is fixed or variable. If labor wins a tough guaranteed-employment contract, are the resulting expenses a fixed cost? More important than cost determination is the fact that simple break-even analysis ignores demand. How does Universal Sportswear know it can sell 4,000 units at $1? Could it sell the same 4,000 units at $2 or even $5? Obviously, this information would profoundly affect the firm's pricing decisions.

19-6 OTHER DETERMINANTS OF PRICE

Other factors besides demand and costs can influence price. For example, the stages in the product life cycle, the competition, the product distribution strategy, the promotion strategy, and the perceived quality can all affect pricing.

19-6a Stages in the Product Life Cycle

As a product moves through its life cycle (see Chapter 11), the demand for the product and the competitive conditions tend to change:

- ▸ **INTRODUCTORY STAGE:** Management usually sets prices high during the introductory stage. One reason is that it hopes to recover its development costs quickly. In addition, demand originates in the core of the market (the customers whose needs ideally match the product's attributes) and thus is relatively inelastic. On the other hand, if the target market is highly price sensitive, management often finds it better to price the product at the market level or lower.

- ▸ **GROWTH STAGE:** As the product enters the growth stage, prices generally begin to stabilize for several reasons. First, competitors have entered the market, increasing the available supply. Second, the product has begun to appeal to a broader market, often lower-income groups. Finally, economies of scale are lowering costs, and the savings can be passed on to the consumer in the form of lower prices.

Exhibit 19.7

COSTS, REVENUES, AND BREAK-EVEN POINT FOR UNIVERSAL SPORTSWEAR

(a) Break-even point

(b) Costs and revenues

Output	Total fixed costs	Average variable costs	Total variable costs	Average total costs	Average revenue (price)	Total revenue	Total costs	Profit or loss
500	$2,000	$0.50	$ 250	$4.50	$1.00	$ 500	$2,250	($1,750)
1,000	2,000	0.50	500	2.50	1.00	1,000	2,500	(1,500)
1,500	2,000	0.50	750	1.83	1.00	1,500	2,750	(1,250)
2,000	2,000	0.50	1,000	1.50	1.00	2,000	3,000	(1,000)
2,500	2,000	0.50	1,250	1.30	1.00	2,500	3,250	(750)
3,000	2,000	0.50	1,500	1.17	1.00	3,000	3,500	(500)
3,500	2,000	0.50	1,750	1.07	1.00	3,500	3,750	(250)
*4,000	2,000	0.50	2,000	1.00	1.00	4,000	4,000	0
4,500	2,000	0.50	2,250	0.94	1.00	4,500	4,250	250
5,000	2,000	0.50	2,500	0.90	1.00	5,000	4,500	500
5,500	2,000	0.50	2,750	0.86	1.00	5,500	4,750	750
6,000	2,000	0.50	3,000	0.83	1.00	6,000	5,000	1,000

*Break-even point

▸ **MATURITY STAGE:** Maturity usually brings further price decreases as competition increases and inefficient, high-cost firms are eliminated. Distribution channels become a significant cost factor, however, because of the need to offer wide product lines for highly segmented markets, extensive service requirements, and the sheer number of dealers necessary to absorb high-volume production. The manufacturers that remain in the market toward the end of the maturity stage typically offer similar prices. At this stage, price increases are usually cost initiated, not demand initiated. Nor do price reductions in the late phase of maturity stimulate much demand. Because demand is limited and producers have similar cost structures, the remaining competitors will probably match price reductions.

▸▸ **DECLINE STAGE:** The final stage of the life cycle may see further price decreases as the few remaining competitors try to salvage the last vestiges of demand. When only one firm is left in the market, prices begin to stabilize. In fact, prices may eventually rise dramatically if the product survives and moves into the specialty goods category, as horse-drawn carriages and vinyl records have.

New releases on *vinyl* can cost from $11 to $30, but rare or collectable records can cost hundreds of dollars!

19-6b The Competition

Competition varies during the product life cycle, of course, and so at times it may strongly affect pricing decisions. Although a firm may not have any competition at first, the high prices it charges may eventually induce another firm to enter the market.

Often, in hotly competitive markets, price wars break out. Amazon.com has been increasing its online presence by offering more than just books, looking to become the go-to online e-tailer. Walmart answered Amazon's expansion by selling its most anticipated hardcovers online for just $10 each (an average hardcover sells for about $25). Later that day, Amazon matched the price. The battle continued until the prices stabilized with books selling for $9 at Amazon, $8.99 at Target, and $8.98 at Walmart.[9] Such rabid debates over pricing of e-books caused Apple and the big six publishers to move to an agency model. In that model, the retailer receives 30 percent of the e-book selling price, and the publisher receives 70 percent of the sale. The major ramification of this model means that discounting books without a publisher's approval loses the retailer money, because it still has to pay the originally agreed-upon price. It also means that Amazon loses money on its aggressively discounted books.[10]

19-6c Distribution Strategy

An effective distribution network can often overcome other minor flaws in the marketing mix.[11] For example, although consumers may perceive a price as being slightly higher than normal, they may buy the product anyway if it is being sold at a convenient retail outlet.

Adequate distribution for a new product can often be attained by offering a larger-than-usual profit margin to distributors. A variation on this strategy is to give dealers a large trade allowance to help offset the costs of promotion and further stimulate demand at the retail level.

Manufacturers have gradually been losing control within the distribution channel to wholesalers and retailers, which often adopt pricing strategies that serve their own purposes. For instance, some distributors are **selling against the brand**: They place well-known brands on the shelves at high prices while offering other brands—typically, their private label brands, such as Kroger canned pears—at lower prices. Of course, sales of the higher-priced brands decline.

Wholesalers and retailers may also go outside traditional distribution channels to buy gray-market goods, as discussed in Chapter 13. Distributors obtain the goods through unauthorized channels for less than they would normally pay, so they can sell the goods

© iStockphoto.com/NoDerog

with a bigger-than-normal markup or at a reduced price. Imports seem to be particularly susceptible to gray marketing. Although consumers might pay less for gray-market goods, they often find that the manufacturer won't honor the warranty.

Manufacturers can regain some control over price by using an exclusive distribution system, by franchising, or by avoiding doing business with price-cutting discounters. Manufacturers can also package merchandise with the selling price marked on it or place goods on consignment. The best way for manufacturers to control prices, however, is to develop brand loyalty in consumers by delivering quality and value.

19-6d The Impact of the Internet and Extranets

The Internet, **extranets** (private electronic networks), and wireless setups are linking people, machines, and companies around the globe—and connecting sellers and buyers as never before. These links are enabling buyers to quickly and easily compare products and prices, putting them in a better bargaining position. At the same time, the technology allows sellers to collect detailed data about customers' buying habits, preferences, and even spending limits so that sellers can tailor their products and prices.

USING SHOPPING BOTS A shopping bot is a program that searches the Web for the best price for a particular item that you wish to purchase. *Bot* is short for *robot*. Shopping bots theoretically give pricing power to the consumer. The more information that the shopper has, the more efficient his or her purchase decision will be.

There are two general types of shopping bots. The first is the broad-based type that searches a wide range of product categories such as mySimon.com, DealTime.com, Bizrate.com, and Pricegrabber.com. These sites operate using a Yellow Pages type of model, in that they list every retailer they can find. The second is the niche-oriented type that searches for prices for only one type of product such as consumer electronics (CNET.com), books (BookFinder.com), or travel-related services (Kayak.com).[12]

Most shopping bots give preferential listings to those e-retailers that pay for the privilege. These so-called merchant partners receive about 60 percent of the click-throughs.[13] Typically, the bot lists its merchant partners first, not the retailer offering the lowest price.

INTERNET AUCTIONS The Internet auction business is huge. Among the most popular consumer auction sites are the following:

» **WWW.UBID.COM:** Offers a large range of product categories. "My page" consolidates all of the user's activity in one place.

» **WWW.EBAY.COM:** The most popular auction site.

» **WWW.BIDZ.COM:** Buys closeout deals in very large lots and offers them online in its no-reserve auctions.

Even though consumers are spending billions on Internet auctions, business-to-business auctions are likely to be the dominant form in the future. Recently, Whirlpool began holding online auctions. Participants bid on the price of the items that they would supply to Whirlpool but with a twist: They had to include the date when Whirlpool would have to pay for the items. The company wanted to see which suppliers would offer the longest grace period before requiring payment. Five auctions held over five months helped Whirlpool uncover savings of close to $2 million and more than doubled the grace period.

Whirlpool's success is a sign that the business-to-business auction world is shifting from haggling over prices to niggling over parameters of the deal. Warranties, delivery dates, transportation methods, customer support, financing options, and quality have all become bargaining chips.

19-6e Promotion Strategy

Price is often used as a promotional tool to increase consumer interest. Marketers at the Pittsburgh Zoo, for instance, have used a series of silly gimmicks to increase attendance. Some of the gimmicks for discounts include "friending" the zoo on Facebook or wearing a tie-dyed shirt. One day, the best mullet won a tour and runners-up earned a free haircut. And if you play along with these gimmicks, you get in to the zoo for $5.[14] The weekly flyers sent out by grocery stores in the Sunday newspaper advertise many products with special low prices.

extranet a private electronic network that links a company with its suppliers and customers

prestige pricing
charging a high price to help
promote a high-quality image

Pricing can be a tool for trade promotions as well. For example, Levi's Dockers (casual men's pants) are very popular. Sensing an opportunity, rival pants maker Bugle Boy began offering similar pants at cheaper wholesale prices, which gave retailers a bigger gross margin than they were getting with Dockers. Levi Strauss had to either lower prices or risk its $400 million annual Dockers sales. Although Levi Strauss intended its cheapest Dockers to retail for $35, it started selling Dockers to retailers for $18 a pair. Retailers could then advertise Dockers at a very attractive retail price of $25. Bugle Boy went out of business in 2001.

19-6f Demands of Large Customers

Manufacturers find that their large customers such as department stores often make specific pricing demands that the suppliers must agree to. Department stores are making greater-than-ever demands on their suppliers to cover the heavy discounts and markdowns on their own selling floors. They want suppliers to guarantee their stores' profit margins, and they insist on cash rebates if the guarantee isn't met. They are also exacting fines for violations of ticketing, packing, and shipping rules. Cumulatively, the demands are nearly wiping out profits for all but the very biggest suppliers, according to fashion designers and garment makers.

Walmart is one of the largest retailers in the world, and the company uses that size to encourage companies to meet its needs. When Walmart decided that its grocery department needed to have everyday low prices instead of periodic rollbacks, it talked to its major suppliers, such as ConAgra, General Mills, and McCormick & Co. to discuss the possibility of offering a consistently lower price to drive business. Some companies, like ConAgra, are struggling to lower costs while grain and other ingredients are steadily increasing in price. Other companies, like Kraft, have been steadily lowering costs and are having an easier time meeting Walmart's demands. The risk of not working with Walmart? Either your product is important enough to driving traffic that Walmart doesn't raise the product price (as happened to Clorox Bleach), or it raises prices and market share drops quickly.[15]

19-6g The Relationship of Price to Quality

As mentioned at the beginning of the chapter, when a purchase decision involves great uncertainty, consumers tend to rely on a high price as a predictor of good quality. Reliance on price as an indicator of quality seems to occur for all products, but it reveals itself more strongly for some items than for others, particularly items geared toward the wealthy.[16] Among the products that benefit from this phenomenon are coffee, aspirin, salt, floor wax, shampoo, clothing, furniture, whiskey, and many services. In the absence of other information, people typically assume that prices are higher because the products contain better materials, because they are made more carefully, or, in the case of professional services, because the provider has more expertise.

Research has found that products that are perceived to be of high quality tend to benefit more from price promotions than products perceived to be of lower quality.[17] However, when perceived high- and lower-quality products are offered in settings where consumers have difficulty making comparisons, then price promotions have an equal effect on sales. Comparisons are more difficult in end-of-aisle displays, feature advertising, and the like.

Knowledgeable merchants take these consumer attitudes into account when devising their pricing strategies. **Prestige pricing** is charging a high price to help promote a high-quality image. A successful prestige pricing strategy requires a retail price that is reasonably consistent with consumers' expectations. No one goes shopping at Gucci in New York and expects to pay $9.95 for a pair of loafers. In fact, demand would fall drastically at such a low price. In addition to prestige pricing, research has found

> People tend to *assume* that higher prices indicate that products contain better materials or are made more carefully.

© iStockphoto.com/Chris Lemmens

two other basic effects associated with the price-quality relationship: *hedonistic* and *allocative effects*.[18] High purchase prices may create feelings of pleasure and excitement associated with consuming higher-priced products. This is the hedonistic effect. Hedonistic consumption refers to pursuing emotional responses associated with using a product, such as pleasure, excitement, arousal, good feelings, and fun.

The allocative effect refers to the notion that consumers must allocate their budgets across alternative goods and services. The more you spend on one product, the less you have to spend on all others. Consumers sensitive to the allocative effects likely prefer low prices. However, managers must be aware that setting low prices or lowering prices with a discount may lower perceptions of product quality, prestige value, and hedonistic value. This is because of the negative cues associated with lower selling prices.[19]

Some companies, concerned about how counterfeits may affect their brands' images, are turning to high-end technology to combat increasingly professional counterfeit products. Companies such as Chanel and True Religion apparel (a high-end denim brand) are protecting their brands' prestige pricing and high-end names by using item-specific identification numbers (Chanel) and inserting security devices into seams in the product (True Religion). Both can be verified at official retailers, and Chanel recommends purchasing only through its Web site or official retailers to ensure authenticity. One company, Applied DNA Sciences, embeds botanical DNA in fibers in its client's products. Each brand receives unique DNA that can be identified under a special light.[20]

Some of the latest research on price–quality relationships has focused on consumer durable goods. The researchers first conducted a study to ascertain the dimensions of quality. These are (1) ease of use, (2) versatility (the ability of a product to perform more functions, or be more flexible), (3) durability, (4) serviceability (ease of obtaining quality repairs), (5) performance, and (6) prestige. The researchers found that when consumers focused on prestige and/or durability to assess quality, price was a strong indicator of perceived overall quality. Price was less important as an indicator of quality if the consumer was focusing on one of the other four dimensions of quality.[21]

STUDY TOOLS 19

↑ **LOCATED AT BACK OF THE TEXTBOOK**
☐ *Rip out Chapter Review Card*

LOCATED AT WWW.CENGAGE.COM/LOGIN
☐ *Review Key Terms Flashcards (print or online)*
☐ *Download audio and visual summaries to review on the go*
☐ *Complete both Practice Quizzes to prepare for tests*
☐ *Play "Beat the Clock" and "Quizbowl" to master concepts*
☐ *Complete "Crossword Puzzle" to review key terms*
☐ *Watch Video on "Ski Butternut" for a real company example*

HOW TO SET A PRICE ON A PRODUCT

Setting the right price on a product is a four-step process, illustrated in Exhibit 20.1 on page 344 and discussed throughout this chapter:

1. Establish pricing goals.

2. Estimate demand, costs, and profits.

3. Choose a price strategy to help determine a base price.

4. Fine-tune the base price with pricing tactics.

> All pricing objectives have trade-offs that managers must weigh.

20-1a Establish Pricing Goals

The first step in setting the right price is to establish pricing goals. Recall from Chapter 19 that pricing objectives fall into three categories: profit oriented, sales oriented, and status quo. These goals are derived from the firm's overall objectives. A good understanding of the marketplace and of the consumer can sometimes tell a manager very quickly whether a goal is realistic.

All pricing objectives have trade-offs that managers must weigh. A profit maximization objective may require a bigger initial investment than the firm can commit to or wants to commit to. Reaching the desired market share often means sacrificing short-term profit because without careful management, long-term profit goals may not be met. Meeting the competition is the easiest pricing goal to implement. But can managers really afford to ignore demand and costs, the life cycle stage, and other considerations? When creating pricing objectives, managers must consider these trade-offs in light of the target customer, the environment, and the company's overall objectives.

20-1b Estimate Demand, Costs, and Profits

Chapter 19 explained that total revenue is a function of price and quantity demanded and that quantity demanded depends on elasticity. Elasticity is a function of the perceived value to the buyer relative to the price. The types of questions managers consider when conducting marketing research on demand and elasticity are key. Some questions for market research on demand and elasticity are:

▸▸ **What price is so low that consumers would question the product's quality?**

▸▸ **What is the highest price at which the product would still be a bargain?**

Chapter 20

Setting the Right Price

Learning Outcomes

After you finish this chapter go to
p358 *for* **STUDY TOOLS**

▶▶ **What is the price at which the product is starting to get expensive?**

▶▶ **What is the price at which the product becomes too expensive to consider buying?**[1]

After establishing pricing goals, managers should estimate total revenue at a variety of prices. Next, they should determine corresponding costs for each price. They are then ready to estimate how much profit, if any, and how much market share can be earned at each possible price. Managers can study the options in light of revenues, costs, and profits. In turn, this information can help determine which price can best meet the firm's pricing goals.

20-1c Choose a Price Strategy

The basic, long-term pricing framework for a good or service should be a logical extension of the pricing objectives. The marketing manager's chosen **price strategy** defines the initial price and gives direction for price movements over the product life cycle.

The price strategy sets a competitive price in a specific market segment, based on a well-defined positioning strategy. Changing a price level from premium to super premium may require a change in the product itself, the target customers served, the promotional strategy, or the distribution channels.

A company's freedom in pricing a new product and devising a price strategy depends on the market conditions and the other elements of the marketing mix. If a firm launches a new item resembling several others already on the market, its pricing freedom will be restricted. To succeed, the company will probably have to charge a price close to the average market price. In contrast, a firm that introduces a totally new product with no close substitutes will have considerable pricing freedom.

Despite its strategic value, pricing research is an underused tool. McKinsey & Company's Pricing Benchmark Survey estimated that only about 15 percent of companies do serious pricing research.[2]

Strategic pricing decisions tend to be made without an understanding of the likely buyer or the competitive response. Managers often make tactical pricing decisions without reviewing how they may fit into the firm's overall pricing or marketing strategy. Many companies make pricing decisions and changes without an existing process for managing the pricing activity. As a result, many of them do not have a serious pricing strategy and do not conduct pricing research to develop their strategy.[3]

Companies that do serious planning for creating a price strategy can select from three basic approaches: price skimming, penetration pricing, and status quo pricing.

PRICE SKIMMING Price skimming is sometimes called a "market-plus" approach to pricing because it denotes a high price relative to the prices of competing products. The term *price skimming* is derived from the phrase "skimming the cream off the top." Companies often use this strategy for new products when the product is perceived by the target market as having unique advantages. Often companies will use skimming and then lower prices over time. This is called "sliding down the demand curve." Hardcover book publishers, such as HarperCollins, lower the price when the books are re-released in paperback. Other manufacturers maintain skimming prices throughout a product's life cycle. A manager of the factory that produces Chanel purses (retailing for over $2,000 each) told one of your authors that it takes back unsold inventory and destroys it rather than selling it at a discount.

Price skimming works best when the market is willing to buy the product even though it carries an above-average price. Airlines tend to use a variation of price skimming surrounding popular travel times or destinations. With the 2012 Summer Olympics in London, prices for travel to Europe initially

Exhibit 20.1

STEPS IN SETTING THE RIGHT PRICE ON A PRODUCT

Establish pricing goals.

Estimate demand, costs, and profits.

Choose a price strategy to help determine a base price.

Fine-tune the base price with pricing tactics.

Results lead to the right price.

© Cengage Learning

rose more than 10 percent and then rose even higher as the games got closer. Because that was an ideal destination for many, travelers were willing to pay the higher prices.[4] Firms can also effectively use price skimming when a product is well protected legally, when it represents a technological breakthrough, or when it has in some other way blocked the entry of competitors. Managers may follow a skimming strategy when production cannot be expanded rapidly because of technological difficulties, shortages, or constraints imposed by the skill and time required to produce a product. As long as demand is greater than supply, skimming is an attainable strategy.

A successful skimming strategy enables management to recover its product development costs quickly. Even if the market perceives an introductory price as too high, managers can lower the price. Firms often feel it is better to test the market at a high price and then lower the price if sales are too slow. Successful skimming strategies are not limited to products. Well-known athletes, lawyers, and hairstylists are experts at price skimming. Naturally, a skimming strategy will encourage competitors to enter the market.

A variation of skimming called anchoring can come into play in pricing a product line. The strategy typically is used by luxury retailers. An anchor is a high-priced product that may never sell but makes everything else look cheap by comparison. Thus, Ralph Lauren priced a "Ricky" alligator bag at $16,995, which made the "Tiffin" bag seem inexpensive at $2,595.[5]

PENETRATION PRICING Penetration pricing is at the opposite end of the spectrum from skimming. **Penetration pricing** means charging a relatively low price for a product as a way to reach the mass market. The low price is designed to capture a large share of a substantial market, resulting in lower production costs. If a marketing manager has made obtaining a large market share the firm's pricing objective, penetration pricing is a logical choice.

Penetration pricing does mean lower profit per unit, however. Therefore, to reach the break-even point, it requires a higher volume of sales than would a skimming

penetration pricing a pricing policy whereby a firm charges a relatively low price for a product initially as a way to reach the mass market

THE PRICE OF SUPER LUXURY

Small, exclusive hotels are all the rage among those with the money to spend. The benefits are myriad—a three-staff-to-one-room ratio is common, a variety of exotic treats and snacks are included with the room, turn-down service provides different treats on your pillow each night, and the hotels have fewer, but larger, rooms. Montage Hotels & Resorts has a property in Deer Valley, Utah, where children are greeted with paintings made by the staff of the hotel's children's program called Paintbox. When you leave to ski (by simply leaving your room), staff members put on your ski boots and lay out your skis. Once you are done skiing, they are waiting there to remove your boots and hand you a hot chocolate. Sound like the dream stay? Expect to pay near $1,000 a night to stay at this type of hotel. After all, such personal service comes at a price!

Source: Andrea Petersen, "What $1,000 a Night Gets You," *Wall Street Journal*, May 2, 2012, http://online.wsj.com/article/SB10001424052702304746604577379944042575320.html (Accessed May 3, 2012).

policy. The recovery of product development costs may be slow. As you might expect, penetration pricing tends to discourage competition.

A penetration strategy tends to be effective in a price-sensitive market. Price should decline more rapidly when demand is elastic because the market can be expanded through a lower price. Also, price sensitivity and greater competitive pressure should lead to a lower initial price and a relatively slow decline in the price later to a stable low price.

Although Walmart is typically associated with penetration pricing, other chains have done an excellent job of following this strategy as well. Fast-food restaurants use dollar menus and low-priced foods to entice customers to visit one chain over another. McDonald's has been successful over competitor Burger King because McDonald's offers a wide range of food at various prices—low-priced snack wraps draw in customers, who may then decide to also get a more expensive item like a smoothie or a salad.[6]

If a firm has a low fixed cost structure and each sale provides a large contribution to those fixed costs, penetration pricing can boost sales and provide large increases in profits—but only if the market size grows or if competitors choose not to respond. Low prices can attract additional buyers to the market. The increased sales can justify production expansion or the adoption of new technologies, both of which can reduce costs. And, if firms have excess capacity, even low-priced business can provide incremental dollars toward fixed costs.

Penetration pricing can also be effective if an experience curve will cause costs per unit to drop significantly. The experience curve proposes that per-unit costs will go down as a firm's production experience increases. Manufacturers that fail to take advantage of these effects will find themselves at a competitive cost disadvantage relative to others that are further along the curve.

The big advantage of penetration pricing is that it typically discourages or blocks competition from entering a market. The disadvantage is that penetration means gearing up for mass production to sell a large volume at a low price. If the volume fails to materialize, the company will face huge losses from building or converting a factory to produce the failed product.

Sometimes, multinational firms will follow a skimming strategy in developed countries and a penetration strategy in developing countries. Procter & Gamble, for example, views low-income consumers in developing countries as crucial to its long-run growth strategy. The company known for its premium razors in developed countries has created the Gillette Guard, which costs 15 rupees (34 cents) and uses blades that cost 5 rupees (11 cents), for the India market. In contrast, P&G's Fusion ProGlide razor system uses cartridges that sell for $16.99. In developing markets, P&G prices its products by determining what the consumer can afford and adjusting features and manufacturing processes to meet the target price. The Gillette Guard features a lightweight handle, which is preferred by Indian men, and eliminates the lubrication strip and colorful handle designs. P&G hopes that, as the Indian economy grows, customers will trade up to more expensive products.[7]

STATUS QUO PRICING The third basic price strategy a firm may choose is **status quo pricing**, also called meeting the competition or going rate pricing (see also Chapter 19). It means charging a price identical to or very close to the competition's price.

Although status quo pricing has the advantage of simplicity, its disadvantage is that the strategy may ignore demand or cost or both. If the firm is comparatively small, however, meeting the competition may be the safest route to long-term survival.

20-2 THE LEGALITY OF PRICE STRATEGY

As we mentioned in Chapter 4, some pricing decisions are subject to government regulation. Among the issues that fall into this category are unfair trade practices, price fixing, price discrimination, and predatory pricing.

20-2a Unfair Trade Practices

In over half the states, **unfair trade practice acts** put a floor under wholesale and retail prices. Selling below cost in these states is illegal. Wholesalers and retailers must usually take a certain minimum percentage markup on their combined merchandise cost and transportation cost. The most common markup figures are 6 percent at the retail level and 2 percent at the wholesale level. If a specific wholesaler or retailer can provide "conclusive proof" that operating costs are lower than the minimum required figure, lower prices may be allowed.

The intent of unfair trade practice acts is to protect small local firms from giants like Walmart, which operates very efficiently on razor-thin profit margins. State enforcement of unfair trade practice laws has generally been lax, however, partly because low prices benefit local consumers.

20-2b Price Fixing

Price fixing is an agreement between two or more firms on the price they will charge for a product. Suppose two or more executives from competing firms meet to decide how much to charge for a product or to decide which of them will submit the lowest bid on a certain contract. Such practices are illegal under the Sherman Act and the Federal

© kontur-vid/Shutterstock.com

Trade Commission Act. Offenders have received fines and sometimes prison terms. Price fixing is one area where the law is quite clear, and the U.S. Justice Department's enforcement is vigorous.

International price fixing by private entities can be prosecuted under the antitrust laws of many countries. In April 2011, P&G and Unilever were fined roughly $450 million by the European Union for price fixing and pricing powdered laundry detergents at anticompetitive prices. The companies had been part of a coalition for reducing the amount of packaging in laundry detergent but instead took the opportunity to protect market share and profit margins by agreeing to maintain prices despite smaller packaging.[8] In 2012, the U.S. Department of Justice sued Apple and five large publishers for price fixing. The charges claim the companies agreed to raise best-seller e-book prices, setting the price point between $12.99 and $14.99. The new business model was then allegedly forced on Amazon.com in order to prevent the company from continuing to sell e-books for $9.99. Hachette Book Group, Simon & Schuster Inc., and HarperCollins quickly settled out of court and now allow all retailers, including Amazon, to discount their books. But Apple, Macmillan, and Penguin claim the charges are false and have not agreed to a settlement.[9]

Most price-fixing cases focus on high prices charged to customers. A reverse form of price fixing occurs when powerful buyers force their suppliers' prices down. Recently, Maine blueberry growers alleged that four big processors conspired to push down the price they would pay for fresh wild berries. A state court jury agreed and awarded millions in damages.[10] Some price-fixing accusations are less clear-cut. For instance, Leegin Creative Leather Products sought to control its brand image by insisting that retailers charge a certain minimum price for its products. Leegin sued a boutique, Kay's Kloset, for offering its products at a lower price. There have been several rulings, new suits filed, and appeals heard, but whatever the outcome, these lengthy cases will influence the pricing and retail strategies of luxury goods companies trying to control their brand image.[11]

20-2c Price Discrimination

The Robinson-Patman Act of 1936 prohibits any firm from selling to two or more different buyers, within a reasonably short time, commodities (not services) of like grade and quality at different prices where the result would be to substantially lessen competition. The act also makes it illegal for a seller to offer two buyers different supplementary services and for buyers to use their purchasing power to force sellers into granting discriminatory prices or services. For a firm to violate the Robinson-Patman Act, it must meet the following six criteria:

1. **There must be price discrimination—that is, the seller must charge different prices to different customers for the same product.**

2. **The transaction must occur in interstate commerce.**

3. **The seller must discriminate by price among two or more purchasers—that is, the seller must make two or more actual sales within a reasonably short time.**

4. **The products sold must be commodities or other tangible goods.**

5. **The products sold must be of like grade and quality, not necessarily identical. If the goods are truly interchangeable and substitutable, then they are of like grade and quality.**

6. **There must be significant competitive injury.**

The Robinson-Patman Act provides three defenses for a seller charged with price discrimination (in each case the burden is on the seller to prove the defense):

▸ **COST:** A firm can charge different prices to different customers if the prices represent manufacturing or quantity discount savings.

▸ **MARKET CONDITIONS:** Price variations are justified if designed to meet fluid product or market conditions. Examples include the deterioration of perishable goods, the obsolescence of seasonal products, a distress sale under court order, and a legitimate going-out-of-business sale.

▸ **COMPETITION:** A reduction in price may be necessary to stay even with the competition.

predatory pricing
the practice of charging a very low price for a product with the intent of driving competitors out of business or out of a market

base price the general price level at which the company expects to sell the good or service

quantity discount
a price reduction offered to buyers buying in multiple units or above a specified dollar amount

cumulative quantity discount
a deduction from list price that applies to the buyer's total purchases made during a specific period

noncumulative quantity discount
a deduction from list price that applies to a single order rather than to the total volume of orders placed during a certain period

cash discount
a price reduction offered to a consumer, an industrial user, or a marketing intermediary in return for prompt payment of a bill

Specifically, if a competitor undercuts the price quoted by a seller to a buyer, the law authorizes the seller to lower the price charged to the buyer for the product in question.

20-2d Predatory Pricing

Predatory pricing is the practice of charging a very low price for a product with the intent of driving competitors out of business or out of a market. Once competitors have been driven out, the firm raises its prices. This practice is illegal under the Sherman Act and the Federal Trade Commission Act. To prove predatory pricing, the Justice Department must show that the predator—the destructive company—explicitly tried to ruin a competitor and that the predatory price was below the predator's average variable cost.

Prosecutions for predatory pricing suffered a major setback when a federal judge threw out a predatory pricing suit filed by the Justice Department against American Airlines. The Justice Department argued that the definition should be updated and that the test should be whether there was any business justification, other than driving away competitors, for American's aggressive pricing. Under that definition, the Justice Department attorneys thought they had a great case. Whenever a fledgling airline tried to get a toehold in the Dallas market, American would meet its fares and add flights. As soon as the rival retreated, American would jack its fares back up.

Under the average variable cost definition, however, the case would have been almost impossible to win. The reason is that like a high-tech industry, the airline industry has high fixed costs and low marginal costs. Once a flight is scheduled, the marginal cost of providing a seat for an additional passenger is almost zero. Thus, it is very difficult to prove that an airline is pricing below its average variable cost. The judge was not impressed by the Justice Department's argument, however, and kept the average variable cost definition of predatory pricing.

20-3 TACTICS FOR FINE-TUNING THE BASE PRICE

After managers understand both the legal and the marketing consequences of price strategies, they should set a base price—the general price level at which the company expects to sell the good or service. The general price level is correlated with the pricing policy: above the market (price skimming), at the market (status quo pricing), or below the market (penetration pricing). The final step, then, is to fine-tune the base price.

Fine-tuning techniques are short-run approaches that do not change the general price level. They do, however, result in changes within a general price level. These pricing tactics allow the firm to adjust for competition in certain markets, meet ever-changing government regulations, take advantage of unique demand situations, and meet promotional and positioning goals. Fine-tuning pricing tactics include various sorts of discounts, geographic pricing, and other pricing tactics.

20-3a Discounts, Allowances, Rebates, and Value-Based Pricing

A base price can be lowered through the use of discounts and the related tactics of allowances, rebates, low or zero percent financing, and value-based pricing. Managers use the various forms of discounts to encourage customers to do what they would not ordinarily do, such as paying cash rather than using credit, taking delivery out of season, or performing certain functions within a distribution channel.[12] The following are the most common tactics:

▸ **QUANTITY DISCOUNTS:** When buyers get a lower price for buying in multiple units or above a specified dollar amount, they are receiving a **quantity discount**. A **cumulative quantity discount** is a deduction from list price that applies to the buyer's total purchases made during a specific period; it is intended to encourage customer loyalty. In contrast, a **noncumulative quantity discount** is a deduction from list price that applies to a single order rather than to the total volume of orders placed during a certain period. It is intended to encourage orders in large quantities.

▸ **CASH DISCOUNTS:** A **cash discount** is a price reduction offered to a consumer, an industrial user, or a marketing intermediary in return for prompt payment of a bill. Prompt payment saves the seller carrying charges and billing expenses and allows the seller to avoid bad debt.

» **FUNCTIONAL DISCOUNTS:** When distribution channel intermediaries, such as wholesalers or retailers, perform a service or function for the manufacturer, they must be compensated. This compensation, typically a percentage discount from the base price, is called a **functional discount** (or **trade discount**). Functional discounts vary greatly from channel to channel, depending on the tasks performed by the intermediary.

» **SEASONAL DISCOUNTS:** A **seasonal discount** is a price reduction for buying merchandise out of season. It shifts the storage function to the purchaser. Seasonal discounts also enable manufacturers to maintain a steady production schedule year-round.

» **PROMOTIONAL ALLOWANCES:** A **promotional allowance** (also known as a **trade allowance**) is a payment to a dealer for promoting the manufacturer's products. It is both a pricing tool and a promotional device. As a pricing tool, a promotional allowance is like a functional discount. If, for example, a retailer runs an ad for a manufacturer's product, the manufacturer may pay half the cost.

» **REBATES:** A **rebate** is a cash refund given for the purchase of a product during a specific period. The advantage of a rebate over a simple price reduction for stimulating demand is that a rebate is a temporary inducement that can be taken away without altering the basic price structure. A manufacturer that uses a simple price reduction for a short time may meet resistance when trying to restore the price to its original, higher level.

» **ZERO PERCENT FINANCING:** During the mid- and late-2000s, new-car sales receded. To get people back into the automobile showrooms, manufacturers offered zero percent financing, which enabled purchasers to borrow money to pay for new cars with no interest charge. The tactic created a huge increase in sales but not without cost to the manufacturers. A five-year interest-free car loan represented a cost of over $3,000 on a typical vehicle sold during a zero percent promotion.

VALUE-BASED PRICING **Value-based pricing**, also called *value pricing*, is a pricing strategy that has grown out of the quality movement. It became very popular during the recent recession. Instead of figuring prices based on costs or competitors' prices, it starts with the customer, considers the competition, and then determines the appropriate price. The basic assumption is that the firm is customer driven, seeking to understand the attributes customers want in the goods and services they buy and the value of that bundle of attributes to customers. Because very few firms operate in a pure monopoly,

In this advertisement, IKEA is using value-based pricing to bring customers into the store and to encourage shoppers to buy as much seating as they need.

however, a marketer using value-based pricing must also determine the value of competitive offerings to customers. Customers determine the value of a product (not just its price) relative to the value of alternatives. In value-based pricing, therefore, the price of the product is set at a level that seems to the customer to be a good price compared with the prices of other options.

Shoppers in competitive markets are seeing prices fall as Walmart pushes rivals to match its value prices. The firm continued to up the ante in 2012 by offering consistently lower prices in its grocery and health and beauty departments.[13] Such reduced prices have conditioned consumers to expect inexpensive goods every day. Customer expectations have pressured regional grocery chains to switch to value pricing. Traditionally, these chains offered weekly specials to attract shoppers and made up the lost profit through higher regular prices. For example, Safeway long banked on customers paying higher prices in return for top-quality fresh produce and upscale ambience. Now, even though it has cut its regular prices, Safeway is still more than 10 percent more expensive than Kroger. The result has been declines in both sales and profitability.[14]

PRICING PRODUCTS TOO LOW Sometimes managers price their products too low, thereby reducing company profits. This seems to happen for two reasons. First, managers attempt to buy market share through aggressive pricing. Usually, however, these price cuts are quickly met by competitors. Thus, any gain in market share is short-lived, and overall industry profits end up falling. Second, managers have a natural tendency to want to make decisions that can be justified objectively.

The problem is that companies often lack hard data on the complex determinants of profitability, such as the relationship between price changes and sales volumes, the link between demand levels and costs, and the likely responses of competitors to price changes. In contrast, companies usually have rich, unambiguous information on costs, sales, market share, and competitors' prices. As a result, managers tend to make pricing decisions based on current costs, projected short-term share gains, or current competitor prices rather than on long-term profitability.

The problem of "underpricing" can be solved by linking information about price, cost, and demand within the same decision support system. The demand data can be developed via marketing research. This will enable managers to get the hard data they need to calculate the effects of pricing decisions on profitability. Parker Hannifin Corporation makes industrial components used in everything from the space shuttle to a mechanism for tilting the model steamship used in the movie *Titanic*. The company was successful, but it was stuck in a profit-margin rut. It couldn't seem to improve its return on invested capital. Like most U.S. manufacturers, Parker used a "cost-plus" pricing method—calculating how much it cost to make a product and adding a flat percentage on top, usually 35 percent. Then its new CEO, Donald Washkewicz, decided to start thinking less like a "widget maker" and more like a retailer.[15] That meant that Parker Hannifin started determining its prices by what a consumer was willing to pay instead of by what a product cost to make. Washkewicz had his new "pricing gurus" determine which products were high-volume commodities with a competitive market and which were customized products with limited or no competition. Then they determined which products offered some unique value, such as faster delivery or better design. Parker's strategic pricing process led to some price cuts for its basic products and to price increases of more than 25 percent for its custom products. Parker's net income soared, from $130 million in 2002 to $830 million in 2007. Its return on investment capital rose from 7 percent to 21 percent over that same period.[16]

20-3b Geographic Pricing

Because many sellers ship their wares to a nationwide or even a worldwide market, the cost of freight can greatly affect the total cost of a product. Sellers may use several different geographic pricing tactics to moderate the impact of freight costs on distant customers. The following methods of geographic pricing are the most common:

▸ **FOB ORIGIN PRICING:** FOB origin pricing, also called FOB factory or FOB shipping point, is a price tactic that requires the buyer to absorb the freight costs from the shipping point ("free on board"). The farther buyers are from sellers, the more they pay, because transportation costs generally increase with the distance merchandise is shipped.

▸ **UNIFORM DELIVERED PRICING:** If the marketing manager wants total costs, including freight, to be equal for all purchasers of identical products, the firm will adopt uniform delivered pricing, or "postage stamp" pricing. With **uniform delivered pricing**, the

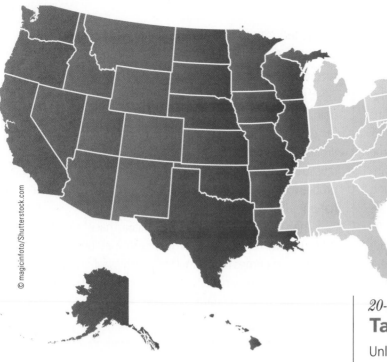

© magicinfoto/Shutterstock.com

Charging customers shipping fees based on the zone in which they are located is a popular GEOGRAPHIC PRICING tactic.

seller pays the actual freight charges and bills every purchaser an identical, flat freight charge.

- ▸ **ZONE PRICING:** A marketing manager who wants to equalize total costs among buyers within large geographic areas—but not necessarily all of the seller's market area—may modify the base price with a zone-pricing tactic. Zone pricing is a modification of uniform delivered pricing. Rather than using a uniform freight rate for the entire United States (or its total market), the firm divides it into segments or zones and charges a flat freight rate to all customers in a given zone. The U.S. Postal Service's parcel post rate structure is probably the best-known zone-pricing system in the country.

- ▸ **FREIGHT ABSORPTION PRICING:** In freight absorption pricing, the seller pays all or part of the actual freight charges and does not pass them on to the buyer. The manager may use this tactic in intensely competitive areas or as a way to break into new market areas.

- ▸ **BASING-POINT PRICING:** With basing-point pricing, the seller designates a location as a basing point and charges all buyers the freight cost from that point, regardless of the city from which the goods are shipped. Thanks to several adverse court rulings, basing-point pricing has waned in popularity. Freight fees charged when none were actually incurred, called phantom freight, have been declared illegal.

20-3c Other Pricing Tactics

Unlike geographic pricing, other pricing tactics are unique and defy neat categorization. Managers use these tactics for various reasons—for example, to stimulate demand for specific products, to increase store patronage, and to offer a wider variety of merchandise at a specific price point. "Other" pricing tactics include a single-price tactic, flexible pricing, professional services pricing, price lining, leader pricing, bait pricing, odd–even pricing, price bundling, and two-part pricing.

SINGLE-PRICE TACTIC A merchant using a **single-price tactic** offers all goods and services at the same price (or perhaps two or three prices). A new startup company called MATTER specializes in quality, in-depth reporting on science and technology. It then publishes one story a month (and will be moving to weekly stories as subscriptions increase) in long-form narrative style over a wide variety of digital platforms. Each story costs 99 cents, or MATTER lovers can purchase a monthly subscription.[17]

Single-price selling removes price comparisons from the buyer's decision-making process. The retailer enjoys the benefits of a simplified pricing system and minimal clerical errors. However, continually rising costs are a headache for retailers following this strategy. In times of inflation, they must frequently raise the selling price.

Sometimes using a single price tactic can open the door for competition. For years, UPS prided itself on charging one price to all its customers. But when FedEx entered the market, one reason for its swift success was its variable pricing, which recognized inherent value differences between customers, orders (parcels versus messages), and times of delivery (8 a.m. versus afternoon).[18]

FLEXIBLE PRICING Flexible pricing (or **variable pricing**) means that different customers pay different prices for essentially the same merchandise bought in equal quantities. This tactic is often found in the sale of shopping goods, specialty merchandise, and most industrial goods except supply items. Car dealers and many appliance retailers commonly follow the practice. It allows the seller to adjust for competition by meeting another seller's price. Thus, a marketing manager with a status quo pricing objective might readily adopt the tactic. Flexible pricing also enables the seller to close a sale with price-conscious consumers.

The obvious disadvantages of flexible pricing are the lack of consistent profit margins, the potential ill will of high-paying purchasers, the tendency for salespeople to automatically lower the price to make a sale, and the possibility of a price war among sellers.

TRADE-INS Flexible pricing and trade-ins often go hand in hand. About 57 percent of all new-car sales involve a trade-in.[19] Trade-ins occur for other products as well, such as musical instruments, sporting goods, jewelry, and some appliances. If a trade-in is involved, the consumer must negotiate two prices, one for the new product and one for the existing product. The existence of a trade-in raises several questions for the purchaser. For example, will the new product's price differ depending on whether there is a trade-in? Are consumers better off trading in their used product toward the purchase of the new one from the same retailer, or should they keep the two transactions separate by dealing with different retailers? Several car buying guides, such as Edmunds.com and Autotrader.com, advise consumers to keep the two transactions separate.[20]

Recent research found that trade-in customers tend to care more about the trade-in value they receive than the price they pay for the new product. Thus, these buyers tend to pay more than purchasers without a trade-in. Analysis of data from the automobile market found that, on average, trade-in customers end up paying $452 more than customers who simply buy a new car from a dealer.[21]

PROFESSIONAL SERVICES PRICING Professional services pricing is used by people with lengthy experience, training, and often certification by a licensing board—for example, lawyers, physicians, and family counselors. Professionals sometimes charge customers at an hourly rate, but sometimes fees are based on the solution of a problem or performance of an act (such as an eye examination) rather than on the actual time involved.

Those who use professional pricing have an ethical responsibility not to overcharge a customer. Because demand is sometimes highly inelastic, such as when a person requires heart surgery to survive, there may be a temptation to charge "all the traffic will bear."[22]

PRICE LINING When a seller establishes a series of prices for a type of merchandise, it creates a price line. **Price lining** is the practice of offering a product line with several items at specific price points. Wireless providers use price lining for cell phones that are purchased with a two-year contract. The top tier is usually priced at $299 (the highest the market will pay), and subsequent tiers are $249, $199, $149, $99, and $49.

Price lining reduces confusion for both the salesperson and the consumer. The buyer may be offered a wider variety of merchandise at each established price. Price lines may also enable a seller to reach several market segments. For buyers, the question of price may be quite simple: All they have to do is find a suitable product at the

$99 $199 $149

© Oleksiy Mark/Shutterstock.com

predetermined price. Moreover, price lining is a valuable tactic for the marketing manager, because the firm may be able to carry a smaller total inventory than it could without price lines. The results may include fewer markdowns, simplified purchasing, and lower inventory carrying charges.

Price lines also present drawbacks, especially if costs are continually rising. Sellers can offset rising costs in three ways. First, they can begin stocking lower-quality merchandise at each price point. Second, sellers can change the prices, although frequent price line changes confuse buyers. Third, sellers can accept lower profit margins and hold quality and prices constant. This third alternative has short-run benefits, but its long-run handicaps may drive sellers out of business.

AT&T has set up a two-tiered price line for its Smartphone broadband users. Instead of charging $30 a month for unlimited use, AT&T now offers 200 megabytes for $15 a month or two gigabytes for $25, with added charges if the customer exceeds the ceiling. AT&T says that 98 percent of its customers consume less than two gigabytes a month.[23] Verizon also uses a tiered access plan. To date, Sprint Nextel and T-Mobile are staying with a flat rate price in an attempt to win market share.[24]

LEADER PRICING Leader pricing (or **loss-leader pricing**) is an attempt by the marketing manager to attract customers by selling a product near or even below cost in the hope that shoppers will buy other items once they are in the store. This type of pricing appears weekly in the newspaper advertising of supermarkets. Leader pricing is normally used on well-known items that consumers can easily recognize as bargains. The trend of geo-social loss leader campaigns is growing in popularity as companies see how successful leader pricing is at enticing people to buy. Daily deal sites Groupon and LivingSocial are some of the biggest leader pricing sources, but some companies are turning to local deal providers to cut down on the cost of the promotion and to avoid deal hunters. For example, Urban Escape Day Spa in Colorado used SaveLocal to send out a coupon for $25 off a $75 massage. While he sold fewer vouchers than he would have through Groupon, the owner retained more revenue from the SaveLocal vouchers and captured more repeat customers.[25]

Leader pricing is not limited to products. Health clubs offer a one-month free trial as a loss leader.

BAIT PRICING In contrast to leader pricing, which is a genuine attempt to give the consumer a reduced price, bait pricing is deceptive. **Bait pricing** tries to get consumers into a store through false or misleading price advertising and then uses high-pressure selling to persuade them to buy more expensive merchandise. You may have seen this ad or a similar one:

REPOSSESSED . . . Singer slant-needle sewing machine . . . take over 8 payments of $5.10 per month . . . ABC Sewing Center.

This is bait. When a customer goes in to see the machine, a salesperson says that it has just been sold or else shows the prospective buyer a piece of junk. Then the salesperson says, "But I've got a really good deal on this fine new model." This is the switch that may cause a susceptible consumer to walk out with a $400 machine. The Federal Trade Commission considers bait pricing a deceptive act and has banned its use in interstate commerce. Most states also ban bait pricing, but sometimes enforcement is lax.

ODD–EVEN PRICING Odd–even pricing (or **psychological pricing**) means pricing at odd-numbered prices to connote a bargain and pricing at even-numbered prices to imply quality. For years, many retailers have priced their products in odd numbers—for example, $99.95—to

leader pricing (loss-leader pricing) a price tactic in which a product is sold near or even below cost in the hope that shoppers will buy other items once they are in the store

bait pricing a price tactic that tries to get consumers into a store through false or misleading price advertising and then uses high-pressure selling to persuade consumers to buy more expensive merchandise

odd–even pricing (psychological pricing) a price tactic that uses odd-numbered prices to connote bargains and even-numbered prices to imply quality

A study at the University of Chicago revealed that a **person's two cents** is worth a lot. When the price of margarine dropped 18 cents, from 89 cents to 71 cents, sales improved 65 percent. But when the price fell again, this time from 71 cents to 69 cents, sales grew by 222 percent![26]

THE REAL DEAL

make consumers feel they are paying a lower price for the product. In addition, Robert Schindler, a professor at Rutgers Business School, conducted a study that revealed the difference between pricing a product at .99 and .00 resulted in the .99 item far outselling the .00 item![27] Even-numbered pricing is often used for "prestige" items, such as a fine perfume at $100 a bottle or a good watch at $500. The demand curve for such items would also be sawtoothed, except that the outside edges would represent even-numbered prices and, therefore, elastic demand.

PRICE BUNDLING Price bundling is marketing two or more products in a single package for a special price. For example, Microsoft offers "suites" of software that bundle spreadsheets, word processing, graphics, e-mail, Internet access, and groupware for networks of microcomputers. Price bundling can stimulate demand for the bundled items if the target market perceives the price as a good value.

Services like hotels and airlines sell a perishable commodity (hotel rooms and airline seats) with relatively constant fixed costs. Bundling can be an important income stream for these businesses because the variable cost tends to be low—for instance, the cost of cleaning a hotel room. Therefore, most of the revenue can help cover fixed costs and generate profits.

Bundling has also been used in the telecommunications industry. Companies offer local service, long distance, DSL Internet service, wireless, and even cable television in various menus of bundling. Telecom companies use bundling as a way to protect their market share and fight off competition by locking customers into a group of services. For consumers, comparison shopping may be difficult since they may not be able to determine how much they are really paying for each component of the bundle. A related price tactic is **unbundling**, or reducing the bundle of services that comes with the basic product. To help hold the line on costs, some stores require customers to pay for gift wrapping. Airlines charge for selecting a good seat, food, and checked baggage, all services that used to be bundled into the price of the ticket.

Clearly, price bundling can influence consumers' purchase behavior. But what about the decision to consume a particular bundled product or service? Some research has focused on how people consume certain bundled products or services. According to this research, the key to consumption behavior is how closely consumers can link the costs and benefits of the exchange.[28] In complex transactions like a holiday package, it may be unclear which costs are paying for which benefits. In such cases, consumers tend to mentally downplay their up-front costs for the bundled product, so they may be more likely to forgo a benefit that's part of the bundle, like a free dinner.

Similarly, when people buy season tickets to a concert series, sporting event, or other activity, the sunk costs (price of the bundle) and the pending benefit (going to see an event) become decoupled. This reduces the likelihood of consumption of the event over time.

Theatergoers who purchase tickets to a single play are almost certain to use those tickets. This is consistent with the idea that in a one-to-one transaction (i.e., one payment, one benefit), the costs and benefits of that transaction are tightly coupled, resulting in strong sunk cost pressure to consume the pending benefit.

A theater manager might expect a no-show rate of 20 percent when the percentage of season ticket holders is high but a no-show rate of only 5 percent when the percentage of season ticket holders is low. With a high number of season ticket holders, a manager could oversell performances and maximize the revenue for the theater.

The physical format of the transaction also figures in. A ski lift pass in the form of a booklet of tickets strengthens the cost–benefit link for consumers, whereas a single pass for multiple ski lifts weakens that link.

Though price bundling of services can result in a lower rate of total consumption of that service, the same is not necessarily true for products. Consider the purchase of an expensive bottle of wine. When the wine is purchased as a single unit, its cost and eventual benefit are tightly coupled. As a result, the cost of the wine will be important, and a person will likely reserve that wine for a special occasion. When purchased as part of a bundle (e.g., as part of a case of wine), however, the cost and benefit of that individual bottle of wine will likely become decoupled, reducing the impact of the cost on eventual consumption. Thus, in contrast to the price bundling of services, the price bundling of physical goods could lead to an increase in product consumption.

TWO-PART PRICING Two-part pricing means establishing two separate charges to consume a single good or service. Airlines have moved to a two-part pricing system, charging the base ticket price, then offering passengers additional perks such as meals, extra leg room, in-flight movies, and trip insurance for additional costs. Last year these fees resulted in approximately $22 billion in revenue for the airline industry.[29]

Consumers sometimes prefer two-part pricing because they are uncertain about the number and the types of activities they might use at places like an amusement park. Also, the people who use a service most often pay a higher total price. Two-part pricing can increase a seller's revenue by attracting consumers who would not pay a high fee even for unlimited use. For example, a health club might be able to sell only 100 memberships at $700 annually with unlimited use of facilities, for a total revenue of $70,000. However, it could sell 900 memberships at $200 with a guarantee of using the racquetball courts ten times a month. Every use over ten would require the member to pay a $5 fee. Thus, membership revenue would provide a base of $180,000, with some additional usage fees throughout the year.

Research has shown that when consumers are thinking of buying a good or service with two-part pricing, they may mentally process the base price, such as a membership fee, more thoroughly than the extra fee or surcharge (playing a game of tennis). Thus, they can underestimate the total price compared with when prices are not partitioned.[30] The researchers also found that low-perceived benefit components should be priced relatively low and vice versa. Consumers find a higher total price more acceptable when the high-benefit component is priced high than when the low-benefit component is priced high. For example, assume John joins a health club and swims at the club four times a month. John really enjoys working out and views being a member of the club as part of a healthy lifestyle (high value). He also swims after a workout once a week to unwind and relax. For John, swimming is not that important but is enjoyable (low value). If the club charges $60-a-month dues and $5 per swim, John perceives this as acceptable. According to the research, John would find it less attractive if the monthly dues were $40 and each swim was $10. Yet the total cost is the same!

PAY WHAT YOU WANT To many people, paying what you want or what you think something is worth is a very risky tactic. Obviously, it wouldn't work for expensive durables like automobiles. Imagine someone paying $1 for a new BMW! Yet this model has worked in varying degrees in restaurants and other service businesses. One of your authors has patronized a restaurant close to campus that asks diners to "pay what you think it is worth." After several years, the restaurant is still in business. The owner says that the average lunch donation is around $8. Social pressures can come into play in a "pay what you want" environment because an individual doesn't want to appear poor or cheap to his or her peers. Panera Bread runs three locations called "Panera Cares," where the customer pays what he or she wants by placing the money in anonymous boxes around the store. The menus have "suggested donation" prices listed (after determining that customers were uncomfortable with the perception they weren't paying enough), and customers also receive that number on their receipt. Panera says that the three restaurants

Many gyms include the price of classes, use of racquetball courts, and other amenities. However, by using two-part pricing, some health clubs have dramatically increased revenue.

© Kzenon/Shutterstock.com

make 75 percent of the retail price. Sixty percent leave the suggested amount and 15 to 20 percent leave more or leave less (or nothing). The businesses have done well enough that Panera plans to open two more locations![31]

20-3d Consumer Penalties

More and more businesses are adopting **consumer penalties**—extra fees paid by consumers for violating the terms of a purchase agreement. Businesses impose consumer penalties for two reasons: They will allegedly (1) suffer an irrevocable revenue loss and/or (2) incur significant additional transaction costs should customers be unable or unwilling to complete their purchase obligations. For the company, these customer payments are part of doing business in a highly competitive marketplace. With profit margins in many companies increasingly coming under pressure, organizations are looking to stem losses resulting from customers not meeting their obligations. However, the perceived unfairness of a penalty may affect some consumers' willingness to patronize a business in the future.

20-4 PRODUCT LINE PRICING

Product line pricing is setting prices for an entire line of products. Compared to setting the right price on a single product, product line pricing encompasses broader concerns. In product line pricing, the marketing manager tries to achieve maximum profits or other goals for the entire line rather than for a single component of the line.

20-4a Relationships among Products

The manager must first determine the type of relationship that exists among the various products in a line:

▸ **If items are complementary, an increase in the sale of one good causes an increase in demand for the complementary product, and vice versa. For example,** the sale of ski poles depends on the demand for skis, making these two items complementary.

▸ **Two products in a line can also be substitutes for each other. If buyers buy one item in the line, they are less likely to buy a second item in the line.**

▸ **A neutral relationship can also exist between two products. In other words, demand for one of the products is unrelated to demand for the other.**

20-4b Joint Costs

Joint costs are costs that are shared in the manufacturing and marketing of several products in a product line. These costs pose a unique problem in product pricing (e.g., the production of televisions that combine televisions and Blu-ray players).

Any assignment of joint costs must be somewhat subjective because costs are actually shared. Suppose a company produces two products, X and Y, in a common production process, with joint costs allocated on a weight basis. Product X weighs 1,000 pounds, and product Y weighs 500 pounds. Thus, costs are allocated on the basis of $2 for X for every $1 for Y. Gross margins (sales less the cost of goods sold) might then be as follows:

	Product X	Product Y	Total
Sales	$20,000	$6,000	$26,000
Less cost of goods sold	15,000	7,500	22,500
Gross margin	$5,000	($1,500)	$3,500

© Cengage Learning

This statement reveals a loss of $1,500 on product Y. However, the firm must realize that overall it earned a $3,500 profit on the two items in the line. Also, weight may not be the right way to allocate the joint costs. Instead, the firm might use other bases, including market value or quantity sold.

20-5 PRICING DURING DIFFICULT ECONOMIC TIMES

Pricing is always an important aspect of marketing, but it is especially crucial in times of inflation and recession. The firm that does not adjust to economic trends may lose ground that it can never make up.

20-5a Inflation

When the economy is characterized by high inflation, special pricing tactics are often necessary. They can be subdivided into cost-oriented and demand-oriented tactics.

COST-ORIENTED TACTICS One popular cost-oriented tactic is *culling products with a low profit margin* from the product line. However, this tactic may backfire for three reasons:

➤ **A high volume of sales on an item with a low profit margin may still make the item highly profitable.**

➤ **Eliminating a product from a product line may reduce economies of scale, thereby lowering the margins on other items.**

➤ **Eliminating the product may affect the price-quality image of the entire line.**

Another popular cost-oriented tactic is **delayed-quotation pricing**, which is used for industrial installations and many accessory items. The price of the product is not set until the item is either finished or delivered. Long production lead times force many firms to adopt this policy during periods of inflation. Builders of nuclear power plants, ships, airports, and office towers sometimes use delayed-quotation tactics.

Escalator pricing is similar to delayed-quotation pricing in that the final selling price reflects cost increases incurred between the time an order is placed and the time delivery is made. An escalator clause allows for price increases (usually across the board) based on the cost-of-living index or some other formula. As with any price increase, management's ability to implement such a policy is based on inelastic demand for the product. Often it is used only for extremely complex products that take a long time to produce or with new customers. Another tactic growing in popularity is to hold prices constant but add new fees.

Any cost-oriented pricing policy that tries to maintain a fixed gross margin under all conditions can lead to a vicious circle. For example, a price increase will result in decreased demand, which in turn increases production costs (because of lost economies of scale). Increased production costs require a further price increase, leading to further diminished demand, and so on.

DEMAND-ORIENTED TACTICS Demand-oriented pricing tactics use price to reflect changing patterns of demand caused by inflation or high interest rates. Cost changes are considered, of course, but mostly in the context of how increased prices will affect demand.

Price shading is the use of discounts by salespeople to increase demand for one or more products in a line. Often, shading becomes habitual and is done routinely without much forethought. To make the demand for a good or service more inelastic and to create buyer dependency, a company can use several strategies:

➤ **CULTIVATE SELECTED DEMAND:** Marketing managers can target prosperous customers who will pay extra for convenience or service. In cultivating close relationships with affluent organizational customers, marketing managers should avoid putting themselves at the mercy of a dominant firm. They can more easily raise prices when an account is readily replaceable. Finally, in companies where engineers exert more influence than purchasing departments do, performance is favored over price. Often a preferred vendor's pricing range expands if other suppliers prove technically unsatisfactory.

➤ **CREATE UNIQUE OFFERINGS:** Marketing managers should study buyers' needs. If the seller can design distinctive goods or services uniquely fitting buyers' activities, equipment, and procedures, a mutually beneficial relationship will evolve. By satisfying targeted buyers in a superior way, marketing managers can make them dependent. Cereal manufacturers have been able to pass along costs by marketing unique value-added or multi-ingredient cereals.

➤ **CHANGE THE PACKAGE DESIGN:** Another way companies pass on higher costs is to shrink product sizes but keep prices the same. By the same token, however, some packaging designs help companies keep prices low. General Mills developed a new, smaller Cheerios box that allows for more cereal and less air. The new box cuts costs and keeps prices down.[32]

delayed-quotation pricing a price tactic used for industrial installations and many accessory items in which a firm price is not set until the item is either finished or delivered

escalator pricing a price tactic in which the final selling price reflects cost increases incurred between the time the order is placed and the time delivery is made

price shading the use of discounts by salespeople to increase demand for one or more products in a line

© Dragana Gerasimoski/Shutterstock.com

» **HEIGHTEN BUYER DEPENDENCE:** Owens Corning Fiberglass supplies an integrated insulation service that includes commercial and scientific training for distributors and seminars for end users. This practice freezes out competition and supports higher prices.

20-5b Recession

As discussed in Chapter 4, a recession is a period of reduced economic activity, such as occurred in the United States in 2007–2009. Reduced demand for goods and services, along with higher rates of unemployment, is a common trait of a recession. Yet astute marketers can often find opportunity during recessions. A recession is an excellent time to build market share because competitors are struggling to make ends meet.

According to pricing strategy consultants Paul Hunt and Greg Thomas, using pricing research to adjust prices during a recession or difficult economic conditions can result in a profit improvement of 20 percent, sometimes more.[33]

Two effective pricing tactics to hold or build market share during a recession are value-based pricing and bundling. *Value-based pricing*, discussed earlier in the chapter, stresses to customers that they are getting a good value for their money.

Bundling or *unbundling* can also stimulate demand during a recession. If features are added to a bundle, consumers may perceive the offering as having greater value. Conversely, companies can unbundle offerings and lower base prices to stimulate demand.

Recessions are a good time for marketing managers to study the demand for individual items in a product line and the revenue they produce. Pruning unprofitable items can save resources to be better used elsewhere.

Prices often fall during a recession as competitors try desperately to maintain demand for their wares. Even if demand remains constant, falling prices mean lower profits or no profits. Falling prices, therefore, are a natural incentive to lower costs. During the past recession, companies implemented new technology to improve efficiency and then slashed payrolls. They also discovered that suppliers were an excellent source of cost savings; the cost of purchased materials accounts for slightly more than half of most U.S. manufacturers' expenses. Specific strategies that companies use with suppliers include the following:

» **RENEGOTIATING CONTRACTS:** Sending suppliers letters demanding price cuts of 5 percent or more; putting out for rebid the contracts of those that refuse to cut costs.

» **OFFERING HELP:** Dispatching teams of experts to suppliers' plants to help reorganize and suggest other productivity-boosting changes; working with suppliers to make parts simpler and cheaper to produce.

» **KEEPING THE PRESSURE ON:** To make sure that improvements continue, setting annual, across-the-board cost reduction targets, often of 5 percent or more a year.

» **PARING DOWN SUPPLIERS:** To improve economies of scale, slashing the overall number of suppliers, sometimes by up to 80 percent, and boosting purchases from those that remain.

STUDY TOOLS **20**

LOCATED AT BACK OF THE TEXTBOOK
☐ *Rip out Chapter Review Card*

LOCATED AT WWW.CENGAGE.COM/LOGIN
☐ *Review Key Terms Flashcards (print or online)*
☐ *Download audio and visual summaries to review on the go*
☐ *Complete both Practice Quizzes to prepare for tests*
☐ *Play "Beat the Clock" and "Quizbowl" to master concepts*
☐ *Complete "Crossword Puzzle" to review key terms*
☐ *Watch Video on "BoltBus" for a real company example*

ANATOMY OF PRODUCT LINE PRICING: McDONALD'S

There would probably be little demand for a menu item that was out of the price/value range established by other items in McDonald's product line. For example, a $10 burger would be well out of the price range that McDonald's customers expect for that product class.

1 ... offers several related products.

2 ... sells related products individually and in combinations.

WHAT WOULD YOU PAY FOR A FAST-FOOD BURGER? $1 $2 $3 $10

3 ... offers a line of products of various sizes, qualities, and prices.

4 ... presents a limited number of prices for all its product offerings.

1

1. Announcement to the AMA Academic Council from Patricia K. Goodrich, Senior Director, Professional Development, American Marketing Association, October 25, 2007.

2. George Anderson, "Satisfied Workers Generate Greater Returns," *Retailwire*, January 16, 2008, www.retailwire.com /discussion/12685/satisfied-workers -generate-greater-returns (Accessed April 16, 2012).

3. "The 100 Best Companies to Work For," *Fortune*, February 6, 2012, 117–127.

4. Philip Kotler and Kevin Lane Keller, *A Framework for Marketing Management*, 5th ed. (Upper Saddle River, NJ: Prentice Hall, 2011), 4–5.

5. Doug Aamoth, "Nintendo Slashes '3DS' Portable Price from $250 to $170," *Time*, July 28, 2011, http://techland.time .com/2011/07/28/nintendo-slashes-3ds -portable-price-from-250-to-170 (Accessed March 27, 2012).

6. Inc. Staff, "10 Ways to Support Your Best Customers," *Inc.*, August 3, 2010, www.inc .com/guides/2010/07/10-ways-to-support -your-best-customers.html (Accessed April 16, 2012).

7. Kathy Grannic, "Zappos.com Tops in Customer Service, According to NRF Foundation/American Express Survey," National Retail Federation, January 11, 2011, www.nrf.com/modules.php?name=News &op=viewlive&sp_id=1067 (Accessed April 16, 2012).

8. George S. Day and Christine Moorman, *Strategy from the Outside In* (New York: McGraw-Hill, 2010), back cover.

9. "The 'Green' Gap between Environmental Concerns and the Cash Register," *Nielsen Wire*, August 31, 2011, http://blog.nielsen .com/nielsenwire/global/the-green-gap -between-environmental-concerns-and -the-cash-register (Accessed April 16, 2012).

10. A.G. Lafley and Ron Charon, cited in Day and Moorman, 235.

11. Day and Moorman, 261–262.

12. Geoff Colvin, "Wal-Mart's Makeover," *Fortune*, December 26, 2011, 50–55.

13. Day and Moorman, 4.

14. Ibid.

15. Daniel Lyons, "The Customer Is Always Right," *Newsweek*, January 4, 2010, 85–86.

16. "2010 Post-Recession Consumer Study," Ogilvy & Mather, March 15, 2010, www.ogilvy.com/News/Press-Releases /March-2010-Eyes-Wide-Open.aspx (Accessed April 16, 2012).

17. Eric Wilson, "Social Shopping: Everybody Wants In," *New York Times*, March 25, 2012, www.nytimes.com /imagepages/2012/03/25/fashion /25SOCIALSHOP_GRAPHIC .html?scp=1&sq=social%20shopping &st=cse (Accessed April 16, 2012).

18. Tim Donnelly, "How to Open a Business in Brooklyn," *Inc.*, June 28, 2010, www.inc .com/guides/2010/06/opening-a-business-in -brooklyn.html (Accessed April 16, 2012).

19. Inc. Staff, "10 Ways to Support Your Best Customers."

20. Phred Dvorak, "Next in Line for Reinvention: The Art of Selling," *Wall Street Journal*, January 28, 2008, B3.

21. Karen Aho, "2011 Customer Service Hall of Shame," MSN, May 18, 2011, http://money .msn.com/investing/the-2011-customer -service-hall-of-shame.aspx?cp-documentid =6821116 (Accessed April 16, 2012).

22. Harley Manning, "How the 'Most Improved' Companies Raised Their Customer Experience Game Last Year," *Harley Manning's Blog*, April 25, 2011, http://blogs.forrester .com/harley_manning/11-04-25-how_the _most_improved_companies_raised_their _customer_experience_game_last_year (Accessed April16, 2012).

23. Jena McGregor, "USAA's Battle Plan," *Bloomberg Businessweek*, February 18, 2010, www.businessweek.com/magazine /content/10_09/b4168040782858.htm (Accessed April 16, 2011).

24. Aho, "The 2011 Customer Service Hall of Fame."

25. Jeff Green and David Welch, "Cadillac Starts Putting on the Ritz," *Bloomberg Businessweek*, June 21–June 27, 2010, 24.

26. Samuel Fromartz, "Good Enough to Eat," *Fast Company*, September 2008, 29.

27. Shalini Ramachandran and Jeffrey A. Trachtenberg, "End of Era for Britannica," *Wall Street Journal*, March 14, 2012, B1.

28. Katherine Barrett and Richard Greene, "Dashboard Confessionals, Eliminating Duplicative Services, and Henry Ford on Innovation," *Governing*, February 17, 2011, www.governing.com/topics/mgmt /Dashboard-Confessionals-Eliminating -Duplicative-Services-and-Henry-Ford-on -Innovation.html (Accessed April 16, 2012).

29. Sharon Edelson, "As Profits Climb, Target Tweaks Mix," *Women's Wear Daily*, November 17, 2011, 8.

30. U.S. Census Bureau, "U.S. & World Population Clocks," February 14, 2012, www.census.gov/main/www/popclock.html (Accessed April 16, 2012).

31. Nina Golgowski, "Average American Consumes One Ton of Food a Year While Equating a Gallon of Soda a Week," *Daily Mail*, January 1, 2012, www.dailymail.co.uk /news/article-2080940/Average-American -consumes-ton-food-year-equating-gallon -soda-week.html (Accessed June 28, 2012).

16. "Our Story," The Chef's Garden, www.chefs-garden.com/our-story (Accessed April 16, 2012); "Research and Development," The Chef's Garden, www.chefs-garden.com/research-and -development (Accessed April 16, 2012).

17. Austin Carr, "Netflix Reacts to Blockbuster's Boasts, iPhone App, and Hulu," *Fast Company*, June 11, 2010, www.fastcompany .com/1659085/netflix-reacts-to-blockbuster -and-ceo-jim-keyes-speaks-on-iphone-app -and-competition-from-hu (Accessed April 16, 2012).

2

1. Sharon Edelson, "As Profits Climb, Target Tweaks Mix," *Women's Wear Daily*, November 17, 2011, 8.

2. Christopher Palmeri, "Disney Takes Aim at SpongeBob and Dora." *Bloomberg Businessweek*, March 26–April 1, 2012, 21–22.

3. Julie Jargon, "Darden Slims Down Its Kids' Meals," *Wall Street Journal*, September 16, 2011, B6.

4. Nat Worden and Stu Woo, "Amazon Goes After Netflix, Adding Movie Subscription," *Wall Street Journal*, February 23, 2011, B1.

5. Clementine Fletcher, "Reckitt Manages Its Heroin Habit," *Bloomberg Businessweek*, November 7–11, 2011, 22.

6. David Lipke, "Ugg Goes Upscale with Men's Collection Line," *Women's Wear Daily*, March 28, 2012, www.wwd.com /menswear-news/clothing-furnishings /ugg-goes-upscale-with-mens-collection -line-5833195 (Accessed April 16, 2012).

7. Bansi Nagji and Geoff Tuff, "A Simple Tool You Need to Manage Innovation," *Harvard Business Review*, May 2015, http://hbr .org/2012/05/managing-your-innovation -portfolio/ar/1 (Accessed June 1, 2012).

8. Peter Burrows and Jim Aley, "Why the iPad's Success May Spell the End of the Computer Industry as We Know It," *Bloomberg Businessweek*, March 26–April 1, 2012, 4–5.

9. Arik Hesseldahl, "Why the Mac Is Still a Rock Star at Apple," *Bloomberg Businessweek*, June 28–July 4, 2010, 30.

10. Austin Carr, "Red Hot Redbox Seeing 40 Rentals per Second: Infographic," *Fast Company*, August 1, 2011, www.fastcompany.com/1770834/red -hot-redbox-seeing-40-rentals-per-second -infographic (Accessed April 16, 2012).

11. "Ben & Jerry's Ice Cream—Ben & Jerry's Mission Statement," Ben & Jerry's, www.benjerry.com/activism/mission -statement (Accessed April 16, 2012).

12. Connie Gugielmo and Aaron Ricadela, "Mulling Options, Dell Considers Going Private," *Bloomberg Businessweek*, June 21– June 27, 2010, 37–38.

© iStockphoto.com/ PeskyMonkey

13. Duane Stanford, "How PepsiCo Refreshed Its SoBe Water Brand," *Bloomberg Businessweek*, June 28–July 4, 2010, 15–16.
14. Keith Bradsher, "Upgraded Pearls of Low Price Flow from China," *New York Times*, August 2, 2011, A1.
15. Molly Prior, "Duane Reade's New Format Steps Up Beauty Battle," *Women's Wear Daily*, July 8, 2011, 1, 8.
16. "Our Story," The Chef's Garden, www.chefs-garden.com/our-story (Accessed April 16, 2012); "Research and Development," The Chef's Garden, www.chefs-garden.com/research-and-development (Accessed April 16, 2012).
17. Austin Carr, "Netflix Reacts to Blockbuster's Boasts, iPhone App, and Hulu," *Fast Company*, June 11, 2010, www.fastcompany.com/1659085/netflix-reacts-to-blockbuster-and-ceo-jim-keyes-speaks-on-iphone-app-and-competition-from-hu (Accessed April 16, 2012).

3

1. Marianne M. Jennings, *Business Ethics*, 5th ed. (Mason, OH: Thomson Higher Education, 2006), 5–6.
2. Edward Stevens, *Business Ethics* (New York: Paulist Press, 1979).
3. Anusorn Singhapakdi, Scott Vitell, and Kenneth Kraft, "Moral Intensity and Ethical Decision Making of Marketing Professionals," *Journal of Business Research*, 36, no. 3, (1996): 245–255; Ishmael Akaah and Edward Riordan, "Judgments of Marketing Professionals about Ethical Issues in Marketing Research: A Replication and Extension," *Journal of Marketing Research*, 26, no. 1, (1989): 112–120; see also Shelby Hunt, Lawrence Chonko, and James Wilcox, "Ethical Problems of Marketing Researchers," *Journal of Marketing Research*, 21, no. 3, (1984): 309–324; Kenneth Andrews, "Ethics in Practice," *Harvard Business Review*, September 1989, 99–104; Thomas Dunfee, Craig Smith, and William T. Ross, Jr., "Social Contracts and Marketing Ethics," *Journal of Marketing*, 63, no. 3, (1999): 14–32; Jay Handelman and Stephen Arnold, "The Role of Marketing Actions with a Social Dimension: Appeals to the Institutional Environment," *Journal of Marketing*, 63, no. 3 (1999): 33–48; and David Turnipseed, "Are Good Soldiers Good? Exploring the Link between Organizational Citizenship Behavior and Personal Ethics," *Journal of Business Research*, 55, no. 1, (2002): 1–15.
4. "A Strong Ethical Culture Is Key to Cutting Misconduct on the Job," Ethics Resource Center, June 23, 2010, http://ethics.org/news/strong-ethical-culture-key-cutting-misconduct-job (Accessed April 16, 2012).
5. Ibid.
6. Terry Mann, "Ethics Training for the Workplace," eHow.com, February 6, 2010, www.ehow.com/facts_5957733_ethics-training-workplace.html (Accessed February 29, 2012).
7. "The View from the Top, and Bottom," *Economist*, September 24, 2011, www.economist.com/node/21530171 (Accessed April 16, 2012).

8. "National Business Ethics Survey 2011," Ethics Resource Center, www.ethics.org/nbes/findings.html (Accessed April 16, 2012).
9. Ibid.
10. Dexter Roberts and Justin Blum, "Bribery Is Losing Its Charm in China," *Bloomberg Businessweek*, July 12–July 18, 2010, 11.
11. Marc Gunther, "Will Social Responsibility Harm Business?" *Wall Street Journal*, May 18, 2005, A2.
12. Preetika Rana, "Reebok Cobbles a Plan for India's Rural Poor," *Wall Street Journal*, November 25, 2011, B7.
13. This section is adapted from Archie B. Carroll, "The Pyramid of Corporate Social Responsibility: Toward the Moral Management of Organizational Stakeholders," *Business Horizons*, 34, no. 4, (1991): 39–48; see also Kirk Davidson, "Marketers Must Accept Greater Responsibilities," *Marketing News*, February 2, 1998, 6.
14. Joe Light, "Sustainability Jobs Get Green Light at Large Firms," *Wall Street Journal*, July 11, 2011, http://online.wsj.com/article/SB10001424052702304793504576433430 1780569100.html (Accessed April 16, 2012).
15. "SAM, Dow Jones Indexes and STOXX, Ltd. Announce Results of Dow Jones Sustainability Review," SAM Media Release, September 3, 2009; see also Marni Evans, "What Is Sustainability?" About.com, June 7, 2010, http://sustainability.about.com/od/Sustainability/a/What-Is-Sustainability.htm (Accessed April 16, 2012).
16. "Globally, Companies Are Giving Back," *HR Magazine*, June 1, 2007, 30.
17. "IBM Global Survey Shows Information Gap in 'Green,' Sustainability Strategies," IBM, June 1, 2009, www-03.ibm.com/press/us/en/pressrelease/27622.wss (Accessed April 16, 2012).
18. Carrie Hall, "United Nations Global Compact Annual Review—Anniversary Edition June 2010," *The United Nations Global Compact*, June 2010, www.unglobalcompact.org/docs/news_events/8.1/UNGC_Annual_Review_2010.pdf (Accessed April 16, 2012).
19. "Secretary-General Opens Global Compact Leaders Summit as Business, Government, Civil Society Leaders Rally for Corporate Citizenship," UNESCAP Press Release No. L/38/2007, July 5, 2007.
20. "Marketing Power—American Marketing Association," American Marketing Association, www.marketingpower.com (Accessed April 16, 2012).
21. Gordon Wyner, "Sustainability Perspectives," *Marketing Management*, 19, no. 2 (2010): 45.
22. "Marketing a Green Product," *Bloomberg Businessweek*, March 5, 2007, www.businessweek.com/smallbiz/content/mar2007/sb20070305_213937.htm (Accessed April 16, 2012).
23. David F. Giannetto, "It's Not Easy Being Green," *U.S. Business Review*, 9, no. 7, (2008): 14–15.
24. Linda Tischler, "Once Returned, a Toothbrush Lives On as a Picnic Table," *FastCoDesign*, August 1, 2011, www.fastcodesign.com/1664638/a-recyclable-toothbrush-that-morphs-into-a-picnic-table (Accessed April 16, 2012).

25. "Consumers Doubt Green Efforts," *Marketing Management*, 18, no. 4 (2009): 5.
26. "Sustainability Marketing Has Legs," *Marketing Management*, 18, no. 4, (2009): 4.
27. Xueming Luo and C. B. Bhattacharya, "The Debate over Doing Good: Corporate Social Performance, Strategic Marketing Levers, and Firm-Idiosyncratic Risk," *Journal of Marketing*, 73, no. 6, (2009): 198–213.
28. "Shelf Awareness for Wednesday, February 29, 2012," *Shelf Awareness*, February 29, 2012, www.shelf-awareness.com/issue.html?issue=1677#m15192 (Accessed April 16, 2012).

4

1. Delia Paunescu,"The Follower's Future: Where Social Media Is Headed In 2012," *VisionMonday*, January 23, 2012, www.visionmonday.com/ViewContent/tabid/211/content_id/31991/catId/183/Default.aspx (Accessed April 17, 2012).
2. Quirk's Staff, "Research Shows Social Networking Site Users More Socially Connected," *Quirk's Marketing Research Review*, August 2011, 8.
3. Ibid.
4. Ibid.
5. "Designing Happiness," *Fast Company*, April 2012, 100–101.
6. Josh Bernoff, "Living in Facebook's Bizarro World," *Marketing News*, March 31, 2012, 11.
7. "How Do You Get to 7 Billion People?" *Wall Street Journal*, October 22–23, 2011, A2.
8. "Population Leaves Heartland Behind," *Wall Street Journal*, April 11, 2011, A6.
9. Ibid.
10. "Marketing and Tweens," *Branding*, June 16, 2010.
11. Kathy Grannis, "National Retail Federation—Back to School Sales Up as Parents Replenish Children's Needs, According to NRF," National Retailing Federation, July 15, 2010, www.nrf.com/modules.php?name=News&op=viewlive&sp_id=966 (Accessed April 17, 2012).
12. Anjali Athavaley, "Make Room for Junior Decorators," *Wall Street Journal*, December 1, 2010, http://online.wsj.com/article/SB100014240527487046792045756466713542109974.html (Accessed April 17, 2012).
13. "Pew Survey: Teens Love Facebook, Hate Blogging, Are Always Online, and Don't Use Twitter," *Fast Company*, February 3, 2010, www.fastcompany.com/blog/zachary-wilson/and-how/pew-survey-finds-increase-social-media-internet-time-decrese-blogging-te (Accessed April 17, 2012).
14. "Teens Slowly Increase Online Shopping," *emarketer*, April 26, 2011, www.emarketer.com/Article.aspx?R=1008359 (Accessed April 17, 2012).
15. Susan Lipston, "Teenage Spending Habits," *Susan Lipston*, January 26, 2011, http://susanlipston.com/wordpress/2011/01/26/teenage-spending-habits (Accessed April 17, 2012).
16. "Teens Slowly Increase Online Shopping."
17. "A Star Customer Falls Back to Earth," *Bloomberg Businessweek*, March 26, 2012, 19–20.

18. "Talk to Me, Not at Me," *Quirk's Marketing Research Review*, February 2012, 10–11.
19. "Demographic Profile: America's GENX," *MetLife Mature Market Institute*, 2009.
20. "Gen X, Y Will Lead Economic Recovery," *Marketing Charts*, April 5, 2010, www.marketingcharts.com/direct/gen-xy-will-lead-economic-recovery-12482 (Accessed April 17, 2012).
21. "Reality Bites," *Bloomberg Businessweek*, September 12, 2011, 84–85.
22. Amy Chozick, "Television's Senior Moment," *Wall Street Journal*, March 9, 2011, http://online.wsj.com/article/SB1000142405 27487035596045761749832726650 32 .html (Accessed April 17, 2012).
23. Beth Bulik, "Boom in Multigenerational Households Has Wide Implications for Ad Industry," *Advertising Age,* August 23, 2010, http://adage.com/article/news /multigenerational-households-implications -marketers/145506 (Accessed April 17, 2012).
24. Chozick, "Television's Senior Moment."
25. Brian Steinberg, "Nielsen: This Isn't Your Grandfather's Baby Boomer," *Advertising Age*, July 19, 2010, http://adage.com/article /mediaworks/nielsen-grandfather-s-baby -boomer/144939 (Accessed April 17, 2012).
26. Sam Fahmy, "Despite Recession, Hispanic and Asian Buying Power Expected to Surge in U.S. According to Annual UGA Selig Center Multicultural Economy Study," Terry College of Business, November 4, 2010, www.terry.uga.edu/news/releases/2010 /minority-buying-power-report.html (Accessed April 17, 2012).
27. Conor Dougherty, "U.S. Nears Racial Milestone," *Wall Street Journal,* June 11, 2010, http://online.wsj.com/article/SB10001424 05274870431210457529851200668106 0 .html (Accessed April 17, 2012).
28. Sean Callebs, "Whites Become Minority in Kansas County," CNN, May 22, 2009, http://articles.cnn.com/2009-05-22 /living/garden.city.kansas.minorities_1 _meatpacking-minority-majority (Accessed April 17, 2012).
29. "Population Leaves Heartland Behind."
30. "New Faces of Childhood," *Wall Street Journal*, April 6, 2011, A3.
31. Pete Born, "Beauty in the Age of Multiplicity," *WWD Beauty Inc.,* March 11, 2011, 8.
32. "Hola: P&G Seeks Latino Shoppers," *Wall Street Journal*, September 15, 2011, B1.
33. "Report Shows a Shifting African-American Population," *Brandweek*, January 11, 2009, 6.
34. Bobbi Bowman, "A Portrait of Black America on the Eve of the 2010 Census," *The Root*, February 10, 2010, www.theroot .com/views/portrait-black-america -eve-2010-census (Accessed April 17, 2012).
35. Authors' projections based upon U.S. Census.
36. "Facts for Features: Asian/Pacific American Heritage Month—May 2011," U.S. Census Bureau, March 8, 2011, www.census.gov /newsroom/releases/archives/facts_for _features_special_editions/cb11-ff06.html (Accessed April 17, 2012); "2005–2009 American Community Survey 5-year Estimates," U.S. Census Bureau, http://factfinder2.census.gov/faces /tableservices/jsf/pages/productview

.xhtml?pid=ACS_09_5YR_DP5YR5& prodType=table (Accessed April 17, 2012).
37. Christine Huang, "GlobalHue Presents: The New Asian American Market," *Slideshare*, May 2010, www.slideshare.net /christinewhuang/asian-american-market -ad-tech-sf (Accessed April 17, 2012).
38. Dennis Cauchon and Barbara Hansen, "Typical U.S. Family Got Poorer during the Past 10 Years," September 14, 2011, www.usatoday.com/news/nation/story /2011-09-13/census-household-income /50383882/1 (Accessed April 17, 2012).
39. Daniel Gross, "You're Rich. Get Over It," *Slate Magazine,* February 3, 2010, www.slate.com/id/2243529 (Accessed April 17, 2012).
40. Robert Longley, "Lifetime Earnings Soar with Education," About.com, February 13, 2010, http://usgovinfo.about.com/od /moneymatters/a/edandearnings.htm (Accessed April 17, 2012).
41. David Wessel, "Did 'Great Recession' Live Up to Its Name?" *Wall Street Journal*, April 8, 2010, http://online.wsj.com/article/SB100 0142405270230359120457516969316635 2882.html (Accessed April 17, 2012).
42. Monica Garske, "Affordable Store-Brand Products Score with Customers," AOLNews, January 21, 2011, www.aolnews .com/2011/01/21/affordable-store-brand -products-score-with-consumers (Accessed April 17, 2012).
43. "Food Firms Cook Up Ways to Combat Rare Sales Slump," *Wall Street Journal*, April 21, 2010, A1, A18.
44. Partially adopted from John Bessant, Kathrin Moslein, and Bettina Von Stamm, "In Search of Innovation," *Wall Street Journal*, June 22, 2009, R4.
45. "U.S. Firms, China Are Locked in Major War over Technology," *Wall Street Journal*, February 2, 2011, B1–B2.
46. "FTC Bureau of Competition," FTC, April 9, 2012, www.ftc.gov/bc (Accessed April 17, 2012).
47. "Pretexting," FTC, www.ftc.gov/bsp/edu /microsites/idtheft/consumers/pretexting .html (Accessed April 17, 2012).
48. "Digital-Privacy Rules Taking Shape," *Wall Street Journal*, March 27, 2012, B1.
49. Ibid.
50. Julie Jargon, "Starbucks in Pod Pact," *Wall Street Journal*, March 11, 2011, http://online.wsj.com/article/SB10001424 0527487048230045761921919589640 06 .html (Accessed April 7, 2012).

5

1. "International Trade Statistics 2011," World Trade Organization, www.wto.org/english /res_e/statis_e/its2011_e/its11_toc_e.htm (Accessed April 10, 2012).
2. "How We Win—2010 Mid-Year Update," Caterpillar, www.cat.com (Accessed April 18, 2012).
3. "SBA Export Express—A Fact Sheet for Small Businesses," http://SBA.gov/content /sba-export-express-fact-sheet-small -businesses (Accessed April 18, 2012).
4. "Exports of Goods and Services (% of GDP)," World Bank, http://data.worldbank

.org/indicator/NE.EXP.GNFS.ZS/countries (Accessed April 18, 2012).
5. Gary Locke and Francisco Sanchez, "Exports Support American Jobs," International Trade Administration, April 2010, http://trade.gov /publications/pdfs/exports-support-american -jobs.pdf (Accessed April 18, 2012).
6. Martin Neil Baily, Matthew Slaughter, and Laura Tyson, "The Global Jobs Competition Heats Up," *Wall Street Journal*, July 1, 2010, A19.
7. Theodore Levitt, "The Globalization of Markets," *Harvard Business Review*, May 1983, 92–100.
8. "What Ever Happened to Tang?" *Fortune*, December 12, 2011, http://features.blogs .fortune.cnn.com/2011/11/29/tang-kraft -sales (Accessed April 18, 2012).
9. Eric Pfanner, "PBS Introduces New Television Channel in Britain," *New York Times*, November 27, 2011, www.nytimes .com/2011/11/28/business/media/pbs -introduces-new-television-channel-in -britain.html (Accessed April 18, 2012).
10. "GNI, Atlas Method (Current US$)," The World Bank, http://data.worldbank.org /indicator/NY.GNP.ATLS.CD/countries (Accessed April 18, 2012).
11. Ibid.
12. Paul Toscano, "The World's Most Expensive Places to Live 2011," *CNBC*, July 12, 2011, www.cnbc.com/id/43729279/The_World_s _Most_Expensive_Places_To_Live_2011 (Accessed April 18, 2012).
13. Laurie Burkitt, "Burberry Dresses Up China Stores with Digital Strategy," *Wall Street Journal*, April 14, 2011, B9.
14. Ibid.
15. Paul Beckett, Vibhuti Agarwal, and Julie Jargon, "Starbucks Brews Plan to Enter India," *Wall Street Journal*, January 14, 2011, http:// online.wsj.com/article/SB1000142405274 87035834045760795935588387 56.html (Accessed April 18, 2012).
16. Peter Coy, "Five Ways Forward with China," *Bloomberg Businessweek*, June 28–July 4, 2010, 4–5; Arnold J. Karr, "Study: China Top Market for Retail Development," *Women's Wear Daily*, June 23, 2010, 2.
17. "Economy Rankings," *Doing Business*, www.doingbusiness.org/rankings (Accessed January 26, 2011).
18. Megha Bahree, "India Unlocks Door for Global Retailers," *Wall Street Journal*, November 25, 2011, http://online.wsj.com /article/SB1000142405297020463090457 7058131832465876.html (Accessed April 18, 2012).
19. Larry Elliott and Heather Stewart, "Doha Trade Round Faces Risk of Collapse after 10 Years of Talks," *The Guardian*, April 24, 2011, www.guardian.co.uk/business/2011 /apr/24/doha-trade-talks-threat-of-collapse -geneva-wto (Accessed April 18, 2012).
20. Loretta Chao, "Huawei: Protectionism Hits Revenue Growth," *Wall Street Journal*, April 27, 2011, http://online.wsj.com/article/SB10 0014240527487039569045762880823572 33172.html (Accessed April 18, 2012).
21. "International Trade Statistics 2011."
22. "North American Free Trade Agreement Fast Facts," North American Free Trade Agreement, April 4, 2012, www.naftanow.org /facts (Accessed April 18, 2012).

23. "U.S. Central America-Dominican Republic Free Trade Agreement (CAFTA-DR) Analysis," (Washington, DC: International Trade Association, Summer 2008), 12.

24. "Countries," European Union, http://europa.eu/about-eu/countries/index_en.htm (Accessed April 18, 2012).

25. Victor Mallet and Peter Spiegel, "Spain and EU Reject Talk of Bailout," *Financial Times*, April 10, 2012, www.ft.com/intl/cms/s/0/2a3f04fc-832a-11e1-9f9a-00144feab49a.html (Accessed April 18, 2012).

26. Gabriele Steinhauser, "EU Fines Procter & Gamble, Unilever over Laundry Detergent Cartel," *Huffington Post*, April 13, 2011, www.huffingtonpost.com/2011/04/13/eu-fines-proctor-gamble-u_n_848508.html (Accessed April 18, 2012).

27. Jonathan Bensky, "World's Biggest Market: European Union Offers Great Opportunities for U.S. Companies, but There Are Also Plenty of Challenges," *Shipping Digest*, July 30, 2007.

28. Harry Papachristou, "Factbox: Greek Austerity and Reform Measures," Reuters, February 19, 2012, www.reuters.com/article/2012/02/19/us-greece-austerity-idUSTRE81I05T20120219 (Accessed April 18, 2012).

29. Ellen Gamerman, "Exporting Broadway," *Wall Street Journal*, July 16, 2010, W1–W2.

30. "International Franchise Association," International Franchise Association, www.franchise.org (Accessed April 18, 2012).

31. Liza Algar, "Abrams & Chronicle Books Announce Sales, Marketing and Distribution Joint Venture to Serve the United Kingdom and Europe Export Markets," Chronicle Books, June 22, 2010, www.chroniclebooks.com/landing-pages/Chronicle/pressroom/A_CB_mediaRelease.pdf (Accessed April 18, 2012).

32. "Korean Dunkin' Donuts," Eat Your Kimchi, March 13, 2011, www.eatyourkimchi.com/korean-dunkin-donuts (Accessed April 18, 2012).

33. Beckett, Agarwal, and Jargon, "Starbucks Brews Plan to Enter India."

34. Nidhi Dutt, "Mobile Tech Brings Big Retail Brands to Rural India," BBC News, March 27, 2011, www.bbc.co.uk/news/business-12841993 (Accessed April 18, 2012).

35. Will Connors and Sarah Childress, "Africa's Local Champions Begin to Spread Out," *Wall Street Journal*, May 26, 2010, B8.

36. "TrustYou Selected by Global Hotel Leader Accor as Social Media Solution," *PR Newswire*, London, March 7, 2012.

37. Tessa Thorniley, "Uniqlo Thrives on Digital Marketing," *Market Leader*, Spring 2011, 50–52.

38. Ibid.

6

1. Lance A. Bettencourt and Anthony W. Ulwich, "The Customer-Centered Innovation Map," *Harvard Business Review*, May 2008, 1–8; also see Anthony W. Ulwich and Lance A. Bettencourt, "Giving Customers a Fair Hearing," *Sloan Management Review*, Spring 2008, 62–68.

2. Eric Bellman, "BlackBerry's Maker Finds Fertile Ground in Indonesia," *Wall Street Journal*, September 12, 2011, A1.

3. Kristina Knight, "User View: 97% of Consumers Research Products Online," *BizReport*, March 11, 2010, www.bizreport.com/2010/03/user_view_97_of_consumers_research_products_online.html (Accessed April 18, 2012).

4. "By the Numbers," *Next*, May 17, 2010, 24.

5. Hui Chen, "The Impact Mechanism of Consumer-Generated Comments of Shopping Sites on Consumer Trust," *Journal of Computers*, 6, no. 1, (2011): 43–50.

6. Jonathan Welsh, "Consumer Reports Drops Civic Recommendation," *Wall Street Journal*, August 2, 2011, B4.

7. Wendy Moe and Michael Trusov, "The Value of Social Dynamics in Online Ratings Forums," *Journal of Marketing Research*, 48, no. 3, (2011): 444–456.

8. Ian King and Ari Levy, "From Chipmaker to Dog Catcher," *Bloomberg Businessweek*, November 21–27, 2011, 49.

9. Jeffrey Inman and Russell Winer, "Impulse Buys," *Wall Street Journal*, April 15, 1999, A1; David Silvera, Anne Lavack, and Fredric Kropp, "Impulse Buying: The Role of Affect, Social Influence, and Subjective Well-Being," *Journal of Consumer Research*, 25, no. 1, (2008): 23–33.

10. Katy Byron, "Was the Recession a Good Thing?" *CNN Money*, July 12, 2011, http://money.cnn.com/2011/07/12/pf/recession_saving_habits/index.htm (Accessed April 18, 2012).

11. Matt Townsend, "Replacing the Extinct Impulse Buyer," *Bloomberg Businessweek*, November 14–20, 2012, 28–29.

12. The material on "types of involvement" was adapted from Barry Babin and Eric Harris, *CB²* (Mason, OH: South-Western Cengage Learning, 2011), 88–89.

13. Allison Aubrey, "Turning to Big Business to Solve the Obesity Epidemic," *NPR*, December 2, 2011, www.npr.org/blogs/thesalt/2011/12/02/143052025/turning-to-big-business-to-solve-the-obesity-epidemic (Accessed April 18, 2012).

14. Ellen Byron, "Hola: P&G Seeks Latino Shoppers," *Wall Street Journal*, September 15, 2011, B1–B2.

15. Alexandra Alter, "Luxury Lit: A Book for $75,000," *Wall Street Journal*, July 16, 2010, W4.

16. Stephanie Clifford, "Even Marked Up, Luxury Goods Fly Off Shelves," *New York Times*, August 3, 2011, www.nytimes.com/2011/08/04/business/sales-of-luxury-goods-are-recovering-strongly.html (Accessed April 18, 2012).

17. Ibid.

18. Ulrich Orth and Lynn Kahle, "Intrapersonal Variation in Consumer Susceptibility to Normative Influence: Toward a Better Understanding of Brand Choice Decisions," *Journal of Social Psychology*, 148, no. 4, (2008): 423–448.

19. Gwendolyn Bounds, "In the New Dream Home, Majestic Boilers and Designer Pipes," *Wall Street Journal*, July 15, 2010, A1, A14.

20. Orth and Kahle, "Intrapersonal Variation in Consumer Susceptibility to Normative Influence: Toward a Better Understanding of Brand Choice Decisions," 429.

21. Peter van Eck, Wander Jager, and Peter Leeflang, "Opinion Leaders' Role in Innovation Diffusion: A Simulation Study," *Journal of Product Innovation Management*, 28, no. 2, (2011): 187–203.

22. Amanda Lenhart, "'How Do [They] Even Do That?' Myths and Facts about the Impact of Technology on the Lives of American Teens," *Pew Research Center*, April 7, 2011, www.pewinternet.org/Presentations/2011/Apr/From-Texting-to-Twitter.aspx (Accessed April 18, 2012).

23. Rama Rao, "Concept Measuring Influence of Spouse Decisions in Purchasing," *Cite Man Network*, March 11, 2010, www.citeman.com/9161-concept-measuring-influence-of-spouse-decisions-in-purchasing (Accessed April 18, 2012).

24. A. Valarmathi, "Children's Influences on Family Decision Making," *Articlesbase*, September 3, 2010, www.articlesbase.com/marketing-tips-articles/childrens-influences-on-family-decision-making-3189980.html (Accessed April 18, 2012).

25. "Charles Schwab's 2011 Teens & Money Survey Sheds Light on New 'Recession Generation,'" *Charles Schwab*, May 24, 2011, www.businesswire.com/news/schwab/20110524005184/en/Charles-Schwab%E2%80%99s-2011-Teens-Money-Survey-Sheds (Accessed April 18, 2012).

26. Anita Manning, "Teach Your Tech-Challenged Parents, Grandparents Well," *USA Today*, March 10, 2011, http://yourlife.usatoday.com/parenting-family/caregiving/story/2011/03/Teaching-elderly-to-come-to-grips-with-gadgets-technology/44700622/1 (Accessed April 18, 2012).

27. Tamara Schweitzer, "Chris Easter and Bob Horner, Founders of The Man Registry," *Inc.*, July 19, 2010, www.inc.com/30under30/2010/profile-chris-easter-bob-horner-man-registry.html (Accessed April 18, 2012).

28. Sue Shellenbarger, "Daunting Task for Mr. Mom: Get a Job," *Wall Street Journal*, May 19, 2010, http://online.wsj.com/article/SB10001424052748703957904575252270698575294.html (Accessed April 18, 2012).

29. Nanette Byrnes, "Secrets of the Male Shopper," *BusinessWeek*, September 4, 2006, www.businessweek.com/magazine/content/06_36/b3999001.htm (Accessed April 18, 2012); also see Xin He, Jeffrey Inman, and Vikas Mittal, "Gender Jeopardy in Financial Risk-Taking," *Journal of Marketing Research*, 45, no. 4, (2008): 414–424.

30. "B&N's Tablet Customer: Marketing to 'Julie,'" *Shelf Awareness*, March 20, 2012, www.shelf-awareness.com/issue.html?issue=1695 (Accessed April 18, 2012).

31. "Ampacet - Managing the Elements of Success," Ampacet, www.ampacet.com (Accessed April 18, 2012).

32. Karyn Monget, "Does Sex Sell?" *Women's Wear Daily*, June 21, 2010, 1, 12.

33. Elizabeth Wilson, "Using the Dollar-metric Scale," in 1987 AMA Educator's Proceedings, ed. Susan Douglas et al. (Chicago, IL: American Marketing Association, 1987), 107.

34. Sarah Nagle, "Four Keys to Creating Products for the Lady Gaga Generation," *Fast Company Design*, June 1, 2011, www.fastcodesign.com/1663954/four-keys-to-creating-products-for-the-lady-gaga-generation (Accessed April 18, 2012).

35. Katherine Boehret, "Making Hotmail Hot Again," *Wall Street Journal*, June 9, 2010, http://online.wsj.com/article/SB10001424052748703302604575294700105749996.html (Accessed April 18, 2012).

36. Judith Aquino, "The 10 Most Successful Rebranding Campaigns Ever," *Business Insider*, February 10, 2011, www.businessinsider.com/10-most-successful-rebranding-campaigns-2011-2 (Accessed April 18, 2012).

37. Ibid.

38. Jyothi Datta, "Aspartame: Bitter Truth in Artificial Sweeteners?" *Business Line*, October 3, 2005, www.thehindubusinessline.com/2005/10/04/stories/2005100404220300.htm (Accessed April 18, 2012).

7

1. Murray Sye, "What Do Most Business Marketers Want from Their Online Marketing Plan?" *WhiteSpace*, December 10, 2010, www.whitespace.on.ca/Blog/bid/56260/What-do-most-business-marketers-want-from-their-online-marketing-plan (Accessed May 21, 2012).

2. Michael D. Hutt and Thomas W. Speh, *Business Marketing Management: B2B*, 10th ed. (Cincinnati: Thomson, 2010), 4.

3. Ibid.

4. Sean Callahan, "Interactive Spending Continues to Climb," *BtoB Magazine*, March 8, 2010, www.btobonline.com/apps/pbcs.dll/article?AID=/20100308/FREE/303049998/1445/FREE (Accessed May 21, 2012).

5. Sean Callahan, "Content Marketing Becoming Vital," *B2B Magazine,* February 13, 2012, 1; 19.

6. "B2B Marketers Gain Ground with Social," *eMarketer*, May 27, 2010, www.emarketer.com.

7. "Emerging Trends in B2B Social Marketing," *BtoB Magazine*, April 2011, www.btobonline.com/section/researchreports5 (Accessed May 21, 2012).

8. Karen Bannan, "YouTube for B-to-B: How to Use the Popular Video Site to Expand Your Branding," *BtoB Magazine*, May 5, 2010 (Accessed May 21, 2012), www.btobonline.com/apps/pbcs.dll/article?AID=/20100503/FREE/305039965/1445/FREE (Accessed May 21, 2012); Paul Gillin, "B-to-B Firmly in Social Media," *BtoB Magazine*, April 12, 2010, www.btobonline.com/article/20100412/FREE/304129965/b-to-b-firmly-in-social-media (Accessed May 21, 2012).

9. Karen Bannan, "10 Great BtoB Sites," *BtoB Magazine*, September 19, 2011, 8.

10. Gabriel Perna, "WWDC: 'Stickiness' Factor Building iCloud Excitement," *International Business Times*, June 7, 2011, www.ibtimes.com/articles/159025/20110607/apple-steve-jobs-icloud-stickiness-iphone-5.htm (Accessed May 21, 2012).

11. Sasthi Sarma, "Measuring Stickiness with Basic Google Analytics' Key Performance Indicators," *Position*[2], June 3, 2010, http://blogs.position2.com/measuring-stickiness-with-basic-google-analytics-key-performance-indicators (Accessed May 21, 2012).

12. Ellis Booker, "B-to-B Marketers Apply Analytics to Social Media," *BtoB Magazine*, April 12, 2010, www.btobonline.com/apps/pbcs.dll/article?AID=/20100412/FREE/304089975/1445/FREE (Accessed May 21, 2012).

13. Brian Hook, "Climbing the B2B Social Media Ladder," *E-Commerce Times*, May 27, 2010, www.ecommercetimes.com/rsstory/70081.html?wlc=1296574575 (Accessed May 21, 2012).

14. Jean Gianfagna, "Four Lessons Big Direct Marketers Can Learn from Small Mailers," *Smart Marketing Strategy*, May 24, 2011, www.gianfagnamarketing.com/blog/2011/05/24/4-lessons-big-direct-marketers-can-learn-from-small-mailers (Accessed May 21, 2012).

15. "Disintermediation," *marketingterms.com*, www.marketingterms.com/dictionary/disintermediation (Accessed May 21, 2012).

16. Roger Cheng and Don Clark, "Cisco Flips Consumer Strategy," *Wall Street Journal*, April 13, 2011, B3.

17. Christopher Hosford, "'BtoB' Leading Edge Attendees Urged to 'Flip the Funnel' toward Retention," *BtoB Magazine*, June 23, 2010, www.btobonline.com/apps/pbcs.dll/article?AID=/20100623/FREE/100629964 (Accessed May 21, 2012).

18. Daisuke Wakabayashi, "Softbank: In Strategic Alliance to Create PayPal Japan," *Wall Street Journal*, May 8, 2012, http://online.wsj.com/article/BT-CO-20120508-724913.html (Accessed May 21, 2012).

19. Karon Snowdon, "Singapore-Virgin Airline Deal Expands Network," ABC Radio Australia, June 8, 2011, www.radioaustralia.net.au/connectasia/stories/201106/s3238843.htm (Accessed May 21, 2012).

20. "MasterCard and Avis Budget Group Announce New Strategic Marketing Alliance," *Financial*, June 8, 2011, http://finchannel.com/news_flash/Banks/88466_MasterCard_and_Avis_Budget_Group_Announce_New_Strategic_Marketing_Alliance (Accessed May 21, 2012).

21. Robert M. Morgan and Shelby D. Hunt, "The Commitment-Trust Theory of Relationship Marketing," *Journal of Marketing*, 58, no. 3, 1994, 23.

22. Ibid.

23. "Suzuki-VW Alliance to Include Hybrids, Management," *Bloomberg*, January 15, 2010, www.bloomberg.com/apps/news?pid=newsarchive&sid=aH4AdlSRfQLE (Accessed May 21, 2012).

24. Mary Morrison, "Getting in with Government," *BtoB Magazine*, May 3, 2010, 13.

25. Ibid.

26. Rebecca Smith and Mike Ramsey, "Rent a Leaf: Enterprise Buys a Fleet," *Wall Street Journal*, July 27, 2010, http://online.wsj.com/article/SB10001424052748704700404575391602609091276.html (Accessed May 21, 2012).

27. Daniel Michaels, "Rivals Race for Tanker Deal," *Wall Street Journal*, July 23, 2010, http://online.wsj.com/article/SB10001424052748704421304575383132903915038.html (Accessed May 21, 2012).

28. "Exostar's Global Customer Base," Exostar, www.exostar.com/Exostar_Customers.aspx (Accessed May 21, 2012).

29. Peter Sanders, "Boeing 787 Lands in Farnborough," *Wall Street Journal*, July 19, 2010, http://online.wsj.com/article/SB10001424052748704196404575374693695488042.html (Accessed May 21, 2012).

30. Marshall Lager, "Listen Up," *Customer Relationship Management*, March 2007, 24–27.

31. "Right-Channeling: Making Sure Your Best Customers Get Your Best Service," Right Now Technologies, June 3, 2009, http://jobfunctions.bnet.com/abstract.aspx?docid=132740 (Accessed March 28, 2011).

8

1. Joseph White, "Retooling Luxury Cars for a Younger Generation," *Wall Street Journal*, September 14, 2011, D2.

2. Sarah Nassauer, "A Season [or 13] for Shopping," *Wall Street Journal*, August 17, 2011, D5.

3. Lynn Finch, "Danger ahead for Free-Spending Teens," *Walnut Row*, May 26, 2011, www.walnutrow.com/2011/05/26/danger-free-spending-teens (Accessed April 18, 2012).

4. Matt Townsend, Ashley Lutz, and Christopher Palmeri, "A Star Customer Falls Back to Earth," *Bloomberg Businessweek*, March 26–April 1, 2012, 19–20.

5. Cathy Yan, "Can Shopping Be Fun Again?" *Wall Street Journal*, May 6, 2010, http://online.wsj.com/article/SB10001424052748704342604575221543926318602.html (Accessed April 18, 2012).

6. Toni Whitt, "Boomers Rewrite Rules for Marketing," *Herald Tribune*, June 25, 2007, www.heraldtribune.com/article/20070625/BUSINESS/706250444 (Accessed April 18, 2012).

7. Leapfrog Interactive, "Social Media Marketing to Women: What Every Brand Needs to Know," *Pontiflex*, May 26, 2011, 2.

8. Ad Age Insights, "Always On Women," *Ad Age*, November 14, 2011, 6.

9. Rachel Brown, "Fashion Gets in the Game: $20 Billion Video Industry Aiming for Female Fans," *Women's Wear Daily*, January 12, 2010, 12.

10. Rosemary Feitelberg, "Russell Simmons to Launch Yoga Brand Tantris," *Women's Wear Daily*, March 29, 2012, www.wwd.com/markets-news/intimates-activewear/russell-simmons-to-launch-tantris-brand-5835915 (Accessed April 18, 2012).

11. E. J. Schultz, "Weight Watchers Picks a New Target: Men," *Crain's New York Business*, April 22, 2011, www.crainsnewyork.com/article/20110422/FREE/110429947 (Accessed April 18, 2012).

12. Christina Binkley, "Post-Recession, the Rich Are Different," *Wall Street Journal*, May 12, 2011, http://online.wsj.com/article/SB10001424052748703730804576317202215630540.html (Accessed April 16, 2012).

13. Rachel Lamb, "Affluent Consumers Demand Top-Quality Customer Service: Experts," *Luxury Daily*, January 12, 2011, www.luxurydaily.com/affluent-consumers-demand-top-quality-customer-service-experts (Accessed April 16, 2012).

14. "The New Mainstream: How the Buying Habits of Ethnic Groups Are Creating a New American Identity," *Knowledge@Wharton*, November 15, 2005, http://knowledge.wharton.upenn.edu/article.cfm?articleid=1270 (Accessed April 18, 2012).

15. Lisa Lockwood, "Hispanics: A Growing Force," *Women's Wear Daily*, March 23, 2011, 2.

16. Doug Anderson and Laurel Kennedy, "Baby Boomer Segmentation: Eight Is Enough," *ACNielsen*, Fall/Winter 2006, 6.

17. Thomas Catan, "To Understand Washington Ads, You've Got to Be a Code Breaker," *Wall Street Journal*, March 7, 2011, http://online.wsj.com/article/SB10001424052748704637704576082212342743824.html (Accessed April 18, 2012).

18. Emily Steel, "Exploring Ways to Build a Better Consumer Profile," *Wall Street Journal*, March 15, 2010, http://online.wsj.com/article/SB10001424052748703447104575117972284656374.html (Accessed April 18, 2012).

19. Mike Esterl, "Coke Tailors Its Soda Sizes," *Wall Street Journal*, September 19, 2011, B4.

20. Lowell D'Souza, "Applying the 80-20 Rule to Marketing," *Marketing Bones*, November 28, 2010, http://marketingbones.com/applying-the-80-20-rule-to-marketing (Accessed April 18, 2012).

21. Kasey Wehrum, "Comic Books for Entrepreneurs," *Inc.*, May 2011, www.inc.com/magazine/20110501/comic-books-for-entrepreneurs.html (Accessed April 18, 2012).

22. Molly Prior, "CVS Retreats from Prestige Beauty," *Women's Wear Daily*, March 29, 2012, www.wwd.com/beauty-industry-news/retailing/cvs-learns-a-lesson-with-beauty-360-5835199 (Accessed April 18, 2012).

23. Eric Wilson, "Social Shopping: Everybody Wants In," *New York Times*, March 25, 2012, www.nytimes.com/imagepages/2012/03/25/fashion/25SOCIALSHOP_GRAPHIC.html (Accessed April 18, 2012).

24. Jeff Green and Alan Ohnsman, "At Subaru, Sharing the Love Is a Market Strategy," *Bloomberg Businessweek*, May 24–May 30, 2010, 18–19.

25. James Hagerty, "Macho Harley Tries Touch of Pink for Women Buyers," *Wall Street Journal*, October 31, 2011, B1.

26. Erick Schonfeld, "Apple's Tim Cook: The iPad Is Cannibalizing Some Mac Sales, But There Are 'A Lot More Windows PCs to Cannibalize than Macs,'" *TechCrunch*, July 19, 2011, http://techcrunch.com/2011/07/19/ipad-cannibalizing-pc (Accessed April 18, 2012).

27. Kasey Wehrum, "Learning from the Customer," *Inc.*, March 1, 2011, www.inc.com/magazine/20110301/customer-service-case-studies-crutchfield.html (Accessed April 18, 2012).

28. Duane Stanford, "Jim Beam's Gender-Bending Adventure," *Bloomberg Businessweek*, October 17–23, 2011, 32.

29. "Our Brands," Gap Inc., www.gapinc.com/content/gapinc/html/aboutus/ourbrands.html (Accessed April 18, 2012).

30. John Pavlus, "'Bumpy Road' Flips Touchscreen Game Mechanics on Their Head," *Fast Company Design*, June 9, 2011, www.fastcodesign.com/1664013/bumpy-road-flips-touchscreen-game-mechanics-on-their-head (Accessed April 18, 2012).

31. Stanford, "Jim Beam's Gender-Bending Adventure."

9

1. Jack Neff, "Pantene Set to Try Again to Reverse Slide," *Advertising Age*, January 17, 2011, http://adage.com/article/news/pantene-set-reverse-sales-slide/148250 (Accessed May 29, 2012).

2. Ellen Byron, "Wash Away Bad Hair Days," *Wall Street Journal*, June 30, 2010, D1.

3. Tim Lynch, "FocusVision Releases 15th Annual Focus Group Index," *PRWeb*, May 18, 2012, www.prweb.com/releases/2012/5/prweb9497403.htm (Accessed May 23, 2012).

4. "Marketers Watch as Friends Interact Online," *Wall Street Journal*, April 15, 2010, B5.

5. Erik Milster, "The Coalition for Innovative Media Measurement Completes Consumer Survey Phase of Its 'USA TouchPoints' Cross-Media Research Study," *CIMM*, June 14, 2011, www.cimm-us.org/mbi_consumer.htm (Accessed May 23, 2012).

6. Raymond R. Burke, "Virtual Shopping: Breakthrough in Marketing Research," *Harvard Business Review*, March/April 1996, 120–131; Valla Roth, "Winning at Retail with Virtual Shopping Research," *Quirk's Marketing Research Review*, June 2011, 46.

7. Roxanne Salen and Susan Stickling, "How the Shopper Is Changing the Retail and Research Landscape," *Quirk's Marketing Research Review*, June 2011, 32.

8. Greg Gates, "Sustainable Compliance within Reach," *Retail-Merchandiser*, June 6, 2011, www.retail-merchandiser.com/current-news/1595-sustainable-compliance-within-reach.html (Accessed June 10, 2011).

9. "US Internet Users," www.emarketer.com, June 4, 2010.

10. Kira Signer and Andy Korman, "One Billion and Growing," *Quirk's Marketing Research Review*, July/August 2006, 62–67.

11. Conversation with Roger Gates, President of DSS Marketing Research, June 2, 2010.

12. "Research in a Petri Dish: Learning from Communities," *Marketing News*, September 3, 2009, 22.

13. Andrew Cutler, "Use These Five Web-Based Approaches to Shrink Your Research Timelines, Costs," *Quirk's Marketing Research Review*, January 2011, 28.

14. "About Consumer-Generated Media (CGM)," Nielsen, www.nielsen-online.com/resources.jsp?section=about_cgm (Accessed October 25, 2010).

15. "BuzzMetrics," Nielsen, http://en-us.nielsen.com/content/nielsen/en_us/product_families/nielsen_buzzmetrics.html (Accessed October 25, 2010).

16. "Products and Solutions: InfoScan Tracking Service," Information Resources Inc., www.usa.infores.com/ProductsSolutions/AllProducts/AllProductsDetail/tabid/159/productid/83/Default.aspx (Accessed December 1, 2008).

17. "IBM Helps Construction Firms Boost Number of Clients by 40% through Mobile Real-Time Trends Analysis," *PR Newswire*, September 1, 2010, www.prnewswire.com//news-releases/ibm-helps-construction-firm-boost-number-of-clients-by-40-through-mobile-real-time-trends-analysis-10196558 38.html (Accessed June 10, 2011).

18. Ibid.

10

1. Karen Weise, "Patagonia Swims Upstream with New Salmon Jerky," *Bloomberg Businessweek*, April 11, 2012, www.businessweek.com/articles/2012-04-11/patagonia-swims-upstream-with-new-salmon-jerky (Accessed April 18, 2012).

2. Ray Smith, "For Men, New Swimsuits with Drawstrings and Dignity," *Wall Street Journal*, April 11, 2012, http://online.wsj.com/article/SB10001424052702304444604577337750372504374.html (Accessed April 18, 2012).

3. Stuart Elliot, "Laundry Soaps Try a Hint of Horror and Some Tough-Guy Talk," *New York Times*, June 15, 2011, www.nytimes.com/2011/06/16/business/media/16adco.html (Accessed April 18, 2012).

4. Bruce Einhorn and Ashlee Vance, "HTC Pins Its Hopes on Music and Software," *Bloomberg Businessweek*, April 5, 2012, www.businessweek.com/articles/2012-04-05/htc-pins-its-hopes-on-music-and-software (Accessed April 18, 2012).

5. Gren Manuel, "Scrabble Rules Are Not Being Changed," *Wall Street Journal*, April 7, 2010, http://blogs.wsj.com/source/2010/04/07/scrabble-rules-are-not-being-changed/ (Accessed April 18, 2012).

6. Ellen Byron, "Wash Away Bad Hair Days," *Wall Street Journal*, June 30, 2010, http://online.wsj.com/article/SB1000142405274870491170457532714193538109 2.html (Accessed April 18, 2012).

7. Susan Berfield, "Marketing Lessons from Brand Oprah," *Bloomberg Businessweek*, May 23–May 29, 2011, 20–22.

8. Tanzina Vega, "Walgreens Launches Campaign to Push Store-Brand Products," *New York Times*, February 10, 2011, www.nytimes.com/2011/02/11/business/media/11adco.html (Accessed April 18, 2012).

9. Hannah Karp, "Store Brands Step Up Their Game," *Wall Street Journal*, January 31, 2012. B1–B2.

10. Ibid.

11. Ellen Byron, "Febreze Joins P&G's $1 Billion Club," *Wall Street Journal*, March 9, 2011, http://online.wsj.com/article/SB10001424 052748704076804576180683371307932 .html (Accessed April 18, 2012).

12. Sarah Nassauer, "Gee, Your Trash Smells Terrific," *Wall Street Journal*, June 9, 2011, http://online.wsj.com/article/SB10001424 052702304432304576369991322977166 .html (Accessed April 18, 2012).

13. "Section 1(a) Timeline: Application Based on Use in Commerce," *United States Patent and Trademark Office*, March 19, 2010, www.uspto.gov/trademarks/process/tm _sec1atimeline.jsp (Accessed April 18, 2012).

14. Deborah L. Vence, "Product Enhancement," *Marketing News*, May 1, 2005, 19.

15. Nathan Olivarez-Giles, "Apple Sued over Its Use of iCloud Name by iCloud Communications," *Los Angeles Times*, June 14, 2011, http://latimesblogs.latimes.com/technology /2011/06/apple-is-sued-by-phoenix-based -icloud-communications-for-use-of-icloud -name.html (Accessed April 18, 2012).

16. David Kesmodel, "U.S. Judge Rules in Bacardi's Favor in Rum Dispute," *Wall Street Journal*, April 7, 2010, http://online.wsj.com /article/SB1000142405270230359120457 5169911818091240.html (Accessed April 18, 2012).

17. Laurie Burkitt and Loretta Chao, "Made in China: Fake Stores," *Wall Street Journal*, August 3, 2011, http://online.wsj.com/article /SB10001424053111904292504576 48408 0863377102.html (Accessed April 18, 2012).

18. Lisa McTigue Pierce, "GE Brings Good Packaging Design to Light," *Packaging Digest*, April 11, 2012, www.packagingdigest .com/article/521468-GE_brings_good _packaging_design_to_light.php (Accessed April 18, 2012).

19. Matthew Boyle, "Even Better Than the Real Thing," *Bloomberg Businessweek*, November 28–December 4, 2011, 25–26.

20. Stephanie Clifford, "Devilish Packaging, Tamed," *New York Times*, June 1, 2011, www.nytimes.com/2011/06/02/business /energy-environment/02packaging.html (Accessed April 18, 2012).

21. Susan Carpenter, "Wasteful Packaging: Do Consumers Care?" *Los Angeles Times*, April 20, 2011, http://latimesblogs .latimes.com/greenspace/2011/04/recycling -packaging-products.html (Accessed April 18, 2012).

22. David Gardner, "How Dell's New Mushroom Packaging and Other Initiatives Are Greening PCs," *Fast Company*, September 6, 2011, www.fastcompany.com/1777672 /dell-corporate-social-responsibility-green -initiatives (Accessed April 18, 2012).

23. Dan Alaimo, "CPGmatters: Nutritional Labeling Provides CPGs, Retailers with Unique Competitive Edge," *Retailwire*, March 22, 2010, www.retailwire.com /discussions/sngl_discussion.cfm/14384 (Accessed April 18, 2012).

24. Ariel Schwartz, "The FTC's New Marketing Rules to Squash Greenwashing," *Fast Company*, June 10, 2011, www.fastcompany .com/1758615/what-will-the-ftcs-new -marketing-rules-mean-for-inauthentic -green-products (Accessed April 18, 2012).

11

1. "The World's 50 Most Innovative Companies," *Fast Company*, www.fastcompany .com/most-innovative-companies/2011 (Accessed April 16, 2012).

2. Neal Ungerleider, "'Virtual Cane' Lets Visually Impaired Navigate via Sonar," *Fast Company*, June 30, 2011, www.fastcompany.com/1764307/new -virtual-cane-lets-visually-impaired-navigate -via-sound (Accessed April 19, 2012).

3. "Moleskine World," Moleskine, www.moleskine.com/moleskine_world (Accessed April 19, 2012).

4. Ira Boudway, "The Brand That Launched a Thousand Chips," *Bloomberg Businessweek*, October 3–11, 2011, 30.

5. Scott McCartney, "An Airier Airplane Takes Off," *Wall Street Journal*, February 24, 2011, D1.

6. Mike Ramsey, "Old Mustang Is Put Out to Pasture," *Wall Street Journal*, April 16, 2012, B1.

7. Joel Rubinson, "Innovating Innovation: The Best Ideas Can Come from Anywhere," *Fast Company*, June 17, 2009, www.fastcompany .com/blog/joel-rubinson/brave-new -marketing/innovating-innovation-best -ideas-can-come-anywhere (Accessed April 19, 2012).

8. "Women's Financial Style," *Adweek Media*, February 16, 2009, 14; Jack Neff, "Package-Good Players Plan New-Product Surge for 2010," *Advertising Age*, December 7, 2009, http://adage.com/article/news/brands -package-good-players-plan-product-surge -2010/140906/ (Accessed April 19, 2012).

9. Bernice Hurst, "Focus Groups Take on New Format," *Retailwire*, January 25, 2010, www.retailwire.com/discussion/14267/focus -groups-take-on-new-format (Accessed April 19, 2012).

10. Rachel Emma Silverman, "For Bright Ideas, Ask the Staff," *Wall Street Journal*, October 17, 2011, http://online.wsj.com /article/SB100014240529702047746045 76631063939483984.html (Accessed April 16, 2012).

11. Sue Shellenbarger, "Better Ideas through Failure," *Wall Street Journal*, September 27, 2011, http://online.wsj.com/article/SB10001 424052970204010604576594671572584 158.html (Accessed April 16, 2012).

12. Anthonia Akitunde, "Nike Unveils Its Big New Paradigm: Shoes Knit Like Socks," *Fast Company*, February 22, 2012, www.fastcodesign.com/1669098/nike -unveils-its-big-new-paradigm-shoes-knit -like-socks (Accessed February 29, 2012).

13. Chris Newmarker, "General Mills Looks Online for Food Innovators," *Minneapolis /St. Paul Business Journal*, November 4, 2009, www.bizjournals.com/twincities /stories/2009/11/02/daily31.html (Accessed April 19, 2012).

14. Andrew Marton, "2006: A Face Odyssey," *Fort Worth Star-Telegram*, February 16, 2006, E1, E8.

15. Pete Engardio, "Scouring the Planet for Brainiacs," *BusinessWeek*, October 11, 2004, 106.

16. "About Ryz," RYZ, www.ryz.com/about (Accessed April 18, 2012); "Threadless Graphic T-shirt Designs," Threadless, www.threadless.com (Accessed April 19, 2012).

17. "Adventures in Test Marketing," *CBS News*, March 25, 2012, www.cbsnews.com/video /watch/?id=7403144n (Accessed April 17, 2012).

18. "Think Big with a Gig: Our Experimental Fiber Network," *Google*, February 2, 2010, http://googleblog.blogspot.com/2010/02 /think-big-with-gig-our-experimental.html (Accessed April 19, 2012); Nancy Gohring, "Majority of US States Request Google Broadband Fibre Network," *Tech World*, July 15, 2010, http://news.techworld.com /networking/3232059/majority-of-us-states -request-google-broadband-fibre-network/ (Accessed April 19, 2012); John Sutter, "Topeka 'Renames' Itself, 'Google, Kansas,'" *CNN*, March 2, 2010, www.cnn.com/2010 /TECH/03/02/google.kansas.topeka/index .html (Accessed April 19, 2012).

19. "P&G Everyday," Procter & Gamble, www.pgeveryday.com/pgeds/index.jsp (Accessed April 19, 2012).

20. Robert Scoble, "PassionPlay," *Fast Company*, November 2008, 90.

21. Kevin J. Clancy and Peter C. Krieg, "Product Life Cycle: A Dangerous Idea," *Brandweek*, March 1, 2004, 26.

22. David Moin, "Madewell Ready for Ramp Up," *Women's Wear Daily*, April 13, 2012, 1, 8.

23. David Goldman, "Are Landlines Doomed?" *CNN Money*, April 10, 2012, http://money .cnn.com/2012/04/10/technology/att-verizon -landlines/index.htm (Accessed April 17, 2012).

24. Ronald J. Baker, *Pricing on Purpose: Creating and Capturing Value* (Hoboken, NJ: John Wiley & Sons, 2006), 338.

12

1. Brian Lavin, "Census Bureau Reports Post-Recession Growth in 10 of 11 Service Sectors," *United States Census Bureau*, February 2, 2012, www.census.gov/newsroom /releases/archives/service_industries/cb12-23 .html (Accessed April 18, 2012).

2. Ibid.

3. Andrea Petersen, "Checking In? Hidden Ways Hotels Court Guests Faster," *Wall Street Journal*, April 12, 2012, D1, D3.

4. Stephanie Clifford, "Would You Like a Smile with That?" *New York Times*, August 6, 2011, www.nytimes.com/2011/08/07 /business/pret-a-manger-with-new-fast-food -ideas-gains-a-foothold-in-united-states.html (Accessed April 18, 2012).

5. Valarie Zeithaml, Mary Jo Bitner, and Dwayne Gremler, *Services Marketing* (New York: McGraw-Hill, 2012).

6. Ibid.

7. Clifford, "Would You Like a Smile with That?"

8. Jena McGregor, "USAA's Battle Plan," *Bloomberg Businessweek*, February 18, 2010, www.businessweek.com/magazine /content/10_09/b4168040782858.htm (Accessed April 19, 2012).

9. Much of the material in this section is based on Christopher H. Lovelock and Jochen Wirtz, *Services Marketing*, 7th ed. (Upper Saddle River, NJ: Prentice Hall, 2010); Christian Gronroos, *Service Management and Marketing: Customer Management in Service Competition*, 3rd ed. (Hoboken, NJ: John Wiley & Sons, 2007).

10. Scott Goryl, "Callaway Golf Introduces Mass Personalization & Customization Options for Its Razr Fit Driver," *PRNewswire*, April 11, 2012, www.prnewswire.com /news-releases/callaway-golf-introduces -mass-personalization--customization -options-for-its-razr-fit-driver-146960885 .html (Accessed April 18, 2012).

11. Larry Magid, "Control Facebook Instant Personalization and Other Privacy Settings (New Video)," *Huffington Post*, May 17, 2010, www.huffingtonpost.com/larry-magid /new-video-control-faceboo_b_578148.html (Accessed April 19, 2012).

12. Lovelock and Wirtz, *Services Marketing*; Gronroos, *Service Management and Marketing*.

13. Ibid.

14. Much of the material in this section is based on Leonard L. Berry and A. Parasuraman, *Marketing Services* (New York: Free Press, 1991), 132–150.

15. Petersen, "Checking In?"

16. "100 Best Companies to Work For," *CNN Money*, February 6, 2012, http://money.cnn .com/magazines/fortune/best-companies/ (Accessed April 18, 2012).

13

1. "Get an Internet Price—2012 Fiesta," Ford, www.quickquote.ford.com/2012-Ford -Fiesta?branding=3&referringsite=4&lang= en (Accessed April 24, 2012).

2. Terry L. Esper, Alexander E. Ellinger, Theodore P. Stank, Daniel J. Flint, and Mark Moon, "Demand and Supply Integration: A Conceptual Framework of Value Creation through Knowledge Management," *Journal of the Academy of Marketing Science*, 38, no. 1, (2010): 5–18.

3. Much of this section is based on material adapted from Donald J. Bowersox, David J. Closs, and Theodore P. Stank, *21st Century Logistics: Making Supply Chain Integration a Reality* (Oak Brook, IL: Council of Logistics Management, 1999).

4. Much of this and the following sections is based on material adapted from the edited volume Douglas M. Lambert, ed., *Supply Chain Management: Processes, Partnerships, Performance* (Sarasota, FL: Supply Chain Management Institute, 2004).

5. "A Machine Running Smoothly," *Economist*, February 5, 2011, 81.

6. John Letzing, "Amazon Adds That Robotic Touch," *Wall Street Journal*, March 20, 2012, http://online.wsj.com/article/SB10001 4240527023047244045772919032447962 14.html (Accessed April 24, 2012).

7. Anjali Cordeiro, "After Buying Its Bottlers, Pepsi Cozies Up to Stores," *Wall Street Journal*, June 21, 2010, B6.

8. Thomas J. Goldsby, Stanley E. Griffis, and Anthony S. Roath, "Modeling Lean, Agile, and Leagile Supply Chain Strategies," *Journal of Business Logistics*, 27, no. 1, (2006): 57–80.

9. John Miller, "Maersk Orders 10 Huge Container Ships," *Wall Street Journal*, February 22, 2011, B3.

10. Letzing, "Amazon Adds That Robotic Touch."

11. Miguel Bustillo, "Wal-Mart Radio Tags to Track Clothing," *Wall Street Journal*, July 23, 2010, http://online.wsj.com/article /SB1000142405274870442130457538321 3061198090.html (Accessed April 24, 2012).

12. Martin Christopher, *Logistics and Supply Chain Management*, 4th ed. (New York: Prentice Hall/Financial Times, 2010).

13. Kate Vitasek, Mike Ledyard, and Karl Manrodt, *Vested Outsourcing: Five Rules That Will Transform Outsourcing* (New York: Palgrave-McMillan, 2009).

14. Chang-Ran Kim, "Toyota Says Supply Chain Will Be Ready by Autumn for Next Quake," March 2, 2012, http://uk.reuters.com/article /2012/03/02/uk-toyota-supply-chain -idUKTRE8210BW20120302 (Accessed April 24, 2012).

15. Matt, "Nylon 3D-Printed Bicycle Featured on BBC," *MakerBot Industries*, March 8, 2012, www.makerbot.com/blog/2011/03/08 /nylon-3d-printed-bicycle-featured-on-bbc (Accessed April 24, 2012).

16. UPS, "Logistics of Sustainability," *Compass*, Spring 2012, 10.

14

1. Eric Savitz, "Apple Screens for iPad3 in Short Supply," *Forbes*, March 1, 2012, 9.

2. James Hagerty, "Whirlpool Expands in China," *Wall Street Journal*, March 20, 2012, B4.

3. Matthias Williams, "India to Levy 10 Percent Import Tax on Power Gear," *Reuters*, August 12, 2010, http://in.reuters.com/article /2010/08/12/idINIndia-50795020100812 (Accessed June 18, 2012).

4. Michael Hughes, "Sweet Green Suppliers," *Industrial Engineer* 43, no. 8, (2011): 6.

5. *Retail Industry Indicators 2012*, National Retail Federation, www.nrf.com (Accessed March 1, 2012).

6. Bureau of Labor Statistics, "Industry at a Glance: NAICS 42–45, Wholesale and Retail Trade," www.bls.gov (Accessed March 1, 2012).

7. *Retail Industry Indicators 2012.*

8. "2010 Retail Report," Stores.org, (Accessed August 12, 2010).

9. "Saks Profits Climb 51%, Sets New Growth Plans," *Women's Wear Daily*, May 15, 2011, 1.

10. Emily Glazer, "Avon Is Late to Social Media's Party," *Wall Street Journal*, April 23, 2011, B1.

11. PRNewswire, "U.S. and Japanese Telemarketing Industry," *The Street*, August 10, 2011, www.thestreet.com/story/11272107/1 /us-and-japanese-telemarketing-industry.html (Accessed June 18, 2012).

12. Direct Marketing Association, "The Power of Direct Marketing: ROI, Sales, and Employment in the US, 2009–10 Edition."

13. Allison Enright, "E-Commerce Sales Rise 14.8% in 2010," *Internet Retailer*, February 17, 2011, www.internetretailer .com/2011/02/17/e-commerce-sales-rise -148-2010 (Accessed June 18, 2012).

14. Louise Lee, "Chained to the Road," *Wall Street Journal*, November 14, 2011, R7.

15. Terry Trucco, "Hospitality Boutiques," *New York Times*, August 9, 2011, B6.

16. Janet Adamy, "Why Wendy's Finds Vanilla So Exciting," *Wall Street Journal*, April 6, 2007, B1–B2.

17. Jeffrey Trachtenberg, "Boutiques at Barnes & Noble, "*Wall Street Journal*, March 11, 2012, http://online.wsj.com/article/SB10001 4240529702039612045772719626696755 68.html (Accessed April 26, 2012).

18. Douglas MacMillan, "Special Deliveries," *Bloomberg Businessweek*, November 28– December 4, 2011, 46.

19. Danielle Kucera, "eBay's Adventures in Brick and Mortar," *Bloomberg Businessweek*, November 28–December 4, 2011, 47–48.

20. Chris Foresman, "Wireless Survey: 91% of Americans Use Cell Phones," *Ars Technica*, March 2010, http://arstechnica.com/telecom /news/2010/03/wireless-survey-91-of -americans-have-cell-phones.ars (Accessed June 18, 2012).

21. "Number of Smartphone Users Jumps by 10%," *Inman News*, August 30, 2011, www.inman.com/news/2011/08/30/number -smartphone-users-jumps-10 (Accessed June 18, 2012).

22. Arnold Karr, "Rate of Mobile Shopping Spikes," *Women's Wear Daily*, December 9, 2011, 10.

15

1. Eric Clemons, Paul Nunes, and Matt Reilly, "Six Strategies for Successful Niche Marketing," *Wall Street Journal*, May 24, 2010, http://online.wsj.com/article/SB10001424052 7487041309045746440842058558424 .html (Accessed May 22, 2012).

2. T. L. Stanley, "Domino's Cooks Up New Pizza, TV Spot," *Adweek*, October 18, 2010, www.adweek.com/news/advertising -branding/dominos-cooks-new-pizza-tv -spot-107900 (Accessed June 20, 2012); Todd Wasserman, "As Domino's Gets Real, Its Sales Get Really Good," *Adweek*, July 11, 2010, www.adweek.com/news/advertising -branding/dominos-gets-real-its-sales-get -really-good-107532 (Accessed June 20, 2012); T. L. Stanley, "Marketer of the Year Runner-Up: Domino's," *Advertising Age*, October 18, 2010, http://adage.com/article /special-report-marketer-of-the-year-2010 /marketer-year-runner-domino-s/146494/ (Accessed June 20, 2012).

3. Valerie Bauerlein and Robb Stewart, "Coca-Cola Hopes to Score with World Cup Campaign," *Wall Street Journal*, June 29, 2010, http://online.wsj.com/article/SB10001 4240527487045692045753289837218652 68.html (Accessed May 22, 2012).

4. Ibid.

5. Ibid; News Release, "The Coca-Cola Company Reports 2010 Second Quarter and Year-to-Date Results," Coca-Cola Company,

July 21, 2010, www.thecoca-colacompany .com/presscenter/nr_20100721_corporate _second_qtr_earnings.html (Accessed June 20, 2012).

6. Jeffrey A. Trachtenberg, "Title + Twitter and YouTube Take Unfinished Book to No.1," *Wall Street Journal*, July 1, 2011, B1, B5.

7. Andrew Johnson, "As Card Firms Try Social Media, Critics Keep Watch," *Wall Street Journal*, March 23, 2012, http://online.wsj .com/article/SB100014240527023047244404 577297860607013698.html (Accessed May 22, 2012); Chase Freedom's Facebook page, October 17–24, 2011, www.facebook.com /ChaseFreedom?sk=wall (Accessed May 22, 2012).

8. The AIDA concept is based on the classic research of E. K. Strong Jr. as theorized in *The Psychology of Selling and Advertising* (New York: McGraw-Hill, 1925) and "Theories of Selling," *Journal of Applied Psychology*, 9, 1925, 75–86.

9. Caroline Waxler, "What You Need to Know about the iPad," *Advertising Age Insights*, August 9, 2010, http://adage.com/trend -reports/report.php?id=27 (Accessed June 20, 2012).

10. Thomas E. Barry and Daniel J. Howard, "A Review and Critique of the Hierarchy of Effects in Advertising," *International Journal of Advertising*, 9, 1990, 121–135.

11. Jack Neff, "Cracking the Viral Code: Look at Your Ads. Now Look at Old Spice," *Advertising Age*, September 27, 2010, http://adage.com/article/digital/viral-ad-hits -p-g-grooming-biz-point-winning-formula /146090/ (Accessed June 20, 2012); Jack Neff, "How Much Old Spice Body Wash Has the Old Spice Guy Sold?" *Advertising Age*, July 26, 2010, http://adage.com/article /news/spice-body-wash-spice-guy-sold /145096/ (Accessed June 20, 2012); Michael Learmonth, "Viral Old Spice 'Responses' Crush Original Ads in Online Views," *Advertising Age*, July 22, 2010, http://adage .com/article/the-viral-video-chart/viral-spice -responses-crush-original-ads-web-views /145015/ (Accessed June 20, 2012); Jessica Shambora, "The Adman behind Old Spice's New Life," *Fortune*, October 18, 2010, 39.

12. Anjali Cordeiro, "Promotions Boost Sales for Food and Beverage Makers," *Wall Street Journal*, July 14, 2010, B5.

16

1. Bradley Johnson, "100 Leading National Advertisers," *Adage*, June 20, 2011, http:// adage.com/article/news/ad-spending-100 -leading-national-advertisers/228267 (Accessed April 19, 2012).

2. Ibid.

3. Tanzina Vega, "Advertising Companies Fret over a Digital Talent Gap," *New York Times*, October 20, 2011, www.nytimes.com/2011/10/31/business /media/ad-companies-face-a-widening-talent -gap.html (Accessed April 19, 2012).

4. Michael R. Solomon, *Consumer Behavior*, 6th ed. (Upper Saddle River, NJ: Prentice Hall, 2004), 275.

5. Reshma Farhat and Dr. Bilal Mustafa Khan, "Importance of Brand Personality to Cus-tomer Loyalty: A Conceptual Study," *New Media and Mass Communication*, Vol. 1, 2011, 4–8.

6. Johnson, "100 Leading National Advertisers."

7. Luisa Zargani, "Backlash Mounts for Benetton Campaign," *Women's Wear Daily*, November 18, 2011, 14.

8. TheKingofBigScreen, "Samsung Smart YV for the New 2012 TVs," YouTube, March 1, 2012, www.youtube.com/watch?v= JV6JLcjVJiA (Accessed April 19, 2012).

9. 21st Century, "'Door Dings' Commercial— 21st Century Auto Insurance: Same Great Coverage for Less," YouTube, November 16, 2010, www.youtube.com/watch?v=I0V -hm2EK-M&feature=relmfu (Accessed June 21, 2012).

10. Ibid.

11. Dr. John Babish, " Ithaca, NY Company, Bionexus, Introduces First Natural Skin Care Lotion for Dogs Containing Standardized Nigella Sativa Extracts," *PRNewswire*, April 17, 2012, www.prnewswire.com/news -releases/ithaca-ny-company-bionexus -introduces-first-natural-skin-care-lotion -for-dogs-containing-standardized-nigella -sativa-extracts-147811745.html (Accessed April 18, 2012).

12. kswissinc, "CEO Kenny Powers," YouTube, July 8, 2011, www.youtube .com/user/kswissinc#p/a/u/0/hgGud5gsbIA (Accessed June 21, 2012).

13. Teressa Iezzi, "Kenny Powers Returns for Second K-Swiss Campaign," *Fast Company*, July 11, 2011, www.fastcompany.com /1766322/kenny-powers-returns-for-second -k-swiss-campaign (Accessed June 21, 2012).

14. Laura Q. Hughes and Wendy Davis, "Revival of the Fittest," *Advertising Age*, March 12, 2001, 18–19.

15. Tim Higgins, "Chrysler's Chief Marketer Finds the Exotic in Detroit," *Bloomberg Businessweek*, December 12–18, 2011, 31–32.

16. Press release, "TNS Media Intelligence Forecasts 4.2 Percent Increase in U.S. Advertising Spending for 2008," www.tns-mi.com /news/01072008 (Accessed February 20, 2008).

17. PricewaterhouseCoopers, "IAB Internet Advertising Revenue Report," Interactive Advertising Bureau, April 2010, www.pwc .com/us/en/industry/entertainment-media /assets/IAB-Ad-Revenue-Full-Year-2009.pdf (Accessed June 21, 2012); Teddy Wayne, "A Milestone for Internet Ad Revenue," *New York Times*, April 25, 2010, www.nytimes .com/2010/04/26/business/media/26drill .html (Accessed June 21, 2012).

18. Higgins, "Chrysler's Chief Marketer Finds the Exotic in Detroit," 31.

19. Shar VanBoskirk, "US Interactive Marketing Forecast, 2011 to 2016," *Forrester Interactive Marketing Professionals*, August 24, 2011, www.forrester.com/US+Interactive +Marketing+Forecast+2011+To+2016 /fulltext/-/E-RES59379?docid=59379 (Accessed May 29, 2012).

20. "Google Talks about Android, Personalized Ads and New Hires," *Wall Street Journal*, July 15, 2010, http://blogs.wsj.com/digits /2010/07/15/live-blogging-google-on-its -earnings (Accessed June 21, 2012).

21. PricewaterhouseCoopers, "IAB Internet Advertising Revenue Report"; Wayne, "A Milestone for Internet Ad Revenue."

22. Vipin Mayar and Geoff Ramsey, *Digital Impact* (Hoboken, NJ: John Wiley & Sons, 2011).

23. Douglas MacMillan, "Farmville? Meet Cheech & Chong," *Bloomberg Businessweek*, June 27–July 3, 2011, 39–40.

24. Mayar and Ramsey, *Digital Impact*.

25. Andrew LaValle, "Start-Ups Find Revenue Source on Hold," *Wall Street Journal*, June 11, 2008, B9.

26. Andrew Hampp, "Cross-Platform Ads: What's Working?" *Advertising Age*, June 26, 2008, http://adage.com/article/media/cross -platform-ads-working/128029/ (Accessed June 21, 2012).

27. "New PQ Media Report Finds U.S. Branded Entertainment Spending on Consumer Events & Product Placement Dipped Only 1.3% to $24.63 Billion in 2009 & on Pace to Grow 5.3% in 2010, Exceeding Most Advertising & Marketing Segments," *Product Placement News*, July 7, 2010, www.productplacement.biz/201007072619 /product-placement-research/new-pq-media -report-finds-u-s-branded-entertainment -spending-on-consumer-events-product -placement-dipped-only-1-3-to-24-63-billion -in-2009-on-pace-to-grow-5-3-in-2010 -exceeding-most-advertising.html (Accessed June 21, 2012).

28. William Chipps, "Sponsorship Spending: 2012 Proves Better Than Expected; Bigger Gains Set for 2011," *IEG*, January 6, 2011, www.sponsorship.com/About-IEG/Press -Room/Sponsorship-Spending--2010-Proves -Better-Than-Expe.aspx (Accessed April 18, 2012).

29 Ibid.

30. Dana Rubenstein, "You Barf, You Lose," *Bloomberg Businessweek*, June 30, 2011, www.businessweek.com/magazine /the-worldclass-eaters-are-getting-full -pockets-07012011.html (Accessed June 21, 2012).

31. Geoffrey Fowler, Ian Sherr, and Niraj Sheth, "A Defiant Steve Jobs Confronts 'Antennagate,'" *Wall Street Journal*, July 16, 2010, http://online.wsj.com/article/SB10001424 052748704913304575371131458273498 .html (Accessed June 21, 2012).

32. NCH Marketing Resource Center, "NCH Coupon Facts Report," www.nchmarketing .com/ResourceCenter (Accessed April 19, 2012).

33. Andrew Johnson, "@AmericanExpress Tries #Deals via Twitter," *Wall Street Journal*, March 7, 2012, http://online .wsj.com/article/SB1000142405297020478 1804577267402969728444.html (Accessed April 19, 2012).

34. Bruce Mohl, "Retailers Simplify the Rebate Process," *Boston Globe*, November 7, 2004; FTC Consumer Alert, "Taking the 'Bait' out of Rebates," www.ftc.gov/bcp/edu/pubs /consumer/alerts/alt059.shtm.

35. Annamaria Andriotis, "Six Rewards Programs Worth Your Loyalty," *SmartMoney*, March 22, 2011, www.smartmoney.com /spend/family-money/the-best-loyalty -programs-1300230426274 (Accessed April 20, 2012).

36. Elizabeth Holmes, "At Bloomies, Loyalty for All," *Wall Street Journal*, February 24, 2012, B5.

37. John Wu, "Effects of In-Store Sampling on Retail Sales: Case Study of a Warehouse Store," FindArticles.com, Spring 2010, http://findarticles.com/p/articles/mi_hb6054/is_201004/ai_n53928748/.

38. "Point-of-Purchase: $17 Billion," *PROMO Magazine*, October 29, 2001, 3; "In Praise of Promotion," *PROMO Xtra*, http://promomagazine.com.

39. Anne Hollard, "MarketingSherpa: Search Marketing and At-Work Coupon Campaigns: Redemption Rate Data and Four Useful Hotlinks," *MarketingSherpa*, www.marketingsherpa.com/article.html?ident=29788.

40. "Internet," CMS, www.couponinfonow.com/Couponing/Internet.cfm.

17

1. Peter King, "Personal Shoppers Find Clothes to Make the Man," *Wall Street Journal*, August 12, 2010, http://online.wsj.com/article/SB10001424052748704164904575421373622725304.html (Accessed June 21, 2012).

2. Michael Beverland, "Contextual Influences and the Adoption and Practice of Relationship Selling in a Business-to-Business Setting: An Exploratory Study," *Journal of Personal Selling & Sales Management*, 21, no. 3, Summer 2001, 207; Gabriel R. Gonzalez, K. Douglas Hoffman, and Thomas N. Ingram, "Improving Relationship Selling through Failure Analysis and Recovery Efforts: A Framework and Call to Action," *Journal of Personal Selling & Sales Management*, 25, no. 1, Winter 2005, 57.

3. Julie Weed, "Getting Closer to Guests," *New York Times*, April 19, 2011, B8.

4. Organic, Inc., "CRM Moves from Elite to Everyman: Four Elements for Creating a Social CRM Strategy," March 16, 2010, www.organic.com/Assets/whitepaper_social_crm_20100312123657.pdf (Accessed June 21, 2012).

5. Barton Weitz, Stephen Castleberry, and John Tanner, *Selling: Building Partnerships* (Burr Ridge, IL: McGraw-Hill/Irwin, 2004), 184–185.

6. Jessica Bruder, "A Customer Loyalty Program (From Some of the Folks Who Brought You Groupon)," *New York Times*, February 21, 2012, http://boss.blogs.nytimes.com/2012/02/21/a-customer-loyalty-program-from-some-of-the-folks-who-brought-you-groupon/ (Accessed June 15, 2012).

7. Brian Rice, "Redbox Proves Creating Customer Loyalty Is as Easy as Saying 'Happy Birthday,'" *Business 2 Community*, July 14, 2011, www.business2community.com/loyalty-marketing/redbox-proves-creating-customer-loyalty-is-as-easy-as-saying-"happy-birthday"-044184 (Accessed June 21, 2012).

8. Donna Fenn, "10 Ways to Get More Sales from Existing Customers," *Inc.*, August 31, 2010, www.inc.com/guides/2010/08/get-more-sales-from-existing-customers.html (Accessed June 15, 2012).

9. Catherine Seda, "The Meet Market," *Entrepreneur*, August 2004, 68; Jim Dickie, "Is Social Networking an Overhyped Fad or a Useful Tool?" *Destination CRM*, January 21, 2005; Kristina Dell, "What Are Friends For?" *Time*, September 21, 2004; Media Releases, www.linkedin.com, December 3, 2007; "About Us," www.linkedin.com/static?key=company_info.

10. Weitz, Castleberry, and Tanner, *Selling*, 198–201.

11. Eileen P. Gunn, "How Twitter Became My Secret Weapon," *Inc.*, June 14, 2011, www.inc.com/eileen-p-gunn/how-twitter-became-my-secret-weapon.html (Accessed June 21, 2012).

12. "Effective Business Presentation—Sales Presentation—Effective Presentation Skill," *Nielsen Business Media*, www.presentations.com.

13. Weitz, Castleberry, and Tanner, *Selling*, 17–22.

14. Oracle, "PeopleSoft Applications," www.oracle.com/us/products/applications/peoplesoft-enterprise/overview/index.htm (Accessed June 15, 2012).

15. Kathleen Joyce, "In the Cards," *PROMO magazine*, September 1, 2003, www.promomagazine.com.

18

1. Brian Solis, *Engage: The Complete Guide for Brands and Businesses to Build, Cultivate and Measure Success in the New Web* (Hoboken, NJ: John Wiley & Sons, 2010), 37.

2. Shanyndi Raice, Mike Ramsey, and Sam Schechner, "Facebook Gains Two Big Advertisers' Support," *Wall Street Journal*, June 20, 2012, B6.

3. Suzanne Vranica, "Knights, Pirates, Trees Flock to Facebook," *Wall Street Journal*, March 26, 2012, B1.

4. "Social Media for Non Profits," *Primalmedia*, February 18, 2009, www.primalmedia.com/blog/social-media-non-profits (Accessed June 23, 2012).

5. Joel Stein, "The Woman Behind @Shaq," *Bloomberg Businessweek*, October 31–November 6, 2011, 89–91.

6. Ibid.

7. Solis, *Engage*.

8. Ibid.

9. Universal McCann, "Power to the People—Wave3 Study on Social Media Trends," March 2008, www.slideshare.net/mickstravellin/universal-mccann-international-social-media-research-wave-3 (Accessed June 23, 2012).

10. Aaron Smith, "Mobile Access 2010," Pew Internet & American Life Project, July 7, 2010, www.pewinternet.org/Reports/2010/Mobile-Access-2010.aspx.

11. Damon Poeter, "Pew: Mobile Helping Narrow Digital Divide, but Not for All," *Pew Internet*, April 15, 2012, http://pewinternet.org/Media-Mentions/2012/Pew-Mobile-Helping-Narrow-Digital-Divide-But-Not-For-All.aspx (Accessed April 30, 2012).

12. Sarah Perez, "iPad Sales May Reach 66 Million in 2012," *TechCrunch*, March 20, 2012, http://techcrunch.com/2012/03/20/ipad-sales-may-reach-66-million-in-2012 (Accessed April 30, 2012).

13. Paul Marsden, "Simple Definition of Social Commerce," *Social Commerce Today*, June 2010, http://socialcommercetoday.com/social-commerce-definition-word-cloud-definitive-definition-list (Accessed June 23, 2012).

14. Lauren Indvik, "How Brands Are Using Promotions to Market on Pinterest," *Mashable*, March 7, 2012, http://mashable.com/2012/03/07/pinterest-brand-marketing (Accessed April 30, 2012).

15. Ibid.

16. Shar VanBoskirk, "U.S. Interactive Marketing Forecast 2009 to 2014," Forrester Research, July 6, 2009, www.forrester.com/rb/Research/us_interactive_marketing_forecast,_2009_to_2014/q/id/47730/t/2 (Accessed June 23, 2012).

17. Jeff Howe, *Crowdsourcing: Why the Power of the Crowd Is Driving the Future of Business* (New York: Three Rivers Press, 2009), 32.

18. Timothy Lloyd, "Beatles Great Paul McCartney Plunges into Crowd Sourcing," *Wall Street Journal*, July 6, 2011, http://blogs.wsj.com/speakeasy/2011/07/06/beatles-great-paul-mccartney-plunges-into-crowd-sourcing (Accessed June 23, 2012).

19. Sean Corcoran, "Defining Earned, Owned and Paid Media," *Forrester Blogs*, December 16, 2009, http://blogs.forrester.com/interactive_marketing/2009/12/defining-earned-owned-and-paid-media.html; Brian Solis, "Why Brands Are Becoming Media," *Mashable*, February 11, 2010 (Accessed June 23, 2012).

20. Ibid.

21. Erik Bratt, "Social Media ROI Success Stories," *MarketingProfs*, 2009, www.marketingprofs.com/store/product/27/social-media-roi-success-stories (Accessed June 23, 2012).

22. David Berkowitz, "100 Ways to Measure Social Media," *Inside the Marketers Studio*, November 17, 2009, www.marketersstudio.com/2009/11/100-ways-to-measure-social-media-.html (Accessed June 23, 2012).

23. Mike Laurie, "How Social Media Has Changed Us," *Mashable*, January 7, 2010, http://mashable.com/2010/01/07/social-media-changed-us (Accessed June 23, 2012).

24. Charlene Li and Josh Bernoff, *Groundswell: Winning in a World Transformed by Social Technologies*, (Boston: Harvard Business Press, 2009).

25. *North American Technographics Interactive Marketing Online Survey*, Forrester Research, June 2009, www.forrester.com/ER/Research/Survey/Excerpt/1,10198,726,00.html (Accessed June 23, 2012).

26. Juan Carlos Perez, "Forrester Notes Social Media Contributor Slowdown," *Computerworld*, September 28, 2010, www.computerworld.com/s/article/9188538/Forrester_notes_social_media_contributor_slowdown (Accessed June 23, 2012).

27. Dan Zarella, *The Social Media Marketing Book* (Beijing, China: O'Reilly, 2010).

28. Roger Yu, "More Companies Quit Blogging, Go with Facebook Instead," *USA Today*, April 20, 2012, www.usatoday.com/tech/news/story/2012-04-19/corporate-blogging/54419982/1 (Accessed May 1, 2012).

29. Lauren Drell, "The Quick and Dirty Guide to Tumblr for Small Business," *Mashable Business*, February 18, 2012, http://mashable.com/2012/02/18/tumblr-small-biz-guide (Accessed May 1, 2012).

30. Olga Khazan, "How Do You Use Twitter and Facebook for Marketing," *Washington Post*, April 22, 2012, www.washingtonpost.com/blogs/on-small-business/post/how-do-you-use-twitter-and-facebook-for-marketing/2012/04/20/gIQA7NXwZT_blog.html (Accessed May 1, 2012).

31. Marketing Profs, *LinkedIn Success Stories*, 2009, www.marketingprofs.com/store/product/37/linkedin-success-stories (Accessed June 23, 2012).

32. Ramya Raghavan, "Using Video to Connect with Your Donors and Prospects," International Fundraising eConference, May 12–14, 2009.

33. Zarella, *The Social Media Marketing Book*.

34. Solis, *Engage*, 54.

35. Solis, *Engage*, 97.

36. David Sax, "Yelp's Online Reviewing Mafia," *Bloomberg Businessweek*, June 2, 2011, www.businessweek.com/magazine/content/11_24/b4232083260194.htm (Accessed June 23, 2012).

37. Solis, *Engage*, 51.

38. Irina Slutsky, "Nothing Casual about This Game Obsession," *Advertising Age*, January 10, 2011, 2.

39. Geekaphone, "Infographic: Mobile Gaming Statistics 2011," *Digital Buzz Blog*, August 2, 2011, www.digitalbuzzblog.com/infographic-mobile-gaming-statistics-stats-2011 (Accessed May 1, 2012).

40. Microsoft Tag, "Infographic: Mobile Statistics, Stats & Facts 2011," *Digital Buzz Blog*, April 4, 2011, www.digitalbuzzblog.com/2011-mobile-statistics-stats-facts-marketing-infographic (Accessed May 1, 2012).

41. "Modify QR Code Watch—Because Simply Reading Time on Your Watch Is So 2011," *Modify Watches*, February 23, 2012, www.modifywatches.com/blog/qr-code-watch (Accessed May 1, 2012).

42. JP Mangalindan, "Barnes & Noble CEO: NFC Coming to the Nook," *CNN Money*, May 1, 2012, http://tech.fortune.cnn.com/2012/05/01/nook (Accessed May 1, 2012).

43. Beth Kanter, "Screencast: Using Widgets to Build Community on Blogs Featured on NTEN Blog," *Beth's Blog*, March 20, 2007, http://beth.typepad.com/beths_blog/2007/03/screncast_using.html (Accessed June 23, 2012).

19

1. Walter Baker, Michael Marn, and Craig Zawada, "Building a Better Price Structure," *McKinsey Quarterly*, August 2010, www.mckinseyquarterly.com/Building_a_better_pricing_structure_2652 (Accessed May 2, 2012).

2. Franziska Volckner, "The Dual Role of Price: Decomposing Consumers' Reactions to Price," *Journal of the Academy of Marketing Science*, 36, no. 3, Fall 2008, 359–377.

3. Ibid.

4. Bruce Einhorn, "A Laptop Maker Looks for Profit in the iPad Era," *Bloomberg Businessweek*, November 14–20, 2011, 47–48.

5. Edward Lotterman, "Why a Great Crop Year Like 2010 Can Be Bad News for U.S. Farmers," *Idaho Statesman*, August 15, 2010, www.idahostatesman.com/2010/08/15/1302125/ed-lotterman-why-a-great-crop.html.

6. Tammo H. A. Bijmolt, Harald J. Van Heerde, and Rik G. M. Pieters, "New Empirical Generalizations on the Determinants of Price Elasticity," *Journal of Marketing Research*, 42, May 2005, 141–156; Christian Homburg, Wayne Hoyer, and Nicole Koschate, "Customers' Reactions to Price Increases: Do Customer Satisfaction and Perceived Motive Fairness Matter?" *Journal of the Academy of Marketing Science*, 33, no. 1, Winter 2005, 35–49; Gadi Fibich, Arieh Gavious, and Oded Lowengart, "The Dynamics of Price Elasticity of Demand in the Presence of Reference Price Effects," *Journal of the Academy of Marketing Science*, 33, no. 1, Winter 2005, 66–78.

7. "Executives Zero In on Pricing," *Wall Street Journal*, September 27, 2010, B7.

8. "What the Traffic Will Bear," *Forbes*, July 3, 2008, 69.

9. Miguel Bustillo and Jeffrey A. Trachtenberg, "Amazon, Wal-Mart Cut Deeper in Book Duel," *Wall Street Journal*, October 17, 2009, B1.

10. Jeffrey Trachtenberg, "E-Book Prices Prop Up Print Siblings," *Wall Street Journal*, September 12, 2011, B1.

11. Joseph Cannon and Christian Homburg, "Buyer–Supplier Relationships and Customer Firm Costs," *Journal of Marketing*, 65, January 2001, 29–43.

12. Yun Wan and Nan Hu, "Comparison Shopping Channel Selection by Small Online Vendors: An Exploratory Study (Abstract)," *IGI Global*, 2009, www.igi-global.com/bookstore/Chapter.aspx?TitleId=6735.

13. "How Shopping Bots Really Work," *MSN Money*, July 11, 2005, http://moneycentral.msn.com.

14. The Associated Press, "Sporting a Mullet Pays Off at Pittsburgh Zoo," *Boston Herald*, July 6, 2010, www.bostonherald.com/news/offbeat/.

15. Martinne Geller and Jessica Wohl, "Analysis: Walmart's Price Push Tests Manufacturers' Prowess," *Reuters*, March 6, 2012, www.reuters.com/article/2012/03/06/us-usa-consumer-walmart-idUSTRE8250GM20120306 (Accessed May 2, 2012).

16. Vicki Young, "Cautions for Luxury: Survey Finds Wealthy Less Keen on Category," *Women's Wear Daily*, September 22, 2009, 20.

17. Katherine Lemon and Stephen Nowlis, "Developing Synergies between Promotions and Brands in Different Price-Quality Tiers," *Journal of Marketing Research*, 39, May 2002, 171–185; also see Valerie Taylor and William Bearden, "The Effects of Price on Brand Extension Evaluations: The Moderating Role of Extension Similarity," *Journal of the Academy of Marketing Science*, 30, no. 2, Spring 2002, 131–140; Raj Sethuraman and V. Srinivasan, "The Asymmetric Share Effect: An Empirical Generalization on Cross-Price Effects," *Journal of Marketing Research*, 39, no. 3, August 2002, 379–386.

18. Volckner, "The Dual Role of Price."

19. Ibid.

20. Elizabeth Holmes, "The Finer Art of Faking It," *Wall Street Journal*, June 30, 2011, http://online.wsj.com/article/SB10001424052702304791204576401534146929212.html.

21. Merrie Brucks, Valarie Zeithaml, and Gillian Naylor, "Price and Brand Name as Indicators of Quality Dimensions for Consumer Durables," *Journal of the Academy of Marketing Science*, 28, no. 3, Summer 2000, 359–374; Wilford Amaldoss and Sanjay Jain, "Pricing of Conspicuous Goods: A Competitive Analysis of Social Effects," *Journal of Marketing Research*, 42, February 2005, 30–42; also see Margaret Campbell, "Says Who?! How the Source of Price Information and Affect Influence Perceived Price (UN)fairness," *Journal of Marketing Research*, 44, no. 2, May 2007, 261–271.

20

1. Keith Chrzan, "An Overview of Pricing Research," *Quirk's Marketing Research Review*, July/August 2006, 24–29.

2. Kent Monroe and Jennifer Cox, "Pricing Practices That Endanger Profits," *Marketing Management*, September/October 2001, 42–46.

3. Ibid.

4. Scott McCartney, "Olympic-Sized Fare Hikes This Summer Make It Important to Book Early," *Wall Street Journal*, April 12, 2012, http://blogs.wsj.com/middleseat/2012/04/12/olympic-sized-fare-hikes-this-summer-make-it-important-to-book-early (Accessed May 3, 2012).

5. "Why the Price Is Rarely Right," *Bloomberg Businessweek*, February 18, 2010, 77–78.

6. Julie Jargon and Gina Chon, "Burger King's Latest Pickle," *Wall Street Journal*, September 1, 2010, http://online.wsj.com/article/SB10001424052748704791004575465961922888040.html (Accessed June 24, 2012).

7. "Gillette's Latest Innovation in Razors: The 11-Cent Blade," *Wall Street Journal*, October 1, 2010, B1.

8. Paul Sonne and Laurence Norman, "EU Fines Unilever, P&G over Pricing," *Wall Street Journal*, April 14, 2011, B1.

9. Thomas Catan, Jeffrey A. Trachtenberg, and Chad Bray, "U.S. Alleges E-Book Scheme," *Wall Street Journal*, April 12, 2012, A1.

10. "How Driving Prices Lower Can Violate Antitrust Statutes," *Wall Street Journal*, January 24, 2004, A1, A11.

11. Evan Clark and Kristi Ellis, "Price-Fixing Plays Out in Supreme Court," *Women's Wear Daily*, June 19, 2008.

12. Bruce Alford and Abhijit Biswas, "The Effects of Discount Level, Price Consciousness, and Sale Proneness on Consumers' Price Perception and Behavioral Intention," *Journal of Business Research*, 55, no. 9, September 2002, 775–778; also see V. Kumar, Vibhas Madan, and Srinin Srinivasan, "Price Discounts or Coupon Promotions: Does It Matter?" *Journal of Business Research*, 57, no. 9, September 2004, 933–941.

13. Martinne Geller and Jessica Wohl, "Analysis: Walmart's Price Push Tests Manufacturers' Prowess," *Reuters*, March 6, 2012, www.reuters.com/article/2012/03/06/us-usa -consumer-walmart-idUSTRE8250GM20120 306 (Accessed May 3, 2012).

14. "Safeway Takes Bullet in Grocery Price War," *Wall Street Journal*, October 16, 2009, B1, B5; "Safeway Says 2010 Profit Could Miss Expectations," *Reuters*, March 3, 2010, www.reuters.com/article/2010/03/03/us -safeway-idUSTRE62251X20100303.

15. Timothy Aeppel, "Seeking Perfect Prices, CEO Tears Up the Rules," *Wall Street Journal*, March 27, 2007, A1, A16.

16. Ibid.

17. Felix Salmon, "Matter's Vision for Long-Form Journalism," *Reuters*, February 23, 2012, http://blogs.reuters.com/felix-salmon /2012/02/23/matters-vision-for-long-form -journalism (Accessed May 3, 2012).

18. "Seven Mistakes of Poor Pricers," *Wall Street Journal*, May 24, 2010, R8.

19. Rui (Juliet) Zhu, Xinlei (Jack) Chen, and Srabana Dasgupta, "Can Trade-Ins Hurt You? Exploring the Effect of a Trade-In on Consumers' Willingness to Pay for a Product," *Journal of Marketing Research*, 45, no. 2, April 2008, 159–170.

20. Ibid.

21. Ibid.

22. To learn more about pricing fairness, see Lan Xia, Kent Monroe, and Jennifer Cox, "The Price Is Unfair! A Conceptual Framework of Price Fairness Perceptions," *Journal of Marketing*, 68, no. 4, October 2004, 1–15.

23. "AT&T Adopts Tiered Wireless Broadband Pricing," *B&C*, June 2, 2010, www.broadcastingcable.com/article/453238 -AT_T_Adopts_Tiered_Wireless_Broadband _Pricing.php.

24. "Sprint, T-Mobile Keep Prices Low on Wireless Broadband," *CNET*, May 4, 2010, http://news.cnet.com/8301-30686_3 -20004054-266.html.

25. David Freedman, "Is SaveLocal a Better Deal Than Groupon?" *New York Times*, March 14, 2012, http://boss.blogs.nytimes .com/2012/03/14/would-you-consider-using -a-groupon-alternative (Accessed May 3, 2012).

26. Martin Lindstrom, "The Psychology behind the Sweet Spots of Pricing," *Fast Company*, March 27, 2012, www.fastcompany.com /1826172/martin-lindstrom-buyology -marketing-psychology-pricing-sweet-spot (Accessed May 3, 2012).

27. Ibid.

28. Dilip Soman and John Gourville, "Transaction Decoupling: The Effects of Price Bundling on the Decision to Consume," *MSI Report*, 2002, 98–131; Stefan Stremersch and Gerard J. Tellis, "Strategic Bundling of Products and Prices: A New Synthesis for Marketing," *Journal of Marketing*, 66, no. 1, January 2002, 55–71; "Forget Prices and Get People to Use the Stuff," *Wall Street Journal*, June 3, 2004, A2.

29. Susan Carey, "Airlines to Load on More Fees," *Wall Street Journal*, March 7, 2011, B1.

30. Rebecca Hamilton and Joydeep Srivastava, "When 2+2 Is Not the Same as 1+3: Variations in Price Sensitivity across Components of Partitioned Prices," *Journal of Marketing Research*, 45, no. 4, August 2008, 450–461.

31. Sarah Nassauer, "A Psychological Twist in Getting Something for Nothing," *Wall Street Journal*, April 23, 2012, http://blogs.wsj .com/health/2012/04/23/a-psychological -twist-in-getting-something-for-nothing (Accessed May 3, 2012).

32. Geller and Wohl, "Analysis: Walmart's Price Push Tests Manufacturers' Prowess."

33. Paul Hunt and Greg Thomas, "Scoring Birdies Instead of Bogies," *Pricing Solutions Newsletter*, 2, no. 2, Winter 2009, www.pricingsolutions.com.

INDEX

KEY TERMS

1-1

marketing the activity, set of institutions, and processes for creating, communicating, delivering, and exchanging offerings that have value for customers, clients, partners, and society at large

exchange people giving up something in order to receive something they would rather have

1-2

production orientation a philosophy that focuses on the internal capabilities of the firm rather than on the desires and needs of the marketplace

sales orientation the ideas that people will buy more goods and services if aggressive sales techniques are used and that high sales result in high profits

marketing concept the idea that the social and economic justification for an organization's existence is the satisfaction of customer wants and needs while meeting organizational objectives

market orientation a philosophy that assumes that a sale does not depend on an aggressive sales force but rather on a customer's decision to purchase a product; it is synonymous with the marketing concept

societal marketing orientation the idea that an organization exists not only to satisfy customer wants and needs and to meet organizational objectives but also to preserve or enhance individuals' and society's long-term best interests

KEY CONCEPTS

LO 1-1 Define the term *marketing*. Marketing is the activity, set of institutions, and processes for creating, communicating, delivering, and exchanging offerings that have value for customers, clients, partners, and society at large. Marketing also requires all facets of a company to work together to pool ideas and resources. One major goal of marketing is to create an exchange. An exchange has five conditions, as listed below. Even if all five conditions are met, an exchange might not occur. People engage in marketing whether or not an exchange happens.

Five conditions of exchange

1 There must be at least two parties.

2 Each party has something that might be of value to the other party.

3 Each party is capable of communication and delivery.

4 Each party is free to accept or reject the exchange offer.

5 Each party believes it is appropriate or desirable to deal with the other party.

Source: Philip Kotler and Kevin Lane Keller, *A Framework for Marketing Management*, 5th ed. (Upper Saddle River, NJ: Prentice Hall, 2011), 4–5.

© Cengage Learning

LO 1-2 Describe four marketing management philosophies. The role of marketing and the character of marketing activities within an organization are strongly influenced by the organization's marketing philosophy and orientation. A production-oriented organization focuses on the internal capabilities of the firm rather than on the desires and needs of the marketplace. A sales orientation is based on the beliefs that people will buy more products and services if aggressive sales techniques are used and that high sales volumes produce high profits. A market-oriented organization focuses on satisfying customer wants and needs while meeting organizational objectives. A societal marketing orientation goes beyond a market orientation to include the preservation or enhancement of individuals' and society's long-term best interests.

© Cengage Learning

1-3

customer value the relationship between benefits and the sacrifice necessary to obtain those benefits

customer satisfaction customers' evaluation of a good or service in terms of whether it has met their needs and expectations

relationship marketing a strategy that focuses on keeping and improving relationships with current customers

empowerment delegation of authority to solve customers' problems quickly—usually by the first person the customer notifies regarding a problem

teamwork collaborative efforts of people to accomplish common objectives

customer relationship management (CRM) a company-wide business strategy designed to optimize profitability, revenue, and customer satisfaction by focusing on highly defined and precise customer groups

LO 1-3 Discuss the differences between sales and market orientations.

First, sales-oriented firms focus on their own needs; market-oriented firms focus on customers' needs and preferences. Second, sales-oriented companies consider themselves to be deliverers of goods and services, whereas market-oriented companies view themselves as satisfiers of customers. Third, sales-oriented firms direct their products to everyone; market-oriented firms aim at specific segments of the population. Fourth, sales-oriented organizations place a higher premium on making a sale, while market-oriented businesses seek a long-term relationship with the customer. Finally, sales-oriented businesses pursue maximum sales volume through intensive promotion, whereas market-oriented businesses pursue customer satisfaction through coordinated activities.

	What is the organization's focus?	What business is the organization in?	To whom is the product directed?	What is the organization's primary goal?	How does the organization seek to achieve its goal?
Sales Orientation	Inward, on the organization's needs	Selling goods and services	Everyone	Profit through maximum sales volume	Primarily through intensive promotion
Market Orientation	Outward, on the wants and preferences of customers	Satisfying customer wants and needs and delivering superior value	Specific groups of people	Profit through customer satisfaction	Through coordinated marketing and interfunctional activities

LO 1-4 Describe several reasons for studying marketing.

First, marketing affects the allocation of goods and services that influence a nation's economy and standard of living. Second, an understanding of marketing is crucial to understanding most businesses. Third, career opportunities in marketing are diverse, profitable, and expected to increase significantly during the coming decade. Fourth, understanding marketing makes consumers more informed.

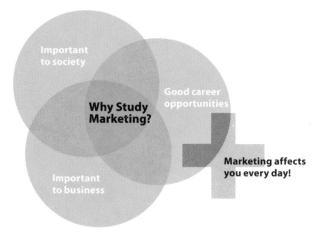

KEY TERMS

© iStockphoto.com/Bill Noll

© iStockphoto.com/OSTILL

2-1

strategic planning the managerial process of creating and maintaining a fit between the organization's objectives and resources and the evolving market opportunities

2-2

strategic business unit (SBU) a subgroup of a single business or collection of related businesses within the larger organization

2-3

market penetration a marketing strategy that tries to increase market share among existing customers

market development a marketing strategy that entails attracting new customers to existing products

product development a marketing strategy that entails the creation of new products for present markets

diversification a strategy of increasing sales by introducing new products into new markets

portfolio matrix a tool for allocating resources among products or strategic business units on the basis of relative market share and market growth rate

star in the portfolio matrix, a business unit that is a fast-growing market leader

cash cow in the portfolio matrix, a business unit that generates more cash than it needs to maintain its market share

problem child (question mark) in the portfolio matrix, a business unit that shows rapid growth but poor profit margins

dog in the portfolio matrix, a business unit that has low growth potential and a small market share

2-4

planning the process of anticipating future events and determining strategies to achieve organizational objectives in the future

KEY CONCEPTS

LO 2-1 Understand the importance of strategic planning. Strategic planning is the basis for all marketing strategies and decisions. These decisions affect the allocation of resources and ultimately the financial success of the company.

LO 2-2 Define strategic business units (SBUs). Each SBU should have these characteristics: a distinct mission and a specific target market, control over its resources, its own competitors, a single business, and plans independent from other SBUs in the organization. Each SBU has its own rate of return on investment, growth potential, and associated risks, and requires its own strategies and funding.

LO 2-3 Identify strategic alternatives. Ansoff's opportunity matrix presents four options to help management develop strategic alternatives: market penetration, market development, product development, and diversification. In selecting a strategic alternative, managers may use a portfolio matrix, which classifies strategic business units as stars, cash cows, problem children (or question marks), and dogs, depending on their present or projected growth and market share. Alternatively, the GE model suggests that companies determine strategic alternatives based on the comparisons between business position and market attractiveness.

LO 2-4 Understand the marketing planning process. A marketing plan should define the business mission, perform a situation analysis, define objectives, delineate a target market, and establish components of the marketing mix. Other elements that may be included in a plan are budgets, implementation timetables, required marketing research efforts, or elements of advanced strategic planning.

LO 2-5 Develop an appropriate business mission statement. The firm's mission statement establishes boundaries for all subsequent decisions, objectives, and strategies. A mission statement should focus on the market(s) the organization is attempting to serve rather than on the good or service offered.

LO 2-6 Describe the components of a situation analysis. In the situation (or SWOT) analysis, the firm should identify its internal strengths (S) and weaknesses (W) and also examine external opportunities (O) and threats (T). When examining external opportunities and threats, marketing managers must analyze aspects of the marketing environment in a process called environmental scanning. The six macroenvironmental forces studied most often are social, demographic, economic, technological, political and legal, and competitive.

LO 2-7 Identify sources of competitive advantage. There are three types of competitive advantage: cost, product/service differentiation, and niche. Sources of cost competitive advantage include experience curves, efficient labor, no-frills goods and services, government subsidies, product design, reengineering, production innovations, and new methods of service delivery. A product/service differentiation competitive advantage exists when a firm provides something unique that is valuable to buyers beyond just low price. Niche competitive advantages come from targeting unique segments with specific needs and wants. The goal of all these sources of competitive advantage is to be sustainable.

LO 2-8 Explain the criteria for stating good marketing objectives. Objectives should be realistic, measurable, time specific, and compared to a benchmark. They must also be consistent and indicate the priorities of the organization. Good marketing objectives communicate marketing management philosophies, provide management direction, motivate employees, force executives to think clearly, and form a basis for control.

marketing planning designing activities relating to marketing objectives and the changing marketing environment

marketing plan a written document that acts as a guidebook of marketing activities for the marketing manager

2–5

mission statement a statement of the firm's business based on a careful analysis of benefits sought by present and potential customers and an analysis of existing and anticipated environmental conditions

marketing myopia defining a business in terms of goods and services rather than in terms of the benefits customers seek

2–6

SWOT analysis identifying internal strengths (S) and weaknesses (W) and also examining external opportunities (O) and threats (T)

environmental scanning collection and interpretation of information about forces, events, and relationships in the external environment that may affect the future of the organization or the implementation of the marketing plan

2–7

competitive advantage a set of unique features of a company and its products that are perceived by the target market as significant and superior to those of the competition

cost competitive advantage being the low-cost competitor in an industry while maintaining satisfactory profit margins

experience curves curves that show costs declining at a predictable rate as experience with a product increases

product/service differentiation competitive advantage the provision of something that is unique and valuable to buyers beyond simply offering a lower price than that of the competition

niche competitive advantage the advantage achieved when a firm

LO 2-9 Discuss target market strategies. Targeting markets begins with a market opportunity analysis (MOA), which describes and estimates the size and sales potential of market segments that are of interest to the firm. In addition, an assessment of key competitors in these market segments is performed. After the market segments are described, one or more may be targeted by the firm.

LO 2-10 Describe the elements of the marketing mix. The marketing mix is a blend of product, place, promotion, and pricing strategies (the four Ps) designed to produce mutually satisfying exchanges with a target market. The starting point of the marketing mix is the product offering—tangible goods, ideas, or services. Place (distribution) strategies are concerned with making products available when and where customers want them. Promotion includes advertising, public relations, sales promotion, and personal selling. Price is what a buyer must give up in order to obtain a product and is often the most flexible of the four marketing mix elements.

LO 2-11 Explain why implementation, evaluation, and control of the marketing plan are necessary. Before a marketing plan can work, it must be implemented—that is, people must perform the actions in the plan. The plan should also be evaluated to see if it has achieved its objectives. Poor implementation can be a major factor in a plan's failure, but working to gain acceptance can be accomplished with task forces. Once implemented, one major aspect of control is the marketing audit and ultimately continuing to apply what the audit uncovered through postaudit tasks.

LO 2-12 Identify several techniques that help make strategic planning effective. First, management must realize that strategic planning is an ongoing process and not a once-a-year exercise. Second, good strategic planning involves a high level of creativity. The last requirement is top management's support and participation.

seeks to target and effectively serve a small segment of the market

sustainable competitive advantage an advantage that cannot be copied by the competition

2–8

marketing objective a statement of what is to be accomplished through marketing activities

2–9

marketing strategy the activities of selecting and describing one or more target markets and developing and maintaining a marketing mix that will produce mutually satisfying exchanges with target markets

market opportunity analysis (MOA) the description and estimation of the size and sales potential of market segments that are of interest to the firm and the assessment of key competitors in these market segments

2–10

marketing mix a unique blend of product, place (distribution), promotion, and pricing strategies designed to

produce mutually satisfying exchanges with a target market

four Ps product, place, promotion, and price, which together make up the marketing mix

2–11

implementation the process that turns a marketing plan into action assignments and ensures that these assignments are executed in a way that accomplishes the plan's objectives

evaluation gauging the extent to which the marketing objectives have been achieved during the specified time period

control provides the mechanisms for evaluating marketing results in light of the plan's objectives and for correcting actions that do not help the organization reach those objectives within budget guidelines

marketing audit a thorough, systematic, periodic evaluation of the objectives, strategies, structure, and performance of the marketing organization

KEY TERMS

3-1

ethics the moral principles or values that generally govern the conduct of an individual or a group

3-2

morals the rules people develop as a result of cultural values and norms

code of ethics a guideline to help marketing managers and other employees make better decisions

Foreign Corrupt Practices Act (FCPA) a law that prohibits U.S. corporations from making illegal payments to public officials of foreign governments to obtain business rights or to enhance their business dealings in those countries

KEY CONCEPTS

LO 3-1 Explain the concept of ethical behavior. Ethics are the moral principles or values that generally govern the conduct of an individual or group. They are standards of behavior by which conduct is judged. Standards that are legal may not always be ethical. An ethics violation offends a person's sense of justice or fairness. Ethics basically constitute the unwritten rules developed to guide interactions. Many ethical questions arise from balancing a business's need to produce profit for shareholders against its desire to operate honestly and with concern for environmental and social issues.

LO 3-2 Describe ethical behavior in business. Business ethics may be viewed as a subset of the values of society as a whole, with a foundation based on the cultural values and norms that constitute a culture's morals. The ethical conduct of businesspeople is shaped by societal elements, including family, education, and religious institutions. As members of society, businesspeople are morally obligated to consider the ethical implications of their decisions. Ethical decision making can be grouped into three basic approaches. The first approach examines the consequences of decisions. The second approach relies on rules and laws to guide decision making. The third approach is based on a theory of moral development that places individuals or groups in one of three developmental stages: preconventional morality, conventional morality, or postconventional morality.

In addition to personal influences, there are many business influences on ethical decision making. Some of the most influential include the extent of ethical problems within the organization, top management's actions on ethics, potential magnitude of the consequences, social consensus, probability of a harmful outcome, length of time between the decision and the onset of consequences, and the number of people affected.

Many companies develop a code of ethics to help their employees make ethical decisions. A code of ethics can help employees identify acceptable business practices, be an effective internal control on behavior, help employees avoid confusion when determining whether decisions are ethical, and facilitate discussion about what is right and wrong.

Studies show that ethical beliefs vary little from country to country. However, there are enough cultural differences, such as the practice of bribery or gift giving, that laws such as the Foreign Corrupt Practices Act (FCPA) have been put in place to discourage and attempt to modify the current acceptance of such practices.

Philanthropic responsibilities
Be a good corporate citizen.
Contribute resources to the community; improve the quality of life.

Ethical responsibilities
Be ethical.
Do what is right, just, and fair. Avoid harm.

Legal responsibilities
Obey the law.
Law is society's codification of right and wrong. Play by the rules of the game.

Economic responsibilities
Be profitable.
Profit is the foundation on which all other responsibilities rest.

© Cengage Learning

3–3

corporate social responsibility (CSR) a business's concern for society's welfare

pyramid of corporate social responsibility a model that suggests corporate social responsibility is composed of economic, legal, ethical, and philanthropic responsibilities and that the firm's economic performance supports the entire structure

sustainability the idea that socially responsible companies will outperform their peers by focusing on the world's social and environmental problems and viewing them as opportunities to build profits and help the world at the same time

green marketing the development and marketing of products designed to minimize negative effects on the physical environment or to improve the environment

3–4

cause-related marketing the cooperative marketing efforts between a for-profit firm and a nonprofit organization

LO 3-3 Discuss corporate social responsibility. Responsibility in business refers to a firm's concern for the way its decisions affect society. Social responsibility has four components: economic, legal, ethical, and philanthropic. These are intertwined, yet the most fundamental is earning a profit. If a firm does not earn a profit, the other three responsibilities are moot. Most businesspeople believe they should do more than pursue profits. Although a company must consider its economic needs first, it must also operate within the law, do what is ethical and fair, and be a good corporate citizen. *Sustainability* is the concept that socially responsible companies will outperform their peers by focusing on the world's social problems and viewing them as an opportunity to earn profits and help the world at the same time. Social responsibility is growing, but it can be costly and the benefits are not always immediate. In addition, some surveys report that consumer desire to purchase responsible products does not always translate to actually purchasing those products. One branch of social responsibility is green marketing, which aids the environment and often the bottom line of a business.

LO 3-4 Explain cause-related marketing. Cause-related marketing is the cooperative effort between a for-profit firm and a nonprofit organization. It is different from philanthropy, which is a specific, tax-deductible donation. Cause-related marketing is very popular because it can enhance the reputation of the corporation and also make additional profit for the company. However, consumers sometimes feel that every company is tied to a cause, resulting in consumer cause fatigue.

KEY TERMS

4-1

target market a group of people or organizations for which an organization designs, implements, and maintains a marketing mix intended to meet the need of that group, resulting in mutually satisfying exchanges

environmental management when a company implements strategies that attempt to shape the external environment within which it operates

4-2

component lifestyles the practice of choosing goods and services that meet one's diverse needs and interests rather than conforming to a single, traditional lifestyle

4-3

demography the study of people's vital statistics, such as age, race and ethnicity, and location

Generation Y people born between 1979 and 1994

Generation X people born between 1965 and 1978

baby boomers people born between 1946 and 1964

KEY CONCEPTS

LO 4-1 Discuss the external environment of marketing and explain how it affects a firm. The external marketing environment consists of social, demographic, economic, technological, political and legal, and competitive variables. Marketers generally cannot control the elements of the external environment. Instead, they must understand how the external environment is changing and the impact of that change on the target market. Then marketing managers can create a marketing mix to effectively meet the needs of target customers.

© Cengage Learning

LO 4-2 Describe the social factors that affect marketing. Within the external environment, social factors are perhaps the most difficult for marketers to anticipate. Several major social trends are currently shaping marketing strategies. First, people of all ages have a broader range of interests, defying traditional consumer profiles. Second, social media, Web-based, and mobile technology change how people and marketers interact by allowing one-to-one, one-to-many, and many-to-many communications. Because Facebook is about human-to-human interaction, companies are turning to it and other forms of social media with ever-increasing speed.

LO 4-3 Explain the importance to marketing managers of current demographic trends. Today, several basic demographic patterns are influencing marketing mixes. The U.S. population grew by 27 million from 2000 to 2010, but growth was unevenly distributed. Marketers are also faced with increasingly experienced consumers among the younger generations such as tweens and teens. And because the population is also growing older, marketers are offering more products that appeal to middle-aged and older consumers.

	Tweens	Teens	Gen Y	Gen X	Baby Boomers
Age	8 to 12 years	13 to 19 years	1979 to 1994	1965 to 1978	1946 to 1964
	20 million	25 million	75 million+	40 million	75 million

© Cengage Learning

LO 4-4 Explain the importance to marketing managers of growing ethnic markets. About one in three U.S. residents is a member of a minority group. By 2050, about one in three U.S. residents will be Hispanic. Many companies are now creating departments and product lines to effectively target multicultural market segments. Companies have quickly found that ethnic markets are not homogeneous.

4-5

purchasing power a comparison of income versus the relative cost of a standard set of goods and services in different geographic areas

inflation a measure of the decrease in the value of money, expressed as the percentage reduction in value since the previous year

recession a period of economic activity characterized by negative growth, which reduces demand for goods and services

4-6

basic research pure research that aims to confirm an existing theory or to learn more about a concept or phenomenon

applied research research that attempts to develop new or improved products

4-7

Consumer Product Safety Commission (CPSC) a federal agency established to protect the health and safety of consumers in and around their homes

Food and Drug Administration (FDA) a federal agency charged with enforcing regulations against selling and distributing adulterated, misbranded, or hazardous food and drug products

Federal Trade Commission (FTC) a federal agency empowered to prevent persons or corporations from using unfair methods of competition in commerce

LO 4-5 Identify consumer and marketer reactions to the state of the economy. In recent years, U.S. incomes have risen at a slow pace. During a time of inflation, marketers generally attempt to maintain level pricing to avoid losing customer brand loyalty. During times of recession, many marketers maintain or reduce prices to counter the effects of decreased demand; they also concentrate on increasing production efficiency and improving customer service.

LO 4-6 Identify the impact of technology on a firm. Monitoring new technology and encouraging research and development (R&D) of new technology are essential to keeping up with competitors in today's marketing environment. Innovation through R&D needs to be stimulated by upper management and fostered in creative environments. Although developing new technology internally is a key to creating and maintaining a long-term competitive advantage, external technology is also important to managers.

LO 4-7 Discuss the political and legal environment of marketing. All marketing activities are subject to state and federal laws and the rulings of regulatory agencies. Marketers are responsible for remaining aware of and abiding by such regulations. Some key federal agencies that affect marketing are the Consumer Product Safety Commission, the Food and Drug Administration, and the Federal Trade Commission. Many laws, including privacy laws, have been passed to protect the consumer as well. In 2012, the FTC called for online data collectors to adopt better privacy policies and asked Congress to pass comprehensive privacy legislation.

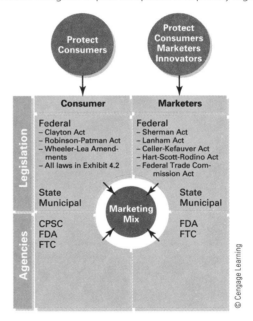

LO 4-8 Explain the basics of foreign and domestic competition. The competitive environment encompasses the number of competitors a firm must face, the relative size of the competitors, and the degree of interdependence within the industry. Declining population growth, rising costs, and shortages of resources have heightened domestic competition.

KEY TERMS

5-1

global marketing marketing that targets markets throughout the world

global vision recognizing and reacting to international marketing opportunities, using effective global marketing strategies, and being aware of threats from foreign competitors in all markets

gross domestic product (GDP) the total market value of all final goods and services produced in a country for a given time period

job outsourcing sending U.S. jobs abroad

5-2

multinational corporation a company that is heavily engaged in international trade, beyond exporting and importing

capital intensive using more capital than labor in the production process

global marketing standardization production of uniform products that can be sold the same way all over the world

multidomestic strategy when multinational firms enable individual subsidiaries to compete independently in domestic markets

5-3

Mercosur the largest Latin American trade agreement; includes Argentina, Bolivia, Brazil, Chile, Colombia, Ecuador, Paraguay, Peru, Uruguay, and Venezuela

Uruguay Round an agreement to dramatically lower trade barriers worldwide; created the World Trade Organization

World Trade Organization (WTO) a trade organization that replaced the old General Agreement on Tariffs and Trade (GATT)

KEY CONCEPTS

LO 5-1 Discuss the importance of global marketing. Businesspeople who adopt a global vision are better able to identify global marketing opportunities, understand the nature of global networks, create effective global marketing strategies, and compete against foreign competition in domestic markets. Large corporations have traditionally been the major global competitors, but more and more small businesses are entering the global marketplace. Despite fears of job losses to other countries with cheaper labor, there are many benefits to globalization, including the reduction of poverty and increased standards of living.

LO 5-2 Discuss the impact of multinational firms on the world economy. Multinational corporations are international traders that regularly operate across national borders. Because of their vast size and financial, technological, and material resources, multinational corporations have great influence on the world economy. They have the ability to overcome trade problems, save on labor costs, and tap new technology. There are critics and supporters of multinational corporations, and the critics question the actual benefits of bringing capital-intensive technology to impoverished nations. Many countries block foreign investment in factories, land, and companies to protect their economies.

Some companies presume that markets throughout the world are more and more similar, so some global products can be standardized across global markets.

LO 5-3 Describe the external environment facing global marketers. Global marketers face the same environmental factors as they do domestically: culture, economic and technological development, political structure and actions, demography, and natural resources. Cultural considerations include societal values, attitudes and beliefs, language, and customary business practices. A country's economic and technological status depends on its stage of industrial development, which, in turn, affects average family incomes. The political structure is shaped by political ideology and such policies as tariffs, quotas, boycotts, exchange controls, trade agreements, and market groupings. Demographic variables include the size of a population and its age and geographic distribution. A shortage of natural resources also affects the external environment by dictating what is available and at what price.

LO 5-4 Identify the various ways of entering the global marketplace. Firms use the following strategies to enter global markets, in descending order of risk and profit: direct investment, joint venture, contract manufacturing, licensing and franchising, and exporting.

RISK LEVELS FOR FIVE METHODS OF ENTERING THE GLOBAL MARKETPLACE

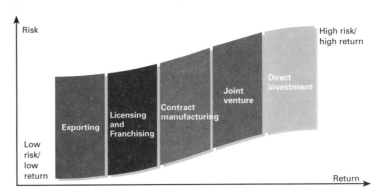

© Cengage Learning

General Agreement on Tariffs and Trade (GATT) a trade agreement that contained loopholes enabling countries to avoid trade-barrier reduction agreements

North American Free Trade Agreement (NAFTA) an agreement between Canada, the United States, and Mexico that created the world's then-largest free trade zone

Central America Free Trade Agreement (CAFTA) a trade agreement, instituted in 2005, that includes Costa Rica, the Dominican Republic, El Salvador, Guatemala, Honduras, Nicaragua, and the United States

European Union (EU) a free trade zone encompassing twenty-seven European countries

World Bank an international bank that offers low-interest loans, advice, and information to developing nations

International Monetary Fund (IMF) an international organization that acts as a lender of last resort, providing loans to troubled nations, and also works to promote trade through financial cooperation

Group of Twenty (G-20) a forum for international economic development that promotes discussion between industrial and emerging-market countries on key issues related to global economic stability

5-4

exporting selling domestically produced products to buyers in other countries

buyer for export an intermediary in the global market who assumes all ownership risks and sells globally for its own account

export broker an intermediary who plays the traditional broker's role by bringing buyer and seller together

export agent an intermediary who acts like a manufacturer's agent for the exporter; the export agent lives in the foreign market

LO 5-5 List the basic elements involved in developing a global marketing mix. A firm's major consideration is how much it will adjust the four Ps—product, promotion, place (distribution), and price—within each country. One strategy is to use one product and one promotion message worldwide. A second strategy is to create new products for global markets. A third strategy is to keep the product basically the same but alter the promotional message. A fourth strategy is to slightly alter the product to meet local conditions.

GLOBAL MARKETING MIX

Product + Promotion	Place (Distribution)	Price
One product, one message	Channel choice	Dumping
Product invention	Channel structure	Countertrade
Product adaptation	Country infrastructure	Exchange rates
Message adaptation		Purchasing power

LO 5-6 Discover how the Internet is affecting global marketing. Simply opening an e-commerce site can open the door for international sales. International carriers, such as UPS, can help solve logistics problems. Language translation software can help an e-commerce business become multilingual. Yet cultural differences and old-line rules, regulations, and taxes hinder rapid development of e-commerce in many countries. Global marketers use social media not only for understanding consumers but also to build their brands as they expand internationally.

licensing the legal process whereby a licensor allows another firm to use its manufacturing process, trademarks, patents, trade secrets, or other proprietary knowledge

contract manufacturing private label manufacturing by a foreign company

joint venture when a domestic firm buys part of a foreign company or joins with a foreign company to create a new entity

direct foreign investment active ownership of a foreign company or of overseas manufacturing or marketing facilities

5-5

floating exchange rates a system in which prices of different currencies move up and down based on the demand for and the supply of each currency

dumping the sale of an exported product at a price lower than that charged for the same or a like product in the "home" market of the exporter

countertrade a form of trade in which all or part of the payment for goods or services is in the form of other goods or services

5-6

blog a publicly accessible Web page that functions as an interactive journal, where readers can post comments on the author's entries

KEY TERMS

7-1

business marketing (industrial marketing) the marketing of goods and services to individuals and organizations for purposes other than personal consumption

7-2

business-to-business electronic commerce (B-to-B or B2B e-commerce) the use of the Internet to facilitate the exchange of goods, services, and information between organizations

stickiness a measure of a Web site's effectiveness; calculated by multiplying the frequency of visits by the duration of a visit by the number of pages viewed during each visit (site reach)

disintermediation the elimination of intermediaries such as wholesalers or distributers from a marketing channel

reintermediation the reintroduction of an intermediary between producers and users

7-3

strategic alliance (strategic partnership) a cooperative agreement between business firms

relationship commitment a firm's belief that an ongoing relationship with another firm is so important that the relationship warrants maximum efforts at maintaining it indefinitely

trust the condition that exists when one party has confidence in an exchange partner's reliability and integrity

keiretsu a network of interlocking corporate affiliates

7-4

original equipment manufacturers (OEMs) individuals and organizations that buy business goods and incorporate them into the products they produce for eventual sale to other producers or to consumers

KEY CONCEPTS

LO 7-1 Describe business marketing. Business marketing provides goods and services that are bought for use in business rather than for personal consumption. Intended use, not physical characteristics, distinguishes a business product from a consumer product.

LO 7-2 Describe the role of the Internet in business marketing. The rapid expansion and adoption of the Internet have made business markets more competitive than ever before. Businesses are integrating content marketing into their B-to-B marketing campaigns, and measurements such as a Web site's stickiness and metrics evaluating social media effectiveness are increasingly important to B-to-B marketers. These trends help B-to-B marketers generate more valuable leads and pull customers into their Web sites.

LO 7-3 Discuss the role of relationship marketing and strategic alliances in business marketing. Relationship marketing entails seeking and establishing long-term alliances or partnerships with customers. A strategic alliance is a cooperative agreement between business firms. Firms form alliances to leverage what they do well by partnering with others that have complementary skills.

LO 7-4 Identify the four major categories of business market customers. Producer markets consist of for-profit individuals and organizations that buy products to use in producing other products, as components of other products, or in facilitating business operations. Reseller markets consist of wholesalers and retailers that buy finished products to resell for profit. Government markets include federal, state, county, and city governments that buy goods and services to support their own operations and serve the needs of citizens. Institutional markets consist of very diverse nonbusiness institutions whose main goals do not include profit.

LO 7-5 Explain the North American Industry Classification System. NAICS provides a way to identify, analyze, segment, and target business and government markets. Organizations can be identified and compared by a numeric code indicating business sector, subsector, industry group, industry, and industry subdivision. NAICS is a valuable tool for analyzing, segmenting, and targeting business markets.

LO 7-6 Explain the major differences between business and consumer markets. In business markets, demand is derived, inelastic, joint, and fluctuating. Purchase volume is much larger than in consumer markets, customers are fewer in number and more geographically concentrated, and distribution channels are more direct. Buying is approached more formally using professional purchasing agents, more people are involved in the buying process, negotiation is more complex, and reciprocity and leasing are more common. And, finally, selling strategy in business markets normally focuses on personal contact rather than on advertising.

Characteristic	Business Market	Consumer Market
Demand	Organizational	Individual
Purchase volume	Larger	Smaller
Number of customers	Fewer	Many
Location of buyers	Geographically concentrated	Dispersed
Distribution structure	More direct	More indirect

(continued)

7-5

North American Industry Classification System (NAICS) a detailed numbering system developed by the United States, Canada, and Mexico to classify North American business establishments by their main production processes

7-6

derived demand the demand for business products

joint demand the demand for two or more items used together in a final product

multiplier effect (accelerator principle) phenomenon in which a small increase or decrease in consumer demand can produce a much larger change in demand for the facilities and equipment needed to make the consumer product

business-to-business online exchange an electronic trading floor that provides companies with integrated links to their customers and suppliers

reciprocity a practice whereby business purchasers choose to buy from their own customers

7-7

major equipment (installations) capital goods such as large or expensive machines, mainframe computers, blast furnaces, generators, airplanes, and buildings

accessory equipment goods, such as portable tools and office equipment, that are less expensive and shorter-lived than major equipment

raw materials unprocessed extractive or agricultural products, such as mineral ore, lumber, wheat, corn, fruits, vegetables, and fish

component parts either finished items ready for assembly or products that need very little processing before becoming part of some other product

processed materials products used directly in manufacturing other products

supplies consumable items that do not become part of the final product

Characteristic	Business Market	Consumer Market
Nature of buying	More professional	More personal
Nature of buying influence	Multiple	Single
Type of negotiations	More complex	Simpler
Use of reciprocity	Yes	No
Use of leasing	Greater	Lesser
Primary promotional method	Personal selling	Advertising

LO 7-7 Describe the seven types of business goods and services. Major equipment includes capital goods, such as heavy machinery. Accessory equipment is typically less expensive and shorter lived than major equipment. Raw materials are extractive or agricultural products that have not been processed. Component parts are finished or near-finished items to be used as parts of other products. Processed materials are used to manufacture other products. Supplies are consumable and not used as part of a final product. Business services are intangible products that many companies use in their operations.

LO 7-8 Discuss the unique aspects of business buying behavior. Business buying behavior is distinguished by five fundamental characteristics. First, buying is normally undertaken by a buying center consisting of many people who range widely in authority level. Second, business buyers typically evaluate alternative products and suppliers based on quality, service, and price—in that order. Third, business buying falls into three general categories: new buys, modified rebuys, and straight rebuys. Fourth, the ethics of business buyers and sellers are often scrutinized. Fifth, customer service before, during, and after the sale plays a big role in business purchase decisions.

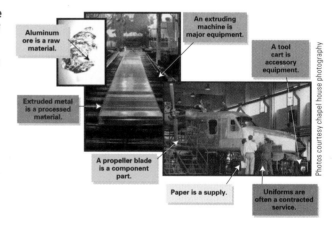

Aluminum ore is a raw material.

An extruding machine is major equipment.

A tool cart is accessory equipment.

Extruded metal is a processed material.

A propeller blade is a component part.

Paper is a supply.

Uniforms are often a contracted service.

business services expense items that do not become part of a final product

7-8

buying center all those people in an organization who become involved in the purchase decision

new buy a situation requiring the purchase of a product for the first time

modified rebuy a situation in which the purchaser wants some change in the original good or service

straight rebuy a situation in which the purchaser reorders the same goods or services without looking for new information or investigating other suppliers

KEY TERMS

10-1
product everything, both favorable and unfavorable, that a person receives in an exchange

10-2
business product (industrial product) a product used to manufacture other goods or services, to facilitate an organization's operations, or to resell to other customers

consumer product a product bought to satisfy an individual's personal wants

convenience product a relatively inexpensive item that merits little shopping effort

shopping product a product that requires comparison shopping because it is usually more expensive than a convenience product and is found in fewer stores

specialty product a particular item for which consumers search extensively and are very reluctant to accept substitutes

unsought product a product unknown to the potential buyer or a known product that the buyer does not actively seek

10-3
product item a specific version of a product that can be designated as a distinct offering among an organization's products

product line a group of closely related product items

product mix all products that an organization sells

product mix width the number of product lines an organization offers

product line depth the number of product items in a product line

product modification changing one or more of a product's characteristics

KEY CONCEPTS

LO 10-1 Define the term *product*. A product is anything, desired or not, that a person or organization receives in an exchange. The basic goal of purchasing decisions is to receive the tangible and intangible benefits associated with a product. Tangible aspects include packaging, style, color, size, and features. Intangible qualities include service, the retailer's image, the manufacturer's reputation, and the social status associated with a product. An organization's product offering is the crucial element in any marketing mix.

LO 10-2 Classify consumer products. Consumer products are classified into four categories: convenience products, shopping products, specialty products, and unsought products. Convenience products are relatively inexpensive and require limited shopping effort. Shopping products are of two types: homogeneous and heterogeneous. Because of the similarity of homogeneous products, they are differentiated mainly by price and features. In contrast, heterogeneous products appeal to consumers because of their distinct characteristics. Specialty products possess unique benefits that are highly desirable to certain customers. Finally, unsought products are either new products or products that require aggressive selling because they are generally avoided or overlooked by consumers.

LO 10-3 Define the terms *product item*, *product line*, and *product mix*. A product item is a specific version of a product that can be designated as a distinct offering among an organization's products. A product line is a group of closely related products offered by an organization. An organization's product mix includes all the products it sells. Product mix width refers to the number of product lines an organization offers. Product line depth is the number of product items in a product line. Firms modify existing products by changing their quality, functional characteristics, or style. Product line extension occurs when a firm adds new products to existing product lines.

LO 10-4 Describe marketing uses of branding. A brand is a name, term, or symbol that identifies and differentiates a firm's products. Established brands encourage customer loyalty and help new products succeed. Branding strategies require decisions about individual, family, manufacturers', and private brands. The table below compares manufacturers' and private brands.

COMPARISON OF MANUFACTURERS' AND PRIVATE BRANDS FROM THE RESELLER'S PERSPECTIVE

Key Advantages of Carrying Manufacturers' Brands	Key Advantages of Carrying Private Brands
• Heavy advertising to the consumer by manufacturers such as Procter & Gamble helps develop strong consumer loyalties.	• A wholesaler or retailer can usually earn higher profits on its own brand. In addition, because the private brand is exclusive, there is less pressure to mark down the price to meet competition.
• Well-known manufacturers' brands, such as Fisher-Price, can attract new customers and enhance the dealer's (wholesaler's or retailer's) prestige.	• A manufacturer can decide to drop a brand or a reseller at any time or even become a direct competitor to its dealers.
• Many manufacturers offer rapid delivery, enabling the dealer to carry less inventory.	• A private brand ties the customer to the wholesaler or retailer. A person who wants a DieHard battery must go to Sears.

(continued)

planned obsolescence the practice of modifying products so those that have already been sold become obsolete before they actually need replacement

product line extension adding additional products to an existing product line in order to compete more broadly in the industry

10-4

brand a name, term, symbol, design, or combination thereof that identifies a seller's products and differentiates them from competitors' products

brand name that part of a brand that can be spoken, including letters, words, and numbers

brand mark the elements of a brand that cannot be spoken

brand equity the value of company and brand names

global brand a brand that obtains at least a third of its earnings from outside its home country, is recognizable outside its home base of customers, and has publicly available marketing and financial data

brand loyalty consistent preference for one brand over all others

manufacturer's brand the brand name of a manufacturer

private brand a brand name owned by a wholesaler or a retailer

captive brand a brand manufactured by a third party for an exclusive retailer, without evidence of that retailer's affiliation

individual branding using different brand names for different products

family branding marketing several different products under the same brand name

co-branding placing two or more brand names on a product or its package

trademark the exclusive right to use a brand or part of a brand

service mark a trademark for a service

Key Advantages of Carrying Manufacturers' Brands	Key Advantages of Carrying Private Brands
• If a dealer happens to sell a manufacturer's brand of poor quality, the customer may simply switch brands and remain loyal to the dealer.	• Wholesalers and retailers have no control over the intensity of distribution of manufacturers' brands. Walmart store managers don't have to worry about competing with other sellers of Sam's American Choice products or Ol' Roy dog food. They know that these brands are sold only in Walmart and Sam's Club stores.

LO 10-5 Describe marketing uses of packaging and labeling. Packaging has four functions: containing and protecting products; promoting products; facilitating product storage, use, and convenience; and facilitating recycling and reducing environmental damage. As a tool for promotion, packaging identifies the brand and its features. It also serves the critical function of differentiating a product from competing products and linking it with related products from the same manufacturer. The label is an integral part of the package, with persuasive and informational functions. In essence, the package is the marketer's last chance to influence buyers before they make a purchase decision.

LO 10-6 Discuss global issues in branding and packaging. In addition to brand piracy, international marketers must address a variety of concerns regarding branding and packaging, including choosing a brand name policy, translating labels and meeting host-country labeling requirements, making packages aesthetically compatible with host-country cultures, and offering the sizes of packages preferred in host countries.

Global Branding Choices	Global Packaging Considerations
One name	Labeling
Modify or adapt one name	Aesthetics
Different names in different markets	Climate

LO 10-7 Describe how and why product warranties are important marketing tools. Product warranties are important tools because they offer consumers protection and help them gauge product quality.

Express warranty = written guarantee

Implied warranty = unwritten guarantee

generic product name identifies a product by class or type and cannot be trademarked

10-5

persuasive labeling a type of package labeling that focuses on a promotional theme or logo, and consumer information is secondary

informational labeling a type of package labeling designed to help consumers make proper product selections and lower their cognitive dissonance after the purchase

universal product codes (UPCs) a series of thick and thin vertical lines (bar codes), readable by computerized optical scanners, that represent numbers used to track products

10-7

warranty a confirmation of the quality or performance of a good or service

express warranty a written guarantee

implied warranty an unwritten guarantee that the good or service is fit for the purpose for which it was sold

KEY TERMS

11-1

new product a product new to the world, the market, the producer, the seller, or some combination of these

11-2

new-product strategy a plan that links the new-product development process with the objectives of the marketing department, the business unit, and the corporation

product development a marketing strategy that entails the creation of marketable new products; the process of converting applications for new technologies into marketable products

brainstorming the process of getting a group to think of unlimited ways to vary a product or solve a problem

screening the first filter in the product development process, which eliminates ideas that are inconsistent with the organization's new-product strategy or are obviously inappropriate for some other reason

concept test a test to evaluate a new-product idea, usually before any prototype has been created

business analysis the second stage of the screening process where preliminary figures for demand, cost, sales, and profitability are calculated

development the stage in the product development process in which a prototype is developed and a marketing strategy is outlined

simultaneous product development a team-oriented approach to new-product development

test marketing the limited introduction of a product and a marketing program to determine the reactions of potential customers in a market situation

KEY CONCEPTS

LO 11-1 Explain the importance of developing new products and describe the six categories of new products. New products are important to sustain growth and profits and to replace obsolete items. New products can be classified as new-to-the-world products (discontinuous innovations), new product lines, additions to existing product lines, improvements or revisions of existing products, repositioned products, or lower-priced products. To sustain or increase profits, a firm must innovate.

LO 11-2 Explain the steps in the new-product development process. First, a firm forms a new-product strategy by outlining the characteristics and roles of future products. Then new-product ideas are generated by customers, employees, distributors, competitors, vendors, and internal research and development personnel. Once a product idea has survived initial screening by an appointed screening group, it undergoes business analysis to determine its potential profitability. If a product concept seems viable, it progresses into the development phase, in which the technical and economic feasibility of the manufacturing process is evaluated. The development phase also includes laboratory and use testing of a product for performance and safety. Following initial testing and refinement, most products are introduced in a test market to evaluate consumer response and marketing strategies. Finally, test market successes are propelled into full commercialization. The commercialization process involves starting up production, building inventories, shipping to distributors, training a sales force, announcing the product to the trade, and advertising to consumers.

NEW-PRODUCT DEVELOPMENT PROCESS

1. New-product strategy
2. Idea generation
3. Idea screening
4. Business analysis
5. Development
6. Test marketing
7. Commercialization

New product

© Cengage Learning

simulated (laboratory) market testing the presentation of advertising and other promotional materials for several products, including a test product, to members of the product's target market

commercialization the decision to market a product

11-4

innovation a product perceived as new by a potential adopter

diffusion the process by which the adoption of an innovation spreads

11-5

product life cycle (PLC) a concept that provides a way to trace the stages of a product's acceptance, from its introduction (birth) to its decline (death)

product category all brands that satisfy a particular type of need

introductory stage the full-scale launch of a new product into the marketplace

growth stage the second stage of the product life cycle when sales typically grow at an increasing rate, many competitors enter the market, large companies may start to acquire small pioneering firms, and profits are healthy

maturity stage a period during which sales increase at a decreasing rate

decline stage a long-run drop in sales

LO 11-3 Discuss global issues in new-product development. A marketer with global vision seeks to develop products that can easily be adapted to suit local needs. The goal is not simply to develop a standard product that can be sold worldwide. Smart global marketers also look for good product ideas worldwide.

LO 11-4 Explain the diffusion process through which new products are adopted. The diffusion process is the spread of a new product from its producer to ultimate adopters. Adopters in the diffusion process belong to five categories: innovators, early adopters, the early majority, the late majority, and laggards. Product characteristics that affect the rate of adoption include product complexity, compatibility with existing social values, relative advantage over existing substitutes, visibility, and "trialability." The diffusion process is facilitated by word-of-mouth communication and communication from marketers to consumers.

LO 11-5 Explain the concept of product life cycles. All brands and product categories undergo a life cycle with four stages: introduction, growth, maturity, and decline. The rate at which products move through these stages varies dramatically. Marketing managers use the product life cycle concept as an analytical tool to forecast a product's future and devise effective marketing strategies.

RELATIONSHIP BETWEEN THE DIFFUSION PROCESS AND THE PRODUCT LIFE CYCLE

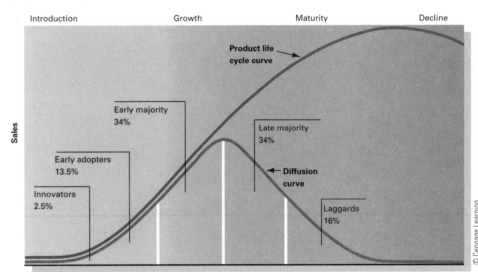

© iStockphoto.com/Bill Noll

© Cengage Learning

KEY TERMS

12-1

service the result of applying human or mechanical efforts to people or objects

12-2

intangibility the inability of services to be touched, seen, tasted, heard, or felt in the same manner that goods can be sensed

search quality a characteristic that can be easily assessed before purchase

experience quality a characteristic that can be assessed only after use

credence quality a characteristic that consumers may have difficulty assessing even after purchase because they do not have the necessary knowledge or experience

inseparability the inability of the production and consumption of a service to be separated; consumers must be present during the production

heterogeneity the variability of the inputs and outputs of services, which causes services to tend to be less standardized and uniform than goods

perishability the inability of services to be stored, warehoused, or inventoried

12-3

reliability the ability to perform a service dependably, accurately, and consistently

responsiveness the ability to provide prompt service

assurance the knowledge and courtesy of employees and their ability to convey trust

empathy caring, individualized attention to customers

tangibles the physical evidence of a service, including the physical facilities, tools, and equipment used to provide the service

gap model a model identifying five gaps that can cause problems in service delivery and influence customer evaluations of service quality

KEY CONCEPTS

LO 12-1 Discuss the importance of services to the economy. The service sector plays a crucial role in the U.S. economy; the U.S. Census's Service Survey found that service industries accounted for 55 percent of U.S. GDP in 2010. Services have unique characteristics that distinguish them from goods, and marketing strategies need to be adjusted for these characteristics.

LO 12-2 Discuss the differences between services and goods. Services are distinguished by four characteristics. Services are intangible performances in that they lack clearly identifiable physical characteristics, making it difficult for marketers to communicate their specific benefits to potential customers. The production and consumption of services occur simultaneously. Services are heterogeneous because their quality depends on such elements as the service provider, individual consumer, location, and the like. Finally, services are perishable in the sense that they cannot be stored or saved. As a result, synchronizing supply with demand is particularly challenging in the service industry.

LO 12-3 Describe the components of service quality and the gap model of service quality. Service quality has five components: reliability (ability to perform the service dependably, accurately, and consistently), responsiveness (providing prompt service), assurance (knowledge and courtesy of employees and their ability to convey trust), empathy (caring, individualized attention), and tangibles (physical evidence of the service).

The gap model identifies five key discrepancies that can influence customer evaluations of service quality. When the gaps are large, service quality is low. As the gaps shrink, service quality improves. Gap 1 is found between customers' expectations and management's perceptions of those expectations. Gap 2 is found between management's perception of what the customer wants and specifications for service quality. Gap 3 is found between service quality specifications and delivery of the service. Gap 4 is found between service delivery and what the company promises to the customer through external communication. Gap 5 is found between customers' service expectations and their perceptions of service performance.

LO 12-4 Develop marketing mixes for services. "Product" (service) strategy issues include what is being processed (people, possessions, mental stimulus, information), core and supplementary services, customization versus standardization, and the service mix. Distribution (place) decisions involve convenience, number of outlets, direct versus indirect distribution, and scheduling. Stressing tangible cues, using personal sources of information, creating strong organizational images, and engaging in postpurchase communication are effective promotion strategies. Pricing objectives for services can be revenue oriented, operations oriented, patronage oriented, or any combination of the three.

12-4

core service the most basic benefit the consumer is buying

supplementary services a group of services that support or enhance the core service

mass customization a strategy that uses technology to deliver customized services on a mass basis

12-6

internal marketing treating employees as customers and developing systems and benefits that satisfy their needs

12-8

nonprofit organization an organization that exists to achieve some goal other than the usual business goals of profit, market share, or return on investment

nonprofit organization marketing the effort by nonprofit organizations to bring about mutually satisfying exchanges with target markets

public service advertisement (PSA) an announcement that promotes a program of a federal, state, or local government or of a nonprofit organization

CORE AND SUPPLEMENTARY SERVICES FOR A UNIVERSITY

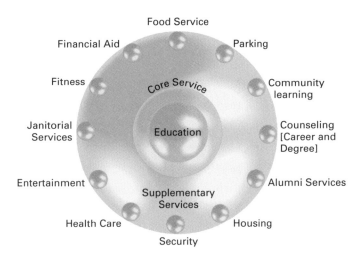

LO 12-5 Discuss relationship marketing in services. Relationship marketing in services involves attracting, developing, and retaining customer relationships. There are three levels of relationship marketing: Level 1 focuses on pricing incentives; level 2 uses pricing incentives and social bonds with customers; and level 3 uses pricing, social bonds, and structural bonds to build long-term relationships.

LO 12-6 Explain internal marketing in services. Internal marketing means treating employees as customers and developing systems and benefits that satisfy their needs. Employees who like their jobs and are happy with the firm they work for are more likely to deliver good service.

LO 12-7 Discuss global issues in services marketing. The United States has become the world's largest exporter of services. Although competition is keen, the United States has a competitive advantage because of its vast experience in many service industries. To be successful globally, service firms must adjust their marketing mix for the environment of each target country.

LO 12-8 Describe nonprofit organization marketing. Nonprofit organizations pursue goals other than profit, market share, and return on investment. Nonprofit organization marketing facilitates mutually satisfying exchanges between nonprofit organizations and their target markets. Several unique characteristics distinguish nonbusiness marketing strategy, including a concern with services and social behaviors rather than manufactured goods and profit; a difficult, undifferentiated, and in some ways marginal target market; a complex product that may have only indirect benefits and elicit very low involvement; distribution that may or may not require special facilities depending on the service provided; a relative lack of resources for promotion; and prices only indirectly related to the exchange between the producer and the consumer of services.

CHAPTER REVIEW

KEY TERMS

13-1

supply chain the connected chain of all of the business entities, both internal and external to the company, that perform or support the logistics function

supply chain management a management system that coordinates and integrates all of the activities performed by supply chain members into a seamless process, from the source to the point of consumption, resulting in enhanced customer and economic value

supply chain agility an operational strategy focused on inducing inventory velocity and operational flexibility simultaneously in the supply chain

13-2

supply chain integration when multiple firms or business functions in a supply chain coordinate their activities and processes so that they are seamlessly linked to one another in an effort to satisfy the customer

demand-supply integration (DSI) a supply chain operational philosophy focused on integrating the supply-management and demand-generating functions of an organization

13-3

business processes bundles of interconnected activities that stretch across firms in the supply chain

customer relationship management (CRM) process allows companies to prioritize their marketing focus on different customer groups according to each group's long-term value to the company or supply chain

customer service management process presents a multi-company, unified response system to the customer whenever complaints, concerns, questions, or comments are voiced

demand management process seeks to align supply and demand throughout the supply chain by anticipating customer requirements at each level and creating demand-related plans of action prior to actual customer purchasing behavior

KEY CONCEPTS

LO 13-1 Define the terms *supply chain* and *supply chain management*, and discuss the benefits of supply chain management. Management coordinates and integrates all of the activities performed by supply chain members into a seamless process from the source to the point of consumption. The benefits of supply chain management include reduced inventory, transportation, warehousing, and packaging costs; greater supply chain flexibility; improved customer service; and higher revenues.

LO 13-2 Discuss the concepts of internal and external supply chain integration, and explain why each of these types of integration is important. In the modern supply chain, integration can be either internal or external. Internally, the very best companies develop a managerial orientation toward demand-supply integration. Companies operating under a DSI philosophy are better at their business because all of the different divisions within the company "play from the same sheet of music." Externally, five types of integration are sought by firms interested in providing top-level service to customers: relationship integration, measurement integration, technology and planning integration, material and service supplier integration, and customer integration.

LO 13-3 Identify the eight key processes of excellent supply chain management, and discuss how each of these processes affects the end customer. The key processes that leading supply chain companies focus on are (1) customer relationship management, (2) customer service management, (3) demand management, (4) order fulfillment, (5) manufacturing flow management, (6) supplier relationship management, (7) product development and commercialization, and (8) returns management. When firms practice excellent supply chain management, each of these processes is integrated from end to end in the supply chain. These processes are made up of bundles of interconnected activities that supply chain partners are constantly focused on when delivering value to the customer.

LO 13-4 Understand which key functional areas of business impact supply chain success, and how. The supply chain team, in concert with the logistics information system, orchestrates the movement of goods, services, and information from the source to the consumer. Supply chain teams typically cut across organizational boundaries, embracing all parties who participate in moving product to market. The logistics supply chain consists of several interrelated and integrated logistical components: (1) sourcing and procurement, (2) inventory control, (3) order processing, (4) production, (5) warehousing and materials handling, (6) transportation, and (7) maintaining supply chain technology. The logistics information system integrates and links all of the logistics functions of the supply chain. Smart RFID tags are another type of advanced computer technology that is helping companies manage their supply chains.

LO 13-5 Discuss new technology and emerging trends in supply chain management. Several emerging trends are changing the job of today's supply chain manager. Some of the business trends affecting supply chain management include outsourcing logistics, maintaining a secure supply chain and minimizing supply chain risk, and maintaining a sustainable supply chain. While these changes exert pressure on managers to change the way their supply chains function, electronic distribution is being used and changed frequently to help make supply chain management more integrated and easier to track.

order fulfillment process a highly integrated process, often requiring persons from multiple companies and multiple functions to come together and coordinate to create customer satisfaction at a given place and time

manufacturing flow management process concerned with ensuring that firms in the supply chain have the needed resources to manufacture with flexibility and to move products through a multi-stage production process

supplier relationship management process supports manufacturing flow by identifying and maintaining relationships with highly valued suppliers

product development and commercialization process includes the group of activities that facilitates the joint development and marketing of new offerings among a group of supply chain partner firms

returns management process enables firms to manage volumes of returned product efficiently while minimizing returns-related costs and maximizing the value of the returned assets to the firms in the supply chain

13-4

logistics the process of strategically managing the efficient flow and storage of raw materials, in-process inventory, and finished goods from point of origin to point of consumption

supply chain team an entire group of individuals who orchestrate the movement of goods, services, and information from the source to the consumer

inventory control system a method of developing and maintaining an adequate assortment of materials or products to meet a manufacturer's or a customer's demand

materials requirement planning (MRP; materials management) an inventory control system that manages the replenishment of raw materials, supplies, and components from the supplier to the manufacturer

distribution resource planning (DRP) an inventory control system that manages the replenishment of goods from the manufacturer to the final consumer

automatic replenishment program a real-time inventory system that triggers shipments only when a good is sold to the end user

order processing system a system whereby orders are entered into the supply chain and filled

electronic data interchange (EDI) information technology that replaces the paper documents that usually accompany business transactions, such as purchase orders and invoices, with electronic transmission of the needed information to reduce inventory levels, improve cash flow, streamline operations, and increase the speed and accuracy of information transmission

build-to-stock a production method whereby products are made in advance of demand based on forecasts and are stored until customer orders arrive

mass customization (build-to-order) a production method whereby products are not made until an order is placed by the customer; products are made according to customer specifications

postponement a hybrid production method whereby basic units of a finished good are manufactured in advance of actual demand and held in strategic form or location until demand occurs, when final customization takes place

materials-handling system a method of moving inventory into, within, and out of the warehouse

logistics information system the link that connects all the logistics functions of the supply chain

smart RFID an inventory handling and tracking system that employs radio-frequency electromagnetic fields to transfer and read product data via an electronic tag

13-5

outsourcing (contract logistics) a manufacturer's or supplier's use of an independent third party to manage an entire function of the logistics system, such as transportation, warehousing, or order processing

third-party logistics company (3PL) a firm that provides functional logistics services to others

fourth-party logistics company (4PL or logistics integrator) a consulting-based organization that assesses another's entire logistical service needs and provides integrated solutions, often drawing on multiple 3PLs for actual service

offshoring the outsourcing of a business process from one country to another for the purpose of gaining economic advantage

nearshoring the transfer of an offshored activity from a distant to a nearby country

supply chain risk any potential disruption that threatens the supply chain's efficient and effective operations

supply chain security efforts made by companies to protect their in-transit inventory or value-transforming assets from external or internal threats

supply chain resilience the ability of a supply chain to return to its ideal operational state after being disrupted

electronic distribution a distribution technique that includes any kind of product or service that can be distributed electronically, whether over traditional forms such as fiber-optic cable or through satellite transmission of electronic signals

three-dimensional printing (3DP) the creation of three-dimensional objects via an additive manufacturing (printing) technology that layers raw material into desired shapes

sustainable supply chain management a supply chain management philosophy that embraces the need for optimizing social and environmental costs in addition to financial costs

KEY TERMS

14-1

marketing channel (channel of distribution) a set of interdependent organizations that eases the transfer of ownership as products move from producer to business user or consumer

channel members all parties in the marketing channel who negotiate with one another, buy and sell products, and facilitate the change of ownership between buyer and seller in the course of moving the product from the manufacturer into the hands of the final consumer

form utility the elements of the composition and appearance of a product that make it desirable

time utility the increase in customer satisfaction gained by making a good or service available at the appropriate time

place utility the usefulness of a good or service as a function of the location at which it is made available

exchange utility the increased value of a product that is created as its ownership is transferred

retailer a channel intermediary that sells mainly to consumers

merchant wholesaler an institution that buys goods from manufacturers and resells them to businesses, government agencies, and other wholesalers or retailers and that receives and takes title to goods, stores them in its own warehouses, and later ships them

agents and brokers wholesaling intermediaries who do not take title to a product but facilitate its sale from producer to end user by representing retailers, wholesalers, or manufacturers

14-2

direct channel a distribution channel in which producers sell directly to consumers

dual distribution (multiple distribution) the use of two or more channels to distribute the same product to target markets

KEY CONCEPTS

LO 14-1 Explain what marketing channels and channel intermediaries are, and describe their functions and activities. A marketing channel is a business structure that helps channel members perform necessary actions to move products to the final consumer. As products move to the final consumer, intermediaries facilitate the distribution process by providing specialization and division of labor, overcoming discrepancies, and providing contact efficiency. Retailers are those firms in the channel that sell directly to consumers as their primary function.

LO 14-2 Describe common channel structures and strategies, and the factors that influence their choice. When possible, producers use a direct *channel* to sell directly to consumers. Alternatively, an *agent/broker channel* may be the best solution. Most consumer products are sold through distribution channels similar to the retailer channel and the wholesaler channel. *Dual distribution* may be used to distribute the same product to target markets, and companies often form *strategic channel alliances* to use already-established channels. Managers must consider the three options for intensity of distribution: intensive distribution, selective distribution, and exclusive distribution.

LO 14-3 Discuss channel relationship types and roles, and their unique benefits and drawbacks. Integrated relationships are closely bonded and explicit but do not offer flexibility; cooperative relationships offer balance and stability but cannot be sustained long term; and arm's-length relationships can satisfy a sudden or unique need but carry a potential for opportunism. Managers must also be aware of the social dimensions that are constantly affecting their relationships.

LO 14-4 Explain the importance of the retailer within the channel and within the national economy. In early 2012, indicators estimated that approximately two-thirds of the U.S. gross domestic product comes from retail activity. The retailing industry is one of the largest employers in the United States. Though most retailers are quite small, a few giant organizations such as Walmart dominate the industry.

LO 14-5 List and understand the different classifications and types of retailers, as well as their different operational models. Retail establishments can be classified according to ownership, level of service, product assortment, and price. Many stores fall into basic categories: department stores, specialty stores, supermarkets, drugstores, convenience stores, discount stores, specialty discount stores, off-price retailers, and in some ways, restaurants. Because consumers demand convenience, nonstore retailing is currently growing faster than in-store retailing. Finally, two basic forms of franchises are used today: product and trade name franchising and business format franchising.

LO 14-6 Explain the major tasks involved in developing a retail marketing strategy. The key tasks in strategic retailing are defining and selecting a target market and developing the retailing mix to successfully meet the needs of the chosen target market. Defining a target market in retailing begins with market segmentation. The retailing mix consists of six Ps: the four Ps of the marketing mix plus presentation and personnel.

LO 14-7 Discuss the roles of CRM and customer data in retailer decision making. The data manufacturers and retailers collect in CRM databases allow them to gain better insight into who is buying their products.

LO 14-8 Describe trends in retail and channel management. M-commerce enables consumers using wireless mobile devices to connect to the Internet and shop.

nontraditional channels non-physical (often electronic) channels that facilitate the unique market access of products and services

strategic channel alliance a cooperative agreement between business firms to use the other's already established distribution channel

intensive distribution a form of distribution aimed at having a product available in every outlet where target customers might want to buy it

selective distribution a form of distribution achieved by screening dealers to eliminate all but a few in any single area

exclusive distribution a form of distribution that establishes one or a few dealers within a given area

14-3

arm's-length relationship a relationship between companies that is loose, characterized by low relational investment and trust, and usually taking the form of a series of discrete transactions with no or low expectation of future interaction or service

cooperative relationship a relationship between companies that takes the form of informal partnership with moderate levels of trust and information sharing as needed to further each company's goals

integrated relationship a relationship between companies that is tightly connected, with linked processes across and between firm boundaries and high levels of trust and interfirm commitment

channel power the capacity of a particular marketing channel member to control or influence the behavior of other channel members

channel control a situation that occurs when one marketing channel member intentionally affects another member's behavior

channel captain a member of a marketing channel that exercises authority and power over the activities of other channel members

channel conflict a clash of goals and methods between distribution channel members

horizontal conflict a channel conflict that occurs among channel members on the same level

vertical conflict a channel conflict that occurs between different levels in a marketing channel, most typically between the manufacturer and wholesaler or between the manufacturer and retailer

channel partnering the joint effort of all channel members to create a channel that serves customers and creates a competitive advantage

14-4

retailing all the activities directly related to the sale of goods and services to the ultimate consumer for personal, nonbusiness use

14-5

independent retailer a retailer owned by a single person or partnership and not operated as part of a larger retail institution

chain store a store that is part of a group of the same stores owned and operated by a single organization

franchise a relationship in which the business rights to operate and sell a product are granted by the franchisor to the franchisee.

gross margin the amount of money the retailer makes as a percentage of sales after the cost of goods sold is subtracted

scrambled merchandising the tendency to offer a wide variety of nontraditional goods and services under one roof

factory outlet an off-price retailer that is owned and operated by a manufacturer

nonstore retailing shopping without visiting a store

automatic vending the use of machines to offer goods for sale

direct retailing the selling of products by representatives who work door-to-door, office-to-office, or at home sales parties

direct marketing (direct response marketing) techniques used to get consumers to make a purchase from their home, office, or other nonretail setting

telemarketing the use of the telephone to sell directly to consumers

shop-at-home television network a specialized form of direct-response marketing where shows display merchandise for viewers to purchase over the telephone with a credit card

online retailing (e-tailing) a type of shopping available to consumers with personal computers and access to the Internet

franchisor the originator of a trade name, product, methods of operation, and the like that grants operating rights to another party to sell its product

franchisee an individual or business that is granted the right to sell another party's product

14-6

retailing mix a combination of the six Ps—product, place, promotion, price, presentation, and personnel—to sell goods and services to the ultimate consumer

destination store a store that consumers purposely plan to visit

atmosphere the overall impression conveyed by a store's physical layout, décor, and surroundings

layout the internal design and configuration of a store's fixtures and products

14-7

data mining the process of discovering patterns in large data sets for the purposes of extracting knowledge and understanding human behavior

14-8

m-commerce the ability to conduct commerce using a mobile device for the purpose of buying or selling goods or services

KEY TERMS

15-1

promotion communication by marketers that informs, persuades, and reminds potential buyers of a product in order to influence an opinion or elicit a response

promotional strategy a plan for the optimal use of the elements of promotion: advertising, public relations, personal selling, sales promotion, and social media

competitive advantage one or more unique aspects of an organization that cause target consumers to patronize that firm rather than competitors

15-2

communication the process by which we exchange or share meaning through a common set of symbols

interpersonal communication direct, face-to-face communication between two or more people

mass communication the communication of a concept or message to large audiences

sender the originator of the message in the communication process

encoding the conversion of a sender's ideas and thoughts into a message, usually in the form of words or signs

channel a medium of communication—such as a voice, radio, or newspaper—for transmitting a message

noise anything that interferes with, distorts, or slows down the transmission of information

receiver the person who decodes a message

decoding interpretation of the language and symbols sent by the source through a channel

feedback the receiver's response to a message

KEY CONCEPTS

LO 15-1 Discuss the role of promotion in the marketing mix. Promotional strategy is the plan for using the elements of promotion—advertising, public relations, sales promotion, personal selling, and social media—to meet the firm's overall objectives and marketing goals. Based on these objectives, the elements of the promotional strategy become a coordinated promotion plan. The promotion plan then becomes an integral part of the total marketing strategy for reaching the target market along with product, distribution, and price.

LO 15-2 Describe the communication process. The communication process has several steps. When an individual or organization has a message it wishes to convey to a target audience, it encodes that message using language and symbols familiar to the intended receiver and sends the message through a channel of communication. Noise in the transmission channel distorts the source's intended message. Reception occurs if the message falls within the receiver's frame of reference. The receiver decodes the message and usually provides feedback to the source. Normally, feedback is direct for interpersonal communication and indirect for mass communication. Social media have increased the amount of feedback received by marketers.

LO 15-3 Explain the goals and tasks of promotion. The fundamental goals of promotion are to induce, modify, or reinforce behavior by informing, persuading, reminding, and connecting. *Informative promotion* explains a good's or service's purpose and benefits. Promotion that informs the consumer is typically used to increase demand for a general product category or to introduce a new good or service. *Persuasive promotion* is designed to stimulate a purchase or an action. Promotion that persuades the consumer to buy is essential during the growth stage of the product life cycle, when competition becomes fierce. *Reminder promotion* is used to keep the product and brand name in the public's mind. Promotions that remind are generally used during the maturity stage of the product life cycle. *Connection promotion* is designed to form relationships with customers and potential customers using social media. Connecting encourages customers to become brand advocates and share their experiences via social media.

LO 15-4 Discuss the elements of the promotional mix. The elements of the promotional mix include advertising, public relations, sales promotion, personal selling, and social media. *Advertising* is a form of impersonal, one-way mass communication paid for by the source. *Public relations* is the function of promotion concerned with a firm's public image. *Sales promotion* is typically used to back up other components of the promotional mix by stimulating immediate demand. *Personal selling* typically involves direct communication, in person or by telephone; the seller tries to initiate a purchase by informing and persuading one or more potential buyers. Finally, *social media* are promotion tools used to facilitate conversations among people online.

LO 15-5 Discuss the AIDA concept and its relationship to the promotional mix. The AIDA model outlines the four basic stages in the purchase decision-making process, which are initiated and propelled by promotional activities: (1) attention, (2) interest, (3) desire, and (4) action. The components of the promotional mix have varying levels of influence at each stage of the AIDA model. Advertising is a good tool for increasing awareness and knowledge of a good or service. Sales promotion is effective when consumers are at the purchase stage of the decision-making process. Personal selling is most effective in developing customer interest and desire.

15-4

promotional mix the combination of promotional tools—including advertising, public relations, personal selling, sales promotion, and social media—used to reach the target market and fulfill the organization's overall goals

advertising impersonal, one-way mass communication about a product or organization that is paid for by a marketer

public relations the marketing function that evaluates public attitudes, identifies areas within the organization the public may be interested in, and executes a program of action to earn public understanding and acceptance

publicity public information about a company, product, service, or issue appearing in the mass media as a news item

sales promotion marketing activities—other than personal selling, advertising, and public relations—that stimulate consumer buying and dealer effectiveness

personal selling a purchase situation involving a personal, paid-for communication between two people in an attempt to influence each other

paid media a category of promotional tactic based on the traditional advertising model, whereby a brand pays for media space

earned media a category of promotional tactic based on a public relations or publicity model that gets customers talking about products or services

owned media a new category of promotional tactic based on brands becoming publishers of their own content in order to maximize the brands' value to customers

15-5

AIDA concept a model that outlines the process for achieving promotional goals in terms of stages of consumer involvement with the message; the acronym stands for attention, interest, desire, and action

LO 15-6 Discuss the concept of integrated marketing communications. Integrated marketing communications is the careful coordination of all promotional messages for a product or service to ensure the consistency of messages at every contact point where a company meets the consumer—advertising, sales promotion, personal selling, public relations, and social media, as well as direct marketing, packaging, and other forms of communication. Marketing managers carefully coordinate all promotional activities to ensure that consumers see and hear one message. Integrated marketing communications has received more attention in recent years due to the proliferation of media choices, the fragmentation of mass markets into more segmented niches, and the decrease in advertising spending in favor of promotional techniques that generate an immediate sales response.

LO 15-7 Describe the factors that affect the promotional mix. Promotion managers consider many factors when creating promotional mixes. These factors include the nature of the product, product life-cycle stage, target market characteristics, the type of buying decision involved, availability of funds, and feasibility of push or pull strategies. As products move through different stages of the product life cycle, marketers will choose to use different promotional elements. Characteristics of the target market, such as geographic location of potential buyers and brand loyalty, influence the promotional mix as does whether the buying decision is complex or routine. The amount of funds a firm has to allocate to promotion may also help determine the promotional mix. Last, if a firm uses a push strategy to promote the product or service, the marketing manager might choose to use aggressive advertising and personal selling to wholesalers and retailers. If a pull strategy is chosen, then the manager often relies on aggressive mass promotion, such as advertising and sales promotion, to stimulate consumer demand.

15-6

integrated marketing communications (IMC) the careful coordination of all promotional messages for a product or a service to ensure the consistency of messages at every contact point at which a company meets the consumer

15-7

push strategy a marketing strategy that uses aggressive personal selling and trade advertising to convince a wholesaler or a retailer to carry and sell particular merchandise

pull strategy a marketing strategy that stimulates consumer demand to obtain product distribution

KEY TERMS

16-1

advertising response function a phenomenon in which spending for advertising and sales promotion increases sales or market share up to a certain level but then produces diminishing returns

16-2

institutional advertising a form of advertising designed to enhance a company's image rather than promote a particular product

product advertising a form of advertising that touts the benefits of a specific good or service

advocacy advertising a form of advertising in which an organization expresses its views on controversial issues or responds to media attacks

pioneering advertising a form of advertising designed to stimulate primary demand for a new product or product category

competitive advertising a form of advertising designed to influence demand for a specific brand

comparative advertising a form of advertising that compares two or more specifically named or shown competing brands on one or more specific attributes

16-3

advertising campaign a series of related advertisements focusing on a common theme, slogan, and set of advertising appeals

advertising objective a specific communication task that a campaign should accomplish for a specified target audience during a specified period

advertising appeal a reason for a person to buy a product

unique selling proposition a desirable, exclusive, and believable advertising appeal selected as the theme for a campaign

16-4

medium the channel used to convey a message to a target market

KEY CONCEPTS

LO 16-1 Discuss the effects of advertising on market share and consumers. Advertising helps marketers increase or maintain brand awareness and, subsequently, market share. Typically, more is spent to advertise new brands with a small market share than to advertise older brands. Brands with a large market share use advertising mainly to maintain their share of the market. Advertising affects consumers' daily lives as well as their purchases. Although advertising can seldom change strongly held consumer attitudes and values, it may transform a consumer's negative attitude toward a product into a positive one. Finally, advertising can also change the importance of a brand's attributes to consumers. By emphasizing different brand attributes, advertisers can change their appeal in response to consumers' changing needs or try to achieve an advantage over competing brands.

LO 16-2 Identify the major types of advertising. Advertising is any form of nonpersonal, paid communication in which the sponsor or company is identified. The two major types of advertising are institutional advertising and product advertising. *Institutional advertising* is not product oriented; rather, its purpose is to foster a positive company image among the general public, investment community, customers, and employees. *Product advertising* is designed mainly to promote goods and services, and it is classified into three main categories: pioneering, competitive, and comparative. A product's place in the product life cycle is a major determinant of the type of advertising used to promote it.

LO 16-3 Discuss the creative decisions in developing an advertising campaign. Before any creative work can begin on an advertising campaign, it is important to determine what goals or objectives the advertising should achieve. The objectives of a specific advertising campaign often depend on the overall corporate objectives and the product being advertised, and are often determined using the DAGMAR approach. Once objectives are defined, creative work can begin (e.g., identifying the product's benefits, developing possible advertising appeals, evaluating and selecting the advertising appeals, executing the advertising message, and evaluating the effectiveness of the campaign).

LO 16-4 Describe media evaluation and selection techniques. Media evaluation and selection make up a crucial step in the advertising campaign process. Major types of advertising media include newspapers, magazines, radio, television, the Internet, and outdoor media such as billboards and bus panels. Recent trends in advertising media include shopping carts, computer screen savers, DVDs, CDs, interactive kiosks, advertisements run before movies, posters on bathroom stalls, and "advertainments." Promotion managers choose the advertising campaign's media mix on the basis of the following variables: cost per contact, reach, frequency, characteristics of the target audience, flexibility of the medium, noise level, and the life span of the medium. After choosing the media mix, a media schedule designates when the advertisement will appear and the specific vehicles through which it will appear.

LO 16-5 Discuss the role of public relations in the promotional mix. Public relations is a vital part of a firm's promotional mix. A company fosters good publicity to enhance its image and promote its products. Popular public relations tools include new-product publicity, product placement, consumer education, sponsorship, and company Web sites. An equally important aspect of public relations is managing unfavorable publicity in a way that is least damaging to a firm's image.

LO 16-6 Define and state the objectives of sales promotion and the tools used to achieve them. Marketing managers can use sales promotion to increase the effectiveness of their promotional efforts. Sales promotion can target either trade

media planning the series of decisions advertisers make regarding the selection and use of media, allowing the marketer to optimally and cost-effectively communicate the message to the target audience

cooperative advertising an arrangement in which the manufacturer and the retailer split the costs of advertising the manufacturer's brand

infomercial a thirty-minute or longer advertisement that looks more like a television talk show than a sales pitch

advergaming placing advertising messages in Web-based or video games to advertise or promote a product, service, organization, or issue

media mix the combination of media to be used for a promotional campaign

cost per contact (cost per thousand or CPM) the cost of reaching one member of the target market

cost per click the cost associated with a consumer clicking on a display or banner ad

reach the number of target consumers exposed to a commercial at least once during a specific period, usually four weeks

frequency the number of times an individual is exposed to a given message during a specific period

audience selectivity the ability of an advertising medium to reach a precisely defined market

media schedule designation of the media, the specific publications or programs, and the insertion dates of advertising

continuous media schedule a media scheduling strategy in which advertising is run steadily throughout the advertising period; used for products in the later stages of the product life cycle

flighted media schedule a media scheduling strategy in which ads are run heavily every other month or every two weeks to achieve a greater impact with an increased frequency and reach at those times

or consumer markets. Trade promotions may push a product through the distribution channel using sales contests, premiums, P-O-P displays, trade allowances, push money, training, free merchandise, store demonstrations, and business meetings. Consumer promotions may push a product through the distribution channel using coupons, rebates, premiums, loyalty marketing programs or frequent buyer programs, contests, sweepstakes, sampling, and point-of-purchase displays. The biggest trend in sales promotion on both the trade and consumer side has been the increased use of the Internet.

pulsing media schedule a media scheduling strategy that uses continuous scheduling throughout the year coupled with a flighted schedule during the best sales periods

seasonal media schedule a media scheduling strategy that runs advertising only during times of the year when the product is most likely to be used

16-5

public relations the element in the promotional mix that evaluates public attitudes, identifies issues that may elicit public concern, and executes programs to gain public understanding and acceptance

publicity an effort to capture media attention, often initiated through press releases that further a corporation's public relations plans

product placement a public relations strategy that involves getting a product, service, or company name to appear in a movie, television show, radio program, magazine, newspaper, video game, video or audio clip, book, or commercial for another product; on the Internet; or at special events

sponsorship a public relations strategy in which a company spends money to support an issue, cause, or event that is consistent with corporate objectives, such as improving brand awareness or enhancing corporate image

crisis management a coordinated effort to handle all the effects of unfavorable publicity or another unexpected unfavorable event

16-6

sales promotion the marketing communication activities, other than advertising, personal selling, and public relations, in which a short-term incentive motivates consumers or members of the distribution channel to purchase a good

or service immediately, either by lowering the price or by adding value

trade sales promotion promotion activities directed to members of the marketing channel, such as wholesalers and retailers

consumer sales promotion promotion activities targeted to the ultimate consumer market

trade allowance a price reduction offered by manufacturers to intermediaries such as wholesalers and retailers

push money money offered to channel intermediaries to encourage them to "push" products—that is, to encourage other members of the channel to sell the products

coupon a certificate that entitles consumers to an immediate price reduction when the product is purchased.

rebate a cash refund given for the purchase of a product during a specific period

premium an extra item offered to the consumer, usually in exchange for some proof of purchase of the promoted product

loyalty marketing program a promotional program designed to build long-term, mutually beneficial relationships between a company and its key customers

frequent buyer program a loyalty program in which loyal consumers are rewarded for making multiple purchases of a particular good or service

sampling a promotional program that allows the consumer the opportunity to try a product or service for free

point of purchase (P-O-P) display a promotional display set up at the retailer's location to build traffic, advertise the product, or induce impulse buying

KEY TERMS

17-2

relationship selling (consultative selling) a sales practice that involves building, maintaining, and enhancing interactions with customers in order to develop long-term satisfaction through mutually beneficial partnerships

17-3

customer-centric a philosophy under which the company customizes its product and service offering based on data generated through interactions between the customer and the company

learning an informal process of collecting customer data through customer comments and feedback on product or service performance

knowledge management the process by which customer information is centralized and shared in order to enhance the relationship between customers and the organization

interaction the point at which a customer and a company representative exchange information and develop learning relationships

touch points areas of a business where customers have contact with the company and data might be gathered

point-of-sale interactions a touch point in stores or information kiosks that use software to enable customers to easily provide information about themselves without feeling violated

campaign management developing product or service offerings customized for the appropriate customer segment and then pricing and communicating these offerings for the purpose of enhancing customer relationships

17-4

sales process (sales cycle) the set of steps a salesperson goes through in a particular organization to sell a particular product or service

KEY CONCEPTS

LO 17-1 Describe personal selling. Personal selling is direct communication between a sales representative and one or more prospective buyers in an attempt to influence each other in a purchase situation. Broadly speaking, all businesspeople use personal selling to promote themselves and their ideas. Personal selling offers several advantages over other forms of promotion. Personal selling allows salespeople to thoroughly explain and demonstrate a product. Salespeople have the flexibility to tailor a sales proposal to the needs and preferences of individual customers. Personal selling is more efficient than other forms of promotion because salespeople target qualified prospects and avoid wasting efforts on unlikely buyers. Personal selling affords greater managerial control over promotion costs. Finally, personal selling is the most effective method of closing a sale and producing satisfied customers.

Personal Selling Advantages

- ✓ Detailed explanation or demonstration
- ✓ Variable sales message
- ✓ Directed at qualified prospects
- ✓ Controllable adjustable selling costs
- ✓ Effective at obtaining sale and gaining customer satisfaction

© Cengage Learning

LO 17-2 Discuss the key differences between relationship selling and traditional selling. *Relationship selling* is the practice of building, maintaining, and enhancing interactions with customers in order to develop long-term satisfaction through mutually beneficial partnerships. *Traditional selling*, on the other hand, is transaction focused. That is, the salesperson is most concerned with making a one-time sale and moving on to the next prospect. Salespeople practicing relationship selling spend more time understanding a prospect's needs and developing solutions to meet those needs.

Sales Increases Result from Creating Value

| Initial Sale | Repeat Sale | Successive Sales |

Traditional Sales

Relationship Selling

© Cengage Learning

LO 17-3 Describe customer relationship management. Companies that have a CRM system have a customer-centric model and learn ways to enhance their product and service, and often use knowledge management systems to centralize customer information. When managing interactions with customers, companies manage touch points. Interactions between the company and the customer facilitate the collection of large amounts of data. Companies can obtain contact information and data pertaining

lead generation (prospecting) identification of those firms and people most likely to buy the seller's offerings

referral a recommendation to a salesperson from a customer or business associate

networking a process of finding out about potential clients from friends, business contacts, coworkers, acquaintances, and fellow members in professional and civic organizations

cold calling a form of lead generation in which the salesperson approaches potential buyers without any prior knowledge of the prospects' needs or financial status

lead qualification determination of a sales prospect's (1) recognized need, (2) buying power, and (3) receptivity and accessibility

preapproach a process that describes the "homework" that must be done by a salesperson before he or she contacts a prospect

needs assessment a determination of the customer's specific needs and wants and the range of options the customer has for satisfying them

sales proposal a formal written document or professional presentation that outlines how the salesperson's product or service will meet or exceed the prospect's needs

sales presentation a formal meeting in which the salesperson presents a sales proposal to a prospective buyer

negotiation the process during which both the salesperson and the prospect offer special concessions in an attempt to arrive at a sales agreement

follow-up the final step of the selling process, in which the salesperson ensures delivery schedules are met, goods or services perform as promised, and the buyers' employees are properly trained to use the products

17–5

quota a statement of the salesperson's sales goals, usually based on sales volume

to the customer's current relationship with the organization. Companies that leverage customer information use that information for campaign management, retaining loyal customers, cross-selling other products and services, and designing targeted marketing communications.

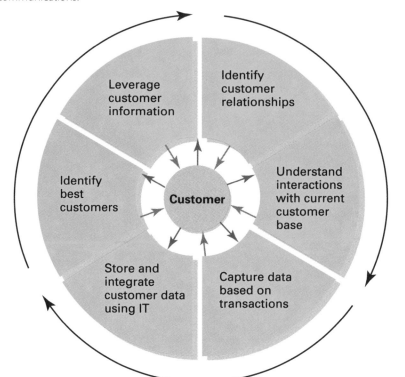

LO 17-4 List the steps in the selling process. The selling process is composed of seven basic steps: (1) generating leads, (2) qualifying leads, (3) approaching the customer and probing needs, (4) developing and proposing solutions, (5) handling objections, (6) closing the sale, and (7) following up.

LO 17-5 Describe the functions of sales management. The sales manager's basic job is to maximize sales at a reasonable cost while also maximizing profits. The sales manager's responsibilities include (1) defining sales goals and the sales process, (2) determining the sales force structure, (3) recruiting and training the sales force, (4) compensating and motivating the sales force, and (5) evaluating the sales force.

CHAPTER REVIEW

KEY TERMS

18-1

social media any tool or service that uses the Internet to facilitate conversations

social commerce a subset of e-commerce that involves the interaction and user contribution aspects of social online media to assist online buying and selling of products and services

crowdsourcing using consumers to develop and market products

18-2

owned media online content that an organization creates and controls

earned media a public relations term connoting free media such as mainstream media coverage

paid media content paid for by a company to be placed online

social media monitoring the process of identifying and assessing what is being said about a company, individual, product, or brand

18-5

blog a publicly accessible Web page that functions as an interactive journal, whereby readers can post comments on the author's entries

corporate blogs blogs that are sponsored by a company or one of its brands and maintained by one or more of the company's employees

noncorporate blogs independent blogs that are not associated with the marketing efforts of any particular company or brand

microblogs blogs with strict post length limits

social networking sites Web sites that allow individuals to connect—or network—with friends, peers, and business associates

media sharing sites Web sites that allow users to upload and distribute multimedia content like videos and photos

KEY CONCEPTS

LO 18-1 Describe social media, how they are used, and their relation to integrated marketing communications. Social media, commonly thought of as digital technology, offer a way for marketers to communicate one-on-one with consumers and measure the effects of those interactions. Social media include social networks, microblogs, and media sharing sites, all of which are used by the majority of adults. Smartphones and tablet computers have given consumers greater freedom to access social media on the go, which is likely to increase usage of social media sites. Many advertising budgets are allotting more money to online marketing, including social media, mobile marketing, and search marketing.

LO 18-2 Explain how to create a social media campaign. A social media campaign should take advantage of the three media categories: *owned media*, *earned media*, and *paid media*. To use these types of media in a social media campaign, first implement an effective listening system. Marketers can interact with negative feedback, make changes, and effectively manage their online presence. Paying attention to the ways that competing brands attract and engage with their customers can be particularly enlightening for both small businesses and global brands. Second, develop a list of objectives that reflects how social media dynamically communicate with customers and build relationships.

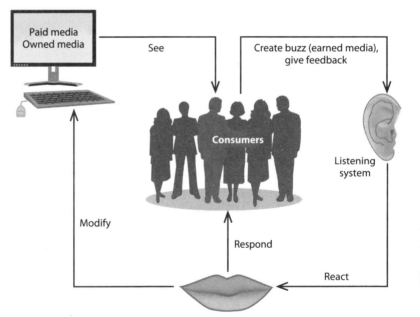

© Cengage Learning

LO 18-3 Evaluate the various methods of measurement for social media. Hundreds of metrics have been developed to measure social media's value, but these metrics are meaningless unless they are tied to key performance indicators.

LO 18-4 Explain consumer behavior on social media. To effectively leverage social media, marketers must understand who uses social media and how they use those media. If a brand's target market does not use social media, a social media campaign might not be useful. There are six categories of social media users: creators, critics, collectors, joiners, spectators, and inactives. A new category is emerging called "conversationalists," who post status updates on social networking sites or microblogs.

social news sites Web sites that allow users to decide which content is promoted on a given Web site by voting that content up or down

location-based social networking sites Web sites that combine the fun of social networking with the utility of location-based GPS technology

review sites Web sites that allow consumers to post, read, rate, and comment on opinions regarding all kinds of products and services

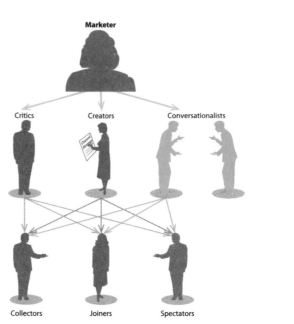

LO 18-5 Describe the social media tools in a marketer's toolbox and how they are useful. A marketer has many tools to implement a social media campaign. However, new tools emerge daily, so these resources will change rapidly. Some of the strongest social media platforms are blogs, microblogs, social networks, media creation and sharing sites, social news sites, location-based social networking sites, and virtual worlds and online gaming. Blogs allow marketers and consumers to create content in the form of posts, which ideally build trust and a sense of authenticity in customers. Microblogs, allow brands to follow, repost, respond to potential customers, and post content that inspires customers to engage the brand, laying a foundation for meaningful two-way conversation. Social networks allow marketers to increase awareness, target audiences, promote products, forge relationships, attract event participants, perform research, and generate new business. Media sharing sites give brands an interactive channel to disseminate content. Social news sites are useful to marketers to promote campaigns, create conversations, and build Web site traffic. Location-based social networking sites can forge lasting relationships and loyalty in customers. Review sites allow marketers to respond to customer reviews and comments about their brand. Virtual worlds are fertile ground for branded content, and online gaming allows marketers to integrate their message onto a game platform.

LO 18-6 Describe the impact of mobile technology on social media.
There are five reasons for the popularity of mobile marketing: (1) mobile platforms are standardized, (2) fewer consumers are concerned about privacy and pricing policies, (3) advertising can be done in real time, (4) mobile marketing is measurable, and (5) there is a higher response rate than with traditional advertising. Because of the rapid growth of Smartphones, well-branded, integrated apps allow marketers to create buzz and generate customer engagement. Widgets allow customers to post a company's information to its site, are less expensive than apps, and broaden that company's exposure.

LO 18-7 Understand the aspects of developing a social media plan The social media plan should fit into the overall marketing plan and help marketers meet the organization's larger goals. There are six stages in creating an effective social media plan: (1) listening, (2) setting social media objectives, (3) defining strategies, (4) identifying the target audience, (5) selecting the appropriate tools and platforms, and (6) implementing and monitoring the strategy. Listening and revising the social media plan to accommodate changing market trends and needs is key to an effective social media plan.

KEY TERMS

19-1

price that which is given up in an exchange to acquire a good or service

revenue the price charged to customers multiplied by the number of units sold

profit revenue minus expenses

19-2

return on investment (ROI) net profit after taxes divided by total assets

market share a company's product sales as a percentage of total sales for that industry

status quo pricing a pricing objective that maintains existing prices or meets the competition's prices

19-3

demand the quantity of a product that will be sold in the market at various prices for a specified period

supply the quantity of a product that will be offered to the market by a supplier at various prices for a specified period

price equilibrium the price at which demand and supply are equal

elasticity of demand consumers' responsiveness or sensitivity to changes in price

elastic demand a situation in which consumer demand is sensitive to changes in price

inelastic demand a situation in which an increase or a decrease in price will not significantly affect demand for the product

unitary elasticity a situation in which total revenue remains the same when prices change

19-4

yield management systems (YMS) a technique for adjusting prices that uses complex mathematical software to profitably fill unused capacity by discounting early purchases, limiting early sales at these discounted prices, and overbooking capacity

KEY CONCEPTS

LO 19-1 Discuss the importance of pricing decisions to the economy and to the individual firm. Pricing plays an integral role in the U.S. economy by allocating goods and services among consumers, governments, and businesses. Pricing is essential in business because it creates revenue, which is the basis of all business activity. In setting prices, marketing managers strive to find a level high enough to produce a satisfactory profit.

$$\text{Price} \times \text{Sales Units} = \text{Revenue}$$

$$\text{Revenue} - \text{Costs} = \text{Profit}$$

Profit drives growth, salary increases, and corporate investment.

LO 19-2 List and explain a variety of pricing objectives. Establishing realistic and measurable pricing objectives is a critical part of any firm's marketing strategy. Pricing objectives are commonly classified into three categories: profit oriented, sales oriented, and status quo. Profit-oriented pricing is based on profit maximization, a satisfactory level of profit, or a target *return on investment* (ROI). The goal of profit maximization is to generate as much revenue as possible in relation to cost. Often, a more practical approach than profit maximization is setting prices to produce profits that will satisfy management and stockholders. The most common profit-oriented strategy is pricing for a specific return on investment relative to a firm's assets. The second type of pricing objective is sales oriented, and it focuses on either maintaining a percentage share of the market or maximizing dollar or unit sales. The third type of pricing objective aims to maintain the status quo by matching competitors' prices.

LO 19-3 Explain the role of demand in price determination. *Demand* is a key determinant of price. When establishing prices, a firm must first determine demand for its product. A typical demand schedule shows an inverse relationship between quantity demanded and price: When price is lowered, sales increase; and when price is increased, the quantity demanded falls. For prestige products, however, there may be a direct relationship between demand and price: The quantity demanded will increase as price increases.

Marketing managers must also consider demand elasticity when setting prices. *Elasticity of demand* is the degree to which the quantity demanded fluctuates with changes in price. If consumers are sensitive to changes in price, demand is

19-5

variable cost a cost that varies with changes in the level of output

fixed cost a cost that does not change as output is increased or decreased

average variable cost (AVC) total variable costs divided by quantity of output

average total cost (ATC) total costs divided by quantity of output

marginal cost (MC) the change in total costs associated with a one-unit change in output

markup pricing the cost of buying the product from the producer, plus amounts for profit and for expenses not otherwise accounted for

keystoning the practice of marking up prices by 100 percent, or doubling the cost

profit maximization a method of setting prices that occurs when marginal revenue equals marginal cost

marginal revenue (MR) the extra revenue associated with selling an extra unit of output or the change in total revenue with a one-unit change in output

break-even analysis a method of determining what sales volume must be reached before total revenue equals total costs

19-6

selling against the brand stocking well-known branded items at high prices in order to sell store brands at discounted prices

extranet a private electronic network that links a company with its suppliers and customers

prestige pricing charging a high price to help promote a high-quality image

elastic; if they are insensitive to price changes, demand is inelastic. Thus, an increase in price will result in lower sales for an elastic product and little or no loss in sales for an inelastic product.

LO 19-4 Understand the concept of yield management systems. *Yield management systems* use complex mathematical software to profitably fill unused capacity. The software uses techniques such as discounting early purchases, limiting early sales at these discounted prices, and overbooking capacity. These systems are used in service and retail businesses and are substantially raising revenues.

LO 19-5 Describe cost-oriented pricing strategies. The other major determinant of price is cost. Marketers use several cost-oriented pricing strategies. To cover their own expenses and obtain a profit, wholesalers and retailers commonly use *markup pricing:* They tack an extra amount on to the manufacturer's original price. Another pricing technique is to maximize profits by setting the price where marginal revenue equals marginal cost. Still another pricing strategy determines how much a firm must sell to break even; this amount in turn is used as a reference point for adjusting price.

Markup: Cost + x% = Price
Profit maximization: Price set at point where MR = MC

Break-even: Price set at point where total costs = total revenue

LO 19-6 Demonstrate how the product life cycle, competition, distribution and promotion strategies, customer demands, the Internet and extranets, and perceptions of quality can affect price. The price of a product normally changes as it moves through the life cycle and as demand for the product and competitive conditions change. Management often sets a high price at the introductory stage, and the high price tends to attract competition. The competition usually drives prices down because individual competitors lower prices to gain market share. Adequate distribution for a new product can sometimes be obtained by offering a larger-than-usual profit margin to wholesalers and retailers. The Internet enables consumers to compare products and prices quickly and efficiently. Price is also used as a promotional tool to attract customers. Special low prices often attract new customers and entice existing customers to buy more. Large buyers can extract price concessions from vendors. Such demands can squeeze the profit margins of suppliers. Perceptions of quality can also influence pricing strategies. A firm trying to project a prestigious image often charges a premium price for a product. Consumers tend to equate high prices with high quality.

KEY TERMS

20-1

price strategy a basic, long-term pricing framework that establishes the initial price for a product and the intended direction for price movements over the product life cycle

price skimming a pricing policy whereby a firm charges a high introductory price, often coupled with heavy promotion

penetration pricing a pricing policy whereby a firm charges a relatively low price for a product initially as a way to reach the mass market

status quo pricing charging a price identical to or very close to the competition's price

20-2

unfair trade practice acts laws that prohibit wholesalers and retailers from selling below cost

price fixing an agreement between two or more firms on the price they will charge for a product

predatory pricing the practice of charging a very low price for a product with the intent of driving competitors out of business or out of a market

20-3

base price the general price level at which the company expects to sell the good or service

quantity discount a price reduction offered to buyers buying in multiple units or above a specified dollar amount

cumulative quantity discount a deduction from list price that applies to the buyer's total purchases made during a specific period

noncumulative quantity discount a deduction from list price that applies to a single order rather than to the total volume of orders placed during a certain period

KEY CONCEPTS

LO 20-1 Describe the procedure for setting the right price. The process of setting the right price on a product involves four major steps: (1) establishing pricing goals; (2) estimating demand, costs, and profits; (3) choosing a price policy to help determine a base price; and (4) fine-tuning the base price with pricing tactics. A price strategy establishes a long-term pricing framework for a good or service. The three main types of price policies are price skimming, penetration pricing, and status quo pricing.

LO 20-2 Identify the legal constraints on pricing decisions. Government regulation helps monitor four major areas of pricing: unfair trade practices, price fixing, price discrimination, and predatory pricing. Many states have enacted unfair trade practice acts that protect small businesses from large firms that operate efficiently on extremely thin profit margins; the acts prohibit charging below-cost prices. The Sherman Act and the Federal Trade Commission Act prohibit both price fixing, which is an agreement between two or more firms on a particular price, and predatory pricing, in which a firm undercuts its competitors with extremely low prices to drive them out of business. Finally, the Robinson-Patman Act makes it illegal for firms to discriminate between two or more buyers in terms of price.

LO 20-3 Explain how discounts, geographic pricing, and other pricing tactics can be used to fine-tune the base price. Several techniques enable marketing managers to adjust prices within a general range in response to changes in competition, government regulation, consumer demand, and promotional and positioning goals. Techniques for fine-tuning a price can be divided into three main categories: discounts, allowances, rebates, and value-based pricing; geographic pricing; and other pricing tactics.

- The first type of tactic gives lower prices to those who pay promptly, order a large quantity, or perform some function for the manufacturer. Additional tactics in this category include seasonal discounts, promotion allowances, and rebates (cash refunds).

- Geographic pricing tactics—such as FOB origin pricing, uniform delivered pricing, zone pricing, freight absorption pricing, and basing-point pricing—are ways of moderating the impact of shipping costs on distant customers.

- A variety of "other" pricing tactics stimulate demand for certain products, increase store patronage, and offer more merchandise at specific prices.

More and more customers are paying price penalties, which are extra fees for violating the terms of a purchase contract. The perceived fairness or unfairness of a penalty may affect some consumers' willingness to patronize a business in the future.

LO 20-4 Discuss product line pricing. Product line pricing maximizes profits for an entire product line. When setting product line prices, marketing managers determine what type of relationship exists among the products in the line: complementary, substitute, or neutral. Managers also consider joint (shared) costs among products in the same line.

cash discount a price reduction offered to a consumer, an industrial user, or a marketing intermediary in return for prompt payment of a bill

functional discount (trade discount) a discount to wholesalers and retailers for performing channel functions

seasonal discount a price reduction for buying merchandise out of season

promotional allowance (trade allowance) a payment to a dealer for promoting the manufacturer's products

rebate a cash refund given for the purchase of a product during a specific period

value-based pricing setting the price at a level that seems to the customer to be a good price compared to the prices of other options

FOB origin pricing a price tactic that requires the buyer to absorb the freight costs from the shipping point ("free on board")

uniform delivered pricing a price tactic in which the seller pays the actual freight charges and bills every purchaser an identical, flat freight charge

zone pricing a modification of uniform delivered pricing that divides the United States (or the total market) into segments or zones and charges a flat freight rate to all customers in a given zone

freight absorption pricing a price tactic in which the seller pays all or part of the actual freight charges and does not pass them on to the buyer

basing-point pricing a price tactic that charges freight from a given (basing) point, regardless of the city from which the goods are shipped

single-price tactic a price tactic that offers all goods and services at the same price (or perhaps two or three prices)

LO 20-5 Describe the role of pricing during periods of inflation and recession. Marketing managers employ cost-oriented and demand-oriented tactics during periods of economic inflation. Cost-oriented tactics include dropping products with a low profit margin, using delayed-quotation pricing and escalator pricing, and adding fees. Demand-oriented pricing methods include price shading and increasing demand through cultivating selected customers, creating unique offerings, changing the package size, and heightening buyer dependence.

To stimulate demand during a recession, marketers use value-based pricing, bundling, and unbundling. Recessions are also a good time to prune unprofitable items from product lines. Managers strive to cut costs during recessions in order to maintain profits as revenues decline. Implementing new technology, cutting payrolls, and pressuring suppliers for reduced prices are common techniques used to cut costs.

flexible pricing (variable pricing) a price tactic in which different customers pay different prices for essentially the same merchandise bought in equal quantities

price lining the practice of offering a product line with several items at specific price points

leader pricing (loss-leader pricing) a price tactic in which a product is sold near or even below cost in the hope that shoppers will buy other items once they are in the store

bait pricing a price tactic that tries to get consumers into a store through false or misleading price advertising and then uses high-pressure selling to persuade consumers to buy more expensive merchandise

odd–even pricing (psychological pricing) a price tactic that uses odd-numbered prices to connote bargains and even-numbered prices to imply quality

price bundling marketing two or more products in a single package for a special price

unbundling reducing the bundle of services that comes with the basic product

two-part pricing a price tactic that charges two separate amounts to consume a single good or service

consumer penalty an extra fee paid by the consumer for violating the terms of the purchase agreement

20-4

product line pricing setting prices for an entire line of products

joint costs costs that are shared in the manufacturing and marketing of several products in a product line

20-5

delayed-quotation pricing a price tactic used for industrial installations and many accessory items in which a firm price is not set until the item is either finished or delivered

escalator pricing a price tactic in which the final selling price reflects cost increases incurred between the time the order is placed and the time delivery is made

price shading the use of discounts by salespeople to increase demand for one or more products in a line